South Carolina State University

South Carolina State University

A BLACK LAND-GRANT COLLEGE IN JIM CROW AMERICA

William C. Hine

The University of South Carolina Press

Published by the University of South Carolina Press
Columbia, South Carolina 29208

www.sc.edu/uscpress

Manufactured in the United States of America

27 26 25 24 23 22 21 20 19 18
10 9 8 7 6 5 4 3 2 1

Library of Congress Cataloging-in-Publication Data
can be found at http://catalog.loc.gov/

ISBN 978-1-61117-851-7 (cloth)
ISBN 978-1-61117-852-4 (ebook)

This book was printed on a recycled paper
with 30 percent post consumer waste content.

For Darlene

The burden of racially segregated public schools,
poverty, and limited opportunities did not suppress
our determination to succeed in America.

Philemon Washington
The Class of 1957

Contents

Acknowledgments

Historians do not work alone. They depend on archivists, librarians, and colleagues as they research and write about the past. That has certainly been the case with *South Carolina State University.* Many people have contributed their knowledge, skills, and time to the preparation of this history.

The University Archives—otherwise known as the Historical Collection—was discovered relatively recently thanks to a tip in the late 1980s from M. Maceo Nance Jr., the former president of S.C. State. Nance recalled that there might be some college papers and records located in a small storeroom in the large Crawford-Zimmerman complex, where the college maintained a warehouse with vast supplies of everything from paper towels to cleaning products. Sure enough there in a windowless room were cardboard boxes of papers stacked haphazardly amid metal file cabinets, their drawers bulging with papers and correspondence dating back nearly a century. Some had been damaged years earlier by water when the records were kept in the basement of Wilkinson Hall. But these were the materials that became the core of the Historical Collection.

Thanks to the determined efforts of Barbara Williams Jenkins, the dean of the library, the documents were moved to the Miller F. Whittaker Library, where they joined the annual reports, college yearbooks, newspapers, and photographs that had been serving as a less-than-complete archive of the college. Today that Historical Collection represents the most important repository of information on a single African American institution in South Carolina. When Nelson C. Nix and John Potts wrote their histories of South Carolina State College years ago, they did not have access to most of these records.

Several archivists have worked diligently for more than two decades to transform those unprocessed, disorganized, raw records into a usable institutional archive. Yet it remains a work in progress. Lela Johnson Sewell, Aimee R. Berry, Ashley Till, the late Barbara Keitt, and Avery Daniels have labored hard to develop this splendid collection, and each of them has been extraordinarily helpful in making those records available for this history.

Following the retirement of Barbara Williams Jenkins, Mary L. Smalls and then Adrienne C. Webber have served as the dean of the library and information services. Too often in recent years, the Miller F. Whittaker Library has been compelled to cope with severe financial constraints. But each of the deans has recognized the importance of the Historical Collection, and they have made certain that it was not neglected.

Several other librarians at the Miller F. Whittaker Library have gone out of their way to assist in acquiring materials for this study. They are Doris Johnson Felder, Cathi Mack Cooper, Sherman Pyatt, Ruth Hodges, Beatrice McDonald, and Wanda Priester. The consortium of South Carolina college and university libraries that make up PASCAL (Partnership among South Carolina Academic Libraries) greatly facilitated the acquisition of library materials.

Archivists at other institutions have also been generous with their assistance. No one helped more over the years than Allen Stokes, the longtime director of the South Caroliniana Library at the University of South Carolina. Now retired Stokes is librarian emeritus. But historians from across the nation know him as an archivist exemplar. He has an unrivaled knowledge of South Carolina history and its resources. (And he is also strikingly well informed on major league baseball, particularly a team that plays in Cleveland.) At the Caroliniana Stokes has been ably assisted by Henry Fulmer, now the director; Beth Bilderback, the visual materials archivist; and Elizabeth West, who presides over the archives related to the University of South Carolina; and Herb Hartsook, the director of the Ernest Hollings Political Collection at the Thomas Cooper Library.

In recent years the South Carolina Department of Archives and History has suffered massive and deplorable reductions in its state appropriations. This has resulted in a loss in personnel, and that fine facility is now open to the public for far fewer hours each week than it was in the 1970s and 1980s. But the services provided by people like Rodger Stroup, W. Eric Emerson, Charles Lesser, J. Tracy Power, Alexia Helsley, and Steven R. Tuttle have remained at a consistently high level. They have been exceedingly cooperative in making state documents and governors' papers involving S.C. State available.

Many years ago the Rockefeller Archive Center made a grant available to travel to North Tarrytown, New York, to examine the General Education Board records that pertained to South Carolina State College. Darwin Stapleton, Ken Rose, and the archive staff helped to navigate those important materials.

There have been many other people willing and eager to share information about South Carolina State. Not only has Barbara Williams Jenkins been a fine librarian and administrator; she also possesses an incredible knowledge of the African American community in South Carolina. It is only a slight exaggeration to insist that Barbara seems to have known every person who attended or worked at S.C. State in the twentieth century. Deborah Blackmon helped track down elusive information and expedite the publication of this history. Richard Reid has an abundant store of information based on his research on S.C. State presidents as well as his extensive excursions into the history of African Americans and their institutions in Orangeburg. Eugene "Gene" Atkinson is well acquainted with the history of Orangeburg and its many leaders and personalities. Heather J. Gilbert, the digital scholarship librarian at the College of Charleston, helped with images from the 1901–2 South Carolina Interstate and West Indian Exposition as did Joyce Baker of the Gibbes Museum of Art. Bill Barley readily offered access to photographs that he took at the time of the Orangeburg Massacre in 1968. Cecil J. Williams has been South Carolina's preeminent civil rights photographer, and he has been unfailingly generous in sharing photos and information on that movement.

William "Bill" Hamilton, the now retired sports information director, assisted with information on athletics. Mary Hill offered some key data on the participation of women in the Bulldog athletic program. Oliver "Buddy" Pough and Willie Jeffries readily shared some of the abundant wit and wisdom they accumulated in the years they have been associated with their alma mater.

Departmental colleagues in history and political science have been willing to offer advice and suggestions—frequently unsolicited—on S.C. State. On more informal occasions, and with some liquid refreshments in hand, they have been known to provide some especially keen insights into the intricacies of South Carolina State's history and leadership. Therefore much appreciation is extended to Willie Legette, Larry Watson, Stanley Harrold, and Millicent Brown. A sizable debt of gratitude is owed to former chairs of the Department of Social Sciences beginning in 1967 with Rubin F. Weston and continuing through Edward R. Jackson, Rickey Hill, Barbara Woods, Learie Luke, Larry Watson, and Benedict Jua.

Further up the academic chain, Presidents Leroy Davis Sr. and Andrew Hugine Jr. expressed ongoing interest in this project, and they consistently extended support as well as patience as this history slowly came to fruition. More recently President Thomas J. Elzey offered essential help as this study neared publication. What is even more important, not one of them made any attempt whatsoever to interfere with or influence the contents of this history.

There have also been colleagues at other institutions who have made major forays into the lives of African Americans in South Carolina who have assisted with this study. They include Edmund L. Drago and Bernard Powers in the history program at the College of Charleston. W. Lewis Burke, who has retired from the faculty of the University of South Carolina law school, has dug deeply into the history of black attorneys in South Carolina. Eric Burgeron at the University of South Carolina and Harlan Greene at the College of Charleston Archives assisted with information on Thomas E. Miller. Robert Moore kindly shared files he maintained as a member of the Blackwell Committee in 1967 and as the state president of the Association of American University Professors (AAUP) in 1967–68. He is a retired professor of history at Columbia College. Thanks too to Jack Dodds, former professor of English at S.C. State and Harper College.

Three people have written valuable dissertations that deal with important figures in the history of South Carolina State. Carmen V. Harris completed a large and well-informed study of the black extension agents in the state. Jean Weingarth has written a fine biography of President Robert Shaw Wilkinson, and Travis Boyce examined the leadership style of President Benner C. Turner.

A number of individuals were cooperative as they provided information about various programs, events, and people at S.C. State. Fred Henderson Moore and Rudolph Pyatt were able to recall in fascinating detail the 1955–56 student protests. Delbert Foster has gone out of his way to explain recent developments in the 1890 program. Leo Twiggs discussed the inception of the I. P. Stanback Museum and Planetarium. John Stroman revealed much about "the Cause" in 1967 and the events leading to the Orangeburg Massacre in 1968. Frank Beacham also provided insights into the massacre and the "official" reaction to it. Jack Shuler shed light on the impact that the massacre had on people in the Orangeburg community. Joel Timmons did not hesitate to share the lyrics of "Orangeburg," a song he wrote and recorded with Sol Driven Train in 2009 about the 1968 massacre. Sara Aiken Waymer was extremely helpful in explaining the history of the home demonstration house that was built in Williamsburg County in the early 1950s. She also provided decades-old photographs of extension agents as well as a U.S. Department of Agriculture brochure that was created to publicize that demonstration home.

Other individuals closely associated with the history of South Carolina State graciously offered recollections, reminiscences, assessments, and sometime hilarious stories about their connections to the institution. Unfortunately too many of them are no longer with us. Their contributions to this history are immeasurable. They include Lewie C. Roache, James E. Sulton, Ruby Sulton, Charles Roberts, Clemmie E. Webber, Gracia Waterman Dawson, Altemease B. Pough, Sara Aiken Waymer, T. J. Crawford, John Wrighten, M. Maceo Nance Jr., Isaac "Ike" Williams, Geraldyne P. Zimmerman, Modjeska Simkins, Philip G. Grose, and Blinzy Gore.

The friendship of Jack Bass, Emma McCain, Cleveland Sellers, and Jordan Simmons III has meant more than they realize. They know only too well what it was like to have been born and raised in a South Carolina that did not treat each of its people fairly and justly.

Historians can be eccentric people, and it is the members of their families who are most often compelled to tolerate their peculiarities. Carol Hine, Thomas Hine, and the late Peter Hine are only too aware of having an odd older brother who sometimes spent an inordinate amount of time dwelling on footnotes. Although Peter dearly enjoyed New York City, he was especially curious about the history of a black college in the South. It is sad he did not live to see that history become a reality. He is missed.

This is not a perfect history of the institution that became South Carolina State University. But it is definitely better than it would have been were it not for the knowledge, wisdom, and encouragement of Darlene Clark Hine. Thank you, Darlene!

Preface

No public institution in South Carolina has meant more to the state's African American residents than the school that became South Carolina State University. This is a history of that institution that concentrates on the ninety years from its founding in 1896 to the "official" end of segregation in higher education in South Carolina in 1988. Black politicians struggled in 1895 to extract an agreement from white leaders at that year's constitutional convention to establish the "Colored Normal, Industrial, Agricultural and Mechanical College of South Carolina." Designated a land-grant institution under the terms of the 1862 and 1890 Morrill Acts, it was for seven decades the state's only public institution of higher education open to black people. But during its first thirty years it functioned primarily as a secondary school that offered vocational training in agricultural and mechanical subjects and prepared teachers for the black public schools.

Since the English established South Carolina as a colony in 1670, education and race have been volatile issues. And those two issues collided repeatedly during the history of the college. The institution was buffeted again and again by the whims and prejudices of the state's white political leadership. For seventy years its board of trustees consisted solely of white men. South Carolina's politicians saw little reason to expend the state's limited financial resources on a school that served, in their judgment, an inferior race of people incapable of mastering the elements of a genuine college education. Better, those leaders believed, to train black people in practical skills and then devote the greater portion of the state's money to the four public institutions of higher education that served white people: the University of South Carolina, Clemson, Winthrop, and the Citadel.

In an era of intense dedication to white supremacy, black leaders lacked political influence and had little choice but to accept what the state provided—or mostly did not provide. But because by law S.C. State could enroll and employ only black people, it became "their" college. They developed an affinity for it, they were proud of it, and they could exert a measure of control over it. The state's miserly funding meant that faculty and students built most of the original campus facilities. They operated the campus farm and consumed much of what it yielded in the dining hall. The college benefited from essential financial assistance from the federal government, and in time from major philanthropic organizations. But for decades it consistently received insufficient financial support and lacked ample dormitories, classrooms, and agricultural facilities. It did not have a separate library building until forty years after the college opened. Every year for more than sixty years students were turned away who wanted to attend.

Students, faculty members, and administrators did not openly challenge white supremacy or publicly criticize white people. Rather than jeopardize the tenuous state support for the college by such criticism, students and faculty members highlighted and praised the contributions and achievements of African Americans. From the school's beginning, college programs, observances, celebrations, and course offerings were often devoted to stressing the accomplishments of previous and current generations of black people and the obstacles that they had endured and overcome. These were occasions to present an image of African Americans that represented a sharp contrast to the views of black people promoted by most white people. People who made up the college community cherished their culture and celebrated their heritage.

Simultaneously, however, college administrators and faculty members placed even greater emphasis on molding mostly rural and young African Americans into models of middle-class propriety. They were determined to instill Victorian morality, Christian beliefs, and a commitment to knowledge among students. They wanted students to conform to rigid codes of behavior. Students were subjected to countless rules regarding dress, when and where they could go on campus, and how they spent their leisure time, and especially to regulations prohibiting encounters with members of the opposite sex.

Students were just as determined to resist these relentless efforts to regiment their lives. Young men and women invariably sought ways to socialize with each other. They did not always spend study and leisure time productively. They strayed from the campus. They evaded rules by playing cards, cursing, and sometimes consuming alcohol. They did not always curb their exuberant (or was it loud and boisterous?) behavior. Appalled by what they considered unrefined, unsophisticated, and immature conduct, the members of the faculty and administration routinely suspended and expelled students with little or no regard for due process. Still the harsh enforcement of disciplinary measures did little to create the austere academic atmosphere that college authorities so desired.

Although a stultifying authoritarian climate pervaded the campus for many decades, students as well as faculty members found satisfying and acceptable diversions in many activities, including athletics, music, drama, and debate. Students joined the YWCA, the YMCA, literary societies, religious groups, and fraternities and sororities. But the officers and advisors of the various student organizations also toiled to shape "proper" behavior among their members.

Beginning in the second decade of the twentieth century, college leaders waged a long and remarkable public service campaign to improve the lives of rural farm families through the federal government's cooperative extension program. With the black extension program headquartered on the S.C. State campus (the white extension program operated out of Clemson) and directed by the college president, farm and home demonstration agents eventually worked in more than thirty South Carolina counties. For a half century, they dispensed advice and information on improving agricultural production and enhancing homemaking skills. They also coordinated the 4-H programs. What is perhaps most important, they offered encouragement and moral support to some of the most destitute and isolated people in South Carolina and the nation.

By the late 1920s, S.C. State had evolved into a full-fledged college that awarded bachelor's degrees. It largely shed its image as a secondary school that focused on vocational training. Although hampered by a lack of accreditation and low faculty salaries, the college managed to survive the severe hardships brought on by the Great Depression thanks to the assistance of New Deal programs and with financial support provided by the Rosenwald Fund and the Rockefeller-sponsored General Education Board.

Most students and members of the faculty responded patriotically to World War I and World War II. Many of them fought in a segregated military in both conflicts to preserve an American way of life that did not treat people of color fairly or justly. In fact, by the 1940s, white South Carolinians were utterly determined that there would be no disruption to the system of segregation nor any reforms implemented that might expand the number of black voters and their political influence.

White leaders rallied in defense of Jim Crow as black people pressed for a more meaningful role and equitable treatment in American society. Rather than allocate state funds on undergraduate education and housing facilities at S.C. State following World War II, those state officials chose to perpetuate segregation through the establishment of the law school and graduate programs at the black college in 1947. Many military veterans who wanted to enroll under the G. I. Bill of Rights were consequently rejected because the college lacked classrooms and dormitories. Politicians led by Governor Jimmy Byrnes were determined to make "separate but equal" a reality in public and higher education to undermine the legal assault on segregation. Byrnes called on influential friends in high places, successfully appealing to the Rockefeller Foundation and its affiliate, the General Education Board, for sizable sums of money to erect new facilities at South Carolina State in the 1950s. The result was a massive building boom on the campus. But the strategy of white political and philanthropic leaders to strengthen and maintain Jim Crow failed within a decade.

South Carolina State students joined the thousands of college and high school students who helped launch the civil rights movement in the 1950s and 1960s that would ultimately destroy Jim Crow and change the face of America. Scores of students were arrested in demonstrations and protests in Orangeburg. S.C. State students also boycotted classes in 1956 as they challenged the authoritarian manner in which the college was administered. Several young people were suspended and dismissed because they had defied the autocratic rule that prevailed on the campus. In the meantime the all-black law school founded at S.C. State to maintain segregation produced attorneys who went to court and challenged segregation laws as they defended hundreds of students who had been arrested in marches and protests against Jim Crow across South Carolina.

Segregation eventually crumbled with the intervention of the federal government and the passage of the Civil Rights Act of 1964. Renewed campus protests against the autocratic administration of the college that included another boycott of classes by students in 1967 finally forced the departure of the longtime college president. But the persistence of segregation in the community led to another round of student protests in 1968, this time with tragic consequences. South Carolina highway patrolmen shot more than thirty young men—killing three of them—on the edge of the campus in the Orangeburg Massacre.

Seven decades as a black-only institution ended with the abolition of Jim Crow. S.C. State was no longer an institution that by law was confined solely to black students and employees. Asian and white faculty members were hired. Small numbers of white students enrolled. The first two black members of the board of trustees were elected in 1966. But the student body remained overwhelmingly black, and the college retained its legacy as a historically black institution in the decades that followed. The Voting Rights Act of 1965 greatly expanded the political clout of the state's black voters and compelled white lawmakers to pay increased attention to black constituents. Black voters also elected African American state legislators for the first time in the modern era, and those leaders were usually sympathetic to the concerns and needs of South Carolina State.

The profound changes in the racial order also produced remarkable changes on the campus. The college was fully accredited for the first time by the Southern Association of Colleges and Schools in 1960. With African Americans admitted to the University of South Carolina law school, the S.C. State law school closed in 1966. The separate cooperative extension program for black South Carolinians ended and was integrated into the Clemson extension service. Agriculture—what had been the life blood of the land-grant college—was also a casualty of segregation's demise. The program in agriculture was discontinued, and the campus farm was transformed into a city recreation complex and golf course. Vocational programs including tailoring and automobile mechanics were terminated. But there were new programs such as speech and hearing audiology, computer science, and music merchandising.

The federal government began to play a more significant role in higher education in the 1960s and 1970s as funds were made available for research and facilities. What is most important, financial aid for students in the form of loans and Pell Grants became available. The Title III program for developing institutions brought a helpful infusion of funds. Federal money for research and extension work was established and expanded through the 1890 program. For the first time in its history, the college had adequate dormitory space. New classrooms and laboratories were added. By the 1980s the campus featured a museum, planetarium, and FM radio station.

Federal authorities insisted in 1980 that the State of South Carolina eradicate the remaining vestiges of segregation from its system of higher education. The state's political leadership created a blue ribbon committee to draft a plan to integrate the colleges and universities more effectively. S.C. State was at the heart of that plan. To attract white students to the college, S.C. State began offering a doctorate in educational administration as well as new programs in agribusiness, nursing, and, in time, nuclear engineering. The legislature appropriated $14 million to the college, and much of that money went to hire new faculty and to augment the salaries of current faculty members that had lagged well behind those of their peers at the other state institutions. But the desegregation plan was not intended to deprive South Carolina State College of its heritage or its character as a black institution, and it did not. The federal government's approval of South Carolina's efforts to eliminate segregation in higher education in 1988 coincided with the emergence of a black majority of members on the college board of trustees. The long era of Jim Crow finally came to an end.

As S.C. State approached its centennial in 1996, new and formidable challenges confronted the historically black college—which had become a university in 1992. The institution went through a succession of presidents and administrators as it began its second century. The crisis in leadership aroused grave doubts among many people about the management of the institution and its prospects for the future. But for a university that had struggled to survive and overcome the humble and lean years that characterized so much of its early history, the problems of the twenty-first century seem to pale in comparison.

In the history that follows, there are several matters worth noting. For more than a half century—from 1896 until 1954—the legal and demeaning name of South Carolina State University was the "Colored Normal, Industrial, Agricultural and Mechanical College of South Carolina." But for most of that time it was commonly referred to as "S.C. State," "State College," and "South Carolina State College," and those are the terms used here. The honorific titles of Mr., Mrs., Miss, Ms., and Dr. have been mostly excluded from this account. When "Negro" was not capitalized in direct quotes, it remains in the lower case.

Then there is the important issue of color consciousness among African Americans. People with a light complexion, straight hair, and European facial features had advantages and privileges often denied to darker members of the race. Many were the descendants of white men and enslaved women. While this was a recurrent subject for discussion on the campus and in the community, it went unmentioned in correspondence, documents, minutes, or articles in the campus newspaper, the *Collegian.* But a cursory examination of photographs in the yearbooks or in the *Collegian* reveals that a disproportionate number of administrators, faculty members, student leaders, and campus queens were lighter members of the race. Of course there were exceptions. Benjamin E. Mays was a notable example of a prominent and successful dark man. His wife, Sadie, was, however, much lighter than he was.

In his reminiscences of student life at South Carolina State in the 1950s, Philemon Washington pointed out this near-obsession with light color. "The president of the college, his wife, top administrators and professors, Miss State College and others represented this stereotype. We even had a white Bulldog as our mascot. Was this a coincidence?"[1]

Prologue

On Monday, September 28, 1896, President Thomas E. Miller and eleven faculty members greeted the first students to enroll at the Colored Normal, Industrial, Agricultural, and Mechanical College of South Carolina. On that warm fall day the 116-acre campus barely resembled the academic institution that it would eventually become. It consisted of a few buildings, including several under construction, a dirt road, and a landscape crisscrossed with gullies. Within the next days and weeks, 960 students would make their way to the Orangeburg campus and register for courses.[1]

The establishment of what would ultimately become South Carolina State University was not as simple or straightforward as its founding in 1896 implies. It arose out of conflicting interests and concerns in the highly charged racial and political climate in the late nineteenth century to become the most important public institution serving the state's black residents in the twentieth century. It was founded out of a deep desire on the part of several of the state's black leaders to exercise greater control over the education of black youngsters.

EARLY EDUCATIONAL EFFORTS

Long before 1896 descendents of Africans in South Carolina demonstrated an awareness of the importance of education and a desire to learn. From its settlement as an English colony in 1670, Carolina's leaders and slave owners recognized both the capacity of Africans to learn and the dangers inherent in trying to maintain a servile labor force that had access to knowledge and an understanding of the world around them. Therefore the colony and the state's slave codes outlawed and then periodically strengthened legislation that prohibited teaching slaves to read and write.

But there were always people of color who found the ways and means to overcome the law and acquire at least a rudimentary education. Some slaves surreptitiously learned to read and write. Free black people taught small numbers of slaves until state authorities cracked down in 1834. Free black teacher Mary F. Weston was arrested twice in Charleston for instructing black children. She avoided further harassment when she agreed to stop teaching slaves and permitted a white person to observe her instructing classes of free black pupils.[2]

When the Civil War concluded and slavery ended in 1865, education was nearly as precious to black people as freedom itself. Even during the war, black and white missionaries and schoolteachers from the North arrived in the wake of white and black Union troops who occupied the South Carolina lowcountry. The educators and church people began to instruct black people, young and old. In 1862 two white women, Laura Towne and Ellen Murray, organized Penn School on St. Helena Island, and it provided education and training for generations of black people. Charlotte Forten, a young black woman from a prominent Philadelphia family, was one of the first teachers at Penn. By the war's end, ten thousand students were enrolled in forty-eight schools in South Carolina.[3]

In 1865 the American Missionary Association established Avery Normal Institute in Charleston under the leadership of Francis L. Cardozo, a black man who had grown up free in the city. Cardozo went on to serve as secretary of state and as South Carolina's treasurer during Reconstruction. Avery went on for nine decades as a private elementary and high school that served the more prosperous and often lighter members of the black community. Normal schools like Avery emerged across America in the late nineteenth and early twentieth centuries. They prepared young people—typically women—for careers as teachers. Their students pursued one- or two-year courses of study and earned a licentiate of instruction rather than a bachelor's degree.[4]

Institutions that identified themselves as colleges and universities also opened shortly after the Civil War and during Reconstruction in South Carolina. Because most slaves had no more than a rudimentary education, these institutions functioned mostly as primary, secondary, and normal schools. In 1870 the African Methodist Episcopal Church established Payne Institute in Newberry. It moved to Columbia in 1880 and was renamed Allen University. Benedict Institute was founded in Columbia in 1870 by the New York-based American Baptist Home Mission Society. Benedict was essentially a secondary school with a department of theology until it became a college in 1894.[5]

CLAFLIN UNIVERSITY AND THE A&M SCHOOL

Claflin University was by far the most important immediate predecessor to South Carolina State, and it would play a crucial role in the formation of the public college. In 1869 northern white Methodists affiliated with the Freedmen's Aid Society established Claflin on property that had been occupied by the Orangeburg Female Institute before the Civil War. Methodist clergymen Alonzo Webster and Timothy W. Lewis provided the initiative while abolitionists Lee Claflin and his son William—who was the Republican governor of Massachusetts—contributed financial support. Although open to black as well as white people and designated a university, Claflin was a primary school for freedmen. Of the 309 students enrolled in 1870, none were in the college curriculum.[6]

The Reverend Alonzo Webster, a native of Vermont, was the first president of Claflin. He was a dedicated, energetic, and paternalistic leader. During Reconstruction Webster developed close ties to black and white Republican leaders in the state legislature. In 1872 Webster persuaded legislators to take advantage of the 1862 Morrill Land-Grant Act to create an agricultural and mechanical institute that would be connected to Claflin.

The Morrill Act was one of the most far-reaching pieces of legislation enacted by Congress in the nineteenth century. It made federal land grants available to assist in the support of at least one college or university in each state. The act promoted instruction in "such branches of learning as are related to agriculture and mechanical arts" as well as military tactics, but "without excluding other scientific and classical studies." Eventually more than seventeen million acres of public lands (over twenty-six thousand square miles) were distributed to the states. Each state received thirty thousand acres for each representative it was entitled to in Congress. South Carolina had six members of the U.S. House and Senate in 1870, and it received the financial benefits from the sale of 180,000 acres.[7]

Webster subsequently purchased 116 acres adjacent to Claflin for $9,000 for the new agricultural and mechanical college. However, the Claflin president's success in securing passage of the 1872 legislation created a most peculiar educational arrangement in attaching the new A&M school to Claflin. By the terms of the measure, the supervision and control of the land-grant institution would be "vested in a Board of Trustees of Claflin University to be known by the name, style and title of the Board of Trustees of the South Carolina Agricultural and Mechanical Institute." Paradoxically the same legislation stipulated that: "The [Agricultural and Mechanical] College shall have no connection whatever with, nor be in any way controlled by, a sectarian denomination." It was an educational anomaly that defied explanation and was a curious amalgamation of church and state that persisted for twenty-four years. Webster and his two successors served as president of both schools. Each institution had the same students and faculty. In 1876 Webster observed that "the college and Claflin were not separated; students belonged to both." The A&M school was identified in 1883 as "The Claflin College of Agricultural and Mechanical Arts" and as "a co-ordinate with Claflin University."[8]

In 1889 there were twelve members of the "joint faculty" including the president. There were also six assistant faculty members, and fourteen superintendents of industry. The teaching staff was responsible for 945 students. Twelve students were enrolled in the college curriculum and twenty-three were normal school students. There were also students in the Baker Theological School, in a night school, and in law courses taught by former associate justice of the South Carolina Supreme Court Jonathan J. Wright.[9]

Claflin embraced the A&M ideal so prevalent in late nineteenth-century America. "Claflin University is fully committed to industrial education. The time has now come when most boys and girls must get their preparation for their life-work in the schools." In 1891 Claflin's farm produced sixteen hundred bushels of corn, seventeen hundred bushels of sweet potatoes, and twenty-five hundred quarts of milk. Most of these commodities were served in the dining hall.[10]

HIGHER EDUCATION IN LATE NINETEENTH-CENTURY SOUTH CAROLINA

As Claflin and the A&M school coexisted and cooperated awkwardly in Orangeburg during the last quarter of the nineteenth century, the state's political leaders fought a series of battles over the direction and future of South Carolina College (now the University of South Carolina). South Carolina's politicians fundamentally disagreed on whether public funds were spent more wisely on agricultural and mechanical training or on traditional and classical collegiate education.

Closed during the Civil War, the South Carolina College reopened in Columbia in 1866 to a few students and faculty as it struggled to regain its prewar status as a respected institution that offered young white men a classical education. When black and white Republicans gained political power during Reconstruction in 1868 they swiftly increased financial support for the college's programs in Latin, Greek, sciences, law, and pharmacology, but they did not immediately press for the admission of black students or the employment of black faculty. Although two black Charlestonians—Dr. Benjamin A. Boseman and Francis L. Cardozo—were elected to the institution's board of trustees in 1869, the student body and faculty remained all white for four more years.[11]

In 1873 South Carolina College began to admit black students, and many white students and faculty members fled. The college hired Richard T. Greener, Harvard's first black graduate, to teach mental and moral science. He also served briefly as the college librarian. Several black men who would become prominent figures in South Carolina enrolled in the Columbia institution in the 1870s. Thomas E. Miller took courses in the law, was later elected to Congress, and would become the first president of South Carolina State in 1896. George W. Murray also became a U.S. congressman. Joseph W. Morris would serve as president of Allen University. William D. Crum became a physician and then was appointed by President Theodore Roosevelt as collector of customs in Charleston. Johnson C. Whittaker went from South Carolina College to the U.S. Military Academy, where he became embroiled in a highly publicized controversy in 1881 and was subsequently court-martialed and discharged from the army. T. McCants Stewart, who became a lawyer, was an associate of Booker T. Washington and would spend time in Liberia, the Virgin Islands, and Hawaii.[12]

As soon as conservative Democrats regained political control of the state in 1877, they closed South Carolina College. They then decided to create a dual system of higher education. Nearly two decades before the U.S. Supreme Court declared in the *Plessy v. Ferguson* decision that "separate but equal" facilities did not deprive black people of their civil rights, South Carolina's white leaders decided to determine the feasibility of establishing separate institutions of higher education for black and white residents. They created a commission "to inquire into and devise plans for the organization and maintenance of one university or college for the white youths and one for the colored youths of the state," but with the stipulation that "said universities or colleges shall be kept separate and apart, but shall forever enjoy precisely the same privileges and advantages with respect to standards of learning and amounts of revenue to be appropriated by the state for their maintenance."[13]

But South Carolina College remained closed until 1880 because Democrats could not agree on what sort of education was most suitable for young white men. Insurgent Democrats led by Martin W. Gary and Benjamin R. Tillman insisted that the state furnish its white sons with practical and agricultural training that would enable them to derive a comfortable living from the soil. Mainline Democrats who were aligned with Wade Hampton favored reopening the college with a traditional curriculum that featured languages, literature, history, and the sciences.

The insurgent Democrats won a short-lived victory in 1880 when the Columbia campus reopened as a three-year agricultural and mechanical institute that offered neither a bachelor's degree nor programs in the liberal arts or classics. The trustees of the new venture diverted Morrill land-grant funds from Claflin's A&M institute to support the Columbia school. They claimed that adequate funds were available for both institutions. "The Agricultural College fund [Morrill money] . . . is sufficient to maintain the present efficient establishment at Orangeburg and to maintain an institution of a much higher order at Columbia" than had previously existed in the state capital.[14]

While the A&M school at Claflin never enjoyed prosperity, it certainly thrived more than the new A&M program in Columbia. By 1884–85 the agricultural enterprise at South Carolina College had all but ceased to exist. Seven of the college's 122 students were enrolled in agriculture. The trustees revived the programs in history, languages, political economy, and mental and moral sciences. The law program was reestablished. In 1887 the college became a university.[15]

Martin Gary, Benjamin Tillman, and their followers were enraged at this shift in the mission of the South Carolina College. Tillman dismissed graduates of the Columbia school as "drones and vagabonds" and lashed out at the recently reopened Citadel as "that military dude factory." The *Greenville News* joined in the attack on the "new" South Carolina College, condemning it as "atheistic, aristocratic, extravagant, and useless."[16]

Defeated in his quest to transform South Carolina College into an A&M school, Tillman advocated the creation of a separate agricultural institution to provide young white men with a practical education. He desperately wanted a facility in which students would be, as he put it, "required each day to hoe, to ditch, to fork manure, to make butter, to feed stock, to graft, to bud, to prune." Tillman and the many Carolinians who agreed with him saw their hopes take a dramatic and positive turn in 1888 with what they could only regard as the timely death of Thomas G. Clemson.[17]

Clemson, who was the son-in-law of John C. Calhoun, was a longtime advocate of agricultural education. He bequeathed Fort Hill, the 814-acre Calhoun family plantation in Pickens County, and $81,529 to the State of South Carolina to create an A&M school for young white men. Clemson A&M College admitted its first students in 1893. Although South Carolina was hardly a prosperous state and the nation was in the throes of a devastating depression in the mid-1890s, the new school endured little economic privation. In addition to Thomas Clemson's financial legacy, the institution received land-grant funds from the 1862 Morrill Act as well as from the recently passed 1890 Morrill Act. It also received federal funds for agricultural experimentation from the 1887 Hatch Act. Furthermore Clemson was the direct beneficiary of a state sales tax on fertilizer, the so-called Tag tax.[18]

With Tillman's election as governor in 1890, the future of Columbia's South Carolina University appeared bleak indeed. Tillman announced in his inaugural address that the liberal arts school's best days were behind it. "The people," he proclaimed, "have decided that there is no use for a grand university." The new governor presided over legislation to terminate the institution's status as a university and to abolish its graduate programs and its school of pharmacy.[19]

BLACK LEADERS INSIST ON A BLACK LAND-GRANT COLLEGE

While white politicians debated the future of collegiate education, several black leaders grew increasingly disenchanted with Claflin and the A&M school associated with it.

Before Tillman's ascendancy to power there had been, according to black lawmaker Thomas E. Miller, a commitment made by conservative white Democrats led by Governor Wade Hampton to establish a state-supported college for young black people. That commitment went unfulfilled. "In the State Senate in the early 1880's," Miller recalled, "the Hampton faction promised Bruce Williams and myself when we voted to return the South Carolina College in Columbia, to the Whites and to open the Military College in Charleston, that in the near future they would give the Negro a College, but they failed to do so."[20]

South Carolina's black leaders were not happy with the Methodist Claflin's control of the state A&M institution, and they were even less pleased that Claflin's administration and faculty consisted mostly of white people. In 1872 several members of Claflin's board of trustees complained that only white teachers served at the institution. In 1878 prominent black leaders representing students and citizens drafted a petition protesting the leadership of Edward Cooke, who was Claflin's second president and a white man. Two of South Carolina's most influential black leaders during Reconstruction—Robert Brown Elliott and Daniel A. Straker—presented the petition to the trustees in which they accused Cooke of making disparaging remarks about Republican leadership during Reconstruction. There was an allegation that Cooke had blurted out, "All colored people will steal." Cooke survived the controversy but finally left Claflin in 1884.[21]

Cooke's successor was Lewis M. Dunton, a white Methodist and native of New Hampshire who was a graduate of Wesleyan University and had served as the president of Wisconsin's Lawrence University. Dunton had closer ties to Republican leaders than Cooke. Still black leaders chafed at white influence over Claflin. Not only did white people exercise authority in the day-to-day affairs of the university and the A&M school, but officials of organizations that included the Freedmen's Aid and Southern Education Society of the Methodist Episcopal Church, the Peabody Fund, and the John F. Slater Fund were also involved in the activities of both Claflin and the A&M school. Although these philanthropic agencies provided much needed financial assistance, they also dictated the way in which funds would be spent on teacher training and industrial education.[22]

Several black leaders—led by Thomas E. Miller—began to agitate for the separation of the A&M school from Claflin. They wanted a black land-grant college supervised by black men and women. It was consequently a bitter irony that when a new state constitution was framed in 1895 to deprive black men of the right to vote, the same document also authorized the establishment of the black college favored by Miller and other black leaders.

Benjamin R. Tillman, who had been elected to the U.S. Senate in 1894, was determined to disfranchise the several thousand black South Carolinians who continued to vote in the 1890s. Few political figures in American history were more determined to make white supremacy a reality than Benjamin Ryan Tillman. The senator and his fellow Democrats had to find a "legal" way to evade the Fifteenth Amendment to the U.S. Constitution that explicitly stated the right to vote could not be denied on the basis of "race, color, or previous condition of servitude." Tillman would have preferred that the amendment simply be repealed, but that was an impossibility.[23]

THE 1895 CONSTITUTIONAL CONVENTION

By the narrowest of margins—31,402 to 29,523—Tillman persuaded the state's voters to call a constitutional convention to draft a new constitution to replace the document adopted during Reconstruction in 1868. The 1895 convention met in Columbia, and Tillman served as presiding officer and as the chair of the Committee on Suffrage. The convention adopted a lengthy and complex set of restrictions on voting that never mentioned race or color. In fifteen paragraphs the new constitution established residency requirements, mandated proof of payment of the poll tax, and disqualified prospective voters who had been convicted of burglary, arson, perjury, forgery, robbery, assault with intent to ravish, and several other crimes regarded as offenses that black men were likely to commit. Conviction for homicide or embezzlement—crimes white men had a tendency to commit—were not disqualifications for voting.[24]

What is most important, the new constitution stipulated that a prospective voter either had to have paid taxes on property assessed at no less than $300 or had to be able to read the constitution "or understand and explain it when read to them by the registration officer." With this "understanding clause," illiterate white men would invariably be eligible to vote while the registration official would almost always determine that the black applicant could not "understand" the constitution.[25]

The six black delegates at the convention—of the 160 men elected to serve—vigorously and courageously protested disfranchisement. Led by Thomas E. Miller but ably supported by Robert Smalls, William Whipper, James Wigg, Isaiah Reed, and Robert B. Anderson, they delivered ringing addresses that defended their race against the loss of voting rights. Miller insisted that black people neither sought to control government nor wanted to socialize with white people. They merely wanted to vote and hold political office. "The negroes do not want to dominate. They do not want and would not have social equality, but they do want to cast a ballot for the men who make and administer the laws." Miller concluded with a plea and hope for racial reconciliation. "I stand here pleading for justice to a people whose rights are about to be taken away with one fell swoop.... I want a united people." The other black delegates followed in a similar vein, but it was all for naught. The suffrage provisions were incorporated in the 1895 constitution.[26]

The eloquent speeches of the black delegates forced Tillman to respond. He was justifiably concerned with the perception effectively conveyed by the black leaders that potential black voters would be unfairly disfranchised. Tillman insisted that there would be no fraud in the enforcement of qualifications for voting, although he did concede that registration officials might "just [be] showing partiality, perhaps or discriminating" as they decided whether or not black applicants "understood" the new constitution.[27]

William Henderson, a delegate from Berkeley County, was not as circumspect as Tillman when he bluntly observed during the debate over suffrage: "We don't propose to have fair elections. We will get left at that every time. . . . I tell you, gentlemen, if we have fair elections in Berkeley we can't carry it. There's no use to talk about it. The black man is learning to read faster than the white man. And if he comes up and can read you have got to let him vote. . . . We are perfectly disgusted with hearing so much about fair elections. Talk all around, but make it fair and you'll see what'll happen."[28]

Although the speeches of the black delegates landed some telling blows, the political influence of the black men did not match their oratorical skills as the white delegates easily swept aside the black opposition to the voting restrictions. Without specifically referring to race or color, the new constitution eliminated thousands of black voters as well as many white voters. By the early twentieth century in South Carolina, politics was the exclusive preserve of white men.

THE CONSTITUTION AND THE BLACK COLLEGE

As strongly opposed as he was to disfranchisement, Thomas E. Miller did not devote all his time at the 1895 convention to that effort. He was also determined to include a provision in the new constitution to separate the twenty-four-year-old A&M institute from Claflin. Black delegate Isaiah Reed strongly supported Miller, but there was formidable opposition to removing the A&M school from Claflin's control. Lewis M. Dutton, Claflin's president as well as several of the institution's white faculty members joined with black delegates Robert Smalls, Robert B. Anderson, and William Whipper to oppose Miller's plan for separation.

Remarkably Miller turned for assistance to his fiercest political foe and the convention's dominant figure, Benjamin R. Tillman. Miller later recalled that it would have been futile to attempt to separate the A&M school from Claflin without the support of Tillman. This occurred in spite of Tillman's long-standing opposition to public education for black people. He had declared in 1886 that "when you educate a negro you educate a candidate for the penitentiary or spoil a good field hand."[29]

Tillman's support had a price. He would back Miller's effort so long as Miller agreed to "leave national politics and head the [new] college." Miller accepted the bargain. He could hardly do otherwise. In 1895 Miller no longer served in Congress. He had lost his bid for reelection to the U.S. House in 1892. He had been elected to the general assembly from Beaufort in 1894, but with the disfranchisement of black voters looming, his chances of winning a national or state office in the future seemed remote.[30]

Miller wrote and distributed to convention delegates a leaflet listing twelve reasons why Claflin should no longer operate the land-grant institution. Miller cleverly and effectively played to the racial, regional, and religious anxieties of the state's white leaders as he justified the establishment of an autonomous A&M institution. Miller charged that the Methodist Episcopal Church ran Claflin as well as the A&M school, and he implied that public money was used for political and sectarian ends. "The Church which practically controls all the funds, elects President, Professors, and Instructors in Mechanical and Agricultural Departments (three Southern white Professors excepted) is unwilling to employ colored persons who will not voice her politics nor regard the South as their enemy, no matter how acceptable they may be to their own race and the Southern whites."

He added that northern white people affiliated with Claflin were motivated by mercenary and not missionary motives: "it has been proved beyond the shadow of a doubt that they are here for the dollars and cents." Miller suggested that students were misled and deceived by these greedy outsiders with their northern points of view. "Students are not taught by percept nor example to be in sympathy with the great interests of the South."

Miller claimed that a separate A&M school would appeal to black people because it would serve the South and not promote northern interests. In the new A&M institution, "Southern men" would supervise and teach—not for partisan political reasons—but for "the best interests of the South." Perhaps exaggerating only slightly, he concluded that the formation of an independent A&M college might even help alleviate the race problem. "Old issues would die out, strife and confusion between the races would cease, and a better era would dawn on the South."[31]

Miller sought to have the faculty and administrators of the new A&M school limited to "Southern Negroes." This brought a sharp rebuke from Robert Smalls, who insisted that color should not be a factor in employment. "And I for one, want the best man for the place, whether he is black or white." Tillman intervened with a compromise of sorts that restricted the faculty and staff to men and women of the Negro race with no reference to region.[32]

Thus Thomas Miller got his way. With the backing of Tillman and his supporters, the provision for education in the new constitution authorized the general assembly to separate "as soon as practicable" Claflin College from Claflin University and to "provide for a separate corps of professors and instructors therein, representation to be given to men and women of the negro race." It would be inconveniently and unfortunately known as the Colored Normal, Industrial, Agricultural and Mechanical College of South Carolina.[33]

Was the inclusion of a public college for black South Carolinians in the 1895 constitution an acceptable political compromise for a constitution that also contained provisions that would deprive black men of the right to vote? The five black delegates who were present at the convention's final session were emphatic in their opposition to that document. They refused to sign South Carolina's new constitution.[34]

OPPOSITION TO THE NEW COLLEGE

Although the new constitution mandated the separation of the A&M school from Claflin, that did not mean that the new institution would be established quickly or painlessly. The South Carolina General Assembly would have to enact legislation to create the school, and for a time that seemed an unlikely prospect. Governor John Gary Evans announced in his annual message to the general assembly in January 1896 that while the constitution required the A&M school to be severed from Claflin, "much time" would be needed to carry out that separation, and that "the necessity is not urgent." In the meantime Claflin president Lewis M. Dunton recommended that the division "take place in two, three, or four years . . . we see no reason for a hasty separation."[35]

However, Thomas Miller, representing Beaufort County in the South Carolina House of Representatives, was working furiously to guide a measure through the legislature to establish the separate A&M school. And once again Miller would seek the assistance of the state's foremost foe of black people, Benjamin R. Tillman. Conservative Democrats and opponents of both Tillman and Miller wanted the new school to be "a part of the white state college at Columbia." Furthermore Tillman supporters who were members of the Orangeburg delegation in the general assembly attempted to modify Miller's pending legislation by striking "all negro teachers" so that white faculty could be employed at the new college. Some white politicians and their followers were quite willing to look the other way when it came to the strict observance of segregation if it created opportunities for the employment of white people at a black institution. Several white faculty members then working at the A&M school attached to Claflin hoped to retain their positions at the new institution.

Thoroughly dedicated to white supremacy and segregation, Tillman would have none of it. At Miller's request the U.S. senator pressured the Orangeburg delegation led by state senator William Samuel Barton to get rid of "the old crowd of white professors" who were Claflin faculty members. The Orangeburg legislators exacted a compromise from Tillman and Miller, however, by insisting that two of the six members of the board of trustees come from Orangeburg and that the new school hire four black Claflin employees.[36]

Claflin president Lewis Dunton appealed to Governor Evans to reject Miller's measure, which the Claflin leader regarded as an unseemly bid for power by black leaders. "The colored men, including Mr. Miller, who are pushing for this immediate separation [of Claflin and the A&M school] have already announced themselves as candidates for the various positions." As an alternative Dunton suggested that either the president of Clemson or the president of the university should administer the new school.[37]

Dunton's wife in a separate letter marked "*strictly confidential*" blamed the impending separation on "a few col.[ored] peo.[ple]." They were, she alleged, "unscrupulous men [who] have dishonored our work + by dishonoring it succeeded in breaking it up." Mrs. Dunton begged the governor for help. "*Can we not claim your protection?* I breathlessly await your action." President Dunton wrote Evans again, insisting that the separation could not be quickly achieved because there would be "no chance of opening a college in two or three years," but their pleas were to no avail.[38]

THE NEW PUBLIC COLLEGE

On March 3, 1896, Thomas Miller's legislation was enacted. It severed the A&M school from Claflin and established "a Normal, Industrial, Agricultural and Mechanical College for the Colored Race." It explicitly called for an all-black faculty and a black president: "The Principal or President and corps of instructors shall be of the negro race." The law also stipulated that the institution would be "a branch of the University of South Carolina" but that it would be under the direction of a separate board of trustees. The new college never functioned as a branch of the white institution, and legislation that had placed S.C. State, the Citadel, and Winthrop under the university's authority was repealed in 1906.[39]

Miller later recalled the joy of his achievement. "Thank God," he exclaimed, "the College is in the hands of Negroes." However, he acknowledged and even praised white authorities who—although they were entirely unsympathetic to the aspirations of most black people—were also willing to have a black college run by black people. "[Coleman] Blease, Gov. [John Gary] Evans, [Benjamin] Tillman, [S. G.] Mayfield, [D. J.] Bradham, [J. W.] Floyd, and all the state officers assisted me in the fight, and were it not for Governor Evans, Blease, Tillman, and Chief Justice [Eugene B.] Gary, a white president and white professors would be in the State College today."[40]

On March 6, and one day before Miller resigned his seat in the house, he nominated in a joint session of the general assembly three of the six white men who were elected to the new institution's board of trustees. It was taken for granted that only white men would serve the black college as trustees. At least Miller had a part in determining who those white men would be. It would not be until 1966 that black men would be elected to serve as trustees of the black college.[41]

The new college was no longer connected to Claflin. But whether it was "in the hands of Negroes," and under genuine black control—as Miller claimed—is doubtful. By law its administrators, faculty, and staff were black. But its board of trustees and the state's political hierarchy were made up exclusively of white men. For seven decades they would pay careful attention to the college, and they exercised considerable influence and authority over its policies and even over many mundane matters. Furthermore the new board created a local committee made up of two trustees who were Orangeburg residents. They observed the day-to-day activities of the college and frequently involved themselves in campus concerns and the decision-making process.

Thomas Miller had been able to exploit a racial environment in 1896 that was decidedly hostile to black people and their interests to create an all-black college. At the same time Miller was urging the exclusion of white people from the faculty and administration of the college, the U.S. Supreme Court was deliberating the constitutionality of segregation in public facilities in the case of *Plessy v. Ferguson*. It announced its decision on May 18, 1896, and declared that "separate but equal" facilities did not deny black people equal protection of the law guaranteed by the Fourteenth Amendment to the U.S. Constitution. The Supreme Court's ruling opened the floodgates for states and municipalities to pass laws mandating racial segregation. Miller shrewdly took advantage of these prevailing racial sentiments to gain support for the creation of the state's only public institution of higher learning for its black residents.[42]

The new board of trustees met for the first time on April 10 with Governor John Gary Evans serving as chair. They proceeded to make arrangements with Claflin president Lewis Dunton to transfer real estate and other property to the new institution that had belonged to Claflin's A&M school. Dunton—still insisting the removal of the A&M school was premature—denied for a time that he had the authority to relinquish the property. But the board demanded, and Dunton finally and then graciously turned over control of 116 acres—much of it farm—and several agricultural facilities to the new school.[43]

On June 10 the board named Thomas Miller the president of the college. In a matter of minutes, Miller was interviewed, nominated, had the nomination seconded, and was appointed. There was no discussion or debate. The men who Miller had helped select for the board of trustees in March elected him president in June.[44]

CHAPTER ONE

The Early Years

As South Carolina State opened its doors in 1896, other doors were slamming shut on African Americans throughout the South and across the nation. Segregation laws mandating the separation of the races on railroad coaches, trolley cars, and steam boats, and in parks, auditoriums, and rest rooms proliferated in the aftermath of *Plessy v. Ferguson* decision. Black men were excluded almost entirely from the political system in South Carolina with the adoption of the 1895 constitution. Following the departure of John W. Bolts from the general assembly in 1902, there were no longer any black men serving in the state legislature. Because only qualified voters were eligible to serve on juries, very few black men and no women were summoned for jury duty.[1]

The epidemic of racial violence so closely identified with the South in the late nineteenth century continued unabated. One hundred and thirteen black men, four black women, and three white men were lynched in South Carolina between 1889 and 1918. On December 28, 1889, eight black men accused of killing a local merchant were forcibly removed from the Barnwell County jail and lynched. Frazier B. Baker, the newly appointed postmaster of Lake City, was killed in February 1898 by a mob of three hundred to four hundred people who did not want a black man supervising the town post office. During the Phoenix riot in Greenwood County later that year an unknown number of black men—perhaps a dozen—were slain after a white Republican candidate for Congress made an issue of black voting rights.[2]

Ten black men and one white man were lynched in Orangeburg County between 1880 and 1924. On January 6, 1897, a young black man, Lawrence Brown, was lynched less than three miles from the recently opened college. Brown allegedly burned a barn belonging to R. E. Wannamaker. Brown's body was found along the railroad track near present-day State A&M Road between St. Matthews Road and Route 601 in close proximity to land S.C. State would acquire some four decades later for a campus farm. Brown's family filed a lawsuit against Orangeburg County to recover damages, but a local judge dismissed it.[3]

It was in the midst of this depressing racial climate that Thomas Miller assembled a faculty and staff in Orangeburg to undertake the creation and operation of an educational institution that would serve the state's nearly eight hundred thousand black residents. But the appearance of the buildings and grounds that had been acquired from Claflin did not impress the first students who arrived at the new college that September and October 1896. James A. Pierce, one of those students, later recalled that it was "a very unattractive place with roads running in every direction and ending up

The first of three Bradham Halls was built in 1897 in part by students with timber harvested from the campus. It served as an academic building and dormitory, and it contained administrative offices. Named after one of the first members of the board of trustees, Major D. J. Bradham, it burned to the ground on November 24, 1909. Courtesy of Historical Collection, South Carolina State University

at no particular place. Deep gullies made by heavy rains were all through the center of the campus."[4]

The eight-acre campus had no running water, no sewer system, and no electricity. Fenn Cottage was a six-room structure inherited from Claflin, and it needed renovations before it became the president's residence. In the meantime Miller and his wife resided in town while their children remained with an aunt in Grahamville in Beaufort County. After Fenn was remodeled, the Miller family occupied one room that served as a bedroom, kitchen, dining room, and pantry. The five remaining rooms housed female teachers by night and were transformed into classrooms by day. For three months in 1896, twenty-five young men lived on the second floor of an eighteen-by-thirty-foot laundry building known as the Old Red Inn. It was an annex of the industrial building that had also been acquired from Claflin. For a brief time the first floor served as a chapel.[5]

Bradham Hall was completed in early 1897. It was an impressive three-and-a-half-story structure built largely of pine and oak timber that had come from trees cut down on the campus. Miller had acquired a used sawmill, and students and faculty members contributed much of the labor in the construction of Bradham. The multipurpose facility would serve as a dormitory for men, women, and female teachers. It included a dining hall, a chapel, classrooms, a library, an accountant's office, and President Miller's office. The new college also had a 130-acre farm that featured a barn, two mules, a small herd of dairy cattle, and a flock of chickens.[6]

THE A&M MISSION AND THOMAS E. MILLER

The college was a land-grant institution that would offer instruction in agricultural and mechanical skills as well as teacher training. Because so many of the state's black youngsters did not have access to primary and to secondary education, S.C. State would serve as a public school and a normal school during its earliest decades rather than as a bona fide college. There was a desperate need to provide basic education to a large portion of the state's black youth. As of 1900, 53 percent of the adult black population in South Carolina was illiterate, and just 45 percent of black children between the ages of ten and fourteen were enrolled in school.[7]

As an A&M institution, South Carolina State would offer instruction in keeping with the models established by Samuel Chapman Armstrong in 1868 at Virginia's Hampton Institute and by his disciple, Booker T. Washington, at Alabama's Tuskegee Institute in 1881. Students would master agricultural and vocational skills as well as a dedication to hard work, thrift, and morality that would enable them to become productive members of society. In an address at the Bamberg County Colored Fair in 1897 President Thomas Miller explained the mission of S.C. State. "The work of our college is along the industrial line. We are making educated and worthy school teachers, educated and reliable mechanics, educated, reliable and frugal farmers. We teach your sons and daughters how to care for and milk the cows, how to make gilt-edged butter, how to make cheese, what kind of fertilizer each crop needs, the natural strength and productive qualities of the various soils, and last to make a compost heap and how to take care of it. We teach them how to make a wagon, plow and hoe, how to shoe a horse and nurse him when sick. We teach your children how to keep books and typewrite, we teach your girls how to make a dress or undergarment, how to cook, wash and iron. We teach your boys how to make and run an engine, how to make and control electricity, we teach them mechanical and artistic drawing, house and sign painting."[8]

Miller's commitment to agricultural and mechanical training belied his own educational experiences and career. He was a lawyer and a politician who had a curious and intriguing upbringing. He was born in 1849 in Ferrebeeville in Beaufort District. His mother was Mary Bird, a slave with a very fair complexion and blue eyes. She was owned by Proctor Scriven, who was also Miller's father. Scriven was stabbed to death in 1850, and Miller would then take the name of his stepfather, Richard Miller. Mary Bird died when he was nine. He attended schools for free black children in Charleston and, by his recollection, mostly raised himself.

Thomas Miller has the dubious distinction as the only person ever employed by S.C. State who wore a Confederate uniform during the Civil War. As a youngster he was employed to ride the train and deliver the *Charleston Mercury* to railroad stations between Charleston and Savannah. In 1864, with the Confederacy facing grave manpower shortages, he was employed at the ripe age of fifteen as assistant conductor on the railroad. With the railroad under the direct control of the Confederate government, Miller was compelled to wear the gray uniform. In early 1865 he was captured by Union troops and briefly imprisoned near Savannah. After his release he accompanied the Twenty-Fourth New York Regiment, a black unit, when they returned to their home state, where he enrolled in public school for a time in Hudson, New York.[9]

He attended Howard University and graduated from Pennsylvania's Lincoln University in 1872. Then Miller enrolled in law courses at South Carolina College (now the University of South Carolina) during Reconstruction, when black men were admitted

By education and experience, President Thomas E. Miller was a lawyer and politician. As the president of a land-grant institution, he had to familiarize himself with the campus farm and several of its four-legged residents. Notice he has his right hand extended in a "V for victory" salute. Courtesy of Historical Collection, South Carolina State University

to that institution. He was admitted to the bar in 1875 and practiced law in Beaufort, where he had been elected school commissioner in 1872.

Miller served in the state house of representatives and then the state senate from 1874 to 1882. He became chairman of the state Republican Party in 1882. He lost election to the U.S. House in 1886 but defeated William Elliott in 1888 after a prolonged electoral controversy. Miller served in the U.S. House in 1890 and 1891. He lost his bid for reelection in 1890 in another contentious election dispute. In 1892 he lost to George W. Murray, another black man, who made a campaign issue of Miller's light complexion. Murray denigrated Miller as "Canary" because of his fair color. While continuing to practice law in Beaufort, he ran successfully for the state house of representatives in 1894, and in 1895 he was elected as one of the six black delegates to the constitutional convention in which he played such a pivotal role.[10]

FACULTY AND STUDENTS

With one exception the faculty that Miller assembled in 1896 lacked agricultural and mechanical training. Robert Shaw Wilkinson, a native of Charleston, was a graduate of Oberlin College. He taught at the black State University in Louisville and received a honorary Ph.D. from that institution in 1898. He would be a professor of mathematics, mechanics, and physics at S.C. State. William R. A. Palmer, who had taught at Claflin, attended Howard University and Drew Theological Seminary. He was a professor of ancient and English classics. Isaac N. Cardozo attended Oberlin and taught mental and moral science as well as pedagogics. Matthew W. Gilbert attended Benedict College and Colgate University. He taught history, political science, and modern languages.[11]

The only ranking faculty member in 1896 who possessed agricultural training was John Wesley Hoffman, who taught agriculture and agricultural chemistry. He claimed a Ph.D. and had attended Howard University, Michigan Agricultural College (now Michigan State University), and Harvard University. Hoffman taught with Wilkinson at the State University in Louisville in the early 1890s. Nelson C. Nix was a Claflin graduate who taught mathematics. Louise Bonneau Fordham graduated from Charleston's Avery Institute and earned a bachelor's degree while first teaching art and drawing and then history at S.C. State. Henry P. Butler taught literature, logic, and Latin. He was a graduate of Lincoln University. In addition there were several faculty members who had little or no college education who taught many of the agricultural and industrial courses.[12]

More than 80 percent of the students who made their way to S.C. State in its early years came from farm families. Although by 1900 black people were amassing land at a more rapid rate than white people and by 1910 over one-quarter of black farmers cultivated their own land, most of them held small parcels. Black families owned 84.1 percent of farms between three and nine acres. But black farmers possessed only 28.6 percent of the value of all farm property in South Carolina. Still most rural black families in South Carolina did not possess even small farms. They struggled to survive as sharecroppers and tenant farmers. Poverty and not prosperity marked their lives.[13]

However, those young people who were able to attend S.C. State in its formative years came mostly from families who owned land and were on the upper economic margins among rural black residents. In 1904 W. T. B. Williams, who was a black field agent for the General Education Board, visited the college and reported landownership among student families. "For instance, in one class 31 out of 54 came from farms of more than 10 acres. 19 of these came from farms over 100 acres. 1 had 400 acres, 1 had [indecipherable] and 1 had 800 acres. 11 of the remainder owned homes in towns and cities."[14]

The most education that most of the state's black youngsters could aspire to—including those from land-owning families—amounted to little more than basic instruction in reading, writing, and arithmetic. The chance to attend secondary school was exceedingly remote. There was not one black public high school in South Carolina in 1900. The state spent a paltry $1.30 for each black child actually attending school, and 55 percent of black children were not even enrolled. The state spent a comparatively generous $5.55 on each white pupil. The average annual salary for a black teacher was $80.68, about $1.00 per day for a school term that lasted about eighty days. Twenty-two percent of the state funds for education went to black public schools in 1900.[15]

And these grim statistics do not begin to offer a meaningful glimpse into the lives of the people represented by the numbers. What was the impact of the ramshackle schools and poorly prepared teachers on children whose parents had had little or no

Table 1. Enrollment at South Carolina State College, 1896–97

College	27
Preparatory	26
Normal	89
Special students	**36**
Total	178
Kindergarten to 8th grade	855
Grand total	1,033

Source: *Catalogue and Special Announcements of the Colored Normal, Industrial, Agricultural and Mechanical College of South Carolina, 1896–1897* (Orangeburg: Parks and Cannon, 1897), 68–69.

access to education themselves? The likelihood that a young black person might acquire a secondary education and then attend college seemed like a wild impossibility to all but the most perseverant youngster. Those black youth who did manage to escape the sun and the soil of rural South Carolina were typically prepared to continue their primary schooling or possibly embark on secondary education. They were not ready for genuine college work.

Thus at the dawn of the twentieth century, South Carolina's black institutions—S.C. State, Benedict, and Allen—were each identified as colleges, but they served mainly as primary, secondary, and teacher-training schools. Young Benjamin Mays typified the black child from rural South Carolina who yearned for more education. He had attended the one-room Brickhouse School in Greenwood County, "so I wanted to go to Benedict College in Columbia, South Carolina, or State College in Orangeburg," where he could continue his education. In 1911 he applied to their high school programs. "I chose State College because it was less expensive."[16]

Young people applying for admission to S.C. State in its earliest years were expected to "have a knowledge of the ordinary branches of an English education." Prospective students were administered an entrance exam and then, based on their performance, placed in one of the higher or lower grades. Benjamin Mays took the test and was told that he belonged in the eighth grade.[17]

Of the 1,033 students who attended State College during its first year, 855 were enrolled in kindergarten through eighth grade. About one-third of the students were Orangeburg children. Local parents enrolled their youngsters in the primary program because the college charged no tuition. There were only twenty-seven students registered in the college curriculum. Olive Sasportas, who had transferred from Claflin, was the first graduate of the college program in 1897.[18]

In 1898 the general assembly authorized S.C. State to award graduates of the normal program a licentiate of instruction diploma, which qualified them to teach in the

Ernest E. Just was among the first students to enroll at S.C. State in 1896. He came from Maryville on James Island near Charleston. He completed the preparatory program in 1899. He went on to Kimball Union Academy and graduated from Dartmouth College. After earning a Ph.D. at the University of Chicago, he became an acclaimed marine biologist. He taught for many years at Howard University, where he was among the founders of Omega Phi Psi fraternity in 1911. Courtesy of Historical Collection, South Carolina State University

state's black public schools. Students had to be at least fourteen years of age to enroll. The normal program expanded from two to three years in 1908–9. The following year the faculty asked the board of trustees to increase the normal program to four years to "give the students more time for thorough preparation in the several trades and in agriculture." The board agreed, "in order to better equip the graduates to teach their race, inasmuch as the great majority of the students never return for higher degrees." In the meantime the kindergarten was abolished in 1904.[19]

Ernest E. Just was one of the first students to enroll at S.C. State in 1896, and he was among the first to earn a licentiate of instruction. He was also one of the exceptional few who did go on to earn a higher degree, but not at S.C. State. Just was thirteen years old when he arrived in Orangeburg from Maryville, a small community on James Island near Charleston. He was four when his father died. His mother worked in the phosphate mines and organized a local school that her son attended before he came to S.C. State. After he received his L.I. in 1899, he decided against teaching in the public schools. Instead he journeyed to Meriden, New Hampshire, where he enrolled in Kimball Union Academy. He graduated magna cum laude from Dartmouth College in 1907 and earned a doctorate in zoology from the University of Chicago in 1916.

Just taught at Howard University in Washington, D.C., and conducted research at the Marine Biology Laboratory at Woods Hole, Massachusetts. He received a research grant in 1928 from the Rosenwald Fund, which enabled him to pursue research in Italy,

Germany, and France. He published dozens of scientific papers and was the author of *Biology of the Cell Surface* and *Basic Methods for Experiments on Eggs of Marine Animals*. He died of cancer in 1941.[20]

A PRACTICAL EDUCATION

For much of its early history, the college—its white trustees and black administrators—made a concerted effort to persuade and even compel young men and women to participate in vocational training associated with the A&M program. By the first decade of the twentieth century, every student—except those in the primary school—was required to select an agricultural or industrial course of study and pursue it while they attended S.C. State.

Among those A&M courses of study available to students were agriculture and dairying; blacksmithing and ironworking; wheelwrighting, carpentry and woodworking; sewing, dressmaking, and millinery; cooking and domestic economy; and nurse training. By 1904 tailoring, shoemaking, and harness making had been added to the program. Students who mastered these skills were awarded a certificate, but they were not classified as graduates. College trustees were convinced that "students that leave this school will be self sustaining and not parasites on the body politic."[21]

William T. B. Williams, the black representative of the General Education Board, offered an evaluation of the various vocational programs during his 1904 visit. He was not impressed with carpentry. "It is not scientifically done, and will not produce carpenters of a high order, I believe." The masonry program was better, and "the blacksmithing department does very good work." "There were several good wagons" on display as examples of the skills taught in wheelwrighting. The tailoring program was new and "not yet well developed." The students in tailoring were making uniforms for the baseball team during Williams's visit. He believed that the vocational program needed supervision by "a specially trained director of industries."[22]

S.C. State was the only public institution in South Carolina that educated large numbers of both males and females. Students in the agricultural and trades courses tended—not surprisingly—to be segregated by sex. Only men enrolled in ironworking, wheelwrighting, masonry, and harness making, while only women took courses in domestic economy, sewing, and dressmaking. There were, however, males and females in dairy courses, cheese making, architectural drawing, and mechanical drawing. For a time females were encouraged to enroll in tailoring. "Young women are admitted to this department as equals of men, and many of them show real aptitude." In 1904–5 there were eighty-seven males and eleven females in tailoring. But by 1909–10 there were fifty men and no women in tailoring.[23]

To foster an appreciation of manual labor and to contribute significantly to the expansion and development of the campus, students were required to work for the college. In 1896 students over the age of twelve had to work for two hours per week for five cents per hour in addition to any labor required in their courses of study. By 1906–7 the minimum age for labor increased to fourteen, and the catalog indicated that especially industrious students might earn as much as $3 to $5 a month.[24]

The campus sawmill prepared timber to construct Bradham and Morrill Halls as well as other campus buildings. It offered students an opportunity to work and acquire vocational skills. President Thomas Miller is on the right. Courtesy of the Historical Collection, South Carolina State University

Student labor literally built the campus. Under faculty supervision students aided substantially in the construction of every new building erected during the college's first quarter century. In 1896–97 the student-operated sawmill processed eighty thousand feet of timber, most of which was used in the construction of Bradham Hall. They prepared 130,000 feet of flooring, weather boards, molding, trim, window, and door frames. Students built twenty dining-hall tables, seventy-five washstands for the dormitory, and benches for classroom use. In 1904–5 students built a new boiler plant and installed all the equipment needed to operate the steam plant. The two-story 120-by-90-foot industrial hall was built of brick, "everyone of which was laid by student labor." By 1910 students had installed a generator that provided electricity to the college, and they built a much-needed sewage system. Were it not for thousands and thousands of hours of student labor, the college might not have developed much less endured.[25]

Students not only worked on campus; many were called home in the middle of the school term to labor with their families in harvesting crops in the fall and planting them in the spring. Enrollments fluctuated wildly during the school year as students continuously arrived and departed from the campus. College regulations merely required that students attend and pay their boarding fees in no less than one-month increments, and that they could leave only if a parent or guardian notified the college president in writing.

It was difficult to maintain a formal academic schedule under such an arrangement. With the school year for so many students severely limited by the necessity to work at home, the college did not close for the Christmas holidays. Students continued to attend class, perform labor, and take examinations through December. School was suspended most years only on Christmas and New Year's days. The first commencement was held May 5, 1897, because the college had to conclude its initial year "to accommodate those who must return home to work."[26]

Most students pursued their education erratically. Often they were unable to meet the requirements for a college degree, a licentiate of instruction, or even a diploma from the preparatory program. By 1906 seventy-eight hundred young people had attended South Carolina State, but just 298 had graduated from one of the programs. Benjamin E. Mays was typical of many students during the early years of the college. He arrived from the tiny community of Epworth in Greenwood County in 1911 and enrolled in the eighth grade at age sixteen. "For the first two years at State College I was called home at the end of February, according to custom, to work on the farm. I was vividly aware that time has swift wings. I was nineteen and not once in my life had I been able to remain in school more than four months in any year."[27]

Mays graduated at age twenty-two from the preparatory (or high school) program in 1916. He spent a year at Virginia Union College before enrolling at Bates College in Lewiston, Maine, where he earned a bachelor's degree in 1920. He married Ellen Harvin—"a beautiful, well balanced, charming girl"—shortly after he finished at Bates. The couple had met more than four years earlier while they were students at S.C. State. Unfortunately Ellen Harvin Mays suffered a miscarriage and died in 1923 following unsuccessful surgery. She was buried near her Pinewood home in Manning, South Carolina.[28]

Unlike Mays most students at S.C. State did not graduate from the preparatory academy. Still they benefited from the knowledge that they did acquire—often haphazardly—at the college. Many undoubtedly enrolled without the intention of securing a diploma or degree, but instead they wanted to learn a skill or acquire sufficient knowledge to improve themselves and their families. To that extent the college fulfilled its mission.[29]

LAND-GRANT INSTITUTIONS

The emphasis on agricultural and mechanical training that figured so prominently in the early development of South Carolina State fit—but not always comfortably—into the educational environment that prevailed across the nation as America entered the twentieth century. Students at land-grant institutions would be armed with the practical knowledge and useful skills that would enable them to contribute to an expanding and more complex economy based increasingly on science, engineering, and technology.[30]

By 1896 there were fifty-seven land-grant schools with thirteen hundred faculty and fourteen thousand students. Between 1880 and 1899, twenty-four additional land-grant colleges had been established, including eleven separate black land-grant institutions. Many of these institutions began to shed their narrow nineteenth-century mission as mere A&M schools that confined themselves largely to preparing students for farming and homemaking.[31]

But this expansion of the land-grant institutions into full-fledged comprehensive universities that included more diverse course work, research, and experimentation did not include the black land-grant colleges. Most white Americans accepted the tenants of social Darwinism and white supremacy at the dawn of the twentieth century, and thus there was no reason for black land-grant schools to offer sophisticated and advanced course work. Their faculty could not teach it, and their students could not comprehend it. Even those white political and educational leaders who stressed the importance of education for African Americans typically doubted the capacity of black youngsters to learn much more than rudimentary academic subjects as they mastered manual labor. Students at South Carolina State would learn harness making, wheelwrighting, sewing, and cheese making rather than the engineering, veterinary medicine, or architecture that emerged at the white A&M schools.

When state superintendent of education W. D. Mayfield spoke on campus at the dedication of Bradham Hall in 1897 he advised students and faculty members to avoid the humanities and to focus on vocational education. "One pupil with a practical education and skilled hands sent out from your college will be worth more to the community in which he locates than a dozen you may send out with a smattering of Greek and Latin or of the higher branches, and with unskilled hands."

Mayfield also endorsed segregation and recommended that those black people associated with the new college not only accept Jim Crow but that they actively promote racial separation. "You can do no greater service to your State than to turn out from your walls those who will appreciate the necessity and propriety of keeping the races separate and distinct, and who will impress this on your people at all times wherever they go, and who will not attempt or permit others to attempt social equality between the races."[32]

EDUCATION FOR SUBORDINATION?

This emphasis on practical training for African Americans combined with tolerance for the racial status quo reflected the educational ideology of Samuel Chapman Armstrong, Hampton Institute's white founder, and his prize pupil, Booker T. Washington. Both men were convinced that African Americans—but a few short decades removed from slavery—would be best prepared to advance themselves and their people by learning agricultural and mechanical skills and by combining those skills with hard work, thrift, and Christian virtues.[33]

Booker T. Washington, a former slave who attended Hampton Institute and founded Tuskegee Institute, articulated his program for racial advancement in his remarkable 1895 address at the Cotton States Exposition in Atlanta. He urged black people to seek their fortunes in the South. "It is in the South that a Negro is given a man's chance in the commercial world." In three short sentences, he praised agricultural training, dismissed literary pursuits, and told black people not to complain. "No race can prosper till it learns that there is as much dignity in tilling a field as in writing a poem. It is at the bottom of life we must begin, and not at the top. Nor should we permit out grievances to overshadow our opportunities."

Then in a striking metaphor, Washington went on to urge acceptance of segregation. "In all things that are purely social we can be as separate as the fingers, yet one as the hand in all things essential to mutual progress." He condemned political protest. "The wisest among my race understand that the agitation of questions of social equality is the extremist folly, and that progress in the enjoyment of all the privileges that will come to us must be the result of severe and constant struggle rather than artificial forcing." Few words uttered by an African American have ever struck a more responsive chord among white Americans as well as among many black people than Washington's impassioned willingness to accept the prevailing economic and racial views.[34]

Not everyone, however, shared these sentiments. Writing in 1903 black scholar and activist W. E. B. Du Bois did agree with Washington that vocational training and the values linked to it were suitable for most black people. "So far as Mr. Washington preaches Thrift, Patience, and Industrial Training for the masses, we must hold up his hands and strive with him." But Du Bois felt compelled to oppose Washington and most other Americans because they tolerated the harmful effects of white supremacy and were unwilling to support genuine collegiate education for black people. "But so far as Mr. Washington apologizes for injustice, North or South, does not rightly value the privilege and duty of voting, belittles the emasculating effects of caste distinctions, and opposes higher training and ambition of our brighter minds,—so far as he, the South, or the Nation, does this,—we must unceasingly and firmly oppose them."[35]

Du Bois demanded that the more gifted members of the race—those he characterized as the Talented Tenth—should have access to educational opportunities that would allow them to become scholars and leaders. "If white people need colleges to furnish teachers, ministers, lawyers, and doctors, do black people need nothing of the sort?" Black youngsters, Du Bois asserted, need to possess sharp minds as well as skilled hands. They needed opportunities for introspection, reflection, and creation. Such young men and women would assist in resolving America's race problem, and the black college would play a critical role in that effort. "The function of the Negro college, then, is clear: it must maintain the standards of popular education, it must seek the social regeneration of the Negro, and it must help in the solution of problems of race contact and cooperation."[36]

Students and faculty at S.C. State neither openly embraced nor categorically rejected the views of either Washington or Du Bois. It was more complicated than that. They accepted agricultural and mechanical training, but they also opposed attempts to limit their access to the liberal arts. Of the 1,033 students enrolled in 1896–97 from kindergarten through college, 553 were taking A&M classes that ranged from woodworking and agriculture to cooking and domestic economy. The sizable number of students in the lower grades of the elementary program did not take A&M classes. The small number of students in the college curriculum in agriculture were required to take a curious combination of courses by their senior year that included Chemistry of Plant Growth, Soils and Fertilizer, History of Political Economy, Spraying of Plants, Pedagogics, and Constitutional Law.[37]

Booker T. Washington paid a visit to Orangeburg during a whirlwind one-week tour of South Carolina in March 1909. According to the local newspaper, he told several hundred black people assembled at Claflin that he had come to "inspire the negroes to higher and better things in life and to cement the already friendly relations existing between the two races in the South, especially South Carolina."[38]

THE HUMANITIES

Faculty members who taught literature, language, history, political science, math, and natural sciences reflected W. E. B. Du Bois's appreciation for Western culture as well his dedication to the heritage of African Americans. Only weeks after the college opened, the faculty agreed to organize a celebration of Emancipation Day on January 1, 1897. Professor Matthew W. Gilbert, who taught history, political science, and modern languages, would be the featured speaker. But the faculty disagreed over the propriety of commemorating Robert E. Lee's birthday, which was a state holiday. Robert S. Wilkinson offered a resolution to celebrate the Confederate general's birthday. Isaac N. Cardozo and William R. A. Palmer objected to such recognition. A few months later literature professor William R. A. Palmer recommended that the institution set aside December 17, 1897, to honor New England poet John Greenleaf Whittier. In 1905 the faculty agreed to observe Frederick Douglass Day on February 14 at the same time they would honor the birthdays of Abraham Lincoln and George Washington.[39]

With faculty encouragement students formed two literary societies—the Pierian and the Douglass—by 1904. These organizations, which met each Friday and Saturday evening, stressed "training in self-restraint and self-command, in parliamentary procedure, and in aptness of studied and impromptu speech." Members were required to attend and to participate actively in the meetings. At the end of the school term, the two societies competed against each other as members made formal presentations.[40]

The first commencement exercises were held over several days in early May 1897, and a number of students delivered a series of speeches that had more to do with African American history than with agriculture or trades. Second-year normal student Ella Robinson delivered a speech entitled "The Negro in History," and first-year normal student Florence Price spoke on Frederick Douglass. A speech by A. C. Garrison, a second-year preparatory student, was entitled "Manliness among Students," and first-year preparatory student P. D. Sims delivered the speech "The Negro in the American Revolution."[41]

By the time that Benjamin E. Mays arrived on the campus more than a decade later, the interest in literary and historical subjects was discouraged in favor of the college's A&M mission. "At commencement if the valedictorian had majored in English or history, the president saw to it that some boy or girl always gave a speech extolling the glories of agriculture and the trades."[42]

The evolving role of President Thomas E. Miller reflected the gradually greater importance that agriculture and mechanical subjects assumed at the college. As a lawyer and politician, Miller had no background or training in agriculture or trades. In 1896 he was designated "President and Professor of Constitutional Law." In 1900 he took on the task of teaching agriculture; by 1906–7 he was listed as "President and Director of the Agricultural, Industrial and Mechanical Departments, and Professor of Agriculture."[43]

When the first students were admitted in 1896 they were required to complete two years of Latin if they were enrolled in the college, normal, preparatory, or agricultural programs. Moreover college students embarked on the classical course of study had to take two years of Greek as well. But the all-white board of trustees insisted that the college focus on its A&M mission, and they quickly abolished the classical languages—but not without a protest. Thomas Miller acknowledged the dissatisfaction. "One or two preachers in the State may tell you that the State colored college is not the place to send your children because they cannot learn Latin and Greek, but such is not the case." He explained that the two languages were taught privately with the approval of the trustees.

The academic faculty petitioned the board in 1904 to restore Latin to the curriculum. The board hesitated until the alumni association appealed for the restoration of both Latin and Greek in 1905. The board partly relented and agreed to require Latin in the last two years of the normal program. This uneasy relationship between the humanities and the vocational curriculum would persist for decades because there were invariably students and faculty members who looked to life beyond the field and farm and hoped for a future that might embrace science, the law, religion, or medicine.[44]

William T. B. Williams did not much care for what he saw of the academic program during his 1904 visit. He noted that there was a steady turnover of faculty members that weakened the institution because "from year to year that uniformity and continuity of effort is almost impossible." The program needed more teachers, more money, and smaller classes.[45]

BEYOND THE CLASSROOM

Life at South Carolina State involved more than learning and labor. There were extracurricular activities. From its inception college authorities considered athletics integral to the development of students, especially young men. "The college athlete of to-day is neither a coward nor a dullard, he is both manly and studious." By 1898 students had organized an athletic association, but football was considered too violent and was initially forbidden.[46]

The ban on football was lifted in 1907 as S.C. State teams competed against other black schools on the gridiron. In one of their first games, S.C. State defeated Georgia State (which is now Savannah State) in Savannah. W. C. Lewis not only coached the team; he played and was injured in what was described as a "tough battle." (After that rugged contest, Lewis might have had second thoughts about lifting the ban on football.) John Mitchell, who was an end on that first team, later recalled that they played Howard High School of Columbia, Biddle College (which became Johnson C. Smith), Shaw, Livingstone and Haines Institute of Augusta. Henry P. Butler assisted Coach Lewis.[47]

Baseball and tennis were also part of the athletic program. A modest athletic complex had been built that included a track and areas for jumps, the pole vault, and the hammer throw. The two coaches who also served on the faculty, Lewis and Butler, administered the athletic association under President Miller's supervision. Lewis would play a particularly influential role in the emergence of the athletic program. College officials soon felt compelled to defend themselves against accusations that sports received undue emphasis. "It is the opinion of the Faculty that whatever excesses there may be in college athletics may best be held in check by sympathetic rather than repressive government."[48]

Religious activities and spiritual beliefs assumed a far larger role in the lives of most students and faculty than did athletics. The college may have been a public institution, but it was not a secular one. For many Americans—especially African Americans—the church was not separate from the state but was more important than the state. Certainly African Americans took a greater interest in and derived more satisfaction from religious activities at the turn of the century than they did from involvement in politics or government. The first college catalog declared emphatically that although there was to be "no hypocritical pretension toward imparting religious culture, it is the aim of those in authority to inculcate in the minds of students the teachings of Christ as exemplified on the cross, untrammeled by creeds." Therefore Bible study was mandatory, as was attendance at religious services.[49]

Several of the early annual reports identified the religious affiliation of the students. The overwhelming number of them were Baptists and Methodists. President Miller was a devout Presbyterian who played a key role in the founding of St. Luke Presbyterian Church. Nelson C. Nix, the dean of the faculty, was a minister at Mount Pisgah Baptist Church.

The YMCA was perhaps the most important student organization—religious or otherwise—during the college's first half century. Active on campus since 1896, it offered students an opportunity to participate in activities among themselves as well as with YMCA students at other institutions. S.C. State students regularly attended regional and national meetings of the YMCA. There was also the Young People' Society of Christian Endeavor, which met every Sunday evening. It enabled students to join together and "to throw around them[selves] the safeguards of religion" to protect against those sinful and predatory influences that might afflict youth on a college campus.[50]

By the terms of the 1862 Morrill Act, land-grant institutions were required to offer military training to male students. S.C. State offered that training to young men who would have no more than very limited opportunities to use their military knowledge and experiences to serve in the U.S. armed forces. The U.S. Army was rigidly segregated following the Civil War. Black men were permitted to enlist only in the all-black Twenty-Fourth and Twenty-Fifth Infantry Regiments and the Ninth and Tenth Cavalry Regiments, which distinguished themselves as the Buffalo Soldiers on the western frontier in the late nineteenth century. When the S.C. State board of trustees asked the War Department to furnish a black officer to take charge of military training in 1896, they were informed that no black officer was available. As a result physics professor Robert S. Wilkinson was placed in command of the college battalion. Although he had no formal military experience, he had qualified for admission to the U.S. Military Academy at West Point before he was rejected because he could not meet the physical requirements.[51]

Table 2. Religious Affiliation of South Carolina State Students, 1907–8

Denomination	Number
Baptist	310
African Methodist Episcopal	228
Methodist Episcopal	80
Presbyterian	17
Episcopal	6
Congregational	2
AME Zion	2
Roman Catholic	1
Unknown	5
Total	651

Source: Thirteenth Annual Report of the Board of Trustees of the Colored Normal, Industrial, Agricultural and Mechanical College of South Carolina, *Reports and Resolutions of the General Assembly of South Carolina* (Columbia: Gonzales and Bryan, 1909), 1120.

All physically able male students over the age of fourteen were required to take part in military exercises and ceremonies. The college battalion consisted of four companies as well as a signal corps and band. Military exercises took place for one hour per day, three days a week, during the first thirteen weeks of the fall term and the last thirteen weeks of the spring term. Students were also required to participate in recitations, and senior cadets had to write an essay on a military subject. Cadets had to purchase a dark-blue uniform with state of South Carolina buttons and a cap. The cost of the uniform ranged from $8 to $15 depending on the quality of the fabric. The cap was $1.50, and an optional overcoat was $15. By 1906 students in tailoring classes were making the uniforms. Although they were not part of the military program, female students were also required to purchase and wear a blue dress uniform and a cap.[52]

In 1900 Johnson C. Whittaker joined the faculty and took over the military science program. He also taught chemistry and mathematics and later became principal of the preparatory department—the high school. Whittaker had been born a slave in 1858 near Camden and was a student at South Carolina College during Reconstruction before he was admitted to the U.S. Military Academy in 1876. He became involved in one of the most controversial and disgraceful cases in the history of the military academy in 1880 when he was found slashed, bloody, and bound in his barracks room. He demanded a court martial to clear his name and reputation, but he was found guilty of mutilating himself to draw attention away from an allegedly mediocre academic record. President Chester Arthur overturned the verdict, but Whittaker was expelled from the academy anyway. He did not receive his commission in the U.S. Army until it was awarded posthumously by President Bill Clinton in 1995.

S.C. State academic faculty of the early twentieth century. From left to right, first row: Otis Cecil Davenport Council, model school teacher; Louise B. Fordham, instructor in art; Julia A. McClain Douglass, instructor in elementary teaching; Olive Sasportas, instructor in English. Second row: Eugene F. Mikell, band and orchestra; Alice B. McCloud, instructor in English; Lillian C. Mack, instructor in English; Johnson C. Whittaker, professor of math and commandant of the cadet corps. Courtesy of the Historical Collection, South Carolina State University

Following his dismissal from West Point in 1882, Whittaker returned to South Carolina, married, studied and practiced law, and taught school for several years in Sumter. He then spent eight years in Orangeburg on the faculty of South Carolina State before moving with his wife and two sons to Oklahoma City in 1908, where he taught and eventually became the principal of all-black Frederick Douglass High School. He then returned to State College in 1925 and was still on the faculty when he died in 1931.[53]

As commandant of the corps at S.C. State, Whittaker was a stern disciplinarian who would brook no nonsense but almost never raised his voice. He rarely mentioned his West Point experience. He would walk the campus with a ramrod-straight military bearing, often humming a hymn. He opened his classes in mathematics with a brief prayer.[54]

Francis Eugene Mikell was the director of the marching band from 1898 to 1906. This was a military ensemble that regrettably did not appear at the intermission of football games. It accompanied male students who participated in military drills, and it sometimes led students as they marched to the dining hall. Mikell was a talented musician who assumed leadership over the band while still in his early twenties. Born in Charleston in 1880, he attended Avery Institute and helped direct the renowned Jenkins Orphanage Band.

Before his marriage in 1903, Mikell became involved with an unnamed female student who had been suspended from the college. In May 1901 Mikell admitted to President Miller and the board of trustees that he had been missing from the campus for several days and that he "had been more or less intimate" with the young woman for "the entire session." The board treated his absence and indiscretion leniently, reprimanding and suspending him for one week without pay.[55]

By 1906 Mikell had left S.C. State, and he went on to a prominent career as a conductor and composer. After directing the band and orchestra at Tuskegee and overseeing the girl's band at Cookman Institute in Daytona Beach, Florida, he settled in New York City. Mikell was commissioned a first lieutenant during World War I and led the Fifteenth Regiment Band for six weeks in Paris. Involved with several musical organizations, he also conducted the Clef Club Orchestra. He composed several works including the "State College Cadet March," the "369th Regimental March," and the "Great Camp Meeting" that was created for the 1921 black Broadway musical "Shuffle Along," starring Noble Sissle and Eubie Blake.[56]

THE CAMPUS

The development and construction of physical facilities for the new college was agonizingly slow and exasperatingly difficult. That gradual but steady progress occurred is testimony to the tenacity of Miller and the faculty, staff, and students. While the board of trustees was generally—but not always—supportive, the general assembly was invariably reluctant to appropriate funds for the black college. Even providing basic necessities proved daunting.

It took more than a decade to bring electricity, an adequate water supply, and a sewage system to the campus. Kerosene lamps initially provided illumination but posed a danger of fire until they were replaced by acetylene gas in 1907. Miller complained, however, that the gas was harmful to the eyes and that it was expensive. As early as 1896–97, the president had asked the legislature to appropriate funds to generate electricity. It was not until 1909 that a generator was installed to light the campus and to furnish power for the vocational program in electricity.[57]

There was not an ample supply of cheap water. The college relied on water furnished by the city of Orangeburg and by a campus well. The industrial machinery, the farm, and the students required several thousand gallons of water each day. Water was also needed in the event of fire. By 1909 it cost the college $800 a year for city water. Miller asked the general assembly for $2,000 to dig another well and to install pumps and tanks to reduce the reliance on city water. The trustees endorsed Miller's request as a cost-reduction measure, but the legislature did not appropriate the funds.[58]

Beginning in 1903–4 the college began to install indoor plumbing and a sewage system to replace outdoor facilities. Student labor laid thirteen hundred feet of twelve-inch pipes that drained the sewage into a ditch "dug down to the swamp." In 1908 the city of Orangeburg mandated the installation of flush toilets, and Miller asked for and

Designed by William Gruber, Morrill Hall's imposing six-story frame structure was built in 1899 and was destroyed by fire on October 21, 1916. It was named for Republican senator Justin Morrill of Vermont, the lawmaker credited with passage of the 1862 and 1890 Morrill Land-Grant Acts. Courtesy of the Historical Collection, South Carolina State University

received $3,500 from the legislature to connect the campus to the city sewage system. In spite of the city regulations, the system was not finished for several years, and the young men living in Morrill Hall lacked indoor plumbing. However, this disagreeable state of affairs presented young Benjamin E. Mays with an opportunity for a job. He cleaned outhouses after midnight. "This was nauseating work, but it paid six dollars a month," he recalled.[59]

Bradham Hall and Morrill Hall were the first two major buildings erected on the campus. Both were frame, constructed largely of extremely flammable pine timber. Bradham, finished in 1897, contained fifty-six dormitory rooms that housed 250 students, a dining room, six classrooms, and Miller's office. Wood stoves furnished heat. Like Bradham, Morrill Hall was a three-and one-half-story structure. William Gruber, who was the superintendent of woodwork and machinery, designed it. It consisted of fifty-two dormitory rooms, a chapel, sixteen classrooms, and "three tower rooms for astronomical and observatory purposes." It was completed in 1899 and had a system of steam heat installed by students.[60]

With no indoor plumbing, the young men who resided there took a bath once a week. L. M. Tobin, who arrived on campus in 1915, explained that each dormitory room had a tin bathtub. "Our hot water for the weekly bath was brought from the boiler room. From seven to eleven o'clock each Saturday night the bucket brigade would be in process. In passing the girls' dormitory the boys would take the opportunity to call, the ladies from the windows, thus reminding them that the weekly ablution was about to be made."[61]

Fire was a constant worry. President Miller repeatedly warned that—with mostly timber construction, wood stoves, kerosene lamps, and the absence of a reliable water system—there was a serious danger of a campus conflagration. Fire drills were held regularly. By 1907 fire escapes had been added to Bradham and Morrill halls. The college purchased five hundred feet of fire hose, and students built a hose wagon.[62]

In spite of the precautions, Miller's fears were justified. On November 24, 1909, Bradham Hall burned to the ground. There were no injuries or loss of life. The fire began in the space between the ceiling of the second story and the floor of the third story, and it was detected just after 6 P.M., when most students were dining. The fire could have been contained. But chemical fire tanks proved almost useless, and there was insufficient water pressure when fire hoses were connected to the city system. In two hours the building and its contents as well as the adjoining dining hall and kitchen "were a bed of ashes." There had been time to remove college records from the president's and the accountant's offices. The 130 female students housed in Bradham were sent home because there were no accommodations available on campus. The loss was estimated at $17,000. There was inadequate insurance coverage because underwriters refused to insure fully such a flammable structure.[63]

It would cost considerably more than $17,000 to replace Bradham. Miller and the board of trustees appealed to the state legislature for an emergency appropriation of $40,000 to construct a new facility. To impress legislators with the gravity of the situation, board members J. W. Floyd and A. L. Dukes—and not Thomas Miller—appeared before the House Ways and Means Committee to appeal for the funds. The general assembly agreed to provide $28,000: $14,000 in 1910 and $14,000 in 1911. The new brick building with two wings attached to a central structure was completed in 1911 on the site of the original building. It provided accommodations for three hundred women.[64]

Miller was immensely pleased to report to the trustees and to state officials that the new Bradham Hall was a genuine bargain. "If the building had been given out to a competent contractor, it would have cost the State of South Carolina not less than $55,000." However, with the assistance of faculty and student labor as well as savings in the purchase of materials, "the building will be furnished and your Honorable Board [of Trustees] will not have to ask the Legislature for one cent more than was appropriated."[65]

Unfortunately Miller neglected to mention that the second Bradham Hall was built without steam heat, and its shivering residents had to rely on wood stoves located in the halls. This, trustees later admitted, was not acceptable because "the girl students are therefore not properly cared for [when] the weather is cold, and their health and general well-being very much endangered." The trustees asked the general assembly to allocate $8,000 to provide heat for Bradham and an additional $1,000 to overhaul the heating system in Morrill Hall, but legislators declined to make the appropriation.[66]

Insurance monies collected on the loss of Bradham enabled the college to build Floyd Hall, a brick dining hall and kitchen that was located adjacent to the new Bradham Hall. Several other facilities were also erected during the first decade of the twentieth century. The industrial hall built of brick in 1902 and the steam power plant were especially critical to the trades programs. In 1905 a new and separate two-and-a-half-story frame home replaced Fenn Cottage as the president's residence. Miller F. Whittaker was among the students who helped construct the house. He would later occupy that home as the third president of the college.[67]

The legislature provided $1,000 in 1909 to construct a model school for teacher training. There were also two barns, a dairy, a farm equipment storage facility, new fences for the farm, and a new laundry building. The campus was a far more impressive and imposing place in 1910 than it had been when the college opened in 1896. Nevertheless the facilities and resources available to students and faculty barely represented more than what was absolutely essential for a land-grant college to function.[68]

THE SOUTH CAROLINA INTERSTATE AND WEST INDIAN EXPOSITION

Eager to promote an economic renaissance in the city of Charleston and to usher in the new century, community leaders organized and built an immense fair, the South Carolina Interstate and West Indian Exposition. Amid much anticipation and enthusiasm, the exposition opened on 250 acres along the east bank of the Ashley River on December 1, 1901. S.C. State students and faculty members as well as President Miller contributed to the Negro Department of the exposition. As segregation expanded across the South in the early twentieth century, it was taken for granted that racial separation would prevail at the fair. Thomas J. Jackson, the black secretary and field agent of the Negro Department, declared, "It would not be the part of wisdom to mix the Negro exhibits with those made by the white race."[69]

The Negro Building as well as the Women's Building were built on the fringe of the fair, away from the choice location, the Court of Palaces. The Negro Department featured black inventions and displays on manufacturing and agriculture as well as the African American exhibit that had been shown at the 1900 exposition in Paris. Several black schools, including S.C. State, provided agricultural and technical exhibits. Faculty member and architect John R. Steele designed the arch that served as the entrance to the Negro Building. He was the superintendent of brickwork, plastering, and stone fitting at the college.[70]

Controversy erupted over the erection of *The Negro Group,* an eight-foot statue mounted on an eight-foot pedestal in front of the Negro Building. Black Carolinians intensely disliked the stereotypes conveyed by the sculpture. It depicted three black figures: a black woman with a basket of cotton on her head; a kneeling black man with a plow in one hand and his other hand on an anvil; and a black boy strumming a banjo. It suggested black people were suitable for manual labor and entertainment. Thomas E. Miller vilified the statue in a letter to Booker T. Washington. "The group is being condemned by every hopeful, aspiring, self respecting Negro of both sexes; and if it remains there it will bring our work into reproach and make the Negro end of this magnificent Exposition a loathsome thing and a byword." He insisted that the young banjo player looked like "a black idiot." Charles A. Lopez, a New York City sculptor, had created *The Negro Group* at the request of the fair's designer and architect Bradford L. Gilbert, who was also a New Yorker.[71]

White Carolinians were surprised and not at all pleased that Black Carolinians took offense to what white people considered a moving and fitting tribute to the black population. Rather than accept black demands that *The Negro Group* be dismantled and

South Carolina State faculty member John R. Steele designed the arch at the entrance to the Negro Building at the South Carolina Interstate and West Indian Exposition, 1901–2. The sign above the arch reads: "Built by the Students Colored N I A and M College of S.C." As an architectural feature, arches would become an enduring motif on the campus in the years that followed. Courtesy of Gibbes Museum of Art/Carolina Art Association

discarded, fair organizers moved it to a more prominent location at the Court of Palaces. So much for a positive response to the complaints of black people.[72]

The same fair organizers who cared so little about the concerns of African Americans were, nevertheless, eager to attract black people to the exposition. They designated January 1, 1902—Emancipation Day—as "Negro Day." The Negro Building would be formally dedicated. They hoped to draw twenty thousand paying black fairgoers.

But despite the band from S.C. State and a keynote speech by Thomas E. Miller, only seventy-seven hundred people purchased tickets. President Miller delivered a conservative and peculiar address in which he praised white authority while simultaneously observing that black people had made significant progress since slavery, but that their opportunity to fulfill their destiny as a people could not occur under white domination.[73]

"The white man of the South is the white man of the Northeast; the white man of the South is the white man wherever the American eagle spreads its wings. He was

African Americans including Thomas E. Miller bitterly complained about the sculpture *The Negro Group,* which was placed in front of the Negro Building at the South Carolina Interstate and West Indian Exposition in Charleston in 1901–2. Offended because black people took exception to this portrayal of African Americans, exposition managers moved it to a more prominent location at the Court of Palaces. Courtesy of Samuel Lord Hyde Papers, Special Collections, Addlestone Library, College of Charleston

born so. He claims the right to rule and it is better that he should—better for the civilization of the world, for the uplifting of humanity; better for the white man and better for the negro." Miller continued that the black man "is stronger, more self reliant, more capable of good work in profitable occupations, and yet not strong enough or with sufficient training, means or experience to make him the leader in any field of industrial endeavor. He never can be in this country, or in any other country which the white man controls." Better, Miller seemed to suggest, that black people dwell in their own nation.[74]

Overall the six month exposition, which closed May 31, 1902, was a financial disappointment. No foreign nations sponsored exhibits. The early months of 1902 were unusually cold and wet, and attendance totaled only 675,000—far fewer than organizers had hoped for and expected. *The Negro Group* aroused animosity among black people. The exposition had, however, helped publicize the college, and it contributed to the growing reputation of John R. Steele, who had designed the arch. In 1908 Steele took an examination in Charleston for senior architectural draftsmen with the U.S. Army Quartermaster Corps. He scored among the three highest candidates of the twenty men who took the exam. He spent the next two decades as a draftsman with the Quartermaster Corps.[75]

For much of the college's history, South Carolina's all-white legislature was reluctant to allocate money to the black institution and did so only grudgingly when lawmakers were assured that the school remained enthusiastically devoted to agricultural and industrial education. Thus Thomas Miller and the trustees dutifully and repeatedly reminded legislators of the college's A&M mission. In 1911 the trustees offered what had become an annual declaration. "We propose to lay stress on industries and yearly to better equip them [students] and secure better results."[76]

Because of the general assembly's parsimonious financial support of the college during its early years, S.C. State would be more accurately identified as a federal institution than a state institution. The school relied more on Morrill money—the 1862 land-grant funds and the appropriations through the 1890 act—than on state assistance. The two Morrill Acts were crucial to the survival of South Carolina State. The college received an annual grant of $5,754 based on the sale of federal lands through the 1862 Morrill Act, and it collected an annual appropriation from the 1890 Morrill Act that periodically increased. The 1890 legislation prohibited racial discrimination in the admission of students to schools that received the federal A&M funds. But an exception permitted southern states to establish and maintain "such colleges separately for white and colored students." Consequently the 1890 act hastened the development of the black land-grant colleges although it would be many decades before these black land-grant institutions began to receive adequate funding.

The 1890 Morrill Act stipulated that federal funds were to be distributed to the black and white land-grant colleges in "a just and equitable" manner. But that did not

Table 3. Funding Sources for South Carolina State College, 1898–1912

	1898	1903	1908	1912
U.S.				
Morrill Acts				
(1862)	$5,754	$5,754	$5,754	$5,754
(1890)	$10,717	$12,441	$12,893	$22,499
Subtotal	$16,471	$18,195	$18,647	$26,253
S.C.	$10,000	$8,500	$7,800	$19,000
Farm revenue	$1,022	$968	$929	$1,664
Total	$27,483	$27,663	$27,376	$48,917

Sources: *Reports and Resolutions of the General Assembly of the State of South Carolina* for each of the years listed: 1898, 276; 1903, 905; 1908, 1066; 1912, 963. The 1862 funds are based on the federal land grants made available to each state. In 1909 the federal government significantly increased funds appropriated through the 1890 Morrill Act. The funds made available by the state that were reported in 1912 include $14,000 appropriated to replace Bradham Hall.

mean that the funds had to be divided equally between the black and white schools. Within a decade of its passage, seventeen southern states were dividing Morrill money between black and white A&M colleges. In most cases the Morrill assistance was disproportionately allocated in favor of the white institutions. South Carolina law, however, did require that the federal funds be split equally between Clemson A&M College and South Carolina State. But South Carolina failed to divide its own funds equally when state monies were provided to the two land-grant colleges.[77]

South Carolina State was the only state educational institution that enrolled sizable numbers of both men and women. South Carolina College in Columbia (now the

Table 4. Demographic Profile of South Carolina's State Colleges and the University

	Total Students		College Students	Faculty	
	Male	Female		Male	Female
1899					
Clemson	302	0	143	25	0
Univ. of S.C.	166	18	184	12	0
Citadel	123	0	123	8	0
Winthrop	0	324	213	4	20
S.C. State	643	390	27	20	12
1906					
Clemson	673	0	518	44	0
Univ. of S.C.	179	8	187	19	4
Citadel	149	0	149	9	0
Winthrop	0	421	516	6	33
S.C. State	369	446	NA	12	10
1910					
Clemson	665	0	592	47	0
Univ. of S.C.	286	12	249	26	3
Citadel	229	0	229	13	1
Winthrop	0	535	495	7	38
S.C. State	309	337	15	15	11

Sources: Data derived from tables in the State Department of Education reports for the years listed in the *Reports and Resolutions of the General Assembly of the State of South Carolina:* 1898, 86–87; 1906, 480; 1910, 934–35, The enrollment figures are for the previous year. Thus the 1910 data are for the 1908–9 school year.

Table 5. State Funding for Public Colleges and Universities

	1902	1906	1910
Clemson	$84,936	$118,820	$168,115
Univ. of S.C.	$28,000	$39,750	$85,776
Citadel	$22,500	$26,250	$30,000
Winthrop	$44,052	$52,989	$70,103
S.C. State	$11,180	$7,500	$12,000

Sources: The appropriations are from the State Department of Education tables contained in *Reports and Resolutions to the General Assembly of the State of South Carolina:* 1902, 878–79; 1906, 480–81; 1910, 934–35. The figures represent state funds only. Federal, private, and tuition monies are not included. The appropriations are for the previous fiscal year. Thus the amounts for 1910 cover the 1908–9 academic year.

University of South Carolina) was the only other public institution of higher education that admitted men and women, although the number of female students was very small.

Each of the other state colleges in South Carolina had access to more money than S.C. State. Clemson, for example, received Morrill funds but also derived income from an endowment of more than $80,000 provided by the estate of Thomas G. Clemson. That endowment furnished the Pickens County school with $3,500 in 1911. The state sales tax on fertilizer known as the Tag tax went to Clemson. A portion of the Tag tax revenue went to Clemson to analyze the chemical composition of commercial fertilizer sold in the state, and any excess funds went for construction and maintenance. These tax monies fluctuated from year to year but went solely to Clemson and in 1911 amounted to over $200,000. Clemson collected far more tax revenue in one year than S.C. State did in fifteen years from state appropriations. Although thousands of black farmers purchased fertilizer, all the taxes they paid were used to support the education of white men at Clemson.[78]

STUDENT COSTS

South Carolina State was the only public college that did not charge tuition in the early twentieth century, thereby making education more accessible to black youngsters. But in 1911 funds that derived solely from student fees ranged from $3,200 at Clemson to $26,577 at Winthrop. However, education was not free at S.C. State. Students who resided on campus paid a boarding fee of $6 a month (or $42 for the school year) in 1911. That fee included food, fuel, lighting, and medical care. There was no charge for occupying dormitory rooms, but students who resided on campus were required to pay the boarding fee and eat in the dining hall. There was a $1 incidental fee, and textbooks cost an average of $7 a year. Students also had to purchase uniforms.[79]

Student and faculty labor significantly subsidized S.C. State. It reduced costs and dramatically relieved the state of financial responsibility for the school. Many thousands of hours of student labor built and maintained the campus infrastructure and increased production on the campus farm. Thomas Miller pointed this out again and again to the state's political leaders. In 1905 in discussing the construction of a steam power plant and renovations to two steam engines, Miller explained the savings. "The work in hand could not be done, if mechanics were employed or the work given out to a contractor, for less than $7,000; but as my labor saves the contractor's cost, and the work of my instructors saves the cost of skilled mechanics; and we work students, many of whom we have made skilled mechanics, for 50 cents and 75 cents a day, we are able to do the work for about one-third of what it would cost were it given to a contractor and skilled mechanics."[80]

The college farm was also an important financial resource. Farm products were served in the dining hall and sold to provide income. In 1897 fifty-five acres were cultivated with the assistance of five mules. Ten cows provided milk and cheese, and there were twenty-five hogs and a flock of chickens. Nine bales of cotton sold for $299.65. Surplus milk and corn brought in $144.98. Sweet potatoes, hay, and fodder were also cultivated. A five-acre truck garden furnished vegetables for the dining hall as well.[81]

The farm grew to sixty-nine acres in 1898 to seventy acres in 1903 and to nearly eighty-five acres by 1911. Agricultural revenue rose and fell depending on crop prices (see table 3). By the first decade of the twentieth century, income from the farm paid the last month's board for more than two hundred students. Without this financial assistance many students would have had a difficult—if not impossible—time remaining in school until the end of the term.[82]

THOMAS E. MILLER AND THE BOARD OF TRUSTEES

Thomas Miller was the president of S.C. State, but white state officials and the trustees of the institution were unwilling to grant him broad and sweeping authority over the college. From 1896 until 1911, Miller often deferred to the trustees, who did not hesitate to interfere in routine affairs and mundane matters affecting the institution. By law South Carolina's governors were members of the board and until the late 1960s, and it was not unusual for the state's chief executive to involve himself directly in college issues and personnel. The trustees initially insisted on considering and adopting textbooks for each course. In 1897 Miller had to ask for the board's permission to operate the sawmill during the summer and to paint the interior of Bradham Hall. In 1909 the legislature, after several requests from Miller, finally appropriated funds to acquire two mules. Perhaps doubting the president's negotiating skills, trustee Archie L. Dukes accompanied Miller to purchase the animals.[83]

The board took particular interest in hiring faculty members who would not challenge white supremacy and Jim Crow. In 1909 the board met in Governor Martin Ansel's Columbia office "for the purpose of electing faculty." After Louise Fordham, who taught history as well as drawing, resigned in 1910, Thomas Miller recommended the Reverend P. P. Watson as her replacement, assuring board members that they would find the clergyman acceptable. "Watson is a good English and Historical Scholar, a clean man, a devout christian. He understands the relation of the two races in the South, and stands for the good of the state."[84]

FACULTY MEMBERS CHALLENGE MILLER

Miller bristled under this close supervision. Faculty and students in turn resented and resisted Miller's attempts to exercise authority over them. Miller could be haughty and demanding, and he sometimes had a contentious relationship with faculty members. At the end of the first school year two faculty members, William R. A. Palmer and Matthew W. Gilbert, publicly opposed Miller's leadership, and the dispute went to the trustees. Gilbert was professor of history, political science, and modern languages. Palmer was professor of ancient and English classics and literature. He was also dean of the faculty. Palmer had been on the faculty at Claflin, and in 1895 he leveled accusations against President Lewis M. Dunton that were taken to the Claflin board. Palmer was one of the Claflin employees who Miller had been compelled to accept in the political compromise involving Senator Benjamin R. Tillman and the Orangeburg legislative delegation that led to the establishment of South Carolina State following the 1895 constitutional convention.[85]

Palmer and Miller had a turbulent relationship during the three years that Palmer served on the S.C. State faculty. The exact charges Palmer and Gilbert made against Miller were not revealed, but the board asked the two faculty members as well as Miller to present their grievances. With Governor William H. Ellerbee presiding, board members ended the dispute—or so they thought—when "reprimand was given" to certain faculty and officers. Miller was forced to share the blame. His annual salary was reduced from $1,800 to $1,500 for 1897–98.[86]

A few months later Miller asked the board to clarify his authority, but the board granted him only vague powers. "The President of the College shall have a general direction and control of the College, subject to the rules of the Board of Trustees made from time to time." The following year the trustees made it clear that they would keep ultimate control when they declared that the local board had the authority "to temporarily suspend any teacher or employee of the College for misconduct, neglect of duty, incapacity or insubordination." The local board consisted of trustees from the Orangeburg area who could keep an eye on the daily activities of the college. At the time, those local trustees were Archie L. Dukes and William R. Lowman.[87]

The dispute between Miller and Palmer flared up again a year later, this time nastier than ever. Miller laid out a litany of charges against Palmer, who was one of the three highest-paid faculty members at $900 per year. Miller claimed that the professor made disparaging and false remarks about the president and his leadership "for the purpose of injuring my work with the citizens." He alleged that Palmer refused to preside over student study hours, that he criticized the college faculty "to citizens of this town and state," that he denounced two board members, that he criticized Miller in the presence of a white Orangeburg educator, and that he had "never been loyal" to the college or its president.[88]

Palmer denied every accusation except he admitted that he had spoken critically of Miller to the unnamed white educator. The board, by a 3–2 vote with two abstentions, fired Palmer as of January 1, 1900. But the matter was not closed. An enraged Miller later notified the board that Palmer had incited a student rebellion, enlisted support from the faculty, and escalated his attacks on Miller's character and leadership. Miller informed the trustees that Palmer appeared before male students assembled in chapel and appealed to them "to rebel against my orders." He added, "Students are now in rebellion and I am powerless to punish them with Prof. Palmer in the faculty." Miller explained that Palmer also appeared at a faculty meeting and "with no provocation" confronted the president and condemned Miller in vitriolic language: "You are a low villain, you are a coward, you are a contemptible scoundrel, you are a vile liar."

Charges and countercharges flew at the ensuing board meeting in October 1899. Palmer defended himself with the assistance of three attorneys—to no avail. The board suspended Palmer immediately without pay. Painting instructor James A. Tolbert, who had been implicated with Palmer, was suspended indefinitely for insubordination. The cases involving the student rebels were sent to the faculty for disposition. Thus ended William R. A. Palmer's career at South Carolina State.[89]

Once again Miller asked the board to define his authority, in this instance in the case of a defiant professor, instructor, or employee who "attack my acts in the presence of students." He asked, "What power has your Honorable Board given me to protect myself from this class of wanton insolence?" The board told him to warn the offender, and if that was not sufficient, to report him or her to the board. The trustees in effect informed Miller that he had no power to compel obedience. Challenges to his authority would be reported to the executive committee of the board, and that committee "shall suspend [the offender] if charges are sustained." The board denied Miller the authority to discipline faculty and staff who he considered obstreperous and unmanageable.[90]

In the summer of 1906 Miller became so frustrated with the board that he tendered his resignation. Miller had charged two faculty members—professor of history and drawing Louise B. Fordham and English instructor Lillian Mack—with altering the contents of a letter that Miller sent to the board asking the trustees to approve his decision to expel a student, Marie Mack. (Perhaps Marie Mack was related to Lillian Mack.) Miller evidently wanted the two faculty members severely punished. Instead the board considered the erasure in the letter "due to an error in judgment" and simply suspended the two women for July without pay.[91]

Miller then submitted a letter of resignation. The trustees declined to accept it because, they believed, it had been hastily conceived and that "it will be for the best interests of the state colored college that said resignation be withdrawn." Miller remained. Two years later the board rewarded him with his first and only pay raise. His salary was increased from $1,800 to $2,000 a year.[92]

On one occasion a personal disagreement between the president and a faculty member turned bloody. Late in 1909 Miller and Nelson C. Nix took part in a noisy verbal altercation that ended in an exchange of blows. Nix, who was a professor of mathematics and vice chair of the faculty as well as the pastor at Mount Pisgah Baptist Church, accused the president of lying. "This morning at chapel," Miller explained,

"Prof. Nix called me a liar and grabbed a chair to hit me and I struck him in his mouth with my fist." At that Nix's fifteen-year-old son, James, seized the chair and struck Miller in the face. Miller summoned Dr. William R. Lowman, who was a pharmacist and one of the local members of the board of trustees. After Lowman treated Miller for a bruised nose, Miller immediately dispatched a letter to board chair and Governor Martin Ansel demanding a full investigation. Miller even offered to pay the expenses of the investigation to save taxpayer money.[93]

Governor Ansel subsequently appointed board member Dr. G. B. White and Aiken attorney Claude E. Sawyer to determine what had happened. A contrite Nix was willing to forgive and forget, but Miller was not. He believed that his honor as well as his authority over students was at stake. He wanted Nix suspended, if not fired. "Do this," he wrote the governor, "and you will stamp out all disorder and division amongst the students, should I fail to control them my influence for good will be gone."[94]

Sawyer, who was white, considered the matter "ridiculous." He lavished praise on Miller but said problems would persist unless there were changes in campus personnel. "I recognize that Miller is a man of remarkable executive ability and wonderfully resourceful and industrious, and he has performed miracles there, but I am afraid that the College can not prosper longer under him unless many of the professors and instructors are changed."[95]

Nix was suspended without pay for one month. Extremely grateful that he had not lost his job, he wrote the governor and humbly pledged that he would not cause any more problems for the college. "I have the Institution at heart, and regard it my sacred duty to help conduct the affairs of the College to the satisfaction of the white and colored people." Making certain that he would not be labeled as a radical or troublemaker, Nix reiterated that he accepted the prevailing racial system in South Carolina. "I fully understand the relation of the two races, and shall ever let my teaching be such as to develop industrious and honorable citizens that will endeavor to keep out of the meshes of politics and secure the best friendship between the races."[96]

The professor of mathematics certainly did not bear a grudge. Three decades later in his unpublished history of the college Nix commended Miller—and never mentioned their unpleasant altercation. "With unfaltering courage President Miller shaped the early destiny of the Colored Normal, Industrial, Agricultural and Mechanical College, and carried it through trying experiences. He successfully combatted every effort to curtail the growth of the College with pleas for perpetual expansion, and left to the Negro youths of South Carolina a well-shaped Institution of true College grade."[97]

Miller and the faculty did not spend all their time engaged in acrimonious disputes. They could and did cooperate with each other. Miller sometimes even deferred to the faculty. In 1903 he asked the faculty to permit John Mitchell to graduate from the preparatory program although Mitchell had failed to meet the requirements for graduation. The president explained that he had asked Mitchell to "have charge of the sports" and that athletics had consumed much of Mitchell's time. Professor Robert L. Douglass immediately objected to Miller's request and pointed out that Mitchell fell below the minimum requirement of a 70 average in three separate subjects. Douglass added that athletic activities should not detract from classroom work. Miller relented and did not pursue Mitchell's case.[98]

When William T. B. Williams visited S.C. State in 1904 he took note of Miller's sometimes overbearing leadership. "The president does not have such loyalty as would ensure the best results from the teachers. It is probably just as true that he does not inspire such loyalty. It seems a difficult matter for strong, capable men to work in harmony with the president."[99]

STUDENT DISCIPLINE

While the trustees carefully managed the president and faculty, they did permit Miller and the teaching staff almost complete control over the students. The board granted the faculty and president the authority "to use such measures as they deem best" to govern student conduct, and that included the use of corporal punishment on the children enrolled in the model school.[100]

Miller, the faculty, and the staff spent enormous amounts of time on student conduct and discipline. Promoting academic knowledge and vocational skills was important, but it was equally important—and in some instances more important—to impart Victorian values that could be combined with refined behavior. Students should be shaped, molded, and even coerced into becoming ladies and gentlemen who would exhibit middle-class manners and morality.

Few students came from Victorian families or homes. Many were young and not a little immature. Females as young as fourteen and males who were at least fifteen were permitted to reside on campus to attend the preparatory and normal programs. They tended to be rambunctious and sometimes had difficulty coping with surging hormones. Faculty and administrators were unrelenting in their efforts to limit contact between the sexes, but they met with only partial success. Catalogs for the college's first three decades contain long lists of rules and regulations governing students that were so rigid and so strict that they must have been impossible to enforce consistently and fairly.

Students regularly tried to evade the draconian measures, and the members of the faculty spent more time in meetings attempting to determine innocence or guilt and proper penalties than they did on academic issues. Today some of the transgressions might seem trivial, absurd, or even comical, but others were quite serious. Nettie Tolbert was suspended for three weeks in 1899 for leaving campus without permission. For laughing during chapel a month later, W. W. Griffin was reported to the president. Four young men wrote "vulgar notes" to young ladies in 1898. One was expelled, two were required "to cut 4 cords of wood or be suspended," and one was "to be punished with whipping by president." College officials were not amused on April Fools' Day in 1899 when three young men yelled "Fire," nearly "causing panic" in Bradham Hall. In 1901 a student named Bouknight was "accused of having ridiculed and belittled the position of the president," and he was suspended for thirty days.[101]

In 1905 George C. Augerly and Tilley M. Grant "were expelled for improper, unmanly and unwomanly conduct." During the next school year two young men were suspended for the remainder of the term "for passing indecent picture cards in classroom." Four young women in the class were required to do extra work because "they looked at them." L. A. Goode was suspended for the balance of the term for writing an "improper note" to Ella Danley in which he proposed "you be my girl tell me how about it I want to know at once and I want you to say yes and I will give you all the money you want and anything you want."[102]

Thomas Williams was suspended in 1897 for the term for "fighting with and cutting B. N. Bradley." Norman Talley was charged after calling A. W. Smith "a M-F-S-O-B." The next month Talley was suspended indefinitely for stealing a guitar from a visiting circus. Frank Peterson was accused in 1905 of giving whiskey to three young women in Morrill Hall. He was suspended indefinitely, and the women were suspended for the school term.[103]

Young women were more closely supervised and often punished more severely than young men. In 1899 a student identified as Nalley was charged with insubordination and with attempting to strike President Miller. He was suspended for one month. In 1910 James Nix—Nelson C. Nix's fifteen-year-old son—did hit Miller in his father's confrontation with the president. Young Nix was suspended indefinitely. Two student rebels incurred Miller's wrath in 1906 with different results. Miller accused male student L. H. Walker of "inciting his class and all the other students he could influence against the president." Walker denied the charges, but the faculty voted 4–1 to suspend him for the rest of the school year. At the same faculty meeting, an angry Miller claimed that Miss Eliza Simmons was "tauntingly insolent to the president" and that she "belittled my position in the presence of her classmates" and attempted to arouse other students against him. He confessed that he nearly lost control of himself in his confrontation with Simmons and angrily had threatened her. "You saucy heifer if you repeat a word of your insolence I would put you out of this institution tonight." By a unanimous vote, the faculty suspended Simmons indefinitely. Thus the young men who threatened to strike Miller openly or had opposed him were suspended temporarily while a young woman who spoke harshly to him was indefinitely suspended.[104]

Or consider the case of Ethel Massey and William Wallace. In 1902 Massey was permitted to practice the piano on Saturday morning in the chapel of Morrill Hall. William Wallace visited her during practice, and President Miller later charged that Massey "changed her mission from legitimate work to that of entertaining and being entertained by student William Wallace for not less than one hour nor more than two and one-half hours." Student witnesses offered conflicting testimony on how long Massey and Wallace were alone and on their behavior together. Ethel Massey denied an allegation that she kissed William. "People are making these things up on me." She claimed, and at least one witness agreed, that she and Wallace had read the Bible together.

The faculty voted to suspend Ethel Massey indefinitely, and William Wallace—who was the son of Professor J. E. Wallace—was sentenced to six days' labor and deprived of social privileges. Miller placed the blame squarely on Massey, insisting that young Wallace "was enticed into the chapel by Miss Massey." Furthermore Massey's sister, Ada, was suspended for the remainder of the term for attempting to eavesdrop on the November 6 faculty meeting where the case was heard. Professor Wallace protested to no avail that the punishment of the Massey sisters was "too severe for the offense."[105]

Thomas Miller expended much energy attempting to define and enlarge his authority as president and to control faculty members and students who he considered disobedient. In an effort to demonstrate the authority that he did possess, he could be ruthless and harsh in dealing with students and faculty. In his relationship with trustees and state officials he could be insistent, but also deferential and accommodating. He made certain they were kept aware of even the most trivial matters affecting the school. Thus he won the confidence and respect of trustees who took it for granted that they ran the institution.

THOMAS E. MILLER AND WHITE SUPREMACY

Miller understood that the state's political leaders would not permit a black college to function with any significant degree of autonomy. He bowed to the racial realities of the era, and he adhered closely to the ideology promulgated by Booker T. Washington. Both men eschewed political activity and advised black people to avoid protest against segregation. Miller and Washington seemed willing to capitulate to white supremacist ideology. The same Thomas Miller who had fought so forcefully against disfranchisement in the 1895 constitutional convention had decided by 1902 that voting rights for black men were no longer relevant. In his Emancipation Day speech at the South Carolina Interstate and West Indian Exposition in Charleston on January 1, 1902, he declared: "We do not believe now, and never have believed, that the negro should have the right to vote. We believe that it is not in his interest that he should have that right." He added that black people should be protected in their civil and property rights and that when murdered, "his murderer should be hanged." But "we do not believe that he should be made an equal sharer with the white man in the affairs of government and that every effort to confer upon him the franchise will result, as all such efforts have resulted, in his disadvantage."[106]

Like Booker T. Washington, Miller would praise southern white men and criticize black people because they constantly complained. "The only thing that surprises," Miller pointed out, "is that we have fared so well at the hands of the Southern white man." There would be more progress among black people, he added, were it not for them "croaking and fault finding, and whining and pining [and] . . . by resolving in meeting or in making bitter speeches." Miller put the blame for the problems that black men and women experienced on black people themselves. He condoned segregation by claiming that social equality between the races was not possible; "there is no such thing as social equality anywhere in the world. . . no sensible negro aims at it or expects it. But we do aim and expect to achieve all the enjoyment of domestic happiness that belongs to a free and untrammeled citizenship."[107]

President Miller's cautious position in 1902 stands in stark contrast to the blunt words uttered by Congressman Thomas E. Miller in 1891 in an address to the U.S. House of Representatives. As he pleaded for passage of legislation to protect black voting rights, he scorned white southerners for their arrogance: "There is no people in the world more self-opinionated without cause, more bigoted without achievements, more boastful without a status, no people in the world so quick to misjudge their countrymen and to misstate historical facts of political economy and to impugn the motives of others. History does not record a civilized people who have been contented with so little and who can feed so long on a worthless, buried past. While crying for mercy and attempting to speak as ambassadors of peace, there are no people in the world more vituperative than her leaders." They lacked a commitment to democratic ideals. "It is not fear of negro supremacy in the South that causes the Southern election officers to suppress the negro vote, but it is the fear of the rule of the majority regardless of race." And he blamed white Democratic leaders for atrocities inflicted on black South Carolinians. "Lynchers of the innocent are elected to office in my state."[108]

Perhaps Thomas Miller, the college president, had over time succumbed to the prestige and trappings of his office. No longer did he speak out boldly and courageously against racial discrimination and for the right of African Americans to engage in politics. By his restrained public comments and his subservient relationship to the board of trustees, Miller appeared to have sacrificed his principles for his position. But had he sold out himself and his people?

Although Miller advised black men to shun politics, Coleman Blease was as serious a threat to black people and their interests as anyone in South Carolina's history. A native of Newberry and a perpetual candidate for office, Blease considered African Americans an "order of lower animals." He opposed the education of black youngsters, regarding it as a reckless waste of state funds. "Instead of making an educated negro, you are ruining a good plow hand and making a half-educated fool." He supported lynching as "necessary and good." He claimed black people had "absolutely no standard of morality" and that the rape of a black woman was not possible because black women possessed no virtue.[109]

Incredibly in 1902 the general assembly had elected Blease to a six-year term as a trustee for S.C. State. Blease seems to have taken little interest in the institution and participated only casually in board matters before he resigned in 1904. Blease spent much of 1906 and 1908 in unsuccessful campaigns for governor.[110]

Coleman Blease's campaign for governor in 1910 prompted Thomas Miller to contradict his own advice against involvement in politics. President Miller opposed the demagogue although he was well aware that a Blease victory might mean Miller's termination. Blease won the election, and one of his first acts following his inauguration was to appear at a board of trustees meeting to demand Miller's resignation for "pernicious political activity."

Miller almost relished the opportunity to resign and informed Blease that principle took precedence over the presidency. "I am guilty of having begged the voters not to vote for you. I counted the cost before I opposed you, hence I am prepared for the blow of your official act." Miller added that he counted among his supporters Republicans and Democrats, members of the judiciary, state legislators, members of Congress, and two U.S. senators. He concluded and spoke directly to Blease. "Honored Sir, I have never slandered you for there was no malice in my opposition to you. I felt your announced policy against the negro was not founded upon justice and the best interest of the State; for that reason I tried to bring about your defeat." Thomas Miller's fifteen-year tenure as the first president of South Carolina State came to an end.[111]

To preserve his presidency and to protect the fledgling college, Miller for years had acquiesced in white supremacist ideology and delivered several obsequious tirades in its support. But the prospect of Coleman Blease as governor was beyond the pale. Rather than silently accept the election of such a virulent racist, Miller courageously spoke out, and it cost him his position. He put the welfare of S.C. State and the future of his people before his own ambition and pride.

As if his opposition to Blease was not enough to insure his reputation as a race leader, Miller also simultaneously had immersed himself in the first legal case involving the National Association for the Advancement of Colored People (NAACP). Pink Franklin was a twenty-two-year-old tenant farmer who shot and killed an Orangeburg constable in 1907 after that constable barged into Franklin's dwelling unannounced in the middle of the night and shot and wounded both Franklin and his wife, Patsy. Franklin—who managed to evade a lynch mob—was found guilty of homicide by an all-white, all-male Orangeburg jury and sentenced to death. After appeals to the South Carolina Supreme Court and the U.S. Supreme Court failed, Miller worked closely in 1910 with the newly formed NAACP and its white executive secretary, Frances Blascoer, to persuade Governor Martin Ansel to commute Franklin's sentence to life in prison. Ansel agreed only to grant a reprieve that would delay the execution until January 27, 1911.

But that reprieve would surely guarantee Franklin's execution. By January 27, the newly elected Governor, Coleman Blease, would have been inaugurated. If Ansel failed to commute Franklin's sentence before then, there was no doubt that Blease would allow the execution to be carried out. Owing largely to the intervention of Miller and Blascoer as well as a massive petition campaign, Ansel commuted Franklin's sentence on January 5, 1911—three weeks before Governor Blease demanded that Miller step down as S.C. State president.[112]

THOMAS E. MILLER: AN ASSESSMENT

Miller derived much satisfaction from and was pleased with his leadership as president. The college had secured its place as a land-grant institution devoted to the agricultural and mechanical training of black youngsters. Although Thomas Miller possessed limited authority, he was able to marshal sufficient support for the development and growth of the A&M college to insure its survival and continued expansion. The outlook for the college was far more promising in 1911 after fifteen years of his leadership than it had been when he assumed the presidency in 1896.

As Miller prepared to depart, student enrollment continued to fluctuate. By 1910–11 there were 592 students, ten fewer students than the previous year. Of those, 297 were in the elementary program. Only one student earned a college degree that year. There were 564 students from South Carolina and 227 from Orangeburg County.[113]

The trustees remained firmly committed to vocational education. "We propose to lay stress on the industries and yearly to better equip them [the students] and secure better results." Every preparatory, normal, and college student was required to master a skill. Masonry was the most popular program for males with seventy-one young men enrolled. Sewing and dressmaking attracted 188 young women.[114]

The faculty had expanded from thirteen in 1896–97 to thirty in 1910–11. Several of the original faculty members were gone. Isaac N. Cardozo, who taught mental and moral science, died in 1898. English and literature professor William R. A. Palmer had been forced out in 1899. History teacher Matthew Gilbert left the same year. J. E. Wallace replaced Palmer, but he left in 1903. Louise Fordham taught drawing and then history, and she departed for a teaching position in Kansas City in 1910. Two of President Miller's children were also briefly affiliated with the college. Mary J. Miller was librarian and her father's secretary from 1896 until 1899. She left after her marriage but later returned and served as the dean of women. Anna Miller became the college accountant and director of the commercial department, but she departed in 1903 after her marriage to Wilson Cooke.[115]

The physical plant expanded dramatically under Miller. The buildings inherited from Claflin in 1896 were worth $50,000. By 1911 campus structures were valued at $250,000. The newly constructed facilities included Morrill Hall, a laundry, the boiler house, the steam and electric plant, a dairy, two barns, a storehouse for farm equipment, the president's house, six houses for teachers, and the model school. Bradham Hall had been consumed by fire, but a second Bradham Hall replaced it. In spite of the remarkable capital improvements, the state never increased its annual appropriation of $5,000 for maintenance, insurance, repairs, and care of the buildings. In 1911 the trustees again requested $5,000 as a portion of the $18,000 they asked the general assembly to provide. However, $8,000 of that amount was a special request for the steam heating plant for Bradham Hall.[116]

Contemporary evaluations of Miller's leadership vary. William T. B. Williams, the black GEB agent, regarded him in 1904 as a "good businessman" and an "organizer of men and forces" but thought he lacked the ability to work effectively with the faculty. A three-member legislative team visited the college in 1906, and they praised Miller for his financial acumen. "He is very watchful of the interests of the College, and has made every cent of the appropriations granted tell in good results." In 1908 in a report to the General Education Board, a man who was identified only as Mr. Savely visited the campus and reported that Miller did well considering the lack of legislative support that the institution received. "I have a most favorable impression both of President Miller and of the State Normal and Industrial School." He added that while the farm needed improvement, "I rather admire a school that can get down and take hold of the bottom and give education at a rate which is within the reach of the average colored man."[117]

Miller retired to Charleston, where he remained active in community affairs. He chaired an all-black subcommittee that promoted the sale of Liberty Bonds during World War I. He also spearheaded a successful but contentious NAACP campaign in the general assembly in 1919 for legislation to remove white teachers from Charleston's black public schools. It was reminiscent of his effort in the 1895 constitutional convention to create an all-black college where students would be removed from the baleful influence of white Claflin faculty members and administrators. If schools were to be segregated by race, then black students would be taught by black teachers. Miller moved to Philadelphia in 1923 but returned to Charleston in 1927, where he died on April 8, 1938. His tombstone in the Brotherly Association Cemetery reads: "I served God and all the people, loving the white man not less, but the Negro needed me most."[118]

CHAPTER TWO

The Struggle to Grow

Following the forced departure of Thomas E. Miller, Robert Shaw Wilkinson would lead South Carolina State as its second president from 1911 to the depths of the Great Depression in 1932. For most of those two decades, the primary educational role of the institution did not change significantly. It was still not a four-year college, and very few students pursued or earned bachelor's degrees. Instead young people would continue to learn skills and absorb values that would enable them to earn a living in a segregated world.

In 1915 Wilkinson aptly but inelegantly summarized the *un*collegiate mission of the school. "The desired aim here to influence real life by making it practical along all lines, thereby increasing the number of intelligent, active and productive farmers, as well as mechanics will be accomplished as these boys and girls return to their homes and carry with them lessons of thrift and industry to be woven into the existence of their communities."[1]

Wilkinson deserves much of the credit for moving the college forward at a time when white supremacy reached a high-water mark in the United States and the South. Lynching continued, and there were a series of bloody race riots in metropolitan areas including Houston, East St. Louis, Chicago, Tulsa, and nearby Charleston during and after World War I. Jim Crow continued to mark daily life. And despite the ratification of the Nineteenth Amendment and the adoption of women's suffrage in 1920, politics in South Carolina remained the province of white men.

That Wilkinson was able to accomplish what he did is testimony to his leadership. It would be easy to dismiss him as an overly cautious and conservative black man who had neither the fortitude nor the desire to speak out forthrightly on behalf of the black institution. Wilkinson did not openly challenge racial separation—although at least on one occasion he privately complained about segregated accommodations. Ever mindful of his predecessor's fate at the hands of Coleman Blease, Wilkinson still would speak candidly in defense of the college when he felt that its interests were jeopardized.

Considering the unpromising racial environment, S.C. State did reasonably well during the second decade of the twentieth century in gaining legislative support and appropriations. The number of faculty members grew, and their academic preparation improved. Perhaps most notably Wilkinson was able to persuade the board of trustees to grant him more authority over faculty, students, and routine matters than Thomas Miller had exercised.

However Wilkinson's ascendancy to the presidency in 1911 was not a foregone conclusion. Several possible successors to Miller emerged including—oddly enough—Miller himself. Three South Carolina State faculty members—Robert S. Wilkinson, Nelson C. Nix, and J. E. Wallace—were considered. C. G. Corbett Jr., the president of Allen University in Columbia, was also discussed, but he showed little interest in the position. For a time thirty-two-year-old Nathaniel J. Frederick was regarded as Miller's most likely replacement. Frederick was the supervisor of Columbia's Howard graded school. He was a graduate of Claflin, and he had earned a bachelor's degree in history and Latin from the University of Wisconsin in 1901. Most important to the white community, Frederick and his father, the Reverend B. G. Frederick, were Democrats in a state where the overwhelming number of black men who identified themselves politically were Republicans. The Fredericks were also natives of Orangeburg.[2]

But there were black and white people who thought that Thomas Miller ought to be retained. The Reverend Richard Carroll was a prominent and conservative black Baptist minister in the early twentieth century who admired Booker T. Washington's program of self-help and the Tuskegee leader's reluctance to challenge segregation. In the pages of the *Southern Ploughman,* which Carroll edited, he not only trumpeted the virtues of rural life and agricultural training for his black brethren; he also recommended that Thomas Miller remain the president of S.C. State, proclaiming that "it will be hard to find a man to be the equal of Dr. Miller."

The Orangeburg *Times and Democrat* agreed with Carroll and endorsed Miller as well. "Miller has made a success of his work at the college, and we doubt if a better colored man can be found in the state for the position." Several weeks later the newspaper conceded that it had once supported Nathaniel Frederick as "thoroughly qualified for the presidency," but that "if the trustees want to re-elect Miller president, and he will accept the place, we have no objection."[3]

As talk of Frederick and Miller swirled, Robert Shaw Wilkinson quietly waged a determined effort to gain the presidency. The day after Blease ousted Miller, Wilkinson wrote the president of Clemson College, Walter M. Riggs, who was a native of Orangeburg, and he asked Riggs to recommend him for S.C. State presidency, "as I feel that such an endorsement from you would be a very great help to me." But Riggs, who had been serving as Clemson's interim president since 1909, politely declined to support Wilkinson publicly. "Certain circumstances make it unwise for me to take part in the election of Miller's successor. However, you are at liberty to give my name as a reference, and if called upon, I will be glad to say what I can on your behalf. I would like to see you get the place."[4]

On March 29, 1911, the trustees met in the statehouse office of Governor Coleman Blease and elected Wilkinson to be the second president of S.C. State. Given Blease's intense dislike of Miller, there was no chance the first president would be reinstated. Moreover Blease did not want black men involved in politics even as Democrats, and Frederick, therefore, was not a likely choice either. Two years later Frederick was admitted to the bar, and he went on to become an accomplished South Carolina lawyer.

He abandoned the Democratic Party and became a Republican. In one of his many legal cases, Frederick filed suit to register black voters. In the meantime, on March 7, the Clemson board named Walter Riggs as their president. Over the next decade, Wilkinson and Riggs would develop a close and respectful working relationship that was unique among presidents of black and white land-grant colleges in the early twentieth century.[5]

ROBERT SHAW WILKINSON

Robert Shaw Wilkinson was born in Charleston on February 18, 1865, three days before black soldiers of the Fifty-Fifth Massachusetts Regiment occupied the city and only weeks before the Civil War ended. He was named after Robert Gould Shaw, the white commanding officer of the black Fifty-Fourth Massachusetts Regiment. Shaw and many of his men had been killed in the courageous but failed assault on Fort Wagner on Morris Island near the entrance to Charleston harbor in July 1863. Wilkinson's parents, Charles H. and Lavinia Brown Wilkinson, were free people of color before the Civil War. Charles Wilkinson, who died when Robert was sixteen, had operated a butcher shop and later became a janitor at the Porter Military Academy and at the Church of the Holy Communion.

Young Wilkinson attended Shaw Memorial School and Avery Institute. He received an appointment to the U.S. Military Academy at West Point. Because of his small stature, academy officials declined to admit him. But Wilkinson's race may have had as much to do with that decision as his size. He enrolled in the preparatory program at Ohio's Oberlin College and went on to earn an A.B. in 1891. Wilkinson embarked on a teaching career at the all-black State University of Kentucky in Louisville, where he taught Latin, Greek, and political science. He subsequently received a honorary Ph.D. from that institution in 1898. When S.C. State opened in 1896, Wilkinson became one of its first faculty members. He taught physics and chemistry and served for a time as military commandant.[6]

Wilkinson would serve twenty-one years as president. Immaculately dressed, he was a rather reserved man who chose his words carefully. Unlike Miller he avoided confrontations. He was, however, an insistent advocate for the college and for black South Carolinians. Considering the racial atmosphere that prevailed in South Carolina, he was remarkably effective in dealing with trustees, legislators, and philanthropists. The college made steady strides under his leadership.

He enjoyed baseball more than football, and he closely followed the fortunes of the college baseball team. While visiting New York City in 1923 he visited the newly opened Yankee Stadium and watched the New Yorkers and Babe Ruth defeat the Washington Senators 4–2 in what he described as a "fine game." But it would be nearly a quarter century before Jackie Robinson would break the color barrier in major league baseball in 1947.[7]

Because he was of fair complexion Wilkinson could sometimes avoid the indignities of segregation. But in 1923 on that trip to New York City, he took time to note briefly one instance where he was the victim of racial discrimination. "Took Pullman

Robert Shaw Wilkinson was born in Charleston in 1865 and would lead South Carolina State as its second president from 1911 until his death in 1932. Courtesy of the Historical Collection, South Carolina State University

SoRy station 11:30 with party. Stopped at Columbia 4:30. Party increased to large number. Fight by a rowdy at Pullman door. Car "Jim Crowed" on train in an unusual place." He did not specify what he meant by "unusual place." The prevailing custom in segregation, however, was to exclude black passengers entirely from Pullman cars.[8]

He married Marion Birnie in 1897, and they were the parents of two boys, Robert Shaw and Frost Birnie, and two girls, Helen Raven and Lula Love. Marion Birnie Wilkinson would become a formidable leader in her own right. They were active Episcopalians, and he was a Republican. He served as president of the State Negro Business League, and treasurer of the Knights of Pythias. He and his wife were also closely involved in the YMCA and YWCA.[9]

As president the diminutive Wilkinson first had to contend with an irascible and temperamental governor who was openly hostile to the black institution. Governor Coleman Blease, as chairman of the board of trustees of the college, was well aware that the trustees had agreed to pay former president Thomas Miller's salary through September 1911. Yet when Wilkinson, as the newly installed president of the college, asked Blease to approve vouchers to compensate Miller, a plainly irritated Blease replied, "If you are performing the duties of President, I think you are entitled to the pay of President. However, if you are willing to certify your pay to another man when he has not done the work, I have no objection."[10]

Blease, who detested Miller, had already threatened to have Miller arrested if the former president ever returned to the college: "if he goes back on that campus, and I find out, I will have him indicted for trespass and prosecuted." And Blease vowed that Wilkinson would be removed if he "does not attend to his duties." He added that "I am getting tired of the way that negro college is being handled, and if it cannot be straightened out one way it will have to be another." In spite of Blease's nasty opposition, Miller was paid $499.98. But it is not certain whether this was the entire balance of his salary in keeping with the agreement that had accompanied his resignation.[11]

Wilkinson's and the college's troubles with Blease were not over. When the chairman of the local board, William R. Lowman, submitted a bill for $175 for two hogs purchased by Wilkinson, the governor was furious. "I am not much of a judge of hogs," he wrote, "but it seems to me that these are outrageous prices to pay for a Boar and Sow. I will sign the bill, however, but will be forced to call the matter to the attention of the legislature." He added, "I hope that you will, in the future, see that Wilkinson does not go to such extravagance."[12]

A year later, in 1913, with his memory of Thomas Miller fading, Blease seemed to moderate his view of the college and endorsed its budgetary request that included $1,000 for extension work and $500 for summer school. "This institution has made wonderful improvement since it has been freed from cheap Negro politics, and is now doing some good for the colored Youth. And this [budget] request is not unreasonable." A few weeks later the mercurial Blease vetoed the funds set aside for extension work and summer school. For good measure he added, "I am opposed to negro education, but you have a good board of trustees for this institution; they are honest, and they are trying their best. If you must have your negro college, have it, but as for me, I think it is a curse to Orangeburg and to the people of South Carolina." The general assembly sustained the two vetoes.[13]

Another year passed, and the governor decided once again that the college was not doing so badly. "The College is now, under President Wilkinson, doing good work in its line. He should be encouraged in his work for his race." But Blease's newfound affection for Wilkinson did not result in increased appropriations for college operating expenses or salaries. With the state enjoying a flush economy, however, Wilkinson and the trustees had been successful in gaining legislative support for several sorely needed additions to the agricultural and mechanical programs including those $175 hogs.[14]

CAMPUS EXPANSION

By 1916 the swine herd included registered Berkshires, Poland Chinas, and Tamworths. The dairy herd consisted of nine cows and two registered bulls. A Jersey bull had recently been acquired to keep the heifers company. There was a new cow barn to house the animals. With the assistance of the Federal Bureau of Animal Industry, the college installed a dipping trough and vat that permitted local black and white farmers to rid their animals of ticks.[15]

In 1912 a long-overdue $8,000 central heating plant was built. According to Wilkinson President Walter Riggs of Clemson College supervised the project and "cheerfully rendered invaluable service in that connection." Riggs reviewed the plans, made suggestions about the bidding process, and came to Orangeburg in October to assist in testing the new system. It provided warmth to dormitories, the dining hall, and industrial facilities.[16]

Beekeeper Benjamin F. Hubert tends to the campus beehives in about 1920. He would lead the agricultural program at S.C. State until he was named president of Savannah State in 1926. Courtesy of the Historical Collection, South Carolina State University

The construction of driveways, walks, and new landscaping improved the campus and its appearance. A new blacksmith shop cost $2,000. A shed was built to protect new farm machinery including a manure spreader, a cutter and binder for corn, a grist mill, an oil engine, and a two-horse disc plow. By 1917 there was also a new incubator facility for chickens and ducks. A new peach orchard was added to the farm.[17]

Instruction was offered in twenty eight trades by 1914–15. New equipment, facilities, and courses in electronics, radio, and auto mechanics were subsequently added. There was a new commercial program that became part of the curriculum, and it served as the predecessor to what would eventually become business administration.[18]

Benjamin F. Hubert joined the faculty in 1913 and introduced beekeeping to the agricultural program, and by 1918 Hubert presided over twelve colonies of bees. What is more important, he assumed leadership over the agricultural program as its director and was the highest-paid faculty member. He earned $1,200 in 1918. Only President Wilkinson at an annual salary of $2,000 earned more than Hubert. Hubert was born in Hancock County, Georgia, and earned a bachelor of arts degree from Morehouse. He then earned a bachelor of science at Massachusetts Agricultural College (now the University of Massachusetts) and later pursued a master of science in agriculture at the University of Minnesota. A talented administrator, Hubert left S.C. State in 1926 to become the president of Savannah State College, which he led until 1947.[19]

Women students—and at least two men—learn the art of typewriting during the second decade of the twentieth century. Courtesy of the Historical Collection, South Carolina State University

The trustees and President Wilkinson were unceasing in their determination to reassure white political and educational leaders that the college was committed to agricultural and mechanical training. "The agricultural work is stressed as never before," the trustees repeated year after year in their annual reports to the general assembly. They noted again and again that every senior in the preparatory program and every first-year student in the normal curriculum was required to take either agricultural, industrial, or home economics course work. Additionally a student could specialize in one of the trades, which would entitle them to earn a certificate upon the completion of that program. President Wilkinson proclaimed in 1917 that the college found it difficult to meet the demand for trained labor. "We are constantly receiving calls for trained workers, especially in the domestic science course to fill appointments in rural school work and homes." He continued, "People everywhere are looking to us for the training of the colored youth of our State along industrial lines."[20]

TROUBLE WITH THE FEDERAL GOVERNMENT

Only five months after he had been named president, Wilkinson received a letter from federal authorities charging S.C. State administrators with misusing land-grant funds. P. P. Claxton, the commissioner of education, informed Wilkinson that in 1910—and

The class of 1913 was the seventeenth class to graduate from the college, and it consisted of slightly more men than women. S.C. State was the only public institution in South Carolina that had a student body made up of substantial numbers of both men and women. Courtesy of the Historical Collection, South Carolina State University

before Wilkinson became president—federal money had been used to pay all or portions of salaries to faculty members and administrators who did not provide instruction in agricultural and mechanical subjects as required by the 1862 and 1890 Morrill Acts. For example Thomas Miller was not eligible to be paid out of federal money because he did not teach. P. P. Watson taught history and economics, and he should not have been paid out of federal funds. "Louisa Blanding's salary must be divided according to the time devoted to dairying and music." Altogether nine individuals had been compensated with funds that they had not been eligible to receive. Moreover federal money had been improperly used to purchase blackboards and a $196 adding machine. Claxton asked Wilkinson to resubmit the 1910 report and to indicate specifically "the number of actual hours of instruction" individuals devote to teaching practical subjects as well as the time they spent on noninstructional duties.[21]

In his reply Wilkinson matter-of-factly explained that the college had been following the same reporting format in 1910 as it had in previous years. He reassured Claxton that in the future he would take the "greatest care" to conform to the more rigorous requirements "and avoid the mistakes to which my attention has been directed by your letter."[22]

That response was unacceptable. Wilkinson was instructed to draft a new report carefully enumerating the disbursement of federal funds. Thus chastised Wilkinson conveniently solved that difficulty by indicating that the questionable expenditures actually had conformed to federal mandates. As for President Miller's teaching duties, "his instruction in the Department of Agriculture was regular and of a thoroughly practical nature; and consisted of lectures, hearing recitations, and giving practical demonstrations on the farm." P. P. Watson's salary supported by federal money went exclusively for teaching political economy. "He drew no salary for history he taught." Similarly Louise Blanding was paid only as a teacher of dairying to which "she devoted her entire time." Her tasks in music "were given outside of her regular time of teaching." Wilkinson stated that the $196 adding machine was used for instruction "and therefore is a just charge against the Morrill fund." He apologized for the incomplete and inaccurate earlier report. Wilkinson could hardly have done otherwise. It is inconceivable that S.C. State was in a financial position to return money to the federal government that had not been spent properly.[23]

ENROLLMENT

Overall enrollment rose and fell dramatically in the second decade of the twentieth century. There were 592 students enrolled in 1911, 826 in 1912, and 607 in 1920. There were thirty-five faculty members in 1912, and that number increased to fifty-four by 1921. Elementary grades one to four were eliminated, and the funds that had been used to pay the elementary teachers were shifted to the A&M program. The number of students who earned a bachelor's degree remained exceedingly small. Far more students pursued a licentiate of instruction certificate.

In 1915 the State Board of Education announced that the licentiate of instruction certificate that students in the normal program earned would not be accepted as a qualification to teach in the state's public schools after July 1, 1916. Wilkinson explained that henceforth S.C. State students would be required to enroll in the collegiate program and earn a bachelor's degree in public instruction to be eligible to teach.[24]

But the attempt to abandon the licentiate of instruction proved premature. In 1918 there was an educational conference at South Carolina State that brought together the state superintendent of schools, J. E. Swearingen, and black college presidents and high school principals. They agreed to restore the L.I., thereby granting "the graduates of seven accredited colored schools and colleges the privilege of teaching without further examination, in the public schools of the State."[25]

Table 6. Graduates, 1914–21

	1914	1915	1916	1917	1918	1919	1920	1921
College	0	0	5	1	9	1	1	3
Licentiate of instruction	48	67	59	56	79	43	53	37

Sources: Compiled from annual reports, *Reports and Resolutions of the General Assembly:* 1914, 2: 587; 1915, 2: 594; 1916, 7–8; 1917, 8; 1918, 7; 1919, 8; 1920, 7; 1921, 8.

Had the L.I. not been reinstated, it would have presented a severe hardship to black schools and black students. Institutions, such as Avery Normal Institute, that did not offer a bachelor's degree would no longer have been able to provide teachers for the state system. Moreover there simply were not a sufficient number of black students, including those at S.C. State, with the necessary academic preparation to pursue a bachelor's degree. The state would have lacked an adequate number of teachers for the black public schools. The licentiate of instruction remained part of the academic program until 1928.

FIRE

Two serious fires in 1916 had a disastrous impact on the campus and its residents. Shortly before 1 A.M. on Monday, March 20, a blaze erupted in Bradham Hall, a women's residence hall that also contained administrative offices. This was the second Bradham Hall. The first, a frame structure, had burned to the ground in 1909. The second Bradham fire, of undetermined origin, spread so rapidly through the U-shaped brick structure that dozens of students and at least two faculty members were forced to jump from second-floor windows. There were no fatalities among the nearly three hundred residents, but forty-six students suffered injuries that ranged from superficial sprains to broken limbs and serious burns. Two instructors, Mattie J. Battiste and Julia Mae Williams, were also hurt. All the injured women were taken to President Wilkinson's residence, where Orangeburg physicians and nurses worked through the night to treat them.

Bradham Hall was destroyed in ninety minutes at a loss estimated at $40,000. Insufficient water pressure hindered fire department efforts to contain the blaze. Claflin University and its president, Lewis Dutton, generously offered to house the displaced students for the remainder of the session. It would not be until the following school year that many of the injured would recover and return to school. It took more than a year before Mattie J. Battiste resumed her teaching duties in September 1917.[26]

During the next school year, on Saturday night, October 21, 1916, a fire of suspicious origin began about 9 P.M. in Morrill Hall on the fifth floor of an unfinished portion of the southwest tower. Morrill Hall was the most imposing and impressive building on the campus. The nearly two-decade-old, five-story wooden structure was reportedly the largest frame building in the state at the time of its destruction. The 243 young men who lived in Morrill fled the flames, and there were no injuries or fatalities. The fire endangered several nearby homes before it was extinguished. Arson was strongly suspected in the Morrill blaze. The *Times and Democrat* reported that "a suspicious negro" was arrested, but that he was later released because of a lack of evidence. No one was ever charged in the loss of Morrill. In 1914 there had been an earlier attempt to burn Morrill when fires were set in three locations in the building.[27]

At the time Morrill Hall seemed irreplaceable. It was one of the first buildings constructed after the college opened in 1896. It provided the only housing for men, and it served as the primary academic facility. It contained sixteen classrooms, laboratories, a chapel, a library, and two towers—one of which was seven stories and served as an observatory. It also housed a host of memories. College officials and students were hard pressed to make arrangements to continue the school year following its destruction. Men were compelled to live with city residents while administrators and faculty scrambled to make classrooms and laboratories available. President Wilkinson explained: "Temporary provisions have been made to overcome meagerly these inconveniences, but it is hoped the general assembly will come to our relief at this time in a substantial manner and replace our lost properties." Because Morrill was constructed of timber, insurance companies would cover it for no more than $19,300 although it was valued at $35,000.[28]

NEW CONSTRUCTION

The general assembly agreed to appropriate $50,000 in two annual installments of $25,000 to cover the losses of Bradham and Morrill. The insurance settlement and the first appropriation of $25,000 enabled the college to construct a trio of separate three-story brick dormitories—Manning and Bradham Halls for women and Lowman Hall for men. Architect and college instructor Miller F. Whittaker designed the three facilities while student labor was responsible for much of the construction. But costs escalated, and the trustees and President Wilkinson were forced to ask that the legislature increase the second annual appropriation to $35,000. New and larger water mains were installed that connected to the city system on both the front of the campus and along Russell Street, and a campus water tank was built to increase water pressure in the event of another fire.[29]

Student and faculty labor remained critical to the growth and operation of the college. Over the first three decades of the college's history, the state and the college continued to save untold sums of money by utilizing student labor. In 1916 President Wilkinson asked for faculty cooperation in permitting students to miss class so that they could work. "When boys are needed to assist in the necessary work of the campus the students should be excused from their classes in academic work."[30]

While supervising students during the construction of Lowman Hall in July 1917, ironworking instructor Solomon M. Boston suddenly died, apparently of a heart attack. He had taught at the college since it opened in 1896. He was buried on campus among the pines in Wilkinson Park, where Oliver C. Dawson–Bulldog Stadium is currently located. His remains were later removed to the Orangeburg Cemetery near Edisto Gardens.[31]

White Hall was built in 1918–19 to replace Morrill Hall. Students did all the electrical work and painting. Overall students were responsible for about one-fifth of the work on the building. "Without this arrangement, which reduced costs considerably," Wilkinson explained, "it would have been impossible to complete the structure on time." Students were paid ten cents an hour and worked two days a week. If school was not in session, student laborers received regular wages of $3 to $5 per day. The eight skilled carpenters who came from Charleston to work on White Hall were paid eighty-five cents an hour for a nine-hour day.

Wilkinson advised, however, that the spiraling costs of labor and materials during World War I would require an additional state appropriation to complete White Hall.

Both students and full-time laborers worked as bricklayers on the erection of Lowman Hall, a men's dormitory, shown here about 1917. Faculty members and students played a major role in the construction of campus facilities during the college's first three decades. Courtesy of the Historical Collection, South Carolina State University

There were shortages of brick and railcars to deliver it. "Lumber not only increased in price 300%, but could not be secured even from our regular dealers." Prices of furnishings such as desks, blackboards, and chairs had gone up 125 percent. Wilkinson asked for and received an additional $30,000 to finish White Hall. At the time of its completion, White Hall was a splendid academic facility that had eight classrooms, an auditorium that would seat 970, and an unfinished basement. The total cost was $90,000.[32]

Despite the college farm's modest size of eighty-five acres, it produced an amazing quantity and diversity of commodities, which were sold to the public or consumed in the dining hall. Agricultural revenues were not large, but they did augment state and federal financial support for S.C. State. Depending on the weather and on commodity prices, the college received between $1,000 and $1,500 annually from the sale of agricultural goods during the World War I era. For example in 1919 the farm furnished 850 bushels of corn, four bales of cotton, one and a half tons of cotton seed, forty tons of hay, 240 bushels of potatoes, three bushels of peanuts, and fifty bushels of oats. It also provided tomatoes, okra, butter beans, string beans, peaches, squash, and huckleberries. The livestock included three horses, four mules, eighteen hogs, 126 chickens, thirteen ducks, one bull, thirteen cows, five calves, and Professor Hubert's twelve hives of bees.[33]

Completed in 1920, White Hall replaced Morrill Hall, which had gone up in flames in 1916. It served as the major academic building for decades. It consisted of twelve classrooms and a spacious auditorium, and it was the home of the Wilkinson organ. Named after G. B. White, a member of the board of trustees, it was demolished in 1974 following the construction of M. Maceo Nance Jr. Hall. Courtesy of the Historical Collection, South Carolina State University

NO SCHOLARSHIPS FOR S.C. STUDENTS

While the farm and especially student and faculty labor subsidized the college, the State of South Carolina would not subsidize the college's students. Students at each institution of higher education in South Carolina benefited from a system of county scholarships underwritten by the state legislature—with the notable exception of the students at South Carolina State. Again and again President Wilkinson appealed to the general assembly to remedy this inequity, and again and again legislators ignored him. In 1915 he simply stated: "This is the only institution supported by the State in which no scholarships have been established for the support of worthy young men and women whose future services would be of great benefit to the State as teachers and leaders among the people." He asked that the legislature set aside $50 for a scholarship for an S.C. State student from each county in South Carolina. He repeated the request in 1916. By 1921 Wilkinson was appealing for two scholarships of $100 each to be awarded to a pair of students from each of the state's forty-six counties at a total cost of $9,200. "This," he noted, "would be an appreciated investment in the colored youth of South Carolina." He suggested that recipients be required to teach in South Carolina's public schools. The members of the general assembly were unmoved by such pleas.[34]

Wilkinson made a far more pathetic, if not demeaning, appeal to state legislators in 1917. Learning that many members of the general assembly were traveling from Columbia to Charleston to visit the Citadel and that their train would pass in front of the S.C. State campus, the president asked faculty and students to organize displays so that legislators could catch a fleeting glimpse of the college and its endeavors. "All departments were asked to arrange an exhibit on the front of the campus so that they [legislators] might be able to see something of the work of the college and its needs." If they even happened to glance at the display as their train rumbled through Orangeburg, what must the white legislators have thought and said about S.C. State?[35]

STUDENT DISCIPLINE

As they had been during the college's early years, administrators and faculty members were obsessed with student behavior and discipline. Had it been possible at a coeducational institution, college officials would have completely segregated male and female students. Because young people had a tendency to talk with each other, in 1914 "Profs [N. C.] Nix, [H. P.] Butler, and [B.] Levister were asked to keep a sharp lookout for students to prevent them from associating (boys and girls) at 8:15 and 1:15 near chapel, and on the way to class. It was decided to have boys and girls line up and march in by classes morning and noon." A month later Wilkinson appealed to faculty "to prevent as far as possible the wholesale note writing carried on between boys and girls."[36]

In 1916 separate doors were set aside for male and female students who were entering and leaving the academic building. With exams approaching in 1917, faculty members were cautioned that young men and women might try to study together, a decidedly unwholesome development. "Mention made of the fact that girls and boys are apt to try and get together these days—teachers asked to be on watch and see that the rules of the institution are kept."[37]

A PARTIAL LIST OF RULES AND REGULATIONS, 1917

Each student is required to have a Bible and the Chapel Hymnal.
All students, whether campus or town boarders, found lounging about restaurants, stores or questionable places will be disciplined by the President and for the second offense will be suspended from the College.
No young woman is permitted to leave the grounds of the College unless accompanied by the matron or a lady teacher.
The use of intoxicating drinks or tobacco are strictly forbidden.
Dice playing, card playing and checker playing are positively prohibited.
Low or profane language will subject a student to severe discipline.
All students must be in bed, with lights extinguished, by 10:30 P.M.
Communication in any form with the opposite sex is prohibited.
Every student over 15 years of age must do two hours manual labor per week under the direction of the President of the College.[38]

Students who were caught in the company of other students of the opposite sex were dealt with swiftly and severely. In 1911 Hattie Hunter, who was from Laurens and Luther Samuels of Spartanburg were expelled for "conduct unbecoming students."

On a spring day in 1915 two young ladies—Beatrice Thompson and Edmona Lewis—said that they were going to Claflin to meet two young women who were students there. Instead they met Russell Coleman and George Lawrence, "who took [the] girls on a ride around town" by horse and buggy. The young men were promptly dismissed, and the parents of the young women were asked "to send for them."[39]

Perplexed and a little uncertain as to how to manage students, especially young women, Wilkinson decided to employ a dean of women in 1918. She could then deal with the "intricate problems" of female students, and furthermore a dean could arrange the various activities of the young ladies and "organize them into efficient forces for the development of womanly character." C. S. Boykin was hired at an annual salary of $900.[40]

Aside from contact between young men and women, there were other transgressions that required intervention and adjudication by the faculty. In 1913 Robert Dendy was apprehended on New Year's Day in Morrill Hall matching coins with J. L. Lundy. He was also accused of calling Julia Barksdale, a student, "a dirty wretch" who had "cut the hog." The faculty found that "he was no longer worthy of a place in the institution." He was suspended indefinitely.[41]

In 1916 two unnamed students were suspended after they were caught playing cards for a second time. Nine male students left the campus without permission in 1918 and were subsequently seen "loitering in the café at the corner of Russell street—Railroad avenue." They were sentenced to three days of hard labor on the campus under the supervision of D. C. Lewis, who taught ironworking and who also had worked as an orderly.

Years after he had been a student, L. M. Tobin recalled what it had been like to serve one of those terms at hard labor. "For breaches of campus laws the boys were put under the discipline of the stern D. C. Lewis. The boys referred to him as "D. C." He sent us to the rock pile. Odd jobs on the campus with a two wheel cart drawn by a stubborn mule was the task. D. C. always managed to get work for us in a most conspicuous place in sight of the girls' dormitory."[42]

Under Wilkinson, students and faculty members were all but compelled to take part in religious observances. In 1916 the president appealed to all teachers to "assist in carrying on the religious work of the institution," and they were asked "if possible" to teach Sunday school. Moreover "teachers should attend weekly prayer services as often as possible." Given the importance that most African Americans attached to their Christian faith, these requests were not considered arbitrary, nor was there open opposition to a state institution mandating religious beliefs or behavior.[43]

Wilkinson briefly—very briefly—permitted students to form a student government. In early 1913 a delegation of students approached the president with a proposal to organize a student college senate. Wilkinson responded favorably and considered the idea "very timely." The senate met, and Wilkinson quickly decided that it was not such a timely idea after all. "The president announced that he had ordered the college senate of the student body to dissolve." No explanation was offered for his hasty change of mind.[44]

ACADEMIC ACCOUNTABILITY

Faculty and administrators perennially contended with the twin problems of their students' weak academic backgrounds that combined with an indifferent attitude toward their studies. Too often students arrived at S.C. State from rural and impoverished schools without sufficient grounding in the basic skills. Not having been exposed at an early age to learning that aroused curiosity and excited an interest in books and ideas, many of the same students demonstrated little motivation and lacked a genuine concern for schoolwork.

As a student Benjamin E. Mays was one of the exceptions. He was the valedictorian of the normal class in 1916. But he noticed the lack of appreciation for education among his fellow students. "The vast majority of the students at State in my day did not really apply themselves; few students had any desire to learn. The boys had their minds on the girls; the girls had their minds on the boys. The boys would sit on campus looking at their girl friend for hours at a time; for hours at a time the girls would parade the campus, the better to be looked at. Study or no study, however, most of them passed their work. The few students who did apply themselves and studied were considered odd and called bookworms."[45]

Wilkinson and the faculty vacillated on how to grapple with poorly prepared and insufficiently motivated students. One approach was to bear down and demand at least a minimum level of competence. Those who could not meet the requirements would suffer the consequences. As the school year concluded in 1913–14, Wilkinson reminded faculty to maintain rigorous standards. "Teachers [were] warned not to be lenient with students' records but see that no one was issued a promotion card unless he deserved the same by examination and general average."[46]

On the other hand and in recognition of the lack of meaningful educational opportunities afforded most students, perhaps some concessions might be made to compensate for student inadequacies. When the school year began in 1914–15, Wilkinson appealed to faculty not to be too strict in their academic demands. "Teachers were asked by the President to be lenient in assigning lessons—not to make the assignments too long." For decades at South Carolina State faculty and administrators would struggle to find a workable approach to academic requirements that took into account the educational deficiencies of their students while simultaneously insisting that students measure up to sound academic standards.[47]

AFRICAN AMERICAN HISTORY

At least a portion of these academic difficulties stemmed from the emphasis the college placed on teaching agricultural and vocational skills at the expense of liberal arts subjects. Acquiring technical expertise and providing labor often took precedence over intellectual development. But this was not always the case. To incite interest among students in the past and in their heritage, the college introduced two Negro history courses in 1918–19. A course entitled History of the Negro in America was required for juniors in the normal program. "The aim of this course is to give historical perspective for the understanding of the present conditions, an appreciation of the honored names of the Negroes in the past, and an estimate of the genuine contributions the Negro people have made to the labor force, military strength, musical culture, etc., of American civilization." The course began at the slave trade and concluded at "the present day."[48]

The second course, Problems of Negro Life, was mandatory for senior normal students. "It is the aim of this course to use all available data to acquaint the student with the part the Negro has in the developing life of America and with the economic, political, intellectual, and religious forces that enter into the relations of the Negro and white people in America." Apparently history instructor Julia Mae Williams taught both courses until the arrival of Asa H. Gordon on the campus the following year.[49]

Gordon was the first college faculty member to write a book. A native of Monticello, Georgia, he graduated from Atlanta University and earned a law degree from Hamilton College in 1920. At five feet five inches, he was a short man who described his primary health problem as "underweight." He had an abiding interest in African American history, and he took over the course the History of the Negro in America. Gordon increased it from a one-hour to a two-hour class. The textbook was Benjamin Brawley's *History of the American Negro.* (Brawley was a native of Columbia, South Carolina, and a prolific historian, critic, and social commentator.) Gordon also offered for the first time a course in the history of South Carolina. But the course Problems in Negro Life was dropped.[50]

Gordon wrote and then in 1929 published *Sketches of Negro Life and History in South Carolina.* It is a rich and fascinating account of the struggles and accomplishments of black men and women in the Palmetto State. There are essays on slavery, Reconstruction, education, business, and agriculture. He made it plain that despite what most white South Carolinians believed, "South Carolina's Negro population was never contented, satisfied and happy to be in slavery, but struggled to be free." There is a splendid chapter devoted to African American women, "The Gifts of Womanhood in Ebony." He asked his friend and colleague Benjamin E. Mays to contribute an essay, "The New Negro Challenges the Old Order." B. B. Barnwell, one of South Carolina's first black extension agents, assisted Gordon with the chapter on the Negro farmer. In the meantime Gordon left the college and joined Benjamin F. Hubert at Savannah State College. For a time he served as dean of the faculty. He also taught at Southern A&M College in Baton Rouge, at Delaware State, and at Alcorn in Mississippi. The current library at Savannah State is named in honor of Asa H. Gordon.[51]

WILKINSON'S AUTHORITY

Wilkinson encountered fewer problems with obstreperous faculty members than had his predecessor. Thomas Miller tended to take disagreements personally, and he intensely disliked criticism, especially from subordinates. He often reacted sharply to any perceived affront. In contrast Wilkinson possessed a calm demeanor and usually responded coolly rather than angrily to critics or challenges to his authority. Wilkinson did attempt to deal quietly with one faculty member who he came to regard not only as troublesome, but as a threat to his authority as president and to the reputation of the college.

Andrew Simkins had been hired in 1913 to teach wheelwrighting. For reasons that are not clear, Wilkinson eventually came to despise Simkins, but he was unwilling to take action against him either privately or publicly. In 1923 he explained to board of trustees member Dr. F. W. P. Butler of Columbia that he was trying to handle "a certain matter . . . with all possible patience" and "adroitly and with tact." But there was no way to mollify Simkins. Wilkinson explained that "on all sides, wherever I travel, I can hear from someone his threats and evil designs." The president never identified the reasons why Simkins was so upset with him, but Wilkinson asked Butler, who was a white medical doctor, to intervene diplomatically so that Simkins's attacks on the college president would cease. "I think he ought to be called down by you in a positive way, for if he continues to think he can do as he wants to, the result after all will be disastrous to the college from the viewpoint of notoriety or perhaps in some other way." Wilkinson went on, "It would be well to send for him, and let him know that he cannot afford to continue to hurt the College by keeping up this fuss and abuse." Wilkinson refused to respond to the Simkins criticism and allegations. "On many sides folks (colored) have asked me 'What is the trouble with you and Simkins?' I am handicapped, for I have promised not to break the peace."[52]

Simkins finally did leave the college, apparently of his own volition. He became a prosperous owner of real estate in Columbia. He also opened several liquor stores in the 1930s after prohibition ended. What is most important, Simkins married Modjeska Montieth in 1929. Modjeska Simkins became a pivotal figure in the twentieth-century civil rights struggle. This was another case where the wife was far more significant historically than her husband.[53]

In 1916 the board of trustees granted Wilkinson more authority and thereby demonstrated that they had more confidence in his ability to govern the college than they had shown Thomas E. Miller. Meeting in the office of Governor Richard I. Manning, the board revised its bylaws and permitted Wilkinson greater control over routine matters. "The Board of Trustees shall determine the general policy of the College, make laws for its government, approve its courses of study, and direct the expenditure of its funds. The President of the College, as chief executive and administrative officer of the Board, shall execute and control the administration. The Board shall not undertake to direct details of executive action except through the President, who is expected to act with perfect freedom within the line of general policy laid down by the Board." The board also let it be known that henceforth faculty, staff, students, and community residents were not to communicate directly with board members. They were to make any inquiries through the president. The implication was that individuals had avoided Wilkinson and had been in the habit of consulting with board members.

Moreover the trustees gave Wilkinson the authority to suspend or dismiss any employee including faculty members, but only on the approval of the two local members of the board. The revised bylaws also stipulated that faculty members were required to attend chapel programs every Monday through Friday unless excused by the president. Five years after selecting Wilkinson to replace Miller, the members of the board of trustees were confident that they had chosen the right man to lead the college. Wilkinson had shown sufficient deference to them and to state officials while at the same time skillfully managing students, faculty, and the affairs of the institution. There had been no unseemly or disruptive public controversies.[54]

THE COOPERATIVE EXTENSION PROGRAM

On May 8, 1914, President Woodrow Wilson signed the Smith-Lever bill into law. This measure enabled S.C. State over the next several decades to develop—in spite of very limited financial support—an impressive extension program to provide information and advice to thousands of black families in rural South Carolina. But the Smith-Lever legislation was not the first effort by the college to reach out to rural residents of the state. As early as 1897, President Thomas Miller and professor of agriculture John W. Hoffman organized conferences on and off campus for the benefit of black farmers. In the summer of 1901 fifteen farmers' institutes were held across the state in communities such as Bishopville, Camden, Gaffney, Adams Run, and Georgetown.[55]

The college also published and distributed by mail extension work bulletins "giving to the colored farmers of the State much valuable information on topics relating to farm work and domestic life." President Wilkinson, who like President Miller had no agricultural training, took the lead in agricultural outreach. In 1912 he asked the legislature for a "small appropriation" of $2,500 to continue "in instructing and interesting the Negro farmers and students in newer and more scientific methods of farm work and production."[56]

The legislature provided $2,000 in 1913, and Wilkinson personally directed all but five of a series of twenty-two conferences and institutes held across South Carolina that attracted 19,462 farmers. The largest crowd, of three thousand, turned out at Elloree on July 24. Wilkinson boasted that "not only have the farmers of this section, both white and colored, been helped by the College, but our workers have assisted them in all sections by correspondence, periodic visits, and bulletin service.[57]

In 1903 the U.S. Department of Agriculture in cooperation with the General Education Board (GEB), a philanthropic enterprise established by John D. Rockefeller, dispatched demonstration agents to the rural South to assist farmers. This initial federal extension effort did not include the land-grant colleges and universities. The GEB provided the money and the Department of Agriculture, through special agent Seaman Knapp, provided the direction. From its inception, a small number of black agents were included in this early program. South Carolina had five or six black agents in 1905–6, and there were twenty-six black agents working across the South by 1911.[58]

In 1911 Department of Agriculture officials approached Clemson College administrators with a proposal that Clemson undertake extension work in South Carolina. Federal authorities made it clear that they expected Clemson to hire black agents to work with black farmers. The Clemson board of trustees wanted no part of that arrangement.

In early 1912 Clemson president Walter M. Riggs explained to Bradford Knapp, who had succeeded his father as federal supervisor of the extension program, that the college was unwilling to employ black people in such positions. The trustees were willing to have Clemson work with black farmers, but not if it meant putting black men on the Clemson payroll: "they were not willing that the College should undertake it, because of the necessity of having negroes in our employ."[59]

When the Smith-Lever legislation went into effect in 1914, it made no specific provision for black demonstration agents or for black land-grant colleges. In that respect it signaled a retreat from the Morrill Act of 1890, which specifically required states that had white-only land-grant schools to make funds available on an equitable basis to black land-grant colleges. Because Congress declined to include African Americans and their institutions in the Smith-Lever bill, the five-year-old NAACP had unsuccessfully opposed its passage.[60]

The Smith-Lever Act vastly enlarged the federal government's commitment to cooperative extension work (while simultaneously excluding the GEB from extension activities). Named after Georgia senator Hoke Smith and South Carolina representative Asbury F. Lever, who was also a member of the Clemson College board of trustees, the law provided funds to each state to establish or to expand on cooperative extension programs through that state's land-grant institution: "cooperative agricultural extension work shall consist of giving instruction and practical demonstrations in agriculture and home economics to persons not attending or resident in said colleges." No funds could be used to construct buildings or offer courses on the college campuses.[61]

With the Smith-Lever Act, Congress for the first time in history compelled states to allocate matching funds. States had to appropriate "an equal sum" to that provided by the federal government to support extension work. The amount that each state would be required to match was based on the proportion of rural residents in that state in comparison to the total rural population of the United States. By this formula South Carolina would receive 2.61 percent of the total Smith-Lever funds appropriated by Congress each year through 1922.[62]

How much of this combined federal and state funding for extension work would S.C. State receive? Not a penny. Shortly after passage of the Smith-Lever legislation, President Wilkinson wrote to President Riggs and to Clemson director of extension work W. W. Long and suggested that black agents be employed to work with black farmers under the authority of S.C. State College.[63]

Riggs agreed that black extension agents should work out of S.C. State, but he declined to make any commitment to Wilkinson. Riggs as well as Wilkinson were well aware that Governor Coleman Blease was no friend of extension work, regarding it as a waste of taxpayer money. The two college presidents also knew that Blease was willing, if not eager, to stir up racial animosity. Extension work among black people would provide Blease a perfect excuse to lash out against both the extension program and African Americans. Riggs wrote Wilkinson that "demagogues in opposition to our getting the State to make appropriations to meet the Lever bill" might thwart efforts to secure matching funds. He asked Wilkinson to "give careful consideration to the present state of politics in South Carolina." Privately Riggs despised Blease and supported the governor's opponent, Ellison D. "Cotton Ed" Smith, in the 1914 U.S. Senate Democratic primary race, an election Blease lost.[64]

In 1915 the general assembly agreed to accept the terms of the Smith-Lever Act, and to furnish the necessary matching funds. As expected, legislators assigned Clemson exclusive responsibility for administering the extension program. But federal authorities through the offices of Bradford Knapp then insisted that Clemson retain black men for extension work. Riggs resisted and suggested instead that the Department of Agriculture should hire and direct the black agents.[65]

Although Coleman Blease was no longer governor or a political threat to Clemson or South Carolina State in 1915, Riggs still had to contend with a board of trustees that opposed the employment of black agents. The Clemson president explained to the chairman of the Clemson board, Alan Johnstone, who was also a state senator: "We are having a little trouble with the Washington authorities in regard to our policy of negro demonstration work. The Washington people want to insist that we use some negro agents, where as we do not think this is best." Finally, after further negotiations with U.S. Department of Agriculture officials, including secretary of agriculture David Houston, Riggs and the Clemson board agreed to include black agents in the extension program, provided those agents worked from the S.C. State campus in Orangeburg.[66]

South Carolina State and Clemson leaders drafted a memorandum of agreement in April 1915, and President Riggs and director of extension work W. W. Long visited Orangeburg a few weeks later to work out the details of the program with President Wilkinson. Clemson maintained overall control of extension work while S.C. State would direct the black farm demonstration agents. Riggs and Long largely gave Wilkinson free reign over the agents but not over the money.[67]

South Carolina State received no federal, state, or county funds for extension work. In 1919, for example, $282,599 was allocated to Clemson for extension work by the federal and state governments and several county governments. In turn Winthrop College in Rock Hill received $105,282 from Clemson for home demonstration work among rural white women. S.C. State simply managed the work of the eight black farm demonstration agents and the one home economics worker who were then paid by Clemson.[68]

In 1919 Wilkinson pointed out that participation in the extension program cost the college money because it received no funds from Clemson. "The Smith-Lever Farm Demonstration Work among colored farmers was given over to the college about five years ago. Since then the college has been directing the agents, collecting the weekly reports, inspecting he field operations, holding the semi-annual conferences of workers and farmers, and making out the annual reports on the work accomplished. The college has borne the expenses of these operations annually without receiving any compensation from Clemson College, which is charged by the Federal authorities with the responsibility of State work."[69]

The situation continued to aggravate Wilkinson, who cordially but firmly complained in 1921: "The College directs six local demonstration agents among the colored farmers, but does not handle the funds. We have no part whatever in the Home Economics work. . . . It is hoped that by some means an opening may be created whereby the college will participate in this very important work among the people." (The number of agents had been reduced to six because Congress had failed to pass an emergency agricultural bill the previous year.)[70]

Wilkinson and Charles F. Brooks, a member of the board of trustees, decided to travel to Washington to appeal to Department of Agriculture authorities in May 1921 to discuss the college's exclusion from Smith-Lever funds. The trip was cancelled, however, and the meeting never took place. Either Wilkinson and Brooks changed their minds, or, more likely, they were informed that such a visit to federal officials on behalf of a black college to complain about neglect at the hands of white leaders would not be in the best interests of the college or the state of South Carolina.[71]

Not surprisingly the white farm demonstration agents also earned considerably more than their black counterparts. In 1919 the white agents earned an average of $1,965. (Wilkinson's salary was $2,100.) The black agents earned an average of $809 each. Moreover several of South Carolina's counties contributed $97,381 to the work of the white men and women who were county agents. No South Carolina county contributed funds for black demonstration work.[72]

W. W. Long, Clemson's director of extension service, made no mention of this disparity as he extolled the contributions of black farmers to South Carolina agriculture and to the state's economy in 1919. He pointed out that there were ninety-six thousand black farmers who owned nearly four million acres of land that was worth $189 million. During the previous decade those black farmers had increased their land holdings by more than two hundred thousand acres. Black farm families raised 45 percent of the state's cotton crop.[73]

South Carolina State also received no federal funds for agricultural experimentation and research through programs established by the Hatch Act (1887) and the Adams Act (1906). Once again Wilkinson courteously asked that some of those funds, which totaled nearly $95,000 in 1919—and that went entirely to Clemson and Winthrop—be redirected to Orangeburg. "If we could secure from Clemson a part of the Hatch and Adams funds, our experimental work in Agriculture could be better equipped and developed." He suggested that "some inquiry [might] be made through the presidents of Clemson and Winthrop colleges as to the possibility of such a course." No such inquiry was made.[74]

STATE FUNDING FOR THE COLLEGE

Not only was S.C. State excluded from sharing in federal funding for agriculture programs (except for the Smith-Hughes Act, which supported educating teachers in agricultural and vocational subjects), but it also received significantly less state funding than other public colleges and universities during the years surrounding World War I. The funding inequity persisted despite the larger number of students at South Carolina State than any other institution except Winthrop. Most S.C. State students still were not enrolled in the college curriculum. They were vocational students enrolled in the preparatory (secondary) and normal programs. President Wilkinson noted in his 1917 annual report: "We hold high rank among the institutions of the State as a well equipped trade school."[75]

Table 7. Enrollments in South Carolina Public Colleges and Universities

	1912–13	1915–16	1919–20
Clemson	811	803	886; 23 graduate students
Univ. of S.C.	453; 74 in law school, 25 in grad school	578; 73 in law school, 23 in army program	579; 101 in law school
Winthrop	745	1,021	1,053
Citadel	229	251	314
S.C. State	826	978	683

Sources: *Reports and Resolutions of the General Assembly of South Carolina, State Department of Education Report:* 1912, 1: 531, 665, 721, 697, 805; 1916, 20: 3, 9, 3, 21; 1920, 2: 16, 3, 11, 3, 7. In the 1916 and 1920 reports, each report was paged separately. South Carolina State admitted males and females. Clemson and the Citadel admitted white men. Winthrop admitted white women. The University of South Carolina had a predominantly male enrollment. The enrollments do not include summer school enrollment.

For reasons that are uncertain, military service during World War I caused S.C. State's enrollment to decline more precipitously than that at the state's white institutions. Wilkinson reported in the 1918–19 school year, "the draft took at least 80% of our boys and the influenza [epidemic of 1918] prevents 50% of our girls from attending school this year." Enrollment was down by over three hundred students from the previous school year.[76]

As had been the case earlier in the history of S.C. State, enrollments fluctuated during the school year as students arrived and departed, depending on the need for their labor at home. The overwhelming number of students came from farm families. Of 887 students in 1913–14, 697 came from farms. In 1914–15, there were 934 students enrolled, but only 579 were still in attendance at the end of the school year in May.[77]

Clemson continued to rely heavily on the proceeds from the state tax—the so-called Tag tax—collected on the sale of commercial fertilizer. Clemson received an average of $237,000 per year during the second decade of the twentieth century from the Tag tax. The upstate land-grant college had a huge financial advantage over the other state schools. In 1913–14, for example, Clemson received $276,000 in Tag tax revenues and spent $102,000 of it on fertilizer inspection, analysis, and several other small agricultural programs. The remaining $174,000 went into Clemson College coffers.[78]

WORLD WAR I

Amid much patriotic fervor, Congress declared war on Germany on April 6, 1917, and the United States entered World War I. As they had in previous wars, many African Americans eagerly supported the war effort while reminding white Americans that they were loyal to their country despite the racial prejudice they experienced. Ten days after the declaration of war, black residents of Beaufort County expressed deep devotion to America while simultaneously lamenting their unjust treatment. "We, as loyal citizens of the United States, in spite of the discriminations, injustice and lack of protection under the laws, both local and national, feel that we are still citizens of this great country, whose flag is as much our flag as it is the flag of every other citizen."[79]

A delegation of South Carolina black leaders, led by the Reverend Richard Carroll, met with Governor Richard I. Manning to pledge their commitment to the cause while asking the governor to permit black men to enlist in the all-white state militia. Manning (who was the chair of the college's board of trustees) appreciated the show of black support but indicated that the racial makeup of the militia would not change.[80]

Former S.C. State president Thomas E. Miller served on an eight-man black subcommittee that assumed responsibility for organizing the state's black population in support of the war effort. This subcommittee functioned as an adjunct to the all-white Central Committee of Civic Preparedness. The Reverend Richard Carroll chaired the subcommittee, and Miller was the only committee member who had been connected in any way to South Carolina State.[81]

Although the South Carolina Militia—soon to be the National Guard—refused to enlist black men, the U.S. government had no such reservations about the enlistment or conscription of black men. When the newly created Selective Service system began to register and then draft men for military service in the summer of 1917, large numbers of those young men in South Carolina were black men. With a small black majority of the state's population, it is not surprising that slightly more than half of the fifty-four hundred men drafted in South Carolina during the war were black. As black men joined the military, the enrollment at South Carolina State plunged from 803 in 1917, to 649 in 1918, to 448 in 1919.[82]

Four faculty members also left the college for military service. Grover Harden, who was commandant for military training at the college, departed, as did William T. Calhoun, who taught plumbing. Benjamin F. Hubert, the director of agriculture, went to France, where he supervised agricultural instruction to black soldiers while serving on the staff of the University of Beaune. Miller F. Whittaker, the architect and the director of the mechanical department, was commissioned a second lieutenant. He served in France in the Intelligence Section of the 371st and 368th Infantry with the all-black Ninety-Second Division of the U.S. Army.[83]

In 1918 the War Department created the Student Army Training Corps (SATC) to prepare 150,000 young men on five hundred college campuses for military service. They would enroll in academic courses and receive military instruction as well as uniforms before joining the U.S. Army or, in some cases, the U.S. Navy. They would then receive commissions as officers. At South Carolina State, the War Department contracted with the college to establish a Student Army Training Corps—but with a difference. The black students who enrolled at S.C. State would not prepare for military service; they would be trained in various vocations. Beginning on a provisional basis in July 1918, S.C. State registered 247 young men for instruction in such subjects as woodworking, ironworking, truck driving, and auto mechanics. There was no military training, and there were no uniforms. Those who completed the program could be expected to contribute to the productivity of the nation's wartime economy. The presence of the men in the program helped the college offset the loss of students who had enlisted or were drafted.[84]

The initial SATC program at S.C. State proved so successful that four instructors were sent to Howard University for additional vocational instruction. Then in October 1918 the War Department announced that the program would be extended until June 1919 with men eighteen to twenty years old enrolling for training that would range from three months, to six months, to a full year. They would receive $30 per month, the same as an army private. The military would pay their tuition and $1 per diem per student. Those who finished the program would be inducted into the army as privates.[85]

When the war ended a month later in November 1918, the War Department abruptly cancelled the SATC program and left the college holding the financial bag. With the program scheduled to continue well into 1919, college officials had invested in equipment and supplies with the expectation that they would recoup the funds. The college was responsible for $7,089. Because the Department of War "refused to take over or pay for such general equipment as they deemed could be of future use to the college," President Wilkinson reluctantly and futilely appealed to the general assembly to reimburse the college.[86]

S.C. State also had an unpleasant experience when it agreed to provide rehabilitation training for black South Carolina military personnel who had been injured in World War I. The college contracted with the Federal Board for Vocational Education to accept twenty disabled soldiers for vocational instruction. But for unexplained reasons, the program did not function effectively. "The experiment proved unsatisfactory for many reasons, hence the engagement was cancelled after consultation with the local committee of the board [of trustees]."[87]

In agreeing to create a rehabilitation program for injured black military personnel, President Wilkinson had observed that it was college's "patriotic duty to assist the Government in whatever may be possible for the prosecution of the war." As commendable as these public-spirited intentions were, S.C. State's involvement with the federal and state programs linked to World War I had been far from an ennobling or gratifying experience. Black South Carolinians and the college had willingly supported and contributed to the war effort, convinced that a war waged to advance American ideals abroad would promote democratic values at home. But whatever hopes black people had that white South Carolinians would realize the injustice inherent in their treatment of black citizens were shattered after the war.

PRESERVING JIM CROW

Oblivious to the hypocrisy of their attitudes and behavior, white southerners were determined to maintain Jim Crow and white supremacy no matter how devoted and patriotic black people had been during the war. South Carolina State history professor Asa H. Gordon captured the bitter resentment of African Americans several years after the war ended. "The Negro had enlisted or had been conscripted into a war which he was told was being fought 'to make the world safe for democracy.' Very naturally and logically he thought the process of democratization should begin at home, in South Carolina, or at least be applied after the war was over and he had done his bit 'to save civilization.' But, alas! the South Carolina he found when he returned from the trenches of blood-stained France was very much the same as the South Carolina he had left singing 'We'll hang Bill Kaiser on the sour apple tree.' He returned to find his white fellow citizens ready to hang him without a trial on the limbs of the pines of his native state if he made the slightest sign of resisting 'the old order.'"[88]

As World War I concluded in late 1918, an influenza pandemic swept the nation, killing nearly seven hundred thousand Americans. S.C. State administrators were alarmed about the impact it would have on the college: "the influenza epidemic threatens the whole institution because of the lack of [a] proper health conservation facility." On the verge of desperation, the trustees pleaded with legislators to appropriate $25,000 to construct a hospital on the campus.

But perhaps because of its rural and isolated location, there was only one influenza fatality at the college, a young man enrolled in the SATC program. One unnamed faculty member also contracted influenza but survived. Although enrollments plunged at the college, the institution was exceptionally fortunate because more than fourteen thousand South Carolinians succumbed to the pandemic. Meanwhile the general assembly quickly set aside $25,000 in 1919 for the campus hospital.[89]

PHILANTHROPIC SUPPORT

It was not until South Carolina State approached its third decade that it was able to attract even modest philanthropic support. There were several major philanthropic organizations during the first half of the twentieth century that made funds available for southern black education. The John F. Slater Fund, which stressed the development of agricultural and mechanical skills among African Americans, was one of those philanthropies. In 1897 S.C. State trustee J. W. Floyd and state superintendent of education W. D. Mayfield—and not President Thomas Miller—traveled to Washington and New York City to enlist financial support from officials at the Slater Fund, but they were unsuccessful.[90]

In 1914 James H. Dillard of the Slater Fund provided $100 toward the salaries of faculty who taught summer school. That amount was increased to $150 in 1915. Summer school had become an important component of the college's role as a teacher-training institution. Teachers from the state's black public schools—and not regular students—enrolled in summer school courses at S.C. State to expand their knowledge and to strengthen their teaching skills.[91]

During a six-week summer session in 1921, 560 teachers enrolled from forty-two of South Carolina's forty-six counties as well as from North Carolina, Georgia, and Florida. Teachers in the Smith-Hughes program were required to attend. The State Department of Education granted teachers a two-year renewal to their teaching certificates if they completed three courses during the summer session. The General Education Board (GEB) contributed $1,000 to the growing summer school program that year. The GEB replaced the Slater Fund by 1920 in providing financial assistance for summer classes.[92]

The General Education Board had been established in 1902 with a gift of $1 million from John D. Rockefeller. By 1921 he had contributed over $129 million to the GEB. In 1920 the GEB agreed to contribute $40,000 toward the construction and operation of a practice or training school on the S.C. State campus that would serve as a local elementary school for black children. The proposal to erect the school was spearheaded by state superintendent of education J. E. Swearingen, and it involved the collaboration of President Wilkinson; William R. Lowman, a member of the college board of trustees; A. J. Thackston, the superintendent of the Orangeburg city schools; and Orangeburg Board of Education member W. W. Wannamaker; as well as Jackson Davis, the field representative for the General Education Board. Davis was an especially eager proponent of the project. He had visited the campus in late 1919 and was impressed. "The whole plant is one of the best of the State institutions, and South Carolina has recently been far more generous to the school than any of the other states in her group."[93]

State superintendent Swearingen worked to persuade doubtful Orangeburg school officials who did not look with favor on the plan to build the practice school on the black campus and place it under the authority of the college and its president. In a letter to Orangeburg school superintendent Thackston, Swearingen pointed out: "The work of this College must set the standard for negro education in South Carolina." He added that "the benefits of such a [teacher-education] program would be immediate and far-reaching on the state-at-large."[94]

The participants in the practice school proposal drafted a memorandum of agreement at a meeting of the college board of trustees in May 1920. They decided that the school would indeed be built on the campus and that it would enroll four hundred students in grade one through either grade seven or grade eight (they preferred grade eight). The Orangeburg School Board would furnish $2 per student per year from its state education funds as well as $5,000 toward construction costs, and it would assume financial responsibility for teachers' salaries. S.C. State would hire the teachers and determine their individual salaries. The General Education Board would share a portion of the construction costs with the State of South Carolina. The GEB would also contribute $5,000 per year for the first ten years of the school's operation.[95]

Jackson Davis urged his superiors at the GEB to support the proposed school. "I do not think we could spend any money for the training of colored teachers in South Carolina more effectively than in giving assistance to this project."[96] Davis provided the figures:

Costs	Sources of Funding
$115,000 construction	$45,000 GEB
$25,000 desks, furnishings, etc.	$90,000 State appropriation
	$5,000 Orangeburg city schools
$140,000 total	$140,000 total

The college, Davis explained, would supervise construction. Faculty member and architect Miller F. Whittaker would design the facility after first examining a similar school that had been built at Winthrop College. Students would serve as part of the labor force during construction as they had with previous campus facilities.[97]

However, this promising project never materialized. The sticking point was the anticipated state appropriation of $90,000. Supporters of the school expected that the legislature would approve of the use of funds for the school that already had been allocated for the erection on the campus of a World War I memorial to black servicemen. In 1919, after the Allied triumph in First World War, the general assembly had set aside $100,000 to construct a memorial building at S.C. State. It would be dedicated to "the military and naval exploits and brave men and patriotic deeds of South Carolinians who have shared the dangers and the glories of the great war on land and sea and in the air." The memorial would include an archive to house books, manuscripts, and other materials concerning the war. A memorial commission was established at S.C. State, and it included the college president, who would serve as the commission chair. The commission was responsible for supervising a fund-raising effort—"a drive to raise $100,000.00 among the colored people of the state to supplement the $100,000.00 provided by the legislature."[98]

That fund-raising effort netted a meager $1,190—a mere $98,810 short of the goal. By 1921 Wilkinson, the memorial commission, and the backers of the practice school believed that despite the fund-raising failure, the proposed practice school could be incorporated into the memorial building by utilizing the $100,000 appropriated by the legislature in 1919. But by that time the state's economy was in distress, and the legislature would not reallocate the memorial funds to build the practice school. The funds were never spent—on the memorial or on the school. The $45,000 grant from the GEB lapsed, and the project collapsed.[99]

THE GREAT MIGRATION

The prosperity of the war years had given way to a growing economic crisis in South Carolina as cotton and tobacco prices dropped dramatically. Overproduction followed by drought and the infestation of the boll weevil led to huge losses among the state's farmers. The 1922 harvest was one of the worst in the state's history. In desperation thousands of people fled the state, especially African Americans. During the 1920s fifty thousand black farmers (as well as many white farmers) left. Twenty-four of the state's forty-six counties lost population during the decade. South Carolina's population, which had had a black majority since the early nineteenth century, lost that

Table 8. Percent of Nonwhite Residents in South Carolina

1910	1920	1930
55.2%	51.4%	45.7%

Source: *Encyclopedia of South Carolina,* ed. Walter Edgar (Columbia: University of South Carolina Press, 2006), 744.

distinction during the twenties. For many South Carolinians, the Great Depression began in the 1920s.[100]

Even before the economic collapse, African Americans had begun to leave South Carolina en masse. Drawn by opportunities for employment in northern cities during the war years, they left the fields in Edgefield, Bamberg, and Williamsburg for the factories in Philadelphia, Pittsburgh, Cleveland, and Detroit. The exodus of so many black people worried some white leaders. In welcoming the National Association of Teachers in Colored Schools to the S.C. State campus on July 31, 1919, Orangeburg mayor W. A. Livingston told his listeners that a better future awaited them in the South, and not in the North, where a wave of race riots had erupted in several cities including East St. Louis, Chicago, and Washington, D.C. "In Orangeburg we don't have any trouble like you read of in Washington and Chicago. Negroes and white people are on the best of terms and both look forward to a happy future." Livingston neglected to mention the riot that had been instigated by white sailors in Charleston in May 1919 that that left three black men dead, seventeen black people injured, seven white men hurt, and many black businesses damaged or destroyed. The "happy future" described by the mayor was not quite as rosy as he and others anticipated.[101]

CHAPTER THREE

Becoming a College

By the 1920s S. C State had emerged as the most important public institution for African Americans in South Carolina. Black Carolinians demanded much of the college that they came to consider "their own." They insisted that the school do more than simply serve as an educational facility. It was a secondary school and a college and more. It would provide programs in liberal arts and business administration. It would include vocational training. It offered extension programs to rural black farmers and their families, including 4-H clubs. For a time it assisted with the State Colored Fair and the Orangeburg Negro County Fair, and with Fairhold, a home for young black women who had run afoul of the law. It also provided employment opportunities for African Americans. With only limited financial resources, the college spread itself thin as it tried to offer such an array of educational programs and public services to the state's black population.

Most significantly, during its third decade, S.C. State gradually began to make the transition from primarily a secondary school to a bona fide four-year college. Despite the financial restraints, the curriculum expanded, the faculty grew and improved, and the extension program continued to develop through the 1920s. Because state authorities were convinced that S.C. State could operate satisfactorily on limited appropriations, students and faculty members continued to spend large amounts of time maintaining the campus, operating the farm, and constructing new facilities. Public financing expanded enough from 1922 to 1929 to keep the institution functioning. But college administrators felt compelled to impose new fees on students to support assorted programs and building projects.

In the meantime thousands of black South Carolinians left the state in the 1910s and 1920s and migrated elsewhere for more meaningful employment opportunities. The outward migration cost the state its black majority. By 1925 and for the first time since the early nineteenth century, there were more white people residing in South Carolina than black people. An estimated one hundred thousand black people deserted South Carolina in the early 1920s. More than thirty-seven hundred left Orangeburg County. "This exodus," President Wilkinson observed in 1923, "is largely the result of economic depression, caused by boll weevil devastation."[1]

Yet the loss of black Carolinians did not reduce enrollments at S.C. State because the college lacked ample facilities for the number of young people who wanted to enroll, especially young men. Although the number of students ebbed and flowed during the 1920s, enrollment exceeded one thousand in 1921 and remained above that figure

The arch not only served as the entry to the campus, but its attractive design was in keeping with the arch at the entrance to the Negro Building at the South Carolina Interstate and West Indian Exposition. It was also a prominent feature of White Hall and later Dukes Gymnasium. Architect and later President Miller F. Whittaker was drawn to the use of brick arches. White Hall and the campus water tower are in the background. Courtesy of the Historical Collection, South Carolina State University

for a decade. Notably, more students enrolled in the college program. There were 295 young people in the college curriculum by 1926. In 1928 the normal program ceased, and the licentiate of instruction was abolished and briefly replaced by a junior college program.[2]

There was inadequate housing for students and faculty, and the academic facilities were insufficient. "Our dormitories and class rooms are overcrowded," Wilkinson pointed out. "We, literally 'packed them in' until the point of turning away over one hundred was reached." In 1922 Wilkinson noted that several courses were "very badly overcrowded" with "numbers running as high as eighty and compelling instructors practically to resort to lecturing, a form of instruction ineffective in any case and particularly unfortunate with students of the age and character of those in the State Colored College."[3]

Had it not been for the contributions of students and faculty as well as financial assistance from the Julius Rosenwald Fund and the General Education Board, there would have been no new facilities constructed on the campus in the 1920s. Even with that philanthropic support, no new dormitories were built between 1917 and 1938. Therefore many youngsters who might have wanted to continue their education at South Carolina State were unable to do so.

STATE FINANCIAL SUPPORT

State appropriations for S.C. State, which reached $73,380 in 1920, declined in 1921 and 1922 with the economic downturn but increased gradually for the remainder of

Table 9. State Appropriations, Colleges and Universities, 1916–32

	Clemson	Winthrop	Citadel	USC	S.C. State
1916	NA	$147,605	$40,500	$98,524	$15,000
1920	$168,070	$416,616	$398,853	$211,515	$115,880
1924	$91,813	$418,108	$161,143	$476,025	$101,150
1928	$223,234	$449,352	$201,666	$439,877	$124,320
1932	$141,000	$292,000	$175,000	$312,000	$73,000

Sources: *Acts and Joint Resolutions of the General Assembly of South Carolina:* 1916, 1043–44; 1920, 1171–72; 1924, 1239–40; 1928, 1340–53; 1932, 1581–82. Owing to expenditures for new construction, annual appropriations for individual institutions sometimes spiked. In 1920 S.C. State received additional funds to build White Hall and a new infirmary. The Citadel received additional money in 1920 to construct new barracks. Clemson continued to receive funds from the tax on fertilizer, the so-called Tag tax. But with the depression in agriculture, the revenue from the Tag tax declined significantly in the 1920s. These state appropriations also include funds for scholarships for each institution except for S.C. State.

the decade. By 1928 the general assembly allotted a relatively generous $124,320 to the college. Compared to other state schools, however, S.C. State continued to receive disproportionately less funding. The Citadel, for example, got $40,500 in 1916, and that rose to $201,666 in 1928. Furthermore each of the white state institutions received funds within their appropriation to award scholarships to state residents. The disparity in funding was reflected in the salaries allotted for the presidents of the state institutions. In 1929 the presidents of the University of South Carolina and Winthrop each received $9,000 per year while the Citadel president was paid $7,500. Robert Wilkinson earned $3,600. (The salary of the Clemson president was not disclosed.)[4]

WILKINSON AND THE POLITICIANS

Following the construction in 1917 of Lowman Hall, a dormitory for men, and the completion in 1920 of White Hall, an academic building, the state provided few funds for major capital improvements at South Carolina State in the 1920s and the 1930s. The general assembly agreed only to provide matching funds for capital projects initiated and paid in part by the Rosenwald Fund and the General Education Board. State appropriations during the two decades were not even adequate in many instances to provide routine maintenance and to make minor improvements.

In 1925 President Wilkinson acknowledged that the previous year the college had been able to tend to several routine matters with the installation of a new laundry machine, repairs were made to a dishwasher, horses and mules received new shoes, and fences were erected around the poultry facility. However, he enumerated fourteen other items that needed repair or maintenance at a total cost of $28,000. White Hall needed painting. The dining hall needed a new floor. The laundry building needed repairs. The steam line needed to be extended as well as repaired. But the state consistently failed to appropriate funds needed to meet the institution's infrastructure needs. The trustees pleaded to legislators for more state funds. "We call your attention to additions and improvements made with meager appropriation available. We would stress constructive needs and accommodations that are elemental, if the College is to meet immediate requirements for training along practical lines."[5]

Wilkinson summed up the college's financial plight perhaps more positively than the situation merited. "I must say that South Carolina is expending generously for the maintenance of this institution, but the Legislature is slow in caring for permanent improvements. We are still in need of a library, agricultural, home economics, science, gymnasium and administration building as well as homes for teachers."[6]

Year after year President Wilkinson was placed in the difficult position of waging unceasing efforts to extract more money from legislators who did not consider black higher education a matter of significance, much less a priority. Still he felt compelled to express gratification to political leaders for their support as he reassured them that the funds they did allot were well spent and that the college was doing a fine job. In 1924 Wilkinson thanked the general assembly that had been "very sympathetic towards the College and its needs." Yet in that same report he expressed considerable concern that the overcrowded dormitories were "inimical to health as well as mental progress" of the students. He also pointed out that it was increasingly difficult to keep buildings and equipment in proper repair. Wilkinson consistently balanced praise with firm but courteous requests for more money.[7]

Wilkinson worked tirelessly to persuade state legislators to allocate more money to the black college. Mostly it was a thankless and unrewarding task. White politicians could easily ignore appeals to support the black institution. No legislator depended on black votes to win election, and there were, of course, no black legislators in the general assembly to support the school. Only those political leaders who felt a kindly or paternalistic obligation to the college were inclined to take an interest in it.

South Carolina State and Wilkinson had a friend and unique ally in Walter M. Riggs, the president of Clemson and a native of Orangeburg. In 1923 Riggs invited Wilkinson to join him and the presidents of the other South Carolina public colleges and universities at a meeting in Columbia to plot strategy to try to get a bond bill through the legislature. Riggs was the only white college president from South Carolina in the first half of the twentieth century who collaborated in a meaningful way with a president from S.C. State. But as Riggs explained to Wilkinson as they attempted to arouse support among legislators, "I feel we all ought to keep pretty close together." But that interracial cooperation ended a year later with the death of Riggs.[8]

In 1926 Orangeburg senator W. Claude Martin, who was a member of the Senate Finance Committee, helped restore funding to S.C. State to assist in the construction of a new agricultural building (which would become Hodge Hall). Wilkinson promptly expressed gratitude on behalf of the black community while also telling Martin that black people still had much progress to make. "The Negroes of Orangeburg County and the entire State feel deeply your friendly interest in them and we realize your liberal friendship and support in our upward struggle towards civic, moral and material betterment."[9]

The next year another legislative crisis over money erupted, and Wilkinson again appealed to Martin. The state senate had slashed nearly $14,000 from the college appropriation. The senator succeeded in having the $13,900 reinserted in the budget bill "as per your request." But he remained concerned, informing Wilkinson, "I do not know that I will be able to get this through [the] Free Conference [Committee], but it is my purpose to do all I can to carry out your wishes in the matter."[10]

In 1931, as the national and state economies collapsed, the State Budget Commission reduced the college's 1930 appropriation of $106,588 to $91,806. Wilkinson relied on his contacts in the black community in an attempt to persuade a powerful legislator to restore those cuts. Wilkinson wrote J. B. Beck, who was the principal of all-black Howard High School in Georgetown, to ask Beck to approach state senator Samuel M. Ward. The Georgetown senator was the chair of the Senate Finance Committee and also the chair of the State Budget Commission and the State Sinking Fund Commission.

Wilkinson carefully instructed Beck in two letters sent five days apart. "When Senator Ward returns home this week end from Columbia, I would appreciate your forming a small committee of three representative colored citizens of Georgetown and call on him to show your interest in State College." Wilkinson went on, "I am sure Senator Ward, who knows me quite well and is well disposed to the institution, would appreciate this display of interest on the part of yourself and friends." The college president reminded the high school principal that the senator "is the most powerful man today in the Legislature, but of course his policy will be limited to some extent on account of economic conditions."

President Wilkinson also dispensed a bit of wisdom by explaining that the best way to deal with white people was to agree with their perceptions of black people. "I have always found it true that white people appreciate an endorsement of their opinion of racial matters by leaders of our group. They want to know what we think of ourselves." Presumably Beck told the senator what he wanted to hear, and $5,000 of the $15,000 reduction was restored to the college's appropriation for the next year. Senator Ward, it is worth noting, was also the chairman of the Georgetown County White Supremacy League and the local Prohibition Law and Order League, and a longtime parishioner of Prince George Winyah Episcopal Church.[11]

Wilkinson also did not hesitate to ask members of the board of trustees to intervene with legislators. When the college appropriation was reduced in the senate in 1927, Wilkinson had asked for Senator W. Claude Martin's assistance, but he also turned to the board and asked the chair, Charles F. Brooks of Laurens, for aid. "Unless something is done," Wilkinson advised, "it will probably be necessary to curtail teachers next year."[12]

Brooks confessed that he had not been paying attention. "I had not noticed the several reductions you made mention of. I regret the reduction in salaries especially." Brooks suggested that board members appeal to legislators on behalf of the college. "What do you think," he asked Wilkinson, "about bringing your entire local board to Columbia with Mr. [Adam] Moss at the head, and lets make a 'days lobby' of it with Senate members?" Four of the six members of the board—Moss, Wallace C. Bethea, Frank Limehouse, and Archie L. Dukes—were Orangeburg residents, and they did make the trip to Columbia. The cuts were restored thanks to the board members and with the helpful intervention of Senator Martin.[13]

Vulnerable for decades to the casual indifference of white leadership, S.C. State College administrators sought any conceivable advantage that might benefit the black institution. They curried favor with white officials by presenting them with small and large gifts that were invariably and gratefully accepted. As a Christmas gift in 1929, Wilkinson dispatched one of the Home Economics Department's highly regarded fruit cakes to Claude E. Sawyer, an Aiken attorney and former member of the board of trustees. Sawyer thanked Wilkinson for the "luscious fruit cake" and then took the opportunity to praise the president. "I do wish that everybody could know what you are doing down there in Orangeburg." Wilkinson used that opening to ask Sawyer if he would have a "friendly talk" with Senator John F. Williams regarding the college's appropriation for 1930. No doubt such a conversation occurred because Williams was Sawyer's law partner.[14]

For many years faculty member Charles E. Waterman and students enrolled in his tailoring classes provided custom-made suits and shirts to state leaders and board members at no cost to the recipient. Governor I. C. Blackwood conveyed his appreciation to new president Miller F. Whittaker in 1933, explaining that the chief executive intended to wear the new suit on a forthcoming trip to New York City. Lieutenant Governor James C. Shepard expressed gratitude to Whittaker "for the beautiful suit . . . it fits perfectly." He added that "I am satisfied that the college is doing fine work in training our young colored men to be tailors."[15]

Unfortunately these gifts of appreciation from a college that was hardly awash in funds came to be expected and then demanded by some of the beneficiaries. In 1927 the college sent a typewriter as well as a hog—"a fine animal"—from the campus farm to board chairman Charles F. Brooks. The college could ill afford to dispense with its limited resources, but Wilkinson had little choice than to do what white leaders insisted on.[16]

Then in 1930 in a poorly composed letter scribbled in pencil, board member E. D. Hodge asked Wilkinson where the shirts he had been promised were. "Dr. I asked to have 2 dress shirts made for me & you said you wood when the sewing class met + had [Professor Charles] Waterman take my measure so get him to attend to it + get them to me as earley as convenient." Wilkinson courteously replied that the shirts would soon be sent and, furthermore, that Hodge's portrait was scheduled to be hung in the newly constructed building that had been named in honor of the insistent board member from Alcolu.[17]

Almost a year later in a response to Hodge, Wilkinson wrote that the work that Hodge wanted college personnel to do at his Alcolu farm would be undertaken as soon as instructor William W. Wilkins completed raising the steel trusses for the new campus gymnasium. Wilkinson also assured Hodge that his order for clothing was almost finished. "I am pushing Prof. Waterman on the clothes for your other son, urging him to finish them up this week so that he may have them."[18]

The most perplexing and troublesome of Wilkinson's political relationships was with that unabashed white supremacist Coleman Blease. Wilkinson necessarily had to deal with politicians who had less than admirable views of black people. But Blease

For decades Charles Waterman's students in tailoring measured, cut, and sewed suits and shirts for political leaders as well as for members of the board of trustees. Most of these men gratefully accepted the "gifts," but Governor Strom Thurmond insisted on paying for his apparel. Courtesy of the Historical Collection, South Carolina State University

was an exception even among avowed white supremacists. As governor Blease had forced Thomas Miller out of the college presidency in 1911 and had acceded to the appointment of Wilkinson to succeed Miller. But Blease, who casually and publicly ridiculed black people in the most vitriolic terms, had involuntarily abandoned politics after failed election campaigns in 1914, 1916, 1918, and 1922. Then in 1924 Blease won election to the U.S. Senate, and Wilkinson dealt with the temperamental leader in an uncharacteristically obsequious and unctuous manner unbefitting even a conservative college president.[19]

During the holiday season in 1926, Wilkinson dispatched a fruitcake prepared by students in home economics to Blease. In gratitude Blease asked for two more of the delicacies to share with fellow senators. Wilkinson sent the additional fruitcakes and reminded Blease that he owed his position as college president to the former governor, "my success thusfar, is based upon your good will in selecting me for this place. Your friendship during the first sixteen years has constantly been an inspiration in developing the College to a point of usefulness not only to my Race, but to all the people of South Carolina." Two weeks later Wilkinson asked Blease to put in "a good word" to Governor John G. Richards in support of appropriations for the college. In his reply Blease said he would take up the matter with Richards but complained that the fruitcakes had been underbaked. He told Wilkinson not to tell the home economics students, because "they would feel badly about it."[20]

Wilkinson continued to shower praise on Blease. He asked the senator to visit the campus and the Orangeburg Colored Fair in 1927, but Blease declined the invitation. Then in 1929 he wrote the senator to ask a personal favor. He explained that he understood that President Herbert Hoover intended to appoint a commission to investigate conditions in Haiti and that one black person would be designated to serve on the commission. He asked Blease to suggest that he be appointed. Blease answered that if a Negro were to be named, "they could not find a better one in America than Bob Wilkinson." However, nothing came of it, and Blease lost his bid for reelection in 1930, freeing Wilkinson from further contact with the reprehensible politician.[21]

THE FACULTY

Wilkinson never failed to commend the faculty in his annual reports to the general assembly. "Harmony and cooperation" accompanied their devotion to hard work. But, he reminded legislators, South Carolina State faculty members were underpaid compared to their peers at other black colleges. Wilkinson worried that if such low salaries persisted, "either we will have to pay more money or we will have to replace experienced and efficient men with others who cannot give the service required."[22]

Many of these "experienced and efficient men" did not possess bachelor's degrees. After a federal evaluation of the college six years later revealed that only seventeen of thirty-three faculty members had a bachelor's degree and that just four of them possessed graduate degrees, Wilkinson recommended that those faculty members who taught college courses possess at least a bachelor's degree by 1933. There were concerns that the quality of instruction was compromised not only by the lack of educational attainments. Through the 1920s faculty members continued to devote considerable time, not to teaching, but to labors outside of the classroom. Miller F. Whittaker, the head of the Mechanical Department, observed in 1927 that much of the maintenance work on the campus had "taken instructors time that well [could] have been given for instruction purposes."[23]

Since 1896 students also had had a mandatory obligation to work on the campus. But the requirement that all students over the age of fifteen provide at least two hours of manual labor each week was dropped after 1923. However, many students—most of them males—were "persuaded" to work by their being paid small sums of money. But

Table 10. Salaries of Black College Administrators and Faculty Members

Presidents	Deans	Professors	Assoc. Profs.	Assoc. Profs.	Inst.
Inst. Averages for 17 Negro State Colleges					
$8,800	$2,000	$1,800	$1,600	$1,400	$1,320
S.C. State Averages					
$8,000	$1,800	$1,600	$1,400	$1,200	$900

Source: *Twenty-Eighth Annual Report of the Board of Trustees* (Columbia: Joint Committee on Printing, 1924), 19.

Technology and the curriculum had changed by the time this photo of the automobile shop was taken in 1924. Wheelwrighting and harness making had been taught at S.C. State since it opened in 1896, but they were no longer marketable vocational skills. Students in Elliott Jamison's class are applying paint to this vehicle with a brush. Courtesy of the Historical Collection, South Carolina State University

even a bit of cash was not a sufficient inducement to work for many young men, leading Wilkinson to complain in 1927 that "there has been a gradual decline of interest in industrial work by our boys." Therefore he recommended increasing their compensation from eight cents an hour to ten cents an hour.[24]

Young men could also find employment in the city. They utilized their vocational skills as carpenters, masons, and painters. They could do manual labor as well as janitorial and maintenance work for white businesses and employers. They were encouraged to do so to supplement their income. "Male students," the catalog extolled, "have a splendid chance to secure work in the City of Orangeburg in various occupations."[25]

STUDENT AND ALUMNI SUPPORT

Although S.C. State did not charge tuition, the cost of attending the college doubled in the 1920s as administrators found it impossible to maintain and expand the institution by relying on the parsimonious general assembly. Students were charged an increasing assortment of fees. The entrance or enrollment fee was the major academic charge, and

Table 11. Annual Student Fees: 1917–18 and 1928–29

1917–18	1928–29
Entrance fee $3.00	Enrollment fee $17.00
Laundry fee $1.00	Library fee $3.00
Textbooks $7.00	Medical fee $2.00
Board (8 months) $64.00	Room $16/semester $32.00
	Student publication $.50
	Board (8 months) $105.00
	Textbooks $10 to $20
Total	
$75.00	$169.50–$179.50

Sources: Catalogue of State Agricultural and Mechanical College of South Carolina for 1917–1918 (Orangeburg: 1918), 21–22; Catalogue of State Agricultural and Mechanical College of South Carolina for 1928–1929 (Orangeburg: 1929), 23.

it may as well have been called tuition. The college also began to charge room rent, which had previously been calculated with the fee for boarding.

The college collected these fees in part to support capital improvements. To construct a desperately needed gymnasium, $5 was added to the enrollment fee in 1923. This "would relieve the College of a necessity which the Legislature would be slow to provide for." By 1928–29 the fund had accumulated over $20,000. Construction began although funds to equip the building were not yet available. Dukes Gymnasium was finished in 1931. It was designed by John H. Blanch as a student project his senior year. Blanche graduated in 1929, and he collaborated on the gym with college architect and the head of the Mechanical Department, Miller F. Whittaker. The two men would work together on several other architectural projects over the next two decades.[26]

The gym, built of red brick with a tile roof, featured attractive arches similar to those that graced the entrance to White Hall. It contained a 70-by-114-foot floor, and a 20-by 60-foot sixty-thousand-gallon swimming pool. It cost $54,000. Student fees amounted to over $23,000 while additional funds came from a loan from the State Sinking Fund Commission. Like virtually every other building constructed on the campus in its first four decades, the gym was named after one of the members of the board of trustees. Archie L. Dukes was from Orangeburg. The only early building not named after a board member had been Morrill Hall.[27]

The college also added a library fee to raise $2,000 in order to match a $1,000 contribution by the Julius Rosenwald Fund for the purchase of books. Unfortunately there was no separate library building to house the volumes. Space in White Hall had been set aside for the college library. Benjamin E. Mays, the president of the alumni association, led a spirited effort in 1926 to raise $25,000 "for an up-to-date library." Mays was

Miller F. Whittaker and his student John Blanche designed Dukes Gymnasium, shown here about 1930, which features familiar red brick and a tile roof. It was the home of Bulldog men's and women's basketball games until the Smith Hammond Middleton Memorial Center was completed in 1969. Courtesy of the Historical Collection, South Carolina State University

confident that the legislature would match that sum "if we ourselves had already raised that amount." But the alumni failed to rally to the cause.[28]

S.C. State students also engaged in charitable efforts to benefit the college. Women students held a series of fund-raisers to pay the cost of materials to construct what came to be known as the Y-Hut. Young men under faculty supervision provided the labor to build the modest red brick structure. It was finished in 1927 at a cost of $10,000. It served for decades as the equivalent of a student union. It had a lounge with a piano and a reading room. There were also rooms for student activities and for Bible study. Wilkinson explained that the Y-Hut "typifies the spirit of self-help and group cooperation between the faculty and students in promoting Christian ideals" of the YWCA.[29]

Students were not alone in contributing materially to the college for critical needs. The alumni donated funds in the early 1920s to construct concrete sidewalks, add a drinking fountain, and install decorative electric lights at the entrance to White Hall. Still money was not available for something as basic as screens for doors and windows. State health inspector Dr. A. H. Hayden repeatedly complained to state authorities. "I again call your attention to the law requiring that all educational institutions be screened throughout. This institution has no screens whatever, except in the Culinary Department and toilets." He added that such screens would cost about $3,000, but that an appropriation for screens had been deleted from the 1929 budget.[30]

ACCREDITATION?

South Carolina State had never been formally evaluated or accredited during its first three decades. In 1927, however, Wilkinson asked the state superintendent of education, James H. Hope, about the college's "rating." Wilkinson explained that outside agencies—presumably the General Education Board and the Rosenwald Fund—had asked about the college's standing. Hope easily dismissed Wilkinson's concern by simply stating that the college was highly regarded: "your State Agricultural and Mechanical College is rated by the State Board of Education as a standard four-year college of the highest type. Your curriculum, apparatus and equipment were inspected by members of this Board and were given the rating as above indicated." Hope went on to add: "Personally, I regard your institution as one of the best, if not the best of its kind, in the South."[31]

North Carolina education officials did not share Hope's optimistic assessment. Wilkinson subsequently submitted data and a college catalog to James E. Hillman, the director of certification for the North Carolina Department of Education. With no on-site visit or consultation, Hillman gave S.C. State's degree programs a B rating, except for the normal program, which received a C. The North Carolina evaluator identified two major weaknesses: the college had department heads who lacked master's degrees, and the institution accepted students for the college program who had not graduated from high school.[32]

The college did indeed have two of five programs with supervisors who lacked not only a master's degree, but even a bachelor's degree. J. Irwin Washington, the head of the commercial program and the college business manager, did not have a bachelor's degree. Marian J. Gardiner, who was the head of home economics, also did not have a bachelor's degree. But Nelson Nix, who was the "dean" of the collegiate program; Miller F. Whittaker, the head of the mechanical arts; and Walter Buchanan, who oversaw agriculture, each possessed a master's degree.[33]

And South Carolina State could hardly be faulted for accepting students who were not high school graduates. There were few public high schools for black youngsters to graduate from in South Carolina. In 1927 there were only ten public high schools for young black people in the state (there were 279 high schools for white youngsters). Just 104 black students earned high school diplomas in South Carolina in 1930. Had S.C. State been compelled to admit only high school graduates, it either would have ceased to exist or would have been a very small college. Instead prospective students who were not graduates of accredited high schools were required to take entrance examinations and provide records of their previous education.[34]

A one-page application form for admission was included in the college catalog. It asked for the name of the applicant, parents' names, schools attended, years attended, and grade completed. It also requested information on who would be responsible for college bills and whether the applicant would reside on campus. The prospective student was asked to have a teacher certify attendance at school and the work completed.[35]

Neither Wilkinson nor faculty members were pleased with the quality of academic preparation of those students who did graduate from the black high schools. Through its history the college accepted (and also rejected) students who were not capable of college work. In 1925 Wilkinson wrote Benedict College president C. B. Antisdel to complain that high school principals permitted weak students to graduate. The S.C. State president called on the black college presidents to "all stand together" in promoting higher standards for incoming students. "It will have a salutary effect upon most High School Principals to make them check up on their work and turn out better material for us, as some of them have not done for years. Most of them have been asleep on their jobs."[36]

In an attempt to attract better qualified high school students, in the late 1920s the college began to sponsor a declamation contest held on campus, usually as part of the commencement week festivities. High school students spoke on a variety of topics as guests of the institution. They came from Avery, Penn School, Schofield Academy, Booker T. Washington High School in Columbia, Wilson High School in Florence, Sumter's Lincoln High School, and Howard High School of Georgetown.[37]

BENJAMIN E. MAYS

Benjamin E. Mays returned to S.C. State in 1925 to join the faculty and teach English. In possession of a bachelor's degree from Maine's Bates College, Mays had begun work on a master's degree in theology at the University of Chicago. He was disappointed to learn that students had not changed much since his graduation from the high school program nine years earlier. Students were still indifferent toward their studies. He lamented that "there was little if any improvement in the level of academic interest and achievement." Moreover Mays was incensed that fellow faculty members had decided by a margin of one vote to allow a senior "who had failed all qualifications for graduation" to earn a college degree.[38]

On a brighter note, Mays met his second wife, Sadie Gray, while the two of them served on the faculty in 1925–26. She was a native of Georgia and taught sociology. By coincidence they were both graduate students at the University of Chicago. They married in the summer of 1926 and hoped to continue as S.C. State faculty members. But college rules prohibited the employment of husband and wife. Benjamin and Sadie Mays reluctantly resigned after President Wilkinson rejected their appeals to make an exception. They took positions in Tampa with the National Urban League and the Family Service Association. Nevertheless Mays remained deeply devoted to S.C. State until his death in 1984. He wrote in his 1971 autobiography that "South Carolina State College at Orangeburg is very dear to my heart."[39]

THE FEDERAL SURVEY OF BLACK COLLEGES

The federal government sponsored a survey and evaluation of four-year public and private black colleges and universities that was published in 1928. Each institution was measured on its own merits, and there was little comparison among the institutions. Fourteen pages of the 965-page report were devoted to S.C. State. *Survey of Negro Colleges and Universities* offered a generally positive assessment of S.C. State,

This photo from the yearbook, the *Wilkinsonian,* shows the academic faculty from 1926. Benjamin E. Mays is right of center. His soon-to-be wife, Sadie, is at the top to the right of center. Asa H. Gordon is second from the bottom on the left. To Gordon's right is Johnson C. Whittaker, and to Whittaker's right is Nelson C. Nix. Courtesy of the Historical Collection, South Carolina State University noting the attractive campus and the "exceptionally clean" buildings. Academic records were "unusually complete," and "the work in the different departments of instruction is well organized, and the teaching tasks are well distributed." Faculty members were not teaching in disciplines in which they lacked training. The library was remarkably free of "old and useless volumes," but its "1,800 well-selected books" were housed in "one very small room."[40]

The most serious criticism, and one that persisted through a significant portion of the college's history, was the lack of academic training among members of the faculty. Nearly half of them (sixteen of thirty-three) did not possess a bachelor's degree. Of those sixteen, seven were in vocational subjects, three were in home economics, two were in commerce, two were in music, one was in physical education, and one was in teacher training. The survey recommended that the administration require those faculty members without degrees to obtain the education.[41]

The survey also found fault with the excessive number of honorary degrees granted by S.C. State, although most of them had been awarded as part of the commemoration of the twenty-fifth anniversary of the founding of the institution in 1921. Twenty-two honorary degrees were granted in 1921–22, and just four since. Eighteen of the honorary degrees were master's degrees—"and the master's degree should not be granted for honorary purposes." Sensitive to the criticism, the college stopped awarding honorary degrees for the next six decades. The sole exception was the fiftieth anniversary celebration in 1946.[42]

The most important and most controversial finding of the survey was the growth in the liberal arts program and the declining interest in agriculture. The number of college students in liberal arts had swelled from eighteen in 1922–23 to slightly over one hundred by 1926–27. At the same time, the number of students in agriculture grew from seventeen to only thirty. This waning interest in agriculture, according to the authors of the survey, was regrettable. "It is the opinion of the survey committee that the administration should encourage in every manner possible the entrance of students to this course. South Carolina is an agricultural State. Many of its farmers are negroes, and the training of the younger members of the race in agricultural science is an important mission that should not be neglected."[43]

In calling for a renewed dedication to the agricultural mission of the college, the survey's authors were countering the historical tide. Black (and white) people were abandoning the rural South by migrating to economic opportunities in the urban North. While many African Americans remained devoted to an agricultural way of life, more and more of them were breaking their ties to the soil in an effort to secure jobs and careers not connected to the land. Generations of black people had come to associate agriculture with slavery, dependence, and manual labor.

The most serious shortcoming of the survey was its failure to recommend increased state funding for the college and its programs. Instead it avoided even mildly chastising public officials by blandly and inaccurately observing: "Through public taxation the institution is beginning to obtain the support it needs." It was not receiving adequate public support to remedy its outstanding weaknesses. The college needed a significant increase in funds. It needed a library building with a larger collection of books and materials. New dormitories were needed, and the academic credentials of the faculty demanded improvement.[44]

Lorenzo Dow Turner was the first faculty member employed at S.C. State with an earned doctorate. However he was merely a visiting instructor in summer school in 1929 and 1930. Turner had a Ph.D. from the University of Chicago and taught full time at Howard University before he moved on to Fisk and to Chicago's Roosevelt University. His summers in South Carolina, however, propelled his academic career in an entirely new direction after he visited African Americans living in the lowcountry. He was struck by their language—Gullah—and he was the first scholar to take seriously their way of speaking, pronunciation, and vocabulary. Scholars and nonscholars alike regarded Gullah as nothing more than a garbled, crude, and incoherent corruption of standard English. Turner determined that it was a lilting mixture of English and African speech patterns and words that had evolved and survived for more than two centuries among the isolated black communities on the sea islands. He devoted much of the remainder of his academic life to the research and investigation of Gullah.[45]

COLLEGE TRADITIONS

Befitting an emerging college, in 1927 the institution adopted a new alma mater that replaced "Hail, Hail Carolina." Although President Wilkinson has been long identified as the author of the words for the new composition, the *Collegian* credited music instructor Theodore D. Phillips with composing both the words and the music. He was an Oberlin graduate who also played the pipe organ. Over several decades wording in the first stanza of the alma mater changed. Today most students and alumni sing "Let us rally to her calls." But the original version was "Let us rally to her cause."[46]

"Sing the praise of Alma Mater
Let us rally to her cause
Lift our voices, send them ringing
Thru the groves and classic halls."

The *Collegian* decided in 1927 that S.C. State needed a mascot too. For a month the newspaper polled students to determine which imposing animal best represented school spirit. The candidates were: tiger, lion, wildcat, bear, bulldog, and greyhound. Students decided on the bulldog because of its "fighting tenacity." They had already settled on garnet and blue as the college colors.[47]

STUDENT CONDUCT

The conduct of students continued to preoccupy faculty and administrators. They worried that unruly students could jeopardize the public image of the college. Black educators maintained their determination to instill middle-class morality and virtues in the younger generation. They were convinced that they could coerce notions of "good" behavior among students by maintaining and enforcing an extensive list of rules, any violation of which subjected the offender to prompt punishment.

They remained obsessed with the behavior and appearance of female students. The institution had a strict dress code by the late 1920s that applied exclusively to women. There were no corresponding restrictions on the day-to-day apparel of men. The code for women was ostensibly to blur the differences between young ladies who could afford more expensive clothing and those who came from less-than-prosperous backgrounds. "To promote economy and avoid distinctions and embarrassments that arise from different conditions, all young women except Juniors and Seniors of College rank, are required to wear a uniform dress, consisting of a navy blue skirt and white middy."

But there may also have been some anxiety that younger women could fall prey to the provocative attire linked to the "flappers," the so-called loose women who wore scanty dresses, smoked, drank illegal liquor, and engaged in other illicit activities during the Roaring Twenties. Only white or navy-blue sweaters were allowed. There would be no colorful outfits. "The coats of the young women shall be suited to the individual taste of the wearer, with the regulation that they be not of bright and conspicuous hue, but of conservative color. Coats of flashy color are disapproved." Hats also had to be "conservative." Women needed to appear somber and serious, not exuberant and eye-catching.[48]

Since its inception S.C. State students had been forbidden from communicating "in any form with the opposite sex," or from leaving the campus more often than once every two weeks except to attend church, and young women who left the campus had to be accompanied by a chaperone. After 1925–26 the five-page list of regulations was largely deleted from the college catalog and replaced by a fifteen-page booklet of rules and regulations distributed to students and available to parents. Of the fifteen pages, eleven were devoted to behavior and four to academic regulations including cheating. It included rules for dormitories, the dining hall, dress, and punishment. Student rooms were subject to weekly inspections as was their luggage.[49]

The Discipline Committee was made up of senior faculty and administrators that included the dean of men, the dean of women, the dean of the college, the faculty member in charge of chapel absences, and the director of the academy (high school). This committee devoted considerable time and energy to adjudicating the cases of students charged with violating rules and regulations. It met as often as once a week and, in the event of an epidemic of misbehavior, even more frequently.

Committee members took their task seriously, and they were determined to treat students fairly but firmly by the imposition of swift punishment of the guilty. Faculty members and administrators believed that such proceedings would serve to deter potential offenders. Students were permitted to appear and provide their account of what had happened. The committee then deliberated and dispensed justice. Occasionally students were acquitted. Far more often they were given demerits for minor violations, and suspended or expelled for major transgressions. Students who communicated with the opposite sex without permission were subject to ten demerits. Card playing or profane language brought thirty demerits. Unauthorized absence from the campus was thirty demerits. Students found guilty of stealing, gambling, or habitually lying were liable to receive sixty demerits. Sixty demerits meant suspension from the college. However, no student could be suspended or expelled without the president's consent. As with every major matter at the college, Robert S. Wilkinson paid close attention to the work of the committee and its deliberations.[50]

Because of the mutual attraction between the sexes, the Discipline Committee spent much of its time deliberating various offenses committed by young men and women. In 1923 Thomas Anderson and Eva Mae D'Oyley were caught kissing and in a "compromising situation" on the rear stairs of White Hall by the dean of women, Mrs. Olive Benson. After a hearing Anderson was suspended indefinitely, and D'Oyley was given forty demerits.[51]

Four couples went joy riding in a Dodge touring car on a Sunday morning in November 1924. They insisted that they had been in church, but their story collapsed because they claimed to have worshiped at Mount Pisgah Baptist Church, where Dean Nelson Nix served as pastor. Instead of enjoying spiritual renewal, the young people went to the woods, "where illicit intercourse was involved in." The eight students were suspended for the remainder of the school year.[52]

In the spring of 1926, three young ladies—Florence Taggart, Rebecca Bingley, and Florence Sampson—left the campus without permission and met two young men—Orleans Reid and Elliott Naggles—and had their photograph taken. The young women lost all social privileges, were suspended from school for two weeks, and were assigned to do housework. The young men also lost social privileges and were fired from their jobs in the dining hall. A month later a male student was apprehended by a night watchman as he descended the fire escape in Bradham Hall, a women's dormitory. The love-struck young man, U. S. Rice, had gone to the room of Margaret Jervay at 1 A.M., where he frightened Jervay and her two roommates. He later told the Discipline Committee, "I don't know why I was so crazy to do what I did." Not finding craziness a plausible explanation, the committee expelled him.[53]

Clandestine meetings of men and women did not violate the U.S. Constitution, but the consumption of alcoholic beverages did. The Eighteenth Amendment to the Constitution and the accompanying Volstead Act led to the prohibition of beer, wine, and liquor in the United States from 1918 until the amendment's repeal in 1933. Nevertheless the Discipline Committee did not consider the consumption of alcohol as much of a problem as a rendezvous between the sexes.

Lee Holman was charged with disorderly conduct in Lowman Hall on Christmas night in 1926. He admitted that he had been drinking wine and "was feeling good." He received thirty demerits because he had no previous offenses. Nearly two years earlier, three young men were suspended for drinking off campus "in a questionable place." In another instance the offenses seem benign, even if the punishment was not. William Mason was suspended in 1928 for erecting a fountain in the dining hall for the junior-senior reception without permission. Morgan's fellow students rallied to his defense in a polite and respectful letter in which they informed President Wilkinson that Morgan was not solely responsible for the fountain, but that he had carried out the wishes of the junior class. Therefore, the students reasoned, they should all share in the penalty. The record does not indicate whether Wilkinson accepted their appeal or not.[54]

Johnson C. Whittaker, the head of the academy, was so bothered by the behavior, deportment, and failure to abide by regulations of three young men in 1928 that he wrote Wilkinson and asked the president to "look into the matter." Willie Jordan did not attend English, history, or mathematics. Livingston Butler "is cutting campus duty[,] is not regular at any class, and when in my classes is very disorderly—a very menace to the pupils." Mr. Bovian was "very disorderly, and disobedient, and trifling."[55]

At least twice in the 1920s, students openly defied college authorities. Unfortunately very little information about these student insurrections has survived. Seniors went on strike in 1923. "The whole affair will be left in the hands of Dr. [Nelson] Nix who will make a thoroinvestigation and report findings to the faculty." What Nix learned or shared with the faculty is unknown. In the course of his investigation, Nix found one student, Henry Sutton, uncooperative. The young man was suspended for the remainder of the term for insubordination. There was a revolt in the academy (high school) in 1925. "Pinckney Davis is thought to have [been] the chief promoter among the boys." He was summoned to the Discipline Committee and charged with "impudence and rudeness." He and Edna Richards were subsequently denied the privilege of going home for the Christmas holiday as their punishment.[56]

Less frequently students were brought before the Discipline Committee for academic infractions. At the end of the 1923–24 term, seventeen students in the academy were charged with cheating on final exams. They received no credit for the semester as their penalty. Two young women were found to have used notes on an exam in 1929, and they were suspended for two weeks. President Wilkinson wrote Mrs. Josephine Jordan in 1930 to explain that her daughter, Melba, had been suspended for a year. She had not attended an English course and then attempted to forge records to show that she not only had attended, but had passed.[57]

Wilkinson and the faculty were almost as firm with parents and guardians as they were with their children. Parents were told not to ask routinely that their children come home. "The right is reserved to the President to refuse such request when in his judgment it would be unwise to grant it. The College authorities do not recognize the rights of parents or guardians to withdraw students from any academic duty expect for reasons approved by the President." In keeping with the principle of in loco parentis (in place of the parent), Wilkinson announced that "the President's authority over the conduct of students continues until they return to their homes and parents." S.C. State remained open during the Christmas holiday, and parents were told not to expect their youngsters to spend Christmas and the New Year holiday at home.[58]

President Wilkinson demonstrated a more sensitive side when he sent a young woman home after a campus physician learned that she was eight months pregnant. Wilkinson commiserated with her father: "It is needless to assure you of our deep sympathy in a matter of this kind." He went on to explain, "Your daughter has been a very good student and we are extremely sorry that she has been overtaken by this misfortune." But Wilkinson also took care to explain that she had been pregnant since the previous summer, and thus her condition was not a consequence of any lack of supervision while she was enrolled at S.C. State.[59]

REFORMING STUDENT REGULATIONS

Across America in the aftermath of World War I and with increased access to the automobile, jazz, alcohol, and cigarettes, a generation of young people challenged their elders' assumptions about morality and what older people defined as acceptable behavior. Even in isolated, rural, and racially segregated South Carolina, black college students chafed under the authoritarian domination of campus authorities. An estimated 90 percent of the male S.C. State students smoked by the late 1920s, and no doubt some of the females did so covertly. There were more than a few students who—at their peril—continued to evade and violate one or more of the many college regulations. Finally some students decided that they would no longer submit to rigid restrictions on their conduct.[60]

The turning point came in 1929. The Discipline Committee renamed itself the Faculty Council. Shortly thereafter senior college students submitted a respectful but emphatic letter to the council asking that specific changes be made in rules affecting them. They requested that college juniors and seniors be excused from Sunday school, prayer meetings, and study hall. They wanted males and females who were seniors to be permitted to sit together on "senior" benches on the campus. They wanted senior women to be able to attend the movie theater and "other wholesome entertainment" during the day in town without a chaperone. But they did not go so far as to ask that male students be permitted to accompany them.[61]

Remarkably the faculty and Wilkinson agreed to these as well as other requests for a relaxed discipline policy. They decided to allow a student to participate in the Faculty Council hearings, but the student member could not take part in the council's deliberations. Seniors would also be permitted to skip meals in the dining hall—something many of them had already been doing. Lights on the second floor in Lowman Hall would be left on until 10:30 P.M. rather than turned off at 10:00 P.M.[62]

Perhaps to the aggravation of Wilkinson and the faculty, these concessions only incited requests for even more changes. Junior women promptly asked that they, like the seniors, no longer be confined to the campus by the white lines that were painted on the perimeter. They asked that they too have access to town and to attend entertainment without chaperones. The Faculty Council turned down the junior women, except that the young ladies would be allowed to go shopping unaccompanied if they returned to the campus by the supper bell. And perhaps to test the limits of the new policy, a few days later eight young men who were not athletes decided to attend an S.C. State football game against Clark in Atlanta. They were quickly suspended for departing the campus without permission.[63]

FREEDOM OF THE PRESS?

Students may have been freed from some of the onerous restrictions that defined their lives on campus, but they did not have freedom of speech or freedom of the press. The trustees and President Wilkinson were not about to let students speak their minds on issues that affected and concerned them. The institution's image took precedence over the rights of students. Any student or students who wished to speak, write, or petition had to obtain approval of the president before doing so. There was no pretense of academic freedom or the open exchange of ideas and opinions. "All recitations, essays, etc., to be delivered by students in public or designed for publication, are subject to control and revision by the President. All programs for celebration or other public occasions at the College must be submitted to the President for approval before printing. All communications for the public or petitions of any kind must be submitted to the President." No doubt Wilkinson as well as other administrators and faculty members genuinely feared the consequences of a student publicly criticizing the college, condemning white supremacy, or assailing one of the state's political leaders.[64]

Freedom of the press became an issue in 1929 when changes were made in the publication of the campus newspaper, the *Collegian*. The advisor for the paper, Mabel James, persuaded administrators to begin awarding credit for writing, editing, and producing the paper. James was an instructor of English, but what is more important, she served as Wilkinson's executive secretary. For a time young James lived with the Wilkinson family. The *Collegian* would be supervised by James and what was termed the College Club. There would also be a five-person Faculty Censorship Committee, which would be made up of three representatives from the College Club and two members designated by the president.[65]

Almost immediately a controversy erupted. President Wilkinson asked that a copy of the *Collegian* be "placed on his desk" before its distribution to students and faculty. This smacked of prior censorship, and the student journalists refused to comply and resigned en masse. A flurry of meetings and discussions ensued. The newspaper staff had a change of heart and sent letters to the Censorship Committee rescinding their resignations and agreeing to serve again. The Faculty Council intervened and initially declined to permit the student journalists to return. But James, who was a member of the College Club and the Censorship Committee, urged that the students be given a second chance. At that point the Faculty Council split and was unable to reach a decision for or against the newspaper staff.

President Wilkinson intervened and declared that the students would not return to their positions with the *Collegian*. Demonstrating that authoritarianism had not vanished from the campus, Wilkinson explained that "he felt to have the students return would be a reflection on the [Faculty] Council as well as on him because of their [the newspaper staff's] previous attitude." The students "could not serve again." Faculty and students would assemble a new staff and continue the publication of the *Collegian*.[66]

Less controversial was the yearbook, the *Wilkinsonian*. It made its initial appearance in 1925, and it offered "a faithful delineation of college life, a life of simplicity, of strength and beauty." Like most yearbooks of the era, it contained individual photographs of seniors accompanied by witty comments and nicknames. There was a class history and a class prophecy. There were group photos of organizations and athletic teams as well as photos of each faculty member. The yearbook concluded with advertisements sponsored by local black and white businesses. The *Wilkinsonian* appeared again in 1926, and never reappeared. The next yearbook, the *Bulldog,* was published in 1938.[67]

REGULATING THE FACULTY

Wilkinson was understandably more flexible with the faculty than the students. If he was in town, he routinely attended the regularly scheduled faculty meetings. For the most part, he implored faculty to keep a watchful eye on students. He told faculty members in 1924, "Our greatest problem is the control of the students so that we will have no breaks in the moral rectitude." He also continued to worry about the commitment of students to their academic work. Faculty members had developed a habit of dismissing students from class who had failed to prepare for class or who were disruptive in class. No doubt this served as an incentive for some students not to do their academic work. They received a free class cut when told to leave the room. Wilkinson asked that the practice cease except in extreme cases.[68]

President Wilkinson urged faculty members to attend events that were mandatory for students. He complained in 1923 about participation in religious services including Sunday school and vespers. "There is a great slumping off in attendance of all the religious services. Absence of members of the faculty is much in evidence. It does not look good." In 1926 he asked that faculty members sit among the students during Sunday night vespers "to help preserve order." Four years later he reminded the faculty that "the example would be good" if they attended chapel as well as various religious services.[69]

It would also be good, Wilkinson informed faculty members, if they remained on campus on the weekends. He asked that they discontinue the practice of weekend departures, "for it would eventually lead to criticism from students and others." In 1930 he told faculty members that they could not miss class and leave the campus unless they had made arrangements for a substitute teacher and also had informed the department head and the president.[70]

While it was necessary to keep a watchful eye on students, faculty members were cautioned not to become too friendly or too familiar with the younger generation. Wilkinson warned against dancing with students or associating "with students in [an] unwholesome manner." Members of the faculty walked a fine line between too little and too much involvement with students.[71]

Then there were those occasional instances where faculty members and administrators were accused of the very conduct that was not tolerated among students. President Wilkinson was embarrassed to learn—from students no less—that the dean of women, Mrs. V. G. Brock, and engineering professor Marron W. Fort were alleged to have engaged in immoral conduct. Wilkinson assembled a committee composed of himself, board of trustees member Wallace Bethea, and English professor Leon C. James to probe the matter. After an investigation and interviews, the charge of immorality could not be sustained, but the committee determined that the conduct of Brock and Fort had been indiscrete. Neither the dean nor the professor was invited to return for the next academic year.[72]

The faculty held a series of forums regularly in the 1920s in which one of their members made a presentation on an academic topic or educational issue. These gatherings, which Wilkinson usually attended, often led to lively discussions. They were an attempt to keep the teaching staff intellectually alert and mentally alive in a climate where it was all too was easy to sink into academic doldrums. E. Horace Fitchett was on the Claflin faculty but taught periodically at S.C. State, and he would become a nationally recognized black sociologist. In 1928 he gave a paper entitled "Sociology: The Science of Human Nature" before a group of Claflin and S.C. State faculty. English professor Leon C. James made a presentation entitled "Thought and Expression" later in 1928 in which he focused on reading and vocabulary skills.

President Wilkinson, in a 1930 address that may have reflected the telling effects of toiling in Orangeburg for over three decades, gave a lecture entitled "Failures in Modern Education." Less than two weeks later, science professor Paul V. Jewel gave a talk entitled "The Mathematics of Astronomy." More than a year later, the college registrar, William Spann, weighed in on the problem of student retention. He pointed out that only 8 percent of students enrolled in the first year of school were enrolled in college through the sophomore year.[73]

A CHRISTMAS HOLIDAY

For three decades S.C. State students and faculty did not enjoy a Christmas vacation. Ordinarily classes were held every week day in December except for the twenty-fifth. In 1921 Wilkinson informed faculty that "the work must go on. Therefore, please do not make any plans to go home" for the holiday. But in 1925, bowing to pressure from students and faculty and in recognition that other colleges and universities took an extended break for the holiday, Wilkinson agreed to an unprecedented Christmas break of five days, from 4:15 P.M., Wednesday, December 23, to 8:15 A.M., Tuesday, December 28.[74]

The college did not have a Christmas holiday in 1926, but the extended break resumed in 1927 and continued thereafter. The advent of a Christmas vacation did not mean, however, that students could simply leave the campus for the yuletide. There were more rules to be observed. A parent or guardian had to provide a letter asking that the student be excused for the vacation. Lest the student not return, no one could leave for Christmas who was in debt to the institution. Students were required to identify substitutes who would work for them in their absence. No young lady could leave to visit friends or family members, except her parents.[75]

Many students consequently remained on the campus during the holiday. On Christmas morning in 1927 student members of the Social Service Committee of the Y took sixty packages of fruit, candy, cigarettes, and handkerchiefs to the poor farm and the city jail. They distributed the gifts and sang carols. The Y students also "adopted" a six-year-old girl and provided her with meals and clothing to help the youngster and her family.[76]

COMMENCEMENT

Commencement each May was the highlight of the school year. This extravaganza lasted over a week and was unlike any other occasion at the college or in the community. It was a pageant, a county fair, a religious ceremony, and a solemn academic exercise all in one. Students, faculty, and staff spent an enormous amount of time planning and preparing for this annual event. Commencement provided favorable publicity for the college in the black community as hundreds of people flocked to the campus to enjoy the abundance of festivities.

In 1926 it included a play—*Daddy Long Legs*—presented by the seniors in the academy on Monday, May 17. Tuesday featured a demonstration of physical training. The high school declamation contest was held on Friday. Baccalaureate services were on Sunday. There were class presentations and a concert, "Once in a Blue Moon," on Monday, May 24. The alumni sponsored a program on Tuesday night in which faculty member and alumnus Benjamin E. Mays presided. Finally graduation ceremonies for twenty college seniors were held on Wednesday morning, May 26, with Governor Thomas G. McLeod as the featured speaker.[77]

AFRICAN AMERICAN LIFE AND CULTURE

No open opposition to racial discrimination, Jim Crow, or disfranchisement surfaced at the black college. Any student, faculty member, or visitor to the campus who expressed reservations, much less hostility, toward white supremacy would have created serious if not catastrophic consequences for the public institution. There was, however, a continued commitment in the 1920s to recognize and to celebrate the achievements and legacy of black people. The desire to enjoy and promote the cultural, artistic, and political achievements of African Americans was part of campus life. January 1—Emancipation Day—was an annual celebration "in keeping with traditions of the college."[78]

Rare was the college program after the mid 1920s that did not include the Negro national anthem, "Lift Every Voice and Sing." It was, for example, part of the observance of the opening of Education Week in 1925. It was included in the alumni program that was part of commencement exercises in 1926. Rosenwald School Day in 1928 featured both "Lift Every Voice and Sing" and "America." The anthem was also part of the high school declamation contest in 1930. But there were exceptions. "Lift Every Voice and Sing" was not on the program if prominent white politicians and educators were present. When Dukes Gymnasium and Hodge Hall were dedicated, it was not featured. Nor was it sung at commencement in 1926 when Governor Thomas G. McLeod spoke. "The Star Spangled Banner" was rarely played or sung, but it was not formally designated the national anthem until 1931.[79]

Negro Week was organized by history professor Asa H. Gordon in 1921, five years before the "Father of Black History," Carter G. Woodson, initiated Negro History Week in 1926. Gordon discussed the Reconstruction era in the 1927 observance while Professor H. D. Gregg appeared in uniform to talk about the Negro soldier in the U.S. military. Frederick Douglass Day was held regularly on February 14. In 1928 President Wilkinson informed faculty members that they were expected to join the Association for the Study of Negro Life and History at their earliest convenience. Woodson had founded the association in 1915, and by the 1920s it had begun to flourish in many black communities.[80]

There were also several programs held in 1928 to observe Negro History Week. Students led the discussions. Anjarone Young gave a lecture entitled "Why We Celebrate Negro History Week." Marie Burch read Clarence Darrow's essay on John Brown from the NAACP publication the *Crisis*, and Carrie Mae Spears gave a lecture entitled "The Kind of Democracy the Negro Wants." In 1929 student B. W. Gallman wrote an essay in the *Collegian* pleading for more interest in African American history. "It is unfortunate that the outstanding achievements of Negroes have not been in American history." He appealed to students to take a greater interest in their past. "Why should we not develop that race pride that has been developed so completely by other nations and races?" The campus newspaper regularly carried a feature about prominent people and episodes in a column called Facts about the Negro.[81]

Negro history courses continued to be part of the academic curriculum even after the departure of Asa Gordon for Savannah State College. The course in Negro history at S.C. State was one of thirty-three such courses offered at black colleges and universities by 1935.

The inclusion of African American history and culture as a vital part of campus life served to demonstrate that black people commemorated those people in their past who challenged the racial status quo and, by implication, demonstrated that the current generation did not accept their status in America with equanimity. They took pride in themselves and in their heritage and looked with measured optimism toward the future. It was optimism grounded in the belief they could overcome formidable racial barriers just as their predecessors had.[82]

While not engaged in studies or work, students were encouraged to take part in an array of campus activities. The literary societies that had been founded two decades earlier—the Philosophian, the Pierian, the Lincoln, the Douglass, the Dunbar, the Garnett, and the Washingtonian—continued to function and meet Friday evenings. They examined a range of intellectual and literary topics as well as exposing students to parliamentary procedure. For example the Douglass Literary Society met in February 1928 to discuss the overemphasis on examinations in the nation's colleges.[83]

STUDENT ACTIVITIES

Intercollegiate athletics and professional sports surged in popularity in the 1920s as people like "Red" Grange, Babe Ruth, Knute Rockne, and Jack Dempsey became American icons. Negro league baseball under the sure-handed guidance of Rube Foster and his Chicago Americans enabled black men to make a living—tenuous at times—as professional athletes. Football and the revenue it produced tended to drive the nation's intercollegiate athletic programs. Not surprisingly S.C. State football aroused much interest in the local black community, but it did not generate enough money consistently to support a robust athletic program.

Men participated in football, basketball, tennis, track, and baseball while women took part in basketball, tennis, and track. In 1913 S.C. State joined the newly formed Georgia–South Carolina Intercollegiate Athletic Conference, which competed primarily in football, baseball, and women's basketball. State played and defeated Benedict

This photo from the practice field in about 1920 depicts an earlier era of gridiron history. No numbers on the uniform. No faceguard on the helmet. And no marching band to play at halftime. Courtesy of the Historical Collection, South Carolina State University

in the first game between the two schools in 1912. But S.C. State lost in 1914 in a game played at the Orangeburg County Fairgrounds. Years later John Dorman, who took part in that game, recalled that a safety playing for State was distracted when a horse-drawn fire engine galloped by, and a Benedict receiver got behind the defender to score the winning touchdown.[84]

William C. Lewis, who also taught leatherwork and harness making, had been involved in coaching football since the sport was introduced in 1907. Head coaching responsibilities changed from time to time. In 1921 President Wilkinson appealed for faculty members to support the team coached by Professor Turner. “He is the coach of the team. His judgment is supreme and final.” Lewis coached again in the 1920s, but after he compiled a poor but unspecified record in 1924, he stepped down. S.C. State’s first “big time” opponent was Tuskegee in 1923, a game that S.C. State lost 13–6. Luther Cottingham scored the only touchdown for State on a long pass.[85]

Faculty members were asked to contribute financial as well as moral support to the football team. President Wilkinson asked them to donate $5 each to the program in 1921. To supplement the diet of football players in 1928, faculty members were among those asked to make a monetary contribution to training table. Thirty-three people provided $225 for the hungry athletes.[86]

Money woes continued to plague athletics. Because of the paucity of funds in 1927, the men’s basketball season was jeopardized. Players were asked to provide their own equipment. In 1929 a football game with Tuskegee was moved from Saturday, October 26, to Friday afternoon, October 25, "so as to give local State [College] people an opportunity to see the game." Many fans would be unable to get away from their businesses and jobs for a Saturday game.[87]

To increase revenue the S.C. State football team played Morris and Benedict at the Orangeburg County Colored Fair in 1926. Students who wanted to attend paid fifty cents. S.C. State also played regularly on Thanksgiving Day in the 1920s. They met Allen in Columbia in 1928. There was some discussion in 1929 of playing Claflin on four consecutive Thanksgiving holidays, but apparently the agreement never materialized. In 1930 State played Paine College on Thanksgiving. The football program enjoyed a rare surplus of $367 on total revenues of $2,889 for seven home games in 1928.[88]

Few scores or results of athletic contests from the early decades have survived. There are scanty records of who played and who coached. But surely one of their best football teams was in 1927 when they outscored their eight opponents 276–18 under coach A. C. Smith. They lost one game, 6–0, to Paine. In 1928 the Georgia–South Carolina Athletic Association renamed itself the South Atlantic Conference, and S.C. State won the championship with an unblemished record in the league. State won the conference championship again in 1930, compiling a 7–1–1 record. In 1931 South Carolina State joined the Southern Intercollegiate Athletic Conference (SIAC), which had been organized at Morehouse College in 1913. In their first year in the SIAC in 1932, S.C. State was 7–2 in football, losing only to Morris Brown and Tuskegee. It was also the first year that the Bulldogs played Claflin in football. They defeated the Panthers on Thanksgiving, 13–10. English professor Robert A. Brooks had assumed the head coaching duties, and he was assisted by William C. Lewis, Harold W. "Crip" Crawford, and Paul V. Jewell. Many of the players on these early Bulldog squads were tagged with colorful nicknames including "Broad River" Dawkins, "Sweet" Gilliam, "Wildman" Harris, "Papa" Whittaker, Larkin "Slipalong" Walker, Allen "Highchest" Ford, and Bennie "Honkey" Taylor.[89]

Under Coach Frank M. Staley, the women's basketball team lost only three games from 1919 to 1925. Two of those losses were to Paine College, and the third was to Tuskegee Institute. Typically the women played between five and ten games each year. The team won conference championships in 1927, 1928, and 1929. Among the outstanding Lady Bulldogs were Mozelle Taggart, Eloise Wilkerson, Isla Jordan, and Cammie Fields. Isabelle M. Hurlong was assistant coach under Staley. Frank Sheffield and Staley coached State College baseball teams to first- and second-place finishes from 1923 to 1927. Wilkinson boasted in 1930 that S.C. State athletic teams "were both feared and admired by our opponents." But baseball was dropped in 1932 for financial reasons.[90]

S.C. State students also participated in intercollegiate debates in a triangular league with North Carolina A&T and Virginia State College. In their seventh annual tournament in 1928, the three teams debated federal support for public education: "Resolved: The U.S. Government should establish a Department of Education with its Secretary in the President's Cabinet." Admission to the Friday night debate cost twenty-five cents. A week later the debate team took on Claflin, and the subject was foreign affairs. "Resolved: That the intervention of the United States in Nicaragua is unjustifiable." The

The women's basketball team was spectacularly successful in the 1920s, first under Coach Frank M. Staley and then under Coach Isabelle M. Hurlong. Note that most of the players are taller than Coach Staley. Courtesy of the Historical Collection, South Carolina State University

S.C. State debaters were Wayman Johnson and Burnett Gallman. History professor Asa H. Gordon coached the team.[91]

Music was an essential component of student life. The college had a band and an orchestra as well as several choral groups. These musical ensembles gave concerts around the state, often to white audiences. In 1926 the men's quartet sang at the Orangeburg Rotary Club luncheon. Board of trustee member and local businessman Wallace C. Bethea informed Wilkinson that the appearance by the young men impressed the Rotarians. "The State College was again 'sold' to the businessmen of Orangeburg who had apparently forgotten that it was located in our city." Guests also entertained students and faculty. The Penn Harmonic Quartette of Penn School on St. Helena Island visited the campus in 1928 and offered a program of Negro spirituals as well as popular music. Famed contralto Marian Anderson gave a recital in White Hall Auditorium in early 1926. She returned in 1927 and sang in German, French, and English. She also included several Negro compositions in her concert.[92]

The Student Council first formed in 1913 and then hastily disbanded by Wilkinson was reconstituted in the 1920s. But it was mostly a cosmetic organization. It had little authority over students or their activities. It was to "uphold, defend, and regard the good name of the College . . . and to transmit to all future generations of students the principals of love and devotion for the College." Many students regarded the organization with suspicion, convinced that members of the council were "stool pigeons" who kept college officials informed on student conduct and activities. Wilkinson and the faculty were not about to concede even a small share of influence to students, and students never fully trusted administrators.[93]

The first national Greek letter organizations were established at S.C. State in 1927. The state legislature had lifted a ban on fraternities at state colleges in 1926. Alpha Phi Alpha and Omega Psi Phi were the first fraternities on campus, followed by Kappa Alpha Psi in 1931, and Phi Beta Sigma in 1937. Alumnus Benjamin E. Mays presented the petition for the Omega Psi Phi chapter at the national organization's meeting in New York City in December 1927. S.C. State graduate Ernest E. Just, who would become a famed biologist, was among the founders of Omega Psi Phi at Howard University in 1911. Alpha Phi Alpha had been founded at Cornell University in 1906. Kappa Alpha Psi had begun at Indiana University in 1911. The first undergraduate sororities were installed in the mid-1930s with Delta Sigma Theta in 1934 and Alpha Kappa Alpha in 1938. Both sororities had been founded at Howard University.[94]

Even before the undergraduate chapters were installed, graduate members of the national fraternities had sponsored programs on the campus. In 1924 Omega Psi Phi held a chapel program to honor the memory of Colonel Charles Young, who had died in 1922. Young was an 1889 graduate of the U.S. Military Academy at West Point, and he had served with distinction in the Spanish-American War, and the Mexican campaign in 1916. Because of his color, War Department officials would not permit Young to serve in World War I. A similar tribute to Young was held in 1928, and it featured President Wilkinson and Miller F. Whittaker. Possibly in response to the initiative of the Omegas, Professor Walter Buchanan discussed Alpha Phi Alpha at a faculty forum in April 1924.[95]

By 1932 campus regulations for the Greek letter organizations were devised and implemented. Fraternities were limited to two initiations each year. A prospective pledge had to have spent one semester on campus and have a C average before he was eligible for a pledge club. Membership in the organizations grew. By 1931, Omega Psi Phi had twenty-three members, Alpha Phi Alpha had twenty-two, and Kappa Alpha Psi had seventeen.[96]

Much of collegiate life revolved around religious activities as administrators and faculty members remained determined to instill Christian values at a state institution that functioned in an increasingly secular world. Attendance was mandatory at "religious services of a simple character" that were held in the college chapel every day except Saturday. At times it must have seemed to students that they spent more time praying than they did studying. And it was not as if students lacked exposure to religion and Christianity at home. Most came from families where spiritual life and religious activities were stressed. A survey of students in 1930 revealed that nearly 50 percent were Methodists, 36 percent were Baptists, 3 percent were Presbyterians, and 1 percent were Episcopalian. Of those who were Methodists, 33 percent were part of the Methodist Episcopal church, while 15 percent were in the African Methodist Episcopal Church (AME), and slightly more than 1 percent were in the African Methodist Episcopal Zion church (AMEZ), and another 1 percent were affiliated with the Colored Methodist Episcopal church (CME). Fewer than 1 percent were Roman Catholic. Somewhat surprisingly—given the emphasis on religion—over 7 percent of the students indicated that they had no church affiliation.[97]

The YMCA and the YWCA played pivotal roles in the religious and social lives of S.C. State students in the 1920s. The YMCA had a spacious room for its activities in Lowman Hall while the YWCA occupied the new Y-Hut. Periodically speakers were invited to the campus to enlighten and inform students. In 1927 among the visitors were Republican senator R. W. Means of Colorado; H. L. Williams, the headmaster of the English School in the British colony of Nigeria; and Dr. Franklin O. Nichols, of the American Hygiene Association, who delivered a lecture on what was described as "personal sanitation" to the male college students.[98]

MARION BIRNIE WILKINSON

With the exception of Benjamin E. Mays, no person associated with South Carolina State College had more influence or more prominence over a longer period of time than Marion Birnie Wilkinson. A native of Charleston, she married Robert S. Wilkinson in 1897 and became a dynamic leader among black women. She remained intimately associated with the college until her death in 1956. She was born in 1870 to the well-to-do Birnie family. Her father, Richard, and his brother Charles were cotton agents. Of fair complexion she graduated with honors from Avery Institute in 1888, and she then taught for several years at the private Charleston school.[99]

Mrs. Wilkinson exemplified the values of middle-class black women who committed themselves to reform and racial progress during the first half of the twentieth century. In 1909 Marion Wilkinson joined with twenty-seven other women who represented Orangeburg's black elite to organize the Sunlight Club. Many of these refined ladies were connected to S.C. State and Claflin as faculty or the spouses of faculty and administrators. Others were the wives of ministers, attorneys, and local black businessmen. The Sunlight Club was one of hundreds of similar organizations founded by black women across the country during the early years of the twentieth century. There was a Culture Club in Columbia, and a Phillis Wheatley Club and later a Modern Priscilla Club, both in Charleston. Across the country the National Association of Colored Women (NACW) was active in coordinating the activities of the local groups.[100]

Mrs. Wilkinson immersed herself in the work of the club women. She was president of the South Carolina Federation of Colored Women's Clubs (SCFCWC), and she became the third vice president of the NACW. She cooperated closely with other prominent black women including Mary McLeod Bethune, Charlotte Hawkins Brown, Margaret Murray Washington (Booker T. Washington's widow), and Lugenia Burns Hope, who was the wife of Morehouse College president John Hope. With the mantra "Lifting as We Climb," these women and others like them threw themselves into a variety of causes, large and small. They were especially eager to assist black women who lacked economic and educational resources as they stressed proper behavior and virtue among their lower-class sisters.[101]

Mrs. Wilkinson donated books so that the Sunlight Club could open a small library. She supported women's suffrage. She made certain that black women including Charlotte Hawkins Brown were invited to speak to students and faculty at S.C. State. She helped organize the YWCA on the campus and pushed for the construction of the Y-Hut in the mid-1920s. She served as one of the seven black women on a committee with the Commission on Interracial Cooperation (CIC). As an indication of how much interracial progress was yet to be made, the CIC had separate seven-member committees of black and white women. Wilkinson was also a vice president of the International Council of Women of the Darker Races (ICWDR), which had been founded by Margaret Murray Washington in 1920 to promote the cause of women of color across national frontiers.[102]

One of Marion Birnie Wilkinson's enduring legacies was Fairwold Home. Although the State of South Carolina provided separate reformatories for young black and white men as well as young white women who violated the law, it offered no such facility for young black women. During World War I both black and white women were charged with prostitution involving soldiers stationed at Camp Jackson (later Fort Jackson) in Columbia. To reduce if not eradicate prostitution, the federal government awarded state authorities $80,000. The state spent the entire amount to build a facility to house white women charged with selling sexual favors while simply ignoring the black women who were prostitutes. No state-run facility for black women was established until 1949.

Assisted by the Commission on Interracial Cooperation, the Episcopal Church, and black businessmen including I. S. Leevy, the South Carolina Federation of Colored Women purchased a farmhouse and thirty acres a dozen miles north of Columbia that became the Fairhold Home for Delinquent Girls. It served as a refuge and an alternative to jail for wayward and homeless black girls and women who had committed misdemeanors. Fairwold's residents were taught to raise crops and take on domestic chores, and they learned hygiene and cleanliness as well as good manners and proper behavior. Etta Rowe, a Claflin faculty member and SCFCWC leader, explained that Fairwold girls were instructed in "how to make an honest living by their own efforts." Unfortunately the first Fairwold burned to the ground in 1925.[103]

The SCFCWC then purchased a three-story brick building in Cayce, west of Columbia, for $12,000 to replace the farmhouse. At the suggestion of Marion B. Wilkinson, S.C. State students helped with efforts to redesign and remodel the building. Funding for Fairwold was a perpetual problem. Mrs. Wilkinson donated $100 in 1925, and the Sunlight Club contributed to its operation. Mary Earle, the daughter of former president Thomas E. Miller, went on a fund-raising expedition across the state in 1927. The Duke Foundation also provided financial assistance.[104]

Mrs. Wilkinson was devoted to Fairwold. She contributed not only money but also much time to the facility. Periodically she brought Fairwold residents to Orangeburg to visit S.C. State and take part in campus activities. She was determined that the impoverished young women would gain exposure to a wider world that would afford them opportunities to improve themselves. In 1931 Fairwold was renamed the Marion Birnie Wilkinson Home for Underprivileged Orphans.[105]

THE COOPERATIVE EXTENSION PROGRAM

Through the expansion of the extension program in the 1920s, S.C. State enlarged its role as a public agency devoted to serving the state's black population. Just as the institution began to emerge as a full-fledged college during the decade, it also extended its reach well beyond Orangeburg into rural South Carolina to assist and uplift black farm families. With limited financial and human resources, this was no easy task, and even an expanded program failed to touch the lives of most poor black people. The number of farm demonstration agents increased from nine men serving in eight counties in 1922 to twelve men in 1933. What is more important, black women who served as home demonstration agents joined the extension program for the first time in 1922, and by 1933 there were nine home demonstration agents.[106]

Under the 1914 Smith-Lever Act, Clemson College was responsible for extension programs in South Carolina. Clemson, however, had delegated farm demonstration work among black farmers to S.C. State and home demonstration work to Winthrop College in Rock Hill. In 1922 Winthrop and Clemson officials agreed to allow S.C. State to establish a home demonstration program for black farm women. But Clemson and Winthrop retained ultimate authority and fiscal control over black extension work.

In 1923 Clemson allotted $14,000 to S.C. State for farm demonstration work, and Winthrop provided $4,567 for black home demonstration work. Three counties—Beaufort, Richland, and Orangeburg—began to contribute funds to supplement the salaries of black extension workers in those counties. S.C. State also contributed $1,380 as well as office equipment to the program that year.[107]

The men who served as agents were invariably paid more than their female counterparts. Dora E. Boston, who headed the home demonstration program for black women, had an annual salary of $1,200 while the three agents under her supervision earned $1,100 each. The lowest salary any of the men earned was $1,200. Two of the men made $1,600, and another received $1,500. Harry Daniels, who supervised the black farm agents, was paid $1,500 and received an expense allowance of $500. Not surprisingly the white agents earned more—much more—than the black agents. The Clemson and Winthrop extension personnel earned on average twice what the S.C. State agents did during the 1920s.[108]

The extension program became a key source of jobs and influence for Wilkinson as Clemson and Winthrop administrators granted the S.C. State president considerable latitude in supervising black extension activities. W. W. Long, who administered extension work for Clemson, and Lonny Landrum, who supervised home demonstration work at Winthrop, gave Wilkinson nearly compete autonomy in personnel matters. They rarely, if ever, took exception to his recommendations for hiring and firing black agents.

By 1924, 90 percent of the men and women in extension work were graduates of the college. In 1930 Wilkinson was pleased to point out: "The extension work among colored people in this State is almost entirely in charge of graduates of our College. They are given preference when appointments are considered. The supervisor of Negro extension work, Smith-Lever and Smith-Hughes reside here and are directed by the President of the College." The extension program provided Wilkinson with patronage that he carefully dispensed to those who supported the college.[109]

Wilkinson attempted to use the migration of rural black residents as well as the danger posed by the boll weevil infestation of the cotton crop to leverage more money for black extension work. He pointed out that such work has been "an influence in the right direction in the matter of Negro migration to Northern industrial centers."[110]

What exactly did these agriculture extension workers do as they circulated through more than a dozen rural counties during the mid- and latter 1920s? They literally demonstrated how to grow cotton, corn, wheat, rye, sweet potatoes, and other crops more productively. They taught farmers how to till the soil and apply fertilizers and insecticides. To entice farmers to participate, they held contests to see which farmers could grow the largest quantities. Eighty-six farmers entered the five-acre cotton contest in 1928, which was won by Berry Cunningham of Reidville. He grew nine thousand pounds of cotton. There were 202 farmers who took part in the corn contest, averaging thirty-four bushels per acre while the state average was only seventeen bushels per acre. Tucker Millet of Clarendon County won the two-acre sweet potato contest with a yield of 208 bushels per acre. Agents also encouraged youngsters in the 4-H program to take part in similar contests. In Spartanburg County, Bernard Walker grew 1,350 pounds of cotton at a cost of $12, which he sold for $103. Jasper Singleton in Sumter County grew 157 bushels of corn on 1¾ acres.[111]

Farm demonstration supervisor Harry E. Daniels was pleased with the 4-H clubs. "The effects of club work on the boys will result in more knowledge, a broader vision, a keener intellect, a more sympathetic attitude toward constructive progress, and a more wholesome rural life. If the club does nothing more than to get boys started off on the right track in their life's work, it will be a great factor of future good."[112]

Dora Boston was equally pleased with the many achievements in home demonstration work. Black women and girls canned almost forty-six thousand quarts of fruits and vegetables, and there were 4,160 quarts of jelly and preserves prepared. They made 2,636 dresses and coats as well as 117 hats. Home demonstration work involved 2,864 women in nine counties, although only six of the counties had agents. Four of those counties were metropolitan areas: Charleston, Richland (Columbia), Greenville, and Spartanburg.[113]

The 4-H girls devoted themselves to food, shelter, gardens, and raising poultry. Boston singled out the poultry program for praise but also identified a nettlesome problem. "We have 237 girls and 30 boys interested in raising poultry. They own 276 hens (very few own more than one hen), raised 2475 fryers and had 1375 dozen or 16,500 eggs." "The difficulty was parents who confiscated the chickens as soon as they were large enough to eat."[114]

These glowing testimonials notwithstanding, extension work among rural black South Carolinians was an extraordinarily daunting task that had the most limited of tangible results among some of the most impoverished people in American society. That was because extension work extended largely to only the more prosperous black farmers, those who owned their own land. President Wilkinson explained that those rural counties with a sizable number of black landowners were the most likely to have extension agents assigned to them. "The selection of a county for Farm demonstration is determined largely by the proportion of colored farm owners therein, since better results may be accomplished with owners than with tenants. Generally speaking, the latter are not in position to carry out demonstration, but to a large extent must comply with plans of landlords." Thus black sharecroppers and renters—those who could benefit the most from the extension service—were rarely exposed to the program.[115]

The companion program to extension work was the Smith-Hughes vocational agricultural education effort. It offered instruction in the public schools to boys and men by faculty members who were prepared and supervised by South Carolina State. However, comparatively few black males were able to take advantage of such instruction. According to 1925 census figures, there were 90,581 black farm operators in South Carolina with 132,326 adult males residing on those farms. Only 2,751 were enrolled in Smith-Hughes vocational agricultural classes.[116]

Many, if not most, black farm families never saw an extension agent. There were not enough agents. There was opposition from white landholders. Then there were black people themselves who were reluctant to take advantage of these federally sponsored programs. It was hard to convince some people that they could indeed improve their lives and the lives of the people around them. Nettie L. Kerner, who replaced Dora Boston in 1928 as the state supervisor of home demonstration work, lamented that it was difficult to make some folks see the relevance of extension work. People were demoralized by poverty, enmeshed in ignorance, and plagued by diseases including pellagra, typhoid, malaria, and tuberculosis.[117]

People were bound by tradition—as outmoded as tradition might sometimes be—and they were unwilling to change their ways. In 1928 Dora Boston found it hard to convince people to diversify their diets. "A big item in food preparation is getting the people to eat different kinds of food" so that they would have better balanced diets. Boston was frustrated that some black families who had truck gardens would sell their produce, but they would not consume it themselves.[118]

By 1930 the extension work program at S.C. State had made such a favorable impression on federal authorities and on executives with the Rosenwald Fund that the college was selected as one of three black institutions to host a major conference on extension work. Tennessee State, Prairie View A&M, and S.C. State shared $20,000 provided by the Rosenwald Fund to support the summer programs. The conference proved to be in the words of President Wilkinson "one of the most remarkable achievements in the history of the institution." It brought together U.S. Department of Agriculture officials and white faculty members and staff from southern land-grant schools as well as faculty from the black land-grant institutions including S.C. State. The "students" were 129 black men and women from the extension programs in Maryland, Delaware, Virginia, North and South Carolina, Georgia, and Florida.[119]

The two-week conference held in early August included instruction in gardening, dairying, and poultry science. There were programs on home sanitation, home improvement, and marketing farm and homemade products. Food preparation, health care, and the eradication of pellagra were also covered. Near the campus, participants completely remodeled and furnished an abandoned farmhouse into an attractive home during the two-week gathering.[120]

The conference concluded with the "Feast of the Tomato," a program held at President Wilkinson's residence. Tomato punch and tomato sandwiches were served to guests, who were entertained with a play produced by the participants. The "drama" featured a rural family that "used very primitive and unscientific methods in home making and agriculture." Their miserable lives were characterized by superstition, filth, indolence, and ignorance. They suffered from malnutrition, pellagra, and malaria. Then through "Education and Extension Work," their lives were remarkably transformed and improved.[121]

But federal authorities later grumbled that the conference at S.C. State had been too expensive. E. H. Shinn wrote Wilkinson that the cost "at your institution was considerably in excess of that of either of the other two schools" in Tennessee and Texas. Wilkinson replied that such comparisons were not fair because "situations of this nature should be judged by local conditions." The president did concede, however, that there were some irregularities in the initial efforts to organize the conference. In 1931 the Rosenwald Fund reduced its funding, and two rather than three extension work conferences were held. One was at Virginia State in Petersburg and the other took place at Pine Bluff, Arkansas. Wilkinson expressed considerable disappointment "in not having the privilege of carrying on this remarkable undertaking again."[122]

WILKINSON AND THE LAND-GRANT INSTITUTIONS

In the meantime Wilkinson had assumed a more prominent role as a leader in the land-grant movement. In 1924 President Wilkinson, responding to an invitation, wrote "Education in Negro Land-Grant Colleges," which was included in a series of essays on land-grant education published by the federal government's Bureau of Education. Wilkinson's was the sole essay on the black land-grant colleges. In it he praised the land-grant schools for their commitment to "scientific training in agriculture, mechanics, and home economics" and for accomplishing so much with so little. While conceding that the southern states had expanded funding for the black land-grant colleges between 1910 and 1920 compared to the previous decade, he called for more state funds. "It would seem desirable that the Southern States should greatly increase their financial support of these institutions."

He went on to insist that the huge gap in salaries between faculty and administrators in the black and white land-grant institutions needed to be closed. The average salary for a full professor at the white land-grant schools was $3,392 while the full professor "of similar training, ability, and service" at the black institution received $1,500. The S.C. State president also pointed to the need for improved libraries so that "these colleges [could] do first-grade college work."[123]

Wilkinson also served on the executive committee of the Association of Land-Grant Colleges for Negroes in 1926 and was subsequently elected president of the organization. The black college land-grant association met each year in conjunction with the larger Association of Land-Grant Colleges and Universities. At the annual meeting in Chicago in November 1927, Wilkinson was selected to serve on an advisory committee to survey and examine the land-grant institutions. The other committee members were the secretaries of agriculture and the interior (the Department of the Interior included the Bureau of Education); the presidents of the University of Maryland, the University of Minnesota, Colorado State University, and the Massachusetts Institute of Technology; the Illinois state superintendent of public instruction; and the director of the New York State College of Home Economics. Wilkinson was the only black person and the only southern member of the committee.[124]

President Wilkinson ran the extension program in the same way he ran the college —in a firm and authoritarian manner. Dora E. Boston was the state supervisor for Negro home demonstration. As such she served under Wilkinson and Lonny I. Landrum, the state home demonstration agent at Winthrop. In 1928 Boston informed Wilkinson that she intended to marry George Daniels, who was a farm demonstration agent in Orangeburg and also an employee in the cooperative extension program. "I am planning to get married next week, I have been trying to tell you for the last month, but each time I attempted it my nerves failed," she wrote Wilkinson. Because S.C. State (and the state government and public schools) did not employ married women, Boston would have to resign.[125]

Neither Boston nor George Daniels had been honest with Wilkinson. They had already been married for ten months when she informed the president of her matrimonial intentions. Wilkinson learned of the deception and insisted that Boston quit as soon as possible and vacate her residence on the campus. "Under the circumstances, and according to our custom[,] it would be the best thing for you to tender your resignation." Of course there was no hint that George Daniels should resign.[126]

Mrs. Daniels, who apparently wanted to remain employed for a few more weeks, later let Wilkinson know that she did not appreciate the way he treated her. "I hope you are getting an extra amount of pleasure out of writing me the type of letters that I have received from you within the last month, but it pays one to be mindful of the fact that he does himself more harm in such a project than the person he is trying to hurt. For personal gain, if nothing else, be as big hearted as the world, or a part of it, thinks you to be. I have lost many friends defending your character, and I would like to always truthfully say to the public that I believe you are a broad-hearted decent man." She continued, "I am not angry with you, I dont suppose you care whether I am or not, but you have done somethings that make me see you in a different light."[127]

Nettie Kenner replaced Dora Boston Daniels as the supervisor of home demonstration work. Kenner then resigned in 1930 to marry, aggravating Lonny Landum because Kenner failed to give the expected sixty days' notice. Landrum asked Wilkinson to suggest a replacement for Kenner. He recommended Marian B. Paul, and she became the third home demonstration supervisor in less than a decade.[128]

REDUCTIONS IN THE EXTENSION PROGRAM

As the economy worsened in the early 1930s, white authorities proposed reductions in and consolidation of the black cooperative extension program. President Wilkinson strongly resisted these developments and insisted that black people and the agents who served them be treated fairly and equitably. The Greenville County legislative delegation eliminated $900 from the 1931 county budget that supported the position of county home demonstration agent Delphenia Wilkerson. Wilkinson wrote E. W. Biggs, a black leader in Greenville, that the "action of the delegation is quite a surprise and I may say somewhat unfair to the Negroes of Greenville County." The loss of $900 would mean an end to the county home demonstration work.[129]

Wilkinson also asked Lonnie Landrum, the director of the home demonstration program at Winthrop, to intervene to save Wilkerson's position. He explained that it "would seem almost a tragedy" to eliminate the home demonstration program in Greenville. Landrum agreed to do so and thought that Wilkerson had done "fine work" and "we would regret exceedingly to have it discontinued."[130]

President Wilkinson then dispatched Marian Paul to Greenville. Wilkinson directed Paul to contact "our leading colored citizens" and to have them try to persuade Greenville legislators to restore the funds. Paul followed up and met with the mayor, a white clergyman, and the legislative delegation. But the effort failed, and the $900 was not returned to the budget. The home demonstration program for black people in Greenville ended in October 1931.[131]

In the meantime in Beaufort, the local Taxpayers League organized a campaign either to eliminate the agent for farm demonstration work among black people or to place that agent under the direct supervision of the white county agent. Beaufort County had contributed $600 to the salary of Benjamin Barnwell, the black agent. The league complained that Barnwell spent too much time at the Penn School on St. Helena Island and did not devote enough time to traveling throughout the entire county. Wilkinson absolutely opposed removing the black agent or putting him under the direction of the white agent. But he did concede that Barnwell did not get around the coastal county "cut up as it is by the tide rivers."[132]

In a letter to Rosa B. Cooley, who was a white woman and the principal at Penn School, Wilkinson stated emphatically that having a white agent supervise the black agent was unacceptable. "We are entirely opposed to the placing of the colored work under the white agent and shall resist it to the end. We feel that such an arrangement would entirely destroy the morale and efficiency of our workers." It would also destroy Wilkinson's authority over the extension program among black people. Wilkinson told Cooley that he was working with the Beaufort County legislative delegation led by state senator Brantley Harvey to preserve Barnwell's position and to maintain the autonomy of the black extension program.[133]

Wilkinson's political efforts paid off, and Barnwell remained the Beaufort County agent under Wilkinson's supervision. Nearly a year earlier when Clemson officials had made some initial inquiries about putting black agents under the supervision of white agents, Wilkinson had written Harry E. Daniels: "They are seeking to place the Negro work under the white County agents, it would be well for me as head of the College to be in a position to protest influence and secure permanency of our present organization. I therefore th[i]nk a change at this time would be inadvisable." The Clemson administrators, however, were not especially eager to manage the black agents, and the matter was dropped.[134]

DISCRIMINATION AGAINST BLACK FARMERS

The refusal of white extension agents to provide loan applications to black farmers in 1931 was an even more serious issue and an obvious example of racial discrimination. Wilkinson would not have it, and he complained to both federal authorities and Clemson officials. He sent a telegram to C. W. Warburton, the secretary of the Federal

Drought Relief Commission, objecting to the treatment of black farmers. Warburton brushed aside Wilkinson's concerns by indicating that fewer loan applications were available in 1931 than in 1930 and 1929, and that, as a consequence, fewer applications were distributed. He told Wilkinson that discrimination was not much of a problem.[135]

Wilkinson also wrote W. W. Long, Clemson's director of extension work, to complain of racial discrimination and to ask Long to take action. Unlike Warburton, Long replied and promised to "see that no discrimination is made." He lamely tried to explain that black farmers had been excluded because white farmers had been the first to apply for the loans, which were used to make seed and fertilizer purchases. Long enclosed a memo to Wilkinson that he said had been sent to all the white county agents informing them that they were not to discriminate against black farmers: "It seems," the memo stated, "that little attention is being paid to the needs of our colored farmers. I sincerely trust that such a situation not prevail."

Long added: "Every farmer should be given an opportunity to make application for this loan, regardless of color or for any reason." Long neglected to mention, however, whether or not the applications from black farmers would be as readily accepted as those submitted by white farmers. Wilkinson promptly expressed gratitude to Long for agreeing to tackle the loan problem, and he reminded him of his commitment. "I thank you for the explanation regarding the situation in the matter of loans to farmers for seeds. We appreciate your interest in them as a whole and realize fully your wish as far as possible equal opportunity be given to all."[136]

THE COLORED STATE FAIR

If discrimination by white authorities were not enough, Wilkinson also had to contend with the black men who ran the Colored State Fair in Columbia. S.C. State College and its extension program had participated in and provided an exhibit for the annual event. But at some point in the mid-1920s, a dispute developed between fair organizers and Wilkinson, and the college withdrew from involvement in the fair. In 1929 one of the fair's leaders, I. S. Leevy, suggested at a meeting of the fair's board that Wilkinson, the college, and the county agents "would be glad to come back" to that year's fair if only asked. But Wilkinson curtly dismissed the proposition: "The actions of the State Fair people are amusing." He wrote J. E. Dickson, the Richland County farm demonstration agent, that few people took I. S. Leevy very seriously. "You know I. S. Leevy pretty well, so does everybody else. Most of his public statements carry little weight."[137]

On more than one occasion fair organizers attempted to have Clemson's extension officials intervene and compel Wilkinson to have the college return to the colored fair. But the Clemson people declined to do so and sided with Wilkinson—as Wilkinson knew they would. They "know the State fair organization pretty well," Wilkinson explained, "and they are already confident in the belief that there must be something wrong that causes us to drop relations with them [the fair's leaders]."[138]

Two years later, in 1931, fair organizers appealed again to Clemson, contacting W. W. Long, the director of extension work. An exasperated Long refused to be drawn in and supported Wilkinson. "I have nothing whatever to do with the administration of the Colored Agricultural College in the extension work that they are doing. I might add that I have always found President Wilkinson disposed to do whatever was best for the interest of the colored citizens of the state."[139]

Wilkinson subsequently explained to Long that money was the critical problem between the college and the men who ran the fair. "They would not agree to the expense suggested but tried in every roundabout way to have us put an exhibit without definite guarantee or promise." He stressed that the college was willing to take part in the fair, "but there are many things connected with its administration that need correction."[140]

Having served as president of South Carolina's only black public institution for two decades, Wilkinson had developed considerable confidence in his ability to deal with white politicians and leaders. He was sure in his judgments and the decisions he made about black people to white authorities. In 1931 Asbury F. Lever of the Federal Farm Board (and the congressional cosponsor of the 1914 Smith-Lever Act) urged Clemson's assistant director of extension, D. W. Watkins, to ask Seymour Carroll to speak at a series of meetings sponsored by the extension program in black communities. Rather than simply invite Carroll, Long first consulted Wilkinson.

Carroll was held in high esteem by many white South Carolinians. He was the son of popular Baptist minister, the Reverend Richard Carroll, who had favored retaining Thomas E. Miller as college president in 1911, and the elder Carroll—who had died in 1929—had been regarded as a very conservative spokesman on racial matters in the Palmetto State. Seymour Carroll was one of the founders of the State Colored Fair and a veteran of World War I. Wilkinson strongly opposed inviting Carroll. He wrote Watkins: "*Confidentially* we would prefer not to have Dr. Carroll of Columbia associated in any way with our meetings. There is an old saying that 'no one knows the Scotch like a Scotchman.' It is equally true that no one knows the Negro like a Negro. Mr. Lever does not know Carroll." Carroll did not receive an invitation.[141]

WILKINSON'S AUTHORITY OVER THE EXTENSION PROGRAM

When longtime black extension agent E. D. Jenkins had his claim for a disability rejected, Wilkinson rose to his defense. Jenkins had been among the nation's first farm demonstration agents, black or white. He had worked in Bamberg County since 1905. He suffered a stroke in 1930 that left him partially paralyzed. There was no state insurance coverage and no state workmen's compensation program, and Clemson's insurance company declined to indemnify Jenkins on the dubious grounds that he could still work. Long and Watkins accepted the insurance company's verdict. Wilkinson did not. By pressing Clemson officials and the insurer, negotiations ensued on Jenkins's behalf. The former agent eventually received a $2,000 settlement, thanks in no small part to Wilkinson's persistence.[142]

There is little doubt that Wilkinson dominated South Carolina's extension program for its black residents. In large measure Clemson and Winthrop extension leaders deferred to Wilkinson. They conceded to him considerable leeway in decisions involving the appointment, termination, and activities of the black extension staff. What Wilkinson could not do as effectively was to coax more money out of those officials as well as state legislators and county leaders for the black extension program.

A small but revealing example of the money difficulties Wilkinson encountered involved legislation in 1931 that authorized Clemson to borrow $50,000 to erect homes for extension directors. Wilkinson promptly wrote Clemson president Enoch W. Sikes to ask if some of those funds "may be set aside for erection of a home at this institution for the assistant district agent of Negro work." Sikes informed Wilkinson that the houses would be built on the Clemson campus, and financed through rental income. He added that there was no expectation that any homes would be constructed off their campus. The unwillingness of Clemson to share even a small portion of borrowed money for housing for a black administrator was symptomatic of the larger financial constraints the black extension program and its staff labored under.[143]

Far less money was set aside for extension work among black farm families than white families. In 1930, $56,335 of $670,063 (or 8.4 percent) was allocated for extension work among black people. Furthermore extension work among black men totaled $37,325 while work among black women totaled $19,030. Although black residents of South Carolina were slightly less than a majority of the state's population in 1930, black people did constitute 54 percent of South Carolina's rural population.[144]

During the 1920s Wilkinson vainly attempted to use the outward migration of black South Carolinians to gain more funding for extension work among rural black residents. Wilkinson asked for two additional extension agents in 1923 at a cost of $1,200 each. He claimed that "there is a widespread desire among the people of the state for more agents." He then sounded an oblique warning. "Taking into consideration also the Negro Exodus I think something along this line should be attempted to allay the unrest among the colored people." Wilkinson's rationale persuaded Clemson president W. W. Riggs, who replied that "the conditions existing at present among the negro farmers would justify everything possible being done to keep them in South Carolina by advising and helping them." The only problem was, Riggs told Wilkinson, funds were not available for the two new agents.[145]

THE ROSENWALD FUND

Julius Rosenwald was one of twentieth-century America's leading philanthropists. He was cofounder with Richard Sears of Sears, Roebuck and Company, and he was the longtime chief executive of the retail giant. Rosenwald donated millions of dollars to a variety of causes, including black education. But the Rosenwald Fund failed to achieve the philanthropic prominence of either the Rockefeller Foundation or the Ford Foundation because Julius Rosenwald would not permit his sizable contributions to be invested to create a gigantic financial legacy that would continue in perpetuity. The cash and stock in Sears that made up the Rosenwald Fund were rapidly dispersed in the 1920s and 1930s, and the fund spent itself out of existence by 1948.[146]

Rosenwald is best remembered for the more than five thousand Rosenwald schools erected across the South between 1912 and 1932. But the Sears executive did not cavalierly dispense money to build the tidy little schoolhouses. He insisted that black and white southerners themselves contribute cash, labor, and material to construct the facilities. In South Carolina Rosenwald provided $435,600 to erect 481 schools, eight teachers' homes, and eleven shops. Black South Carolinians exceeded Rosenwald's gift by contributing $508,000. White South Carolinians provided $224,800 for the black schools.[147]

While Julius Rosenwald responded generously to the pathetic plight of black education, he was no racial egalitarian at the vanguard of the struggle to eradicate segregation in public education. Rather he hoped—futilely as it turned out—that his contributions would shame the white South into improving black schools. They accepted Rosenwald's money, but they made only modest attempts on their own to advance the quality of black education.[148]

Rosenwald's philanthropy extended to South Carolina State in the 1920s when the fund collaborated with the Rockefeller-sponsored General Education Board to provide $7,000 to build a teacher-training school on the campus. The GEB had agreed in 1919 to furnish $45,000 to build that facility. But that grant had lapsed when the state failed to match the GEB funds.[149]

S.C. State's training school—unlike most Rosenwald schools—was built of red brick, which was consistent with most of the campus buildings constructed after the disastrous fires in 1916. The school was named for Joseph B. Felton, a white educator

The Felton Training School, shown here about 1924, was a Rosenwald School. Unlike most Rosenwald schools, this four-classroom building was constructed of red brick and located on a college campus. It survived until the current Felton Laboratory School was completed in 1964. Courtesy of the Historical Collection, South Carolina State University

from Anderson, who served as the state agent for Negro schools from 1919 to 1947. Felton's salary came from funds provided by the General Education Board. Completed in 1924, the school provided S.C. State students in the normal program with an opportunity to do practice teaching under the supervision of one of the four veteran teachers assigned to the school. By 1928, 124 students (seventy boys and fifty-four girls) from the Orangeburg community were enrolled. In the meantime Rosenwald also furnished $1,000 to build a cottage for teachers adjacent to the school.[150]

Julius Rosenwald and the executives of the fund demonstrated a genuine and personal interest in the children enrolled in the Felton School when they contributed Christmas gifts to the youngsters in 1928 and 1929. There was a stipulation, however, that college authorities select the gifts from the Sears catalog and that the total value not exceed $75. In 1928 those gifts included a baseball and bat for the boys; and a doll, an eight-piece pantry set, and a woman's handkerchief for the girls. On behalf of the children, President Wilkinson expressed appreciation, explaining that the gifts represented "in a very large part of all the Christmas happiness that will come to these children."[151]

The Rosenwald Fund (and later the General Education Board) provided scholarships for S.C. State faculty for additional study and to complete degree programs. Walter Buchanan was able to earn a master's degree in agriculture at Ohio State. Alfred W. Shute attended Iowa State in farm management while O. C. Williams studied home economics at the same institution. Harry Daniels went to the University of Connecticut to study agriculture. C. V. Bing went to the University of Minnesota in vocational agriculture. The chair of Economic Science Department at Iowa State praised Shute as "one of our first rank graduate students." But Harry Daniels had to withdraw from the University of Connecticut because of sickness in his family in South Carolina. Former S.C. State student Ernest E. Just also received Rosenwald assistance to pursue pure scientific research, and he became the Julius Rosenwald Fellow in Biology.[152]

Not everyone who sought Rosenwald aid received support. Harold Crawford, who had graduated in 1927 with honors in building construction, was denied assistance, apparently because of his youth and inexperience. Wilkinson's efforts to secure help for his executive secretary, Mabel C. James, to attend the University of Michigan also failed as did his attempt to gain funds for the head of the home economics program, Marian J. Gardiner, to return to Hampton to finish a bachelor's degree.[153]

The Rosenwald Fund also agreed to donate $1,000 for the purchase of library books if the students, faculty, and alumni would provide an additional $2,000. It took more than two years, but the matching money was eventually raised, mostly through small contributions of $5 or less. Among the larger donations, the college Sunday school gave $200, the student body donated $126, and there was an anonymous gift of $100.[154]

The generosity of Julius Rosenwald combined with the willingness of African Americans to contribute funds for the benefit of education—whether the money was for library books or a Rosenwald school—is testimony to the value that the black community placed on education. It also reveals how little white state political and educational leaders valued black education through their inability and perverse reluctance to provide such basic educational needs as decent school buildings and adequate numbers of books.

With money provided by the Rosenwald Fund S.C. State purchased this panel truck, for mobile education, shown here about 1930. W. W. Wilkins, the supervisor of agricultural education, traveled throughout South Carolina offering advice and demonstrating skills in everything from woodworking to crop management. Courtesy of the Historical Collection, South Carolina State University

In 1930 the Rosenwald Fund allocated money to purchase a panel truck, grandly described as "the agricultural engineering car." William W. Wilkins, who was the supervisor of agricultural education, traveled the state for the next several years dispensing advice and information and teaching technical skills to teachers and students in rural schools. Wilkins was a 1922 graduate of S.C. State, and he kept a detailed journal as he toured South Carolina demonstrating methods in the construction of farmhouses and barns, the erection of fences, and the installation of sanitary outdoor toilets.[155]

With the stock market crash in 1929, the Rosenwald Fund began to restrict its commitments and grants. The fund's assets were largely in cash and Sears stock, and the value of that stock plunged from $190 a share before the crash to $32 a share in 1932. S.C. State and its faculty members would no longer receive Rosenwald support. Attempts by Wilkinson to elicit Rosenwald money to complete Dukes Gymnasium were unsuccessful. The fund stopped providing Christmas gifts to the Felton School children. No Rosenwald schools were built after 1932, which was coincidentally the year that Julius Rosenwald died.[156]

The emphasis that Julius Rosenwald and his fund placed on agricultural and industrial education bolstered the argument that northern philanthropists like Rosenwald and Rockefeller were mainly interested in educating black southerners for menial positions in society. They would be the farmers and laborers as well as teachers who would work with their hands and teach others to do so in order to make America a more productive society. Thus few African Americans would be prepared for the professions, and most would remain largely confined to a subservient status in society aided and abetted by the misguided, if not racist, intentions of the philanthropists.[157]

There is at least an element of truth to the charge so far as the Rosenwald Fund and South Carolina State are concerned. Faculty members affiliated with the agricultural program received more financial assistance for additional study than academic faculty did. The fund combined with the U.S. Department of Agriculture to sponsor the 1930 program for black extension and home demonstration agents held at the college. Rosenwald money also purchased the vehicle used by Wilkins to aid in vocational instruction around the state. On the other hand, the Rosenwald Fund certainly did not designate money solely for agricultural and mechanical purposes. Rosenwald administrators also offered money for library books as well as for the construction of Felton School in collaboration with the General Education Board. But S.C. State was a land-grant school, and the faculty most in need of more education came from the vocations rather than the academic disciplines.

THE GENERAL EDUCATION BOARD

The General Education Board was more important as a philanthropic organization in the history of South Carolina State than the Rosenwald Fund. Founded in 1902 at the behest of John D. Rockefeller Sr., the General Education Board would spend $325 million on the promotion of education in the United States. Over $41 million of that went to historically black colleges and universities by the time the GEB depleted its funds in 1960.[158]

In the 1920s GEB administrators decided to devote more of its financial resources to black education. There was a concern that the economic, educational, and social situation of black people in the South was so grim that it endangered the future of white people. In a 1922 report, the GEB assessed the prospects of African Americans. "Aside from any concern which may on humanitarian grounds be felt for the Negro for his own sake, it is clear that the welfare of the South, not to say the whole country—its prosperity, its sanitation, its morale—is affected by the condition of the Negro race."[159]

The board subsequently spent most of the $25 million that it allocated for black schools between 1924 and 1931 on private black colleges and secondary schools. But some of those funds were directed to black public institutions such as South Carolina State where state authorities were extremely reluctant to appropriate money to black institutions.[160]

In 1924 President Wilkinson asked GEB officials for financial help in building a facility "especially equipped for the teaching of science." Shortly thereafter Jackson Davis visited the campus accompanied by Joseph B. Felton. Davis was a white Virginian, and he would serve nearly three decades as a field agent for the GEB, winning the support and admiration of black and white educators alike. He was already familiar with S.C.

State. In 1920 he had recommended that the GEB grant $45,000 toward the construction of the practice school that was never built. In 1924 Jackson was favorably disposed toward the request for the science building, but he believed that Wilkinson's plans for the project were "rather hastily" conceived.[161]

Nevertheless the GEB agreed to furnish $25,000 toward the construction of the new science building. Even with that commitment of private assistance, the legislature declined to provide sufficient funding to complete the structure. In 1925 the general assembly allotted $25,000 toward the estimated $75,000 cost of the building. In the meantime Miller F. Whittaker had drafted plans for the facility—drawings that would help Whittaker earn a master's degree in architecture from Kansas State. But the board of trustees disagreed on the propriety of breaking ground without all the funds in place.[162]

By a vote of 4–2, the board decided in 1926 to begin construction. Fortunately in 1927 the general assembly appropriated an additional $25,000. Once again faculty members as well as students contributed to the erection of a campus building. "The instructors of woodworking, ironworking, masonry, plumbing, electric wiring, painting, auto-mechanics and other branches devoted their entire time to the work." Wilkinson estimated that the final cost of the building would have been $120,000 without faculty and student assistance. President Wilkinson also expressed gratitude to local board member Wallace C. Bethea for his help in purchasing materials and in executing contracts for construction.[163]

Built mainly of brick, steel, and concrete, the building was completed in 1928 and named for E. D. Hodge, a farmer and board member from Alcolu. Hodge Hall was dedicated during commencement week in May 1928. Clemson president Enoch W. Sikes delivered the main address. The new building housed more than science classrooms and laboratories. It contained facilities for teaching agriculture. It also furnished extension work offices and provided space for the headquarters of the Orangeburg County Negro Fair Association.[164]

ROBERT SHAW WILKINSON: AN ASSESSMENT

Robert Shaw Wilkinson had not been in the best of health, but his death March 13, 1932, shocked black and white South Carolinians. He was sixty-seven and succumbed to pneumonia. As the state's foremost black leader, he had driven himself relentlessly for years, and it contributed to his ill health. He had been hospitalized in New York City in 1925 for an undisclosed illness. In 1930 former member of the college board of trustees Claude E. Sawyer cautioned Wilkinson about overexerting himself. "Therefore, I again wish to urge you to take a rest. No man can stand it forever to be grinding as you are day in and year out from day to day forever." Later that year Wilkinson suffered what he described cryptically as a "severe breakdown." But he rarely stopped pushing himself.[165]

For years Wilkinson had immersed himself in the details of management of the college as well as in an array of other civic and religious activities. Whether it involved disciplining students, contacting legislators, or administering the cooperative extension program, President Wilkinson was directly involved. He traveled the state almost continuously on behalf of the college and to participate in nonacademic organizations. He had served for six years as the president of the all-black Palmetto State Teachers' Association. He was an officer in the Knights of the Pythias. He was a member of Omega Psi Phi Fraternity, the Elks, and the Odd Fellows. He was a thirty-third-degree Mason and the deputy grand master for South Carolina. He served as secretary for the Voorhees College board of trustees. He had become a member of the Episcopal Church and was working diligently at the time of his death to have a black Episcopal church built in Orangeburg.[166]

Despite less than satisfactory support from the state, Wilkinson had presided over the transformation of S.C. State from a vocational school to its emergence as a four-year college. Although he did not draw attention to it, there was also somewhat less emphasis on agriculture and home economics than there had been when he assumed the presidency in 1911. In the meantime the cooperative extension program expanded steadily in the 1920s.

There were several major capital improvements under Wilkinson's leadership including White Hall, Felton Training School, the Y-Hut, Dukes Gymnasium, and Hodge Hall. There were also three new dormitories—Manning Hall, Bradham Hall, and Lowman Hall—completed during World War I. Each of these structures was designed and erected in part by faculty and students. Felton and Hodge could not have been built without the financial assistance of the Rosenwald Fund and the General Education Board.

The most serious blemish on Wilkinson's presidency was his willingness to flatter and appeal to the notorious Coleman Blease. Wilkinson's overtly obsequious behavior toward the state's most reprehensible racist was deplorable and difficult to fathom. Wilkinson's eagerness to cultivate favor with Blease to secure a federal appointment on the Haiti commission befitted neither the college nor Wilkinson.

Although Marion Birnie Wilkinson would survive her husband by nearly a quarter century, as a couple they had devoted nearly three decades to S.C. State and to African Americans in South Carolina prior to his death. The Wilkinsons were proud of themselves and proud of their race. They were conscious of their privileged status within that race, and that they had earned a measure of respect from the state's white leadership. They certainly did not risk that hard-won status by openly challenging white supremacy although they clearly did not accept it.

Like virtually all black leaders in the early decades of the twentieth century, they embraced middle-class ideology that rested on hard work, education, religious faith, and morality. Those values prevailed, they believed, whether a person was a farmer, a teacher, a small business owner, or a medical doctor. The Wilkinsons also accepted the notion that the lack of commitment to education, loose behavior, and irresponsible conduct displayed by many poorer African Americans could be altered through schooling and involvement in church and other civic organizations. By eradicating that undesirable conduct, black people would gain greater acceptance from the white population.

Of course the Wilkinsons themselves effectively demonstrated middle-class values, and yet they were never fully accepted by white people who judged them not by their knowledge, sophistication, and refinement, but by their color. Furthermore there were many white South Carolinians who exhibited precisely those lower-class characteristics rejected by people like the Wilkinsons. But those poorly educated white Carolinians enjoyed privileges not available to black people in a Jim Crow society.

CHAPTER FOUR

The Great Depression

Robert Shaw Wilkinson's death occurred in the midst of nation's descent into the worst economic crisis of the twentieth century. Even during a more robust economic environment, S.C. State had not benefited from generous state support. While other state institutions suffered devastating cuts in the 1930s, S.C. State absorbed even greater reductions over a longer period of time. Had it not been for the calm and reassuring leadership of President Miller F. Whittaker combined with the federal financial assistance of New Deal programs and the philanthropic support of the General Education Board, the college would have had a far more difficult time surviving as a viable institution into the 1940s.

Even with that federal and philanthropic aid in the mid- and latter 1930s, the college endured a grave situation. For a time state funding ceased altogether. Faculty members who resigned, died, or were dismissed were not replaced. Money was not available for maintenance and the purchase of supplies. The campus high school was eliminated. To make matters worse, the college's dairy herd was decimated by Bang's disease.

MILLER F. WHITTAKER

Miller Fulton Whittaker would guide the college through the Depression, World War II, and the early stages of the civil rights movement. Two days after Wilkinson died on March 13, 1932, the board of trustees named Whittaker the acting president. Two months later the thirty-nine-year-old leader let Charles F. Brooks, the chairman of the board, know indirectly that he aspired to the permanent position. "I hope you will keep in mind the fact that I am completing my nineteenth year as an employee of the college, and that above all during this time I have been loyal and worked always for the interests of the administration."[1]

Benjamin E. Mays, the president of the college alumni association, contacted graduates in several states including Georgia, North Carolina, Texas, Pennsylvania, and New York and then wrote the board to support the elevation of Whittaker to the presidency. "I can truthfully say there is a strong desire on the part of these graduates to see Professor M. F. Whittaker succeed Dr. Wilkinson."[2]

With Governor I. C. Blackwood presiding as the ex officio chairman, the board of trustees convened in the supreme court room of the state capital in Columbia on May

30, 1932, and Whittaker was formally named and introduced as the third president of the college. Although the trustees had received applications for the presidency from several individuals who they did not identify, the board conducted no formal interviews before selecting Whittaker.[3]

Whittaker had been associated with the college since childhood. His father taught at the institution from 1902 until 1908. Johnson C. Whittaker and his wife and two sons then left Orangeburg when the elder Whittaker assumed a position as teacher and later became the principal at all-black Frederick Douglass High School in Oklahoma City. In the meantime Miller F. Whittaker graduated from Douglass High School and then Kansas State College (later University) with a degree in architecture. He returned to Orangeburg as a faculty member in 1913. Except for military service during World War I, he remained with the college for the rest of his life. He was named dean of mechanical arts in 1925, and President Wilkinson periodically called on Whittaker to serve as acting president in Wilkinson's absence.[4]

Whittaker, who never married, devoted himself to the college and to his profession as an architect. His mother, Page, lived with him in the president's residence until her death in 1944. Although not a physically imposing man at five feet seven inches and about 150 pounds, Whittaker thrust himself into the economic calamity in 1932 and quickly asserted himself. He took careful measure of the critical problems facing the college and rarely openly complained about the plight of the institution. Rather he seemed to relish the opportunity to confront such formidable challenges.

THE ECONOMIC COLLAPSE

And formidable were those challenges. Prior to Wilkinson's death, state appropriations to the institution were slashed. The college received $96,000 from the legislature in 1931, and it would be over a decade before state funding reached that level again. In 1932 the college was allocated $73,000—a 24 percent reduction from the previous year. The appropriation sank to $49,667 in 1933. College employees saw their salaries reduced again and again. In 1931 salaries were cut between 5 percent and 7 percent, and they were reduced another 10 percent on January 1, 1932. As the Depression's grip tightened in 1933 and appropriations dwindled, employees making over $1,000 per year took a 25 percent reduction while those earning less than $1,000 took a 20 percent cut. Overall faculty salaries were reduced an average of 34 percent between 1929 and 1934. The number of faculty members dropped from seventy-five to fifty-four during Whittaker's first two years as president.[5]

Then the financial situation worsened. In March 1932 the state appropriation was delayed, and the board of trustees authorized acting president Whittaker and secretary of the board Wallace C. Bethea to negotiate a $4,000 loan from a local bank. The money would pay for animal feed, water, electric power, and telephones, and the loan would be repaid when state funds arrived. Then late that same year, the state was unable to provide $10,950 (or 15 percent) of the $73,000 appropriated to the school. As a result faculty and staff received half pay in November 1932, and they were not paid at all in December. The college had no money. Whittaker grimly explained: "The College is without funds of any kind and has been in this condition since the middle of November. It does not appear that the legislature will be very liberal with us and we are finding it necessary to curtail our work in many instances."[6]

Something close to panic ensued shortly after Whittaker became acting president in 1932 when information reached the campus that President Herbert Hoover's director of the budget had recommended that all federal aid to the states be suspended. This would mean the elimination of Morrill land-grant and scrip funds—about $31,000 annually—for S.C. State. That represented about 40 percent of the institution's budget. Whittaker hurriedly dispatched telegrams to South Carolina's six members of the U.S. House of Representatives and to the state's two U.S. senators—Ellison D. "Cotton Ed" Smith and James F. Byrnes—asking them to intervene to preserve the federal funds.[7]

Whittaker did not point out that such a loss in funding might mean that the college would cease to exist. Instead he couched it in terms that might be more amenable to political leaders, explaining that such a cut "would almost totally destroy practical training for Negroes in this state." He asked that those funds be restored. But the fears that federal funds would vanish was more a sign of the uncertainty and even hysteria generated by the Depression than political reality. Federal authorities reassured Whittaker and officials at other land-grant schools that Morrill money would continue without reduction.[8]

Yet federal funds that had been appropriated were not readily available because of the financial crisis. Money that was ordinarily allocated to pay staff engaged in agricultural and mechanical instruction in the public schools through the Smith-Hughes program was inaccessible. Joseph B. Felton, the state agent for Negro schools, informed Whittaker that William W. Wilkins, who toured the state providing instruction in various vocational skills, would not receive his salary or expenses. The South Carolina National Bank had closed, "and it will be impossible for us to send you a check for same until the bank is opened, if it does open."[9]

A year later, in April 1933, Whittaker attempted to pay employees with federal Morrill land-grant funds only to find that the bank crisis prevented it. State comptroller-general A. W. Beattie explained to Whittaker that "the [Morrill] fund is deposited by the state treasurer in banks that are now closed, and is, therefore, not available." By 1934 Whittaker pointed out that "the College is commencing to suffer materially and educationally on account of reduced appropriations." With the loss of faculty, the lack of supplies, and the inadequate maintenance, the institution had fallen to "mediocre standards."[10]

With reduced income and then no income, faculty and staff members were hard pressed to meet their personal financial responsibilities. In opening the school year in September 1932, Whittaker uncharacteristically showed little sympathy to an assembly of faculty and staff. He said that he had been "besieged on all sides this summer with letters, bills, merchants and collectors seeking to collect debts contracted by employees of the college." He callously informed them that they were harming the reputation of the college by their financial laxity, and that those who did not pay their bills might not be retained. Whittaker offered no advice on how people who had suffered repeated reductions in pay—and that was when they were paid—were expected to meet their

Table 12. State Appropriations for South Carolina State, 1931–39

1930–31	$96,000
1931–32	$80,929
1932–33	$73,000
1933–34	$49,667
1934–35	$66,000
1935–36	$72,000
1936–37	$82,500
1937–38	$90,000
1938–39	$83,125
1939–40	$89,997

Sources: *Thirty-Fifth Annual Report,* 18; *Thirty-Sixth Annual Report,* 8, 16–17; *Thirty-Seventh Annual Report,* 5, 11; *Thirty-Eighth Annual Report,* 24; *Thirty-Ninth Annual Report,* 31; *Fortieth Annual Report,* 31; *Forty-First Annual Report,* 35; *Forty-Second Annual Report,* 27; *Forty-Third Annual Report,* 27; *Forty-Fourth Annual Report,* 29.

financial obligations. Whittaker tried to leaven his blunt comments by offering some encouraging platitudes in the face of continued adversity. "The work of the college, the business of the state must go on, with funds available but somehow by faith, faith in God that He wants the work to go on, done, and having no doubt as to our ultimate success."[11]

THE QUEST FOR HELP

Moreover, and to his credit, Whittaker did more than simply offer empty words of solace. He made concrete efforts to assist beleaguered members of the faculty. The Depression and the salary reductions exacerbated a housing crisis for a number of faculty families. Finding convenient and affordable housing was a perennial problem for people employed by the college. Unmarried faculty members usually lived in the dormitories with students, which meant less housing was available for students. But those faculty members who were married with families had a difficult time finding accommodations in the community.

During the 1920s President Robert S. Wilkinson had invested his own funds, and seven modest rental homes for faculty were built on Lovell Street adjacent to the campus. But when faculty salaries were reduced in the early 1930s, the occupants of the homes could no longer afford the rent. Presumably Robert S. Wilkinson's widow, Marion Birnie Wilkinson, was responsible for the mortgage payments on the dwellings.

Miller F. Whittaker submitted a proposal to the General Education Board recommending that the GEB purchase the seven homes and lots for a total of $18,500. The staff of the GEB took Whittaker's request seriously and sent field agent Walter B. Hill to Orangeburg in March 1933 to examine the homes, several of which were vacant by that time. But the executive committee of the GEB finally decided not to purchase the real estate on behalf of the college.[12]

Because the GEB appeared to be the sole private agency with any money at its disposal during the Depression, Whittaker had already appealed to the Rockefeller-sponsored fund to assist in paying the salaries of college employees after the state appropriation failed to materialize in late 1932. He explained that it was "the first time in the history of the institution that we shall be unable to pay our teachers." But the GEB's Walter Hill, while expressing sympathy for the plight of the faculty, told Whittaker that the board could not provide funds for basic operations or for payroll. If the GEB would not help with salaries, would it aid the institution in purchasing land for the college farm? The college had been renting fifty acres of land primarily to provide forage for its farm animals. But those rental funds had evaporated. Once again GEB authorities declined to support Whittaker's request.[13]

In the midst of these economic woes, the college lost most of its dairy cattle. The state veterinarian found half of the cows infected with Bang's disease (*Brucilla abersus*), and the affected animals were destroyed. Only four cows remained, and just two of those produced milk. The college had relied on its dairy herd to provide milk for the dining hall and for cheese making. To replace the cows, Whittaker turned to Clemson president Enoch W. Sikes and asked if S.C. State might borrow or lease some of Clemson's cows, and Clemson agreed to lend the animals to the college.[14]

This was not the first time that a college president had asked to borrow from another state agency. Less than a year earlier and only a month before his death, Robert S. Wilkinson had written to Benjamin M. Sawyer, the chief of the State Highway Commission, to ask if S.C. State could temporarily use highway department equipment that was in storage because of the weak economy. Wilkinson wanted transits, levels, and rods that could be put to use in the instructional program. However, there is no record that the Highway Commission responded to the inquiry.[15]

THE HIGH SCHOOL

In 1933 the campus high school closed. It had been a key component of the academic program at S.C. State since 1896. The deplorable state of the economy was one of several factors that contributed to the demise of the secondary program. Most of the high school students resided in the Orangeburg area. Fewer students from around the state came to Orangeburg for high school by the 1930s because there were twenty-nine high schools for black students, and the graduates of these schools were admitted to the state's private and public black colleges. When S.C. State opened in 1896, there were no public high schools for black youngsters. Of 232 high school students enrolled on the campus in 1932–33, 155 were local students, and only twenty-seven high school students resided on campus. Moreover the high school was a fiscal drain on the college, and the U.S. Office of Education recommended in 1930 that federal land-grant funds not be expended on secondary education.[16]

Initially there was much dissatisfaction among parents and students with the decision to terminate the high school. But its loss benefited the college in the short and long terms. More of the institution's exceedingly limited resources could be devoted to the undergraduate program. However, arrangements had to be made for the students currently enrolled in the secondary program. Its ninety-one sophomores and forty-eight juniors could transfer to Claflin's high school. Students who were entering their senior year could elect to remain at S.C. State, where they would be classified as "sub freshmen." Of the fifty-six eligible seniors, only sixteen (eleven males and five females) availed themselves of that opportunity. The college also retained three of the six high school teachers: Joseph W. Harper, Sara B. Henderson, and Mamie Jones.[17]

THE FACULTY

The floundering economy cost the college valued faculty members. The 34 percent reduction in salaries between 1929 and 1934 was not enough to keep all the faculty and staff employed. The number of faculty members had declined by twenty-one between 1931 and 1935. Like student enrollment the size of the faculty recovered modestly during the second half of the 1930s. The figures can be somewhat misleading because Whittaker included the high school faculty members until that facility closed. He also counted summer school faculty in the totals although they did not belong to the regular faculty who taught during the academic year.

Despite the Depression the academic preparation of the faculty improved as more faculty members earned master's degrees and pursued course work beyond the master's level. In 1931 seven faculty members possessed a master's degree, and by 1939 seventeen faculty members had a master's and six of them had completed one year of graduate work beyond the master's degree. However, no member of the S.C. State faculty had earned a doctorate.[18]

As bleak as the situation was for the teaching staff, it could have been worse. The passage of the Bankhead-Jones Act in 1935 increased federal land-grant funds beginning with $5,000 in 1936 and increasing in annual increments of $1,000 to $10,000 in 1941. This enabled the college to hire four additional faculty members in 1935–36. They were Myrtle Dejoie in physical education, Grace Postles in English, Gladys Thomson in music, and Bryant Blakemon in business and economics.[19]

In a segregated world it was a difficult challenge for faculty members at the black colleges to earn graduate degrees. Except for Howard University in Washington, D.C., no black college offered graduate programs, and southern white institutions did not admit African Americans to their graduate programs. Most northern universities accepted limited numbers of black students to their master's and doctoral programs, but they rarely employed people of color. The black colleges represented the sole teaching opportunity for the vast majority of African Americans who earned graduate degrees in the first half of the twentieth century. As thousands of African Americans migrated north for jobs in urban areas, small numbers of black men and women with academic credentials journeyed south to secure teaching positions at the only colleges that would employ them.

Table 13. The Number of Faculty Members at S.C. State Including Administrators and Professional Staff, 1930–39

1930–31
49 college faculty members
15 summer school
7 high school
4 Felton Training School
75 total
1932–33
54 college faculty members
15 summer school
6 high school
3 Felton Training School
78 total
1934–35
44 college faculty members
3 summer school
4 Felton Training School
51 total
1936–37
48 college faculty members
8 summer school
4 Felton Training School
60 total
1938–39
54 college faculty members
11 summer school
3 Felton Training School
68 total

Sources: College catalogs, 1930–31, 7–11; 1932–33, 7–8; 1934–35, 7–8; 1936–37, 8–11; 1938–39, 8–12.

Faculty members at schools like S.C. State usually could afford to pursue graduate work in the North only during summer sessions. If they had families, they had to teach during the regular academic year to support them. Then it became an arduous academic, economic, and logistical burden to attempt to earn a master's degree or a doctorate by spending several summer sessions or regular academic terms in the North.

Therefore the financial support of the General Education Board for faculty fellowships was of incalculable benefit. GEB aid permitted S.C. State faculty members to pursue graduate study at northern universities, something most of them could not have done without such assistance. The GEB funds also enabled the college to retain valuable faculty members during the Depression by letting them take a leave of absence and thereby temporarily relieve the institution of the responsibility for their salaries.[20]

In 1932 the GEB awarded fellowships to biology professor Edward Ferguson, to modern languages and history professor Frederick M. Sheffield, and to education professor Rosamond Alston. Ferguson went back to the University of Illinois, where he had already received his bachelor's degree. Sheffield attended New York University, and Rosamond Alston continued graduate work at the Teachers' College of Columbia University. Each of them earned a master's degree.[21]

Other faculty members including Helen Sheffield, Dudley Zimmerman, James H. Birnie, and Joseph W. Harper would subsequently receive GEB aid. Helen Sheffield was the daughter of Robert S. and Marion B. Wilkinson, and she was the wife of Frederick Sheffield. She earned an M.S. in chemistry at New York University. James H. Birnie had a bachelor's degree from Morehouse College and a master of science from Brown University. GEB support permitted Birnie to work on a Ph.D. in biology at Cornell University. Zimmerman and Harper used GEB aid to attend summer programs, but they did not earn degrees.[22]

The GEB refused to offer a fellowship to Mabel C. James. She had served as President Wilkinson's executive secretary, and she was closely involved in the day-to-day administration of the college. In 1931, with the strong support of Wilkinson, James sought GEB financial help to pursue a bachelor's degree in business management that would strengthen her knowledge of fiscal affairs. But GEB officials made it clear that while her proposal had merit, they were not about to assist a woman who wanted to earn a degree in business. Jackson Davis, the field agent for the GEB, explained to Wilkinson. "The general idea is excellent but our committee does not feel warranted in providing fellowships for women for work in this field. This is no reflection whatever upon Miss James' ability, but I am obliged to write you that we cannot offer her any encouragement for a fellowship."[23]

Rebuffed by the GEB, James enrolled at her own expense at the University of Michigan shortly after the death of Wilkinson. Perhaps discouraged by the GEB's dismissive attitude toward her interest in business administration, she received a bachelor's degree in education and went on to earn a master's degree in education in 1934. She married Frederick B. Payton, who had taught music at the college in the 1920s, and they moved to Philadelphia where she died in 1979.[24]

President Whittaker also benefited from GEB assistance. During the summer of 1933, Whittaker spent six weeks at Cornell University in Ithaca, New York, with the presidents of five other black land-grant colleges. The GEB paid for tuition and travel. (The total sum for the six presidents was less than $1,000.) Each president was responsible for his own living expenses. They stayed in Cornell dormitories. The six men enrolled in a variety of regular summer courses in education and business. In addition they participated in seminars on agriculture, college finance, curriculum, food services, and more. They also took a field trip to the New York State Agricultural Experiment Station at Geneva, and they were invited to a meeting of the Ithaca Rotary Club.[25]

THE CONFERENCE OF PRESIDENTS OF NEGRO LAND-GRANT COLLEGES

From the 1920s through the 1940s, Robert S. Wilkinson and then Miller F. Whittaker played key roles within the Conference of Presidents of Negro Land-Grant Colleges. Established in 1923 at Tuskegee Institute as the Association of Negro Land-Grant Colleges, it was renamed shortly thereafter. It continued to function until it merged in 1954 with the larger Association of Land-Grant Colleges and Universities. The seventeen presidents of the black land-grant schools constituted the membership of the organization, but non-land-grant schools including Central State, Howard, and Texas Southern participated as associate members. Meeting informally without a constitution or bylaws, the group gathered once a year in November. The presidents discussed mutual problems including finances, facilities, faculty, and curriculum.[26]

With such a small membership, the presidents had frequent opportunities to make presentations. Wilkinson delivered a talk in 1928 in Washington entitled "Constructive Tendencies in Our Land-Grant Colleges," and he discussed extension work at the 1930 gathering that also met in the nation's capital. In 1935 Whittaker offered a presentation

The presidents of the black land-grant colleges met at Howard University in November 1937. Miller F. Whittaker is standing at the center of the front row. Courtesy of the Historical Collection, South Carolina State University

called "Study of Occupational Opportunities of Negroes." The next year he moved on to a more sensitive subject in a lecture entitled "The Ability of Southern States to Pay for an Adequate Program of Public Education for Negroes." He told the other presidents assembled at Virginia State College in Petersburg what they already knew: the South's lack of wealth made it difficult to support one system of public education, and it was impossible for the region to support segregated and parallel systems of education. Wilkinson served as president of the conference in 1927, and Whittaker was elected its chief executive nearly a decade later in 1936.[27]

ACADEMIC CHALLENGES

The economy and career opportunities elsewhere made it difficult for S.C. State to retain several key faculty members. William H. Bell, the dean of liberal arts and a history professor, was appointed the president of Alcorn A&M College in 1934. Bell's wife, Thelma, who taught music, resigned to join him in Mississippi. Alfred W. Shute and his wife, Beulah, left Orangeburg for Florida A&M. He taught dairy science and agricultural economics, and he had conducted a research project involving black farmers in Sumter County. His wife taught nutrition.[28]

The persistence of inadequate salaries—low even among the historically black institutions—made it difficult to keep valued faculty members. Whittaker and Wilkinson repeatedly pointed out the problem of compensation to state authorities. But their pleas went unheeded year after year. In 1938 Whittaker included, without comment, a table in the annual report of the college comparing salaries at the black land-grant colleges.

This weak salary structure combined with the lack of solid academic credentials among many S.C. State faculty members prevented the college from attaining an A rating from the Association of Colleges and Secondary Schools of the Southern States. The association maintained a separate A-B-C rating system for black colleges and universities through the era of segregation. S.C. State kept a B rating through the 1930s. In 1938 Fred McCuistion, the executive agent of the association, informed Whittaker that

Table 14. Annual Salaries at the Seventeen Black Land-Grant Colleges, 1937–38

Position	Median Salary	S.C. State Salary
Deans	$2,094	$1,800
Professors	$1,795	$1,485
Associate professors	$1,586	$1,350
Assistant professors	$1,419	$1,320
Instructors	$1,193	$1,136 to $1,246

Sources: *Forty-Second Annual Report, 1937–1938,* 18. Whittaker cited the 1937 report from the U.S. Office of Education.

Table 15. Expenditures per Student at South Carolina Public Colleges and Universities, 1934–35

Institution	Expenditure
Citadel	$306.91
Clemson College	$277.20
University of South Carolina	$257.50
Winthrop College	$231.00
S.C. State College	$138.08

Source: *Thirty-Ninth Annual Report, 1934–1935*, 12.

the association's Committee on Approval of Negro Schools "felt it would be necessary for you to further strengthen the training of the faculty and increase your salary schedule before they would feel justified in recommending the Class 'A' rating." It grated on Whittaker and others closely connected to S.C. State that two peer institutions, North Carolina A&T and Florida A&M, had earned the coveted A rating.[29]

There was little Whittaker could do about the matter of faculty compensation. The state legislature had reduced funding during the Depression, and S.C. State remained woefully underfunded in comparison to the other four public colleges. In his annual report in 1934–35 Whittaker included without comment a list of the funds the general assembly appropriated per student to each public college.

Presumably Whittaker expected the numbers to speak for themselves. He did not use the figures to make a plea for a more equitable distribution of the limited funds that were available. Whittaker may have believed that legislators staring at such a stark disparity would be embarrassed into corrective action. If so he was wrong. The entire system of Jim Crow was predicated on the assumed inferiority of Negro people, who needed less and got less than white South Carolinians. Had a comparison among the state schools revealed something even close to equal funding for S.C. State, it would have been cause for concern in the general assembly. To the vast majority of white political leaders and their constituents, S.C. State deserved precisely what it received and no more.

While state support languished, S.C. State benefited significantly from private and federal funds as the Depression took its toll on the institution. The General Education Board and several of the "alphabet agencies" created as a part of Franklin Roosevelt's New Deal were vital in helping sustain the college through the grim days of the economic crisis. Since 1896 federal money had substantially aided the land-grant institution. That was even more the case during the 1930s. The college consistently received more revenue from the federal government and its own internal sources than it did from the state. In 1937–38, for example, S.C. State collected $51,385.91 in land-grant money. It generated $42,915 from student fees including tuition, and earned an additional $19,850 from the farm, dairy, cafeteria, summer school, and other internal sources. The state appropriation was $90,000. The following year state funds were reduced to $83,125.

Table 16. S.C. State College Revenue for 1937–38

Federal Sources	
Morrill fund	$45,631.91
Land scrip	$5,754.00
S.C. State College Sources	
Student fees	$42,915.00
Farm, dairy, cafeteria	$19,850.00
State appropriation	$90,000.00
Total	$204,150.91

Source: *Forty-Second Annual Report, 1937–1938,* 28.

THE NEW DEAL AND S.C. STATE

Almost from the inception of the New Deal in 1933, S.C. State received funds from the newly created agencies. The Federal Emergency Relief Administration (FERA) provided $500 million in grants to the forty-eight states for food and clothing for the destitute as well as for projects that employed people. The federal money was administered in the Palmetto State by the South Carolina Emergency Relief Administration. Governor I. C. Blackwood appointed Malcolm Miller to run the SCERA.[30]

The subsequent appointment of S.C. State trustee Wallace C. Bethea to the state planning board of the SCERA was of enormous benefit to the college. The planning board determined which proposed projects would be awarded SCERA funds in the form of loans. Bethea was a prominent Orangeburg businessman who served as the secretary to the board of trustees. His membership on the planning board gave the college the sort of leverage that the black institution rarely possessed during its history as it dealt with federal and state bureaucrats. The SCERA quickly approved $45,000 for S.C. State to construct a much-needed laundry and to make general repairs. The laundry project would employ thirty-three men for four months at thirty-five cents per hour. Bethea suggested that new steam lines be included in the request, and they were added to the grant at an additional cost of $15,000.[31]

The Orangeburg administrator for the Emergency Relief Administration, P. B. Kortjohn, agreed to assign one man to work two days a week on the campus. Several weeks later Whittaker invited Kortjohn to drive through the campus to see the new farm road that had been paved and the new dairy barn that had been built by the Civil Works Administration (CWA).[32]

Students received part-time employment through the FERA beginning in early 1934. S.C. State was able to put thirty-four students to work as clerical and laboratory assistants, on janitorial jobs, and in farm labor and painting. They were paid thirty cents per hour. Most of them worked twenty-five hours a week and earned a respectable

$7.50. (When Congress passed the Fair Labor Standards Act in 1938, it established a minimum wage of twenty-five cents an hour for full-time work.) The thirty-four college students worked 826.6 hours in February at a cost of $248. Young people pleaded for these jobs. Rosa Lee Irby's letter to President Whittaker was typical. "I am one of your college students in the freshman class, but my father informs me that he is not going to be able to keep me in college unless I can get some work to help him pay my expenses." She continued, "I am willing and will be glad to accept a job from you that will help me through college. I will do any kind of work that is common."[33]

The new agencies and programs created during the New Deal did little to challenge the racial status quo. Jim Crow continued to prevail. But there were uneven efforts by the Roosevelt administration and by New Deal administrators to accommodate African Americans by setting aside jobs and funds for black people and their institutions. For example the Civil Works Administration specifically allotted a portion of its resources to black colleges. However, the black schools were then compelled to compete against each other for that small slice of the pie. Paul V. Jewell, who had succeeded Whittaker as dean of mechanical arts, hoped that S.C. State could obtain access to some CWA jobs for students to help boost enrollment of first-year students. "Then too," he wrote Whittaker, "if we were able to get the proportion of the Negro allotment here we may be able to so arrange it that it may serve to draw freshmen here."[34]

THE LIBRARY

The General Education Board and federal programs enabled the college to undertake its first significant capital projects in nearly a decade. During the late 1930s, a library, a men's dormitory, and a new structure to teach mechanical trades were erected. Since its founding S.C. State had never had a separate library building. By the 1930s the college housed its collection of some twelve thousand volumes in three classrooms in White Hall. In 1936 President Whittaker asked General Education Board officials if they might be receptive to underwriting one-half of the cost of a $40,000 library. The GEB had taken a special interest in college libraries in the 1930s. The board extended more than sixty grants to colleges and universities for libraries and supported the construction of nineteen library buildings. Thirteen of those new libraries were built on the campuses of black colleges.[35]

GEB administrators were, therefore, very much interested in S.C. State. They considered a "new library the greatest need at State College," but they were incredulous that Whittaker, an experienced architect, thought a library could be built for a mere $40,000. GEB field agent Jackson Davis wrote Leo Favrot, "I just can't believe that $40,000 would be a sufficient sum to build and equip the library building they require."[36]

After a conference with Davis, Whittaker revised the cost of the library upward to $80,000. GEB staff member Leo Favrot visited Whittaker on December 12, 1936, and on December 13 Whittaker formally requested $40,000 from the GEB to cover one-half of the library's cost. On December 19 Whittaker received a postal telegram from the GEB's W. W. Brierly indicating that the board had approved the request.[37]

Table 17. College Bond Bill, 1937

Institution	Authorized Amount	Purpose
Clemson	$300,000	Textile building
University of S.C.	$325,000	Library or admin. building
Winthrop	$350,000	Auditorium or classroom building
Citadel	$300,000	Barracks
S.C. State	$75,000	Library/dormitory

Source: "Copy of Act to Provide for the Construction at State Educational Institutions," Folder 1, Library Building, HCSCSU.

Whittaker was elated at the generosity of the GEB. "Coming as it did at Christmas time, it was a wonderful surprise for students and faculty." What was not so wonderful was the difficulty Whittaker experienced in his attempt to secure funding for the balance of the library's cost. Initial efforts to come to an agreement with the federal government's Public Works Administration failed, and the library was delayed temporarily.[38]

Instead it was the South Carolina General Assembly that matched the GEB's $40,000 contribution. It was not, however, a case of legislators and Governor Olin D. Johnston suddenly developing a desire to deal generously with the long-neglected black college. On the contrary, in legislation enacted in 1937 to authorize the sale of bonds to permit the state's five public colleges to undertake major capital improvements, S.C. State was once again the recipient of far fewer dollars than the other four institutions. The college would receive $75,000 from the sale of bonds—$40,000 would go to the library, and $35,000 would assist the Public Works Administration in the construction of a dormitory.[39]

Whittaker thoroughly immersed himself in the construction of the library. He had already assumed a major part in the design and erection of previous campus projects, including Lowman Hall, Hodge Hall, and Dukes Gymnasium. The architectural firm for the library, Lafaye and Lafaye of Columbia, retained Whittaker as an advisor on the construction of the library as well as on the new men's dormitory. While Whittaker derived considerable satisfaction as well as financial benefits from this arrangement, it raised the specter of a conflict of interest. The Public Works Administration, in fact, would not permit Whittaker to serve as the architect for the new dormitory. But George Lafaye, one of the architects of that building as well as the proposed library, informed Whittaker that he could be a paid consultant: "we could then employ you as our resident superintendent at a stated fee or salary." Lafaye insisted that PWA administrators would not object.[40]

Once construction of the library began in early 1938, Whittaker involved himself in the minutest details of the project. There are dozens of pieces of correspondence

With the General Education Board providing $40,000 and a state bond bill furnishing an additional $40,000, S.C. State was able to erect its first library building, Wilkinson Hall. Dedicated in 1939 it also housed the business office, the bookstore, and the president's office. Courtesy of the Historical Collection, South Carolina State University

that reflect his attention to detail in the engineering and erection of the building. He shopped around for construction supplies. "Please quote me a price on 5000 lineal feet of Reinforcing Rod, ⅜" in diameter." "Please quote me a price on 50 cu. yards of bank sand." He told the architects to redraft plans for the ground floor to include enough room for an office for the college president. He wanted venetian blinds in all ground floor windows. He also asked that a room be set aside as a "Negro Literature Room."[41]

With the nation's economy still stagnant, President Whittaker wanted friends and students employed in the construction of the library. He implored the general contractor, J. S. Heslep of Columbia, to hire Leroy Sulton as an electrical contractor. "He is a graduate of State College and fully capable of electrical installations. He also has the backing of J. J. Sulton and Sons, lumber manufacturing, one of the oldest firms in Orangeburg." Whittaker wanted Thomas Nelson and Clifford Hooper given "any kind of work" that is available. "Nelson is indebted to me and Hooper is indebted to the college and promises to pay if they can get any kind of work."[42]

Whittaker made repeated requests to the general contractor to employ students, telling Heslep that the young people "are willing to work for whatever they are worth" in order to remain enrolled in college. Heslep made no promises but told Whittaker that his requests would be considered. "We will endeavor to work this out to our mutual benefit, and our Mr. Heslep on his next visit to Orangeburg will stop and discuss the matter with you."[43]

The new library opened on February 7, 1939, and it was named in honor of Robert Shaw Wilkinson, the second president. Together with the new dormitory, the library was formally dedicated on the second annual Founders' Day, March 3, 1939. Benjamin F. Hubert, a former faculty member and the president of Savannah State College, was the featured speaker at the dual dedication ceremony. The alumni association president, Harold W. Crawford, presented $1,000 to the college to purchase books written by and about African Americans.[44]

Even before its dedication, there were problems with the new library. The final cost exceeded the $80,000 estimate by a paltry $1,367.09. Whittaker asked the GEB for $683.54 to cover one-half of that over run—a request that was quickly rejected. The president appealed to the Rosenwald Fund for money for books for the new facility, and that brought another hasty rejection. The Rosenwald Fund had ceased grant activity by 1939. There were delays in the arrival of desks and chairs for the library, which irritated Whittaker. "We are being unduly delayed by the Southern Desk Company's failure to deliver furniture." He continued in a letter to company officials, "This will certainly influence any further purchase of equipment from your company." The company sales director apologized, but it did not expedite delivery.[45]

There were construction defects in the new building that went unresolved much to the dissatisfaction of Whittaker and the board of trustees. The roof had major leaks. Whittaker dispatched letter after letter to the architect, the general contractor, and the roofing contractor in 1939, 1940, and 1941 in an attempt to remedy the problem—all to little effect. Either the leaks defied solution or—more likely—the contractors were not inclined to heed the complaints from the black college. Finally in late 1940, the trustees threatened legal action against the general contractor, J. C. Heslep.[46]

MILLER HALL

Before construction began on the library, work was already underway on a new men's dormitory. For nearly two decades, there had been a severe shortage of housing for students. The completion of Manning, Bradham, and Lowman Halls during World War I helped alleviate the housing problem, but did not entirely solve it. In 1923 President Wilkinson stressed that large enrollments "make it necessary to appeal to the Legislature for at least a boy's dormitory." Year after year the general assembly ignored pleas to provide more housing.[47]

Nor did the decline in enrollment during the Depression lessen the need for campus housing. Many students resided in town, and some prospective students were turned away because there was no place for them to live. Lowman Hall, the only residence hall for men, was badly overcrowded. Built to house 187, it was bursting at the seams with 229 residents by 1936. Three to eight men lived in each of Lowman's rooms. The running water and toilets all were located in the basement. Fire was a serious hazard. There was no fire alarm, there were no exit signs, and the fire escape was inadequate.[48]

Finally with the passage of the state bond bill in 1937, the Public Works Administration (PWA) agreed to provide slightly over $27,000 in funding for the new men's dormitory. The estimated cost for the three-story structure was $61,000. It would create jobs for black and white laborers, and thus give a boost to the local economy. The six-month building project employed between forty and one hundred men per month. Skilled carpenters, bricklayers, and electricians earned seventy-five cents an hour. Apprentice bricklayers and electricians helpers received forty cents an hour while the unskilled workers were paid twenty-five cents per hour. With this federal project, employees were guaranteed the right to organize and bargain collectively. Those individuals who were unemployed and on "the public relief rolls" were to be given preference in hiring. Whittaker asked federal officials to designate students as "unemployed" so that they would be eligible to work on the dormitory. As a New Deal project, there was to be "no discrimination because of race, creed, color, or political affiliation" in employment. But PWA projects such as this one did not challenge segregation. The contractor was required to furnish "two privies . . . one for the exclusive use of the colored men and one for the use of white men."[49]

Construction began in late 1937. The cornerstone was laid in mid-December, and it encased a copper box that housed college mementos and served as a time capsule. Whittaker intended to name the new dormitory after Thomas E. Miller, only to learn that the PWA would not permit a facility to be named in honor of a living person. But before construction was finished, the first president of the college died at his home in Charleston on April 9, 1938, and the new dormitory was named Thomas E. Miller Hall.[50]

Work on Miller Hall was not finished before Whittaker began to complain of defects in workmanship. The biggest problem was a large leak in the roof that permitted heavy rains to flood the basement with six inches of water. Whittaker was also upset that the electrical contractor had installed a used condensation pump and passed it

Lowman Hall had been the sole men's dormitory until the completion of Miller Hall in 1938. During World War II, Miller Hall was converted to a women's dormitory and remained so thereafter. Courtesy of the Historical Collection, South Carolina State University

off as new. The president demanded that the general contractor, J. C. Heslep, repair the roof and that the pump, which had burned up, be replaced. The addition of Miller Hall relieved the housing crisis but did not eliminate it. The college now offered living space for 553 students. Miller Hall housed ninety-one men, and Lowman's occupancy was reduced to 183. Bradham Hall had 181 women residents and Manning Hall had ninety-eight women. Fifty men had to live in the city because of the lack of campus housing.[51]

THE MECHANICAL INDUSTRIES BUILDING AND THE WPA

With the construction of both Miller Hall and the library already underway, work on a new facility for mechanical arts had also begun. The Works Progress Administration is perhaps the best remembered of the New Deal agencies, and it helped fund campus projects and offered employment to students. The WPA was created in 1935, and it eventually provided jobs for eight million people and spent $11 billion on thousands of construction projects and other employment programs across the nation. By the time Congress abolished the WPA in 1943, it had built or renovated 2,179 schools in South Carolina. It constructed 1,267 county and municipal buildings, sixty-nine water and sewage treatment plants, 122,932 sanitary privies, and numerous playgrounds, parks, and athletic fields across the state. WPA teachers offered instruction to 53,357 illiterate adults. It had paid $95 million in wages to the state's residents. Were it not for the WPA, thousands of South Carolinians would have endured destitution and starvation during the Depression.[52]

The WPA provided partial funding for the construction of the mechanical industries building. It replaced the thirty-year-old trades building. The WPA contributed $74,000 while the college furnished $24,362 in nonstate funds and supplies. Faculty members Paul V. Jewell and John Blanche helped design the facility and assisted with engineering supervision. After a fire partially destroyed the building before construction was complete, the State Sinking Fund Commission loaned the college an additional $40,000 in 1940 to finish the project.[53]

In late 1938 Whittaker asked the General Education Board for $10,310 to equip a physics laboratory in the proposed mechanical industries building. GEB director Dr. Robert J. Havighurst, a scientist who had visited the campus and inspected its facilities, was not receptive. He recalled that there were few students enrolled in physics and that the college "had a fair amount of equipment which was not being taken care of very well and which was very poorly housed."[54]

Informed of GEB doubts, Whittaker vigorously defended his request, explaining that the Works Progress Administration would provide no funds toward the cost of equipping the new facility, and that enrollment in physics classes was indeed large because all students in mechanical arts were required to take a physics course. However, he reduced the request to $5,451. The GEB awarded $5,000 to the college for equipment and furniture for the laboratory.[55]

Several months later GEB officials were annoyed to learn that Whittaker had acquired a Westinghouse x-ray machine with a portion of those funds. Havighurst rejected Whittaker's contention that it would stimulate interest among students in careers as x-ray technicians. He bluntly informed Whittaker that the device was wasted on S.C. State students. "First, I doubt that there are many vocational opportunities for Negro x-ray technicians; second, I think that $500 would be spent more effectively for other forms of vocational stimulation and guidance; third, I doubt that undergraduates could learn to operate this x-ray outfit unless they were given a special course in its use."[56]

Whittaker refused to back down as he justified the purchase of the machine. "There is not a colored school in South Carolina with an x-ray outfit and we think we should give our students in physics some idea of this valuable apparatus." GEB officials relented by agreeing to pay for the machine because, as Fred McCuistion put it condescendingly to Whittaker, "We don't want to embarrass you."[57]

Before the fire in 1940 delayed the completion of the mechanical industries building, Whittaker asked the GEB for $10,000 of the estimated $20,000 that would be needed to equip the facility with tools and machinery to teach woodworking, plumbing, heating, auto mechanics, painting, printing, tailoring, and shoemaking. GEB staff members were more than mildly displeased that the college president had not asked the State of South Carolina to make those funds available. "Why didn't he ask [the] State for all [of the $20,000]?" Nevertheless the GEB agreed to provide the $10,000, and Whittaker once again expressed gratitude to the board for its confidence in "the work which we are doing and planning to do in the field of mechanical industries."[58]

The General Education Board kept a watchful eye on S.C. State as the library, dormitory, and mechanical industries building transformed the campus. Days after the dedication of the library and the dormitory, the GEB sent President L. H. Foster of Virginia State College to Orangeburg to assess S.C. State. Foster was not exactly overwhelmed by what he observed. He wrote that "the new buildings, while good, are not as good as they might be." He was dismayed that the facility built as a library also housed the president's office, the office of a dean, the registrar, the business manager, a post office, and the bookstore. Foster repeated what Whittaker had already noted—the book collection was weak. Despite the unenthusiastic evaluation, the GEB was prepared to consider additional funding for the college.[59]

THE MARINE BIOLOGY LABORATORY

In 1938 biology professor James H. Birnie formulated perhaps the most imaginative and exciting proposal that the GEB ever received from South Carolina State. Birnie asked GEB officials if they would be willing to provide $15,000 to develop a marine biology laboratory on the Carolina coast near Georgetown, South Carolina. The college would own and administer the facility, but it would be open to students, faculty, and scientists from the South's historically black colleges and universities.

Birnie, who was just twenty-seven years old, had graduated from Morehouse College and earned a master's degree from Brown University. He was within an academic session of completing a Ph.D. from Cornell. He was the half brother of Marion Birnie Wilkinson, although she was thirty-one years older. He had taught for two years at

Biology professor James H. Birnie in Hodge Hall Laboratory. He, to the left, and chemistry professor T. J. Crawford, near the center, preside over an intent group of science students in the mid-1930s. Courtesy of the Historical Collection, South Carolina State University

Morehouse and for three years at S.C. State. He spent a summer at the marine biology facility at Woods Hole in Massachusetts and four summers at the laboratories at Cold Spring Harbor in New York State.[60]

GEB officials were intrigued by Birnie's proposal, and they invited him to their headquarters in New York City in August 1938 to spell out in greater detail his goals and plans for the marine biology laboratory. He arrived with a ten-page document, a map, and additional plans. He enthusiastically revealed his vision for the facility. The real estate where the laboratory was to be located would be provided to the college at no cost. James Birnie's brother was C. W. Birnie, a medical doctor who practiced in Sumter, and he was the owner of the property. Dr. Birnie was willing to donate as many as nine acres to S.C. State for the laboratory. The tract of land was located on the Atlantic Ocean, thirteen miles north of Georgetown near Highway 17. James Birnie described it in idyllic terms. "The shore is varied by necks, points, flats, gutters, bays and islands; there are numerous fresh water ponds, lakes and rivers in the vicinity; there is no sewage to pollute the sea water; the fauna and flora are exceptionally favorable; the climate is excellent for summer work; the place is free from the inconveniences and distractions of a summer resort."[61]

Birnie went on to explain that the facility would include a twenty-by-eighty-foot laboratory with the necessary scientific equipment. There would be two six-room cottages with kitchen facilities to serve as residences. There would be a pumping station and a storage house. Among the courses that would be offered were Marine and Fresh Water Biology, Marine and Fresh Water Botany, Protozoology, and Experimental Embryology. He also provided a tentative list of faculty members who would teach the courses including biologists from West Virginia State, Spelman, Tuskegee, Prairie View A&M, and New York University. Birnie intentionally excluded famed scientist and S.C. State graduate Ernest E. Just because, he said, "I doubt seriously that his services could be obtained."[62]

The GEB's Jackson Davis supported Birnie and was drawn to the possibilities for the laboratory. "Mr. Birnie makes an excellent impression." However, he thought that Birnie had underestimated the cost of such a facility at $15,000. Yet Davis seemed committed to it. "This proposal deserves careful consideration. There is undoubtedly need for something of this sort for Negro biologists."[63]

It was not to be. Other members of the GEB staff were not as enthralled as Davis was with Birnie and his proposed laboratory. They raised concerns but failed to enumerate specific and serious objections. There were questions about the Georgetown location. Birnie had not included any faculty members from Howard, Fisk, or Atlanta University. They suggested it might be more economical simply to have black biologists spend time at Woods Hole or Cold Stream Harbor rather than erecting a separate laboratory—although Birnie had already hinted that black scientists did not exactly receive a warm and cordial welcome when they arrived at those laboratories, which were also located far from the southern institutions.[64]

Without stating it explicitly, the GEB seemed to doubt both the capacity of S.C. State to operate such a facility and the ability of black scientists and students to make effective use of it. The GEB was far more accustomed to supporting traditional programs in the trades and teacher training for the black colleges. The failure to fund Birnie's marine biology laboratory was a sorely missed opportunity in the history of South Carolina State as well as the General Education Board.

PENN SCHOOL

The GEB was more comfortable supporting programs to prepare black public school teachers, especially those who would teach in the most isolated and impoverished areas of the rural South. In 1936 the board endorsed a cooperative teacher training program between S.C. State and the Penn School on St. Helena Island near Beaufort. Penn School had been established during the Civil War by Quaker missionaries from the North to help freed men and women learn to read and write as they made the transition from slavery to freedom. Penn had remained an important educational institution and community center for more than seven decades after emancipation.[65]

Penn School leaders and S.C. State administrators fashioned a program to have S.C. State students travel to Penn to learn to teach children who lived in the Carolina lowcountry and on the Sea Islands. The GEB furnished a grant of $15,200 for three years to assist the venture. The funds would be used primarily to employ a faculty member to supervise the program as well as to purchase a station wagon for transportation, and to construct housing at Penn for the college students.[66]

THE NATIONAL YOUTH ADMINISTRATION

The National Youth Administration was another New Deal program established in 1935 as an agency within the WPA. The NYA created part-time jobs for high school and college students. Students received thirty cents an hour and typically worked ten to twenty hours a month. The NYA jobs went to students who would not otherwise have the resources to attend college. As had been the case a year earlier with the Federal Emergency Relief Administration's jobs program, students and their parents besieged Whittaker with pleas for employment.[67]

Attalee Pickens wrote a postcard from Bennettsville to Whittaker to explain that he had two children in college and that they needed financial help. "When Judge Kinney written you concerning Oliver Pickens getting aid, you said you would place his application on file. And after you received his transcript you written him and said it had been approved that is why I sent him. For I am not able to pay his and his sister Alice C. Pickens board as we are farmers and not making much that is why I sent $41.00 for Alice C. and $35.00 for Oliver. I am asking you please if any chance to please help me with one I am thanking you in advance."[68]

Juanita Williams, a student, wrote the president to ask for work. "I am a very poor girl my parents are not able to put me through College, and I am very interesting in College, but if I am not able to work my way through I will have to discontinue my school work, and if I am successful to get a job, I will assure you that you won't regret one time I really don't mind work."[69]

Occasionally parents and students attempted to use their connection to influential white South Carolinians to pressure or intimidate Whittaker. Francis Pendarvis, a student, informed the college president that he had talked to the secretary of the board of trustees, Wallace C. Bethea, and that Bethea wanted him to be employed. "Having talked to Mr. Bethea, a trustee of State College and explaining to him my condition and the general income of my home, he then told me to come to you and explain to you and tell you he said to give me something to do." Pendarvis went on to remind Whittaker that "I have been to you over and over again and I hope this time you will fulfill your promise as you have promised me for a long time." In red pencil Whittaker wrote across the top of the letter, "file for consideration."[70]

MARY MCLEOD BETHUNE

Mary McLeod Bethune, who was a native of Mayesville, South Carolina, and the president of Bethune Cookman College, had been appointed the director of the Division of Negro Affairs in the NYA. She wrote Whittaker to solicit his help in securing work for a family member. "My grandnephew, James Murray, is applying to State College for NYA assistance for the next school year. Mrs. [Marion Birnie] Wilkinson has talked with you about him. I hope it will be possible for you to give him the maximum of $20.00 a month because he has nobody to help him." Whittaker's gracious reply assured Mrs. Bethune that he would assist the young man. "We shall be glad to do anything possible for your grand nephew, James Murray, when he comes to State College next year." Wilkinson assured Bethune that Murray would get a NYA job as well as work with Mrs. Wilkinson in the dining hall.[71]

The NYA assisted dozens and dozens of S.C. State students in the late 1930s and the early 1940s. By 1940–41 eighty-nine students were employed through the NYA, and the college received $11,052 from the federal government for the academic year. Whittaker described it as a "most satisfactory" program in which students had been "selected on the basis of need." To keep their NYA jobs as library assistants, laboratory assistants, tutors, messengers, and recreation workers, they "have been required to maintain good scholarship." Whittaker pointed out that overall the NYA students had slightly higher academic averages than did non-NYA students.[72]

More than twenty thousand high school and college students in South Carolina received aid amounting to well over $1 million. To what extent these funds were distributed equitably between black and white students is unknown. But Mary McLeod Bethune did provide supplemental aid to S.C. State beyond the funds that were allotted through the NYA. In 1939 the college employed an additional four students who would otherwise have not received NYA help.[73]

STUDENTS

Although the elimination of the high school in 1933 reduced the number of students who were fourteen, fifteen, and sixteen years of age, student deportment and behavior remained no small matters of concern to administrators and faculty. Rules—especially those affecting women—were relaxed again ever so slightly, as they had been under President Wilkinson. In 1935 a new twelve-page booklet of student regulations was issued. Some previous rules remained in effect. For example women could attend church only if accompanied by a chaperone. However, young ladies could now walk to and from class in the company of young men as long as they remained on the sidewalks and did not stop to loiter. Women could also attend campus plays, concerts, and social affairs with members of the opposite sex. But they were forbidden to participate in religious services with young men.

Students were still not permitted to make any public pronouncements, either oral or written, nor were they allowed to draw up petitions without the permission of the president. Students continued to be responsible for performing "duty work" on the campus each week. They were not to leave Orangeburg without presidential permission. Students found lounging about restaurants, stores, and "questionable places" were subject to punishment. Although prohibition had ended in 1933 with the repeal of the Eighteenth Amendment, no alcoholic beverages were permitted in dormitories, nor were students allowed to play games of chance.[74]

Students were required to attend chapel every Monday, Wednesday, and Friday morning. Chapel on Mondays was devoted to religion. On Wednesday music was usually featured. Friday's chapel was for student organizations, pep rallies, and somewhat less serious matters. But even with the modest revision in regulations, many students were unhappy with the proliferation of rules and their enforcement. Student leader (and later professor) Nevin Austin wrote President Whittaker in November 1935 to voice concern that students were not permitted to sit on campus benches or to gather informally from 8:30 A.M. to 12:30 P.M. and from 2:00 P.M. to 4:00 P.M. on class days. Whittaker agreed to some concessions. Seniors could sit and visit each other on the benches except during evening study hours. Seniors were also exempted from dining hall duty. Senior women could henceforth attend away athletic events with parental permission.[75]

The Faculty Council continued to hold hearings for students charged with violations of campus regulations. If they were found guilty, punishments or demerits or both were administered. When several students were found in Floyd Dining Hall after hours on a Sunday night in 1933, they were each given forty demerits and required to "husk and shell 5 bushels of corn." In 1934 Herman Frazier was expelled for a host of offenses. He had neglected his school work, he had been drinking, and he had visited "houses of ill repute in the city." Three young men—Alphonso Dix, Robert Walker, and George Wilson—were suspended in May 1936 for the remainder of the school year for entering a woman's dormitory at Claflin "with an implied illicit intention."[76]

Although Faculty Council afforded students the right to a hearing and to deliberations, this judicial arrangement was hardly a sterling example of due process. Moreover faculty and administrators took advantage of the summer recess to inform students—without any judicial proceeding whatsoever—they would not be permitted to enroll for the next school term. In some cases students were placed on probation or expelled for academic deficiencies. In other instances they were deemed guilty of offenses that were loosely defined. In 1932 Nelson C. Nix, the chair of the Faculty Discipline Committee, compiled a list of students who either could not return the next semester or were given formal warnings that their conduct was unacceptable. Among them Edgar Martin and Thelma Dawkins were not to return to S.C. State because their "influence [was] bad." Ruth Mills and Edward Grimes were merely warned because they were "inclined to be insubordinate." Charles Coleman was also warned. He was "thought to drink and sell whiskey." Other students were charged and punished for having been "disrespectful," for "using vulgar language," and for a "spirit of insubordination."[77]

Very few students had access to automobiles, but the small number who did were not permitted to bring them to school. There was an exception made, however, for young men who needed transportation for jobs they held. In 1934 B. F. Collier was one of those young men. He had an arrangement with Marion Birnie Wilkinson to keep his car in her garage off campus. One evening he visited a local prostitute and wound up in an altercation with her. The "lady of the evening" proceeded to set fire to Collier's car that at the time was parked in Mrs. Wilkinson's garage. The car and the garage went up in flames, and Collier's career as an S.C. State student ended that night. Although he appealed his expulsion, his presence on the campus was "deemed detrimental" to the institution.[78]

In 1935 six young men brought automobiles to the college. Four were ordered to take them home, and two were permitted to keep them for transportation to jobs.

Morgan R. Gibson lost that privilege in November following a collision with a post in Orangeburg. City police brought him to the campus infirmary with a head laceration, and they charged him with driving drunk. The court suspended his driver's license for sixty days, and the Faculty Council revoked his right to keep the car on campus for the remainder of the year. But he was neither suspended nor expelled from the institution.[79]

Aside from infractions involving their academic and personal conduct, students in the 1930s were quiescent and little inclined to take part in political and racial controversy. The campus newspaper, the *Collegian,* ran a story in October 1936 on the upcoming presidential election between Republican challenger Alf Landon and Democratic incumbent Franklin D. Roosevelt. The Cabot Lodge Debating Union held a lively discussion and straw poll among its members. Cecil Whittaker (President Whittaker's niece) presented the programs of the two candidates. The students then voted to support "the man" rather than the party. Fourteen of them backed Roosevelt while three sided with Landon. The 1936 presidential election marked the beginning of the shift of black voters from their historical allegiance to the Republican Party to support for the Democratic Party. The small poll of S.C. State students seemed to reflect that change.[80]

The *Collegian* mostly confined itself to stories concerning fraternity and sorority social affairs, YMCA and YWCA activities, accounts of football and basketball games, and advertisements for local black and white businesses. Editorials steered clear of controversy. In 1933 the editor, E. Franklin Page, took about as bold a position as any student journalist would at that time when he wondered if a college degree was worth pursuing in light of the nation's economic woes. He answered affirmatively, optimistically, and a bit incoherently. "These conditions are not final but are signs of the great transition and are tokens of the dawn of a new order based upon a social minded philosophy."[81]

In 1935 editor Lawrence Bowen appealed to students to shed their apathetic ways in an editorial that was typical of the era. The language was grandiose and the meaning minimal. "It behooves us therefore fellow students to awaken ourselves from this lassitudinous state of coma in which we now repose and rededicate and reconsecrate ourselves to the ideal of making this a bigger and better institution for higher education of the Negro youth of the State of South Carolina."[82]

SUPPORT FOR THE RACE

Occasionally sparks of insight and discontent flew from the pages of the *Collegian.* There was a long summary of an address delivered in 1935 by Dean Kirkland W. Green during Negro History Week. He was the dean of liberal arts, and he deplored the status of black people in America. He asked if the United States was really a Christian nation. "What kind of gospel can a minister preach to a congregation of lynchers?" If black people were treated fairly, there would be no alleged Negro problem. "If the game of life was played square the so-called race problem would solve itself." Green proceeded to list six specific issues that demanded resolution if there was to be racial progress.

The Negro wants to vote.
The Negro wants justice in the courts.
The Negro wants to serve on juries.
The Negro wants better educational opportunities.
The Negro wants lynching abolished.
The Negro wants Christianity respected at home before it's propagated abroad.

Green did not explicitly call for an end to Jim Crow. Perhaps he believed that segregation would disappear if black people gained meaningful political influence. He went on to describe eloquently the pain endured by people of African descent in America and their unyielding hope for a better day. "The Negro has traveled through four hundred years of American history amidst thorns of torture, ridicule, scorn, degradation and shame. These thorns have torn his flesh and wounded his soul. Bathed in blood and tears he prayed and sang for the coming of a new day when he would come into his own, into possession of his birthright, freedom, recognition and a man's chance—the right to live his own life to his best self and to fulfill his God given mission. Millions waited for that day and died."[83]

Two years later the same Kirkland W. Green who had spoken so powerfully on the inequities experienced by Africans in America unleashed a torrent of criticism at labor unions. Congress had enacted the National Labor Relations Act in 1935, affording unions the right to organize and to bargain collectively. Green was not pleased and said so in words that any southern textile operator could embrace. "Unions are," Green insisted, "a social menace," and "they promote violence and racketeering." Moreover "the philosophy of organized labor is fallacious and serious." Green's antiunion invective may have been related to the refusal of most labor unions to accept black members.[84]

There is little doubt that Miller F. Whittaker—like his predecessors—took pride in his role as a race leader. As the president of the sole public college devoted to the education of black people, he extolled the legacy of South Carolina State. Whittaker had spent a significant portion of his life on the campus. He had the last name of the first president bestowed on him as his first name.

One year into his presidency Whittaker invited Thomas E. Miller to return to the college that he had helped to establish nearly four decades earlier. It must have been an emotional visit for the eighty-three-year-old man. Apparently it was the first time Miller had returned to the college since his removal by Governor Coleman Blease in 1911. Miller had not enjoyed a cordial relationship with his successor, Robert S. Wilkinson, and Wilkinson had never extended a welcome to the first president. On May 15, 1933, Whittaker introduced Miller to students and faculty. There were several faculty members present to greet him who had been students while Miller was president. Among them was James Pierce. At least two of the early members of the faculty—Nelson C. Nix and William C. Lewis—were still teaching. The program ended with the gathering singing "Lift Every Voice and Sing."[85]

The previous year Whittaker had hired Miller's daughter, Mary J. Miller Earle, to serve as the dean of women. She replaced Willie Mae King. Mary Miller had already worked for the college during the first decade of the twentieth century when she served as a bookkeeper during her father's presidency.[86]

S.C. State continued its zealous observance of Negro History Week under Whittaker. In fact, by the mid 1930s, it took most of February to celebrate the week. Such an extended practice was justified by the need to provide a balanced perspective of the past. "The objective is to secure for the study of Negro culture the same consideration which is given to other elements of the population in educating all the youth of America." In other words there must be more emphasis on black history as a corrective to the stress laid on the heritage of white people.[87]

Among the highlights of that 1934 program were musical selections by Negro composers and the reading of a story by Paul Laurence Dunbar. One unidentified student claimed a first place award of $3 for correctly answering the most questions on a one-hundred-question Negro history quiz. The prize for second was $2. In addition students debated on whether or not the recently created New Deal agency the National Recovery Administration (NRA) was beneficial or detrimental to the Negro.[88]

Four chapel programs were devoted to Negro history in 1936. Negro poets including Paul Laurence Dunbar were featured in the first program. The second compared Booker T. Washington to W. E. B. Du Bois. Annette Lewis discussed Washington: "The Philosophy of a Realist"; and Mary Thomas examined Du Bois: "The Philosophy of an Idealist." The third program was devoted to the Negro press. The final chapel program of Negro History Week was a presentation of Negro music that featured Maceo Miller singing Negro spirituals. In February 1937 students and faculty recognized "Outstanding Negroes of South Carolina," including Ernest E. Just, Mary McLeod Bethune, Benjamin Brawley, William Pickens, Kelly Miller, Nelson Nix, Marion Birnie Wilkinson, and Edwin Harleston, "for they proved to us and the world that the Negro was capable physically, spiritually, morally, and socially to bear the burdens placed upon them by their white brothers."[89]

In 1938 President Whittaker announced that the college would celebrate its first Founder's Day with an elaborate program on March 3. Robert L. Douglass was the featured speaker. He was among the first faculty members employed in 1896 when he moved from Claflin to the new agricultural and mechanical college. He taught math at S.C. State until 1903 and then went to Johnson C. Smith College in Charlotte. Altogether he had dedicated nearly a half century to teaching. He gave a lecture entitled "Education: The Hope of Democracy."

That first Founder's Day witnessed the unveiling of a likeness of Thomas E. Miller that had been created by his grandson, Willis Earle II. (Miller did not attend the ceremony, and he would die a month later in Charleston.) Whittaker also decided to use the occasion of that initial Founders' Day to recognize faculty and staff members who had devoted twenty-five or more years of service to S.C. State. William C. Lewis had taught shoemaking and harness making since 1905, and he spent considerable time coaching football and guiding the early athletic program. Nelson C. Nix had taught math since 1896, and he had served as the dean of liberal arts. He also wrote an unpublished history of the college that he completed in 1937. Phillip Nott Harris had served as an instructor in electricity since 1912. Marion Birnie Wilkinson had directed the dining facilities since 1911. Charles Watermann arrived on the campus in 1908 and taught tailoring. James A. Pierce was a graduate of S.C. State who had been among the first students to attend the college in 1896. He returned in 1909 to teach woodworking and carpentry. Unfortunately Pierce died two months prior to Founder's Day. Accepting recognition on his behalf was his daughter Geraldyne Pierce Zimmerman. The Pierce family remained closely connected to the college from 1896 until the death of Geraldyne in 2011.[90]

In 1938 Whittaker invited Benjamin E. Mays, the dean of religion at Howard University, to deliver a sermon at an Easter service in the White Hall Auditorium sponsored by the YMCA and the YWCA. Mays, who would become the president of Morehouse College in 1940, thus began a long and cherished tradition of returning to the campus almost every year for three decades with his wife, Sadie, to deliver an Easter sermon.[91]

College administrators and faculty members remained devoted to the agricultural and mechanical mission of the institution. Whittaker seemed to echo that commitment in remarks delivered to the faculty to open the 1936–37 school year. He stated that many parents mistakenly believed that their sons were destined to be lawyers or physicians and that their daughters would be schoolteachers. Many students, however, lacked the academic skills and experiences necessary for those professions. Still in those same remarks Whittaker insisted that the college had an obligation to foster intellectual development "to solve the supreme problems of education as they confront the welfare of the race." If African Americans lacked access to education, the race problem in America would continue to fester. Students must be taught, Whittaker stressed, to "realize and appreciate the unselfish attempt of mankind to improve civilization through experience, science, and art." Faculty, in turn, "must stimulate, and in many cases drive the intellectual activities of the student far beyond the ordinary 'passing' aspect."

THE INSTITUTION'S IMPACT

But with the Depression still lingering, the college continued to confront a burden that was far beyond its means to solve. S.C. State was able to address the educational needs of only a miniscule portion of the state's black population. There were over eight hundred thousand black residents of South Carolina. The state had twenty-seven accredited black high schools that enrolled four thousand students. There were an additional seven thousand youngsters who attended unaccredited high schools. S.C. State had received 229 applications for its freshmen class entering September 1936. It was uncertain how many of the 229 might actually register for classes. Regardless of the number, it would represent a mere fraction of those who needed an opportunity for further schooling. But in his annual report later that year, Whittaker saw a silver lining in these dismal figures because the college would have an impact far beyond the campus. By providing education for "those few fortunate individuals who come within [the college] walls, it will benefit those thousands through the service which they can render the society in which they live."[92]

As the New Deal evolved during the decade, there were increases in appropriations for the nation's A&M colleges and universities. For S.C. State these funds were of enormous benefit in offsetting the reductions in state funds. Furthermore additional money for extension work gradually permitted the college to expand its public service commitment to rural black residents in the 1930s. Although this support from Washington was of critical importance at a time of severe economic stress, S.C. State received no more than morsels and crumbs from federal programs, which dispensed far larger amounts of money to the white land-grant schools. The Bankhead-Jones Act of 1935 provided an annual series of increases in funding for extension programs, for agricultural research, and for instruction in agriculture. The State of South Carolina would at the end of five years in 1941 annually receive $230,000 for extension activities, $15,000 for research programs, and $20,000 for instructional purposes—a total of $265,000. Of these funds the extension and research money went to Clemson. Extension officials at Clemson would then set aside a portion of those funds for farm and home demonstration work at Winthrop and S.C. State. Clemson retained all the research funds. S.C. State received no funding for agricultural research. Of the $20,000 allocated for instruction, Clemson and S.C. State split it equally, and each institution received $10,000.[93]

Miller F. Whittaker and the faculty were grateful for the Bankhead-Jones money S.C. State would receive directly beginning in 1936 with $5,000 and increasing by increments of $1,000 over a five-year period to $10,000. Still it was only a tiny portion of the money that had been allotted through the Bankhead-Jones legislation. The college's extension program also enjoyed increased funding through the same legislation, but those funds were distributed to the institution at the discretion of Clemson president Enoch W. Sikes and Clemson director of extension D. W. Watkins.[94]

THE DEPRESSION AND THE EXTENSION PROGRAM

Following the precedent established by President Wilkinson, Miller F. Whittaker managed the extension program with the funds controlled by Clemson. Funds for home demonstration work first went to Winthrop and the state director for home demonstration work, Lonny Landrum. Despite this awkward arrangement and the limited funds made available, extension work among black Carolinians expanded significantly by the end of the 1930s. Over the decade, and after some reductions in personnel early in the 1930s, the number of black farm and home demonstration agents increased. In 1929 there were twenty agents—twelve men and eight women—working in counties with large numbers of rural black residents. By 1939 there were nineteen men and fifteen women, a total of thirty-four black agents at work in twenty-five counties. In eight of those counties, there was a farm demonstration agent and a home demonstration agent. By comparison Clemson had farm and home demonstration agents in every one of the state's forty-six counties—ninety-two agents.[95]

To be sure, there were more white residents of the state. By 1940 white people represented 57 percent of the population. Although African Americans continued to migrate from the state in the 1930s, it was at a much slower rate than in the 1920s. Despite that out migration, there was a net gain of nearly twenty-one thousand black people in South Carolina from 1930 to 1940. Thus the black population of 815,015 in 1940—even accounting for urban residents—was underserved by the thirty-four black extension agents.[96]

Far more personnel and resources were devoted to extension work among rural white Carolinians. The Clemson extension program had specialists devoted to dairying, entomology, horticulture, livestock, and poultry among others, while Winthrop had home demonstration specialists in clothing, poultry, nutrition, child development, and home management. S.C. State had no specialists, and there were twenty-one rural counties with no black farm or home demonstration agent including Abbeville, Edgefield, Laurens, Horry, Hampton, and Jasper. Marian Paul, who directed the program, also assisted with home demonstration work in Florence and Lexington counties where no black agents were assigned.[97]

The black extension agents did have an opportunity to draw on the expertise of Clemson and Winthrop specialists in livestock, poultry, or nutrition at the cooperative extension conferences that were held annually at S.C. State. The black farm and home demonstration agents attended sessions on a variety of topics that featured specialists from Clemson and Winthrop as well as from black land-grant colleges and the U.S. Department of Agriculture.

Aside from these yearly events, there was little day-to-day cooperation between South Carolina's black and white extension agents. Occasionally specialists would meet with black agents and farmers. In 1932 a Clemson agronomist spoke to black farmers in Spartanburg. But the black agents were largely on their own as they dispensed advice and offered instruction. In 1935 the farm and home demonstration agents met among themselves on February 4 on campus in a one-day series of sessions. There was, moreover, little in the way of infrastructure or a reasonably well equipped bureaucracy as they went about their tasks.[98]

Two administrators directed the extension program from Hodge Hall on the S.C. State campus. Harry E. Daniels ran the farm demonstration program, and Marian Baxter Paul was in charge of home demonstration work. It was not until the late 1930s that either of them had clerks to assist them with paperwork and day-to-day activities. The county agents had no help at all. They not only lacked secretarial assistance; they did not have offices, desks, chairs, or file cabinets except for those that they provided for themselves in their own homes. No agent had access to a typewriter.

Marian Paul explained the burden assumed by home demonstration agents. "For years and years the agents used their bed rooms or a part of their houses as offices. Often her lap was her desk, card board boxes her filing cabinets, an orange crate her bulletin rack and the trunk of her car her supply cabinet. These conditions not only handicapped the agents from properly preparing her work, but was most inconvenient and embarrassing to callers." Black extension agents were denied office space in public buildings such as courthouses, post offices, and agricultural centers that made room for Clemson agents. The Beaufort home demonstration agent, Willie Mabel Price, did have an office at the Penn Center while the Greenville agent, Delphenia Wilkerson, was able to work out of the Phillis Wheatley Center until the Greenville program was terminated following the loss of county funding.[99]

The black agents were not paid merely less, but much less than the white agents. Typically they received only 30 to 40 percent of the salaries earned by their white counterparts. Marian B. Paul, who was in charge of the black home demonstration program, was paid 58 percent of what the white county agent for Charleston took home. Like black public school teachers, extension agents were not beneficiaries of salary equalization. Most of the extension agents were S.C. State graduates. In 1932 twenty-one of twenty three agents were S.C. State alumni.[100]

As the Great Depression worsened, extension agents worked among rural residents to bring a ray or two of hope and a measure of economic relief to people whose meager lives had known little but poverty. In some instances the black agents could not make contact with destitute Carolinians. There were more than a few landowners who would not permit extension workers to offer information to sharecroppers, tenant farmers, and renters. They worried that extension agents and their programs might incite dissatisfaction or create expectations among people who constituted a dependent work force. It was usually the landowner who determined which crops would be planted, how they would be tended, and what kind of living quarters would be made available to the farm family.

There were, Miller F. Whittaker pointed out in 1937, 18,294 black-owned farms in South Carolina. But there were also 75,537 black farmers who worked someone else's land. In most cases the thirty-four extension agents had to confine their activities to those farm people who owned their land. Yet even among these black landowners, there were very few who possessed extensive acreage or had mastered the necessary skills and knowledge to prosper.[101]

MARIAN BAXTER PAUL

No one in twentieth-century South Carolina offered more compelling descriptions and insights into the plight of rural African Americans than Marian Baxter Paul. For more than two decades, Paul carefully and astutely assessed the lives of impoverished black Carolinians in her lengthy annual reports. These were not dry bureaucratic accounts, crammed with tedious tables and endless statistics. In graceful and clear prose that deserved a much larger readership, Paul provided marvelous, poignant, and disturbing descriptions of people who had been almost completely ignored as they endured generations of poverty.

These were Americans who had little or no access to education. They had never been introduced to such "conveniences" as electricity, plumbing, or even outdoor toilets. They survived on inadequate diets and lived in the most rudimentary housing. Their lives did not change and—most of them believed—would not change in the foreseeable future. They lived essentially as their parents and grandparents had. They had no prospects and no hopes for progress. In fact they often resisted offers of help or assistance.

Marian Baxter was born in 1900 in Georgetown County. She attended Howard School in the community before enrolling at Howard University and then Cheyney College in Pennsylvania. She also attended the University of Minnesota before embarking on a career teaching clothing and sewing, first in Birmingham, Alabama, and later at Booker T. Washington High School in Columbia, South Carolina. She worked for a time as a home demonstration agent in Georgetown County. Her husband, Robert, was a tailor and also operated a shop for cleaning and pressing in Columbia in partnership with Henry T. Owens. President Robert S. Wilkinson hired Paul in December 1930 to head the home demonstration program following Nettie Kerner's resignation.[102]

Paul had an abiding affection for the people she served, and she was convinced that extension agents could transform the lives of black South Carolinians. She traveled the state tirelessly at a time when it was difficult to negotiate the primitive network of roads and highways. She met with county agents, visited rural residents, and counseled with them. For example, in February 1933, Paul spent nine days in her Orangeburg office and fifteen days on the road. She visited nine agents, gave nine talks, went to twenty-nine homes, and wrote ninety-six letters. That month the home demonstration agents emphasized the importance of poultry. "It is our aim," Paul wrote, "to encourage the raising of more poultry, better breeds, and the building of poultry houses."[103]

Three months later, in May, the home demonstration agents were pursuing a "sanitary toilet" campaign. In many locations people did not have outdoor facilities—"we found none at all just [a] poor, rough unsanitary shanty." Their goal in Greenville County was to install one outdoor sanitary toilet in each community that would serve as a model. Diagrams and directions would then be distributed so that other hygienic toilets could be built.[104]

Borrowing from remarks made by President Wilkinson, Paul asserted that the three Rs were no longer as relevant as the three Bs. "The 3 Rs in education are now changed to the 3 Bs—Bread, Brotherhood and Beauty. That seems to express our ultimate goal and policies; to teach our people how to obtain their food, to love each other, and to appreciate everything beautiful." However, this rosy outlook for the future did not necessarily match reality. When Paul visited her home county of Georgetown in 1933, she found people barely surviving. "At Dunbar, Georgetown County, some children are almost starved and most of them nude." She reported that the county agent and several friends assisted by providing food, clothing, and fertilizer to the destitute.[105]

Young people, Paul believed, were more susceptible to change than their parents, and she worked diligently with extension agents on the 4-H program. She compiled a seventeen-page 4-H handbook in 1931. It was a practical guide for girls enrolled in the program. It offered recipes and tips on sewing, canning, and gardening. It contained examples of projects that they could create and then submit in competition for awards among 4-H members. S.C. State sponsored a three-day summer program on the campus for 156 4-H boys and girls in July 1932. It was the first time that many of them had heard a pipe organ or seen a motion picture film. They sold fruit, vegetables, and eggs and joined in other fund-raising projects to be able to afford the trip to Orangeburg.[106]

Marian Paul reveled in small signs of progress, which she took delight in, including in her reports. She wryly wrote in 1932 that "the agent in Georgetown County gave

Grace Smith a pig, Grace named the pig Rosa after the agent [Rosa Gadsden] and Rosa had a litter of 9 pigs—5 of these she gave to other club girls. Next year we expect to have great results from this project." Many farm women did not like milk and refused to keep a cow. But agents showed them how to prepare creamed dishes and make puddings and ice cream. "Now we have 282 women using milk and its products according to the standards."[107]

At Lands End on St. Helena Island in Beaufort County, home demonstration agent Willie Mabel Price and her Better Homes Committee worked with Mrs. Willie Simmons to renovate the ramshackle home inhabited by Mrs. Simmons. "This house had been built years ago of poor construction, and poorer design. The rooms were small crowded and untidy. The hall way was so narrow that a real fat person could not have walked through it, the ceilings were so low that on entering the house you invariably bowed your head. The kitchen was placed on the front and the so-called living room in the rear. . . . There was a porch without a roof on the side, the house had never been painted."

Paul was ecstatic at the transformation worked by Price and her committee. "When I next visited Lands End I did not want to believe my eyes; for there like a miracle stood one of the most attractive homes I had ever seen. The kitchen was placed on the rear, with the pump and a screened in porch. The hall was widened, and the roof raised, the chimney which stood open between two rooms was encased, the walls were painted, a porch with steps on the front and side added and the house painted yellow trimmed in white." After listing the extensive changes, Paul concluded, "I think I was as jubilant over the improvements, comforts, and beauties of that home as Mrs. Simmons was proud of her 'new home.'"[108]

Funds were limited. To remodel Mable Perry's home in Florence, orange crates furnished a table and bed stand. A barrel became a chair. The footstool was made of cans. The curtains and bedspread were tie-dyed. Vases were old bottles. Paul reported, "The room was most attractive and the actual cost was $1.25." When there were insufficient jars available for canning, resourceful home demonstration agents approached county sheriffs and secured jars that had been confiscated from moonshiners—minus the corn liquor.[109]

EXTENSION AGENTS AS COMMUNITY LEADERS

For many of the people who lived in remote and isolated areas of the state, the men and women who served as extension agents ranked with clergymen and schoolteachers as community leaders. Paul pointed out that "the Home Demonstration Agent is looked upon by the County as a sort of 'Fairy God Mother' or 'Magician.' She is often called upon to do the impossible, such as to prescribe for those who are ill, to patch up family quarrels, to find employment for the idle, to aid in building churches and school houses—and . . . to bury the dead. . . . It shows the Agent has gained the confidence and love of her people and her County." Similarly and seven years later, J. E. Dickson—the farm demonstration agent for Richland County—commented that "extension teaching through Negro leadership has grown to the point where the Negro agricultural agent is looked upon as the guiding influence for Negro farm people throughout the county."[110]

The professional lives of the directors of extension work, Marian Paul and Harry Daniels, paralleled each other. But the monthly and annual reports prepared by Daniels were more succinct, lacked the extensive descriptions, and were absent the passion that Paul took such care to include. For example, in his monthly report of February 1933, Daniels explained what he accomplished in Greenville County. "February 3–4 was spent in Greenville assisting the agent in outlining the program of work. We completed two poultry houses with a brood of 400 chickens. Outlined suitable hay crops and pasture grasses on Mr. Harris' dairy farm." In 1934 farm demonstration agents visited eighteen hundred farms, and black farmers called on agents for information on more than fourteen thousand occasions. Sidney McClary Jr., a 4-H member from Sumter County, raised 133.5 bushels of corn on a one-acre demonstration plot, breaking the record for corn production by a Negro farmer in South Carolina. The enterprising youngster earned a profit of $99.[111]

Considering the miserable state of the economy in 1932, Marian Paul might have been guilty of excessive optimism when she declared that home demonstration agents might eventually lift rural black folk out of grinding poverty to a new status of economic self-sufficiency located in a veritable Garden of Eden. "The ultimate goal of Home Demonstration work in South Carolina is to reach the stage 'where every farmer in South Carolina shall eat bread from his own field, meat from his own pastures, and disturbed by no creditors, shall sit amid his teeming gardens, and orchards, and vineyards, and dairies and barnyards, pitching his crops to his own wisdom and growing them in independence.'"[112]

Although sometimes overexuberant and perennially hopeful, Paul's view of the world around her was firmly attached to reality. She never succumbed to the temptation to blame the people themselves for their ignorance, lack of ambition, and unrefined behavior. She understood that the problems afflicting black South Carolinians emanated from elsewhere. "The Negro is not the problem, but rather the problem is the white man's attitude toward him. The great majority of Negroes live in rural sections of the State and are tenants and sharecroppers. Some, due to ignorance and circumstances are held almost in peonage. The poor, inadequate school facilities, plus the land lords' attitude toward education are partly responsible for the illiteracy among Negroes. The great majority of the people with whom we work are sharecroppers, and are people forgotten by many. Nevertheless, they are individual beings with hopes and longings. It is true that many of these people have accepted the dreary existence that seems to be the lot of the Negro sharecropper, perhaps because that seems to be the simplest and easiest solution to an almost useless struggle."[113]

Paul refused to surrender to apathy as she waged a determined campaign to expand the extension program. In 1932 she was discouraged by the absence of support from South Carolina's political leadership. "Last year I went to 5 Senators and 17 Legislators asking for appropriations to enlarge our work, for it is so greatly needed. They refused because of lack of funds. Oh if they could only go with me thru the rural sections of South Carolina and see the ignorance and suffering, their hearts would be softened. My people are easy followers, all they need is the right leader. And the Home Demonstration agent, who acts as teacher, preacher, doctor, nurse and advisor, has gained the confidence of her people."[114]

As the decade wore on, however, the extension program attracted increased federal support. The extension administrators at Clemson and Winthrop directed some of those funds to the black extension program, and the number of black agents grew from twenty-three to thirty-four. Yet the magnitude of the problems in which race and poverty were so tightly intertwined defied solution. Even had there been a tenfold increase in agents—340 rather than thirty-four—it is not likely that they could have had an appreciable impact on deep-seated economic and racial problems affecting the state. To their lasting credit, however, the men and women in the extension program did through personal intervention and the diffusion of information assist several thousand people to better their lives.

THE A&M MISSION

Is it then any wonder that there were younger people who wanted to escape the bleak and dismal conditions that characterized the lives of so many rural South Carolinians? Whatever education they might manage to acquire could help propel them to more rewarding lives away from the hot sun and parched soil. But South Carolina State and the other historically black land-grant institutions had been established on the premise

Table 18. Survey of the Sixty-Seven Graduates of S.C. State in 1935 and Their Plans for the Immediate Future

Agriculture	5
Mechanical	1
Home economics	5
Academic (teaching)	21
Farm demonstration	1
Business	2
Graduate school	4
Other	12
Unknown	16
Total	67

Source: Miller F. Whittaker, "A Study of Occupational Opportunities of Negroes by the Land Grant Colleges," *Proceedings of the Thirteenth Annual Conference of the Presidents of Negro Land Grant Colleges,* November 18–20, 1935, Washington, D.C., 14–17.

Table 19. Enrollment in Degree Programs

	1929–30	1939–40
B.A. in arts	72	108
B.S. in science	32	70
B.S. in business administration	18	53
B.S. in education	1	164
Total	123	395
B.S. in mechanical industries	29	100
B. S. in agriculture	27	132
B. S. in home economics	16	141
Total	72	373

Sources: College catalogs for 1929–30 and 1939–40. In 1929–30 the bachelor of arts in education was new, replacing the licentiate of instruction. Also there were 430 high school students and almost six hundred unclassified students (many of them in summer school) in 1929–30.

that practical training in agricultural and vocational skills was the most suitable education for those black southerners who hoped to lead productive lives. The S.C. State board of trustees continued to stress the need for the instruction in A&M subjects to maintain the decades-old mission of the college. Since its founding the white men who had served on the college's board of trustees remained committed to the Hampton and Tuskegee models of higher education for black youngsters. In 1937 Wallace C. Bethea, the secretary of the board, repeated the mantra "the most important of these [needs] is the training of teachers; the training of Negro youth in agriculture, home economics and mechanical arts."[115]

However many of the young people who came to the college by the 1930s did not share that vision for their future. They did not want an education that would prepare them to return to the farms and fields from which they fled. In a presentation in 1935 to the Conference of Presidents of Negro Land-Grant Colleges, Miller F. Whittaker noted that many students had no desire to pursue a life in agriculture. He said that in a survey of 178 incoming freshmen 79 percent indicated they intended to become teachers. And, he added, of the sixty-seven graduates in May 1935, fifty-one had determined their immediate plans for the future. For most those plans did not relate to A&M subjects.

Whittaker also drew on a survey undertaken by Mary E. Frayser at Clemson College, "Attitudes of High School Seniors toward Farming." Questionnaires were completed by 924 white students and 566 black students. Just 26 percent of the black students indicated an interest in farm life while 60 percent showed an unfavorable interest in pursuing agriculture. Although large numbers of S.C. State students shied away from the A&M programs, for many others agriculture, mechanical industries, and home economics remained the curriculum of choice.[116]

RESEARCH

No matter what interest students expressed or failed to express in careers in agriculture, mechanics, and home economics, S.C. State would continue as an A&M institution. To that end Whittaker and the faculty hoped to expand that mission beyond providing instruction in agricultural and vocational subjects. They wanted research and experimentation in agriculture to become a component in the college's role as a land-grant institution. However, authorities with the U.S. Department of Agriculture and at Clemson did not share that view.

The black land-grant colleges had never received federal funds designated for agricultural research through the Hatch Act (1887), the Adams Act (1906), and the Purnell Act (1925). In South Carolina those funds went exclusively to Clemson. S.C. State's role as an A&M school was limited to instruction and to extension work. But a modest breakthrough in 1932 opened the possibility of an increased role in agricultural research for the black college.

Alfred W. Shute was a professor of agricultural economics who specialized in dairy science. He had been born and raised in Sheridan, Wyoming, where he attended high school. He earned an undergraduate degree at the University of Minnesota and a master's degree from Iowa State University. He and his wife, Buelah—who he met while they were students at Minnesota—joined the S.C. State faculty in 1929–30. Like many African Americans with an advanced education, their only prospect for meaningful employment was at a southern black college. Shute wanted to undertake a study of organization and management techniques utilized by black farmers. He wanted to determine which crops bought them the largest financial returns and the extent to which they pursued diversification among crops and livestock they raised.[117]

Edwin R. Embree of the Rosenwald Fund agreed to provide $500 toward Shute's study, and he suggested that the S.C. State professor seek additional sources of funding to complete the project. President Whittaker contacted Clemson officials to see if they might be willing to provide funds to match the Rosenwald money. W. W. Long, Clemson's director of extension work, informed Whittaker that extension work funds could not be spent on research. But Long did agree to consult with Clemson president Enoch W. Sikes to see if there were other ways to support Shute's research.[118]

After Sikes contacted H. W. Barre, the director of the South Carolina Experiment Station at Clemson, Barre informed Whittaker and Shute that research funds could be expended only on projects that originated at the experiment station and had been approved by the Office of Experiment Stations with the U.S. Department of Agriculture. A. F. Woods, the director of scientific work, with the Department of Agriculture, maintained it was very unlikely that the federal agency would offer assistance to Shute. Therefore, and in spite of the Rosenwald funding, it appeared that Shute's proposal was at a dead end.[119]

But not quite. Possibly prompted by the intervention of President Sikes, H. W. Barre gave Shute's project "further consideration" and decided that it would be feasible to conclude a "cooperative agreement" that would enable Shute to undertake the farm management study. Clemson would, however, provide no money. Instead the experiment station would contribute time and work in the form of "services and expenses" that would be equal to the $500 furnished by the Rosenwald Fund.[120]

Rosenwald officials were pleased to learn of the cooperation between the black and white land-grant schools. They considered it a promising development in race relations. George R. Arthur, the associate director for Negro welfare with the Rosenwald Fund, told President Whittaker, "This step in our opinion is one of the most significant that has yet been taken in direct cooperation efforts between experiment stations of white Land Grant colleges and departments of agriculture in the Land Grant colleges for Negroes." Arthur added optimistically that "with such contacts I am sure not only scientific information will result but also better understanding of race attitudes." With the support of Clemson and the Rosenwald Fund, Shute proceeded with his investigation. In 1935 Clemson published the results. Despite an intensive search at S.C. State and at Clemson, no copy of Shute's study has been found.[121]

Unfortunately Shute's research project did not mark the beginning of a fruitful and long-standing relationship in agricultural research between Clemson and S.C. State. It was the first and also the last such effort. Shute and his wife left S.C. State for more lucrative positions at Florida A&M. There were no further attempts by either agricultural personnel at S.C. State or Clemson to follow up on Shute's pathbreaking effort.

THE TRUSTEES

To the contemporary observer, the college's board of trustees did not seem to play a very conspicuous role in the management of the institution. Typically the six white men who served on the board met just twice a year—during graduation week in May and again in October. They rarely intruded publicly or openly in college affairs. They appeared to be little more than casual caretakers who routinely approved the president's proposed budget, ratified the appointment of new faculty members, and agreed to the dismissal of others. They consented to contracts for the construction of new facilities on those infrequent occasions when funds were available for capital improvements. And they sometimes lobbied legislators on behalf of the college. Yet it would be highly inaccurate to regard the board as benign and unobtrusive during the college's first seven decades. Board members took an intense—if paternalistic—interest in S.C. State. They were genuinely concerned with the welfare of the institution, and they believed that the college could not flourish without their guidance. Of course the college barely flourished—at least financially—even with their guidance.

The key member of the board was *not* its chairman, even when the governor actively served as chair. On a day-to-day basis, the chairman of the local committee was the most influential member of the board. From its inception in 1896, the board maintained a local committee that kept a sharp eye on the college. The local committee consisted of the three or four board members who resided in Orangeburg or the surrounding area. They had easy access to the college. Not much that happened on the campus escaped their notice. Until 1970 the secretary of the board also served as the chair of the local committee. Moreover the board secretary was compensated the equivalent of a generous part-time salary, ostensibly for maintaining a record of the board meetings. But this salary was, in fact, paid for the time devoted to chairing the local committee, and not for keeping the minutes. Remarkably, between 1896 and 1966, only two men served in the combined position of board secretary and chair of the local committee. Dr. William R. Lowman was an Orangeburg physician who also operated a local pharmacy. He was one of the original board members elected in 1896, and he served until his death at age fifty-eight in 1925.[122]

Wallace C. Bethea was the most important trustee in the history of S.C. State. Although he never served as chairman, he succeeded Lowman as secretary and as chair of the local committee in 1925 and served in both capacities until 1966. Bethea was born in 1894 in Branchville. He graduated from Wofford College and Trinity University (now Duke University). He came to Orangeburg after serving as an artillery officer in World War I. He married the daughter of J. W. Smoak and became the general manager of J. W. Smoak Hardware. He helped organize the First National Bank during the Depression and became its president in 1941. Even in the warmest weather, the dapper Bethea was neatly attired in a three-piece suit with a fedora. For many years he lived on Russell Street one block from the campus. In less than fifteen minutes, he could walk from his home to the president's office.[123]

In some respects Bethea was the surrogate president of the college. He was a looming presence for more than four decades as he advised three presidents and sometimes intruded on their authority. It was, for example, Bethea—and not President Wilkinson—who wrote the General Education Board in 1926 to ask for $25,000 to aid in the construction of Hodge Hall. When the GEB approved that request, GEB officials wrote to Bethea. On occasion Bethea would assist Whittaker in the preparation of the annual college budget. Bethea's membership on the State Emergency Relief Administration board helped the college obtain funds from the Public Works Administration for the erection of Miller Hall.[124]

Board members like Bethea regarded their service as a public commitment. It was their civic responsibility to oversee the "colored college." Despite their lack of public visibility, trustees certainly could not be accused of failing to pay attention to S.C. State. Until 1927 the governor of South Carolina chaired the board of trustees. Beginning with the administration of Governor John G. Richards, governors subsequently served in an ex officio capacity. But ex officio or not, board meetings were often held with the governor in Columbia. Governors sometimes came to Orangeburg for meetings. In 1927 President Wilkinson suggested to Governor Richards that he could catch a 7 A.M. bus in Columbia for the May 20 board meeting in Orangeburg. But Richards decided not to ride the bus and did not attend the meeting.[125]

Through most of the history of the college, South Carolina's governors played a decisive role in determining who would serve as the college president. In 1911 Governor Coleman Blease, as the new chairman of the board of trustees, demanded and received the resignation of President Thomas E. Miller. Blease later approved the selection of Robert S. Wilkinson as Miller's successor. In 1933 the trustees met in Columbia with Governor I. C. Blackwood to name Miller F. Whittaker as the third president of the college. In 1950 the board met in the office of Governor J. Strom Thurmond to choose Benner C. Turner as the fourth president. Then in 1967, responding to pressure from the black

Table 20. Key Members of the Board of Trustees, 1896–1960

Name	Hometown	Profession	Term	Role on Board
William R. Lowman*	Orangeburg	Physician	1896–1925	Secretary, 1896–1925
Archie L. Dukes*	Orangeburg	Grocer	1902–42	Member
Charles F. Brooks*	Gray Court	School supt./ farmer	1918–50	Chair, 1927–50
Adam H. Moss*	Orangeburg	Attorney	1927–59	Chair, 1950–59
Wallace C. Bethea	Orangeburg	Hardware/ bank	1925–70	Secretary, 1925–66
E. D. Hodge*	Alcolu	Farmer	1917–35	Member
W. Mc. Hodge	Sumter	Unknown	1939–56	Member
William P. Mason*	Westminster	Unknown	1932–50	Member

*Died while serving as a trustee

Sources: Board minutes, annual reports, college catalogs.

community, Governor Robert McNair personally informed Turner that he would have to step down as president. Several months later McNair decided that acting president M. Maceo Nance Jr. should be Turner's successor and so informed the trustees.[126]

The responsibility that board members and governors felt toward the institution derived in no small measure from their determination to make certain that this public institution did not disrupt or interfere with the racial status quo. This was not discussed openly, at least not until civil rights became an issue after World War II. But it was clearly understood by trustees, public officials, and college administrators. The obligation and dedication that board members felt toward the college and what they regarded as its proper role in southern society was reflected in their long terms of service. Several trustees remained board members not merely for years, but for decades, as they were re-elected again and again to six-year terms by the legislators. For more than a half century, there was little turnover in board membership. Most often death ended board service.

Except for governors, board members rarely had political aspirations. They did not use board service as a stepping stone to elected office. Only Adam H. Moss and William P. Mason served in the legislature. Moss served two terms in the house in 1901–4, and that was long before he became a trustee. Mason served four nonconsecutive terms (1917–18, 1927–28, 1931–32, 1939–40) as a representative from Oconee County before and after his election to the board.[127]

On occasion board members solicited legislators for appropriations for the college. They were well aware that the school was not adequately funded by the state. On the other hand, it would be fair to assume that trustees such as Wallace C. Bethea, Charles F. Brooks, Adam H. Moss, and Archie L. Dukes took it for granted that S.C. State would not be funded in fair proportion to the monies allocated to Clemson, the University of South Carolina, or the Citadel. There are simply no instances of white authorities in the South in the first half of the twentieth century insisting that state funds be dispersed in an equal manner between black and white educational institutions.

Although Wallace Bethea was the only board member paid for his services, other trustees derived pecuniary advantages as a consequence of their position. Board members as well as other state officials were the recipients of "gifts" from the college that included food from the home economics program, and farm supplies and labor provided by agriculture students, faculty, and extension personnel. South Carolina's governors, other state executives, and trustees were measured for and received custom-tailored suits courtesy of Charles Waterman's classes in tailoring. E. D. Hodge sought and received assistance from the college in the form of repairs and construction for his Alcolu farm. Charles Brooks drove his vehicles from Gray Court for maintenance and repairs in the college automobile shop.

Trustees took advantage of their board membership to arrange transactions for the college that benefited them personally. By the 1930s the college had its seventy-two acre campus farm and rented an additional fifty acres away from the institution. Whittaker sought funds from the general assembly in 1934 for at least an additional one hundred acres, but the legislators declined to provide the money. Aware that the college needed additional acreage for crops and livestock, local residents tried for years to sell mediocre land to the school. In 1930 President Wilkinson complained to board member E. D. Hodge that "a certain party here" was attempting to dispose of land and "to unload it on the College." Wilkinson extended gratitude to Hodge, however, for blocking that transaction while at the same time enabling Wilkinson to save face. "I am glad that you will handle the matter so as to relieve me of embarrassment. I opposed the deal when it was presented before and do not wish to be put into the same position again."[128]

Five years later and six months following the death of Hodge, trustee and Orangeburg resident Archie L. Dukes offered to sell slightly more than seventy acres of farmland he owned to the college for $10,500. This was, of course, in the midst of the Depression, when the institution's financial situation was precarious. Nevertheless the trustees decided to purchase the Dukes property in four installments. The board retained the law firm of board member Adam H. Moss to execute the transaction. President Whittaker, who apparently had no role in the acquisition of the Dukes land, noted that the additional farmland was located beyond the city limits, about two miles from the campus near the state highway garage on U.S. Highways 21 and 178. The college used the land mostly for forage for the thirteen cows in its dairy herd. It was planted in oats, corn, wheat, and hay.[129]

The trustees failed to acknowledge that the sale of such real estate to the college by a board member while another trustee's law firm handled the legal arrangements was a clear conflict of interest and a serious ethical breach. Two years later, however, when the trustees agreed to a motion to pay $200 to attorney P. F. Haigler for legal work that involved a contract with the Public Works Administration for the construction of Miller Hall, Moss declined to vote. This time he was apparently aware of the appearance of impropriety as Haigler was a colleague in Moss's law office.[130]

THE IMPACT OF THE DEPRESSION

Considering the severity of the economic crisis that the nation, state, and college endured in the 1930s, it is remarkable that S.C. State emerged from the decade in its strongest position in more than forty years of its existence. This is not to suggest that it survived the Depression unscathed. It did not. President Robert S. Wilkinson died in 1932. The college and its employees struggled mightily, especially in the early years of the decade, as salaries were slashed and individuals went unpaid for weeks in late 1932 and early 1933. College facilities were neglected and fell into disrepair. The campus high school closed. The Southern Association continued to impose a B rating on the institution mainly because of the weak salary structure.

Yet by 1940 the college was on relatively solid footing. Miller F. Whittaker, the third president, provided steady leadership. With the termination of the high school, S.C. State became a four-year undergraduate institution. State appropriations reached a pre-Depression level by the end of the 1930s. What is most important, the college benefited enormously from federal aid and philanthropic support. New Deal agencies including the Public Works Administration, the National Youth Administration, and the Works Progress Administration furnished funds that assisted in the construction of Miller Hall and the mechanical industries building. The federal money also supported the part-time employment of students through the NYA and offered full-time work to students and local residents on the building projects. The Department of Agriculture allocated funds through Clemson that permitted the extension program to expand, and a dozen additional farm and home demonstration agents were employed by decade's end.

The Rosenwald Fund and then the General Education Board provided money for faculty members to attend graduate school, and the academic preparation of the faculty improved dramatically. The GEB also contributed $40,000 to aid in the construction of Wilkinson Hall, the first library building, and awarded additional funds to equip a physics laboratory, and to help furnish the new mechanical industries building. The board also backed the creation of a cooperative teacher-education project with the Penn School on St. Helena Island. But the staff of the GEB had a fairly narrow conception of the most appropriate use of its funds by black institutions. The Rockefeller-sponsored philanthropy declined to support the development of a marine biology facility near Georgetown. The GEB would not purchase housing for faculty, and it would not grant a scholarship to Mabel James because she was a woman. Despite these limitations the GEB would continue to be a major source of financial assistance through the 1940s. But the college and the nation had not fully recovered from the Depression before another crisis in the form of a world war loomed on the horizon.

CHAPTER FIVE

The Second World War

World War II brought an abrupt end to the Great Depression as the United States and most of the rest of the globe plunged into the most devastating and costly conflict in history. For African Americans—including students and faculty at S.C. State—the Second World War represented an opportunity for people of color to demonstrate yet again their patriotism and loyalty to a nation that continued to confine them to second-class citizenship. But this war against the totalitarian regimes in Germany, Japan, and Italy heightened expectations among African Americans that the Jim Crow society that they inhabited was vulnerable to change—change that they were resolved to make a reality.

The war dramatically altered life on the campus. The number of men declined drastically as they entered the military or the civilian labor force. Although the institution's financial situation improved markedly in the 1940s compared to the 1930s, the war meant shortages of supplies and materials. And the college still lacked sufficient classrooms and housing for students and faculty.

When the war ended in 1945 and as the college approached its fiftieth anniversary in 1946, state authorities were more committed to maintaining the rigid racial caste system than to remedying the glaring deficiencies at S.C. State. Therefore white leaders insisted on the creation of a separate law school and a graduate program on the campus rather than the construction of badly needed dormitories and undergraduate teaching facilities. That was, they reasoned, a far more sensible priority than admitting black men and women to the professional and graduate programs at the University of South Carolina or at Clemson A&M College.

SHOULD S.C. STATE STUDENTS SUPPORT THE WAR?

Even before World War II erupted in Europe in September 1939, several male students at the college expressed concerns about military service. Months earlier, in February, the *Collegian* had posed a question: "Under what circumstances would you be willing to go to war?" Enoch Jenkins replied, "If I felt the Negro would be helped." Arthur Kirkland said, "If the enemies should invade the United States." Howard Bampfield answered similarly, "Only if my country is attacked." Joseph Brown added two caveats. "If I could be well trained and I felt that there would be no Jim-Crowing." Three young men—Joseph Harrison, Samuel Bacote, and Ronald Pride—said that they were unwilling to serve whatever the circumstances. On a personal level, Julian Dugas was willing to go to war "if my aunt's life was in danger." Robert Johnson attached a monetary value to his life, indicating he would serve "under the condition that I were paid $1,500,000 before I should leave."[1]

As the prospects increased for U.S. involvement in the conflict in 1940 and 1941, concern among students intensified. An editorial in the *Collegian* commented that "the mad dogs of war are running wild in a world filled with international hatred and mistrust." The impending crisis created uncertainty and bewilderment in the editorial writer's mind. "We read and wonder what will happen next."[2]

Following the Japanese attack on Pearl Harbor on December 7, 1941, there was a far more unified response among students and enthusiastic support for the U.S. entry into the conflict. But that patriotism was tempered by the conviction that the war overseas must bring significant changes to the racial climate within the United States. "We are at war!" declared the *Collegian*. "The Negro's traditional loyalty to American has never been questioned." And once again America could rely on the support of black Americans. "We should and will support every military and civilian effort for the defense of America because we are Americans."[3]

But the same editorial insisted that the commitment to the war effort would not weaken the struggle for racial progress—even temporarily. "We, as Negroes, should not halt our demands for all-out equal rights, economically, educationally, and politically." During the war African Americans rallied to the call for a "Double V," that is, a victory over foreign oppressors combined with a victory over racial inequality and injustice in the United States. The *Collegian* echoed that call. "The very thing we are fighting for to defeat abroad is to be defeated at home."[4]

There were already small but meaningful cracks beginning to appear in the edifice of white supremacy. In 1940—a presidential election year—Franklin Roosevelt embarked on a campaign for a third term and promoted Benjamin O. Davis Jr. to the rank of brigadier general. He was the nation's first African American general. Roosevelt also asked William Hastie, the dean of the Howard University law school, to serve as a "Civilian Aide on Negro Affairs" with the War Department.

Harold Wilson wrote an editorial lauding the appointments in the *Collegian* after noting that the black vote had helped to reelect Roosevelt. "Many are attaching political significance to these appointments since they came in a politically important time. The question is debatable but it is highly probable." Wilson went on to add that "whatever the case, we are glad to see the appointments of these Negroes because in them we see a brighter future for Negro youth in the armed forces of the land." In another editorial in the same issue of the *Collegian*, John L. Pendarvis failed to share Wilson's optimism. Pendarvis acknowledged the loyalty of African Americans but cited lynching, the loss of Negro farms, and the racial discrimination that Negro migrants faced wherever they moved to work and settle.[5]

In another important milestone, A. Philip Randolph, the head of the Brotherhood of Sleeping Car Porters, had appealed to President Roosevelt in the summer of 1941 to eliminate racial discrimination in the hiring practices of companies that did business with the U.S. government. Randolph informed the president that unless he addressed the issue, Randolph intended to lead a march of thousands of Negroes on Washington. Roosevelt initially balked at Randolph's demand but finally gave in and issued Executive Order 8802 creating the Fair Employment Practices Commission (FEPC).[6]

In the meantime the NAACP and its lawyers, led by Thurgood Marshall, won court cases in Maryland and Virginia in 1939 and 1940 to bring parity to salaries paid to white and black schoolteachers in the segregated public education systems. In South Carolina Marshall subsequently joined Columbia attorney Harold Boulware as they brought suit on behalf of Viola Duvall against the Charleston School Board in 1943. Federal district judge Waties Waring ruled in early 1944 that the enormous gap in salaries paid to white and black teachers in Charleston violated the equal protection clause of the Fourteenth Amendment.[7]

The *Collegian* in 1941 was pleased that the U.S. Supreme Court had rejected appeals from Maryland and Virginia in the salary equalization cases and with the progress that the high court's rebuff represented. "The ruling is in keeping with every democratic principle and entirely in order." But the newspaper went on to lament the mediocrity of some of the black schoolteachers. "It is an unhappy fact that many of our Negro teachers are not adequately prepared to execute the academic and administrative duties of teachers[.] However, unequal educational facilities, salary inequality, and even lack of personal interest share a part of the responsibility for this condition."[8]

The genuine but limited progress that was represented in the promotion of Benjamin O. Davis Jr., the appointment of William Hastie, and the creation of the Fair Employment Practices Commission, as well as the positive judicial results in the salary equalization cases, helped sustain support for the war among African Americans. But these modest signs of advancement were also reminders that enormous challenges remained.

For the *Collegian* in 1942, there was a cruel irony in the support that African Americans offered for the war. "Colored Americans as usual find themselves in the strange position of defending that which they do not have." The assistant editor of the newspaper, Ernest Lewis, called on graduating seniors to assume the burden of fighting for racial progress. "Now more than ever the destiny of the Black Race will depend on what you do in the next few years. If it is America's duty to fight to save democracy, then it is your duty to fight for a place in democracy."[9]

THE DRAFT

In 1940 Congress had implemented the first peacetime draft in U.S. history. South Carolina governor Burnet Maybank asked Miller F. Whittaker and Seymour Carroll to help oversee the registration of black men. Maybank also appointed three black men in each of South Carolina's forty-six counties to assist in that registration process. But no black men were asked to serve on the local Selective Service boards that determined which men would be called for military service and which men would be deferred temporarily or permanently.[10]

As the campus lost large numbers of men to the war effort, the college experienced a severe but temporary demographic transformation. The institution took on

Table 21. Enrollment during World War II

	Male	Female	Total
1940–41	483	434	917
1942–43	459	634	1,093
1944–45	241	657	898
1945–46	335	749	1,084

Sources: Annual reports, 1940–41, 6; 1942–43, 14; 1944–45, 34; 1945–46, 21. These figures do not include male students enrolled in special training programs or the students in Felton Training School.

the appearance of a black women's college by 1944–45. President Whittaker drafted letter after letter to Selective Service authorities during the war asking that students as well as faculty members be deferred from military service until at least the end of the academic term. The *Collegian* also asked that students be granted deferments until the school year concluded.[11]

According to Whittaker students were uncertain of the immediate future, and this created anxiety, particularly among young men. "The war has materially affected the morale of students, especially males. It has manifested itself by an uncertainty of mental objectives, a lowering of grades, and a general restlessness." Whittaker indicated that students were reclassified by their local draft boards and then called for military service even before a decision had been made on granting or denying them a deferment. He stated, for example, in 1942 that juniors and seniors majoring in agriculture "were drafted before the Selective Service ruled that they might be deferred." Approximately 175 students withdrew from the college during the 1942–43 school year, and 253 young people had joined the armed services since Pearl Harbor. In many cases Whittaker's letters to local draft boards asking that young men be deferred were unsuccessful.[12]

Whittaker had more success in persuading local draft board 62 in Orangeburg and its chairman, W. A. Schiffley, to defer members of the faculty and staff. In April 1943 the president asked that agriculture instructor W. C. Hurley not be reclassified 1-A, which would make him eligible for conscription. Hurley's loss, Whittaker noted, "would seriously handicap instruction of agriculture students and [he is] the Manager of the College dairy which supplies milk and butter for the State A&M College." A few days later Whittaker appealed to Schiffley "respectfully requesting that Prof. J. H. Birnie be deferred." The president explained that Birnie "is professor of biology and as such is one of the principal instructor[s] of Pre-medical students, and his loss at present would seriously handicap our Pre-Medical program." Birnie was deferred, but later in the war he was commissioned an officer in the Maritime Service of the U.S. Navy.[13]

Most faculty members and administrators who were eligible for military service remained on the campus during World War II. Among those who Whittaker wrote letters asking that they be deferred because of their critical importance to the college were Oliver C. Dawson, Thomas J. Crawford, Gabe Buchanan, E. Melvin Adams,

H. W. Crawford, and Dudley M. Zimmerman. Not one of them served in the armed forces. Southern draft boards were especially reluctant to put college-trained black men in uniform, even though U.S. military forces remained strictly segregated.[14]

Two prominent faculty members—Paul V. Jewell and Howard Jordan—did leave the college because of the war. Jordan, a professor of education, was drafted and served as a lieutenant in the army. Jewell, the dean of mechanical arts, left to serve in an unidentified but "a vital war industry" in Indiana. Both men were granted leaves of absence. Jordan returned to the campus following the war, but Jewell did not. However, it was mostly students and not faculty members and staff who departed for the military during the war.[15]

ENROLLMENT

Students who did not enter the military had the option—unlike young people during the Depression—of obtaining jobs in the civilian workforce or furthering their education. Whittaker pointed out that "young men and young women could secure lucrative employment in industry." Carriebelle C. Wright was a case in point. She wrote Whittaker in 1942 from Pittsburg, California, that she would not be returning to S.C. State "until the second semester due to the fact that I am employed at a defense plant here at an attractive wage." But the loss of students to the military and to the domestic economy hardly resulted in empty classrooms and vacant dormitories during the war.[16]

In 1940–41 one hundred would-be students were refused admission, and 131 were rejected in 1943–44 because of lack of space. Another 207 young people were turned away in 1944–45. Many young people asked Whittaker to assure them that they would have a job on campus in order to pay their fees. He declined to make such promises. Furthermore Whittaker wrote to dozens of young women informing them that they could not enroll because of the lack of housing. The absence of adequate facilities would continue to plague the college in the postwar years. Hundreds of African Americans were denied the opportunity to enroll in the only state college in South Carolina that they were—by law—eligible to attend.[17]

The loss of male students and the surge in female enrollment led to the conversion of Miller Hall from a men's dormitory to a women's dorm. But even with female students occupying Miller, many young women were compelled to live off campus in residences in Orangeburg. This was a disturbing situation conceded President Whittaker, because "they cannot receive the proper watch care of the college." With the decline in male students in agriculture and mechanical arts, Whittaker announced plans to increase the number of women students in what had been traditionally male preserves within the curriculum. But these plans for women to enroll in poultry science, automobile mechanics, and other so-called male subjects failed to materialize.[18]

The institution also failed to take advantage of the presence of so many female students to fill the gap in the critical shortage of student labor. Since the college's founding, male students were needed to maintain the campus and its facilities. With the war there were more than enough women to fill part time campus jobs as clerks, as typists, and in the dining hall. But maintenance work involving physical labor on the campus and the farm was neglected because of the lack of men. Although young women were begging for employment on campus, it apparently did not occur to administrators that women could have worked in the barns, painted, and done janitorial work. Also, to make more efficient use of those facilities and conserve resources and supplies, the academic year was reduced by one month. Classes were held on twenty Saturdays, which brought the school year to an end by early May.[19]

TRAINING PROGRAMS, BUT NO ROTC

As had been the case during World War I, S.C. State provided training during World War II for civilian laborers at U.S. government expense. College-level courses in engineering drawing, organic chemistry, office management, statistics, and engineering for women were taught. There were also noncollege short courses lasting three to four months in welding, radio repair, and machine shop offered. The U.S. Office of Education sponsored the classes and loaned the college "many expensive machines" and "valuable equipment" for instruction. With the demands brought by the war, some of the classes were offered on a twenty-four-hour schedule. In 1942–43 there were 131 men and 118 women enrolled in these training classes. The college's agricultural program also conducted an experiment to see if goldenrods could be utilized in the production of rubber.[20]

Whittaker recognized that the college would have to adjust, adapt, and sacrifice for the war effort. S.C. State would offer "staunch support of our government in every effort to win this war." But it deeply disturbed and even angered the normally placid Whittaker—a veteran of World War I—that the college was not permitted to provide military training through an ROTC program. Moreover federal authorities lacked the courtesy to offer an explanation. Whittaker was about as blunt over this lack of respect as he permitted himself to be in dealing with public officials. "We have been disappointed by the failure of the War Department to utilize the facilities of this institution for the training of soldiers. Under the [Morrill] act creating the land-grant colleges this college should offer military training. We anticipated this war several years ago and made repeated requests for the establishment of a Reserve Officers Training Corps. . . . Repeated inquiries have failed to bring any information as to why this college has not been selected to participate in the army specialized training program." But Whittaker and everyone else knew the reason why the black college was not involved in training black men to serve as officers.[21]

FUNDING AND STATE APPROPRIATIONS

Not surprisingly the college had far more funds at its disposal than had been the case during the Depression. State appropriations surged by the mid-1940s. Legislators did the state's institutions of higher learning a big favor in 1943 when they funded the debts of the schools. S.C. State was relieved of repaying the State Sinking Fund $33,150 that it still owed on an original debt of $40,000, which had been its portion of the cost of the construction of the mechanical industries building.[22]

Table 22. S.C. State College Revenue, 1941–46

	State Appropriation	Morrill Land Scrip	Student Fees	Miscellaneous Revenue	Total
1941–42	$90,000	$51,385	$49,150	$31,919	$222,454
1942–43	$100,000	$51,385	$53,350	$37,030	$241,765
1943–44	$107,926	$51,385	$40,300	$34,506	$234,117
1944–45	$146,500	$51,385	$45,000	$25,400	$268,285
1945–46	$195,000	$51,595	$54,400	$35,696	$336,691

Sources: Annual reports for the college: 1941–42, 26; 1942–43, 28; 1943–44, 13; 1944–45, 24; 1945–46, 30. These were funds that would be available in the following academic year, therefore the figures from the 1945–46 annual report are for July 1, 1946, to June 30, 1947.

Nevertheless money for the institution was still tight, and Whittaker was constantly pleading for more funds from the legislature. New construction and maintenance were difficult with wartime shortages in materials and supplies for civilian projects. There was also a scarcity of labor. The most critical and immediate need was for new boilers, a facility to house them, and new steam lines for heating campus structures.

Whittaker pressed legislators for years to replace boilers that had been built and installed in 1912–13 early in Wilkinson's presidency. Those old boilers frequently broke down and were expensive to repair. In 1943 he explained that "the present boiler plant is over thirty years old, inadequate, inefficient, and dangerous." He worried than any additional major breakdowns could "cause the closing of the institution."[23]

Finally the general assembly set aside funds for a new heating system—sort of. The new boilers would cost an estimated $60,000 to $65,000 including the structure to house them and the necessary steam lines. But the lowest bid of $62,470 could not be accepted because the legislature had appropriated only $45,000. Bids were subsequently resubmitted for only the two boilers and the structure to contain them, and a bid of $40,253 was accepted. The new boilers were built and installed in the new building. But they were of no use until they were connected to new steam lines. That required an additional appropriation of $22,970 and an additional year to complete the project.[24]

SALARIES AND ACCREDITATION

Although the legislature increased appropriations during World War II, low faculty salaries persisted. Despite the weak salary structure, the college gained the coveted A rating from the Southern Association in late 1941. Exactly what college administrators and faculty did to raise the institution's rating from B to A among the black institutions is uncertain. Although the number of faculty members with master's degrees had

Table 23. Revised Faculty Ranks and Proposed Salary Schedule, 1945

Rank	Education	Experience	1945–46	1946–47
Dean	—		$2,700	$3,100
Professor	Doctorate or two years grad work	5 years	$2,600	$3,000
Associate professor	Two years grad work	5 years	$2,400	$2,700
Assistant professor	One year grad work and/or master's degree or bachelor's degree	5 years	$2,100	$2,400
Instructor	Bachelor's degree	—	$1,400–$1,700	$1,700–$2,000

Source: *Annual Report, 1944–1945,* 9–10.

increased in the 1930s, not one person in the academic program had an earned doctorate by World War II.[25]

Whittaker pleaded repeatedly with legislators to increase salaries of the teaching staff through the 1940s. He asked for an appropriation that would permit a $5 a month increase for each faculty member in 1943. A few months later he asked that all employees be awarded a 10 percent increase. The following year Whittaker told the general assembly that a number of faculty members remained attached to the college out of sheer loyalty—and the belief that their compensation was about to increase. "Many of our faculty have refused flattering offers to teach elsewhere or in war work because of their love for the institution and the hope that salaries here will soon be made the equal of those in similar institutions elsewhere." Those members of the faculty and staff who held out hope that their compensation was about to increase were disappointed. Salaries remained far less than generous.[26]

In 1945 Whittaker proposed that an individual faculty member's rank be more closely aligned to education and experience. Therefore adjustments in compensation would follow. However, in no case would a faculty member have his or her compensation reduced. The new ranks and proposed pay schedule was contingent, as usual, on legislative financial support, which was, as usual, not immediately forthcoming.[27]

THE RETIREMENT SYSTEM

Faculty and staff benefitted enormously in the short and the long run from the creation in 1945 of a retirement system for state employees. Teachers sixty-five years of age and other employees who were seventy could begin to receive retirement benefits in July 1946. Faculty with thirty-five or more years of service could begin to draw benefits in July 1945. Eight employees of S.C. State were immediately eligible including dean of women Mary J. Miller Earle; instructor of tailoring Charles Waterman; instructor of leatherwork and former athletic coach William C. Lewis; and longtime college physician Lin C. Shecut. (Shecut and board secretary Wallace C. Bethea were the only two white people who were paid employees of the college during its first fifty years.)[28]

Unfortunately two of the institution's most prominent figures had died on the eve of the creation of the retirement program. Nelson C. Nix, who was a charter member of the faculty in 1896, died in December 1944 after forty-eight years of service as dean of the faculty and a professor of mathematics. He had also completed an unpublished history of the college in 1937. Born June 10, 1865, Nix was the son of former slaves. He was also the longtime pastor of Mount Pisgah Baptist Church in Orangeburg. One of Nix's four children, Robert N. C. Nix, was a lawyer in Philadelphia, and he was elected to the U.S. House of Representatives in 1958 and served until 1979. The grandson of Nelson Nix, Robert N. C. Nix Jr. was born in 1928, and he was also a lawyer. He served as an associate justice on the Pennsylvania Supreme Court from 1972 to 1984 and the chief justice until 1996. Harry E. Daniels, the head of the farm demonstration program and a leader in extension work for more than a quarter century, also died in December 1944.[29]

Employees of the college also benefitted from the creation in April 1936 of one of the nation's first black credit unions. K. W. G. Donma, a Liberian immigrant who taught poultry science, spearheaded the effort to found the Edisto Credit Union. With an initial membership of fifteen people, it provided loans totaling $410 in its first year. By 1939 it had 129 members and made loans of $7,356, and no borrowers had failed to repay a loan.[30]

STUDENTS

When faculty member Harold Crawford was asked to contribute an article to the *Collegian* in late 1941 he reminisced nostalgically for those days nearly two decades earlier when he had been a student. He observed how much easier college life was for students in the 1940s than it had been in the 1920s. Current students had fewer restrictions and fewer responsibilities. Of course, he pointed out, there were only a few college degrees granted in the early 1920s while 149 young people were awarded diplomas in 1940. With little regret he noted that the Friday night lyceum programs had vanished. The strict student dress code had all but disappeared. "In the old days they [women students] wore white middies and blue skirts with full length hose and Cuban heels." Twenty years later ladies wore socks, saddle backs, and tweed skirts with a pullover.[31]

It seemed almost incredible to Crawford that by 1941 "almost all male students and many female students go and come almost at will." He informed the younger generation that "twenty years ago a student who frequented 'the corner' at Russell and Boulevard streets would be dismissed from the institution." But earlier that year the College Soda Shop had opened on the corner. Students were free to patronize the popular hangout owned and operated by economics professor Paul Webber and his wife, Clemmie Embly Webber.[32]

Crawford worried that the younger generation had become lackadaisical and unreliable. But students themselves were some of their own sharpest critics. Eugenia

Dean wrote a regular column in the *Collegian* in which she railed against the unsophisticated behavior and lack of refinement among her fellow students. All too often they were not proper ladies and gentlemen. She complained about the informal gatherings of students on the campus. "On a pleasant Sunday afternoon, they assemble on some convenient spot, where their piercing screams and savage guffaws alarm others who maybe near."[33]

Dean took young women to task for their inappropriate use of makeup. "Some girls seem committed to the use of orange rouge and an altogether contrasting color of raspberry lipstick which gives them a carotty look." With no irony intended, she told students in December 1940 to behave properly on the segregated railroad coaches as they traveled home for the holidays. "Of course, this is a free country; you have paid for your seat and transportation, you have the right to talk as loud as you wish and to bring gobs of garbage if you desire, but why characterize yourself as inconsiderate and selfish." She continued, "Don't forget that there is a conductor. Why make extra work for him? He'll control his temper if he finds he is dealing with humans instead of animals." Dean went on in issue after issue of the newspaper in what many students must have regarded as condescending and prudish attempts to have them mend their ill-mannered ways.[34]

Still there were other students who agreed with Dean and objected to the uncouth and anti-intellectual actions of some young people during the lyceum programs when impatient students purposely and repeatedly coughed to disrupt the speaker or artist. There were complaints that Floyd Dining Hall was the scene of "loud and boisterous conversations." In 1943 Lyles Perry, a student, criticized dining hall behavior. "'Mother' [Marion Birnie] Wilkinson isn't just 'kidding' when she says that it isn't necessary to have such rudeness and vociferousness in the dining hall."[35]

With the sharp decline in male enrollment, there were fewer discipline problems. Yet there were still rules to be enforced, and the institution was not quite as lax in the enforcement of regulations as Harold W. Crawford had suggested. Chairman Nelson C. Nix and the Faculty Discipline Committee continued to recommend the dismissal of students. In 1942 the committee asked Whittaker to dismiss four women and sixteen men. Nix's committee asked that Edith Curry be expelled "for leaving campus without permission repeatedly" and for "bad conduct on campus and in the Dorm." Ruby Doyle was told to leave because of "unfavorable rumor and bad conduct on the campus." Harold Abrams and Gordon Alexander were dismissed for "drunkenness and boisterousness." Two males were expelled for "assault on a girl."[36]

The Reverend J. D. Bryan of Seneca, who was an alumnus, could not understand why his seventeen-year-old son had been dismissed from the college in 1942. He asked Whittaker "to disclose the nature of his sins." The president replied that the student and another young man had been caught shoplifting by a local merchant who declined to prosecute. The two young men were then expelled, but they were free to enroll elsewhere "without a black mark" on their records.[37]

Some students were simply given warnings and informed that if their behavior and academic performance did not improve, they would no longer be enrolled at S.C. State. Whittaker wrote a young man from Columbia named Matthew Perry and told him that he was "surprised to see such poor grades from you," and that he was disappointed that Perry's conduct in the dining hall had been "unbecoming a college student." He let Perry know that he needed "to turn over a new leaf." Perry decided to take the president's advice.[38]

Dissatisfied students sometimes dismissed the college, disappointed at the reception they received. In an irate letter, W. M. Kinney of Bennettsville let it be known that his freshman daughter, Ruth, was "toadly disatified with the treatment that have been given her." She had been teased by sophomores, and she had been compelled to live on the third floor of Bradham Hall when the father had made it plain that she wanted to reside on the first floor. He asked for an honorable dismissal and a refund. Whittaker hurried to comply with the request—no doubt relieved to be free of the unhappy father and daughter.[39]

Students complained that there were not enough extracurricular activities available on campus to keep them occupied. Because it was the midst of World War II, perhaps this criticism was a bit unfair. S.C. State was also a small college in a small and segregated town without many options for entertainment. However, Lyles Perry explained that he and other students were interested in more than fun and entertainment. "Something should be done to make week-ends more lively and I say lively not in the sense of the 'flaming youth' but as I said before with interesting and educational views in mind."[40]

There were a variety of concerts, observances, organizations, and athletic events available to the campus and local black community before, during, and after the war. The selection and presentation of the May Queen and her court generated enormous interest in the late 1930s and early 1940s. Many students participated in programs sponsored by the YMCA and the YWCA. The YMCA had a room set aside in Lowman Hall while the Y-Hut served YWCA. The YWCA periodically hosted the local women's organization the Sunlight Club. The YMCA and the YWCA cosponsored the annual Easter program, which featured an address delivered by Benjamin E. Mays, who had assumed the presidency of Morehouse College in 1940.[41]

Fraternities and sororities were integral to campus life although there were complaints that their members had too much influence in student activities to the exclusion of students who did not belong to the Greek letter organizations. The fraternities held smokers to introduce students to their brotherhoods. Kappa Alpha Psi sponsored its annual "Guide Right" program. In 1941 Alpha Phi Alpha brought the famed Earl "Fatha" Hines and his orchestra to Dukes Gymnasium for a benefit dance. Billie Eckstein was the featured vocalist.[42]

Alpha Kappa Alpha brought Ann C. Cooke to the college in early 1941. She was a professor of drama at Howard and the granddaughter of Thomas E. Miller as well as the niece of the dean of women, Mary J. Miller Earle. Cooke delivered a lecture entitled "Religious Themes in Modern Drama." Nearly a year later, Philippa Dukes Schuyler gave a recital that Alpha Kappa Alpha sponsored. Schuyler was a renowned pianist who had been a child prodigy, and she was the daughter of black journalist and commentator George Schuyler. In late 1945 novelist and winner of the Nobel Prize for Literature Sinclair Lewis made a brief and surprise visit to the campus. African American history

This cartoon, *Friday Night in Room 185,* drawn by Eugene Rivers Jr. appeared in the January 1943 *Collegian.* These were some "starving" and bored young men who apparently lacked the financial resources to visit the College Soda Shop. Courtesy of the Historical Collection, South Carolina State University week continued to be commemorated each February. In 1943 the *Collegian* proclaimed in a headline: "18th Negro History Week Observed." There were programs, readings, and a concert given by the Wilkinson High School Glee Club as well as another contest that included a Negro history quiz.[43]

A fleeting controversy erupted in the pages of the *Collegian* in December 1941 over the need among students for the establishment of a genuine Student Council that would replace the long-standing College Club. The club was made up of the entire student body. It had officers, and it selected the editor and staff of the *Collegian.* But it had little real authority over students and their activities. In a poll of seven students, the *Collegian* found—not surprisingly—that six of seven favored the creation of a Student Council to replace the College Club. M. L. Pequette wanted the council to "serve as a discipline committee for students before they are carried before the Faculty Council." R. F. Ledbetter commented that student councils functioned effectively at other colleges, and Margaret E. Bookman thought a council would increase student morale. The sole dissenter quoted by the *Collegian,* Oliver B. Johnson, caustically claimed that S.C. State students were not ready for a council. "Until we as students, expel the bitter venom of partiality from out narrowed and self-centered lives, such a body will not function successfully on our campus." Johnson proved prophetic. No Student Council was established for more than a decade, and even then it lacked influence.[44]

Coach Oliver C. Dawson's football team compiled a record of four wins, three losses, and two ties in 1941 and went 3–2–1 in 1942 before football was suspended until 1946. But there were other sports. The men's basketball team won twenty games and lost four in 1943 in winning the Southern Intercollegiate Athletic Conference title. The squad was led by Henry "Mice" Holden, the center, and Bill "Babyface" Copeland, a guard. Holden led black colleges in scoring with 227 points after seventeen games. Copeland had developed a one-hand shot "which is rapidly replacing the traditional two-hand shot in the S.I.A.C." On three consecutive nights at Dukes Gymnasium, the Bulldogs defeated Xavier 37–35 and 30–27 before losing in overtime to Florida A&M, 46–45.[45]

The campus bell was relocated in 1941. It had been marking the time and calling students to the dining hall since at least the early years of the twentieth century. Located for decades on the original mechanical industries building, that facility was demolished when the new mechanical industries building was completed in 1940. The bell was then moved to a silver tower not far from Floyd Dining Hall. In 1945 the bell became a source of concern when a group of young white men began riding through the campus late at night "ringing the college bell at all hours." Rather than contact local law enforcement personnel himself, President Whittaker asked Orangeburg attorney Adam Moss, who was a member of the board of trustees, to handle the matter. Moss assured Whittaker that he would "confer with [the] chief of police to stop these nocturnal visits."[46]

For more than a half century, S.C. State students did not have a student center, a student union, or even a snack bar. There was no place on or off campus where they could congregate, get something to eat or drink, and socialize. White-owned businesses on nearby Russell Street did not allow African Americans to consume food or beverages on the premises. This lack of an informal social center came to an end in early 1941 when Professor Paul Webber and his wife, Clemmie, opened the College

Paul and Clemmie Webber opened the College Soda Shop on Boulevard Street at the railroad corner just as World War II erupted. It served for many years as a de facto student union. The Webbers opened a second soda shop on Riverside Drive in 1945. Courtesy of the Historical Collection, South Carolina State University

Soda Shop across the street and railroad tracks not far from the entrance to S.C. State. The soda shop instantly became a de facto student union for State and Claflin students. It also offered employment opportunities for scores of students before it closed in 1960. The first two soda jerks were Robert "Wagg" Howard and Leon Coleman. In a world where Jim Crow prevailed, the soda shop allowed African Americans to enjoy a hot dog or hamburger and a milk shake at the twelve-foot-long counter or in booths while listening to popular music on the jukebox. For many younger (and older) people, it was the first time they sat at a counter or sampled a banana split.[47]

Rumors circulated for a time among black and white people that the soda shop was a front for questionable activities. In fact one inquisitive but unnamed member of the board of trustees paid a visit, convinced that he would find illicit sex through a side door to "a special room of 'ill repute.'" Actually the State Theater—"South Carolina's Newest and Most Modern Colored Theater"—was located adjacent to the soda shop, and it was possible to enter the lobby of the theater through a door from the shop—as the relieved member of the board discovered.[48]

CELEBRATING A HALF CENTURY

The college celebrated its fiftieth anniversary during Founders' Day ceremonies in 1946. T. J. Crawford, who had graduated from the campus high school and from the college, chaired the program. He was a professor of chemistry and biology. (Crawford served as the honorary chair of the one hundredth anniversary commemoration in 1996.) The featured speaker was Dr. D. L. Witherspoon, a 1906 graduate, who was the treasurer of the pension department of the African Methodist Episcopal Church in Nashville. The institution used the occasion to award honorary degrees to five African Americans who were natives of South Carolina and closely connected to the college: Benjamin E. Mays, Mary McLeod Bethune, Robert S. Wilkinson Jr., Ernest A. Grant, and Walter H. Aiken. Mays was the president of Morehouse College. Bethune served as president of Bethune Cookman College and was the president of the National Council of Negro Women. Wilkinson was a physician in New York City and the son of the second president. Ernest A. Grant was an authority on agricultural education from Tuskegee Institute, and Walter H. Aiken was a prominent builder and contractor from Atlanta. It was the first time that the college had awarded honorary degrees since 1922, and it was the last time it would do so until 1988.[49]

THE HILLCREST FARM

As state revenues surged during the war, legislators loosened purse strings slightly in 1943 and appropriated $10,000 to S.C. State to purchase additional farmland. Despite the acquisition of the Dukes farm in 1935, the college was again renting acreage by 1940. It was President Whittaker who seized the initiative. He asked board secretary Wallace Bethea to appeal to members of the general assembly for the funds. "Some land is available," Whittaker advised Bethea, "and I am respectfully suggesting that you use your good office to present this matter to the Legislature, requesting a special appropriation for the purchase of farm land." Whittaker added that $10,000 should be sufficient.[50]

Legislators responded favorably, and the trustees formed an agriculture committee consisting of W. P. Mason, W. Mc. Hodge, and newly elected board member Julian Wolfe to oversee the purchase. In the summer of 1943 S.C. State acquired the 109-acre Hughes farm, located about two miles north of the campus. Several weeks later arrangements were completed to exchange the seventy-one-acre Dukes farm and 5.7 acres that the college owned on Russell Street for the 187-acre O'Cain farm, which was located adjacent to the Hughes farm. The college then possessed nearly three hundred acres that came to be known as the Hillcrest Farm.[51]

THE TRUSTEES

Over the years some board members were often more concerned with the personal benefits they could extract from the college than in the advancement of the institution. No one was more eager to take advantage of his position than the longtime chairman of the board Charles F. Brooks. He became a trustee in 1918 and served until his death in 1950. He was a farmer and school superintendent from Gray Court in Laurens County. Although Brooks was nominally the chairman when governors did not attend board meetings, Brooks showed minimal interest in the economic, political, and academic issues that affected the college. An affable man with a pleasant disposition, Brooks besieged President Whittaker with handwritten requests for personal favors.

In 1943 Brooks asked Whittaker if he could purchase a mower and rake that the International Harvester Company had loaned the college. "See what you can find out about it, and advise me. We are needing one very badly. Hope that you will be able to land one for me." Whittaker responded and told Brooks that the mower and rake had already been returned to the company. "We, therefore, have no way to get a mower and rake for you." In the same letter Brooks also indicated that he had sold a calf he had taken from the campus farm and that he would reimburse the college $5 to cover the cost of transferring the registration papers for the animal. It is not clear whether Brooks paid for the calf or considered it a "gift." Brooks also acquired two young pigs from the college in 1945, but both died soon thereafter. "Certainly sorry to lose them," he told Whittaker, "—had hoped to raise some fine meat."[52]

Prior to a board meeting in October 1946, Brooks informed Whittaker that he needed Raymond Clagett to provide automobile repairs in the campus shop. "I'll want a little work done on my Packard when I come down—My brakes need lining—I guess Prof. Clagett can do that while I am there." He also asked Whittaker to delay the meeting of the trustees' planning board so that Brooks could attend the Orangeburg County Fair. "I always enjoy taking in the fair—it[']s the only one I go to see."[53]

In the meantime Brooks's term on the board neared an end, and he instructed Whittaker to make sure that he and Wallace Bethea were reelected by the legislature. "Mr. Bethea's and my place [on the board] expires at this time. See to it that we are retained on the board. Speak to Mr. Bethea and Julian [Wolfe] in our behalf—I'll appreciate your influence and help."[54]

The next year Brooks solicited medical assistance from S.C. State. He wanted the college physician, Dr. James Shecut (who was a white man), to give him a physical. Shecut should "give me a good 'look over'—I think I need it." Brooks complained that his knees were giving him trouble. So was his vehicle. He wanted the college automotive shop to repair his Dodge pickup truck, and he promised to pay for any parts the truck needed. Other trustees occasionally took advantage of their positions as well. In 1946 two college employees, Clarence Clinkscales and Florella Fordham, assisted at the Orangeburg wedding of Julian Wolfe's daughter.[55]

Professor Charles Waterman and the students enrolled in tailoring classes made a suit for Brooks in 1946. For three decades the campus tailoring shop had measured, fit, and prepared suits for governors and other public officials. In 1948 Governor Strom Thurmond received such a suit. Thurmond, unlike most recipients, insisted on paying for his new apparel. Occasionally favors were returned. Charles Brooks sent a tie to President Whittaker in 1947—"just wanted you to know I was thinking about you."[56]

Too often S.C. State presidents had little choice but to accede to the requests (demands?) of trustees and other public officials. But in some instances it was college administrators who displayed generosity in an effort to curry favor among those whose support the institution needed. On occasion such acts of kindness had unforeseen consequences. For many years students in home economics prepared fruitcakes as Christmas gifts for friends of the college. During one holiday season in the early 1950s

Clarence Clinkscales was delivering one of those cakes to the Orangeburg home of trustee Adam H. Moss. But when Mrs. Moss's small dogs began yapping and snapping at Clinkscales's heels, he attempted to kick them away, but she sharply reprimanded him. "Don't you hit my damn dogs!" He responded, "I'm just trying to keep 'em from biting me." "Well damn it," Mrs. Moss exclaimed, "let 'em bite you."[57]

Long before meetings of public officials became open meetings, administrative bodies like the S.C. State board of trustees—and particularly its local board—met when and where they pleased. Often those gatherings were held off of the campus. They met in the office of the governor, in the office of Wallace C. Bethea at the First National Bank, or in the law office of attorney Adam H. Moss. When General Alvin C. Gilliam, the commander of the Third U.S. Army, was invited to deliver the commencement address in 1948, the trustees entertained him at lunch at the all-white Orangeburg Country Club.[58]

THE EXTENSION PROGRAM

The Second World War led to an unprecedented and rapid expansion of the extension program as federal authorities rushed to increase the nation's agricultural production. Department of Agriculture funds funneled through Clemson College permitted S.C. State to hire additional extension agents. On the eve of World War II in 1940 there were nineteen farm demonstration agents and fifteen home demonstration agents. President Whittaker regarded this as a thoroughly insufficient number of extension workers needed to serve the state's black population. "For a reasonable service to the people," he insisted that "there should be an agent in each county."[59]

By 1945 the black extension program had grown dramatically, but not nearly enough to assign one farm demonstration agent and one home demonstration agent to each of South Carolina's forty-six counties. Ten emergency farm demonstration assistants joined the nineteen agents, and twenty emergency home demonstration assistants had been added to the force of fifteen home demonstration agents. For the first time—and temporarily as it turned out—there were thirty-five women in the home demonstration program and twenty-nine men in farm demonstration work.[60]

This expanded extension force fanned out across South Carolina to urge farm families to contribute to the war effort by boosting production and becoming more self-sufficient. Propaganda was considered essential to that mission. The black agents showed films produced by the U.S. government including *Planes, Plows, and Peace; The Heritage We Guard;* and *The Negro Farmer.* M. L. Wilson, the director of the nation's extension program, spoke in Orangeburg and appealed to the audience to support the defense of America.[61]

Black and white leaders were eager to instill pride and patriotism among disfranchised and dispossessed farm families. In 1942 at a meeting that combined Farm and Home Demonstration Week with 4-H Conservation Week held on the S.C. State campus, President Whittaker admonished the gathering to help win the war or "lose our freedom forever." At the same meeting, adults and 4-H members from Spartanburg presented a short play, *4-H March to Victory.*[62]

In the words of farm demonstration director Harry E. Daniels in 1942, "production of food is wartime work." One of the national goals of the Department of Agriculture was to convince farm families to raise 75 percent of the food they consumed and to grow 75 percent of the feed needed for their animals. But attaining even partial self-sufficiency among rural black Carolinians was a formidable, if not impossible, task. Extension agents found farm families did not have adequate knowledge, land, equipment, and housing. Many of them could not even meet their basic needs.[63]

They lacked even a rudimentary awareness of food and nutrition. "It seems as if the average home maker has been accustomed to preparing and serving only a limited variety of food . . . and as a result many families are slowly starving from lack of many foods." There was a critical need for vegetables, milk, and milk products. Most black families did not have a cow, and of those that did, few of them had electricity and refrigeration.[64]

Extension efforts and the 4-H program continued to benefit the moderately prosperous black families more than those who were impoverished. But in 1942 farm demonstration agents persuaded 440 farmers to take and tend a cow for the first time. Another 1,478 raised pigs for the first time while 170 planted their first peanut crop for oil, and incredibly 1,460 farmers were convinced to plant their first garden. The agents also cooperated with farmers in planting demonstration plots of cotton, corn, and wheat.[65]

There were 4,396 4-H members who took part in the "Food for Victory" program. By 1945, 4-H members raised over 154,000 fowl. They planted 2,290 acres of gardens, raised 907 pigs, canned 192,284 quarts of fruit and vegetables, made 4,826 garments, and refashioned another 3,843 garments. There were 407 4-H clubs with just 935 boys taking part while 8,913 girls were involved. The 4-H program and its activities appealed most to youngsters who had remained in school. It offered competitive projects that represented an opportunity for young people to gain knowledge and to derive a sense of satisfaction from what they were able to accomplish.[66]

Because of the abysmal condition of many rural schools attended by 4-H members, they worked to improve their own educational facilities. The 4-H club in Little Mountain in Newberry County raised $475 to install a stove in their school lunchroom, and 4-H participants in Jalapa, which was also in Newberry County, raised $190 to paint the interior of their school. In Allendale County 4-H clubs cleaned and beautified twelve schools. Three 4-H girls in Pleasant Falls in Spartanburg County sold enough peaches and vegetables to buy pianos for their schools so that they and eleven other 4-H girls could take instructions to learn to play the instruments that they had purchased.[67]

As an example of what black farm families could achieve, Harry Daniels proudly pointed to B. C. Andrews, his wife, and eight children in Florence County. They lived in a six-room house that was painted and had screens. Electricity had been added in 1942, and the Andrewses acquired a refrigerator. The farm had chickens, pigs, and cows. Andrews had plows, a disc harrow, cultivators, and a mower. The family grew corn, wheat, vegetables, sweet potatoes, fruit, and cane for syrup. Four of the children were in 4-H and active in the Victory Garden campaign. But the Andrews family and their circumstances were hardly typical of the state's rural black residents. Rather they were held up as an example of what less affluent families could aspire to.[68]

Many rural residents hoped to escape the desolate and poverty-stricken way of life that they endured as sharecroppers, renters, and agricultural laborers. World War II afforded them that opportunity as they fled the land for the relative prosperity of towns and cities. While some of them entered the military and others found civilian employment, white farmers and state officials became alarmed at the loss of cheap farm labor to industry. An unskilled industrial worker could earn $60 a week compared to the miniscule $4 a week a rural laborer took home. This loss of labor was offset partly by mechanization. Still there was an acute shortage in the farm workforce.[69]

Marian Paul, the head of the home demonstration program, was terribly disappointed when the end of World War II brought the elimination of the agents who had been hired for the wartime emergency. Paradoxically Congress had passed the Bankhead-Flannigan Act in 1945 to expand the county extension work programs. Instead the black extension program in South Carolina suffered reductions. But those reductions could have been even worse. The farm demonstration program kept twenty-nine agents, but Paul lost twelve of the twenty agents employed during the war as emergency food specialists. "The magnificent results obtained by these workers made us optimistically hope they would be employed permanently," she lamented. But they were not. The Bankhead-Flannigan legislation did permit Paul to retain six of the twenty-two agents who remained with the home demonstration program.[70]

Moreover Paul insisted that black agents should assist black people. White agents and specialists could be helpful, but black extension workers were in a better position to address the needs of poor black South Carolinians. Paul preferred, for example, the retention of black food specialists—the very people who had been terminated at war's end. "Although the white specialists are most kind and cooperative, we feel that there's a kindred and understanding spirit among persons of our own race which can not be comprehended by others."[71]

THE WAR AND RACIAL PROGRESS

For African Americans like Paul, the issue of race took on increased significance as the Second World War drew to a close. The war against those fascist nations that had proclaimed their racial and cultural superiority had ended with their surrender. With Americans of all backgrounds celebrating the Allied triumph, many black people—although certainly not all of them—optimistically believed that Jim Crow's days were numbered.

President Miller F. Whittaker contemplated "a new world [that] will demand justice and freedom through interracial cooperation." But trepidation and anxiety tempered that optimism. The vast majority of white southerners showed no inclination to abandon segregation or jettison white supremacy. Alarmed that the NAACP had mobilized legal assaults against Jim Crow, South Carolina's white leadership had begun to move vigorously prior to World War II to stem the tide of racial change. In 1938 Charles B. Bailey applied for admission to the University of South Carolina law school. Bailey was a black resident of Columbia and a 1932 graduate of Morehouse College.

Bailey informed NAACP special counsel and former dean of the Howard University law school, Charles H. Houston, of his intentions, and Houston in turn encouraged Bailey to pursue his effort to get a legal education.[72]

While Bailey waited for a reply from the university's law school, the U.S. Supreme Court ruled in late 1938 that Lloyd Gaines, a black applicant to the University of Missouri law school, would have to be admitted to that institution unless the state provided him with a separate legal education that was "substantially equal" to that which the University of Missouri already offered to white residents. The Missouri legislature subsequently appropriated $200,000 to open a separate law school in St. Louis under the control of the state's historically black college, Lincoln University.[73]

Bailey's application and the Supreme Court's decision in the Gaines case alarmed South Carolina's political leadership. But Solomon Blatt, who was the speaker of the South Carolina House of Representatives and a member of the University of South Carolina board of trustees, reassured citizens of the Palmetto State that neither Charles Bailey nor any other black person would ever grace the halls of the university. "The white people of South Carolina need not have any fear as to what the outcome of this application is going to be. The board of trustees will do everything in their power to maintain the University of South Carolina for white students only."[74]

A BLACK LAW SCHOOL?

Rather than admit Bailey or any other Negro to the university, the state's educational and political leadership decided to establish a separate law school at S.C. State. As early as 1936, the dean of the university's law school, J. Nelson Frierson, recommended the creation of a law department at State College. Frierson advised university president Leonard T. Baker that the new law program did not have to be equal to that operated by the university. "I believe, however, that if reasonably good facilities are offered there, the Courts will not be too keenly critical and would not (in view of the present development of the two races in this State) require exact equivalents in facilities furnished."[75]

In early 1939 Solomon Blatt introduced legislation in the South Carolina House of Representatives to create a legal program at South Carolina State. Blatt conceded, "We know of no other way to meet this than to establish a chair of law at the State Colored college." Blatt's measure easily passed in the house. But the state senate resisted demands for a separate law school because of the cost that it would entail. The senate devised alternative legislation—in keeping with the Gaines decision—to admit any applicant to the university's law school "regardless of race, color, creed, or sex." Did the state's senators seriously intend to admit *any* applicant regardless of race? Not quite. There was a huge loophole in the senate proposal. All applicants to the law school would be required to present a certificate signed by two members of the general assembly testifying to that applicant's "good moral character." Obviously no black applicant would ever secure such a certificate, and the law school would remain an all-white institution. The house, however, declined to accept the senate measure, and the attempt to create a law program at S.C. State in 1939 failed.[76]

In the meantime Charles Bailey waited—and waited. He received no reply after writing to the law school dean; to the new university president, J. Rion McKissick; and to the institution's board of trustees. Bailey's efforts to enlist the legal assistance of the NAACP were no more successful. In 1940 Bailey wrote NAACP special counsel Thurgood Marshall, who had replaced Charles H. Houston, to ask if his legal case against the university was still viable. Marshall insisted that it was, but he acknowledged that the NAACP was overwhelmed with criminal cases, segregation cases, and teacher salary equalization cases. With the passage of time, Bailey lost interest. He took a job with the U.S. Post Office in Columbia and gave up on his quest to become a lawyer.[77]

LEGISLATORS TAKE AN INTEREST IN S.C. STATE

There matters stood until World War II ended. Fully expecting African Americans to renew demands that they be admitted to the University of South Carolina, the general assembly seized the initiative and reinvigorated their defense of the racial status quo. The state house of representatives dispatched a delegation of ten legislators to the S.C. State campus on March 20, 1945, to evaluate the postwar needs of the college. In their report of slightly more than three pages, the lawmakers indicated that they were pleased with what they saw and who they met. President Whittaker's demeanor struck them as especially appropriate. "We were particularly impressed by the very apparent ability of the President and the equally apparent determination on his part to keep himself in the background with the idea that the Trustees should take the initiative and that he would be called when wanted."[78]

They visited an "efficiently managed shoe-making and repair shop," a tailoring class, a course in radio repair, and premedical students who were at work in a science class. They also toured the new Hillcrest Farm north of the campus. The level of maintenance and care that they saw on the campus genuinely surprised committee members. "Some of us are individually of the opinion that we have never seen public buildings of any description which appear to be better cared for or as highly regarded by the users as is the case with buildings of this Institution." They concluded with fulsome praise as well as an oblique confession that the needs of the state's black population had been badly neglected. "We cannot put in too strong language the impression of purposefulness that comes to a visitor observing the work of the faculty and of the students of this college. To fully appreciate the handicap and the background of many of these people requires personal observation."[79]

The committee recommended the appropriation of $250,000 for permanent improvements at the college. The most pressing needs were completion of the heating plant; barns and buildings to house animals and equipment at the farm; and dormitory space. Whittaker had informed the legislators that two hundred "perfectly qualified applicants" had been rejected for admission because of the lack of campus housing. The general assembly did not heed these recommendations. Instead legislation was introduced and passed to offer legal and medical education at the college. But no money was appropriated for a law school or a medical school for black South Carolinians.[80]

THE CALCOTT REPORT

The S.C. State board of trustees reacted to this legislative initiative by asking W. H. Calcott, the dean of the graduate school at the University of South Carolina (and a former professor of history) to evaluate the feasibility of providing graduate and professional education at S.C. State. Calcott visited the campus on June 7, 1945, and submitted his six-page report in October. He recommended the creation of a graduate program that would offer master's degrees to black public school teachers. There could be, Calcott suggested, programs in four areas: English, chemistry/biology, history/political science, and economics/sociology. The students who might enroll in these programs would be encouraged to take agriculture or home economics as a minor. Calcott stressed the need to expand the book and periodical collection in the library by spending $25,000 over a five-year period. The college should also hire at least "two men" with a Ph.D. to teach graduate courses. To provide graduate classes in science in "badly overcrowded" Hodge Hall would be an impossibility. Thus an addition to Hodge or an entirely new science facility was needed.

Although the legislature had already authorized the formation of a law school at the college, Calcott assumed that only a small number of students would enroll. Because it would require "a heavy initial outlay" in funds to establish a reasonably well equipped law library, Callcot indicated that the state of South Carolina would be better served by providing scholarships for the small number of aspiring black lawyers to attend law school out of state. Similarly he recommended that medical school students obtain out-of-state scholarships.[81]

THE PEABODY SURVEY

Almost simultaneously there was yet another assessment of higher education that prescribed the implementation of "a limited amount of graduate work at S.C. State." In 1945 the general assembly retained the Division of Surveys and Field Services at the George Peabody College for Teachers in Nashville to conduct a study of public colleges and universities in South Carolina to create a "an adequate, efficient and progressive system of coordinated and unified higher education for the state."[82]

The research staff from George Peabody College assembled a fourteen-member team of experts in higher education from other southern states, and they proceeded to compile a 428-page report that included a range of specific recommendations. In examining the resources, programs, and management of the state's six institutions of higher education, there was no consideration given to dismantling segregation among the colleges and universities in order to promote the development of an "efficient and progressive system."[83]

Rather than question the merits of operating separate collegiate institutions based on race, the survey team assigned S.C. State a monumental educational responsibility: "to upgrade the life of the great mass of Negroes who live in South Carolina." Thus the historically underfunded black college was saddled with the herculean task of improving the standard of living for 43 percent of the state's residents. In the thirty-seven-page chapter devoted to S.C. State, the survey team gave only passing attention to creating graduate and professional programs for black South Carolinians. For those who wanted to pursue advanced degrees, the state could provide scholarships at modest cost to study at institutions out of state. The main mission of S.C. State was to prepare highly qualified public school teachers, especially in agricultural and vocational subjects. Those teachers would serve as the vanguard that would improve the quality of life among black South Carolinians.[84]

"The major purpose of the College," according to the survey staff, "is to provide leadership training for the great number of Negroes who cultivate the soil of South Carolina and who are employed as mechanics and artisans in its various industries." To that end the Peabody report recommended that the state appropriate $880,000 for critical needs at the black college, which included two new dormitories, a home economics facility, a hospital, a farm shop, and an addition to Hodge Hall. The report also called on the state to set aside an additional $820,000 for future needs at the institution—a total of $1.7 million. This was an impressive and unprecedented sum of money in the history of the college. Yet it represented a mere 8 percent of the $22.5 million total that the survey team suggested that South Carolina spend on higher education for immediate and long-term needs in the postwar era. The five white institutions were entitled to 92 percent of the funds for the 57 percent of the population that they served.[85]

S.C. STATE'S FUTURE IN THE POSTWAR ERA

Although no one in a position of authority in the Palmetto State seems to have discussed it, or perhaps even considered it, South Carolina had reached a crossroads in higher education for African Americans as World War II ended. With its very limited financial resources, the state could significantly increase funding for undergraduate programs and facilities at S.C. State—as the legislative committee and the Peabody report each suggested. *Or* the state's political leaders could create separate and costly graduate and professional programs for black South Carolinians in order to fend off legal challenges initiated by the NAACP. But it could not do both. And, in reality, it was never a meaningful dilemma for most white South Carolinians. They would defend Jim Crow.

The maintenance of segregation was by far the more pressing problem in 1945 and 1946. For nearly a decade, supporters of white supremacy had been compelled to mobilize their defenses against the growing attacks on Jim Crow. The NAACP had won the lawsuits to equalize the salaries of public school teachers. In 1944 the U.S. Supreme Court declared that the all-white Democratic primary elections in Texas were unconstitutional in another legal victory for the NAACP. But in South Carolina, Democrats decided to circumvent that Supreme Court decision. Governor Olin D. Johnston and the general assembly repealed all state laws pertaining to primary elections. They believed they could thereby establish the Democratic Party as strictly a private organization that could legitimately prohibit Negro membership and voting in the party's elections.[86]

In the meantime a group of black men and women—most of them NAACP members—organized the Progressive Democratic Party (PDP) in 1944. The PDP challenged the admission of South Carolina's all-white delegation to the Democratic National Convention in Chicago that summer. The national party refused to seat the PDP, but the black Democrats led by John McCray and Osceola McKaine did cause considerable concern among the state's white Democrats. The PDP's presence and NAACP influence may also have been factors in President Franklin D. Roosevelt's decision not to choose powerful South Carolina Democrat James F. Byrnes as his vice presidential candidate. Roosevelt decided on Missouri senator Harry S. Truman as his running mate. Meanwhile McKaine, a Sumter native and World War I veteran, ran with PDP support against Olin Johnston in the U.S. Senate election in 1944. McKaine lost, but it was the first time a black man had run for statewide office in South Carolina since Reconstruction ended in 1877.[87]

Nor could most white South Carolinians have been comforted by the strike of mostly black and white women at the American Tobacco Company's cigar factory in Charleston. In October 1945 nine hundred black and white women walked out of the rigidly segregated facility after two black employees were fired. Organized by the United Cannery, Agricultural, Packing and Allied Workers of America, the strike stretched on for nearly six months. Complaints and grievances that involved pay and the filthy, degrading working conditions helped to generate union solidarity. Initially the union followed the customary practice of segregation and held separate meetings for black and white workers on separate nights. But it was not long before joint meetings became more practical, efficient, and less time consuming. Still many of the striking women could not hold out during the long and chilly winter into 1946, and they returned to work. When the strike finally ended in March, it was less than a complete victory for the union and workers. Yet they did get a pay raise of eight cents an hour.[88]

Osceola McKaine was astonished at this demonstration of racial and labor unity in one of the Old South's leading cities. "Deep in the grass roots democracy is beginning to work effectively in the South. For the first time in 80 years, the laboring classes of both races" were merging "to discuss their problems—as equals." But for numbers of white South Carolinians this imperfect example of racial cooperation was yet another sign that Jim Crow's security was threatened.[89]

No one had a better grasp of the doubts and hopes of rural black people than Marian Paul, the head of the home demonstration program. In 1946 Paul explained how these mostly impoverished people looked to the future with very mixed expectations. "There are three distinc[t] attitudes or schools of thought found among the rural Negroes of South Carolina. First, there are those, who through years of exploitation, toil, poverty and ignorance, have become discouraged and self satisfied and are resigned to their plight. Second, there are those who have served in the armed forces of our country or have had their loved ones fighting for democracy. Now they are frustrated by intolerances, injustices and intimidations, and we find hatred and rebellion within their minds. Third, there are those who are ambitious, tenacious, and determined, yet are thwarted by poor and inadequate educational facilities and the denial of rights of full citizenship. These three groups, comprising fifty per-cent of the population of South Carolina, if given opportunities for proper educational advantages, suitable housing conditions, economical security, and full participation as citizens, could pull South Carolina out of its undesirable and deplorable position as the State at the bottom of all States of the United States in illiteracy, housing and health."[90]

On the campus President Whittaker worried in 1946 about the impact that segregation in the small community of Orangeburg might have on a new administrator, a forty-three-year-old native of Connecticut who had earned a doctorate in education from the Teachers College of Columbia University. Whittaker was contemplating the appointment of Ethna B. Winston as the dean of women, and he sought the advice of his friend and colleague Benjamin E. Mays, the president of Morehouse College. Whittaker wondered if Winston "will be able to fit into the life, proscribed as it is, in a small Southern town. In other words, can she take 'jim-crow' as we experience it in Orangeburg?" Mays knew Winston because she had been the dean of women at Atlanta's Clark College, and Mays was confident that she had adjusted to Jim Crow. "Doctor Winston will fit in very well in Orangeburg. You know Atlanta has more nasty jim crow and discrimination than Orangeburg. I do not think jim crow will disturb her." He added that Winston had been able to accept the recent election of rabid segregationist Eugene Talmadge as Georgia governor. "I think she has taken Talmadge's victory calmer than I. I doubt if she thinks much about it." Reassured by Mays, Whittaker hired Winston. She and history professor Lewis McMillan were the first two people with doctorates employed full time by the college.[91]

Most white South Carolinians were alarmed at even the slightest hints of black dissatisfaction with their subordinate status in society. Some white people struck back in fury at unwelcome signs of racial change. Black U.S. Army sergeant Isaac Woodard was beaten and permanently blinded by Batesburg police chief Lynwood L. Shull in February 1946. Woodward had spent four years in the U.S. Army including fifteen months in the South Pacific. He was beaten on the day he had been discharged at Fort Gordon in Augusta, Georgia. While still in uniform and traveling by bus to his home in Winnsboro, South Carolina, Woodard got into an argument with the bus driver who summoned the police. Shull subsequently described Woodard as "very abusive." Federal authorities later brought charges against Shull, and he was tried in federal court in November. It took an all-white and all-male jury thirty minutes to acquit the law enforcement officer.[92]

JOHN WRIGHTEN AND HIS LEGAL CASE

While Woodard was recovering from his injuries in a veteran's hospital, a black veteran from Charleston was preparing his application for admission to the law school at the University of South Carolina. It certainly should have come as no surprise to white political and educational leaders in South Carolina when John H. Wrighten, a twenty-four-year-old senior at S.C. State College, who had served with the Army Air Corps, applied to the all-white law school. Wrighten had been born on Edisto Island and had graduated from Avery Institute in Charleston. University authorities swiftly rejected his application because of his race.[93]

With the support of the South Carolina Conference of the NAACP, Wrighten went to court. The NAACP Legal Defense Fund dispatched Thurgood Marshall and Robert Carter to Columbia, where local black attorneys Harold R. Boulware, Esau Parker, and W. F. Robinson assisted them. This legal team filed a civil action in federal district court, *Wrighten v. Board of Trustees of the University of South Carolina, et al.* They asked the court to order Wrighten's admission to the law school and for $20,000 in compensatory damages.[94]

The legal case did not hinge on the issue of segregation because the state did not provide a separate law school for black residents. Instead Wrighten's case was based on the state's refusal to admit him to its sole law school. This constituted, NAACP attorneys would argue, a violation of the equal protection clause of the Fourteenth Amendment to the U.S. Constitution. The state offered its white residents the opportunity to attend law school while denying black South Carolinians the same opportunity.[95]

With Wrighten's suit pending, the general assembly rushed to appropriate $60,000 to establish a graduate program and a law school at South Carolina State for the 1947–48 academic year. Federal district judge J. Waties Waring then heard Wrighten's case in Columbia on June 5–6, 1947. The State of South Carolina's legal position was that it was fully prepared to provide legal training to John Wrighten and other black people at the yet-to-be established law school at S.C. State. South Carolina and its lead attorney, David Robinson, based their argument on the precedent established nearly a decade earlier in the Gaines case, when Missouri created a separate law school for its black residents.[96]

College president Miller F. Whittaker was called to testify for the State of South Carolina. Because he was a state official—its highest-ranking black state leader—Whittaker was expected to support the state's legal claim that Wrighten should be denied admission to the university's law school inasmuch as the aspiring lawyer would be afforded the opportunity to gain his legal education in Orangeburg. That placed the fifty-four-year-old president in the unpleasant predicament of opposing Marshall and the NAACP, and he complained privately, "They are putting me in the middle between the plaintiff and the defendants in this Law School business."[97]

In response to a sharp series of questions posed by Thurgood Marshall, Whittaker readily conceded that no legal education was currently available in South Carolina for its black citizens. He further testified that no funds had been allocated for a law school at S.C. State in 1945–46 or 1946–47, and that the college had hired no law professors and had no law library. Marshall asked Whittaker if adequate classroom, library, and office space was currently available for a law school. Whittaker answered affirmatively. "They could be made available, yes."

Marshall then drove to the heart of the NAACP's case and asked Whittaker if in view of "the fact that you don't have faculty yet, nor a dean, nor a librarian, do you, in your own mind believe you can set up a law school by September that would be the full and complete equal of the law school at the University of South Carolina?" Whittaker firmly replied, "No, I don't think so."[98]

Judge J. Waties Waring announced his decision in the Wrighten case on the same July day in 1947 that he rejected the South Carolina Democratic Party's attempt to maintain all-white primary elections. The outcome of that case, *Elmore v. Rice,* attracted far more attention than Wrighten's case because it would enable the state's black voters to participate in primary elections that had previously been closed to them.[99]

Although Waring has a well-deserved reputation as a progressive southern federal judge, he essentially agreed with white state leaders in his ruling in the Wrighten case. Despite the obvious fact that South Carolina State College had no law school, no law library, and no law professors, Waring—citing the Gaines case as precedent—decided to give the Orangeburg school and the state until September to establish such a facility. He declared, "I feel that due faith and deference must be given to the assurances that the law school will be in active operation, equipped, fitted and staffed, and ready for the giving of instruction on a complete parity with the University Law School." Waring warned, however, that if a law school was not established for black South Carolinians that was substantially equal to the university's law school, then Wrighten would be admitted to the all-white law school or legal education would be abolished in South Carolina for black and white residents.[100]

THE NEW LAW SCHOOL

Improbable as it may seem, within two months of Waring's decision, S.C. State did indeed have a law school. But it was hardly "on a complete parity" with the University of South Carolina's law school as Waring had demanded. Following a long interview with Whittaker and local board members Wallace C. Bethea and Adam H. Moss, Benner C. Turner was hired as the dean of the new law school at a salary of $5,000. Turner was a law professor at the all-black North Carolina College of Law in Durham, North Carolina. He possessed superb academic and legal credentials. A native of Columbus, Georgia, he was a graduate of Phillips Andover Academy, and he had an undergraduate as well as a law degree from Harvard University. He had been a lawyer with Raymond Pace Alexander in Philadelphia, one of the nation's foremost black law firms. Most important to white leadership, Turner was not likely to disrupt the racial status quo. College board of trustees chairman Charles F. Brooks described Turner as "an outstanding and highly qualified man." He added, "We want nothing less than a man of ability, character, and with a correct understanding of the American way of life—especially here in South Carolina."[101]

Whittaker and Turner then proceeded to hire two additional law professors, Leo Kerford and the only black woman lawyer in the state—Cassandra Maxwell—who also initially served as law librarian. One classroom, bookshelves, and student desks were set aside in Wilkinson Hall, which was the college library. But Wilkinson Hall also housed the president's office, the business manager, and the campus bookstore. Office space for the law school dean and the two faculty members was made available across the street in Manning Hall, a women's dormitory. Hundreds of law books were hastily acquired. Five full-time and four part-time students enrolled. There were eight men and one woman taking five law courses when classes began in September 1947, eight weeks after Waring delivered his decision.[102]

Thurgood Marshall regarded the outcome in the Wrighten case and the creation of the new law school a significant defeat. He considered the establishment of the all-black law school as nothing more than a capitulation to segregation. Furthermore Marshall grew increasingly impatient with Wrighten. Marshall told him more than once not to enroll in the S.C. State law school: "I had advised you not to go to the Jim Crow law school which has been set up in one room in the Administration Building in Orangeburg with practically no library and three teachers without any previous law school teaching experience."[103]

Marshall subsequently decided not to appeal the Wrighten case because he did not believe that he could depend on John Wrighten as a client. Marshall informed Columbia attorney Harold Boulware in a "confidential" letter to "withdraw without prejudice, the last motion we filed in this case and to leave it as it is." Marshall explained: "The main reason for this is that I think all of us are in agreement that Wrighten has demonstrated that he is not the type of reliable plaintiff necessary to proceed further in this type case."[104]

Marshall was not the only black leader who opposed the state's determination to create a law school and graduate program at S.C. State. As disgusted as they were with white political leadership, there were black Carolinians who were even more furious with those black people who supported and enrolled in the separate "Jim Crow" programs. Modjeska Simkins was a Columbia civil rights advocate who supported the Progressive Democratic Party and was active in the NAACP. She harshly criticized S.C. State College leaders and aspiring graduate students in a newspaper column she wrote in 1947 for the Norfolk *Journal and Guide.*

"The disrespect and scorn which thousands of Negroes in the Palmetto State hold for most of the legislators can be surpassed only by the utter contempt many of the same persons hold for the administrative officials of the so-called *"Graduate School"* at State A. and M. College at Orangeburg. Nothing in recent weeks has so nauseated and infuriated them as the expensive newspaper ads highlighting the "department" which this summer is offering "graduate" study in education, English, and the social and natural sciences. As long as administrative officials at the college consort with legislative and education department officials in hoodwinking the few shortsighted Negroes who will fall victim to this asinine scheme, they are being bought for a cheap and inglorious price. The only persons who could become even more pronounced objects of derision would be the persons who, knowing the score, deliberately walk into these chump courses."[105]

To Thurgood Marshall's dismay, John Wrighten did enroll in the new law school in 1949 and graduated in 1952. But in fairness to Wrighten, he had experienced considerable financial distress largely as a result of his participation in the case, and he did want to become a lawyer. Furthermore there were black South Carolinians who, although they adamantly opposed segregation of the races, did welcome the opportunity to operate and control a law school. Black people, so often entirely excluded from

The law school at South Carolina State opened in 1947 and closed in 1966. This photo of faculty and students is from 1948 or 1949. Seated left to right: Cassandra E. Maxwell, associate professor and law librarian; Benner C. Turner, professor and dean; Eloise Vaughn, administrative assistant; and Leo Kerford, professor. Standing left to right are students: Alfred Pearson, three unidentified individuals, Willie Smith, Matthew Perry, and unidentified student, and Oliver C. Dawson. (Two of the unidentified students are Julius Williams and Albert Kennedy. They were the first two graduates of the law school. The other two unidentified students are Raymond White and A. W. Brown.) Courtesy of the Historical Collection, South Carolina State University

most American institutions and their management, believed that the creation of a black law school—though not necessarily the equal of a long-established white law school—would furnish opportunities for black law professors and law students that would not otherwise exist.

Marshall did not care much for Wrighten, but the NAACP attorney was captivated and won over by President Miller F. Whittaker and his courtroom remarks in the case. In a letter to Frank A. DeCosta, who was the acting head of the graduate program at S.C. State, Marshall praised Whittaker. "I hope that you will also tell your President that we were more than impressed with his frank testimony on the witness stand, which testimony certainly required courage. You know, at times you have to make up your mind as to whether you are going to be a man or a mouse, and more and more, we are getting tremendous respect for certain educators in the South."[106]

It is, therefore, no small paradox that white leadership was equally enthralled with Whittaker's performance in the law school case. With the solid support of the board of trustees, legislators increased Whittaker's annual salary from $4,500 to $6,000. At the time of Whittaker's increase in salary, the presidents of the other state colleges and universities were each earning $7,500. Still how many African American leaders simultaneously pleased both black and white leaders for actions they took and words they spoke on the subject of racial segregation during the emerging civil rights movement?[107]

In 1948 the general assembly appropriated $200,000 to erect a law school building that would also house the graduate program. Members of the board of trustees conceded that undergraduate programs and facilities—already under severe strain because of burgeoning post war enrollments—would have to be sacrificed to develop the new graduate and law programs. "While the college is overcrowded in all departments and also needs several dormitories, the Board feels that we must immediately have a Law and Graduate building." The board solicited bids from contractors and construction of the new law building began in early 1949.[108]

OUT-OF-STATE SCHOLARSHIPS

To avoid admitting black men and women to professional programs in medicine, pharmacy, dentistry, and veterinary science, the State of South Carolina allocated money that furnished scholarships for black students to attend out-of-state institutions. The Regional Education Council coordinated the programs among southern states that provided black students with these scholarships. In 1948 Governor Thurmond asked President Whittaker to serve as a consultant on the Regional Education Council, and he accepted the appointment. Whittaker and his successor, Benner C. Turner, were given almost complete latitude in determining which black people would be awarded the scholarships. In this instance the effort to maintain segregation created a patronage system among black people. In 1946–47, fifteen students received $6,000 to attend school outside of South Carolina. By 1957–58, there were 239 students who were awarded $55,000 in scholarships so that they could go to an out-of-state institution.[109]

THE G.I. BILL OF RIGHTS

Creation of the law school and the graduate program at S.C. State and the implementation of the out-of-state scholarship program did sustain segregation in higher education. But doing so diverted funds that were desperately needed for undergraduate education after World War II. The G.I. Bill of Rights brought a huge surge in enrollments in the latter half of the 1940s. The college lacked dormitories, classrooms, laboratories, and library space and resources. There were not enough faculty members, and those who were on the teaching staff were not adequately compensated. Hundreds of young people including many military veterans were rejected for admission because there was nowhere to house or to teach them. This dramatic increase in enrollment spurred by the G.I. Bill was not unique to S.C. State. But because the college was the only state-supported four-year institution for black South Carolinians, those prospective students had few alternatives for their education if they were turned away from S.C. State.

The G.I. Bill of Rights—the Servicemen's Readjustment Act of 1944—provided educational benefits to a generation of young men and a smaller number of women who had served in the armed forces during World War II. The measure provided funds for tuition, housing, and books for those veterans who enrolled in a college or university. But many black veterans who wanted to attend S.C. State could not enroll. Approximately 55 percent of black veterans who sought a college education across the South were rejected by historically black institutions because of lack of space. Enrollments of veterans and nonveteran students at the black colleges and universities mushroomed from twenty-nine thousand in 1940 to 73,174 in 1947. But by 1947 an estimated twenty thousand black veterans had not been accepted by those colleges and universities.[110]

Many of those veterans who came to S.C. State did not register for degree programs. They opted to take short courses in assorted trades and skills. Those courses were open only to veterans at a cost of $125 per semester. The courses included auto mechanics, electricity, masonry, plumbing, tailoring, interior decorating, and landscape gardening. It is likely that many of the veterans who took the short courses were not high school graduates and thus were not eligible to enroll in the undergraduate program.[111]

THE CROWDED CAMPUS

Enrollment nearly doubled at S.C. State between 1941 and 1947. In 1945–46, 250 veterans were attending the college, and there was a waiting list of nearly five hundred veterans for 1946–47. An additional 350 applicants who were not veterans were also turned away. President Whittaker observed that the college could easily enroll two thousand students if it had the facilities to house and teach them. In 1946–47 five hundred veterans did enroll, but another five hundred had been turned away. Whittaker pointed out what had become painfully obvious to those familiar with the institution's postwar predicament. "The College is definitely unable to care for all students who apply. At present, rooms that should be used for undergraduate students are being used for law and graduate work, since no additional space has been allowed for these branches."[112]

The four campus dormitories—Lowman, Bradham, Manning, and Miller—were bursting with residents. There were 354 women in three dorms and 186 men in Lowman. Miller Hall had been built as a men's residence hall, but it had been converted to a woman's dormitory during the war and it would remain so for another half century. Approximately 40 percent of the students lived off campus in and around Orangeburg. Parents as well as college administrators worried about the housing needs of the women students. There was a persistent desire to have them reside on campus where they could be more carefully supervised. President Whittaker acknowledged that many parents of women would prefer that their daughters enroll at another institution if dormitory space was not available at State College.[113]

Bradham Hall was symptomatic of the postwar dormitory problems. It housed 195 women. The thirty-year-old building had five bathrooms, one shower, four bathtubs, seven toilets, eleven sinks, and one drinking fountain. Because of the absence of adequate housing for members of the faculty, single members of the teaching staff were

Table 24. Post–World War II Enrollments

	1945–46	1946–47	1947–48	1948–49	1949–50
Undergraduate					
Men	324	528	636	553	594
Women	678	557	485	450	440
Total	1,002	1,085	1,121	1,003	1,034
Veterans' Short Courses					
Men	123	192	221	193	94
Women	0	0	3	1	1
Total	123	192	224	194	95
Graduate Studies					
Men	0	0	31	34	65
Women	0	0	11	42	66
Total	0	0	42	76	131
Law School					
Men	0	0	7	11	16
Women	0	0	1	0	0
Total	0	0	8	11	16

Sources: Annual reports, 1945–46, 21; 1946–47, 17; 1947–48, 17; 1948–49, 18; 1949–50, 32. These enrollment figures do not include summer school students, elementary school students enrolled at Felton Training School, or students enrolled in study centers off campus. When President Miller F. Whittaker discussed enrollments, he invariably included all students enrolled at any time during the school year on and off campus.

assigned rooms in the men's and women's dormitories reducing the already limited space available for students. In 1949 fifteen male faculty members lived in Lowman Hall, and twenty-four female faculty members resided in the women's dormitories. This elicited a circumspect warning because such a situation might "tend to bring about close associations between faculty members and students other than on a professional basis."[114]

When the war ended, there was almost no housing available on campus for the flood of arriving veterans. As their numbers swelled, they were forced to live on cots placed on the basketball floor in Dukes Gym. They took up residence in private homes, boarding houses, "and any place they could find" until military surplus Quonset huts arrived in early 1947. The huts were placed adjacent to the campus in an alternately muddy and dusty area that came to be known as "Vetville." It housed three hundred veterans at a cost of $8 per resident per month. There were also a limited number of one- and two-bedroom apartments for married veterans that rented for $14 a month.[115]

Table 25. Proposed Spending for Higher Education, 1947

Institution	Amount
University of South Carolina	$1,450,000
Citadel	$600,000
Clemson A&M College	$1,300,000
Winthrop College	$700,000
Medical College of S.C.	$3,100,000
S.C. State College	$350,000

Source: File—State of South Carolina, 1947, Miller F. Whittaker papers, HCSCSU.

STATE FUNDING

The money to assist the college with its rapidly rising enrollments was simply not forthcoming. With little success Whittaker, the board of trustees, and legislators from Orangeburg urged members of the general assembly to increase funding for the black college. In the spring of 1947, just weeks before Judge J. Waties Waring delivered his decision in the law school case, the legislature took up a bill to increase funding for the state's colleges and universities. Lawmakers were responding in part to the 1945 Peabody Report, which called for substantially expanded financial support for higher education in South Carolina.

But when President Whittaker saw the funds projected for each institution, he was not pleased, and he complained to legislators. "This allows State A and M College only 4.6% of the amount set up for higher education. I am sure you will agree that this is a very small proportion of funds to serve all the Negro people of the State." Whittaker dispatched letters to local legislators asking them to try to increase the amount allotted to S.C. State to at least $750,000.[116]

The speaker of the South Carolina house, Solomon Blatt, offered Whittaker an unhelpful response. "I think you should get more than $350,000. I am afraid if we try in the present bill to get the increase the bill will be killed. You notice the fight in the senate. Will look into this when I get back to Columbia." But the college did not get the additional funds for the 1947–48 fiscal year.[117]

There was another attempt to get an increase in funding a few weeks later and shortly after Judge Waring ruled that the state could establish a law school at S.C. State. Julian S. Wolfe, an Orangeburg attorney who had replaced Archie Dukes on the board of trustees in 1942, appealed to Columbia attorney David Robinson for assistance in securing more money for the college for the following fiscal year. Robinson was the lead attorney who defended the University of South Carolina and the State of South Carolina in John Wrighten's lawsuit. Wolfe told Robinson that "many of us down here [in Orangeburg] feel that the Legislature certainly treated the State Colored College most unfairly in the proposed program."[118]

Table 26. Student Fees per Academic Year

	1941–42	1948–49
Tuition	$60.00	$80.00
Laboratory fees	$10.00	$10.00
Books	$6.00 to $12.00	$20.00
Board @ 8.5 months	$102.00	$187.00
Activity		$17.50
Room	$34.00	
Key deposit		$.50
Total	$178.00–$184.00	$349.50

Sources: *State Agricultural and Mechanical College Bulletin,* Announcements 1941–42, 21; *Agricultural and Mechanical College Bulletin;* Announcements, 1948–49, 23.

Hugo Sims, an Orangeburg attorney and member of the South Carolina House of Representatives, also tried and failed to persuade influential political leaders to increase appropriations for the college. Sims's twin brother, Henry, had been a state senator until he resigned in 1944 to become the president of Winthrop College, the state-supported white women's institution in Rock Hill. The Sims brothers owned and published the *Orangeburg Times and Democrat* and owned radio station WTND. Hugo Sims apologized to Whittaker in early 1948. "I am extremely sorry that my efforts were not successful in getting the $1,055,000 appropriation for State College." He pointed out that he had spoken in favor of the appropriation and that five other legislators also made remarks on the house floor supporting the additional funds. Sims noted that thirty-five of the eighty-six lawmakers supported him. But it was not enough.[119]

The lack of adequate financial support at a time of relative prosperity crippled the college and denied hundreds of black South Carolinians the opportunity to further their education. It is not that funding failed to increase in the late 1940s. Appropriations did grow. But sufficient funds were not made available for faculty salaries, undergraduate classrooms, laboratories, and dormitories. Students themselves paid an increasing portion of the institution's budget as their fees nearly doubled in less than a decade.

ROTC

In 1947 the War Department finally agreed to establish a Reserve Officers Training Corps (ROTC) at South Carolina State thus fulfilling a long-standing goal of Miller F. Whittaker. Although his father had been court-martialed and then dismissed as a cadet at the U.S. Military Academy in 1881, Whittaker was an enthusiastic supporter of the military. He had served during World War I as a first lieutenant with the all-black

371st Regiment in France, and he was determined that the college would have a ROTC program.

From the time he assumed the presidency in 1932, Whittaker made periodic and then annual requests beginning in 1937 to the War Department asking that the U.S. Army provide military training in keeping with the college's mission under the 1862 Morrill Land-Grant Act. Whittaker repeatedly pointed out that the nineteenth-century legislation required land-grant institutions to offer courses in agricultural and mechanical subjects as well as military training. Each year the War Department replied evasively or not at all. In 1937 the board of trustees joined the effort after forming a committee chaired by Adam Moss to determine "the advisability of placing a R.O.T.C. unit at the college." Whittaker later mentioned that the college "just missed" getting the program established in 1940.[120]

After the United States entered World War II in 1941, requests for ROTC intensified and enjoyed the support of some of the state's key political leaders. Whittaker specifically credited former governor and U.S. senator Burnet Maybank for intervention on behalf of the college. During World War I, Southern University in Baton Rouge and Howard University in Washington, D.C., had ROTC programs, but they had ceased by the 1930s. In 1941 Tuskegee became the first of the black colleges to have an ROTC program.[121]

South Carolina State, Prairie View A&M, and Southern University were then among the first of the dozen black schools to gain ROTC units following the Second World War. Freshmen and sophomore men were required to enroll in ROTC at S.C. State. Veterans with one or more years of military service were exempt although some joined the program voluntarily. Lieutenant Colonel James H. Robinson was the first professor of military science. He was assisted by two other officers and four noncommissioned officers. In 1947–48 there were 181 first-year students, twenty-eight first-year advanced students, and thirty-nine second-year men in ROTC. The sixty-seven students in the second year and the advanced first year were veterans. The War Department—soon to become the Department of Defense—furnished the officers as well as the uniforms and equipment for the program.[122]

Whittaker and other black leaders regarded ROTC as an opportunity for young black men to enter a profession at a time when many careers and jobs in private enterprise remained closed to African Americans. Whittaker also perceived a more immediate benefit to the college. Participation in ROTC would bring some regimentation and order to young men whose lives often lacked purpose and focus. "I am sure," Whittaker observed, "this training will improve morale, physique, discipline and personality of our male students."[123]

Fred Dowdy Jr. and Rufus Streeter were the first two ROTC students to receive commissions as second lieutenants at commencement in 1948. Shortly thereafter four other cadets earned their commissions and entered the U.S. Army—Spencer Bracey, William Nelson, Richard Williams, and George Wright. Lieutenant General Alvin C. Gilliem Jr., commandant of the Third Army at Fort McPherson, Georgia, was one of the speakers at commencement in 1949, when five more cadets received commissions in

The first South Carolina State students to earn commissions in the U.S. Army through the ROTC program in 1949 were, left to right: Richard A. Williams, William J. Nelson, Spencer Bracey, Fred Dowdy, and George Wright. Courtesy of the Historical Collection, South Carolina State University

the Regular Army and one cadet was commissioned in the Reserves. By 1950 the ROTC program sponsored a military ball, had a twenty-eight-piece band, and supported a rifle team that won nine of fourteen matches.[124]

THE FEDERAL GOVERNMENT AND CIVIL RIGHTS

The nearly simultaneous establishment of the law school, the graduate program, and ROTC came at a time when the federal government began to challenge Jim Crow. On July 26, 1948—one year after ROTC came to the S.C. State campus—President Harry S. Truman ordered the desegregation of U.S. military forces. Executive Order 9981 was in part a response to a threat by A. Phillip Randolph to organize opposition to a new peacetime draft law that was scheduled to take effect on August 16, 1948. Randolph, the president of the Brotherhood of Sleeping Car Porters, was concerned that black men would once again be compelled to serve in a segregated military.

Truman was also responding to the recommendation of the Committee on Civil Rights, which he had appointed in late 1946. That committee's report, "To Secure These Rights," was issued in October 1947 just as the first law school classes were convening at S.C. State. The report charged that America had failed to live up to its professed ideals as a democratic nation. The committee recommended the enactment of a federal antilynching statute, the abolition of the poll tax, stronger enforcement of fair employment practices, and an end to segregation in the U.S. armed forces. "To Secure These Rights" also condemned racial segregation, particularly in Washington, D.C.[125]

Truman, who was eager to win the presidential election in 1948, was sensitive to the shifting political winds. He would need black votes, especially in northern states, if he hoped to retain the White House. Truman was also genuinely outraged by the treatment of African American veterans and incensed at the 1946 beating of Isaac Woodard. After an invitation from the NAACP and its executive director, Walter White, Truman agreed to speak at a rally sponsored by the organization at the Lincoln Memorial on June 29, 1947. Before a crowd of ten thousand and in an address broadcast nationwide by radio, Truman called for the federal government to ensure equal rights and equal opportunities for all citizens. "The extension of civil rights today means, not protection of the people against the government, but protection of the people by the government. We must make the Federal Government a friendly, vigilant defender of the rights and equalities of all Americans. And again I mean all Americans."[126]

The president had already met with black leaders and educators. Truman greeted the presidents of the black land-grant colleges, including Miller F. Whittaker, at the White House on October 22, 1946. They were in the nation's capital for their annual meeting. The fifteen-minute gathering, which was little more than an opportunity for shaking hands and a photograph, was a symbolic gesture. But symbols are important in politics. During the 1948 presidential campaign, Truman visited black neighborhoods in Philadelphia, and he spoke a few days before the election at a rally in Harlem.[127]

With pundits and pollsters predicting his defeat, Truman won the election over his three challengers, the Republican Thomas Dewey, the Progressive candidate Henry Wallace, and the States' Rights or Dixiecrat candidate Strom Thurmond. Black voters were critical to the election outcome. Truman probably would not have carried California, Illinois, and Ohio without the black vote.[128]

Thurmond and the Dixiecrats carried four southern states: South Carolina, Alabama, Mississippi, and Louisiana. But they failed to deny Truman a majority in the Electoral College. A veteran of World War II, Strom Thurmond had been elected governor of South Carolina in 1946, and he had a unique interest in S.C. State. As the state's chief executive, he served as the ex officio chairman of the board of trustees of the institution. Strom Thurmond's daughter was also a student at the black college.

ESSIE MAE WASHINGTON

Essie Mae Washington was born in 1925 in Edgefield to sixteen-year-old Carrie Butler, who worked as a domestic in the Thurmond family household. James Strom Thurmond was an ambitious twenty-three-year old graduate of Clemson A&M College whose political career would eventually span nearly a half century of service in the U.S. Senate. Essie Mae Washington was raised by an aunt and uncle—Mary Washington and

John Henry Washington—in Coatesville, Pennsylvania, a gritty industrial town about thirty miles west of Philadelphia. She attended the local high school during World War II, where the black and white students were educated together, but rarely mingled socially, and never dated.[129]

With her father's financial support, Essie Mae Washington enrolled at S.C. State in 1946, where she found the campus crowded with veterans. She also found students well behaved but largely detached from racial realities including the highly publicized lynching of twenty-five-year-old Willie Earle in Greenville in February 1947. "The students didn't seem interested in changing the world," she wrote nearly sixty years later, "only in *improving their* private worlds. The main focus was on career and marriage."[130]

Her thoughts too turned to romance. She was charmed by a veteran named Matthew J. Perry Jr., who had returned to college in 1946 after he had been drafted in 1943 for military service in World War II. But she fell in love with twenty-eight-year-old Julius Williams. He was a native of Savannah and had served in the U.S. Marine Corps in the South Pacific before enrolling in the new law school in 1947. The couple married secretly in 1948, and she dropped out of college in 1949 after she became pregnant. The following year Julius Williams and Arthur Kennedy were the first two students to earn law degrees at S.C. State. Perry graduated in 1951 with the law school's second class.[131]

Governor Strom Thurmond visited the campus frequently during his daughter's days as a student. She believed that he was sincerely interested in her, her education, and her mother. They would usually meet in President Whittaker's office or an adjacent room in Wilkinson Hall. In Thurmond's first visit during his fall campaign for governor in 1946, he informed her that he was committed to improving S.C. State. "I've got big plans for this school. I'm going to do all I can for it." It was during his administration that the graduate program and the law school were established. But the governor and the legislature were unwilling to do much else of substance for the college.[132]

Essie Mae Washington Williams insisted that Thurmond demonstrated genuine affection for her and her mother, Carrie. But during his presidential campaign in 1948 he became identified as an implacable foe of civil rights and an arch defender of segregation. When Thurmond and his daughter met on campus a month after his defeat and Truman's victory, she asked her father "how he could have said all of those terrible things" about black people? "What things?" he blithely responded. She said, "All this stuff you said about keeping us out of your homes, your churches, your swimming pools." "Essie Mae," Thurmond sternly replied, "there is no man in this country who cares more about the Negro than I do. I think you know that."[133]

She asked him to explain then why Negroes could not dine at the lunch counter at Woolworth's. He answered, "Why would you want to? The food's no good." Exasperated she told him that she and others simply wanted the choice of where to get a meal or snack. She added that many black people were "hurt by what you said" during the campaign. Thurmond answered that much of it was inflated campaign rhetoric and that he strongly supported the advancement of the Negro—as long as it was within the system of segregation. The meeting ended coolly as Essie Mae Washington Williams rejected a hug from her father.[134]

THE POSTWAR CAMPUS

When Essie Mae Washington arrived on the campus in September 1946, she was struck by the earnestness and decorum among the students. There were few signs of lightheartedness or antics so typical of many college students. "Everyone was so serious, so dignified, so proper. . . . They all seemed much more grown-up, like business people more than students. No one was throwing balls or clowning around or having any fun." She assumed that the almost grim level of maturity was due in part to the influx of hundreds of older male students like veterans Matthew Perry and Julius Williams.[135]

Amazingly college administrators attempted to maintain prewar codes of student conduct among postwar students. "The discipline," Essie Mae Washington observed, "seemed more suited to West Point or Annapolis than a regular college." Students, especially women, remained mostly confined to the campus. They could leave Monday, Wednesday, and Friday afternoons but were required to return by 5 P.M. On Tuesdays and Thursdays they were allowed to attend motion picture theaters. No women—including cheerleaders—were permitted to leave campus to attend away football games.[136]

Parties and dances were restricted to the campus. And those ever-so-serious students that Washington referred to were sometimes not so serious. President Whittaker had to inform Mr. and Mrs. Theo Barnes that their daughter had been consuming alcohol at a college dance. "Your daughter was in possession of a bottle of liquor and dropped the same in the gymnasium before a large crowd of students and faculty. She embarrassed everybody concerned." Fortunately for Miss Barnes, she was not expelled or even suspended, but merely confined to the campus and not permitted to go home during the remainder of the semester. But Catherine Franklin was expelled the following year after she was found intoxicated in her dormitory room. She was also cited for poor scholarship and uncooperative behavior.[137]

On the other hand, six veterans who were gambling in a men's restroom in the mechanical industries building were in effect expelled without the benefit of due process. They were invited to withdraw from the institution in order to maintain their benefits under the G.I. Bill. They were allegedly playing blackjack. To terminate six veterans for an innocuous round of gambling—something they no doubt had engaged in frequently in the military—seems excessive in the extreme. Incensed at the treatment of their fellow veterans, a group of them including M. Maceo Nance Jr., Matthew Perry Jr., and Ramsey Weston joined in a protest march through the campus. But it was to no avail. College authorities could point to a pledge that incoming students were required to sign. It gave administrators wide latitude over discipline, and they did not hesitate to punish or expel a student for almost any conceivable reason. The pledge stipulated: "I hereby agree that so long as I shall remain a student of the College, I will endeavor to comply cheerfully with all its regulations and customs in its efforts to maintain a high standard of honor among the students and to further the interests of the College. If I do not live up to this pledge I agree that it is not right for me to remain [a] student at State A&M College."[138]

Even in the face of pressure from a powerful white politician, President Whittaker refused to compromise on student discipline and punishment. Julius Augustus was accused in 1946 of fighting and cutting another student—Arthur Seabrook. Augustus allegedly initiated the fight and was expelled. Seabrook was suspended for the remainder of the semester. Solomon Blatt, the influential speaker of the South Carolina House of Representatives, appealed by telephone to Whittaker to readmit Augustus. Whittaker replied by mail and explained that while he had the authority to overrule the Student Discipline Committee in its decision to dismiss Augustus, he would not do so. Violence among students could not be tolerated, the president advised Blatt. However, Whittaker diplomatically appealed for the continued support of the speaker in spite of his unwillingness to grant the request. "We have appreciated your support in the past, and would like to grant you this favor, but we are afraid it would handicap us in administering discipline in the future."[139]

THE SOUTHERN NEGRO YOUTH CONGRESS

Essie Mae Washington may have overestimated the lack of political consciousness on the campus. Some students and faculty were determined to pursue racial advancement in postwar America, and they found a college president ready to support them in their quest. Quiet and unassuming, Whittaker was hardly the sort of black leader who would be expected to take a strong public stand with those who openly condemned Jim Crow and white supremacy. But when the Southern Youth Legislature of the Southern Negro Youth Congress met in Columbia's Township Auditorium in October 1946, Whittaker not only permitted publicity for the gathering to circulate on the S.C. State campus; he personally sold tickets to the meeting. Founded in Richmond in 1937, the SNYC was a radical but short-lived organization that advocated dramatic changes in racial and class arrangements in the South as the U.S. emerged from World War II.[140]

With workshops and panel discussions held at Allen University and Benedict College, participants denounced segregation, called for a stronger Federal Employment Practices Commission (FEPC), demanded an end to police brutality, and called for the abolition of the poll tax and the restoration of full voting rights. There were discussions of the plight of black working women and verbal attacks on the Ku Klux Klan. Appeals for cooperation among black and white working people were heard again and again. There were pleas for southern white youth to join in the movement for racial progress.[141]

The meeting attracted more than 861 delegates and featured luminaries from the political left including W. E. B. Du Bois, Paul Robeson, and historian Herbert Aptheker. And who was seated among the dignitaries on the platform at the main session of SNYC? President Miller F. Whittaker. He listened as Du Bois rhetorically appealed to South Carolina's most influential native son, U.S. secretary of state James F. Byrnes, to demonstrate as much interest in promoting democracy in South Carolina as he did in appealing for democracy in the Soviet Union. "He must begin to help establish in his own South Carolina something of that democracy which he has been recently so loudly preaching to Russia." Paul Robeson sang and spoke to the common people. "One must understand the unity of struggle," he proclaimed in his booming baritone voice. "We are laboring people. We come from toiling masses and have always seen as allies the toiling masses of the world."[142]

Following the SNYC gathering, the campus newspaper, the *Collegian,* urged students who had not already done so to join the organization. "Muster strength to SNYC's platform which condemns prejudice, discrimination, jim-crow, disfranchisement, Ku Klux Klan, white supremacists, poll taxes and general customs and practices which violate human dignity and rights. Let us strike while the iron is hot. Join the Southern Negro Youth Congress!!!!"[143]

South Carolina's political leadership was appalled with the SNYC and its platform. Governor Ransome J. Williams alleged "that Communistic elements came boldly and brazenly into South Carolina in an effort to undermine Secretary of State Byrnes' position in the councils of the United States." Such harsh conservative opposition spelled the demise of SNYC. The House Un-American Activities Committee (HUAC) and the FBI had already undertaken investigations of the "subversive" organization. By 1949 SNYC ceased to exist.[144]

A year after the SNYC Youth Legislature met, Paul Robeson returned to Columbia for a concert, and tickets for the performance were sold on the S.C. State campus—again with Whittaker's blessing. Robeson was a world-renowned singer, actor, and former All-American football player at Rutgers. He had earned a law degree at Columbia University. By 1947 he had become a lightning rod for controversy by cooperating with the Communist Party and for his endorsement of life in the Soviet Union. Robeson was unwavering in his support of civil rights as he appealed to people of color in Africa, Asia, the Caribbean, and the United States. Increasingly reviled by conservatives as the Cold War intensified, Robeson had his passport revoked by the U.S. State Department in 1950.

Given the racial and ideological climate that prevailed in the state and in the nation in the late 1940s, it is astonishing not only that Whittaker—as the president of a state educational institution—encouraged students and faculty to support those who advocated civil and political rights, but that he would take part himself in those activities.[145]

SENECA JUNIOR COLLEGE

It is not often that someone offers to give away a college and its campus. Yet that is exactly what Miller F. Whittaker was staring at as he opened his mail in late January 1947. The Reverend T. A. Gideon, the chairman of the Seneca Junior College board of trustees, offered to donate the eight-acre campus and it four buildings to South Carolina State.[146]

Seneca Institute had been founded in 1898 by the Seneca River Baptist Convention, a black denomination in Oconee County in the far northwestern corner of South Carolina. The Institute became a junior college in 1926. It managed to survive during the Depression but finally closed in 1939. Eight years later, with no chance of reviving the school, the trustees recommended that S.C. State take it over and operate it as a vocational school or junior college.[147]

Miller F. Whittaker and Charles F. Brooks, the chairman of the S.C. State board of trustees, visited the rustic and dilapidated campus in February 1947. A two-story frame structure was beyond repair. Perhaps two brick buildings and the log cabin library could be renovated. It was estimated that it would cost $75,000 to $100,000 to restore the buildings, erect a new dormitory, and landscape the grounds. Then the annual operating expenses would be approximately $50,000 to $100,000. These were costs that S.C. State could not afford. Whittaker recommended—and the trustees concurred—that the offer to take over Seneca Junior College be rejected.[148]

SHOULD CLAFLIN COLLEGE AND SOUTH CAROLINA STATE MERGE?

Several proposals were put forth over the years that S.C. State and its next-door neighbor Claflin combine into one college. Although Claflin was a private institution supported by the Methodist Church, many outside observers thought that the two black colleges could function more effectively with less duplication of programs if they became one.

Miller F. Whittaker wrote General Education Board (GEB) officials in 1939 asking if the GEB would provide funds to acquire Claflin. "Confidentially," he explained, "there may be an opportunity to purchase Claflin's plant." But the GEB staff was not interested. Three years later there was speculation that Claflin might merge with Clark College, and Claflin's students and faculty members would transfer to the Atlanta institution, opening the way for S.C. State to take over the Claflin campus. Nothing came of it.[149]

In 1950 GEB leaders took the initiative and asked S.C. State's new president, Benner C. Turner, if he would support a merger of South Carolina State and Claflin. Turner was noncommittal, but the GEB persisted. A year later GEB staff members wondered among themselves if the State of South Carolina would be amenable to combing the two schools if the GEB furnished $1 million of the estimated $3 million it would cost to unify them.[150]

Turner was decidedly cool to any amalgamation with Claflin. He told Fred McCuistion of the GEB in 1951 that bringing the two colleges together created a ready-made excuse for South Carolina's political leaders to abandon the allocation of funds for construction and improvements at S.C. State. The politicians would point to the acquisition of Claflin and indicate that its buildings were sufficient, and no additional money was needed for South Carolina State.[151]

Turner was correct. Five years later a special task force created by the Fiscal Survey Commission sought ways to save the state money. The commission strongly recommended to the general assembly that S.C. State purchase Claflin. "A serious effort should be made to acquire the properties of this institution (Claflin) and to incorporate its grounds into those of state college." But like so many recommendations to the legislature, this one was ignored.[152]

MILLER F. WHITTAKER'S DEATH

Miller F. Whittaker's death at the age of fifty-six on November 14, 1949, was not completely unexpected. He had suffered a serious heart attack the previous April that left him incapacitated for several weeks. At the time the board of trustees asked Frank A.

DeCosta, the head of the newly established graduate program, to serve as acting president. Whittaker returned to the presidency on July 1 only to suffer a second and this time fatal heart attack at the president's campus residence four months later.[153]

Whittaker's younger brother Jonathan had died in 1946 at the age of forty-nine, and Jonathan's son and Miller Whittaker's nephew, Peter, would die in 1954 at age thirty-three. Thus Miller F. Whittaker's death at a relatively young age may have been a consequence of family medical history. However, his father, Johnson C. Whittaker, died at the age of seventy-two, and his mother, Page, died in 1944 at the age of seventy-four. It is also possible that Whittaker's death could be attributed to the considerable stress he had endured during his seventeen-year tenure as president.

Whittaker's funeral was held on the campus in the auditorium of White Hall, and it attracted a "who's who" of black and white South Carolinians: Governor Strom Thurmond; House Speaker Solomon Blatt; Congressman Hugo S. Sims and his brother, Henry Sims, the president of Winthrop College; Robert Poole, the president of Clemson; Orangeburg mayor R. H. Jennings; attorney David Robinson, whose legal efforts in opposition to the NAACP and Thurgood Marshall led to the establishment of the law school. Black college presidents including J. J. Seabrook of Claflin, O. B. Reuben of Morris, Charlotte Hawkins Brown of Palmer Memorial Institute, and representatives of the black land-grant colleges attended. Members of the board of trustees and, according to one report, "thousands" of others gathered to pay their respects. Benjamin E. Mays delivered the eulogy, and he characterized Whittaker as "a very, very, very, very good man."[154]

MILLER F. WHITTAKER: AN ASSESSMENT

Throughout the nation college presidents had struggled to steer their institutions through the economic adversity of the 1930s and the war years of the 1940s, and Whittaker was no exception. But as the president of a public college for black people, he faced the daunting and nearly impossible task of guiding an underfunded institution between political leaders who were committed to the preservation of white supremacy and African Americans who wanted "their" college to accept if not embrace changes in society that would disrupt—if not destroy—Jim Crow.

Miller F. Whittaker managed the extraordinarily difficult feat of pleasing black and white people who had contradictory visions of the future of their state and nation. Whittaker never publicly criticized segregation, or the poll tax, or lynching. He supported the creation of separate law and graduate programs at S.C. State while constantly lamenting the state's inadequate financial support for faculty salaries, dormitories, and undergraduate programs. By the time of the Second World War, he firmly hinted that changes among black and white people were in the offing.

Whittaker won the admiration and support of many black Carolinians. He was regarded as a "race man." He was quietly committed to securing the legal and political rights of black people who had long since grown weary and frustrated by the restraints and indignities imposed in a Jim Crow world. Indeed Whittaker had testified in 1947 that a separate law school could be established at S.C. State, but that it would not be the equal of the law school long established at the University of South Carolina. For that blunt testimony, Whittaker earned the warm praise of NAACP legal counsel Thurgood Marshall. But members of the board of trustees and state legislators were so pleased with Whittaker's endorsement of a separate legal program that they gave him a hefty pay raise.

Whittaker devoted considerable time to soliciting legislators for increases in state appropriations for the college during the 1940s. But those efforts were mostly unsuccessful, and this at a time when the state experienced relative prosperity in the aftermath of World War II. He did manage, however, to get new boilers and new farmland for the college. The school continued to rely on student and faculty labor and was increasingly dependent on student fees as a source of funding. With the exception of Moss Hall, which housed the new law school, the state did not contribute any funds for major capital improvements between the Great Depression and the Korean War.

President Whittaker provided leadership for the extension program at a time when it was expanding, although not as rapidly as people like Marian Paul thought necessary to bring long-needed improvements to the lives of rural black Carolinians. Whittaker also managed to pursue his profession as an architect. At the time of his death, work was well underway on a new Lutheran church on Ellis Avenue in Orangeburg. Whittaker and faculty member John Blanche cooperated in executing the plans for that attractive building, which was completed and dedicated in 1950.[155]

If these major concerns were not enough to keep Whittaker occupied, he—like other presidents of S.C. State—had to tend to mundane and even trivial matters that should not have had to consume the time of a chief administrator. Whittaker's files contain dozens and dozens of memos he wrote involving routine maintenance: replacing light bulbs, cutting dead limbs from trees, patching plaster in a dormitory, repairing a leaking drinking fountain, selecting a new textbook for freshmen composition.[156]

The board of trustees met following Whittaker's funeral and designated a five-man committee to run the college until a new president could be selected. The committee was chaired by Kirkland W. Green, the dean of the College of Arts and Sciences. The committee members were Harold W. Crawford, dean of the School of Engineering and Industrial Education; Frank M. Staley, the dean of the School of Agriculture; J. I. Washington, the business manager; and Frank DeCosta, the dean of the School of Graduate Studies. Evidently the trustees had not been altogether pleased with Frank DeCosta's service as interim president during Whittaker's illness earlier in that year. Presumably DeCosta would have been named acting president a second time if they had been satisfied with his previous performance. As it turned out over the next several months, the committee proved to be a less than satisfactory way to manage an educational institution.[157]

CHAPTER SIX

Separate but Equal?

Building on a foundation they created in the 1930s and 1940s, African Americans made civil rights the preeminent issue in American society by the mid-twentieth century. They petitioned, they marched, and they died in a struggle to eradicate segregation and racial discrimination from American life. South Carolina State College students and faculty played an integral role in this movement, which fundamentally changed the legal, political, and interpersonal relationships between black and white people. And these activists who were so determined to make America live up to its principles were themselves transformed by the enormous shift in the racial order.

In the meantime S.C. State College became a political football as white leaders made a serious attempt to improve the institution's infrastructure and its programs in order to preserve the racial "integrity" of the state's white colleges and universities. White politicians were convinced that if S.C. State could be made the approximate equal of the white schools, separation based on race in higher education could be maintained and justified. But to bring about those improvements at S.C. State, sizable sums of money would be needed.

Benner C. Turner was the man who would guide the college during most of this turbulent era. He served as president from 1950 until 1967, and he is often credited with initiating a host of progressive changes on the campus. The physical plant expanded dramatically with the construction of several major facilities. The number of faculty members with doctorates increased, and faculty salaries improved. For the first time, in 1960, the Southern Association of Colleges and Schools (SACS) fully accredited S.C. State.

BENNER C. TURNER

By education and intellect, Turner was exceptionally well qualified to be president. He was the son of Dr. Edwin J. Turner, a prosperous physician in Columbus, Georgia. During the 1920s Turner had attended two of the nation's premier academic institutions, graduating from Philips Andover Academy in Andover, Massachusetts, and earning a bachelor's degree from Harvard University. In 1930 Turner graduated from the Harvard law school, passed the Pennsylvania bar examination, and joined one of the country's foremost black law firms, Raymond Pace Alexander in Philadelphia. Turner left Philadelphia in 1932 and returned to Georgia, where he ran a real estate business

From 1938 until 1967, Benjamin E. Mays delivered an annual Easter address in White Hall Auditorium that was cosponsored by the YWCA and YMCA. Seated in front of White Hall, from left to right: Julia Turner, Marion Birnie "Mother" Wilkinson, and Sadie Mays. Standing, left to right: Benner C. Turner and Benjamin E. Mays. Courtesy of the Historical Collection, South Carolina State University

in Columbus for eleven years. He married Julia Allen, whose father, Benjamin F. Allen, had been the president of Missouri's Lincoln University. In 1943 Turner became a law professor at the law school at North Carolina College for Negroes in Durham. Miller F. Whittaker and the board of trustees invited Turner to become the dean of the new S.C. State law school in 1947.[1]

But Turner's appointment in 1950 as the president of S.C. State had less to do with his academic qualifications and more to do with the mounting anxiety among white leaders over the evolving threat to segregation posed by the impending changes in relations between the races. The U.S. armed forces were desegregated. Jackie Robinson had broken the color barrier in major-league baseball, and the State of Texas had lost a legal battle to prevent a black man—Heman Sweatt—from enrolling at the University of Texas law school.

Frank A. DeCosta was one of several men who had hoped to succeed Whittaker as S.C. State president. Shortly after Whittaker's funeral and sensitive to white concerns, DeCosta—who had served as acting president during Whittaker's illness—asked his academic mentor at the University of Pennsylvania to write a letter to Governor J. Strom Thurmond assuring the state's chief executive that DeCosta was not about to disrupt the racial status quo if he became president. E. D. Grizzell, the dean of the School of Education, informed Thurmond: "I personally would not be interested in suggesting for the position one who had extreme and untried ideas regarding the education of colored people."[2]

DeCosta was one of eleven men the trustees interviewed on May 25, 1950, to become the fourth college president. They considered the five administrators who had been managing the institution since Whittaker's death: Kirkland W. Green, Harold W. Crawford, Frank M. Staley, J. I. Washington, and DeCosta. They also interviewed three other S.C. State administrators: E. W. Brice, Paul R. Webber, and Benner C. Turner. Three men who were not employed at S.C. State were interviewed as well: Claflin president J. J. Seabrook, former Avery principal John Potts, and James Parler, who was the superintendent of the black public schools in Orangeburg.

In the meantime much rancor had arisen among the members of that five-man committee as they tried to run the college while they contended with each other for the presidency. According to one observer, M. Maceo Nance, "There was a great deal of infighting. The faculty and staff began to choose sides in terms of who they would support, and, of course, as a result little clandestine things started appearing for and against the various candidates." Thus the institution suffered from almost nonexistent leadership as the members of the executive committee spent much of their time bickering. It was, in Nance's words, "almost chaos."[3]

On August 1, 1950, the trustees assembled in the office of Governor Thurmond to conduct a second round of interviews and then choose the president. They had already dismissed Potts as "too ingratiating." Green was considered "ok" but "not too strong." DeCosta was not among the final candidates either. The board interviewed Harold Crawford, James Parler, Turner, and a new candidate, Dr. Thomas P. Fraser, who was a native of Georgetown, a graduate of Claflin, and the head of science education at Baltimore's Morgan State College. Parler was considered "ok," but "faculty and students oppose him." Crawford was rejected because he was "questionable on segregation in education." Fraser was not mentioned.

The board turned to Turner. Adam Moss, longtime board member and an Orangeburg attorney, nominated Turner, and Charles Jones seconded the nomination. Moss was convinced that "attorneys could do everything." Turner became the fourth president of S.C. State. People in the black community and on the campus were stunned at the choice of Turner. M. Maceo Nance recalled that "no one had ever dreamed that he would be the person selected." The other candidates had been "too busy fighting each other."[4]

GOVERNOR JAMES F. BYRNES

If Turner was well qualified for the presidency, then James F. "Jimmy" Byrnes was overqualified to serve as the governor of South Carolina. Three months after the trustees selected Turner, South Carolina voters elected Byrnes the state's chief executive. A native of Charleston, Byrnes was first elected to Congress in 1910. In 1930 he was elected to the U.S. Senate, where he became a strong supporter of President Franklin D. Roosevelt's New Deal. In 1941 Roosevelt appointed Byrnes to the U.S. Supreme Court. At Roosevelt's request Byrnes stepped down from the court to head the Office of Economic Stabilization and then serve as the director of the Office of War Mobilization.

On August 1, 1950, the board of trustees met in Columbia in the office of Governor Strom Thurmond and selected Benner C. Turner to be the fourth president of South Carolina State College. Left to right: Thomas A. Babb; Howard G. Royal; Adam H. Moss, chairman; Governor Strom Thurmond; Wallace C. Bethea, secretary; Charles A. Jones, W. Mc. Hodge. Courtesy of the Historical Collection, South Carolina State University

Working out of the White House and informally referred to as the "Assistant President," Byrnes was considered for the vice presidential nomination in 1944. But labor unions and African American groups including the NAACP and South Carolina's Progressive Democratic Party successfully lined up in opposition to Byrnes. President Harry S. Truman appointed Byrnes secretary of state in 1945, a position he held until 1947. He was *Time Magazine*'s "Man of the Year" in 1946. Byrnes was among the ranking power brokers and most knowledgeable political operators in the nation's capital in the second quarter of the twentieth century.[5]

Byrnes was not only capable of providing a formidable defense of segregation; he was eager to do so. The sixty-eight-year-old governor was confident almost to the point of arrogance that the separation of the races was so time tested and logical that the U.S. Supreme Court was all but certain to reject any challenge to segregation. The only potential weak spot was the long-standing lack of equality in the separate facilities created for blacks and whites—especially in education.

In his inaugural address on January 16, 1951, Byrnes outlined his plans for improving public education while safeguarding segregation. He vowed that every child would receive "at least a graded school education." He wanted appropriations to increase teachers' salaries and to purchase additional school buses. What is most important, he asked for a $75 million bond issue to finance a school construction program. The governor insisted that there should be parity between black and white schools. "It is our duty to provide for the races substantial equality in school facilities. We should do it because it is right. For me that is sufficient reason."[6]

Byrnes cautioned that there was litigation pending in the courts that challenged segregated public education. But the governor reassured white South Carolinians that black people had no interest in integrated schools "except for the professional agitators, what the colored people want, and what they are entitled to is equal facilities in the schools. We must see that they get them." Later that year, however, Byrnes warned that he would close the public schools before he would preside over integration. "Our present system of public schools is a dear possession to us, but the preservation of racial integrity is even dearer."[7]

As the NAACP Legal Defense Fund prepared an assault on segregation in public education, Byrnes moved adroitly to fend off the attack. The NAACP case *Briggs. v. Elliott* originated in Clarendon County, adjacent to Orangeburg County, and Thurgood Marshall and his legal team were determined to demonstrate before a panel of three federal judges in Charleston in May 1951 that segregated schools meant grossly inferior schools for black children. Byrnes's response was to persuade the general assembly to enact a 3 percent sales tax to fund a $75 million school building program. In the ensuing four years, the state spent in excess of $124 million on school construction, and two-thirds of that money went to the black schools.[8]

S.C. State posed a similar challenge to the resourceful Byrnes. The legislature had appropriated an additional $140,000 to the college in 1949, but it was for the graduate program, the law school, and out-of-state scholarships in pharmacy and medicine. Despite the additional state spending and increases in student fees, the college remained woefully underfunded at midcentury. Doak S. Campbell, the president of Florida State University, evaluated S.C. State in 1951, and he was appalled. In a letter to Turner, he cited the institution's deficiencies. "The salaries of your professional staff are notably low." The programs in agriculture and teacher education were "glaring inadequacies." There were serious problems with the physical plant. Campbell concluded, "I consider your needs as urgent as in any institution it has been my privilege to study."[9]

Byrnes was aware of the problems at S.C. State. As governor-elect he toured the campus in November 1950 with Governor Thurmond and the State Budget and Control Board. Having sought and then obtained the 3 percent sales tax for the public schools, Byrnes was reluctant to return to the legislature to ask for additional funds for the black college. He also worried that any request for more funds for S.C. State would prompt the presidents of the state's white public institutions to elevate their demands for money. Byrnes decided that he could not ask the general assembly for appropriations to undertake long overdue construction at S.C. State. "Under the circumstances, I think it extremely unwise to ask for a direct appropriation for a building program solely for the college for colored students."[10]

THE GENERAL EDUCATION BOARD AND SEGREGATION

To secure the money needed to improve the facilities at S.C. State, Byrnes turned to the General Education Board (GEB). The governor was intimately acquainted with several of the members of the board of the Rockefeller Foundation, which sponsored the GEB. Furthermore there was a decades-long relationship between the GEB and S.C. State.

From the 1920s through the 1940s, the GEB had provided funds for facilities, programs, and the faculty.

GEB grants had been instrumental in the construction of Hodge Hall and Wilkinson Hall as well as in purchasing equipment for a physics laboratory. The GEB supported a teacher-education program in cooperation with the Penn School on St. Helena Island near Beaufort. Faculty members were also awarded GEB funds to pursue graduate work at northern universities. But the GEB had also rejected requests from S.C. State. During the Depression the GEB declined to provide money for operating expenses. Professor James Birnie's appeal for money for a marine biology laboratory along the South Carolina coast was turned down. In 1947 the GEB rejected President Whittaker's request for $28,000 to purchase books for the new law library.[11]

Byrnes contacted the GEB in 1951 and met with its vice president and director, Robert D. Calkins, to determine what assistance the philanthropic organization could provide for S.C. State. Byrnes told Calkins that the college needed considerable financial assistance. In December Calkins came to Orangeburg to meet President Turner and Wallace C. Bethea, who was the secretary of the board of trustees and the chair of the local board. Turner was ready with a lengthy and expensive list of overdue capital improvements: agriculture building ($350,000), dairy building ($30,000), greenhouse ($20,000), food center ($75,000), academic building ($750,000), two dormitories for men ($900,000), two dormitories for women ($700,000), and a student union ($150,000). The total was $2,975,000. In addition Turner stated that still more funds were needed to increase faculty salaries and to support teacher training. Undaunted Calkins told Turner to prepare a request for financial support and to send it to Governor Byrnes by year's end. Turner did just that.[12]

With Turner's request in front of him, Governor Byrnes contacted Robert Calkins by telephone and asked that the GEB furnish $1 million to S.C. State for an agricultural facility and a classroom building. Byrnes informed Calkins that he planned to ask the general assembly to approve a loan of $1 million for dormitory construction, and that dormitory revenues would be used to repay the loan.[13]

GEB officials may have been astonished—or even dumbfounded—at the audacity of Byrnes's request. In any event they quickly turned down the governor and confided among themselves that they did not want to create the impression among African Americans that the GEB favored segregation: "we should not make a commitment at this time partly because of the uncertainties regarding the status of the Supreme Court suit and the danger of our getting involved in the segregation issue, in that Negroes would regard this as Board support for Byrnes's public statements regarding his determination to perpetuate segregation even if it meant giving away the schools." The GEB staff considered Byrnes's request excessive, and furthermore it violated GEB policy by not including a provision for matching funds from the state.[14]

The rejection did not deter Byrnes in the least. He pressed Calkins to present the $1 million request to the trustees of the GEB at their next meeting in April. Calkins relented slightly and told the governor that he would ask the board for $500,000. "One-half million would probably be the outside figure we could consider." But he reminded Byrnes that the state still had an obligation to furnish matching funds. "When we appropriate funds to public institutions it has been customary over years of the Board's activities to specify that matching funds provided by the legislature shall be outright appropriations. The proceeds from [dormitory] revenue bonds would not meet our usual terms, especially when the amortization of the bonds would be thrown as a burden mainly on the students and their parents at the institution."[15]

Impatient with the nettlesome GEB staff, Byrnes had already appealed directly to John D. Rockefeller III and asked him for assistance. He explained that he was attempting to provide equal school facilities for both races in South Carolina. "Because so little had been done in previous years, it now requires that much be done." He told Rockefeller that money for the college would foster better race relations and quell smoldering discontent among black people. "I am confident," Byrnes wrote, "that a comprehensive program for the College at this time would go far to allay the unrest among our colored people and contribute to better relations between the races." But Rockefeller declined to intervene and showed little sympathy for the racial crisis that Byrnes said he was confronting.[16]

Byrnes, fully summoning his powers of persuasion and exuding cordiality, turned again to GEB officials and boldly suggested that they simply make an exception to their policy mandating matching funds. In a face-to-face interview in the governor's office that associate GEB director J. Harris Purks described as "a pleasure indeed," Byrnes explained that "he wanted help *help for the Negroes,* and not for himself or the whites." Purks, however, held out little hope, informing the governor "that I doubted that we could act favorably on terms suggested, and that, even assuming the recommendation eventually to be made, the probability of action [at the board meeting] in April would be remote."[17]

Although legislators had authorized the sale of $1 million in bonds for dormitory construction at the college, the lawmakers adjourned without appropriating any funds for academic facilities. But Purks and Calkins succumbed to Byrnes's charm and persistence. In early March 1952, they indicated that they would recommend that the GEB trustees approve an unprecedented "outright grant" of $500,000, of which $400,000 would finance the construction of an agriculture building and $100,000 would be devoted to the erection of an academic building. The latter structure was contingent on the legislature providing $100,000 in matching funds, something it heretofore had shown no inclination to do. Purks meanwhile cautioned Byrnes that approval by the trustees was by no means assured.[18]

Unwilling to risk rejection, Byrnes immediately contacted the president of the Rockefeller Foundation and the chairman of the trustees of the General Education Board. In a "Dear Foster" letter Byrnes asked John Foster Dulles for assistance in securing the grant, but he pointed out that the request did involve a departure from GEB policies regarding matching funds. "However, I am hoping you will conclude that rules, like laws, should not be inflexible in administration. If you can be of help in this situation, it will contribute to the improvement of relations between the two races in this State." In a "Dear Jimmy" reply, Dulles diplomatically promised to give "sympathetic consideration" to the proposal. He added that GEB had nearly depleted all its funds as it prepared to terminate its existence as a philanthropic organization.[19]

THE GOVERNOR'S SUCCESS

Less than three weeks later in Princeton, New Jersey, the GEB trustees, "after careful deliberation," approved a $500,000 grant to South Carolina State College, a remarkable amount of money in the waning days of the GEB. If board members deliberated the merits or implications of the Byrnes proposal at length, the minutes do not reveal it. The minutes do indicate that there was some unease in awarding a grant that could be perceived as perpetuating segregation. Among those taking part in the deliberations was Dean Rusk, who would serve as the next president of the Rockefeller Foundation and the last president of the GEB. John Foster Dulles would soon step down to serve as U.S. secretary of state under President Dwight D. Eisenhower.[20]

By dogged determination and through carefully cultivated contacts, Byrnes accomplished what no other southern politician could have done. He had succeeded in persuading one of the nation's foremost philanthropic foundations to violate its own guidelines and award a half million dollars to a rural black college. The grant would improve facilities at the black institution, but it would also strengthen South Carolina's defense of segregation. It is unlikely that the GEB would have parted with such a large sum of money under the terms that it did were it not for Governor Byrnes's personal contacts with John D. Rockefeller III and especially John Foster Dulles.

GEB vice president and director Robert D. Calkins—who soon would depart to head the Brookings Institution—put the best light on the grant in a note to Byrnes. "Its purpose as you so well expressed it over the telephone, is to help the Negroes of the area by improving their educational opportunities." But GEB officials remained worried that there would be a negative reaction among black people. In an interview with Turner shortly before the grant was made, J. Harris Purks asked the college president if NAACP leaders might oppose funds for the construction of the agricultural building. Turner dismissed the NAACP, explaining "that he saw no reason why [the] N.A.A.C.P. should object, but that its objections would make no difference to him; that he had taken criticism from the N.A.A.C.P. before." The grant generated little interest and aroused no controversy in South Carolina.[21]

MORE MONEY

Between its establishment in 1902 and its termination in 1960, the General Education Board spent more than $129 million on education in the United States. Those funds were furnished by the Rockefeller Foundation. The total $640,000 that the General Education Board contributed to South Carolina State over the years represented the largest amount of money that any state-supported black college received during the history of the GEB. But most of that resulted from the intervention of Governor Byrnes in 1951 and 1952.[22]

Byrnes's stunning success with the GEB helped generate vastly increased financial support for the college. After decades of deprivation, there was an unprecedented building boom on the campus in the 1950s. In excess of $3 million was spent on construction—more than had been expended since the school's founding in 1896. Political

Table 27. Funding Sources for Campus Construction, 1952–54

Source	Amount	Facility
General Education Board	$500,000	
	$400,000 outright grant	Agriculture building (Staley Hall)
	$100,000 match required	Academic building (Turner Hall)
State tuition bonds	$950,000	
	$650,000 "match"	Academic building (Turner Hall)
	$148,726	Sewage, utilities, land-scaping
	$150,000	Athletic field (Bulldog Stadium)
Sinking Fund Comm. Loan	$1,135,000	
	$700,000	Student dormitory (Bethea Hall)
	$435,000	Faculty housing
State appropriations	$750,000	
	$400,000	Student dormitory (Earle Hall)
	$100,000	Infirmary (Brooks)
	$150,000	Student center (K. W. Green)
	$75,000	Food conservation (Mason Hall)
	$25,000	Dairy building
Total	$3,333,726	

Source: Benner C. Turner to Robert W. July, Assistant Director, General Education Board, 2 December 1954. GEB Records, Series 1, Subseries 3, Box 479, Folder 5098, Rockefeller Archive Center. The Sinking Fund Commission was a self-insurance fund operated by the state. With the approval of the State Budget and Control Board, the commission authorized loans to state agencies and institutions.

Table 28. New Facilities Constructed, 1952–57

Facility	Cost
Agriculture building—Staley Hall	$435,000
Academic building—Turner Hall	$770,000
Boiler plant addition	$142,000
Athletic fields—Bulldog Stadium and baseball field/track	$178,000
Calf barn	$17,000
Cannery—Mason Hall	$75,000
Dairy building	$25,000
Men's dormitory—Bethea Hall	$635,000
Faculty apartments—Henderson and Sheffield Halls	$112,000
Faculty dormitories—Nix and Rowe Halls and 14 houses	$185,000
Paving of campus drives	$12,000
Sprinkler system	$202,000
Women's dormitory—Earle Hall	$239,000

Source: Appendix 7, *Annual Report, 1956–1957*, 93. Funds were shifted after they had been allocated. Money for the boiler plant addition had initially been set aside for the women's dormitory in a loan from the Sinking Fund. Also funds were used to furnish and equip the new facilities.

leaders were determined to improve the college's infrastructure to ward off challenges to the separate-but-equal doctrine in higher education. Nevertheless white authorities could not summon the will or the financial resources to spend very many taxpayers' dollars on the black institution.

The GEB provided $500,000. But much of the remaining funding came from students and their families through tuition, fees, and dormitory charges that were used to pay off bonds that were sold to fund construction. Of the more than $3.33 million spent, just $750,000 came from direct state appropriations. GEB officials had insisted that the State of South Carolina match $100,000 of the $500,000 that the organization provided to S.C. State. But the state failed to fulfill that mandate. Instead tuition bonds were used to underwrite the state's portion—$650,000—of the cost to build the classroom facility that would be named Turner Hall.[23]

FACULTY ISSUES

The massive building program transformed the campus. Equally important were the dramatic improvements in the education and compensation of the faculty. For the first time in the history of the college, there were faculty members on the staff with earned doctorates. Ethna B. Winston, who had an Ed.D. from the Teachers College at Columbia University, had been hired as dean of women in 1946, and she also taught graduate courses in education. She left S.C. State in 1949 for a position at Howard University. Lewis K. McMillan was the first full-time professor with a Ph.D. He was a native of Allendale and had earned a Ph.D. in history in 1932 from the University of Bonn in Germany. He taught at Ohio's Wilberforce University, and in 1946 and 1947 President Miller F. Whittaker invited McMillan to teach summer school at S.C. State. He moved to Orangeburg in 1948 and split his time teaching between Claflin and S.C. State before taking a full-time position at S.C. State in 1950. McMillan in the meantime worked diligently to complete a book on the history of black higher education in South Carolina.[24]

When Turner became president, he made it a priority to hire faculty members who possessed doctorates. This was nearly an insurmountable challenge. Few African Americans had earned doctorates during the first half of the twentieth century, and there was intense competition among historically black institutions to hire those who did possess them. Between 1876 and 1951, 673 African Americans had earned doctoral degrees, and 292 of those degrees had been earned between 1944 and 1951.[25]

On the other hand, a black man or woman with a doctorate stood little more than a slim chance of joining the faculty of a northern white college or university and absolutely no chance of gaining employment at a white southern college or university. There were 133 black faculty members at seventy-two predominantly white colleges and universities in the North and in the West in 1949. Not all were permanent or

Table 29. Black Colleges and Universities and the Number of Individuals with Doctorates on Their Staff, 1943–44

Howard University	70
Lincoln University (Mo.)	19
Atlanta University	12
Wilberforce University	12
Southern University	11
Fisk University	9
Morgan State College	9
Morehouse College	9
Prairie View A&M	7
Tuskegee Institute	5
Hampton Institute	5
Florida A&M	2
S.C. State	0

Source: Harry W. Greene, *Holders of Doctorates among American Negroes*, 216–17. Green's book contains a more complete list of black institutions and number of faculty with doctorates.

tenured members of the faculty. Some were visiting, part-time, and summer school faculty. Because the 1896 legislation establishing S.C. State stipulated that the corps of instructors and the president had to be of the Negro race, Turner and his predecessors could not employ Caucasian or Asian people.[26]

By 1951–52 six of the ninety-four members of the S.C. State faculty had a doctorate, and by the end of the decade thirteen of ninety-three faculty members possessed the terminal degree. Several of these professors would remain at S.C. State for their entire academic careers. And because they had advanced degrees, they quickly rose to administrative positions. It was the degree and not their teaching experience, record of research and publications, or potential for leadership that led to these posts.[27]

Algernon S. Belcher earned a Ph.D. in economics from Catholic University. He ascended though the ranks from chair of social sciences, to dean of arts and sciences, to vice president for academic affairs. George Hunter, with a Ph.D. in chemistry from Penn State, became chair of natural sciences and then dean of arts and sciences. Nettie Parler, with a Ph.D. in English from New York University, was the chair of the Department of English for more than three decades. Laler DeCosta became assistant dean of agriculture and then the dean. He had a Ph.D. in animal husbandry from Cornell. Annabelle S. Sherman was the associate dean of home economics, and she had a Ph.D. from the University of Wisconsin. Ashriel I. Mose earned an Ed.D. from New York University and served as the dean of the School of Education, and then dean of the faculty. George Brooks, with an Ed.D. from Indiana University, chaired social sciences before becoming dean of graduate studies.[28]

Other faculty members with doctorates moved on to positions at other institutions. Edward Ferguson had a Ph.D. in zoology from the University of Illinois. He chaired the Department of Natural Sciences before moving to Grambling in 1956 to become department chair there. J. Irving Scott directed the academic extension courses held off campus in the early 1950s. He had a Ph. D. in educational administration from the University of Pittsburgh. He left to become the supervisor of Negro schools in Jacksonville, Florida. Howard Jordan had an Ed.D. from New York University. He was the dean of the School of Education and then dean of the faculty. He left S.C. State in 1962 to become the president of Savannah State College. (Benjamin F. Hubert, who taught agriculture at S.C. State in the 1920s, served as the president of Savannah State from 1926 to 1947.)[29]

Faculty salaries lagged at S.C. State. In 1951 Turner pointed out that "we are still substantially below the salaries paid by comparable Negro institutions." In 1952 Governor Byrnes persuaded the general assembly to appropriate $100,000 for an increase in

Table 30. Minimum Salaries for Negro Colleges, Twelve-Month Employment

Professors	$4,500
Associate professors	$4,000
Assistant professors	$3,500
Instructors	$3,000

Source: Annual Report, Southern Association of Colleges and Universities, 1951–52, 11.

Table 31. Salaries of Selected Faculty Members, 1951–52

Edward Ferguson	Biology	$6,000
George Hunter	Chemistry	$6,000
Lewis K. McMillan	History	$4,600
Leo L. Kerford	Law	$4,600
Blinzy L. Gore	Law	$4,600
James H. Green	Chemistry	$3,800
Nettie Parler	English	$3,750
Trudelle Wimbush	Education	$3,600
Kathlyn Moses	Library science	$3,600
T. J. Crawford	Biology/chemistry	$3,600
Paul Webber	Economics	$3,600
Alfred Isaac	History	$3,200
Florence Miller	English	$3,200
John H. Blanche	Architecture/engineering	$3,100
Gracia W. Dawson	Librarian	$2,800
Russell E. Williams	Poultry science	$3,600
R. F. Allen	Electrical engineering	$3,600
Edith DeVane	Art	$3,200
Reginald Thomasson	Band/orchestra	$3,000
Geraldyne Zimmerman	Mathematics	$2,880
Carrie H. Ward	Business admin.	$2,800
Mamie E. Thompson	Physical educ.	$2,500
B. A. Moorer	Tailoring	$3,200
E. E. Pinson	Music	$3,000
C. R. Claggert	Auto mechanics	$3,000
Maceo M. Nance	ROTC custodian	$2,700
Alba Lewis	Critic teacher	$2,400
Benner C. Turner	President	$8,100
J. I. Washington	Business manager	$6,100
Lawrence E. Simmons	Coach/athletic dir.	$6,000
Frank A. DeCosta	Dean, grad. school	$5,500

Table 31. *Continued*

Peter H. Whittaker	Acting dean, law	$5,000
Paul King	Comptroller	$4,500
Dudley Zimmerman	Supt. of bld./gnds.	$4,200
M. R. Vernon	Dean of women	$4,000
Maurice Mynatt	Dean of men	$3,600
Althema R. Nix	Head librarian	$3,600
Emma Dawkins	Sec. to president	$3,600
J. C. Shecut	College physician	$3,000
Alpha O. Josie	Clerk, post office	$2,500
Julia Nance	Cashier	$2,160
W. C. Bethea	Board secretary	$2,160

Source: Interview and Accompanying Documents, 1951–52, Series 1, Subseries 3, Folder 5097, Rockefeller Archive Center.

salaries, but it was little more than a short-lived boost. Turner was pleased, but hardly overjoyed. The surge in salaries would mean that S.C. State would meet the minimum requirements for salaries among black colleges established by the Southern Association of Colleges and Schools (SACS). However, Turner indicated that most of S.C. State's peer institutions—the black land-grant colleges—offered "substantially higher salaries" than the minimum set by SACS.[30]

Turner complained, however, that some faculty members who signed contracts in July left for more lucrative positions before school started in September—"they simply walked off the campus." While acknowledging that the majority of teachers "are conscientious," there "are others who are simply peddling the doctorate from school to school to the highest bidder." He lamented in 1957 that an unnamed faculty member in chemistry earning $4,200 at S.C. State left for a position paying $6,100. He admitted that faculty members with doctorates could command $2,000 to $3,000 more at other black institutions.[31]

ACCREDITATION

Furthermore SACS kept raising its standards for minimum acceptable salaries. In 1951 the accrediting organization ended its policy of having separate standards and having separate visiting committees evaluate black and white colleges, thus vastly increasing pressure on black institutions to increase salaries. In the meantime Turner and S.C. State administrators and faculty members submitted detailed reports to SACS in preparation for on-site visits by SACS committees. In 1952 SACS offered a negative assessment to the S.C. State submission. "Instructional expenditures, faculty training, and salaries were below standard, especially in view of offering graduate work."[32]

In 1954 SACS dispatched a biracial team of three white men and one black man to the campus to determine whether the college sufficiently met twenty-one standards for accreditation. The committee made a series of recommendations that included an increase in salaries, better-educated faculty, and faculty with doctorates in areas in which the college offered graduate training. The institution was given time to implement the improvements.[33]

In 1957, and having made an intensive effort to remedy an assortment of problems, S.C. State sought full accreditation from SACS for the first time in its history. It failed and was given probationary status. SACS administrators pointed to inadequate salaries as one of several specific areas where the college did not meet minimum standards for accreditation.[34]

The college also lost facilities and maintenance personnel who could find more attractive wages elsewhere. The federal government's construction of the Savannah River Plant—"the Bomb Factory"—on a 310-square-mile site drew thirty-five thousand workers to the Aiken area in the early 1950s. Laborers who had been employed on the campus departed for the better-paying jobs.[35]

FACULTY HOUSING

Although it was a difficult challenge to compensate faculty members satisfactorily, the construction of campus housing for administrators and the teaching staff helped to some extent to offset the salary inequities. As late as the fall semester of 1954, thirteen male faculty members were living among male students in the recently renovated Lowman Hall. There were single female faculty members dispersed among the three dormitories for women: Manning, Bradham, and Miller Halls.[36]

The lack of suitable housing for faculty in the community and on the campus had been a perennial problem. There were 173 faculty members and staff in 1953. Forty-two resided on campus and forty-five lived in the community. "The remaining 86 have found it extremely difficult to rent adequate housing facilities in the community." President Turner reported that "a marked absence of acceptable housing" was available to them for sale or rent. The shortage of housing compounded the problem of hiring qualified faculty members.[37]

To alleviate the housing shortage, the campus construction program included $435,000 in funds borrowed from the Sinking Fund Commission to erect residences for faculty members and their families. Two faculty dormitories were built for single men and women. Nix Hall housed twenty-four men, and twenty-eight women lived in Rowe Hall. Two apartment buildings—Henderson Hall and Sheffield Hall—were built. Each contained four apartments. There were also fourteen single-family homes constructed in the new faculty residence complex near the rear of the campus. Four of the homes were four rooms each. Six homes contained five rooms, and four had six rooms. The availability of affordable rental housing on the campus quickly became the envy of faculty and administrators at other black colleges.[38]

Turner announced in 1952 that because the college had a graduate program, its faculty should be expected to conduct research and publish the results of their investigations. "Our faculty will not only be enabled to keep abreast of educational developments but will also grow in prestige and status and will make significant contributions to the state's cultural and material progress." But when historian Lewis K. McMillan did precisely what Turner recommended, the president was not the least impressed with the results of McMillan's scholarship. In fact, angered by McMillan's book, Turner reacted vindictively toward the fifty-six-year-old faculty member.[39]

McMillan was regarded by students and faculty colleagues as well informed and personable but a bit eccentric. He greeted nearly everyone with a friendly, "Hi, neighbor." One former student recalled that he was not a large man—"a little small man with a huge bald head." McMillan had been at work on a history of higher education among black South Carolinians for over a decade. He joined the faculty just as the graduate program was initiated in 1947. He subsequently taught graduate and undergraduate history courses and occasionally taught German as well.[40]

Lewis McMillan was born in Allendale County in 1897. He first attended school at age eleven, when he enrolled in the primary program at Voorhees Institute in Denmark, South Carolina. He went to Benedict College in Columbia for the eighth grade and completed high school at the academy affiliated with Howard University. He then earned a bachelor's degree in social sciences from Howard in 1922. In 1925 he earned a bachelor's degree in divinity from Yale University. He taught briefly at Shaw University in Raleigh before traveling to Germany in the late 1920s. He enrolled at the University of Berlin and then the University of Bonn. He earned a Ph.D. in history and philosophy at the University of Bonn in 1933—just as Adolph Hitler and the Nazi Party came to power. McMillan's dissertation was "Die Kunst-Und Geschichts Philosophie Karl Cshaases" [The Art and History of Philosopher Karl Cshaases]. McMillan returned to the United States and taught at Virginia State, Bishop College, and Wilberforce University before coming to Orangeburg.[41]

Given the German commitment to Aryan supremacy during the Nazi ascendancy in the 1930s and 1940s, it is ironic that McMillan was so fond of the German people and their culture. Shortly after World War II ended, he made a nostalgic return to Germany in 1949, where he had an emotional reunion with the family he had resided with while he had been a graduate student in 1931–32.[42]

McMillan got along well with Miller F. Whittaker and then Benner C. Turner—until his book was published. In an effusive New Year's greeting to Turner in late 1951, McMillan thanked the president for bringing "positive good to me personally." Turner responded warmly and thanked McMillan for his support.[43]

When *Negro Higher Education in the State of South Carolina* was published—at the author's expense—in early 1953, McMillan apparently believed that his judicious and pathbreaking study would stimulate genuine reforms and progress in the state's public and private black colleges. In the preface he noted what should have been obvious to many people, but clearly was not: that "the Negro is educable [and] that his education

A native of Allendale, South Carolina, Lewis K. McMillan was the first full-time faculty member with an earned doctorate. After he wrote and published *Negro Higher Education in South Carolina,* President Benner Turner declined to renew his contract in 1953. He never taught full time in a college or university setting again. Courtesy of the Historical Collection, South Carolina State University

is indispensable to the finer growth of the State, and that something will be done about Negro higher education in the state of South Carolina when its terrible plight has been fully known to the people."[44]

In a modest volume of 220 pages, McMillan tried to offer a balanced and careful assessment of that "terrible plight" that was black higher education. He included extensive quotations from primary sources, an ample compliment of statistical evidence, and an additional seventy pages of appendixes. But published on the eve of the *Brown v. Board of Education* decision, the book is less a historical analysis and more an anguished denunciation of racial segregation and an impassioned expose of the abysmal lack of meaningful educational opportunities for the state's black population. McMillan's only unreserved words of praise were for the black and white educators who labored to bring knowledge to former slaves in South Carolina in the decades immediately following the Civil War. These energetic pioneers not only taught the fundamental skills of reading, writing, and basic mathematics; they imparted a desire among their students for more education. What is most important, McMillan insisted, these remarkable educators instilled self-respect and dignity in their students.[45]

McMillan argued that twentieth-century educators utterly failed to build on that nineteenth-century legacy. On page after page he severely criticized administrators and faculty for failing their inadequately prepared students. In his examination of fifteen institutions—nine of them no longer exist—he could find no private or public two- or four-year college that provided a minimally adequate education for its students. On the contrary the educators who supervised these schools accepted and even embraced a system of education that consigned their students (and themselves) to a subordinate status in society. Moreover he indicted white political leaders—and by extension the state's white citizens—for their woeful neglect, indifference, and outright hostility to the education of nearly half of the state's residents, which had prevailed for decades under the guise of the "separate but equal" system.

Negro Higher Education bristles with razor-sharp barbs as McMillan deplores the condition and status of black South Carolinians. He likened the lives of rural black people to those of medieval serfs. "Illiteracy prevails here," he pointed out, as did dependency. "A precarious, childish hand-to-mouth existence characterizes the life of the people for almost all of them are bound through some sort of attachment to a human lord; most often it is the relation of the plantation lord and subservient tenant farmer. Simple toil of 'beasts of burden' marks the level on which the Negro in this section of the Deep South does his work." He added that black residents of rural counties like Allendale and Bamberg had no political influence whatsoever. "Democracy is absolutely foreign to them; exercising the franchise, holding public office, and determining public policy are downright forbidden territory."[46]

In assessing specific institutions, he spared no criticism as he assailed black educators. Columbia's Allen University offered lofty and idealistic aims. But most of it was, McMillan declared, "a monstrous bit of empty prattle." The faculty had no role in devising educational policies. "It initiates nothing; it votes on nothing; it determines nothing." Benedict College, located across the street from Allen, busied itself preparing students to teach and accept the status quo. "One thing is certain, these young people will almost never get in trouble, for they are not taught to bother about anything that is substantial. Nor does the College itself breathe life into the nostrils of a prostrate people."[47]

McMillan reserved his most stern criticism for his employer, S.C. State. The institution badly failed its ill-prepared and unworldly students. "The poor browbeaten, downtrodden persons they are, inevitably seek the shadow of things: membership in fraternities and sororities; 'shining' in athletics, hollow popularity in social affairs; expensive clothes bought on credit by lowly parents; high grades in snap courses, in short, a name! merely a name!"[48]

Ultimately, however, the enormous failure to offer a semblance of satisfactory higher education to students at South Carolina State belonged to the State of South Carolina. "Neither the State's educational leadership nor its political leadership has ever placed it [S.C. State] in the equation of the State's scheme of public higher education. Out there to itself, it serves now and always as a mere make-believe, a thing to point to when legal questions of educational equity are raised."[49]

McMillan concluded that the yawning gap in educational opportunities between black and white South Carolinians had not even begun to close during the first half of the twentieth century. "As one looks to the future, the outlook for public higher education for Negroes in the state of South Carolina is very dark. Practically everything remains to be done; even the beginning has yet to be made." McMillan called for the full inclusion of black people in developing and implementing educational policies for

South Carolina. "The Negro, who has been treated hitherto (and is still being treated now), as a subject people, must be taken into the scheme of things as equal partners both in policy-making and in execution; and also in the enjoyment of the best fruits of the State's wealth, material, and culture."[50]

If McMillan intended his history and analysis to enlighten readers and to provoke them to action, it failed completely to arouse demands for reforms in higher education. Instead McMillan's book infuriated black and white people—including many who never even saw the book—and led to his dismissal from South Carolina State and exile from his native state. Many black South Carolinians were up in arms because McMillan had had the temerity to criticize "their" school and the faculty and administrators who guided those institutions. John McCray, the talented and candid editor of the *Lighthouse and Informer*, a black newspaper published in Columbia, acknowledged that there were people who wanted McCray to put "Dr. Lewis K. McMillan in his place." But the editor defended McMillan's right to free speech and offered cautious praise. "On the whole, I consider [the book] worthy of reading, scholarly presented, though I do not necessarily endorse references to some of the personalities he discusses." McCray added that he was certain "that all of us have known for more than 50 years that our colleges aren't the equal of those operated by and for whites."[51]

The day after a faculty meeting in which McMillan announced that the book would appear in two weeks, President Turner summoned McMillan to his office and informed him that it was a violation of S.C. State policy for any member of the faculty to "vilify" the college or any similar institution in South Carolina. McMillan brushed off Turner's warning, and the book was published in mid-February 1953. Turner took the matter to the board of trustees and recommended McMillan's termination. Three months later in a one-sentence letter, the president informed McMillan that he would not be offered a contract for the 1953–54 school year. He did not bother to thank McMillan for his service. Because S.C. State had no tenure policy, McMillan had few avenues of appeal.[52]

McMillan was stunned. Although Turner had warned him, the history professor simply did not expect that his book would lead to his termination. He pleaded with the trustees to rescind the president's decision. He explained that he and his family had just moved into their "dream house," where they planned to live lives of "nearly first-class citizens." He was convinced that he had the freedom to write the book. "The only language I know now, or ever have known, is the language of FREEDOM—freedom of existence, freedom of thought, freedom of speech. Freedom, gentlemen, is for me a way of life." He implored the trustees to read the book and to reverse "the brutal wrong that has been done to me." The board ignored his impassioned plea.[53]

McMillan also asked the Southern Association of Colleges and Schools (SACS), the American Civil Liberties Union (ACLU), and the American Association of University Professors (AAUP) to intervene. The *Harvard Crimson* and the Academic Freedom Project at Columbia University also inquired about McMillan's termination. The executive secretary of SACS, J. M. Godard, told McMillan as well as President Turner that the organization did not investigate such cases. But Godard did advise Turner that the organization was interested in assuring that proper procedures had been followed and wanted to know if McMillan had had a hearing. Turner wrote Godard and explained that McMillan had not been accorded a hearing because he had not been dismissed while his contract was in effect. His contract simply was not renewed. And it was not renewed because "it is against the policy of this institution for members of the staff to insult, defame, libel, slander or vilify other institutions or their staff members." Turner also insisted that in criticizing S.C. State, McMillan had exceeded the boundaries of academic freedom. "It is not felt that a person hostile and antagonistic to the institution can contribute to its progress and its welfare."[54]

Historian Howard K. Beale of the University of Wisconsin wrote a scathing letter to Turner condemning him for his treatment of McMillan. "I write to protest that instead of dismissing a man for speaking the truth about the wretched discrimination against Negroes that starves them intellectually and deprives them of a chance, you should honor him. It seems to me that you are unworthy to be president of a Negro college in the South if you are not, yourself, ashamed of your college and the terrible discrimination against Negroes in South Carolina and burning with a fire to remedy the wrong." While excoriating Turner for his termination of McMillan, Beale and his colleagues at the University of Wisconsin did not suggest that the beleaguered black historian apply for a teaching position on their faculty or with the faculty of any other majority institution.[55]

McMillan's inquiry to the AAUP languished for three years. Finally, and at McMillan's prodding, Warren C. Middleton, a staff member at the organization, asked President Turner for an explanation of the historian's removal. Middleton admitted that "on account of an enormously heavy work load," he had not pursued McMillan's case in a timely manner. Turner wrote Middleton and said the board of trustees would respond to the AAUP at its next meeting. After another inquiry from Middleton nearly six months later, Turner told Middleton that W. C. Bethea, secretary to the board of trustees, would explain the dismissal of McMillan.[56]

But it was Turner who drafted the letter that Bethea sent to Warren Middleton and the AAUP. Turner said in that draft that the "matter is over four years old," that the membership of the board had changed, and that records regarding the case "are no longer at hand." Therefore the board of trustees at its June 20, 1957, meeting considered the case "closed because of the lapse of time." Thus the AAUP by its lack of diligence and interest had let McMillan down. Clearly, however, it had been Turner—and not the trustees—who took the lead in ousting McMillan.[57]

Lewis K. McMillan's academic career was finished. He never taught full time in college again. He left South Carolina, and by 1958 he and his wife, Kathryn, were living in Stratford, Connecticut. He taught at Bullard Havens Technical High School in Bridgeport, and she was a supervisor of English with the Stratford Board of Education. Lewis McMillan died in July 1974.[58]

ACADEMIC FREEDOM AND TENURE

President Turner suspected that too many faculty members put their personal interests above the welfare of the college. In 1952—before McMillan's book was published—the president of Alabama A&M, a black land-grant college, asked Turner if S.C. State had a manual that spelled out rules and responsibilities that applied to members of the faculty. Turner replied that S.C. State had no such document, and that it had no intention of creating such a manual, because it would just embolden some faculty members. He explained that "a certain type of teacher will try to convert the rules and regulations set forth in a handbook into a Bill of Rights, and insist that the college administration is powerless to admit itself to new or unforeseen situations by modifying or abrogating previously adopted regulations or by enacting new ones."[59]

The college had never had a tenure policy—which suited President Turner. Instead the institution relied on the bylaws of the board of trustees to "safeguard" the employment security and "protect" the academic freedom of faculty members. The bylaws stipulated that: "The election or appointment of teachers shall be for one year, but that faithful and efficient performance of duties, and good behavior shall be recommendations for repeated elections irrespective of change of work, title, or salary." As Lewis McMillan learned, this policy provided no protection if the president recommended that the board not tender the faculty member a contract for the next academic year.[60]

Turner did not mind devising and implementing a new tenure policy as long as it did not prevent him from removing faculty members whose conduct was, in his judgment, injurious to the interests of the college. The new tenure policy, adopted in 1955, afforded faculty members no protection whatsoever against arbitrary administrative authority. Tenured or continuous faculty could be dismissed for:

Misconduct
Failure to perform required duties
Bona fide reductions in staff
Curtailment or discontinuation of a department or school
Conduct detrimental to the best interest of the college.

The president would determine what constituted detrimental conduct. Faculty members who were terminated were to be given thirty days' notice *"when practicable."* They also had the right to ask for a hearing before the board of trustees, and that faculty member would be permitted to defend himself or herself at that hearing. So that there was no possible misunderstanding, the trustees included an additional statement in the tenure policy that further undermined faculty security. *"In implementing the foregoing policy, the Board of Trustees recognizes its inability to make any binding commitment extending over periods of time greater than one year under the laws of South Carolina; and it further recognizes its duty at all times to act in the best interest of the College and the State of South Carolina, which rights and duties are paramount."*[61]

No faculty member could take comfort in this tenure policy. It was no deterrent to Turner, to the trustees, or to the State of South Carolina in the years that followed. Faculty members could be and were dismissed with impunity, just as McMillan had been. But as the civil rights movement began to gain momentum in the mid-1950s, members of the faculty did take a stand for themselves and for the college as white authorities sought to quash activism at the black institution.

In April 1956 the ordinarily quiescent S.C. State faculty rose up in near unanimous opposition to a decision by the general assembly to launch a probe of NAACP involvement among faculty and students at the college. Almost every faculty member signed a resolution protesting the legislative investigation. Such defiance of state authority by the middle-class and professional staff at the black institution was unprecedented. But it occurred only after months of an escalating controversy that divided the Orangeburg community along racial lines and spilled over to the campus.[62]

On July 31, 1955, fifty-seven parents of black children in Orangeburg signed and submitted a petition requesting that the local board of education take "immediate concrete steps leading to early elimination of segregation in public schools" in keeping with the 1954 U.S. Supreme Court decision mandating an end to the "separate but equal" doctrine in public education. The Orangeburg petition was one of about sixty that local branches of the NAACP drafted in the weeks after the Supreme Court declared in May 1955 that desegregation should proceed "with all deliberate speed."[63]

The petition was the work of the NAACP branch president, the Reverend Matthew McCollom, a Methodist minister, and James Sulton, the treasurer of the branch. He was a World War II veteran and the co-owner (with his brother, Roy) of Sulton's Esso service station, which was located adjacent to the campus. Hazel Pierce, a schoolteacher and mother of S.C. State faculty member Geraldyne Pierce Zimmerman, was the NAACP executive secretary. Attorney Newton Pough, who was a graduate of the S.C. State law school, assisted in drafting the petition. The fifty-seven signers represented a cross section of the black community. They were bricklayers, carpenters, domestics, and sharecroppers as well as the owners of a taxi company, a coffee shop, and a funeral home.[64]

According to the *Times and Democrat,* the local newspaper, the petition badly disrupted the racial harmony that had long prevailed in the community. "We have been fortunate in this area to have enjoyed unexcelled relations between the races for many decades. . . . There is a genuine spirit of friendliness between the races." Efforts to merge the separate public schools "with all deliberate speed" was too awful a possibility for white people to contemplate. There would be no tampering with segregation. Although the petition was entirely legal, it was entirely unacceptable. "The people in this state and in this area are not ready for integration. . . . Attempts to use legal means to force people into changing their methods are certain to bring about a worsening of relations between the races, friction, and much ill-will."[65]

To oppose the petition and the NAACP, the white community swiftly closed ranks. They were not prepared to accept changes to the racial environment in the Orangeburg community. Led by local insurance agent W. T. C. Bates and with the enthusiastic encouragement of the mayor, state legislators, the sheriff, the solicitor, and the clerk of courts, they organized a Citizens' Council. They held a rally that drew three thousand people to Mirmow Field, the local baseball park. The council devised a campaign of economic coercion against the black petitioners to force them to withdraw their support for desegregation of the schools.[66]

Mayor Robert H. Jennings was an influential businessman who operated the Palmetto Bakery, Orangeburg Fuel and Ice, Paradise Ice Cream, and the local Coca-Cola franchise. He suspended deliveries to black grocers, barber shops, and restaurants. The black owner of a Shell service station lost his franchise. James Sulton could not get gasoline deliveries to his Esso station for the Labor Day weekend. Coble Dairy stopped deliveries to petitioners. Sharecroppers were evicted. A black mechanic at the local Ford dealer lost his job. Insurance was not renewed and credit denied. The municipal utility department fired an employee who had signed the petition. About one-half of the original fifty-seven petitioners removed their names.[67]

The black community fought back, and an economic war over race ensued in Orangeburg. The local NAACP branch shrewdly developed a selective-buying campaign to divide the white community. Black leaders decided to patronize some white businesses while avoiding twenty-three others. They urged black people not to purchase Coca-Cola, Standard Oil products, or Sunbeam bread, and not to conduct business at Horne Motors, the Ford dealer, or Beckers' store for women. This created bewilderment and consternation among white retailers, especially those on the "don't buy list." They were at a loss to understand why black people continued to patronize their competitors.[68]

The standoff between black and white people in Orangeburg continued for weeks and then months. That August, Emmett Till, a fourteen-year-old youngster from Chicago, was lynched in Mississippi. In December black people in Montgomery, Alabama, began a boycott of buses after Rosa Parks, a local NAACP leader, refused a driver's orders to vacate her seat for a white man. The Reverend Ralph David Abernathy and others involved in the Montgomery boycott asked Orangeburg leaders to travel to Alabama to share advice and suggestions on conducting a mass movement.[69]

Black leaders appealed to South Carolina State students to observe the selective-buying campaign. NAACP treasurer James Sulton met with Fred H. Moore, the Student Government Association president, and the Reverend Francis Donlan, the rector of Christ the King Catholic Church, and asked for their support. A senior from Charleston, Moore was a chemistry major who had graduated from Burke High School. As a child he had contracted polio and walked with a limp. He attended S.C. State on one of the scholarships awarded to black students by the City of Charleston so that those young people would not enroll in the College of Charleston, which was at the time a municipal institution.[70]

Moore was eager to back the NAACP campaign but turned for advice to President Benner C. Turner. Ever cautious and conservative, Turner had a frosty relationship with state NAACP leader James Hinton, and he had developed no close relationships with leaders in the local black community. Turner urged Moore not to get students involved in the campaign. He cautioned the SGA president that "we [the college] had no obligation to protect the community because we were sort of—not alien to it—but at least separate and distinct from the Orangeburg community, and should not be involved in civic matters." Moore feigned agreement with Turner but covertly organized support among students for the NAACP campaign.[71]

Because the dining hall continued to serve products that were forbidden as part of the NAACP selective-buying campaign, students refused to dine on Sunday, March 25, 1956. Here students are shown walking out of Floyd Dining Hall. They staged an ongoing boycott of the dining hall in sympathy with the NAACP struggle. Courtesy of Cecil J. Williams

At S.C. State, Floyd Dining Hall became the focal point of student discontent. For decades that dining hall was operated by Marion Birnie Wilkinson as a private concession. In spite of the selective-buying campaign, the dining hall continued to serve Sunbeam bread from the Palmetto Bakery, milk from Coble Dairy, and Paradise Ice Cream. At Sunday dinner on March 25, 1956, protesting students poured water on the bread, refused to drink the milk, and marched out without eating. Turner appeared at vesper services that evening and pleaded for moderation. He explained, however, that "the College would honor its contracts" with the local businesses and "would not enter into an economic warfare or boycott." Unhappy students responded by scraping their feet on the floor of White Hall Auditorium. The next day 150 students marched to the president's campus residence to present complaints. Unknown to students and faculty, Turner then told a meeting of the local board of trustees that the "students were being exploited by outside forces." The board explicitly instructed the president "to continue using" the products that were the object of the NAACP campaign. Turner's fears that the college could be dragged into the community controversy had materialized.[72]

In the meantime South Carolina's political leadership reacted with fury to the assertive efforts of the NAACP and black leaders. During the early months of 1956 they went on the offensive to make certain that the Supreme Court's decision to implement the *Brown* decision "with all deliberate speed" did not occur then or in the foreseeable future. What is more important, they seemed determined to intimidate black people and to create a climate of apprehension and fear that would curtail the movement to end segregation. The state's politicians were convinced that the state's black population and the NAACP had either naively or purposely allowed themselves to become dupes in the vast communist conspiracy to create turmoil and upheaval in the United States. White leaders could not comprehend the possibility that black South Carolinians were genuinely dissatisfied with the state of racial affairs.

Governor George Bell Timmerman told the state Democratic Party convention in March 1956 that integration was a "very real and very meaningful part of the communist conspiracy." He went on to add that racial integration was an insidious plot. "When we think in terms of racial mixing, remember that it was first advocated in the United States by the Communist Party. It was then and still is a part of the Communist program to create dissension and discord." In what came to be known as the "segregation session," legislators clamored to outdo each other as they introduced a flood of measures to uphold segregation. There were among the dozens of proposals enacted in 1956:

> A bill to close the state's white colleges and universities as well as S.C. State if the courts ordered the integration of any institution of higher education.
>
> A bill to prohibit NAACP membership among state, county, and local employees, including public school teachers.
>
> A resolution drafted by House member Jerry M. Hughes, Jr., of Orangeburg to create a nine-member legislative committee to investigate the activities of the NAACP at S.C. State College.
>
> A resolution to have the federal government designate the NAACP a subversive organization.[73]

The faculty and staff at South Carolina State in 1956 could hardly be characterized as a band of civil rights agitators or rabble-rousers. But the normally quiet and compliant faculty reacted with barely disguised anger at this legislative attack on the NAACP and the college. They took a decisive and public stand for themselves and the institution. Initially an anonymous resolution dated March 23, 1956, had circulated among faculty members. Rather, however, than weakly relying on the nameless document, the faculty drew up a second resolution that was signed by 176 of 177 faculty members and administrators. It was sent to Turner with a copy for each member of the board of trustees. It was also disseminated on April 4, 1956, to the Associated Press, United News Service, International News Service, and the American Negro Press. R. C. Henderson, the chairman of the Faculty Study Commission and a sociology professor, explained that they resented the legislative assault on academic freedom. Faculty members could not teach

Because President Benner C. Turner and Governor George Bell Timmerman cracked down on students following their dining hall protest, students hanged a crude likeness of President Turner from a campus tree in late March 1956. State representative Jerry Hughes of Orangeburg and Governor Timmerman were also subsequently hanged in effigy. Notice that someone had scrawled "brain" on the crotch of the Turner effigy. Courtesy of Cecil J. Williams

effectively "if pressures and attempts at intimidation are leveled at us—no matter from whence they come."

Written evenhandedly and without rancor, the resolution made no explicit requests or demands. Perhaps purposely it lacked rhetorical flourishes brimming with moral outrage or indignation. The resolution calmly pointed out that the U.S. attorney general had not included the NAACP on a list of subversive organizations. They affirmed their support for "law and order," for the U.S. Supreme Court, and for the U.S. Constitution. They concluded by asking—as had previous generations of African Americans—for the defense of their rights. "We believe that history convincingly shows that our constitutional rights need protection."[74]

However, Governor George Bell Timmerman believed that the college was on the brink of insurrection. He announced that SLED—the State Law Enforcement Division—would be dispatched to the campus. Law enforcement personnel would investigate subversive activities among students and faculty. Timmerman's actions only served to incite further indignation among students and faculty.[75]

Student Government Association president Fred H. Moore declared that students would not tolerate the presence of law enforcement officers on the campus. "This is not a mental institution nor a penal institution but an institution of higher learning, attended by free people in a free land." Students proceeded to hang Turner, local state legislator Jerry Hughes, and Governor Timmerman in effigy on the campus. They also scrawled messages and slogans in chalk on campus sidewalks. Turner "made every effort through the college police force, administrative officials, and others," but he failed to determine the "perpetrators of these acts." Then there was an odd lull in the crisis because students went on spring break for five days between April 3 and April 8.[76]

STUDENTS STRIKE AND TURN ON TURNER

When students returned on Monday, April 9, 1956, nearly everyone one of the eleven hundred undergraduates refused to attend class. Moore explained that until Governor Timmerman withdrew his decision to send law enforcement officials to the campus, students would stay on strike. President Turner insisted that "I am in no position to tell the Governor what to do, or what not to do." But Turner did warn students that their failure to return to class would result in expulsion. White leaders threatened to close the college permanently if students continued to defy demands to halt the strike. But instead of returning to class, students were even more determined, and they shifted from opposition to the governor to criticism of the college president and his policies.

Simmering discontent with Turner flared into the open. With the encouragement of several faculty members including psychology professor William N. Smith, biology professor and chair of natural sciences Edward Ferguson, and history professor the Reverend Alfred Isaac, they focused on Turner's aloof and arbitrary leadership. Attention shifted from the community to the campus. Students drew up a list of grievances. They wanted an end to disciplinary hearings that they compared to an "inquisition," the selection of students to serve on committees based on competence and not the president's "petty, personal and private likes and dislikes," a revised publication policy for the *Collegian,* the extension of "common courtesies and fair treatment" to students, and a guarantee that there be no reprisals for participation in the strike. Having made known their dissatisfaction with President Turner, students conducted a vote of confidence on his leadership. Of 716 who voted—over half of the student body—614 voted no confidence, one hundred abstained, and two voted that they did have confidence in him.[77]

With threats to expel students looming, the four-day strike ended. Students agreed to resume classes on Friday morning, April 13. President Turner submitted a report to the trustees six days later and cautioned against disciplinary action because order had been restored and tensions reduced. He worried that punishment "may create additional unrest." Yet Turner promised to discipline any individual "guilty of instigating or creating disturbances in violation of the law or college regulations." But he expressed considerable frustration with his inability to identify those who were responsible for inciting the uprising while he simultaneously admitted that the entire affair was peaceful and orderly. There "was no outward violence, no destruction of property, no open violation of college regulations" except for students who had not attended class.[78]

Retribution was swift, nevertheless. SGA president Fred Moore was brought before the board of trustees on April 25, and Turner recommended his immediate expulsion The trustees quickly—even eagerly—agreed. Moore, a graduating senior, was permitted to retrieve his belongings from the dormitory, and then escorted from the campus. The board characterized the faculty resolutions as "unwise and untimely." They strongly praised Turner for "his sane leadership" during the student protests. White political leaders and journalists were pleased with the resolution of the crisis.[79]

One month later Turner ordered fourteen additional students—eleven of them women—suspended for the 1956–57 academic year. Marie R. Vernon, the dean of women, wrote Turner on May 29 and identified nine female students "who were playing the

On April 25, 1956, the board of trustees and President Benner C. Turner expelled Student Government Association president Fred Moore for his role in leading the student protest and boycott of classes. He was not given a hearing and was denied an appeal. Here his fellow students bid him farewell as he departs the campus. Courtesy of Cecil J. Williams

role of leaders, agitators, and undercover persons" in the student strike. The nine young women "were instrumental in helping women students lose sight of their educational objectives, reject social activities as a base for revenge against the administration." Vernon recommended that they not be permitted to return to S.C. State.[80]

Turner added the names of two women and three men to Vernon's list of nine, and on May 30 he asked the trustees to approve the suspension of the fourteen students, and the board readily concurred. On May 31 President Turner sent separate letters to the students and to their parents or guardians informing them that they could not return to the college for one year. He told the students that they had been unwilling "to conform sincerely and loyally to the usages and regulations of the College." He added that the "decision is based on reports and recommendations made by faculty personnel responsible for student conduct."[81]

The fourteen suspended students:

1. Vivian Lennon, New York City
2. Barbara Harrell, Florence, S.C.
3. Annie Bomar, Spartanburg, S.C.
4. Vera Rhue, Georgetown, S.C.
5. Barbara Brown, Charleston, S.C.
6. Alice Pyatt, Charleston, S.C.
7. Ruthie Mae Sarvis, Conway, S.C.
8. Rochelle Moore, Conway, S.C.
9. Geneva White, Lake City, S.C.
10. Claudia Brown, Conway, S.C.
11. Eugenia Thomas, Columbia, S.C.
12. Alvin Anderson, Charleston, S.C.
13. Earl Bradford, Charleston, S.C.
14. Roosevelt Brown, Southampton, Bermuda

The parents of several students wrote Turner to ask for an explanation. Mr. and Mrs. Rudolph A. Pyatt Sr. wondered why they had not been notified that the conduct of their daughter Alice "was of such a nature as to require her withdrawal." They politely requested a fuller accounting of the entire episode, and they asked why Alice was suspended "without an opportunity to defend herself."[82]

Turner replied cordially that "I deeply regret this matter." He indicated that the suspended students had taken part in acts "designed to harm the institution" and create "student unrest." Without identifying her Turner quoted directly from Dean Marie R. Vernon's letter that members of the faculty regarded Alice Pyatt as one of the students "instrumental in helping students lose sight of their educational objectives." Dean Vernon was not a member of the faculty, however. She was an administrator. In response to a query from Mrs. Roosevelt Brown about her daughter, Barbara Brown, President Turner sent Brown the same letter he sent to the Pyatts. Turner mentioned the recommendation of the unnamed faculty members and quoted again from Dean Vernon's letter.[83]

Alice Pyatt was devastated by her suspension: "When I received the letter that summer saying not to return to state college, I cried practically the whole summer. And I am not a weepy person, I'm not a softie. But it hurt so hard, until I cried and cried and I cried." She enrolled at Allen University that fall and earned a bachelor's degree four years after her graduation in 1955 from Burke High School. She managed to retain her scholarship from the Charleston County schools but carried the scars of her Orangeburg experience for years. She was especially bitter toward the NAACP. Their leaders had encouraged students to support the movement but then abandoned them after they were suspended; those leaders said "they could not help me."[84]

Several of the suspended students including Barbara Brown never returned to S.C. State or managed to enroll at another institution. Suspension was the equivalent of expulsion. In his letter to Alice Pyatt, Turner said that he was hopeful "that you will be able to transfer without difficulty to another educational institution and continue your

President Benner C. Turner sent letters to students who he regarded as ringleaders in the student protest and boycott of classes in April 1956, informing them that they were suspended for the following academic year. From left to right, suspended students Barbara Brown, Alvin Anderson, and Alice Pyatt stare in disbelief at Turner's letter. Courtesy of Cecil J. Williams

college career." But Turner was not candid with Alice Pyatt or the others. In a letter to Robert P. Daniel, the president of Virginia State College, Turner offered to send a list of the students who were told not to return so that Daniel could check the list against applicants to Virginia State. Turner implied Daniel would not want to accept them. In effect Turner had black-listed them.[85]

Fred Moore did graduate from Allen University and earned a law degree at Howard University. Rudolph Pyatt, one of the student leaders, was permitted to graduate. But his sister, Alice, who was a freshman and was not as directly involved in the protest as her older brother, had been suspended. Turner took action against her because Rudolph was scheduled to receive a commission as a second lieutenant in the U.S. Army through ROTC, and his suspension or expulsion would have created complications with the military. In a news conference in New York City in June, Harlem congressman Adam Clayton Powell condemned the expulsion and suspensions, and he called for an inquiry into the affair. One of the suspended students, Vivian Lennon, was the daughter of Powell aide Acy Lennon, who was a graduate of S.C. State. But Powell never pursued the inquiry.[86]

Not surprisingly the response of the media to the student protests broke along racial lines. The conservative *Charleston News and Courier* saw the student uprising as ultimately an attempt to promote integration. Was the college preparing leaders? "Or is it training a corps of discontented agitators whose only aim is to change Negroes into white people by forced association?"[87]

Black journalist John McCray, writing in the pages of the *Baltimore Afro American*, saw it as an all-too-common case of white men and their black agent aligned in opposition to the aspirations of black South Carolinians. "But the collusive trustee-president's actions simply highlight a familiar pattern in the deep south—the white man and his favorite colored employee acting in concert against a sizable group of colored citizens." McCray, however, failed to understand Turner if he believed that the president was the mere pawn of the board of trustees. It was Turner who assumed the initiative and monitored the conduct of students and faculty. He was not forced or even persuaded to make decisions or implement directives that he opposed or doubted. He governed the college, and he made decisions that the trustees were almost always willing to support.[88]

Four faculty members were to varying degrees also casualties of the student strike. William N. Smith, who was a psychology professor as well as the director of student guidance and personnel, had been the faculty member most openly critical of Turner. In his letter of resignation, he complained to Turner that there was a conflict "between what I know to be educationally sound and morally right, and what appears to me to be practices designed for opportunism and expediency." Smith's wife, Vivian, who was a professor of education, also quit.[89]

Professor Edward Ferguson, who chaired the Department of Biology, resigned—he said—because promises for new equipment and supplies had not been kept. Moreover Ferguson, with a Ph.D. from the University of Illinois, was able to command a salary of $9,600 at Grambling State University. No S.C. State faculty member earned an amount close to that figure. The Reverend Alfred Isaacs left his teaching position in history. But he probably would not have been retained regardless, because he had not earned a master's degree in history. Isaacs was a clergyman in Orangeburg at Mount Pisgah Baptist Church.[90]

FLORENCE MILLER'S TERMINATION

The most contentious departure was that of Florence Miller, who had been teaching English at the college for nearly a decade. Her contract was not renewed, but Miller did not depart quietly. She challenged her dismissal and retained a familiar figure as her legal counsel. Cassandra Maxwell Birnie took Miller's case to the board of trustees and insisted that they provide the specific charges that led to her client's removal. Cassandra Maxwell had been on the faculty of the law school before she married James H. Birnie in 1950. She had been the first black woman to practice law in South Carolina, but she had since joined her husband in Atlanta, where he was teaching biology at Morehouse College.[91]

The trustees delayed providing any meaningful response in hopes of wearing down Miller and her attorney. It took almost three years for the board to act. In the meantime

President Benner C. Turner ousted Florence Miller as a professor of English and advisor for the *Collegian* because she had failed to restrain the student journalists on the *Collegian,* particularly Rudolph Pyatt. She took a teaching position at Tuskegee and, with the legal assistance of attorney Cassandra E. Maxwell, successfully sued S.C. State. Courtesy of the Historical Collection, South Carolina State University

Miller had taken a position teaching at Tuskegee Institute. Finally on February 20, 1959, and only after a pointed letter of inquiry from the American Association of University Professors (AAUP), the executive committee of the board held a hearing. The all-day session convened in the law offices of Herbert and Dial in Columbia. R. Beverly Herbert was an attorney and a member of the board of trustees.

Dr. Nettie Parler, the chair of the Department of English, charged that Miller's performance was "unsatisfactory and ineffic[i]ent," and that she did not teach properly and gave too many low grades. But it was Miller's oversight of the *Collegian* that was the real reason for her removal. During the 1954–55 school year she had permitted one of the student journalists, Rudolph Pyatt, "to use the paper to promote a feud with another student (Student Council President Benjamin Payton) and to launch personal attacks upon the administrative and faculty personnel." Turner had summoned Miller to a conference and told her to rein in Pyatt. But she "allowed the practice to continue." She neither changed nor improved her conduct. In fact, Parler alleged, Miller became "belligerent, vituperative, and defiant." But Turner made certain that Pyatt did not write for the *Collegian* in 1955–56. Thus Miller's most grievous offense had occurred the previous year.[92]

The board's executive committee reluctantly conceded that Miller had not been treated fairly. They agreed to award her one year's salary of $4,500 but immediately reduced that to $850 because Miller had been employed at Tuskegee. They did offer to allow her "to resign without prejudice." Miller and attorney Cassandra Maxwell Birnie declined the offer and indicated that they intended to pursue the case to the AAUP. They apparently hoped that the national organization might level sanctions against the college at the very time the institution anticipated earning accreditation from the Southern Association of Colleges and Universities. Several weeks later the trustees authorized a payment of $1,000 to settle the case once Miller agreed to drop her appeal to the AAUP.[93]

THE CONTROVERSY RECEDES

Student resentment toward Turner festered in the months that followed the class boycott and Fred Moore's dismissal. Someone posted a large sign with neat block letters near the president's campus residence: "THIS WAY TO UNCLE TOM'S CABIN." As the academic year ended students suspended social activities. No ceremony to crown the May Queen, Jimmie Payne Grayson, was held. Fraternities and sororities cancelled an assortment of events. Nearly a year after the strike, any mention of Turner's name in student gatherings incited coughing and foot scraping.[94]

Orangeburg and S.C. State gradually returned to what passed for normal. Thirty-one of the fifty-seven people who had signed the NAACP petition in July had removed their names. W. T. C. Bates stepped down from the White Citizens Council. The selective-buying campaign continued into late 1956 before it waned and finally disintegrated. The loss of black customers did force Beckers', a store for women, to close its doors. But the public schools stayed segregated, and Orangeburg remained as deeply divided by race as ever. Legislators who had been so eager to uproot communist influences on the campus lost interest. The nine-member legislative committee made two cursory visits to S.C. State in June and August 1956, but they found no communists lurking among the students and faculty. They were not even able to identify any NAACP members to question among the faculty or students, because there had been no NAACP on the campus since Turner became president. The committee did not pursue the investigation nor issue a report.[95]

In the aftermath Turner repeated the dictum that he had earlier offered Fred Moore—academic institutions should shun controversy, "that a college is an educational institution and cannot expect long to survive if it is allowed to become a political, social or economic battleground." For their backing during the ordeal, he profusely thanked the trustees, "who have supported the administration's efforts to minimize the effects of the difficulties recently experienced here, and to stick to the paths of education." Exactly a half century later in 2006 at a ceremony to mark the fiftieth anniversary of the protests and strike, S.C. State president Andrew Hugine and board chairman Maurice Washington formally apologized on behalf of South Carolina State University to those students who had been expelled and suspended. Fred Moore graciously accepted the apology on their behalf.[96]

Jim Crow may have been as firmly entrenched as ever and Benner C. Turner seemingly well ensconced as president of the college, but S.C. State students in 1955–56 had shed several layers of complacency and demonstrated an activism that would reassert itself again and again over the next decade. Turner managed for a time to squelch student discontent by expulsion and suspension. Often, however, he tried to manage students diplomatically by cultivating the support of their leaders while maintaining an assortment of written and unwritten rules and regulations.

Prior to the selective-buying campaign and the student strike, for example, Turner attempted without success to win the allegiance of student journalist Rudolph Pyatt. As a columnist for the *Collegian*, Pyatt criticized Student Government Association president Benjamin Payton. Turner assumed that Pyatt was a dissident determined to cause trouble. But Pyatt assured him that "I was not a trouble maker" and that he was a member of the male chorus and the track team and belonged to the same fraternity as Turner, Alpha Phi Alpha. Turner tried to cajole and flatter Pyatt, but the young man displayed a streak of independence that dismayed the president. Turner then made certain that Pyatt was not on the staff of the *Collegian* the following year, and the president recommended that Florence Miller's contract not be renewed.[97]

Turner had developed a cordial relationship with Benjamin Payton. During Payton's senior year in 1954–55, Turner urged him to apply to the graduate program at Turner's alma mater Harvard University, and Turner wrote an effusive letter of recommendation. Payton came, Turner explained, from a large family with a small income. Payton's father was a part-time minister and a full-time carpenter. Payton was "a young man of splendid character, initiative, high ideals and unusual ability." Turner was sure that if Payton was admitted, "it will bear good fruit in the future." It did, indeed, "bear good fruit." Payton earned a degree in divinity at Harvard and a Ph.D. in social ethics at Yale. He became the president of Benedict College and then served three decades as the president of Tuskegee University. But then Turner's nemesis, Rudolph Pyatt, did well too. He was commissioned an officer in the U.S. Army. He became the first black journalist with the *Charleston News and Courier* and went on to write for many years as the business editor for the *Washington Post.*[98]

After Payton graduated Turner had tried to create a similar relationship with the next Student Government Association president, Fred Moore. He told Moore that he could follow in Payton's footsteps. Turner promised Moore that he would work to secure the young Charlestonian's admission to the law school at Harvard. But the student strike and Moore's defiance of Turner put that possibility to an end.[99]

Turner fully expected students and faculty to defer to him because of his position and perhaps because of his academic background. He was sensitive to slights and criticism, even when that criticism was unintended. In 1953 Student Government Association president Franklin R. Jackson wrote a letter to Turner politely asking if rumors were true that Lewis K. McMillan and football coach Lawrence Simmons had been terminated. Turner was "grossly offended" that a student—even a student leader—would have the temerity to ask such a question. Of course the rumors were true.[100]

STUDENT CONDUCT

Like Presidents Wilkinson and Whittaker, Turner was much concerned with student conduct and behavior. When Franklin R. Jackson, the SGA president in 1952–53, made three requests of Turner in October 1953, Turner rejected two of them. He did agree to suspend Saturday classes from 11:30 to 12:30 for homecoming. But he would not agree to have the dining hall open early for homecoming. He also refused to permit members of the junior or senior classes to travel to the football game at Tuskegee on November 1.[101]

Turner did agree to a request by the Student Council that students serve on several campus committees. The executive committee of the council was authorized to name students to serve on eight committees as voting members including the Men's Council, the Women's Council, and the religious activities, student activities, entertainment and lyceum, and orientation committees. Students did not serve on the admissions, athletics, catalog, alumni, or discipline committees.[102]

Three students—all veterans and all over the age of thirty—were arrested in early 1951 near the town of North, South Carolina, about twenty miles from Orangeburg. They were charged with drunkenness. Franklin Monroe, James Sanford, and John Sims were driving to Columbia and had stopped for gas in North, where they each consumed a can of beer before continuing their trip. They were stopped outside of town by a South Carolina highway patrolman. Taken to jail, permitted no phone calls, they were held overnight and quickly tried and sentenced the next morning. Sims was also charged with disorderly conduct because he had acted belligerently.

When college authorities learned the whereabouts of the three men, they were at a county work camp wearing striped prison garb. Fines were paid and the three veterans were released. President Turner explained that they "had had a taste of Southern justice." Then they got a taste of S.C. State justice. Even though the incident occurred far from the campus, the Faculty Discipline Committee at Turner's request took action. The three men were in violation of college regulations. Franklin Monroe had not registered his vehicle with college authorities, each of them failed to notify the dean of men that they were leaving the campus, and they had been drinking. The committee suspended them for one semester.[103]

Like their predecessors faculty members and administrators continually vacillated when it came to the intellectual commitment of students. They persistently worried about the impoverished backgrounds and the weak academic training that black youth experienced. They believed students needed considerable encouragement and advice. Etta Rowe mentioned, for example, that one of her advisees was "a fine person, whose grades were fair, except for an 'F.'" But the young woman had become very discouraged primarily because of a lack of understanding on the part of her mother and father. "Her parents are able to keep her in school, but uneducated themselves, they feel that she is staying in school rather long." After some heartfelt conversations with Miss Rowe, the young lady decided to remain in school.

Faculty encountered unsophisticated students from rural areas who were unaware of the need for cleanliness. Rowe mentioned a young woman who had no toilet articles because her parents, who were "progressive farmers," regarded such items as "a luxury." After Rowe had several discussions with family members, the student received a supply of "'toilet articles,' three serviceable, needed dresses, and a warm wrap."[104]

On the other hand, there were students like Jacqueline Jenkins: "Positively an honor student—rated very high on freshman examinations and is keeping up the good work. No problems." But many students could not read very well, and that impeded their ability to study and grasp material. It also left them easily discouraged academically.

Some with "limited experiences" had difficulty adjusting to dormitory life. Hattie R. Dingle, a faculty advisor, reported that freshman students tended to blame themselves for their problems while seniors put the blame for their difficulties on faculty members. There were also senior women, Dingle indicated, who were "concerned with the issue of getting husbands." They "were frustrated over the fact that many of the eligible men were killed in Korea." Five members of the class of 1951 had died in the Korean conflict; four were officers: James B. Miller, Edwin D. Chavous, James N. Parker, and W. Watt McKellar, and one was an enlisted man, Harold S. Thompson.[105]

Aware of the deficiencies of their students, faculty members were sometimes less than demanding and rigorous in their expectations of academic achievement. As a result there were complaints that grades were too high. At a Department of English meeting in 1957, faculty members took note of the large percentage of high grades in composition and literature courses, without specifying the exact number. Department chair Nettie Parler reminded faculty, "It is obvious that our students are very poor in language arts; therefore, there is considerable doubt that the large number of A's and B's accurately represented student performances." Very few students were dismissed for failing grades in the fall of 1954: four of 259 seniors, eight of 209 juniors, thirty-five of 347 sophomores, and twenty-one of 272 freshmen. Charles H. Williams was one of the failures. His grandmother wrote President Turner and asked if her grandson could return to S.C. State that fall. Turner replied that he could not change the rules, but that her grandson could reenroll in spring 1956.[106]

During the same academic year that Charles Williams failed, dean of arts and sciences Kirkland W. Green complained in a meeting that "it appeared teachers had been a little too liberal in grading." The grades for the fall of 1954 in arts and sciences: 676 A's, 2,061 B's, 1,785 C's, 748 D's, 540 F's, and fifty incompletes. Green advised faculty members to take more care in evaluating students lest there be allegations that black people are not equal to white people; "make sure that there is no misrepresentation [in grading], because we did not want to prove by our actions that what is being said about us at this time before the United States Supreme Court by southern white attorneys is correct, that we are an inferior people."[107]

The number of students dismissed because of poor academic performance during the mid-1950s was low. But the high grades that many students received combined

Table 32. Rate of Academic Failures

	Number	Percentage
1952–53	24	2.2%
1953–54	41	3.5%
1954–55	67	6.0%
1955–56	43	3.9%
1956–57	42	4.1%

Source: *Annual Report, 1956–1957*, 30.

with the low failure rate was not an indication of academic excellence or even competence. On the contrary administrators and faculty members regularly bemoaned the poor academic preparation and lack of motivation among their students.

The dean of arts and sciences, Kirkland W. Green, complained of "far too many students who have shown by actual experience inadequate preparation for scholastic work on the college level." Too many freshmen students had to take noncredit remedial courses in reading and math, and that remedial program was costly for the college and time consuming for members of the faculty who taught those basic courses.[108]

ENTRANCE EXAMINATIONS

Dean Green proposed a solution: entrance examinations. These exams would be administered to high school seniors, and inadequately prepared students would be rejected for admission. President Turner endorsed the proposal, and the board of trustees approved it. In 1955 S.C. State began to require prospective high school seniors to take the exam. The results of the exam would constitute one of several criteria including high school grades and class standing to determine which prospective students stood the best chance of achieving academic success on the college level.[109]

More than twenty-eight hundred high school students took the exam in the spring of 1955, at sixty locations around the state. The next year the number dropped to 2,438, but the college accepted a historic high of five hundred applicants for September 1956, and 329 of them actually enrolled. The adoption of the entrance exam seemed to be a relatively simple answer to a difficult problem. New students were tested again during their first week on campus in September to diagnose potential academic difficulties. They were also given personality tests to determine "the degree in adjustment in homes, scholastic, social and business life as well as to find out vocational interests." With test results and personal records at hand, a faculty member or a dean could offer solid advice to a student to help assure his or her academic success. The student who could not meet minimum academic standards after this intense intervention would not be retained. "The faculty," Turner reported, "is making a greater effort to weed out those students who, after having been given the maximum attention, care and assistance, prove themselves to be so deficient academically that it is inadvisable for them to continue their efforts towards a collegiate degree."[110]

The military also adopted testing to aid in determining which ROTC cadets were qualified for the advanced program and eventual commissions as second lieutenants in the U.S. Army. But the initial results in 1954 of the so-called RQ-3 exam created consternation on the campus because there was such "a high rate of failure." The precise number of failures was not revealed, but it led to an immediate effort among military personnel and the academic faculty to improve cadet skills in English and math. Their efforts largely succeeded. By the spring of 1956, eighty-one of ninety-six cadets qualified for the advanced corps.[111]

The reliance on examinations—especially the entrance exam—proved more problematic and less progressive than anticipated. The academic performance of students did not improve dramatically because weaker applicants had been turned away. In 1958

Turner came close to conceding defeat. There was little the college could do inasmuch as its students who were admitted were not prepared for the rigors of collegiate work. "We may as well face the fact that one of our most serious handicaps lies in the problem with which we must contend when so many students come to us with poor foundations in English and in mathematics. It is indeed difficult to build on such foundations. We have struggled in the past with testing, with non-credit remedial classes, with tutoring and with other devices but ultimately it is clear that our students must come to us with stronger foundations."[112]

South Carolina State's reliance on entrance exams not only largely failed to improve the academic performance of students; it was ironically part of a larger statewide trend to utilize entrance exams to restrict the potential admission of black high school graduates to South Carolina's public institutions that were all-white. On May 27, 1954—only ten days after the U.S. Supreme Court declared segregation in public education unconstitutional—University of South Carolina president Donald Russell urged faculty members and the board of trustees to adopt an entrance exam as a requirement for admission to the institution. Faculty members and trustees complied, and political leaders and the media almost uniformly supported the new and widely publicized policy. Thomas Waring, the segregationist editor of the *Charleston News and Courier* was candid in his appraisal, admitting that "there will be some intelligent well-prepared Negroes who would pass the test" and gain admission to the University. However, Waring predicted that the new entrance exam will be "an immediate guarantee that tens of thousands of diploma-bearing Negro high school graduates would not show up next autumn at the gates of our white colleges."[113]

The university turned to the Educational Testing Service (ETS) of Princeton, New Jersey, to provide the test. ETS officials were pleased to comply because no southern public university or college had adopted an entrance exam. But the price of the ETS exams was steep, and USC president Donald Russell urged other public institutions in South Carolina to adopt the exams to reduce the cost. By 1958 every state college and university in South Carolina including South Carolina State was utilizing the ETS exam. During his unsuccessful campaign for governor in 1958, Russell proudly defended the use of the exams "in protecting our Southern way of life."[114]

If entrance exams were adopted by the state's white institutions to exclude black applicants, how could faculty members and administrators at S.C. State justify their use? Of course S.C. State was not about to use the exams to turn away most or many black applicants. But they were ready to turn away black applicants who were unprepared for academic work at the college level. Therefore it is troublesome—to put it charitably—that S.C. State allowed itself to be a part of a larger strategy that the other state schools used to postpone and restrict the admission of black students. Ultimately, however, the tests mostly failed to accomplish their intended purposes. The entrance exams did not keep poorly prepared students out of South Carolina State because there were simply too many black students with weak academic backgrounds who graduated from the state's segregated public schools. To have admitted only highly qualified black applicants would drive the enrollment at S.C. State down to an unsustainable level, and it would deny an opportunity for higher education to young black people who, through no fault of their own, were products of a poorly funded and racially divided system of public education.

The use of the exams by the white institutions proved to be an inconsequential factor in preventing black students from enrolling in the mid- and latter 1950s and early 1960s. For a brief time after the Supreme Court announced the *Brown* decision in 1954, it appeared that some southern white leaders were reluctantly prepared to begin a slow process of dismantling segregation. This was before the onset of massive resistance later in 1955 and in 1956. Once southern whites embarked on a course that absolutely rejected desegregation, then entrance exams made no difference. Dedicated foes of integration were unwilling to have even one black student enroll at a white educational institution no matter how well qualified he or she might be.

Many black and white Americans initially reacted with shocked uncertainty to the U.S. Supreme Court's decision in *Brown v. Board of Education* in May 1954. It would be more than a year before massive white opposition would erupt, and then that opposition did not occur until after African Americans through the NAACP had drafted and submitted more than sixty petitions in southern communities asking that public schools be desegregated. That determination among black parents and the NAACP incited an angry backlash among white southerners.[115]

THE IMPACT OF DESEGREGATION ON BLACK LAND-GRANT INSTITUTIONS

Even before the Supreme Court delivered the death blow to the "separate but equal" doctrine in public schools, black educators began to anticipate the decline and eventual disappearance of segregation in higher education. In 1950 the high court *in Sweat v. Painter* had prohibited Texas from establishing a separate law school for black residents, which is exactly what Judge Waties Waring's district court had sanctioned in the Wrighten case in South Carolina three years earlier. In 1950 the Supreme Court also ordered the University of Oklahoma to open its graduate program to a black man, George McLaurin. The presidents of the black land-grant institutions began to worry about the future of their institutions. They were not certain that the black colleges would survive the abolition of segregation.

In 1952 President Turner wondered what might happen if segregation ended in a state that had a well-financed and well-established white land-grant college and a poorly funded black land-grant school. "If there is to be integration ultimately, and if there is not to be a duplication of offerings in any one state, what effect should this fact have upon a future program of an institution which is now a Negro Land-Grant College in a state which has a Land-Grant College for white students that is already extensively developed?" Turner believed that S.C. State would at least have to eliminate some programs while strengthening others, but he did not identify those programs. Could S.C. State and other black institutions compete with white institutions in a desegregated environment?

The great divide between the black and white land-grant colleges and universities narrowed slightly in 1954. Frederick L. Hovde, the president of Purdue University, invited the presidents of the black land-grant colleges to attend the Association of Land-Grant Colleges and Universities meeting that November. The association had been founded in 1887 to represent the interests and concerns of the predominantly white agricultural and mechanical institutions. The Conference of Presidents of the Negro Land-Grant Colleges had been formed at Tuskegee in 1923 and had met annually for three decades. Following a formal invitation to join the association, four presidents of the black land-grant schools including Turner met on the campus of Michigan State University in November 1955 and agreed to dissolve their conference. Turner had been elected president of the conference for 1954–55, and he was the last presiding officer of the organization. Although the conference ceased to exist, the presidents of the black institutions continued to meet informally on an annual basis on the day before the larger land-grant association convened.[116]

There were also those who believed that with the end of segregation on the horizon, Negro history as a separate scholarly area was no longer needed. Dean of arts and sciences Kirkland W. Green informed Turner in 1953 that the Association for the Study of Negro Life and History had "about outlived its usefulness as a separate organization." Although he believed that Turner would "no doubt disagree," Green explained that black history had lost its claim to legitimate scholarship. "Negro history is being replaced by a more complete and valid United States History, which is to be taught without magnifying or minimizing the contributions of any group, as individuals of all groups made significant contributions to the world's culture in general, and American culture in particular." But the dean's prognosis proved premature even for the immediate future of African American history at S.C. State.[117]

Negro history, as it was commonly called, had first been offered at the college in 1917, and it was continuously part of the curriculum in various forms until World War II. In 1937–38, for example, seven history courses were in the catalog including two U.S. history courses, two modern Europe courses, an English history course, and Negro History. In 1941–42, History of the American Negro (History 202) was listed, but it was dropped by 1944–45. For the next dozen years, there was no black history course. In fact, in 1948–49, there were just five history courses for undergraduates. In 1957–58 History of the Negro (History 311) was restored to the curriculum with a note that there would be special emphasis on the role of the Negro in South Carolina. Since that year African American history in various forms and courses has been offered every year for well over a half century at S.C. State.[118]

Although white politicians—most notably Governor James F. Byrnes—vowed four years before the Supreme Court decision to close the public schools rather than desegregate them, there were some white leaders who initially reacted with a measure of equanimity to the court's ruling. The director of public relations for the South Carolina State Chamber of Commerce, Lane L. Bonner, wrote President Turner less than six months after the 1954 *Brown* decision to ask what local chambers might do to aid Negro people in their efforts to become "useful, self supporting citizens in their respective communities." Turner in turn asked each of the deans at S.C. State to submit concrete suggestions, and their responses reveal their understanding of the obstacles confronting African Americans.[119]

Maybe it was considered inevitable in the weeks and months immediately after the *Brown* decision, but not one of the deans explicitly called for the prompt end to segregation in American society. Yet each of them made it clear that people of color wanted improved economic and job opportunities. Black people should be employed "wherever possible, one or more colored persons in each business or industry in the local community." Salaries and wages should be based on merit, not color. There should be increased educational opportunities accompanied by internships and apprenticeships. School attendance should be compulsory. Increased home ownership among African Americans needed to be addressed as well as improved infrastructure in black neighborhoods including roads, utilities, and street lighting.

Frank M. Staley, the dean of agriculture, and Geraldyne Penn, the head of home economics, stressed the need to create biracial committees in each community to initiate discussion and to facilitate communication between black and white people. Staley wanted to know if members of the chamber of commerce "are sincere in their efforts." And Penn asked if those chamber members were prepared to "examine their own attitudes and willingness to cooperate with Negroes." Kirkland W. Green, the dean of arts and sciences, in perhaps a veiled reference to Lewis McMillan's experience, insisted that black people needed to be assured that they could speak their minds freely "so that competent Negro leaders can encourage their people to strive to become first class citizens without fear of losing their jobs." Given the rise of massive resistance to desegregation that soon overwhelmed the Deep South, the inquiry by the chamber of commerce and the thoughtful rejoinder by the S.C. State administrators seem in retrospect quaint and naive.[120]

A NAME CHANGE

Although it was so cumbersome and demeaning that it was rarely used, the legal name of S.C. State since 1896 had been "The Colored Normal, Industrial, Agricultural and Mechanical College of South Carolina." That designation continued to appear for over a half century on such legal documents as contracts as well as on each diploma awarded by the institution. Some graduates declined to display their diplomas because they regarded the name as inappropriate, if not degrading.[121]

With prodding by President Turner, the legislature considered changing the name. Thomas Babb was a state representative from Laurens County who had served briefly on the college board of trustees from 1950 to 1952. Shortly after his election to the general assembly, Babb introduced a bill in 1953 to rename the institution "Orangeburg State College." Turner advised Babb, however, that the new name should avoid the A&M designation because most students were involved in teacher training and not in agricultural or mechanical pursuits. The president indicated that faculty and students preferred a name with "a local flavor" similar to other black educational institutions including Savannah State, Albany State, and Fort Valley State. Fortunately the general assembly steered clear of that sort of narrow and parochial label. Babb's bill died in the House Education Committee.[122]

In 1954 the name was changed to South Carolina State College. C. Walker Limehouse, a house member from Orangeburg, and J. A. Spruill, a representative from

Chesterfield County, cosponsored the legislation to make the change. The measure passed easily in the house and the senate, and it became law on March 23.[123]

While Turner did not ignore the land-grant mission of the institution, he never displayed the abiding interest in agriculture, vocational training, and home economics that his predecessors had demonstrated. With his Harvard pedigree and with the shifting tides in educational and racial concerns in post–World War II America, Turner was more involved with liberal arts, teacher training, and the newly established graduate and law programs. Furthermore he was consumed with the construction program on campus, improving credentials of the faculty while dismissing those professors who were "uncooperative," and with diffusing student unrest and opposition. Understandably the president was not absorbed with the farm and home demonstration extension programs that penetrated remote areas of the state by the 1950s.

EXTENSION WORK

By the time that Benner C. Turner arrived in Orangeburg in 1947 as the newly appointed dean of the new law school, Marian B. Paul was already in her fifteenth year as the director of the home demonstration program of the extension service. She would remain closely involved in the lives of rural black Carolinians for nearly another fifteen years before she retired. Shortly after World War II—and with President Miller F. Whittaker's blessing—Paul proposed to General Education Board officials that the college erect a demonstration house on the campus to provide a place where farm families, especially women, could experience the conveniences of modern living.[124]

Paul conducted a survey of rural Negro homes in 1946 that revealed the abysmal living conditions of so many poor black people. She was convinced that if these rural and isolated men and women were exposed to quality but affordable housing, they would be willing and eager to undertake improvements in their own dwellings. Whittaker made it clear that in the construction of a modest residence, "the building ought not to be of a type that would seem unattainable to the Negroes who occupy the building for demonstration purposes." GEB administrators were openly receptive to Paul's request.[125]

GEB officials recommended, however, that the home be built in a rural area and not on the campus. Paul agreed, and a site was selected in Williamsburg County—a "thickly populated area of Negro landowners"—about seventy-five miles from Orangeburg. The GEB provided $7,500 of the estimated cost of $15,000. The college would furnish a portion of the labor as well as half of the salary of the supervising home demonstration agent assigned to the house. The extension service would provide the remaining half salary. The Cooper Rural Home Demonstration club of Williamsburg County would contribute $500. The local school board provided three acres of land. Nearby farmers would contribute timber. But there were prolonged delays in construction due in part to Whittaker's death and the lack of assertive leadership while the five-man committee administered the college in 1949–50.[126]

The demonstration home was an immediate attraction following its dedication on May 13, 1952. The one-story frame house had three bedrooms and hardwood floors.

The cooperative extension program spent decades working with rural black residents, encouraging them and showing them how to make improvements in their humble dwellings. Mrs. Maggie Jenkins saved enough money through her home demonstration Christmas club account to enhance her home in 1949. Still there was no indoor plumbing or electricity. Courtesy of Sara Aiken Waymer

It was furnished with a used dining-room suite, reupholstered furniture, and a rug donated by a local business. Textile mills donated fabric for drapes and slipcovers. Another business donated an electric pump for the well. Extension agents were able to purchase a washing machine, refrigerator, stove, and water heater at a 45 percent discount. Home demonstration councils donated a radio, record player, and vacuum cleaner.[127]

The initial plan was to have families reside in the home for a week. But men were reluctant to leave their own farms to live in the house. It became essentially a female affair. Home demonstration agents arranged for groups of four or five women to live in

Table 33. Survey of Rural Negro Homes, November 1946

5.3%	with running water
13.9%	have indoor hand pump
3.8%	possess flush toilet
76.3%	have outdoor toilet
19.8%	have no outdoor toilet or privy
72.4%	have no refrigeration

Source: GEB, Series 1, Subseries 3, Box 479, Folder 5099, Rockefeller Archive Center. Marian Paul did not indicate how many homes were included in the survey.

With the financial assistance of the General Education Board, Marian B. Paul and the cooperative extension program at S.C. State built the Williamsburg County home demonstration house, completed in 1952. African American women from across rural South Carolina spent a week in this modest but modern home. From left to right: Eva Lawrence, home demonstration agent for Williamsburg County; Mabel Price, assistant to Marian B. Paul; Marian B. Paul, state director of Negro home demonstration; and Vannie Thomas, farm demonstration agent for Williamsburg County. Courtesy of Sara Aiken Waymer

the home for a week at a time with their county agent. "For some of these women," Paul explained, "it's their first opportunity to live in a modern house." It had hot and cold running water, a bathroom, a washing machine, a refrigerator, and a lawn and garden. As Marian Paul had predicted, it inspired many farm families to make improvements in their own dwellings.[128]

Within a year rural black families built thirty new bathrooms, and forty families improved their kitchens. The congregation of the church located next to the demonstration home felt either embarrassed or inspired. In any event they planted grass, painted their church, and installed indoor toilets shortly after completion of the house. Within two years 253 women had spent a week in the home. Through the mid-1950s, the extension service and the U.S. Department of Agriculture brought more than eight hundred black and white visitors to see the home, including several from foreign countries.[129]

Paul and the home demonstration agents developed a weekly schedule for the farm women who were in residence. They were given instructions and advice in meal planning, cooking, cleaning, caring for furniture, and gardening. Each day the women alternated tasks and learning experiences. The women and the agents found that it was most convenient to schedule visits during the slack season in agriculture that extended from September to June. Paul was somewhat dismayed by the reluctance of young farm wives and mothers to travel to Williamsburg County for a week. The home had much more appeal for older women.[130]

The demonstration house—like the entire extension program—barely benefited the poorest of the poor. Marian Paul divided farm families into three groups. The sharecroppers were the most poverty stricken. They had little ambition. "This group is a burden to the race and to society in general." They represented the most difficult challenge for extension agents. "To them our program must be attractive and clear enough to motivate them with the desire for self-improvement."

Those who were renters and tenants "form the largest segment of our clientele." They were mostly "alert and ambitious" and hoped to acquire land. But many of them had to seek employment off of the land to make ends meet. They were often, Paul explained euphemistically, "victims of circumstances." In other words they were exploited and cheated and thus dejected. They needed and sought the help and encouragement of the farm and home demonstration agents. The landowners enjoyed the highest standard of living among the black farm families. They had comfortable homes, enough nutritious food, and farms that produced income. They were usually eager to draw on the "advice and guidance" of the extension workers.[131]

On the eve of her retirement after nearly three decades as the director of the home demonstration program, Paul was vividly aware that poverty remained endemic in South Carolina. Nevertheless the extension program and the people who it served had not remained static over the years. In 1958 she observed that "it has been interesting, startling and gratifying to note the changes in the development of my people." There were fundamental alterations occurring in the way people lived and earned a living.

It was a new era. "Gone now are the corduroy or wash board roads, the lean-to cabins, the one-teacher schools that ran three months, the horse and buggy, the one-crop system with cotton planted to the cabin door, the illiterate and superstitious families and eight Negro home demonstration agents to work the entire State." A skillful writer, Paul pointed out that the demonstration agents no longer: "had to corral these poor, poverty stricken illiterate people, gain their confidence and respect, [and] then motivate them with the desire for self-improvement. . . . Our program was simple but sound[,] built upon the theory that 'an enlightened people can be trusted to save themselves.'"[132]

As many of these people struggled to save themselves, they benefited enormously from the information and assistance furnished by extension program personnel. The farm and home demonstration agents were the only public officials rural black people had any contact with. Local and state elected officials were white men who paid little heed to the isolated and impoverished black population in their midst. The extension agents were civic leaders who were knowledgeable, helpful, and sympathetic. They were "half-missionary, half-magician." In times of crisis and despair, black people did not hesitate to call on "their" agents.[133]

By the mid-twentieth century, rural residents were no longer as isolated and as unknowledgeable as previous generations had been. As Paul indicated, roads were improved and more people had access to automobiles and trucks. Men who had been in the military returned home with a greater awareness of global affairs. Radio and television exposed people to a heretofore unknown world of material goods and possessions. The soil bank and farm mechanization largely ended the dependency on cotton. Many younger people fled the countryside for economic advantages elsewhere. But they were often turned away because of their lack of skills or because of the color of their skin or both. "Their desires to improve their standards of living force them to seek employment in industries or jobs in metropolitan areas only to be confronted with technical or racial disadvantages."[134]

During her tenure Paul witnessed and helped preside over major growth in the extension program. By 1958 there were black home demonstration agents in thirty-three of South Carolina's forty-six counties. Every agent except one had a bachelor's degree, and eight counties had assistant agents. County legislative delegations in all thirty-three counties supplemented the funds provided by the U.S. Department of Agriculture for extension work among African Americans in amounts ranging from $300 to $3,000. The additional money was used to increase agents' salaries, to rent office space, to pay for secretarial help, and to assist the 4-H program. Paul was particularly pleased that every agent had office space as well as furniture and a telephone, although in some instances that office was cramped and inadequate. Still it was an improvement over the complete absence of office space for county extension work in the 1930s. Furthermore Staley Hall—the new agricultural building on the S.C. State campus—contained ample offices for the three men, three women, and three secretaries who directed the farm and home demonstration programs from the college.[135]

HELPING PEOPLE HELP THEMSELVES

Paul's gravest concern was the lack of a home demonstration agent in thirteen South Carolina counties. Several of those rural counties had large black populations including Laurens, Dillon, Calhoun, and Jasper. On the other hand, Paul was gratified at the range of services and programs that agents under her supervision offered across much of the state. Each of the thirty-three counties had women's clubs that met regularly to discuss food, nutrition, clothing, health, housing, and community development. The women participated in regional and statewide contests. The agents also organized and administered 4-H clubs, took part in the state fair, and helped with the new demonstration house. The agents also worked to assist individual farm families. Paul proudly recounted the successful examples of intervention.[136]

In the Cherokee Springs community in Spartanburg County, the Moss family consisted of five adults and seven grandchildren. Some were overweight, and some were underweight. The agent, Cammie F. Clagett, worked with sixty-three-year-old Ethel Moss on nutrition and meal planning. Mrs. Moss worked in turn with other families in the community. Poultry, eggs, and milk were added to their diets. More food was conserved. "Each family member cooperated with the diet plans and now there [are] no over-weight nor under-weights in the Moss family."[137]

The agent in Union County, Laura J. Whitney, helped bring routine and responsibility to the daily lives of the Henderson family. There were seven of them: the parents, four adult and married daughters, and an adolescent son. "The family wanted to be self-supporting, but they feared that their resources were insufficient." Whitney encouraged the family to hold a meeting and create a division of labor in which family members would agree to assist each other. "Mother and daughter Johnsie took gardening, Elmer another daughter took sewing, Daisy took a poultry project and Dorothy got a job as secretary in one of the schools. The father operated the farm." Each family member retained profits from products they sold, but each also contributed to a general fund to pay such costs as utilities and insurance. The Hendersons were able to purchase furniture, an electric range, farm equipment, and a used car.[138]

Vesta Harris in Cherokee County learned marketing skills as a member of the local women's home demonstration club. She developed a florist business raising and selling cut flowers, dish gardens, plants, shrubs, and also vegetables. In 1958 she earned a tidy $1,231 from the flowers and another $589 from the produce.[139]

In the four years that followed the *Brown v. Board of Education* decision, Paul believed that the state's black and white extension agents had forged a surprisingly cooperative relationship with each other. She was hopeful that a new day had dawned in racial reconciliation. For decades there had been almost no contact between black and white agents. "The two races scarcely knew each other[']s program [and] they scarcely knew each other."[140]

But that had changed. "We work in perfect harmony and accord and I dare say that in no state with a bi racial staff does there exist a more friendly and sincere relationship as that which we have in South Carolina." She explained that in each county black and white agents met monthly to share information and to discuss programs and problems. Paul can be pardoned for exaggerated claims of racial collaboration. The Department of Agriculture, through the Clemson extension service, required that the meetings take place. Black and white agents may have worked more closely together than they had, but the extension programs remained segregated.[141]

Nationally there was less racial cooperation as segregation and exclusion persisted. Black 4-H members were not permitted to participate in the national 4-H meetings. Instead young black men and women from South Carolina attended an all-black regional camp from 1947 to 1961 while white 4-H youngsters went to the national camp. The regional camps were held at black land-grant colleges including Southern, Tuskegee, Arkansas Pine Bluff, and Howard.[142]

Marian Baxter Paul retired in 1959. No South Carolinian was more intimately acquainted with the lives of despair and poverty experienced by thousands of rural residents of the state. Nor was any one more committed to alleviating the hopeless and harsh existence that characterized their lives. Paul was only too well aware of the terrible toll that inadequate diets, poor health, substandard housing, and inferior education exacted on people. She had a deep and uncommon affection for "her people." She was not put off by their backward and uneducated ways. To Paul they were decent, worthy people who possessed dignity. She dedicated her life to helping them, and help them she did.

As Benner C. Turner approached the end of a decade as the president of S.C. State, he was pleased with the progress that the institution had made under his leadership. He could point proudly to the massive building program. Between 1896 and 1949, buildings costing $954,000 had been erected. Between 1950 and 1957, construction amounting to $4,054,000 had transformed the campus. Most of those improvements, however, could be attributed to the determination of state officials—mainly Governor James F. Byrnes—to create some semblance of equality between the state's black college and the white institutions. Yet Turner noted that much remained to be done. There had been no capital improvements since 1957, and the college desperately needed a new dining hall, dormitories, added science facilities, a classroom building to replace aging White Hall, and a new or expanded library.[143]

Annual state appropriations grew significantly but not dramatically. The legislature appropriated $825,000 to the college in 1951–52 and $1,527,778 in 1959. Lawmakers simultaneously hope to stave off integration in higher education by increasing funding while remaining as parsimonious as they could in sending taxpayer money to Orangeburg.[144]

Enrollment barely increased in the 1950s. Many more students could have and would have attended S.C. State. The problem of inadequate campus housing remained. The dormitories were full. There were two new dormitories—Bethea Hall for men and Earle Hall for women. Lowman Hall had been renovated. The temporary structures that had initially housed veterans finally had been demolished. Some men continued to live in the community, but administrators were reluctant to allow undergraduate women to live off campus.

The adoption of entrance exams had been intended to deny admission to the most ill-prepared applicants—and perhaps it did. Nevertheless Turner and faculty members continued to complain about the weak academic skills of students. The number of faculty with doctorates had increased to twenty-three by 1959. Still the institution was not yet fully accredited. The Southern Association for Colleges and Schools (SACS) had recommended the consolidation of several small academic departments including biology and chemistry into the Department of Natural Sciences.

The student uprising and strike of 1956 had been quelled with no additional protests. The trustees had fully supported President Turner and the stern measures and tough punishment he levied. He hoped to continue to keep the college insulated from the emerging civil rights movement. However he was also concerned, as were other leaders of black institutions of higher learning, about the survival of the historically black colleges if they were suddenly thrown into competition with white colleges and universities once desegregation was implemented. But in 1959 that seemed unlikely as white southerners remained defiant in their defense of Jim Crow.

CHAPTER SEVEN

Civil Rights in the Community and on the Campus

No one would claim that the decade of the 1960s was period of peace, tranquility, and stability in American society. The changes that reverberated through that decade and beyond profoundly transformed South Carolina State College. In 1960 S.C. State was—as it had been since 1896—an all-black institution. By law its students, faculty, and president were confined to members of the Negro race. By 1970 there were white as well as Asian members of the faculty, and the first white students had enrolled. Conversely the first black men took seats on what had been the all-white board of trustees.

Hundreds and hundreds of S.C. State students spent the early 1960s marching and peacefully protesting against segregation in Orangeburg. They were arrested by the score. By 1967 many of those young people switched their attention from the community to the campus. Having absorbed the lessons of civil disobedience in their assault on Jim Crow, students successfully challenged the rigid campus policies of President Benner C. Turner.

On February 1, 1960, four freshmen from North Carolina A&T College in Greensboro sat down at the Woolworth lunch counter and—without intending to—set the sit-in movement in motion. Their attack on racial segregation quickly spread across the South. Small numbers of students from S.C. State and Claflin sat down at the lunch counter at the Kress store on the town square in Orangeburg on February 25 and 26. They were not served, and they were not arrested.[1]

The local newspaper, the *Times and Democrat,* told the student protestors in an editorial, "A Word of Caution," that they were in the minority in opposing segregation although a majority of the residents of Orangeburg County were black—"the majority is not yet ready to change most of the basic customs of the community. We say that knowing full well the percentage of Negroes in the county." Many white people had convinced themselves that black people accepted and even embraced segregation. But young people were energized, and the movement gathered support. On March 1 more than four hundred students quietly proceeded downtown with signs that read "Segregation Must Die." They had prepared and organized for peaceful protest at Trinity United Methodist Church, located across the street from the two campuses. They were given instructions on how to protect themselves if they were physically attacked or beaten.[2]

Well-dressed students from S.C. State and Claflin quietly and peacefully marched down Russell Street on March 15, 1960, to protest segregation. They were arrested by the score. Courtesy of Cecil J. Williams

THE ORANGEBURG MOVEMENT

On March 15, a cold and raw Tuesday, more than one thousand students from S.C. State and Claflin neatly attired in their "Sunday best" walked silently in groups of about seventy-five along Amelia and Russell Streets to the central business area. This time state and local law enforcement personnel and firemen were waiting. Defying orders to turn back, the marchers were drenched by fire department hoses and teargassed by police. Nearly four hundred of the students were arrested and incarcerated in a hastily erected stockade where they sang "God Bless America" and "The Star Spangled Banner." Several students and adults who arrived with dry clothing, blankets, and food were also arrested as they attempted to pass or throw the contraband to the prisoners.[3]

The next day the *New York Times* featured a four-column photograph of the beleaguered students on its front page with an accompanying story by Harrison Salisbury. Several white journalists were impressed by the quiet determination of the marchers. Writing in the *State,* Gus Chigges observed: "Through it all, the young Negroes maintained characteristic blank, passive expressions. For the most part, they stared straight ahead, displaying neither defiance nor fear."[4]

Students took note of their own demeanor. State College student Charles McDew, who would become the second chairman of the Student Non-violent Coordinating

Committee (SNCC), looked up after he was arrested and saw football player and future NFL star David "Deacon" Jones holding an injured young woman who had been knocked down by fire hoses. "The expression on Jones' face was one of peaceful sadness instead of rage."[5]

The black community in Orangeburg, often divided by class and education, rallied in support of the students. Black funeral director T. K. Bythewood; James Sulton, the service station owner; State College professor of education Charles Thomas; and retired farm extension agent George W. Daniels organized prosperous members of the community to post bond. But black people who were not in the middle class also showed their concern. Harold Bardonille, a junior at S.C. State, was visibly moved when a group of poor farmers appeared on the campus to offer assistance. "And I mean these were real tenant farmers—dirt farmers. You know? They went up to one of the profs and said, 'What're you gonna do to help all those chillun that got hosed?' They said they wanted to help, and they'd do anything they could. They didn't know what they can do, but they look to us for leadership. They're eager to be part of this."[6]

President Turner was in a quandary. Less than twenty-four hours after the massive demonstration and arrests he summoned eight members of the Faculty Council and sought their "reactions and advice." The misnamed council was made up not of teaching faculty but solely of administrators. And they were uncertain about how to proceed. These were uncharted waters. Ordinarily college officials had no qualms when it came to disciplining students who had violated campus regulations dealing with class attendance, alcohol, gambling, and women leaving campus without permission. But these were students who stood up and marched for rights they were denied in a Jim Crow society and then were arrested and charged with violating the law. There was admiration mixed with anxiety among administrators.[7]

Two students—Alvin Blank and Artie Brown—had already approached Turner to ask him what he thought of the student protest. Turner told the two young men and then informed the Faculty Council that he had a personal opinion as well as a professional responsibility and that the two did not coincide. "As an individual he wanted equality, justice and civil rights just like everyone else." But he had to place the welfare of the institution above his personal opinions. As president he had to consider the interests of "all the people of South Carolina" including state leaders, students, parents, and alumni. He felt a special responsibility to parents to make certain that no harm came to their children.

The Faculty Council engaged in a lengthy discussion on whether or not Turner should meet with the student body or perhaps a delegation of students. M. Maceo Nance, the business manager, suggested that Turner assemble the students in chapel and address them. But Turner said he "was not in favor of doing this" because the students were too emotional and that one or more rabble-rousers would jump up in such a meeting and embarrass him with questions. So after indicating that he would be uncomfortable speaking to the students, Turner asked the council to vote on whether or not he should meet with the young people. Not surprisingly they voted 8–1 that he not meet with them. It was a missed opportunity to reassure the students and express support for their cause. But neither Turner nor the council had a good grasp of the surging

The Orangeburg County jail, known as "the Pink Palace," was in 1960 a fortress-like relic from the nineteenth century that had been painted pale pink. The Orangeburg Fire Department had doused student protestors, including the 388 arrested that chilly Tuesday, March 15, 1960. It may have been the first time in civil rights history that authorities turned fire hoses on protesting young people. Courtesy of Cecil J. Williams

momentum of the civil rights movement. They agreed as their meeting concluded that "it was the feeling of the group that the demonstrations were over."[8]

The demonstrations had just begun. Turner's public comments were tempered and in keeping with his desire to avoid controversy. He remained committed to the notion that the college could and should isolate itself from community activities and controversy. "Regardless of all other factors that may be involved," he stated publicly, "the college must hold as foremost the safety of its students and the primary purpose of its program, which is education." He told the trustees and the community that he "would make every effort to prevent the continuance of demonstrations." However it was no longer possible that S.C. State could somehow serve as a quiet island in the midst of a remarkable movement to remake the prevailing racial structure of the South.[9]

The trustees were more intransigent than Turner because they were absolutely committed to segregation. On March 17—two days after one thousand students marched—somber and grim members of the board gathered in a hastily called meeting in the office of Governor Ernest Hollings in Columbia. After Wallace Bethea reported on the Orangeburg demonstrations, the trustees quickly and unanimously passed a resolution warning that demonstrations were almost certain to "culminate in violence and riot if the practice continued in the future." The resolution insisted on the need to preserve peace and order, although no one suggested that the demonstrations that had already occurred had been anything but peaceful and orderly.

Board members warned that those students who took part in future public demonstrations without the approval of college authorities would be expelled. In this instance the trustees, who usually secluded themselves and their activities from public scrutiny by meeting privately, issued a press release promising swift disciplinary action in the event of future protests. Students were not intimidated and barely took notice of the trustees' action.[10]

Of the 388 students arrested on March 15, 373 were tried for breach of the peace over the next several weeks, and 373 were found guilty. They were sentenced to thirty days in jail or a fine of $50. All were released on bond pending an appeal based on their claim that they had the right to assemble peacefully. The NAACP retained Matthew Perry, Zack Townsend, Newton Pough, and Lincoln Jenkins to defend the students. With the exception of Jenkins, the lawyers had graduated from the S.C. State law school. Three years later, in 1963, the U.S. Supreme Court reversed the convictions of the students and in doing so overturned a ruling by the South Carolina Supreme Court.[11]

James Clyburne (as the *State* misspelled his name) was in the first group of fifteen found guilty by a six-man jury made up of five white men and one black man in D. Marchant Culler's magistrate's court. Clyburn declared that the purpose of the march had been "to petition city officials for denying us our rights of peaceful assembly." Protests did taper off that spring as the trials for the 388 arrested students were held over several weeks, and the semester ended quietly. By August the ardor and anger of the trustees had cooled, and they rescinded their March resolution, preferring—they said—to leave disciplinary matters to President Turner.[12]

The commitment of students to civil rights did not waver. No one was more dedicated to the movement than sophomore Charles "Chuck" McDew. A somewhat short and stocky young man with a quick wit and a ready smile, McDew looked every bit the football player that he was. He was from Massillon, Ohio—the hotbed of high school football in the Buckeye State—and he came to South Carolina State because his father had attended the college and played football as a Bulldog. But the younger McDew could not adjust to the segregated South. He was arrested three times in South Carolina for flouting Jim Crow restrictions.[13]

When the Student Non-violent Coordinating Committee (SNCC) was organized at Shaw University in Raleigh, North Carolina, in April 1960 under the creative and inspirational leadership of Ella Baker, Chuck McDew was there. He joined young people who would serve among the shock troops of the civil rights movement in the 1960s: Julian Bond, Ruby Doris Smith, Robert Moses, David Dennis, John Lewis, and Diane Nash.[14]

A few months later McDew was in jail in Orangeburg after his arrest at yet another sit-in at the Kress store. Lodged in what was not so fondly referred to as "the Pink Palace," the nineteen-year-old wrote a letter on brown paper towels to Valerie Brown, who was a white student at Texas Christian University. As he sat in his cell, McDew was troubled and perplexed by the irrational response of people to skin color.

> Hi Val . . . Please excuse my stationary, I was arrested over an hour ago along with three other students. We sat down at the S. H. Kress & Co., lunch counter and asked to be served. . . . I can hear singing outside. They are singing "We Shall Overcome" and it sounds so wonderful that I kind of want to cry. Dot, the girl in the next cell, can see them and there are nearly four hundred students outside . . . all singing. Now they are singing the "Star Spangled Banner" and I feel a kind of bitter sick feeling deep inside. I know that singing as well as we who are in here believe that "we shall overcome and the truth will make us free" and trying so very, very hard to believe too that this is the "home of the brave and the free." I keep asking myself just how brave are the people who put me here? . . . Oh, God why must it be this way? Why can't we be a world of blind men. Then we would all be free and equal. Or would a group of blind bigots start discriminating on the basis of tone quality. Would all people with high voices have to live in filthy ghettos and be second class citizens?
>
> Oh, sickness, oh hate. Go and leave the hearts of man. Let me be me, Charles Frederick McDew, man, student, lover of life. I don't want to be that nigger with no personality, no being, just a dark blob. I want to be me with my color that I love, with my eyes, my body, my dreams and aspirations. I better close now. It has been a very trying day and we have trial in the morning. Pray for us, Val, pray for us all. Chuck, or as the fellow in this cell call me, 24771[15]

In 1961 McDew left South Carolina State to commit himself full time to civil rights and SNCC. He went to McComb, Mississippi, to join in protests over the murder of Herbert Lee. Thanks in part to the influence of Ella Baker, McDew was selected as the second chairman of SNCC. He succeeded Marion Barry, the first chair and a chemistry major from Fisk University in Nashville. McDew would be arrested and beaten again and again in Mississippi and Louisiana as he and the other people involved in civil rights risked their lives—and sometimes lost those lives—as they dedicated themselves to making the United States accept and treat African Americans with dignity and respect, and as citizens of the nation that they helped so much to build.[16]

MORE PROTESTS

Demonstrations in Orangeburg had resumed in September 1960, and McDew was one of those incarcerated after another sit-in at the Kress store in October. President Turner was either unwilling or unable to prevent wave after wave of S.C. State students from joining the marches and protests. Students were arrested on the November day that John F. Kennedy was elected president. Later that month Student Government Association president Catherine Peppers was among those arrested. When Turner was asked what he intended to do about the jailed students, he did not reply.[17]

In exasperation the management of the S. H. Kress store removed the seats from the lunch counter. No one could sit and dine. To deny black people the opportunity to eat at the lunch counter, white people lost their right to sit there as well. But seats or no seats, the demonstrations went on into 1962 and 1963. The marches and picketing severely disrupted downtown businesses. White customers stayed away. The chamber of commerce ran advertisements urging people to patronize the local stores. City officials tried to curtail the protests. They required permits for picketing and notarized identification cards that had to be renewed monthly. The city police department and the county sheriff had a difficult time contending with the hundreds of protestors who they felt compelled to control and arrest.[18]

Yet as disruptive and burdensome as the demonstrations were to the community, white people made no concessions on segregation. If anything there was a reactionary backlash as white leaders clung more fervently than ever to Jim Crow. The "Conservative Americans" organized in Orangeburg in 1962 to support constitutional government. They attracted about one hundred dues-paying members. Wallace C. Bethea, the longtime secretary of the S.C. State board of trustees, was elected honorary chair of the organization. Members praised the conservative values espoused by Arizona senator Barry Goldwater and Virginia senator Harry Byrd. Both of those lawmakers strongly opposed proposed civil rights legislation. Conservatives argued that the owners of private businesses that served the public including restaurants, hotels, and bowling alleys had the right as property owners to deny admission to anyone who they did not want as a customer.[19]

In one week in October 1963, 1,350 Claflin, S.C. State, and Wilkinson High School students were arrested. Many of them were arrested more than once. Concern over the unrelenting Orangeburg protests prompted Governor Donald Russell to summon the S.C. State board of trustees, as well as President Turner, Algernon S. Belcher, and M. Maceo Nance to Columbia, where they were joined by attorney general Daniel McLeod, and the director of SLED, J. P. "Pete" Strom. Governor Russell, the former president of the University of South Carolina, was "disturbed with conditions among the students at State College." But after considerable discussion, no action was taken. "The meeting was recessed for a few days to give Dr. Turner and his staff a chance to return the student body from the streets to the class rooms."[20]

With three years of demonstrations behind them, students did not suddenly halt their nonviolent protests. On November 22, 1963—the day President Kennedy was assassinated in Dallas—students in Orangeburg were marching in the streets. It was not until eight months later, when Congress passed and President Lyndon B. Johnson signed the Civil Rights Act of 1964, that the demonstrations finally ended. That legislation outlawed racial discrimination in public facilities.[21]

In the midst of the Orangeburg movement in 1962, James Baldwin, one of the twentieth century's preeminent writers, spoke to students and members of the faculty in the student center, and he discussed America's long-standing racial crisis. He declared that "the Negro slave was not the submissive Uncle Tom as he has often been pictured. But a tough individual able to endure hardship and to face his problems realistically." When asked by a student what had inspired him to write *Another Country,* Baldwin responded sharply that he had not been inspired. Instead "the word that should have been used is tormented."[22]

SACS ACCREDITATION

While the civil rights protests of the early 1960s disrupted the educational equanimity that President Turner so cherished, he as well as the faculty and students were delighted when the Southern Association of Colleges and Schools fully accredited the college for the first time in 1960. It had been a long and trying ordeal. Since 1940 the Southern Association of Colleges and Schools (SACS) had classified S.C. State as an "A" institution. Prior to 1940 it had a B rating. The Southern Association maintained separate and unequal criteria for the accreditation of black and white institutions. In 1951 SACS ended that dual rating system and adopted uniform standards for what it termed full membership in the association.

Almost immediately eighteen of sixty-three eligible black institutions qualified for that coveted membership. These were mostly the private and premier black schools. Among them were Fisk, Bennett, Clark, and Atlanta University. By 1957 eight more were accredited including Xavier, Spelman, Virginia Union, and Texas Southern—but not S.C. State. In 1954 SACS sent a four-man team to the campus to evaluate its programs and faculty. There were three white men, and Alex Manly, the black president of Spelman. The committee praised the college: "The institution is in general meeting very satisfactorily the minimum standards." Those were, however, "minimum standards," and the committee did not recommend S.C. State for full membership. Among the problems: salaries were too low, there was no tenure policy, and the library facility (Wilkinson Hall) was inadequate.[23]

In 1957 SACS recognized S.C. State "as an approved institution" but withheld accreditation and placed it on "probationary status." The college had failed again to meet several SACS standards while there were other standards it met only marginally. The number of faculty without doctorates and low faculty salaries remained major weaknesses. SACS insisted that a faculty member with a doctorate be employed in each area that offered a major. Teaching loads were also unacceptably high. The graduate and professional programs were weak. The graduate program, while offering a concentration in such areas as social sciences and natural sciences, offered only a master's degree in education, and not in specific academic disciplines. The faculty members who taught graduate courses were overburdened because the college offered graduate courses mainly for public school teachers at various extension locations away from the campus. The library was still a problem. The law school was not yet accredited by the American Bar Association.[24]

Turner was determined and desperate to achieve full membership in SACS. He solicited Dr. John A. Hunter, the dean of student services at Louisiana State University to assist with accreditation. Hunter—who would be named the president of LSU in 1961—visited S.C. State twice and made a series of suggestions that were helpful in framing the institution's request for full SACS membership. But no consultant could solve the most critical problem, and that was the lack of black men and women with doctorates who would teach at S.C. State for the salaries offered. That problem, Turner emphasized, was "compounded by the fact that the College is legally authorized to employ teachers of one race only."[25]

Finally in 1960 SACS granted S.C. State full membership—but only after Governor Ernest Hollings intervened with the Southern Association. It is uncertain how critical Hollings's action was in the accreditation process. But as African Americans had intensified their efforts to undermine segregation, political leaders like Hollings (and Governor James F. Byrnes before him) worked diligently to maintain the guise of "separate but equal" in education. However it was hard to claim that something close to separate but equal prevailed in higher education in South Carolina if the state's sole public black college remained unaccredited.[26]

South Carolina State became the forty-first of the sixty-three historically black institutions to gain accreditation. In approving S.C. State, SACS officials made it clear that the college's newly achieved status was not necessarily assured. For three years the association closely monitored S.C. State (as well as other black institutions) and required S.C. State to submit annual reports that indicated the extent to which the college maintained compliance with SACS standards. The two most pressing problems remained the lack of doctorates and low faculty salaries.[27]

THE MISSION OF S.C. STATE

South Carolina State, however, grappled with a larger and more complicated problem than salaries and doctorates. The college needed to define its mission more explicitly and then acquire sufficient funds to sustain that mission. Since its inception in 1896, S.C. State had been mostly all things to all black Carolinians. It was required to fulfill a comprehensive educational mission by offering a proliferation of programs with severely limited faculty and financial resources.

President Turner was well aware of the problem, and he repeatedly implored the state's political leadership to define more precisely the educational and public service role that the college was expected to play. Historically S.C. State was asked to perform many of the same educational and public service tasks for black South Carolinians that the University of South Carolina, Clemson, Winthrop, and the Citadel provided for white Carolinians. Turner pointed out that "this is the only institution of higher learning maintained and operated by the State for its colored citizens and residents and therefore its offerings are spread over a wide area while the enrollment is comparatively smaller because of the limitations of [the] existing physical plant." S.C. State was all but overwhelmed with programs in teacher education, agriculture, liberal arts, vocational skills, and graduate studies, the law school, and extension work.[28]

As Turner saw it, the solution to this problem was not in the hands of the college administrators; "the ultimate responsibility lies in an expression of the opinion, feelings, sentiments, and wishes of the state's population." The people would decide. But rather than wait—and it might be a very long wait—for South Carolina's citizens to take an interest in the college and its mission, Turner recommended that the institution reduce the number of programs it offered while "expanding and improving" its physical facilities. State legislators would have to allocate additional funds for salaries and capital improvements. Turner, moreover, offered the unique suggestion that funds for the college should be based on the number of programs it offered rather than on the number of students it enrolled. Turner may have been disappointed, but he could not have been surprised that the state's white leaders and residents continued to show little interest in the mission and programs at the college.[29]

College administrators abolished engineering in 1957–58 by eliminating programs in architectural, civil, electrical, and mechanical engineering. Those engineering curricula had never possessed the equipment, buildings, and fully qualified faculty needed for a bona fide engineering program. SACS leaders had informed college authorities that the institution would not be accredited as long as the engineering program was so weak. Turner also told the board of trustees that it was impossible to find black engineers to teach in the program. Moreover for decades the engineering program had been attached in an unwieldy way to industrial education, which comprised the vocational programs in woodworking, tailoring, and automotive mechanics among others. Turner explained that technical courses would replace engineering, and that these courses would prepare students as draftsmen, materials testers, land surveyors, and construction workers.[30]

When outsiders proposed the elimination of one long-standing program and educational facility at S.C. State, college officials strenuously resisted. In 1961 consultants retained by the newly created Governor's Advisory Committee on Higher Education recommended that no state college operate an elementary or secondary school. If that recommendation was implemented, it would eliminate the Felton Laboratory Training School. It had eight teachers and slightly more than one hundred students, and it had been housed in a four-classroom brick building since its construction in 1924 with the financial help of the Rosenwald Fund. The college erected a cafeteria and restrooms near the school. But it had been identified in 1954 by the visiting SACS team as a weakness affecting the development of the college.[31]

Turner, faculty members, and people in the black community not only insisted that Felton continue; they wanted the legislature to appropriate $750,000 to build a modern facility to educate as many as five hundred elementary and secondary students. In 1961 the State Budget and Control Board approved the use of $500,000 from a state bond issue for erection of a new laboratory school. But the opposition of the consultants put a hold on the funds pending a decision on Felton's fate. The Governor's Advisory Committee suggested that the new school not be built, and that students who were enrolled at Felton could attend the still segregated local Orangeburg schools. Turner maintained that the laboratory school was an essential element in the college's teacher-training program. Essential it may have been, but the presence of the school on the campus meant that the education of those young people—some of whom were the sons and daughters of faculty members—was exclusively in the hands of black people. Turner explained that deans and faculty members recommended that the proposed new school "be entirely under the College's jurisdiction." The funds to build a new Felton Laboratory School were finally released, and the new school, which would serve grades one through eight, was completed in 1964.[32]

In 1961 Governor Ernest Hollings created an advisory committee on higher education consisting of the presidents of the state's colleges and university that would evolve by the end of the decade into the Commission on Higher Education. Initially it would evaluate the state's institutions to foster greater coordination and less duplication of programs among them. Turner promptly pointed out the obvious. S.C. State had been created expressly in order to duplicate programs for "its colored citizens" that existed for the benefit of white Carolinians. And when that advisory committee suggested the possibility of establishing three junior colleges in South Carolina for Negroes, Turner emphatically opposed the idea. He noted that the three new institutions would dilute already inadequate resources set aside for the higher education of black people in the state.[33]

A year later, when the advisory committee broached the subject of creating a new program at S.C. State to address the needs of inadequately prepared students, Turner seized that opportunity to promote two new programs. The college should hire, he recommended, a reading and language arts specialist at an estimated cost of $11,000 who would formulate a program to prepare college students to teach reading in the public schools. The college would also, he suggested, establish a separate department in special education at a cost of $20,000 to develop teachers who would work in the public schools with "slow learners." Although there was a definite need to confront these problems and S.C. State was the logical institution to do so while South Carolina's public schools remained segregated, the additional programs that were created represented still another burden for the college that—as Turner repeatedly pointed out—was already attempting to do more than it could or should.[34]

INTEGRATION OF THE FACULTY

However people might describe Benner C. Turner, few would characterize him as a civil rights pioneer. But Turner was insistent on the integration of the faculty at S.C. State. It was mainly for academic and administrative reasons, however, and not because he had a keen desire to break down racial barriers in South Carolina. It was because it was so difficult to hire and retain black faculty members with doctorates. The lack of qualified faculty members contributed to the loss of the engineering program. Turner was so determined to employ nonblack faculty that he startled a meeting of the board of trustees held in the governor's office in 1961 by asking them to assist in changing the law that stipulated that the "president and corps of instructors shall be of the Negro race" at South Carolina State. The trustees after "considerable discussion" approved a motion recommending an amendment to the law that would permit the college to employ white and Asian faculty members. But the proposal got nowhere in the legislature.[35]

Turner did not give up in his appeal for "a relaxation of statutory racial restrictions." His efforts led to a unique summit meeting over what should have been a routine issue in the office of Governor Donald Russell on September 11, 1964. Joining the chief executive were attorney general Daniel McLeod; attorney David Robinson; Bruce White, an attorney who chaired the college board of trustees; and President Turner, who was also an attorney. The single topic of discussion was how to replace Carl O. Clark, who taught physics at S.C. State. Clark had a leave of absence to pursue a doctorate. He taught a required course, Thermodynamics and Electricity, and Turner explained that it had been impossible to find a "qualified Negro replacement" for Clark.

The assembled legal minds wrestled with a proposed solution that would have a University of South Carolina physics faculty member teach Clark's class. But to conform to the law, the USC faculty member would be paid by the university, and S.C. State would then reimburse the university and thereby avoid employing a white man to teach. These high-level legal gyrations occurred several weeks after the passage of the Civil Rights Act of 1964. Title VII of that act barred discrimination in employment based on race as well as on sex, religion, and national origin. Either the attorneys were not yet familiar with Title VII or they did not think that its restrictions applied to state institutions. Within several months such restrictions in employment had ended. Turner was pleased as "difficulties in securing qualified personnel have been somewhat reduced." But he would soon conclude that hiring white faculty members with doctorates posed another set of problems.[36]

THE OUT-OF-STATE SCHOLARSHIP PROGRAM

To maintain segregation in South Carolina's public colleges between the end of World War II and the passage of the Civil Rights Act of 1964, state leaders had adopted a two-pronged strategy. They created the graduate program and the law school at S.C. State in 1947. But they also implemented and funded—as did every Deep South state—an out-of-state scholarship program. The scholarships went to black Carolinians who wanted to pursue graduate degrees and professional programs at universities outside of South Carolina. By the late 1950s, this scholarship program had burgeoned into a costly and major enterprise administered from the president's office at South Carolina State. In 1947 the legislature set aside $5,000 for the scholarships. By 1958 it cost taxpayers $60,000, and it had become a bureaucratic nightmare for college officials, who did not need yet another program to manage.

For Emma S. Dawkins, President Turner's executive secretary, the scholarship program evolved into nearly a full-time job. Dawkins was a paragon of efficiency who had worked for Presidents Wilkinson and Whittaker. The program entailed vast amounts of paperwork and demanded attention to detail. Scholarship applicants had to have been accepted at the institution they wanted to attend. They were required to demonstrate that the program that they intended to enroll in was offered by one of South Carolina's white public institutions, but not by S.C. State. They had to verify that they were U.S. citizens and residents of South Carolina. Applications had to be notarized and renewed each semester or term as recipients demonstrated satisfactory progress toward a degree. The amount of aid the applicant could qualify for was based on the difference between the tuition charged to white students in South Carolina institutions, and the instructional cost of attending the out-of-state school. (Medical school students received $500 per term.) The state could pay up to $75 per semester for one round trip to the out-of-state school. But no funds were allocated for books, equipment, or housing.

Mrs. Dawkins had to maintain the records, and the college was responsible for dispensing the funds. No money was available to recover administrative costs. In 1953–54 there were 116 scholarship recipients. By 1956–57 that number swelled to 239 people who attended thirty-four institutions. There were seventy-six in medical school, thirty enrolled in doctoral programs in education, eleven in home economics, and eight in music. There were a few undergraduates in programs such as journalism and architecture. It was all too much for President Turner. He pleaded with the trustees and legislators to relieve the college of the burden of managing the scholarship program either by establishing and funding an office on the campus or by the creation of a separate office in Columbia. In the meantime the City of Charleston operated an "Out of Charleston" scholarship program for black Charlestonians. City funds helped maintain the College of Charleston, but black city residents were prohibited from attending. The city provided scholarships to black Charleston high school graduates who enrolled out of the city.[37]

DESEGREGATION OF HIGHER EDUCATION

Even before the passage of the Civil Rights Act of 1964, segregation in higher education in South Carolina had begun to end. Led by Clemson University, the historically white institutions began—with some reluctance—to admit black students and employ black faculty. Harvey Gantt, an architecture student from Charleston's Burke High School, was admitted to Clemson in January 1963 with the legal assistance of attorney Matthew Perry and the support of the State Conference of the NAACP. Later that year three African Americans enrolled at the University of South Carolina. Segregation in South Carolina's public colleges and universities crumbled.[38]

After seven decades S.C. State College was no longer by law an all-black institution. But it would continue to maintain its character and mission as a historically black college and then university into the twenty-first century. Nevertheless the end of segregation in higher education brought fundamental changes to the college. Two of the prominent programs associated with the institution—the law school and the program in agriculture—were terminated with the elimination of Jim Crow.

THE LAW SCHOOL

The law school simultaneously thrived and withered in the years after it was established in 1947. Judge J. Waties Waring's decision had required the State of South Carolina to establish a law school at S.C. State on "complete parity" with the University of South Carolina law school. That never happened. The all-black law school was never remotely comparable in funding, facilities, resources, or size to the university's law school. Furthermore the new law school never had more than a few students at any one time. The poorly compensated law school faculty members sometimes outnumbered the full-time students, and there were never more than five faculty members and the dean. Although it was not generously funded, the S.C. State law school was still a severe financial drain on the college. Yet it would be a mistake to judge the separate and unequal enterprise as a failure. To the contrary the law school was—despite its shortcomings—a remarkably successful educational effort if judged by the quality and productivity of many of its graduates.

In 1950 the American Bar Association accredited the law school on a provisional basis in anticipation of fully accrediting it once it was fully functional. President Turner, the former dean, worked closely for more than a decade with John G. Hervey to secure ABA accreditation. Hervey was the advisor on legal education and admissions to the bar for the American Bar Association. He had been the dean of the law school at Temple University and served as the dean of the law school at the University of Oklahoma. Hervey and Turner developed a cordial relationship that eventually led Turner to address Hervey in personal terms as "Dear John." (Turner simply did not use first names in correspondence with anyone—black or white—including administrators and faculty members at S.C. State.)[39]

During its two decades, the law school had an excellent faculty. Two were graduates of the Harvard law school—Turner and Paul A. Simmons, who taught from 1949 to 1952. (In 1978 President Jimmy Carter appointed Simmons to the federal bench as a district court judge in Pittsburgh.) Leo Kerford, who taught for all nineteen years of the law school's existence, was a graduate of the University of Kansas law school, and LeMarquis DeJarmon earned a law degree at Western Reserve University in Cleveland. Blinzy L. Gore had a law degree from the University of Iowa. Two Howard University law school graduates taught at S.C. State. Cassandra Maxwell was a native of Orangeburg and the first black woman to practice law in South Carolina. Charles E. Washington was from Beaufort, where his father and grandfather had practiced law. His uncle was J. I. Washington, the longtime business manager at S.C. State.[40]

After Turner's elevation to the college presidency in 1950, Peter H. Whittaker became the law school dean at the ripe age of twenty-nine. Whittaker was the nephew of Miller F. Whittaker and the grandson of Johnson C. Whittaker. After he graduated from high school in Detroit, he followed his sister, Cecil, to S.C. State, where he enrolled in 1938. Like so many young men, he left school for the military during World War II. He was trained as a fighter pilot and became a Tuskegee Airman. Commissioned a lieutenant in 1944 when he received his wings, he was not deployed to Europe. He returned to Detroit after the war and earned a law degree at Wayne University (today it is Wayne State University) and passed the Michigan bar exam in 1949. He then joined the law faculty at S.C. State. In 1951 S.C. State awarded Whittaker a bachelor's degree even though he had never finished the undergraduate program at the college. Unfortunately Whittaker died of heart trouble at the veteran's hospital at Tuskegee in October 1954. Theodis R. Gay, who was also a graduate of the Wayne law school, succeeded Whittaker as dean and served until 1961.[41]

Once the law school was established at S.C. State, the State of South Carolina quickly moved to require graduates of law schools at the university and at South Carolina State to pass the bar examination. Prior to the creation of the black law school, graduates of the university's law school were admitted to the bar by virtue of "diploma privilege." Their law degree brought admission to the bar. As one legislator explained in 1948 in supporting the measure to require the bar exam, it would "bar Negroes and some undesirable whites" from practicing law. The first two graduates of the S.C. State law school in 1950—Albert A. Kennedy and Julius T. Williams Jr.—beat the deadline for the imposition of the exam and were admitted to the bar by "diploma privilege."[42]

Matthew J. Perry, who graduated in 1951, was the first S.C. State law school graduate to pass the bar exam. Some graduates of the law school had difficulty with the exam. John Wrighten, who enrolled in the law school two years after his unsuccessful effort to gain admission to the university's legal program, graduated from the S.C. State law school in 1952. But he did not pass the bar exam until his fourth attempt. Ordinarily candidates for the bar were given three opportunities to pass the exam. But Wrighten threatened to sue the university again for admission to its law school, maintaining that he had received an "inferior" legal education at S.C. State. He was allowed to take the exam one more time, and he passed. Still Turner was pleased with the record of success of S.C. State law school graduates. By 1953 nine of the sixteen graduates had been admitted to the bar in three states, and one other graduate was pursuing a graduate degree in law.[43]

Once dismissed by Thurgood Marshall as a "Jim Crow dump in South Carolina," the poorly funded S.C. State law school produced a remarkable cadre of attorneys over two decades. Matthew J. Perry, after a successful career as a lawyer, went on to serve on the U.S. Military Court of Appeals from 1975 to 1979. President Jimmy Carter appointed Perry to the U.S. District Court in 1979, and in 2004 the new federal courthouse in Columbia was named in his honor. Perry died, still serving on the federal bench, in 2011.

Ernest A. Finney Jr., who received his undergraduate degree from Claflin, graduated from the S.C. State law school in 1954. He served on the South Carolina Circuit Court prior to his election to the South Carolina Supreme Court in 1985. He was the chief justice from 1994 until his retirement in 2004. Other law school graduates ascended the judicial ladder. Daniel E. Martin was a judge on South Carolina's Ninth Circuit Court. Reuben L. Gray was a Family Court Judge. Paul R. Webber III was a Superior Court Judge in the District of Columbia. Talmadge Bartelle was a military lawyer. Colonel Ned Felder was a military judge with the U.S. Army. Bassey Mbrey Bassby practiced law in Nigeria, and Allen A. Christian was a lawyer in Frederikstadt in the U.S. Virgin Islands.[44]

At least twelve of the twenty-seven law school graduates who practiced in South Carolina were involved in dozens of civil rights cases from the 1950s to the 1970s as those black lawyers defended several thousand protestors and demonstrators who had been arrested. They filed actions against school boards, hospitals, and county and city governments, and in job discrimination cases. Matthew Perry was an attorney in at least ninety-three of those cases. Willie T. Smith Jr., W. Newton Pough, Zack E. Townsend, John Wrighten, Ernest A. Finney Jr., and others spent long hours for minimal compensation as they contributed enormously to the transformation of lives of black and white people in South Carolina.[45]

Between 1950 and 1966, fifty men and one woman—Laura A. Ponds—graduated from the law school. The number of students enrolled was never large and made for a legal education program that was not cost effective. There were eight full-time students in 1953–54, and five of them graduated. Five students were enrolled the following year, but there were no graduates in 1955. Those five students were served by a staff of eight people: the dean, the librarian, five professors, and one secretary. In 1956 Turner asked state officials to consider the future of the law school. By that time it had "carried the status of a 'provisional accreditation' longer than any other Law School in the country." Yet it was not going to gain full accreditation until the salaries of the law faculty increased dramatically.

The ABA would not accredit a law school if the median salary for its professors was less than $6,000 per year in 1955. At S.C. State the dean, Theodis R. Gay, earned $5,500, and five faculty members each earned $5,000. South Carolina State ranked 111 out of 119 law schools in median salaries, and it was forty-fifth among forty-five state-supported law schools in salaries. With only five full-time students in 1955, Turner pointed out to John Hervey that if faculty salaries were raised to that ABA minimum of $6,000, then the cost per law student would be an astronomical $9,760.[46]

The ABA continued to withhold accreditation. John G. Hervey visited the campus for at least the fourth time in 1963. His evaluation was even more discouraging than previous assessments. Enrollment remained low. The Law School Admission Test (LSAT) scores and undergraduate records of students were weak. Faculty salaries were still a concern because they were "out of line with what prevails nationally." The law library was a problem. The collection of state statutes was not current, and the law review collection was incomplete. Hervey did offer some praise. The records of the law school were well kept, and "the physical facilities are excellent." He added that faculty morale "appears to be high."[47]

With low enrollment, high costs, and virtually no chance of ABA accreditation, President Turner decided to close the law school in 1965. No new students were admitted to the law school for the 1965–66 academic year. The board of trustees concurred with Turner. The last student, Jasper Cureton, transferred to the University of South Carolina law school and earned a law degree as its first African American graduate in the twentieth century. Robert McC. Figg Jr., the dean of the university's law school, who had worked so diligently in building the state of South Carolina's legal defense of segregation in the 1950s, did not exactly greet the initial black students with open arms.[48]

There was not a ripple of controversy over the elimination of the law school. Faculty members quietly dispersed. Leo Kerford, the fourth and last dean, became the director of financial aid at S.C. State. Earl Coblyn briefly taught business law and worked with Orangeburg lawyer Zack Townsend, who had graduated from the law school in 1963. Blinzy Gore, who had also earned a Ph.D., taught social sciences before moving to Claflin College, where he became a dean. Gore also wrote a history of Claflin. Charles E. Washington maintained a law practice in Beaufort. LeMarquis DeJarmon had already moved to the North Carolina Central law school.[49]

The twenty-one-thousand-volume law library was given to the University of South Carolina's law library under terms of the general assembly's 1965–66 appropriation act. Turner had hoped to sell the library collection and use the proceeds toward the renovation of Moss Hall, which had housed the law school. The School of Business Administration occupied Moss Hall until Belcher Hall was completed in 1986.[50]

The saga of the S.C. State law school represents another one of the genuine paradoxes in African American history. It was the creation of white political and educational leaders who in the 1940s did not want black students in the University of South Carolina law school. It was persistently underfunded, and yet the State of South Carolina spent several hundred thousand dollars to build and equip Moss Hall and finance the law school for nearly two decades. But it was money that could have been more wisely allocated to support the undergraduate education of African Americans. Hundreds of young black people were denied admission to S.C. State from 1947 to 1966 because of the lack of facilities. And yet the "Jim Crow law school" that Thurgood Marshall had so severely disparaged went on to produce a phalanx of attorneys who played essential roles in eliminating segregation in South Carolina. Created to perpetuate segregation, that law school produced graduates who succeeded in helping to eliminate it. Could there be a more enduring legacy?

THE AGRICULTURE PROGRAM

A similar fate befell the agricultural program. S.C. State had been established as an agricultural and mechanical institution in 1896 under the terms of the 1862 and the 1890 Morrill Acts. Agricultural courses and farm production were inextricably linked to the college for seven decades. Following World War II, President Miller F. Whittaker predicted "a new awakening in agriculture." Frank M. Staley, who had taught at S.C. State beginning in the 1920s, became the dean of the School of Agriculture in 1947. Student interest in agriculture held steady for a time during the postwar period. Between 11 percent and 13 percent of S.C. State students (all of them men) majored in agriculture between 1947 and 1957. Approximately fifteen young men graduated each year with degrees in agriculture through the 1950s. Almost all those graduates went on to teach the subject in the public high schools. Of the 119 men who taught agriculture in South Carolina's

Table 34. Enrollments in Agriculture, 1951–65

1951–52	148
1954–55	122
1957–58	101
1960–61	44
1964–65	39

Sources: *Annual Report, 1951–1952,* 12–14; *Annual Report, 1957–1958,* 6; *Annual Report, 1960–1961,* 64; *Annual Report, 1964–1965,* 46.

black high schools in 1953, 105 were graduates of S.C. State. While it is likely that many of those teachers also engaged in farming, there were very few young men who majored in agriculture who believed that their future was tied solely to working the soil. Most young black men who sought a college degree wanted to escape from rural life, and not return to it.[51]

With end of slavery and the inception of sharecropping in the decades after the Civil War, many African Americans wanted to abandon the drudgery and dependence of farming and take advantage of whatever limited but meaningful opportunities industrial America offered to African Americans. Hundreds of thousands of black people migrated from southern fields to northern factories. In 1920 there were 926,000 black farms in the United States. That number fell to 560,000 in 1950, and plunged to 57,000 by 1978. Between 1920 and 1978, 94 percent of African American farmers left the land.[52]

Except for the sympathetic ear of the black farm demonstration agents who worked from the S.C. State campus, South Carolina's black farmers typically experienced a response that ranged from indifference to hostility when they dealt with U.S. Department of Agriculture officials as those black men sought loans, additional acreage, and information. Therefore it is hardly a surprise that fewer and fewer black college students saw a future for themselves and their families in agriculture.[53]

The agricultural program at S.C. State had relied on meager facilities and insufficient farmland for over half of a century. Finally with the financial assistance of the General Education Board (GEB), the Staley Building was erected and opened in 1954. Although the new structure provided offices (including much-needed space for the cooperative extension program), classrooms, laboratories, a lecture hall, sewing and kitchen facilities for home economics, and a dairy-processing area to make cheese, butter, and ice cream, the college still lacked sufficient land, dairy barns, poultry facilities, animals, tools, equipment, machinery, greenhouses, and food- and meat-processing facilities. Mason Hall was built in 1958 at a cost of $75,000, and it served as a food-processing and cannery facility. But the college needed a meat-processing area.[54]

The construction of Staley and Mason Halls on the lower end of the campus left the college short of agricultural acreage. The 160 tillable acres at Hillcrest Farm were not enough. For a time farm superintendent Samuel Pinckney was reduced to borrowing rent free ten acres of private land held by A. J. Hutto to grow hay. But Dean Frank Staley and President Turner were not pleased with this informal arrangement, and it came to an end.[55]

Since its founding, the farm with its student and faculty labor furnished produce and dairy products for the college dining hall. That was no longer the case by the mid-twentieth century. Students did not provide labor for Hillcrest Farm, which was located two miles from the campus. Tenants resided on or near the farm and did most of the work. Tenant labor posed problems. One tenant was alleged to have stolen feed. In 1956 the tenant house of Jonathan Gass was destroyed by fire. The college assisted the Gass family in finding a new residence and replacement furniture.[56]

Unlike most major land-grant universities, S.C. State conducted very little agricultural research or experimentation. The Hatch Act, passed in 1886, did not provide research funds to the black land-grant schools. Faculty did periodically undertake

Table 35. Agricultural Production at S.C. State, 1956–57

Cotton	4 bales
Corn	2,168 bushels
Corn	245 tons
Oats	2,622 bushels
Hay	16.5 tons
Swine	42
Beef	19
Guernseys	23, with 100,221.9 pounds/milk
Holsteins	8, with 57,911.7 pounds/milk

Source: *Annual Report, 1956–1957*, 6–7. The college also maintained poultry, but there was no mention of them in the report.

research projects if they had the time and funds. The School of Agriculture had a research project with the Tennessee Valley Authority (TVA) in the mid-1950s. But the farm's main purpose continued to be as a source of revenue for the college.

In 1952 Dean Frank M. Staley was pleased to report that income from the farm had exceeded by nearly $4,000 the $7,000 it was expected to provide for the 1951–52 fiscal year. The farm "produced an unusually large quantity of hay." With that sizable surplus, Staley asked for permission to purchase a side rake and a rotary baler. Turner and J. I. Washington, the business manager, acceded to Staley's request.[57]

The problem for the agriculture program was not revenue. It was the decreasing number of students and the high cost of maintaining faculty salaries and the various facilities. To attract more students, a proposal was floated in 1956–57 to create a two-year curriculum in agriculture. But it was never implemented. Instead the curriculum in agriculture for undergraduates was overhauled in 1962–63. The program in general agriculture and a combined program in horticulture and agronomy were dropped. They were replaced by a major in plant science and a new curriculum in agricultural economics and business—a precursor to the agribusiness major that was implemented in 1987.[58]

To "sell" these innovative programs the new dean of the School of Agriculture, Laler C. DeCosta—who had succeeded the recently retired Frank M. Staley—visited black high schools around the state. He explained that there were abundant opportunities for young people in agriculture. They could engage in farm management, in businesses that were agricultural enterprises, and in federal and state government. They could become farm extension agents, landscape gardeners, and nurserymen. But most of the young people were not persuaded. The new curricula and the recruitment efforts did not boost enrollment.[59]

The faculty-to-student ratio in agriculture was high—only five students for each faculty member in 1964–65. This, President Turner observed, raised "the question of whether or not the institution is justified in continuing such an area of instruction." Furthermore the program still needed improved facilities for maintaining poultry, and a "substantial sum" was necessary for the installation of irrigation at the Hillcrest Farm. Mason Hall also needed a walk-in cooler for meat and produce.[60]

Agriculture's days at S.C. State were numbered. During the summer of 1966, Turner asked Robert C. Edwards, the president of Clemson, to send two members of that university's agricultural staff to Orangeburg to evaluate the black college's agricultural facilities and program. Edwards leaped at the opportunity. He did not dispatch two administrators. Ten Clemson officials as well as Edwards himself arrived on the S.C. State campus on August 30, 1966. They toured the farm and facilities, and met with faculty and staff in agriculture. Two weeks later they sent Turner a report explaining the needs and the cost of improving teaching and research in agriculture at the college. The Clemson administrators indicated that it would require nearly $8 million ($7,839,395) to improve facilities and salaries at the black college.[61]

As officials from both schools were well aware, that was a cost that state and federal authorities were not prepared to pay. Two S.C. State administrators traveled to Clemson in November. Algernon S. Belcher, the dean of the faculty, and Laler C. DeCosta, the dean of the School of Agriculture, in meetings with the Clemson officials, agreed that the agricultural program at S.C. State would be terminated as soon as it was feasible.

Leaders from both schools drew up a memorandum of understanding that would permit sophomore students in agriculture at S.C. State who possessed a good academic record to transfer to Clemson for their junior and senior years. Sophomores with a weak record of scholarship would have to select a new major and remain at S.C. State. Juniors and seniors at the college were expected to complete their program and graduate by 1969, when the agriculture program would formally end. There were also thirty-seven graduate students in agricultural education at S.C. State, and they were given until May 1969 to complete the graduate courses necessary for a master's degree in education. The memorandum made no mention of the disposition of farm animals, equipment, and machinery owned by S.C. State. There was also no suggestion that any of the faculty members or staff in agriculture at S.C. State would transfer to Clemson. Instead S.C. State personnel would be absorbed into various programs at the college.[62]

DESEGREGATING THE EXTENSION PROGRAMS

Since the passage of the Smith-Lever Act in 1914, South Carolina had operated segregated extension programs. For nearly a half century separate programs functioned among rural South Carolinians. Black farm demonstration agents and home demonstration agents assisted black farm families while white agents worked with white families. The black extension program was administered from South Carolina State College although it was under the control of extension authorities at Clemson University. No one pretended that the separate black and white programs were equal. There were white farm and home demonstration agents in each of South Carolina's forty-six counties. By the 1960s there were black farm demonstration agents in thirty-one counties

Table 36. Counties with a Majority Black Population with No Black Extension Agents

County	Black Percentage of Population
Allendale	63%
Calhoun	67%
Edgefield	58%
Jasper	62%
McCormick	62%

Source: "Clemson University Extension Service: Some Notes and Statistics Relating to Negro Participation," Penn Community Services. Inc., Frogmore, S.C., January 1967.

and black home demonstration agents in thirty counties. Several counties with a majority of black people in their population had no black extension service. There were also several counties including Abbeville (32 percent), Barnwell (43 percent), and Saluda (37 percent) with black populations that represented one-third or more of the total population that had no black extension agents.

The Civil Rights Act of 1964 outlawed segregation in public facilities and prohibited racial discrimination in the administration of federal programs. This landmark law ended the dual extension systems. In the name of integration, the segregated extension programs would be merged immediately but not smoothly or equitably. The supervisors who had directed the black extension program from Orangeburg would move to Clemson, where they were assigned nonsupervisory roles. With the merger, titles and positions were changed at the county level. No longer would there be county farm demonstration and home demonstration agents. Henceforth there would be one county leader would supervise men and women. There would also be subordinates who were designated assistant agents and associate agents.

No black man or woman was placed in charge of a county extension program in 1965–66. White personnel monopolized the management of county programs. Seniority, experience, and education were less important than race in determining salary and rank. One unnamed black associate agent with a bachelor's degree and thirty years experience earned $5,951 while the white home demonstration agent with two years experience earned $6,141

Black extension agents had earned much less during segregation, but Clemson officials began in 1961 to provide greater increases in the salaries of black agents compared to the increases that white agents received in an attempt to "catch up" and achieve parity. But it was a large gap to close, and salaries among black extension employees continued to lag following the merger of the two systems.[63]

Clemson administrators also instituted in 1962 a new university-wide evaluation system for faculty members and professional staff including those in the extension program. As black personnel came under the authority of white supervisors after

Table 37. Comparison of Extension Agent Salaries, 1966

	Number	Average Number of Years	Salary
County agents (all white)	46	21	$9,985
White associate agents	22	16	$8,372
White assistant agents	28	6	$7,226
Black associate agents	23	19	$7,214
Black assistant agents	9	6	$6,455
White assistants and associates with M.S. degree			$7,705
White assistants and associates with B.S. degree			$7,690
Black assistants and associates with M.S. degree			$6,988
Black assistants and associates with B.S. degree			$6,974

Sources: "Clemson University Extension Service: Some Notes and Statistics Relating to Negro Participation," Penn Community Services, Inc., Frogmore, S.C., January 1967, 8. United States Commission on Civil Rights, South Carolina Advisory Committee, Records, 1967–68. South Caroliniana Library, University of South Carolina, Columbia.

desegregation, they received consistently lower evaluations than white extension agents. Eighty-five percent of white personnel received a three or four rating while 46 percent of black extension staff received the same three or four rating.[64]

Three administrators who had managed the black extension program closed their Orangeburg offices in 1965 and moved to Clemson as the two extension programs were consolidated. Sara Aiken Waymer, who had replaced Marian Paul in 1959 as the director

Table 38. Evaluations of Black and White Extension Personnel, 1966

Rating	0*	1	2	3	4	Total
White	0	0	33	162	52	247
Black	1	3	34	32	1	71

*Zero represented the lowest rating and four represented the highest

Sources: "Clemson University Extension Service: Some Notes and Statistics Relating to Negro Participation," Penn Community Services, Inc., Frogmore, S.C., January 1967, 12. United States Commission on Civil Rights, South Carolina Advisory Committee, Records, 1967–68, South Caroliniana Library, University of South Carolina, Columbia.

of the home demonstration program, and Altamese B. Pough and Wayman Johnson, who both had directed the 4-H programs for black youth, made the trek to Clemson. Pough later recalled that she "wanted to see first hand what it [integration] would be like." But Ernest N. Williams, who had directed the farm demonstration program since 1944, opted to retire in Orangeburg rather than transfer to Clemson. Waymer, Pough, and Johnson joined a staff of 134 white extension personnel at the larger land-grant university. And while there was no open hostility directed at the new arrivals, they were not exactly warmly welcomed. "Discrimination can be subtle," Pough observed. The black administrators were given innocuous tasks. Pough remembered that "we worked on simple things."[65]

The difficulties in bringing the two statewide extension programs together stemmed in part from the lack of enthusiasm on the part of Clemson's director of extension. George Nutt had run the program for a decade, and he had grave doubts about the civil rights movement. Nutt was a Mississippi native who had strongly praised Mississippi senator and staunch segregationist John Stennis for his unflagging opposition to the 1964 Civil Rights Act. "It is my belief," Nutt wrote Stennis, "that in time to come the thinking of the people of the nation will see the wisdom of your stand."[66]

Frustrated black county agents compiled a list of fourteen grievances that they submitted to George Nutt. They were dissatisfied with salary inequities, evaluations, the termination of black secretaries, the absence of black representation on the extension senate, and the lack of black specialists on the extension staff. Most of all they were profoundly disappointed with what they perceived as their loss of status within the black community. "It is the feeling of the general public that the Negro agent will lose his identity with his people and serve as flunkies for the county leader."[67]

It took the intervention of Clemson president Robert C. Edwards to expedite the integration of the extension service and to secure fairer treatment of black staff members. Concerned about the lack of progress, Edwards summoned black and white extension personnel from across the state to a meeting at Clemson in July 1965, and he attempted to impress on them the need for change as he explained the spirit as well as the letter of the recently enacted civil rights law.[68]

Despite Edwards's concern and direct involvement, implementation of the legislation remained agonizingly slow. At least three county extension offices had maintained signs designating "white" and "colored" entrances nearly a year after passage of the act. Altamese Pough resigned from the extension program in 1966. She was frustrated with the lack of progress toward genuine integration. But she also had left a young daughter in Orangeburg who needed her care and attention. In 1967 Sara Aiken Waymer also left Clemson and returned to Orangeburg.[69]

White extension administrators grew exasperated at what they considered the incessant complaining of the black staff members. In 1967 a weary and aggravated George Nutt declared, "The Extension Service is not an integration agency. We are the education agency of the USDA [United States Department of Agriculture] for Agriculture, Home Economics, and Youth and related programs." In late 1968 Nutt retired after thirteen years as Clemson's extension director.[70]

In this fowl affair two young people have entered their chickens in a 4-H poultry contest in Horry County. They are flanked by Horry County farm demonstration agent W. P. Johnson on the left and Jean McIver, Horry County home demonstration agent, on the right. Courtesy of Sara Aiken Waymer

Within weeks of Nutt's departure, Clemson president Edwards personally asked Bernice Brown, a black woman, to take charge of the extension program in Dorchester County. Edwards commended Brown because she had "demonstrated clearly the ability to provide leadership and direction that this program needs . . . in providing the very best services possible to the people of Dorchester County." Brown was the first black associate county agent leader. Shortly after her appointment, Bennie L. Cunningham was invited to Clemson to serve as state leader for a program directed at low-income farmers. Cunningham was a graduate of S.C. State and the associate agent in Chesterfield County. In 1970 E. D. Dean, a black veteran of the extension service, was named county agent for Bamberg County. Dean replaced the white agent who had assumed leadership of the extension program in Orangeburg County.[71]

Segregation's demise disrupted 4-H activities across the state. Most 4-H chapters attempted for a time to remain separate organizations. Those 4-H groups that met in public schools had to halt their activities because they were in violation of civil rights provisions attached to federal aid to education. In 1966 at least thirteen South Carolina school districts were in breach of the nonrestrictive racial requirements. Outside of the schools, segregation persisted among the 4-H clubs. In 1968, 275 of 350 4-H clubs in South Carolina were functioning separately. Eighty-six of them served 1,830 white youngsters while 189 were for 6,668 black young people. However, seventy-five clubs had integrated with 1,901 white members and 319 black members.[72]

The 4-H camps were also temporary casualties of desegregation. Two white camps and Camp Harry Daniels for black youngsters closed from 1964 to 1967 rather than have integrated activities. After extensive planning the two white camps—Cooper and Long—were reopened on an integrated basis in 1968. Twenty percent of the campers at the previously all-white camps were black. But fearing possible interference from disgruntled white people, the State Law Enforcement Division [SLED] had been notified and was available if trouble erupted. It did not.[73]

Camp Daniels was not reopened at the time as a 4-H camp. There were discussions of transferring its ownership to Clemson, but that did not happen. However, when the segregated extension programs merged, the ownership of the house for black home demonstration work that had been built in Williamsburg County was transferred from the local home demonstration council to the Peoples' Cooperative of the local community. It no longer functioned as a home demonstration project. It fell into disuse and eventually was demolished.[74]

THE COSTS OF DESEGREGATION

The Civil Rights Act of 1964 ranks among the most important legislative achievements in American history. But too often it was black men and women who had to bear a disproportionate share of the burden in eradicating segregation. The creation of the single extension system in the mid- and late 1960s is a revealing example. African Americans lost control of a major program that they had administered for decades from the campus of S.C. State. They were not assigned leadership roles at the state or county level in the new extension program that were commensurate with their previous positions. The salary gap between black and white agents persisted after segregation formally ended. Black agents were supervised by white personnel, and they invariably received lower evaluations than their white counterparts. Black people employed in extension work must have wondered if eliminating the dual system had been worth it.

White extension officials—well aware of mounting black dissatisfaction with the way in which desegregation was conducted—were convinced, however, that black extension personnel were not as well qualified as white agents. This explained the lack of black leaders and the disparities in salaries and evaluations. The black agents were mostly graduates of S.C. State, and the black college had never had the facilities or funding that Clemson University had received. Therefore white administrators believed that black men and women could not be expected to demonstrate the knowledge or skills that the graduates of white land-grant schools possessed.[75]

Furthermore widely varying perceptions of the role of county extension agents marred the merger of the black and white programs. White people saw the extension service essentially as a vehicle to furnish information and ideas on how to improve agricultural production and homemaking skills. Black agents perceived themselves as community leaders similar to that of the clergy and educators. Rural white residents could turn to local politicians, businessmen, and bankers for assistance. But not most

Over the years women participating in the home demonstration program sponsored a variety of activities. Here women in Hartsville in Darlington County in 1953 are preparing fruits and vegetables as well as canned goods and fresh flowers for the Hartsville Farm Market. Courtesy of Sara Aiken Waymer

black people. Thus the black extension agents were respected, looked up to, and called on by "their people" for more than knowledge of crops, fertilizer, nutrition, and home management. They were needed in the case of family emergencies, personal problems, and with issues affecting the surrounding black community. For generations black agents had been regarded as race leaders. But not anymore.

The end of segregation also led to other difficulties and challenges for those who benefited most from the extension program. For years black and white women had met separately in local home demonstration councils. These councils afforded women an opportunity to exchange information, cooperate with each other, develop leadership skills, and create personal and lasting relationships. These councils often met in the homes of members. With desegregation, many women had no desire to begin meeting with women of the other race in close and intimate confines. It would be, they felt, a very uncomfortable and awkward situation. Black women voted in their annual state meeting of local councils in May 1965 to continue as an autonomous organization. While some leadership sessions and training meetings were held jointly with black and white women, the local councils remained segregated and at least in technical violation of the 1964 Civil Rights Act. In 1968 there were sixty-two white councils and fifty-eight black councils. It would take some time and some adjustment for women of different races to begin meeting together easily and informally.[76]

The civil rights movement profoundly affected American society, and it contributed prominently to major changes that occurred at South Carolina State College. Within half a decade—1965 to 1970—the college closed its law school, terminated the program in agriculture, halted production on the campus farm, and saw its extension program for black farm families merged with Clemson's previously all-white extension service. The loss of these programs ignited no controversy on the campus or in the black community. In fact President Benner C. Turner was quietly relieved by the reduction in major programs. He had complained for years that the college had been saddled with more responsibilities and programs than it could adequately support and manage.

THE BOARD OF TRUSTEES AND THE BOARD OF VISITORS

As the civil rights movement gathered momentum, other notable and overdue changes occurred on the campus. For seven decades the board of trustees had consisted solely of seven white males including the governor. Six trustees, elected by the general assembly, were a tightly knit group whose membership changed infrequently. The board, and especially its local committee, supervised the college. Wallace C. Bethea, Adam H. Moss, and Julian Wolfe (for a brief period) paid careful attention to the institution through the mid-twentieth century and were willing to work with Presidents Whittaker and Turner in expanding state funding and securing philanthropic support. But for the most part the trustees let the president administer day-to-day affairs.

Aware of the growing unhappiness among black South Carolinians with the white male monopolization of the board of trustees, Governor Ernest Hollings in 1959 decided to remedy the situation. But he only exacerbated the dissatisfaction. Hollings, who was the ex officio chair of the board, did not propose naming a black man or woman as a trustee of the black college. Instead the governor recommended the creation of a separate board of visitors made up solely of black Carolinians. The new board would not replace the board of trustees. In fact it had no legal standing whatsoever. It would merely make recommendations to the board and to the college president. Having conceived of this board, Hollings then proceeded to appoint its seven members in early 1960. Dr. Carl A. Green was the chair. C. C. Woodson, Walker E. Solomon, Benjamin Sanders, Allard Allston, Reginald Barrett, and Mrs. Larkin Walker were the other visitors. Mrs. Walker served as secretary.[77]

Many of the state's black residents did not regard the creation of this board as a harbinger of racial progress. John McCray complained in the pages of the *Afro-American* that a racially integrated board of trustees was needed, and "not a buffer, honorary committee without either legal status or authority." But for the next six years the board met annually and functioned—as McCray had suggested—as a convenient rubber stamp. The visitors visited the campus each spring and then issued a glowing report praising what they had seen and endorsing what they had heard. Their recommendations invariably coincided with needs of the institution that had already been identified by President Turner. In 1961 the visitors called for the construction of a new training school, a new physical education facility, and new dormitories. By 1964 they had expressed pleasure at the attractive campus. However they were at least mildly concerned that efforts to raise admission standards might mean the rejection of those "less fortunate." But even this ordinarily timid group politely informed the board of trustees in 1964 and again in 1965 that many students and faculty members wanted black men and women to serve as trustees.[78]

The addition of one or more black men or women to the board of trustees was not as politically easy to accomplish as it might have seemed. The all-white general assembly elected and usually reelected the trustees. Most legislators were not ready to replace a white man on the board with a black man or woman. The solution, therefore, was to expand the board. However, it was not students, the faculty, or administrators who launched the effort to bring about that change. The alumni association asked T. J. Crawford, the director of alumni affairs, to draft letters to legislators imploring them to enact a measure to increase the board from six to eight members with a provision that one of the new members be an alumnus of the institution.

South Carolina's political leadership remained resistant to any hint of change in the racial status quo in the mid-1960s. The state's congressional delegation was unanimously opposed to the passage of the Civil Rights Act of 1964 and the Voting Rights Act of 1965. Nevertheless state legislators in 1966 were mostly amenable to the proposed change that would integrate the college board of trustees. But at least one lawmaker took exception to the notion that one of the new seats go to an S.C. State graduate. Harold Breazeale of Pickens County complained. "I don't like the idea of the alumni association recommending someone to us. It might be the very type of person we wouldn't want on the board and not in the best interest of the school." The measure passed anyway, and several weeks later with no controversy and with only two men nominated, I. P. Stanback and Dr. James Boykin were elected to the board.[79]

Stanback was a graduate of Johnson C. Smith College and the manager of the Columbia District of North Carolina Mutual Life Insurance company. Boykin was a 1949 graduate of S.C. State who had earned a medical degree at Howard University. He practiced medicine in Lancaster. For the first time in its seventy-year existence, the black college had black men on its board of trustees.[80]

Among those closely affiliated with the college, only President Benner C. Turner seemed to regard the change with apprehension. According to T. J. Crawford, who also served as the college public relations director, Turner believed that black board members would take an unseemly interest in the president's personal and family life. "They would," Crawford recalled Turner sourly saying, "want to know what you are cooking for dinner."[81]

At the first board meeting that Stanback and Boykin attended, Wallace C. Bethea resigned as the board secretary after nearly forty years of service. He had succeeded the first secretary, William R. Lowman, in 1926. No trustee had served longer or had been more directly involved in the affairs and management of the college than Wallace C. Bethea. In many respects Bethea had been the de facto chairman of the trustees for decades—serving as secretary and chair of the board's local committee. Living in close proximity to the college and as the only paid member of the board, Bethea monitored the institution and had regularly consulted with Presidents Wilkinson, Whittaker, and

Turner. The integration of the board of trustees effectively ended the decades-old reliance on the local committee of the board. When his final six-year term expired in 1970, Bethea had completed forty-five years as a board member. He died in 1982. Elliott Elam of Aiken, who had been elected to the board in 1960, had taken over as the third secretary in 1966. Elam was the last paid secretary of the board, but he never possessed the influence or cachet of Bethea.[82]

ATHLETICS

For years cynics have insisted that the "A&M" that identified many black and white land-grant institutions did not stand for "agricultural and mechanical," but rather referred to "athletics and music." And it is true that in the post–World War II era, there was far more emphasis on athletics—especially football—and on music—especially marching bands—at colleges and universities across America including South Carolina State. Many black and white Americans, including those who had never set foot on a college campus, closely followed the football fortunes of their favorite school.

After a three-year hiatus during World War II, football resumed at S.C. State under head coach Oliver C. "Ollie" Dawson in 1946. Playing in the segregated world of southern college football, Dawson's teams competed in the all-black Southern Intercollegiate Athletic Conference (SIAC). When teams like S.C. State went to away games in the days long before interstate highways, it was sometimes a lonely and long trip down the two lane highways and byways of the rural South to Tallahassee or Tuskegee. Until the mid- and latter 1950s, no students—including cheerleaders and the marching band—accompanied the team. Dawson made arrangements in advance to eat at all-black diners. While away from Orangeburg, S.C. State teams did not stay in motels or hotels. They were lodged in facilities on the opposing team's campus. When teams came to S.C. State, they usually stayed in Poplar Hall, one of the veterans' dormitories erected after the Second World War.

In the postwar era of college football and before the National Collegiate Athletic Association (NCAA) imposed strict regulations on the eligibility of athletes, prospective football players arrived on the S.C. State campus in August to try out for a place on Coach Dawson's team. Those who were good enough to secure a spot on the squad earned a scholarship. Those who did not make the team could either go home or pay their own way.

On a miniscule budget and with "very little professional assistance," Dawson's 1947 team won six games and tied games against Benedict and Alabama A&M. The team was invited to play Shaw University for the mythical Black National Championship in Washington, D.C. The team traveled by train on the Atlantic Coast Line to Washington and stayed at the YMCA. Shaw won the game, 7–6, on December 6, 1947. But the game was a financial flop as only slightly more than one thousand spectators paid their way into Griffith Stadium.[83]

Coach Dawson's 1949 and 1950 teams fared poorly, and he stepped down as head football coach after the 1950 team compiled a 1–7 record. "Ollie" Dawson's overall record was 30–29–7. After football this man for all seasons continued to coach four other sports—basketball, tennis, golf, and track and field—during his four-decade tenure at the college. He also served intermittently as athletic director from the late 1950s until 1970.[84]

In 1951 Lawrence Simmons succeeded Dawson as head football coach. The forty-year-old Simmons, who had coached at Langston in Oklahoma and at Tennessee State, lasted two years. Although his teams won twelve games and lost only two, he aroused the ire of the Athletic Committee, which was chaired by Frank M. Staley, the dean of the School of Agriculture, and included for a time, business manager J. I. Washington and President Benner C. Turner. Simmons failed to follow proper procedures in ordering athletic equipment and supplies. He was also accused of recruiting tramp athletes who lacked minimum academic credentials. It was a charge he stoutly denied after he was dismissed in 1953. In a letter to the *Collegian,* the former coach maintained that only four young men who he had recruited "flunked out" and that none of his players were expelled for disciplinary reasons.[85]

Frank Staley's Faculty Athletic Committee hired John Martin, the Savannah State head coach, to take over the S.C. State program. Martin lasted just two years before his untimely death. After winning six games and losing three in 1953, Martin had major surgery prior to the 1954 season, and he returned to coaching in October, and the Bulldogs went 7–2. But Martin never fully regained his health, and he died in January 1955. One of Martin's three assistant coaches, W. C. Brown, took over as head coach for 1955 before he was replaced the following year by Roy D. Moore.[86]

Moore compiled a respectable record of twenty wins and thirteen losses in four seasons. But once again off-the field problems plagued a head coach and led the Faculty Athletic Committee to recommend Moore's dismissal in 1960. It seems Moore had failed to pay federal income taxes since 1953, and he was also well in arrears in car payments to a Buick dealer in Nashville, where he had coached prior to coming to Orangeburg. The committee was also perturbed because Moore had not established a cooperative relationship with them.[87]

For all intents and purposes, the Faculty Athletic Committee ran the S.C. State athletic program by the mid-1950s. President Turner, who meticulously supervised most college operations, surrendered control of intercollegiate athletics to the committee and rarely overrode their decisions. He was less interested in athletics (as well as agriculture) than he was in academic issues and student behavior. The Faculty Athletic Committee consisted of three administrators: Frank M. Staley chaired the committee, and he was the dean of the School of Agriculture. Harold "Crip" W. Crawford, the dean of industrial education, was the secretary, and M. Maceo Nance, the business manager, also served on the committee. This powerful trio handled the budget, hired and fired coaches, and scheduled many of the athletic contests. The director of athletics carried out the committee's policies and decisions. In 1956, for example, Staley informed Moore—who was then serving as both athletic director and head football coach—that Moore was not to hire football officials who had graduated from either Benedict or Allen to officiate at S.C. State games.[88]

In the meantime S.C. State unveiled a new football facility. Bulldog Stadium was among the many capital improvements made on the campus in the mid-1950s. Opened for the 1955 season, the new stadium had a capacity of six thousand spectators. It was located on the northeastern edge of the campus in what had been the Wilkinson Woods. It replaced the football field that had existed for decades along with a baseball field behind Dukes Gymnasium.

The new stadium featured lights, and the first home night game in college history was played on a rainy Saturday night in October against the Allen Yellow Jackets. The visitors defeated the Bulldogs before a damp crowd of five thousand fans. In 1959 WPBD broadcast the first S.C. State home football game on the radio as the Bulldogs lost to Florida A&M on Halloween, 34–12. The sponsors were several local black businesses including Webber Motors, Lamar's Restaurant, and Montgomery Insurance.[89]

From 1959 until 1966, the Bulldogs and the Benedict Tigers played the Pumpkin Classic on Thanksgiving Day. The games alternated between Columbia and Orangeburg. The 1963 game in Columbia was played six days after the assassination of President John F. Kennedy, and the Garnet and Blue Marching Band dedicated the halftime show to the slain leader. The Pumpkin Classic ended when Benedict discontinued football. As the last game concluded in Columbia with a Bulldog win, 35–18, the crowd sang "Auld Lang Syne." S.C. State won five of the eight classics.[90]

In 1960 the Faculty Athletic Committee hired William B. Harris from Elizabeth City State in North Carolina to replace Moore as football coach. Harris lasted two years, winning three games and losing fourteen. Florida A&M's legendary coach A. S. "Jake" Gaither had invited S.C. State to meet the Rattlers in a game in 1960 at the Gator Bowl in Jacksonville for a guarantee of $5,000. It was an offer Staley's committee could not refuse. But Gaither's powerful team "treated" the Bulldogs to an 80–0 shellacking. The next year the Bulldogs narrowed the margin of defeat, losing 60–0.[91]

George Bell took over as head coach in 1962. A graduate of Indiana University, Bell went on to guide the Bulldogs to an excellent 20–6 record in three years. But as important as football was to S.C. State students in the 1960s, the civil rights movement took precedence. In 1963 the Bulldogs lost their only game that season, 18–7 to Allen—a defeat that the *Collegian* explained was due to student participation in ongoing protests over Jim Crow in Orangeburg. "The game was played when the majority of students were concerned with the Orangeburg Movement; thus football was far from the cry on South Carolina's State's campus."[92]

In the meantime Emilie Green Bythewood took those same students to task for holding their annual homecoming parade through the streets of Orangeburg. She reminded readers in a letter to the *Collegian* that students had been arrested and soaked with water from fire department hoses in peaceful protests. "How can you spend your parents' hard earned money with merchants who stood aside and permitted town authorities to do such a cruel thing and make no outcry? How can you parade through these streets?" The homecoming parade went on, but so did the protests.[93]

For the first time, in 1964, the football team traveled by aircraft to a game. They flew Delta Airlines to Ohio to take on Central State. They lost, 20–15. A few months later, Coach Bell caught Bulldog fans by surprise when he announced his resignation. The likable Bell was a Seventh-Day Adventist, and Saturday is their Sabbath. The coach decided that he could not violate that Sabbath and continue to spend Saturdays at football games.[94]

Oree Banks, who had been an assistant coach at Grambling State University under famed Coach Eddie Robinson, replaced Bell in 1965. But tragedy struck before Banks's first game. John Devlin, a nineteen-year-old running back from Brewer High School in Greenwood, died of heat stroke during preseason drills in August.[95]

As the football team's fortunes ebbed and flowed in the 1950s and 1960s, the basketball team won eight SIAC (Southern Intercollegiate Athletic Conference) championships and made its first appearances in national championship tournaments. The architect of the basketball program was Edward "Ed" Martin, an easygoing but intensely competitive coach. Born in Allentown, Pennsylvania, in 1925, Martin's first sport was baseball. After graduating from North Carolina A&T, he pitched for the Philadelphia Stars in the fading days of the Negro League in 1951 and 1952 before a shoulder injury cut short his career. He earned a master's degree from Temple University. After a stint teaching and coaching at Avery Institute in Charleston, Martin came to S.C. State in 1955 and succeeded Victor Kerr as basketball coach. He was also the baseball coach and an assistant with the football team.[96]

Martin turned out superb teams and outstanding players during the thirteen years he spent at S.C. State. But he had to overcome the doubts of the ever-vigilant Faculty Athletic Committee because of his close association with football coach Roy D. Moore. In early 1960 when the committee decided to terminate Moore, they expressed reservations about Martin's future with the basketball and baseball teams. But they reluctantly agreed to support athletic director Dr. Jesse L. Parks's recommendation to reappoint Martin.[97]

Martin had already coached the Bulldog basketball team to its first-ever appearance in the NCAA national championship tournament in 1958. The team traveled to Monroe, Louisiana, to take part in the college-level tournament. For the first time in S.C. State history, an athletic team traveled by aircraft. But they lost to Grambling, 100–82, and then defeated Philander Smith 80–70 in the consolation game. The NCAA accommodated to the Jim Crow practices of southern states and did not have black and white colleges compete against each other in tournaments in the South.[98]

The 1958 team was led by sharp-shooting six-foot-one guard Teddy Wright, who averaged over twenty-eight points per game. He had forty-six points against Fort Valley State earlier in the season in a 91–85 Bulldog win. Wright's scoring achievements eclipsed the earlier marks set by "Mice" Holden in the 1940s. Martin's 1961 team won the SIAC championship for the first time since Oliver Dawson's squad took conference honors in 1943. The team was invited to Crawfordsville, Indiana, for the first round of the NCAA tournament. For the first time in S.C. State history, one of its athletic teams competed against a college with a predominantly white student body. The Bulldogs lost to Wabash College 94–83 and then lost the consolation game to Youngstown, 96–82. They finished the year 23–9.[99]

Martin's teams had both the advantage and disadvantage of playing their home games in Dukes Gymnasium. The three-decade-old facility had limited seating that could not accommodate all the students or local fans who wanted to see the Bulldogs play. In the era before magnificent college arenas, Dukes Gym was cramped and alternately drafty and unbearably hot—all to the detriment of visiting teams. It was also the era before southern white colleges and universities recruited black athletes. Martin was able to attract excellent basketball players in the early 1960s to play in the unglamorous confines if Dukes Gym. Lindberg Moody, Bill Morgan, and Ernest "Sonny" Jackson were three Bulldogs who subsequently signed to play professional basketball.

Moody was a quick guard and prolific scorer. He totaled 2,529 career points, an average of 27.8 per game. He was drafted by the Detroit Pistons in the fifth round of the 1962 draft. He was quick with a pencil too, serving as the sports editor of the *Collegian* his senior year. Bill "Hustle" Morgan was a skilled playmaker who signed to play with the Harlem Globetrotters in 1963. Ernest "Sonny" Jackson was a product of Philadelphia's Public League, and he averaged twenty-nine points a game in 1962–63. Eldon Miller, who coached the 1963 college national champions, Wittenberg College, labeled Jackson the best guard they faced during the season.[100]

That 1963 Bulldog team went to Akron, Ohio, for the NCAA Mideast Regional Tournament. They defeated the University of Buffalo, 80–63, but lost a hard-fought game to eventual national champion Wittenberg, 70–63. After winning the SIAC Tournament at Tuskegee in 1964, Martin's squad took part in the NAIA (National Association of Intercollegiate Athletics) District 6 tournament. They lost to Miles College, 103–99, but won against Florida A&M, 91–82, in the consolation game. The NAIA (like the NCAA) created an all-black first-round tournament so that southern white colleges would not have to compete against schools with black players until those schools reached the final round of the NAIA tournament in Kansas City.[101]

Following the 1967–68 season and after having compiled a record of 214–87 at S.C. State, Ed Martin and his wife, Ruby (who taught English), accepted positions at Tennessee State University. In seventeen years at the Nashville school, Martin's teams won 290 games and lost 169. He later served as an assistant coach at Vanderbilt and worked as a scout for the NBA. Coach Martin died in 2002.[102]

Many S.C. State athletes participated in more than one sport. Lindberg Moody played first base on Coach Martin's baseball team. Willie Jeffries was a center on the football team and a pitcher on the baseball team. Running back Wendell Tucker also played baseball. Swimmer Carroll Thompson was the cocaptain of the football team in 1961.[103]

Thompson was one of the many superb athletes who played for S.C. State. He was nearly a one-man swimming team for the aqua Dogs. Ordinarily members of collegiate swimming teams were limited to participation in three events in a meet or tournament. But because the S.C. State swimming team usually had no more than five to seven members, they were sometimes given a waiver that enabled individual swimmers to compete in as many as five and even seven events in what became grueling tests of endurance. In 1961 Thompson took part in seven separate events when only two swimmers traveled to a dual meet at Tuskegee that they lost 89½ to 60½. Five swimmers remained in Orangeburg to take part in Alflamingo.[104]

A year earlier in a triangular meet with Tuskegee and Alabama State, the four members of the Bulldog swim team won by compiling fifty-eight points. Tuskegee had fifty and Alabama State had thirty-one. Lloyd Williams won six events in that meet. But they lost to Morehouse 64–21 when the S.C. State swimmers were each limited to participation in three events. The Bulldog swim team labored under the additional disadvantage of having no home meets. The pool at Dukes Gym was inadequate for intercollegiate competition, and therefore S.C. State swimmers competed only on the road. In 1963 Robert Bradley was one of three S.C. State swimmers to take part in the SIAC tournament at Morehouse, but he earned honors as the "Outstanding Swimmer" in the competition. Bradley went on to become one of the first of several S.C. State students to gain summer employment with the National Park Service when he worked at Yellowstone National Park in 1964.[105]

Carroll Thompson was not only an outstanding swimmer; he was the quarterback and cocaptain of the 1961 Bulldog football team. He graduated in 1962 and was commissioned an officer in ROTC. He was a captain with Special Forces in Vietnam when he was killed by small arms fire in Quang Ngai Province in November 1966. He was twenty-five.[106]

Besides swimming, tennis and golf were two sports that few black youngsters had an opportunity to learn and compete in with each other in the Jim Crow South. Nevertheless tennis had been popular at S.C. State since before World War II. The campus tennis courts were located in front of Dukes Gymnasium in the 1950s and 1960s prior to the expansion of the K. W. Green Student Center. The all-black American Tennis Association national championships took place at S.C. State in 1948. By the 1950s George Stewart, "the Panama Kid," Nelson Brownlee, and Rudolph Glover were playing tennis for the college.[107]

African Americans had almost no access to golf courses or country clubs. Croquet was the sport of choice among male faculty and administrators in the 1950s and 1960s. There was a croquet court located behind Wilkinson Hall, and it attracted Maceo Nance, Oliver Dawson, William C. Lewis, Kirkland W. Green, Edward W. Ferguson, and Dudley Zimmerman among others as they engaged in genial competition and ribald conversation.[108]

When heavyweight boxing champion Joe Louis visited the campus in 1950, he took part in an exhibition of golf with Coach Oliver Dawson. More than a decade later Dawson was instrumental in organizing the college's first intercollegiate golf team. But there was no "home" course available in Orangeburg.[109]

The NCAA did not begin to sanction women's intercollegiate athletics until the 1970s. Although men's athletics had always taken precedence, women had participated in sports for decades at S.C. State. They had competed in basketball since the 1920s. Mamie Thompson coached the 1947–48 Lady Bulldogs to an 8–4 record. But women's sports were barely mentioned in the *Collegian* or in the *Bulldog*. Opportunities for women to participate in sports or receive athletic scholarships were far fewer than for men. A woman at S.C. State in the 1950s and 1960s had a better chance of representing a student organization as "their" queen in the pages of the *Bulldog* than taking part in a sponsored athletic endeavor.[110]

Still for more than a quarter century women from black colleges competed twice a year in sports festivals. In 1965 the Women's Athletic Association winter sports meet was held on the S.C. State campus. Seven colleges entered teams of twelve women to take part in activities that included volleyball, shuffleboard, and bicycle-riding competition. In 1960 women had begun to compete in track and field. There were eight women and fifteen men on the 1961 team. The women lost two dual meets that year, but the *Bulldog* praised sprinter Mattie Johnson as possibly "another Wilma Rudolph." Rudolph was the Tennessee State star who won gold medals at the 1960 Rome Summer Olympics. Shortly after, women's participation in track and field ended for more than a decade.

In 1964 "Bullet Bob" Hayes—the World's Fastest Human—came to Orangeburg to compete with Florida A&M on the track at Bulldog Stadium. He did not disappoint as he won the one-hundred-yard dash in an unofficial 9.1 seconds. S.C. State was leading in the 440-yard relay until Hayes picked up the baton on the anchor leg and won.[111]

As athletics—especially football—aroused greater interest on the campus in the decades after World War II, so did music—especially the marching band. There were a variety of musical organizations that performed during the school year including the men's and the women's glee clubs, the college chorus, the symphonic band, and the concert band. Then there was the Wilkinson pipe organ, which had been installed in White Hall in 1925. This cherished instrument was refurbished in 1961 and rededicated with a concert performed by music professor C. Edourd Ward.[112]

THE MARCHING 101

But it was the marching band—what came to be known as the Marching 101—that created the most excitement and support in the last four decades of the twentieth century. For the first half of the century, there was no well-organized ensemble that played regularly at the halftime of football games. In the early 1900s there was a contingent of students who played in a military-style band directed by Eugene Mikell that accompanied students who were themselves in uniform as they marched to the dining hall. Concert and dance bands entertained on and off campus in the 1920s and 1930s. Harold June's band was perhaps the best known of these groups.

Following the establishment of the ROTC program in 1947, there was a military band that played at football games and on ceremonial occasions such as the funeral of President Miller F. Whittaker. They also played at Friday afternoon retreat. When Republican presidential candidate Dwight D. Eisenhower visited Columbia in October 1952, the ROTC band took part in the parade for the World War II general and future president. The ROTC band, which was made up solely of males, was under the direction of civilian faculty members Reginald R. Thomasson and Shellie Thomas Jr.[113]

As of the mid-1950s, there was no student musical organization that could be dignified by the term "marching band." F. P. Abraham, the chair of the music department, complained that there were just twelve indifferent students in the so-called band after several other students lost interest and quit. The band members lacked uniforms, instruments, and practice facilities. They shared $3,600 in work scholarships that yielded $8.40 per month per student during the school year. President Turner responded to this woeful situation by setting aside $6,170 from the institution's general appropriation for the marching band for the 1955–56 school year. The fifty-member Garnet and Blue Marching Band took the field in September 1955 as the first formally organized and nonmilitary marching band in the college's history. It was also the first home game in the new Bulldog Stadium and the first home night game.[114]

By this time people had started to take note of the spectacular Florida A&M marching band. Organized in 1946 and then directed for more than fifty years by William P. Foster, the Florida A&M Marching 100 became the envy of colleges and universities throughout the country, but particularly of historically black institutions. On November 1, 1958, Foster led the Marching 100 (which had grown to 132 musicians) into Orangeburg. In an unusual display of hospitality, the Garnet and Blue Band stepped aside and let the Marching 100 play the entire pregame and halftime shows. The Bulldogs lost to the Rattlers, 28–8. It was not the last football loss to Florida A&M, but it was the last time that S.C. State allowed Florida A&M to monopolize the marching and music.[115]

With more money and more institutional support, the Garnet and Blue Marching Band developed its own devoted following of fans. In 1963 eighty musicians and five majorettes assembled on Labor Day weekend to begin preparations for that year's performances. They were under the direction of Cornelius V. Troup and Reginald Thomasson.[116]

In a not-so-subtle display of one-upmanship with Florida A&M, the Garnet and Blue Marching Band transformed itself into the Marching 101 in 1964. As a bigger and better musical organization, they began to take to the road. They appeared in Jacksonville at the Gator Bowl Classic for the Bulldog football game against Bethune Cookman College. In 1965 the Marching 101 appeared for the first time on national television during a halftime performance in Washington, D.C., at a Redskins football game against the St. Louis Cardinals. The 115 member band traveled by three chartered busses and spent two nights in a Washington hotel.[117]

WHITE FACULTY MEMBERS

Ironically it was forces set in motion by the civil rights movement that brought Benner C. Turner's presidency to an unhappy end in 1967. Since 1960 students involved in the "Orangeburg movement" had marched, protested, and been arrested month after month and semester after semester in their campaign to end segregation. Although stubborn resistance to opening public facilities in Orangeburg to African Americans persisted following the passage of the Civil Rights Act of 1964, President Turner and college administrators began to employ the first nonblack faculty members. The elimination of segregation in higher education enabled Turner to draw on a larger pool of applicants for faculty positions—and it was Turner who reviewed the applications—to bolster the academic credentials of the teaching staff. But when Turner arbitrarily declined to renew the contracts of two of the first three white faculty members, their dismissal touched off a series of student protests and a boycott of classes that cost Turner his position.[118]

The college had employed three young white faculty members who were Woodrow Wilson teaching interns as part of an effort to "help small struggling colleges upgrade themselves." Thomas Wirth came to S.C. State in 1965 to teach chemistry. He was the institution's first white faculty member. Wirth had a bachelor's degree "with honors" from Cornell University, and he had a Ph.D. in chemistry from the California Institute of Technology. In 1966 Anthony Fanning and Kristin Morrison joined the faculty. Fanning had a master's degree from the University of California at Berkeley and taught mathematics while Morrison had a Ph.D. from Harvard University, and she taught composition and literature.[119]

Wirth, Fanning, and Morrison were young, easygoing, and generally popular among students, most of whom had never been taught by a white person But the white instructors were amazed and appalled at the rigid and stultifying academic atmosphere that pervaded the campus. There seemed to be more emphasis on the enforcement of the extensive list of rules than on creating an open learning environment. However, Turner as well as some black faculty members and administrators were themselves appalled at what they perceived to be the casual and condescending behavior of Wirth, Fanning, and Morrison. They were convinced that the three new faculty members—while well intentioned—were "outsiders" who did not understand the way black colleges functioned. President Turner told Kristin Morrison during her first semester that "her continued presence was unwelcome." Hurt and discouraged she decided to leave, and she had little trouble finding a teaching position for the next academic year at New York University.[120]

In February 1967, the dean of the faculty, Algernon S. Belcher, informed Wirth and Fanning that it was their last semester; their contracts would not be renewed. Belcher stressed that their professional competence was not the issue. Wirth was told that he was "too research oriented," and that he did "not fit into the program." Fanning was let go, according to Belcher, because the college was in the process of hiring two new faculty members who each possessed a Ph.D. in mathematics—unlike Fanning, who had a master's degree. Wirth and Fanning did not have tenure, and even if they had, tenure at S.C. State was meaningless. The college's tenure policy stated: "The College reserves the right, acting through its President, to terminate the appointment of any continuous (or tenure) faculty appointment, prior to its expiration, for . . . conduct detrimental to the best *interest of the College.*"[121]

When word circulated among students that Wirth and Fanning would not be retained, many of them began to complain. They wondered why faculty members who were regarded as effective teachers, who had a passion for their subjects, and who were devoted to students had been summarily terminated. Wirth advised the young people not to protest, lest it jeopardize their status at the college.[122]

Telling college students in Orangeburg in 1967 not to protest was an exercise in futility. They did not hesitate to make their opposition to the removal of Wirth and Fanning known. Building on a legacy of protest, students were no longer challenging Jim Crow. Now they took on the black man who administered the college that they attended. In civil rights protests, white authorities could and did arrest them. President Turner could and did suspend them.

"THE CAUSE"

In what came to be known as "the Cause" (unlike the earlier Orangeburg movement), students in mid-February began with a meeting in the lounge of a women's dormitory. One week later there was a raucous late-night gathering on the front lawn of the president's campus residence that he later characterized as "noisy, discourteous and

In the spring of 1967, students began a boycott of classes to protest the autocratic administration of President Benner C. Turner; their opposition came to be known as "the Cause." Turner had not renewed the contracts of two white faculty members, Thomas Wirth and Anthony Fanning, and then suspended student leaders—Joseph Hammond, John Stroman, and Benjamin Bryant—who protested Turner's action. Courtesy of the Historical Collection, South Carolina State University

disorderly." The next night students occupied the student center until dawn. "The College administration," Turner emphasized, "will not deal with a rowdy and undisciplined mob." Turner had had enough. Three student protest leaders were identified, and the Student Disciplinary Committee suspended John Stroman, Joseph Hammond, and Benjamin Bryant until August 1970 for violating campus regulations that prohibited unauthorized demonstrations and parades.[123]

The suspensions only served to ignite further protests. Student leaders including senior class president Isaac "Ike" Williams met with Turner, who coldly and confidently informed them that they would not prevail. "Mr. Williams, when the students have a problem with the administration, the students cannot win." Turner did, however, agree to a rehearing before the Student Disciplinary Committee, which decided that the three young men could be reinstated in August 1967. But it was too late. Students refused to accept this concession.[124]

On March 2 Ike Williams and other class presidents called for students to boycott classes. Perhaps 60 to 70 percent of students stayed out of class. But there were fractures within the student body. The Student Government Association and its president, Bernard Gaillard (who was Williams's roommate), opposed the boycott. There was a failed attempt to impeach Williams, and it was Gaillard who resigned as support for the boycott expanded. As many as fourteen hundred of 1,695 undergraduates stayed out of class. Stokely Carmichael, the chairman of the Student Non-violent Coordinating

The president of the senior class in 1967, Isaac "Ike" Williams, led "the Cause." Here he addresses students and the media during the boycott of classes. Courtesy of the Historical Collection, South Carolina State University

Committee (SNCC), sent President Turner a telegram demanding the immediate reinstatement of Stroman, Hammond, and Bryant. But student leaders asked that SNCC stay out of what was considered a campus controversy.[125]

"The Cause," which began over Wirth, Fanning, and the three suspended students, quickly evolved into a larger movement that focused on Turner's autocratic leadership and the quality of education that the state of South Carolina provided to black students at S.C. State. Students had long objected to the repressive array of rules and regulations they were expected to abide by. They wanted an end to compulsory class attendance and mandatory participation in Sunday vespers and lyceum programs. They insisted on an end to the dress code for Sunday dinner. And they wanted more: greater student control over student government, student involvement in the selection of faculty advisors for student organizations, student selection of the student representatives of the Student Disciplinary Committee, a wholesale revision of the women's handbook, and "delocalizing" of the faculty through hiring on a nationwide basis. They also wanted Turner to lift the suspensions of Stroman, Hammond, and Bryant.[126]

Uncharacteristically Turner accepted the student demands except for the immediate reinstatement of the three young men. "This," Turner stated emphatically, "is an ultimatum the college cannot accept." Students declined to return to class, and Turner withdrew the concessions. The president instructed faculty members to continue to conduct classes (in virtually empty classrooms) and to maintain a list of the absent students.[127]

The eight members of the board of trustees, including the first two black members —I. P. Stanback and Dr. James Boykin, fully supported Turner. They insisted on the enforcement of class attendance regulations, and they authorized Turner to suspend college operations if order was not soon restored—a peculiar demand in that the class boycott had been entirely peaceful. But the events in Orangeburg attracted the attention of media outlets from across the state as well as the attention of Governor Robert E. McNair.[128]

The governor fully supported Turner and the trustees. He summoned the president and attorney Bruce White, who was chairman of the board, to a meeting in Columbia on March 8 with attorney general Daniel McLeod and SLED chief J. P. "Pete" Strom. There was no sympathy for the students and their demands. The boycott was considered nothing more than defiance of properly constituted authority. Turner had given the students until Friday, March 10, to end their boycott or face expulsion. McNair dispatched twenty state highway patrolmen to Orangeburg, and the FBI sent two agents to the community.[129]

McNair rejected a request from students for a meeting. "I have no intention to meet with any group of students who refuse to attend classes, who fail to abide by rules of responsible conduct, and who fail to recognize the necessity for settling grievances with the authorities who are legally responsible for the operation of the college they attend." McNair's position was widely shared by many South Carolinians, who regarded the students as troublemakers and rebels who were wholly ungrateful for the educational opportunities made available to them. People wondered why students who wanted an education would refuse to attend class.

Students were not intimidated by this nearly solid opposition of black and white authorities. They rejected the ultimatum that they return to class. Ike Williams reassured students at a campus rally. "Let's keep our cool, and keep our hands on the plow. I expected more wisdom from the Governor and trustees." He ridiculed Turner, who "doesn't know how to be a Negro." Junior class president Alexander Nichols questioned the quality of education the college offered and emphasized the need for academic improvements. "They can have their $6 million gymnasium [coliseum] in Columbia [at the University of South Carolina], just give us some competent instructors. That's all we want." Someone in the crowd aroused a cheer by yelling, "Give us a new president." The crisis intensified as Williams announced that as many as one thousand students would travel by car and bus to Columbia on Saturday for a march at the statehouse. The senior class president dismissed Turner as a "white Negro."[130]

Williams's display of braggadocio and the demonstration of student solidarity were not foolhardy or empty gestures. From the beginning of "the Cause," the state NAACP had been aware of the events at the college, and its leaders stood by the students. Ike Williams and Joseph Hammond were far more closely aligned to the NAACP than they were to Turner. Williams was the National Youth Work Committee chair of the organization. He was from Charleston, and while a student at Bonds Wilson High School he had become involved in NAACP activities and protests. Hammond was the president of the state Youth Conference of the NAACP.[131]

Williams was well acquainted with the executive director of the state NAACP, I. DeQuincey Newman. Turner had no relationship with the organization. The NAACP had previously scheduled a statewide meeting for Columbia, and they used the occasion to discuss the Orangeburg situation and to endorse the students' position. Billie Flemming, a longtime NAACP leader from Manning, denounced Turner. "Bernard Turner [*sic*] doesn't know anything about the Negroes' problems. Negroes have nothing to say about how State College is run." Newman complained that black voters had been "kicked in the teeth" by Governor McNair. He had won the previous November's election with strong support from black voters, but he refused to meet with S.C. State students.[132]

With neither side showing any inclination to compromise, McNair abruptly reversed his position. The governor invited four class presidents—Ike Williams, Alexander Nichols, Johnnie Bishop, and Robert Cunningham—to Columbia for a secret meeting on March 9. He listened patiently to their concerns and complaints about Turner and S.C. State. Years later McNair recalled, "They were very frank, very forceful in presenting their views." He was sympathetic to the reforms they sought and agreed to most of the changes they proposed. There would be amnesty for the students involved in the boycott. He was willing to allow the federal court to determine whether or not Stroman, Hammond, and Bryant would be reinstated. The students also insisted that McNair remove Turner, but the governor resisted. He asked Williams and the other three class presidents to let him resolve it. "Now on that item, you gotta trust me to work it out." There was no mention of Thomas Wirth or Anthony Fanning, the two men whose termination touched off "the Cause" in the first place. With McNair's reassurances, students returned to class. The strike ended.[133]

Federal district judge Robert Hemphill ordered Stroman, Bryant, and Hammond reinstated on March 14 after McNair had quietly informed the judge that the state would not appeal such a decision. Attorney Matthew Perry successfully represented the students. His earlier effort to persuade Turner to readmit the young men without going to court failed. In a meeting with Perry, Turner told the civil rights attorney, "Well you're going around suing everybody . . . go ahead and sue if that's what you feel you've got to do." Ironically Turner had been one of Perry's law professors while Perry was in law school at S.C. State.[134]

Political fallout continued long after students returned to class. Not everyone was pleased with Governor McNair's intervention in the campus controversy. One member of the board of trustees resigned in protest. Dr. Howard Royal was a physician from Langley in Aiken County, and he complained that McNair's action was a "usurpation of authority." Republican state senator Marion H. Smoak of Aiken criticized the governor for siding with students. "The impression at this moment is clear that disorders, demonstrations and riots bring results." William D. Workman Jr., the editor of the *State* newspaper, backed Turner and regarded the students' behavior as immature.[135]

The Reverend I. DeQuincey Newman, the executive director of the state NAACP, opposed Turner and defended the role of the civil rights organization in the controversy. In a letter to the *State,* Newman charged that Turner had been handpicked by the all-white board of trustees in 1950 because he did not seem to identify "with the Negro's aspiration for equality of opportunity." Newman claimed that white leaders took it for granted that they could "appoint leaders for the Negro community without first entering into dialogue with the Negro community concerning proposed appointments."[136]

Turner, however, was much relieved and satisfied that the boycott was over and the crisis had ended. "Now we can pick up the threads and get back to work." But his optimism was premature. Although the governor and trustees continued to support him publicly and expressed appreciation for his leadership, he had lost their confidence. McNair had come to realize that Turner had little or no support in the black community. The NAACP drafted a petition asking for Turner's removal. It seemed likely that if Turner remained, there would be future campus protests.[137]

Shortly thereafter McNair invited Turner to the governor's mansion and suggested to the president that he retire. Turner was startled and asked if he had an option. "Doctor," McNair replied, "I hate to say this, but no; you do not have an option." Deeply disappointed Turner announced his retirement at a board meeting on May 10. He admitted in a backhanded way that he could no longer lead the college effectively because "the influence of non-campus organizations and individuals and their effect on the work of the College have become so pervasive and continuous that the situation has become difficult for the faculty, administration and student body to carry on the normal routine of this institution."[138]

BENNER C. TURNER: AN ASSESSMENT

So ended the seventeen-year presidency of Benner C. Turner. He could take pride in the advancement of the college during his tenure. The Southern Association of Colleges and Schools (SACS) accredited S.C. State for the first time in 1960. The qualifications of the faculty had improved substantially with twenty-seven members of the faculty with earned doctorates by 1967. Salaries had increased appreciably although they still lagged behind many historically black colleges as well as the state's white public colleges. Turner and the faculty continued to struggle with the perpetual problem of students who were poorly prepared for the rigors of college work in large measure because so many of them were products of segregated and inferior public schools.

The massive construction program undertaken in the 1950s dramatically altered the campus. But much of the early impetus behind those capital improvements came courtesy of efforts by white leaders—chiefly Governor James F. Byrnes—to maintain segregation in higher education by improving facilities at S.C. State with the financial assistance of the General Education Board. Turner was also responsible for the elimination of the program in agriculture while the law school failed to survive low enrollments, lack of ABA accreditation, and the integration of the University of South Carolina law school. After a half century, the black extension program that operated from the campus ceased to exist.

In many respects Benner C. Turner was a casualty of the end of Jim Crow in public education and southern society. He had been elevated to the college presidency in 1950 following Miller F. Whittaker's death primarily because the board of trustees and the state's political leadership were confident that Turner would assist in maintaining segregation. But African Americans and the civil rights movement succeeded in eradicating the system of "separate but equal" despite massive white opposition. And as black

South Carolinians gained greater political influence through the Voting Rights Act of 1965, Turner's days were numbered.

Turner had never established close or enduring relationships with people in South Carolina's tightly knit black middle-class community. He was reserved and often ill at ease in public. He was not accessible and amiable, and he simply could not speak informally in large or small gatherings. He prepared written remarks for even the shortest introduction or ceremony. He belonged to Alpha Phi Alpha, but he rarely took part in fraternity affairs. Although nominally a Presbyterian, for most of his first decade as president, Turner infrequently attended church. In a personal note in 1958 to Etta Rowe, one of the few faculty members he seemed comfortable with, he told her "that I am going to church regularly which may be you consider a startling event."[139]

As president Turner was rigid and inflexible and tolerated little dissent from students and faculty. He could be abrupt and impatient. During the prolonged and difficult discussions to end the boycott of classes in 1967, Governor McNair asked Turner to remain in his campus office pending another telephone call from McNair. Turner told McNair that he left his office every day at 5 P.M. The incredulous governor told Turner: "I don't think you better leave your office at five o'clock today. I won't leave mine until this matter is resolved. And I don't want to make a phone call to you and find you not in your office."[140]

Once Turner and his family departed from S.C. State, he never returned, and they maintained few contacts with anyone in Orangeburg. He retired with his wife, Julia, to Somersworth, New Hampshire, in 1968. When he died there in 1988, his obituary made no mention that he had served for seventeen years as a college president.[141]

CHAPTER EIGHT

1968

The departure of Benner C. Turner ended nearly two decades of authoritarian administration at South Carolina State. Refreshing winds of change swept the campus. Gone were the countless regulations and the arbitrary discipline that stifled creativity and prohibited dissent. It would be the task of the next president to help foster a new collegial and collaborative atmosphere on the campus while simultaneously guiding a college that was no longer restricted by law to African American students, faculty, and administrators.

Only days after Turner announced his retirement, the board of trustees invited Howard Jordan to become the new president. Jordan was beginning his fourth year as the president of Savannah State College, but he had spent the previous decade at S.C. State as a professor of education and then dean of the faculty. Jordan quickly declined the offer. The trustees then considered the creation of an executive committee to run the college while they conducted a search for a new president. They had followed this process in 1949–50 following the death of President Miller F. Whittaker. But management of the college by a committee had been an unwieldy arrangement that led to unseemly disagreements among committee members, and that recommendation was rejected.[1]

Instead the trustees turned to M. Maceo Nance, Jr., the recently named vice president for business and finance, and asked him to serve as acting president beginning July 1, 1967. Nance was a graduate of the college who had interrupted his education to serve in the U.S. Navy during World War II. Hired as the property custodian of the ROTC program in 1949, he rose steadily through the administrative ranks. He ran the bookstore and then was named the director of the student center after it opened in 1954. He earned a master's degree in student personnel from New York University. In the meantime he married 1947 graduate Julie Washington, who was the daughter of Julius I. Washington, the former college business manager. When Washington retired in 1957, Nance replaced him.

Although Nance lacked an academic background and did not have a doctorate, he had worked closely on the budget, on athletics, and with students. He was familiar with the trustees and had been among the administrators who met with Governor Robert McNair during the student protests a few weeks earlier. He was an outgoing and affable chain smoker who was far more comfortable among students and faculty members than his predecessor had been.

By 1959 M. Maceo Nance Jr. had succeeded his father-in-law, J. I. Washington, as business manager at S.C. State. Here he is with his Fiat coupe, which he affectionately referred to as "Little Willie." Courtesy of the Historical Collection, South Carolina State University

FACULTY GOVERNANCE

As Nance settled into the president's office in Wilkinson Hall, the faculty had already assumed the initiative in promoting change. They formed a nine-member committee to create a faculty senate, which would come to play a critical role in governing the college. It would replace the long standing Faculty Study Commission (FSC), which had been little more than a shell of a meaningful organization. Created in 1937 at the urging of Dean Kirkland W. Green, the FSC took up such issues as faculty research, program evaluation, and graduate study for faculty members who wanted to pursue advanced degrees.[2]

The Faculty Study Commission had no real authority or standing. It neither initiated nor approved academic policies. It was described as a "semi autonomous organization which operates on the basis of certain democratic [principles]." Those democratic principles were not identified. The FSC served "as an organization through which programs of college-wide significance may be presented and discussed by *all* staff members." Essentially the FSC was limited to talking.[3]

That talking was confined to innocuous issues. There was no discussion, for example, of the impact that "McCarthyism" or civil rights had on S.C. State or on higher education. When faculty members Lewis K. McMillan and Florence Miller were terminated in the mid-1950s, the FSC did not get involved. There was never any mention of tenure, promotion, or faculty grievance procedures. Instead faculty members had to be content to listen to their colleagues, visiting speakers, and panel discussions on such timely matters as improving teaching effectiveness and the evaluation of students. The faculty did get an opportunity to approve the creation of a student loan fund. When the future of the law school and the fate of the agriculture program were considered in the mid-1960s, the Faculty Study Commission was not consulted. Still attendance at FSC meetings was mandatory. Faculty members and administrators who missed the meetings without an excuse had their pay docked $5 for each absence.[4]

THE BLACKWELL COMMITTEE

In June 1967 and in the aftermath of Turner's autocratic administration, John K. Cauthen, the chairman of the South Carolina Commission on Higher Education, appointed a twelve-member committee to examine the situation at South Carolina State. With the approval of Governor McNair, Cauthen asked the committee to review policies and to make recommendations that would reform the roles of faculty and students on the black college campus. The committee would assess "campus procedures" and "rules and regulations" at the college so that those practices would be "in keeping with those typical of other state institutions of higher education."[5]

The Blackwell Committee—as it came to be known—was chaired by Furman University president Gordon W. Blackwell. The twelve-member committee included six representatives from South Carolina State: one administrator, two students, and three faculty members. Six members including Blackwell came from Clemson, Winthrop, Voorhees, the University of South Carolina, Columbia College, and Furman. Acting president Nance welcomed the Blackwell Committee to the campus for its first meeting in July, and he informed them that faculty and students had already begun to consider internal reforms. The Faculty Senate Guidelines Committee was at work on creating a meaningful faculty organization. Cochaired by psychology professor Roland Haynes and history professor Rubin Weston, the committee members were ready to expand the role of the faculty in college affairs. Three members of that Faculty Senate Committee—Leroy F. Anderson, Rubin F. Weston, and Marguerite R. Howie—were also asked to serve on the Blackwell Committee. There were also, Nance explained, separate college committees working on student issues and administrative practices.[6]

With overlapping membership, the Faculty Senate Guidelines Committee and the Blackwell Committee worked in tandem over several weeks. A subcommittee of the Blackwell Committee, chaired by Winthrop dean Walter D. Smith, met on July 22 with the Senate Guidelines Committee. Relations between the on-campus and off-campus groups were generally amiable, but there were some tensions and uncertainties. The Blackwell Committee focused on the administration of the academic program and on the appointment, promotion, and tenure of faculty members, as well as on the rights and responsibilities of students. Members of the Faculty Senate Committee understandably worried that the Blackwell Committee—in focusing on academic and student issues—might neglect financial and budgetary resources in comparing S.C. State to other state institutions of higher learning. They feared the Blackwell Committee might be "whitewashing the situation." Without directly addressing the issue of financial disparities, John Cauthen responded to their concerns and promised that there "is nothing to whitewash . . . if the committee comes up with rules, regulations and procedures which are in order." But no mention was made of the gap in funding between the state's white public institutions and South Carolina State.[7]

The Faculty Guidelines Committee completed a faculty senate constitution on the eve of the new school year. They had consulted the senate constitutions of other colleges and universities but relied heavily on the model provided by Western Michigan University. The new S.C. State Faculty Senate Constitution was adopted at a meeting of the entire faculty on August 29, 1967, and it was approved by the Blackwell Committee two weeks later. It was sent to the college board of trustees for final approval.[8]

THE FACULTY SENATE

The new constitution empowered the faculty and served as a stark contrast to the defunct and discredited Faculty Study Commission. The faculty was henceforth delegated broad "legislative powers" that were "subject to the review of the President and Board of Trustees." As the representative body of the faculty, the senate would consider "policies affecting the academic activities of the college, faculty welfare, administration, standards of admission, registration, requirements for degrees, granting of degrees, curriculum, instruction, research, extra-curricular activities, the educational standards and policies of the college, and all other matters pertaining to Faculty Affairs, including the discipline of its own members." Its recommendations were subject to the approval or disapproval of the president. But the veto by the president of a senate recommendation could be overridden with a three-quarters vote of the entire faculty—something that never occurred in the ensuing forty years.[9]

Representation in the twenty-four-member senate would be based on the number of faculty members teaching in the various departments and divisions. But every academic area was entitled to at least one senator. Six senators would be elected at-large, and the college president would appoint three senators. Department chairs were eligible to serve as senators as long as they taught a class.[10]

The senate constitution provided for several standing committees and councils, the most important of which was the Educational Policies Council. This large and sometimes balky bureaucratic body was made up of nine senators, the undergraduate deans, the dean of the graduate program, the director of admissions, the registrar, the head librarian, and the professor of military science. Depending on the changing number of undergraduate deans over the next several decades, there were about twenty members of the council. The vice president for academic affairs chaired the council.

Although this council generally consisted of as many full-time administrators as full-time faculty members, if not more, it was responsible for "explaining to the President and Board of Trustees the views of the faculty." It had broad and extensive powers that included "the allocation of funds," setting enrollment, determining admission and degree requirements, establishing policies for research, and making changes in the curriculum and academic programs. It was, moreover, responsible for "appointments, promotions, and dismissals of faculty members and procedures for tenure."[11]

While the Faculty Senate Constitution did not explicitly state it, the Educational Policies Council would make recommendations to the senate, which would then approve or disapprove. Those it approved would be forwarded to the president for his or her support or rejection. For the first time in the history of S.C. State, the members of the faculty had—on paper at least—a significant and influential role in the governance of the institution.

To protect individual faculty members against arbitrary administrative actions, the newly formed Faculty Senate also created and adopted a statement on appointments, dismissals, ethics, and tenure. That statement was sent to the Blackwell Committee, which made several modest suggestions for changes, which were in turn adopted by the senate. Faculty members finally had meaningful tenure protection that permitted them to teach and to conduct research without unwarranted or capricious interference. But the statement on tenure did not include a formal process, nor did it specify criteria needed to earn tenure. In effect tenure would be granted to faculty members by default.

Any full-time S.C. State faculty member who taught for six years would automatically have tenure. Tenured faculty could be dismissed only "for adequate cause or extraordinary financial emergencies." Adequate cause included moral turpitude, incompetence, and failure to perform duties. Tenured faculty members who were dismissed (and those probationary faculty members who were dismissed after specified deadlines had elapsed for nonrenewal of their contracts) were guaranteed due process either through a formal hearing or mediation. Those hearings would be conducted by a committee on academic freedom and tenure created by the faculty. The faculty member had the right to an advisor of his or her choice, and a transcript would be kept of the proceedings. The faculty member would remain employed and would be compensated until the committee made its recommendation unless the faculty member was an immediate danger to himself or herself, or to others.[12]

The 1940 Statement on Principles of Academic Freedom and Tenure adopted by the American Association of University Professors (AAUP) was incorporated into the S.C. State policy on tenure and academic freedom. That statement underscored the need for free inquiry in research and freedom in the classroom. But it also obligated faculty members to be accurate, to focus on their disciplines while teaching, and to demonstrate respect for others.[13]

The creation of a Faculty Senate that would share governance of the college with the administration was a major and unprecedented advance in the history of South Carolina State. The new and genuine guarantee of tenure for members of the faculty would provide them with academic and economic security to function with a measure of independence from administrative interference and control. Administrators, and especially the president, could no longer intimidate and dominate the faculty with impunity.

STUDENTS

There was a similar transformation so far as S.C. State students were concerned. Following the 1967 student uprising, the departure of President Turner, and the intervention of the Blackwell Committee, repressive control of students came to an end. Turner repeatedly told students and their parents that attending college was a privilege, and not a right. Students, therefore, possessed no rights. The student handbook put it bluntly: "A student whose progress, conduct or attitude is out of harmony with the institution or whose example or influence is found detrimental to its welfare may be dropped at any time without obligation on the part of the officers of the college to state specific reasons for requesting withdrawal." Students were not permitted to hold demonstrations, rallies, parades, or celebrations without the approval of the office of president. Freshmen and sophomores were required to attend chapel on Friday and vespers on Sunday. Students had to dress in proper attire for Sunday dinner. Women were not allowed to wear slacks on campus or in town.[14]

Because the S.C. State faculty had assumed the initiative in creating the senate and drafting a tenure statement, the Blackwell Committee devoted more of its time to reforming regulations that applied to students than with faculty issues. The committee placed special emphasis on freedom of speech, the right to assemble, and free expression in student publications within the campus environment. Of course students were expected to behave responsibly and within the law. But even at an educational institution, freedom of the press had its limits. Student journalists with the *Collegian* and the *Bulldog* were "expected to exhibit good taste" and to exclude material that was "salacious, obscene, or vulgar, and which ridicules religious and minority groups, human infirmities and the like." No beer or whiskey advertising could be published. However, ads for tobacco products were permissible.[15]

Students were permitted, if not exactly encouraged, to invite visiting and controversial speakers to the campus. They had to reserve a meeting space and provide pertinent biographical information about the speaker. If the director of student activities believed that the appearance of that individual posed "a potential threat of unlawfulness," the Student-Faculty Appeals Committee would make a final decision.[16]

Students were guaranteed the right to assemble peacefully, but it was not an unfettered right. Students did have to seek authorization from the director of student activities twenty-four hours in advance. College officials would, depending on the circumstances, make an effort to provide a security officer at the gathering.[17]

DUE PROCESS

The primary concern involving S.C. State students was to insure due process for those young people who were charged with any one of an assortment of campus transgressions. Since the founding of S.C. State in 1896, students had been suspended or expelled by the president or Faculty Discipline Committee with no consistent attempt to safeguard the rights of the accused. For the first time, the rights of students charged with violating college regulations were spelled out. Such students were guaranteed the "right to a fair hearing," they would be informed in writing of the accusations filed against them, they would have a right to present and to question witnesses, they did not have to testify, and they would have the right to an advisor, "preferably from within the College," who would assist them.[18]

To assure due process for students, new judicial policies and student judicial boards were put into effect. Accused students could pursue one of three courses of action. One, he or she could admit guilt and be informed in writing of a penalty. That penalty could be appealed to a judicial board. Two, the student could admit the violation and ask for a hearing before a judicial board. Three, the accused could deny the charge and have the case heard by the appropriate judicial board.[19]

Several layers of student judicial boards were created to replace the decades-old Faculty Discipline Committee. There would be a six-member Residence Halls Association Judicial Board. It would hear appeals from the judicial boards of the individual dormitories. Verdicts rendered by the Residence Halls Association Judicial Board could be appealed to the Student Government Association Judicial Board, and there could be a final appeal to the College Judicial Board. Students who were charged with transgressions that did not involve residence hall conduct would have their cases heard by the Student Government Association Judicial Board, and those cases could be appealed to the College Judicial Board. All the judicial boards were made up of a majority of students with the exception of the College Judicial Board, and it consisted of four faculty members and two students, one a male and one a female.[20]

A CAMPUS TRANSFORMED

A new day had dawned at South Carolina State. It was almost as if the college had been founded for a second time. The opening of the school year in August 1967 was a dramatic departure from the past. Although most of the students, faculty members, and administrators were not new to the college, crucial changes had occurred and would continue. As acting president M. Maceo Nance offered an informal style of leadership that was a sharp break with that of Benner C. Turner. Members of the faculty created a senate, and they were prepared to share power with the administration. For students draconian disciplinary measures had disappeared, and they enjoyed many more rights than they had previously.

Even the local newspaper, the *Times and Democrat,* took note of the changes. Under the guidance of publisher Dean Livingston, the paper ran a special fifty-six-page supplement welcoming students back. It was crammed with feature stories, photos, and advertisements from local businesses. Never before had such a mainline institution in the community offered such an expansive and positive assessment of the college.[21]

For the first time students were able to organize a collegiate chapter of the NAACP. For years many students had belonged to NAACP youth branches in their hometowns. However, President Turner disliked the NAACP and its South Carolina leaders. Even had he favored the organization, however, state authorities would not have permitted what they regarded as a radical and dangerous racial group to function in the 1950s or early 1960s at a state institution. More than three hundred young people joined the NAACP in 1967. George Campbell, a cadet officer in ROTC, was the president. The moderate NAACP sought full rights of citizenship for African Americans and their inclusion in the larger American society. Professor of education Charles Thomas served as faculty advisor.

More militant students were surprised when President Nance permitted them to organize the Black Awareness Coordinating Committee (BACC) that fall semester. It had been established with the encouragement of Cleveland Sellers, the twenty-three-year-old program director for the Student Non-violent Coordinating Committee (SNCC). BACC members were more inclined to reject cooperation with white people and stress Black Nationalism than were students in the NAACP. History professor Rubin Weston was the BACC faculty advisor.[22]

Nance was uneasy with the inflammatory language of BACC. But the acting president was well aware that any attempt to muzzle BACC students would only serve to draw more attention and support to the group. In his first address to students in September 1967, he tried to disassociate himself from BACC's ideology without an outright condemnation of the organization. He asserted that black power advocates did not grasp the fluid and dynamic nature of American society. Rather they saw a racial Armageddon, an "armed conflict of two opposing and unequal camps ready to do violent battle."[23]

BACC's presence ignited controversy on a campus not known for ideological conflicts. There were a series of spirited exchanges in the pages of the *Collegian* in late 1967 and early 1968. Some students and faculty members were alarmed at what they perceived as Black Nationalist rhetoric they heard from BACC members and read in the pages of the periodical *BACC Speaks.* In a tepid editorial in the *Collegian,* its editor, Rebecca Vanderhorst, wondered exactly what BACC stood for. Did they want a separate state or nation? Did they want students to wear their hair in a "natural" or Afro? Did BACC have a connection with SNCC? "Tell us what's up BACC, and tell us true! Tell us as the devoted Stateites whom we feel you are. Tell us something!"[24]

Vanderhorst's words divided the campus. Praise and condemnation followed in letters to the editor. R. C. Gamble, the editor of the yearbook, supported his fellow editor. Betty Edwards shared Vanderhorst's concerns about BACC. "I am a Negro; I am all for *Black Equality,* but until the members of BACC make clear their aims and how they are to achieve them, without personal attacks, I must stand aside." But Emma McCain, a sophomore, strongly defended BACC and denied that it espoused racial intolerance. "Speaking of racial hatred for the white race, well if loving my people and trying to seek ways of helping them makes me a racist, then I know no better name for me. If being anti oppression and anti desegregation made me anti white, the title is worthy."[25]

In another editorial, "Once Again . . . BACC," Vanderhorst tried without much success to defuse the controversy by insisting that most people did not know the precise positions held by members of BACC. "Simply inform the student body of *all the things that BACC does stand for,* and keep us informed of any policy changes." She also still wanted an explanation of BACC's links to SNCC.[26]

Despite the sometimes heated language of the students, the gap between the moderates and militants was not huge. So many people were alarmed by the slogan "Black Power" that they were quick to equate it with a call for black violence. Acrimony often obscured overlapping areas of agreement. So-called moderates might recoil from calls for Black Nationalism, but they still took pride in black heritage and culture. And did the so-called proponents of militancy actually favor violence or separatism? Peculiar ironies surfaced as students tried to navigate through the racial quagmire of the mid- and late 1960s. Kenneth D. Pangburn served as one of the rotating chairman of BACC, but he was also a cadet captain in ROTC who would receive a commission in the Regular U.S. Army.[27]

Few people including students had a carefully conceived and coherent ideology. Their views were evolving in the midst of what appeared to be an ever-deepening racial crisis in America. Deadly and costly uprisings in places like Watts in Los Angeles, Newark, Cleveland, and Detroit left many black and white Americans wondering if or how the nation could bridge the racial divide. The nonviolence championed by Dr. Martin Luther King Jr. now seemed increasingly irrelevant and antiquated to many discouraged young people.

Cleveland Sellers was a thin young man with a massive "Afro," which made him look taller than he was. At age twenty-three, he was a grizzled veteran of the civil rights movement and an inspiration to the members of BACC. Sellers had been born and raised in the nearby town of Denmark, and he had attended Howard University before interrupting his education to become a full-time participant in civil rights. He became a leader in the Student Non-violent Coordinating Committee (SNCC). No one had been more committed, more passionate, and more skilled as a SNCC organizer than Sellers. But he was never as flamboyant or outspoken as other SNCC leaders including John Lewis, Stokely Carmichael, and H. Rap Brown.

After helping SNCC coordinate its role in the 1963 March on Washington, Sellers traveled to rural and impoverished Mississippi, where three young men—James Chaney, Andrew Goodman, and Michael Schwerner—had been murdered in June 1964. In this grim and oppressive atmosphere, Sellers joined college students in organizing poor African Americans. He was later in Alabama for the march from Selma to Montgomery. In 1966 he joined with Stokely Carmichael, Dr. Martin Luther King Jr., and hundreds of others in a march through the Mississippi delta after James Meredith had been shot and wounded during his one-man campaign to promote voter registration. As they strode down the backwoods roads of Mississippi, Sellers had a chance to carry on long and congenial conversations with King. He developed an appreciation and fondness for the civil rights icon that transcended their ideological differences. By that time Sellers had become one of the key figures in the emergence of "Black Power" as SNCC evolved into a more militant organization in 1966 and 1967.[28]

A COMMUNITY DIVIDED

Sellers returned to South Carolina in October 1967 and took up residence in Orangeburg on Boulevard Street across the street and the railroad tracks from Claflin and S.C. State. The Orangeburg that Sellers uncomfortably settled into was a community reluctant to let go of the racial arrangements that had prevailed for generations. For much of a decade, African Americans had boycotted, marched, demonstrated, and been arrested—all to little avail until the passage of the Civil Rights Act of 1964. This watershed legislation prohibited racial segregation and opened public facilities to African Americans. Locally owned white restaurants and motels admitted—if they did not exactly warmly greet—black patrons. Most "white only" and "colored" signs gradually disappeared. The A&P grocery store, which was located in a small shopping center near the town's only bowling alley, hired its first black cashier in 1967.[29]

But Jim Crow had not vanished. Black people were denied admittance to the two drive-in movie theaters. There were separate waiting rooms for black and white patients in the offices of white physicians. The hospital maintained separate emergency rooms. A coin-operated laundry facility a few blocks from the campus still had a "white only" sign on the door. White owners of homes and apartments refused to rent to African Americans. Harry Floyd, the proprietor of the All-Star Bowling Lanes, would not permit black people to bowl. The sign on the entrance had been changed from "white only" to "privately owned."[30]

John Stroman liked to bowl, but that was not possible in Orangeburg. He was a senior majoring in chemistry, and he was one of the three young men who President Turner had suspended the previous spring during "the Cause." James P. Davis was a twenty-six-year-old air force veteran and a freshman student in 1967. When he tried to enter the All-Star Lanes that fall semester, Floyd escorted him out. On January 29, 1968, Stroman asked John C. Bloecher, one of the college's few white students, to see if he could enter the "privately owned" bowling alley. Bloecher agreed and went bowling by himself late that Monday afternoon. Fifteen minutes later Stroman, Davis, and about ten other students showed up to join Bloecher. Several of them entered before Floyd locked the door. Following a brief standoff, all of them left, including Bloecher.[31]

THE SITUATION WORSENS

The following Monday, February 5, Stroman recruited approximately thirty to forty students—most of them freshmen—for a sit-in at the bowling alley. Police chief Roger E. Poston refused to make any arrests because no law had been violated. Instead he infuriated Floyd by ordering the All-Star Lanes closed for the evening as a precautionary measure.[32]

The next night Stroman and about thirty students were back to confront Floyd. But most S.C. State students were not interested in bowling nor were they especially indignant at Floyd's "white-only" policy. As Stroman's group departed the campus, at least two hundred students remained behind to take in a Hollywood film in the White Hall Auditorium. Moreover Cleveland Sellers and BACC students were not concerned about the bowling alley, and they had declined Stroman's invitation to join his protest. BACC's members as well as Sellers believed that the civil rights struggle had moved beyond attempts to integrate with white people. They were insistent that black people determine their own destiny and control their own institutions.[33]

Law enforcement personnel, including Chief J. P. "Pete" Strom of the State Law Enforcement Division (SLED) and Chief Roger Poston, were waiting for Stroman and his supporters at the locked entrance to the All-Star Lanes that Tuesday night. They informed Stroman that students could be admitted but that Floyd could file trespassing charges and have them arrested. But in doing so, Floyd might make himself libel for violating the public accommodations provisions of the Civil Rights Act of 1964 *if* it was determined that bowling alleys were covered by that legislation. All the students then entered the bowling alley, and fifteen of them including Stroman agreed to be arrested. The situation while tense seemed to be well in hand and perhaps open to resolution.[34]

Then, as the arrested students were led out, someone cursed a policeman, who promptly arrested the vocal young man. There was an angry reaction. More students were arrested. At least one student raced back to the campus with news of the arrests. Word quickly circulated among students who had been watching the film and among others who were across the street in Lowman Hall, the men's dormitory. Cleveland Sellers had been out of town, but he had returned and was visiting Lowman Hall when word of the arrests spread. In a matter of minutes, an angry group of three hundred to four hundred young people were milling around the large parking lot in front of the strip mall that included the All-Star Lanes. Sellers arrived, and city authorities later maintained that he quietly circulated among the students and allegedly provoked them to act.

With a volatile crisis looming, several college officials soon arrived including Oscar Butler, director of student activities; Henry N. Vincent, dean of men; history professor Rubin Weston; and Colonel Walter Mebane, professor of military science. To diffuse the situation, Butler suggested to Poston and Strom—and they quickly agreed—that the arrested students be released to Butler's custody, and that the young men be brought back to the parking lot where they could urge those in the crowd to return to the S.C. State campus as well as the Claflin campus.

Suddenly a fire truck roared into the parking lot, setting off new waves of anger punctuated by catcalls, foul language, and people lighting matches and cigarette lighters and sarcastically asking "where's the fire?" As a safeguard Poston had asked for the fire equipment. But he was a recent arrival in Orangeburg and apparently unaware that the fire department had soaked civil rights demonstrators earlier in the 1960s. The fire engine left, but the damage was done. All the while people inside the All-Star Lanes continued to bowl, oblivious to the drama unfolding outside.

There was pushing and shoving near the congested entrance of the bowling alley, located in the corner of the L-shaped shopping center. Then a pane of glass shattered. Police immediately arrested Arthur Dodson Jr., a student. Highway patrolman John S. Timmerman had a caustic liquid sprayed in his eyes, which permanently impaired his sight. Amid the disorder and confusion, pandemonium erupted.

Students threw rocks and bricks. Several young men rocked a police car. Highway patrolmen armed with three-foot wooden batons waded into students, swinging indiscriminately. Two policemen held sophomore Emma McCain while a third beat her. William Stackhouse had a huge wound opened in his scalp by a baton-wielding officer. As dazed and bleeding young people retreated to the campus, others threw nearly any object they could lay their hands on through white-owned businesses along Russell Street including Sutcliffe Furniture, Piggly Wiggly grocery store, and Acacia Flower Shop. At East End Motors, a Lincoln-Mercury dealer, showroom windows were broken, new automobiles scratched, and radio antennas broken off. There was more than $5,000 in property damage that evening. But no looting occurred.[35]

Word of what happened flashed through Orangeburg that night and the next morning, and the reactions in the white and black communities were at polar opposites.

Most white residents were convinced that the town was on the verge of a racial catastrophe brought on by vicious black militants led by Cleveland Sellers. The destruction of property the previous evening was the first step in a black uprising that—if not crushed—would leave Orangeburg in ashes. Weeks earlier white citizens had unsuccessfully urged Chief Poston to force Sellers to leave town although the Denmark native had broken no laws. Now Sellers was promising that if he was arrested, Stokely Carmichael would soon arrive in Orangeburg. In the meantime people in the black community were outraged that the city police officers and state highway patrolmen had beaten young black men and women. In an address to students the next day, and with city officials present, President M. Maceo Nance deplored the destruction of property. "But for the record," he pointed out, "it happened after young ladies were hit."[36]

Governor Robert McNair sent fifty additional highway patrolmen to Orangeburg to join the fifty who were already present. He also called up the 250 members of the 1052nd Transportation Company of the South Carolina National Guard, which was located in Orangeburg. All the highway patrolmen and every one of the National Guardsmen with one exception were white.[37]

On Wednesday city leaders turned down a request from students for a parade permit that would enable them to march downtown to protest police brutality and to deliver a recently drafted list of grievances to town officials. Instead city manager Robert Stevenson and Mayor E. O. Pendarvis agreed to come to the campus to meet with students in an attempt to reduce tensions and to respond to their grievances. What followed that morning in the White Hall Auditorium was a fiasco. The two men had not been given the list of grievances beforehand, and they were ill prepared for the hostility they encountered. They stammered and equivocated as they tried to answer pointed questions about the state of race relations in the community. Students ridiculed Mayor Pendarvis when he uttered "nigra" as he struggled to pronounce "Negro." Stevenson and Pendarvis mistakenly assumed that their chief interrogator was Cleveland Sellers. However it was Wayne Curtis, the current chairman of BACC, who asked several questions. Sellers was present, but he remained silent.[38]

As the crisis worsened, concerns expanded beyond exclusion from the All-Star Lanes. Students framed their grievances in frank but temperate language. They insisted that the bowling alley be closed pending a change in its white-only policy. They wanted, among the other eleven issues of concern: the mayor to oversee the creation of a community human relations commission, the establishment of a city fair employment practices commission, extension of city boundaries into black neighborhoods, "encouraging the Orangeburg Regional Hospital to accept the Medicare program," elimination of segregation in the waiting rooms of white physicians, the integration of drive-in movie theaters, and the acceptance of the Civil Rights Act of 1964. They also deplored the police brutality that had occurred the previous evening.[39]

Surprisingly Harry Floyd did agree that day to shut down the All-Star Lanes for at least one night. South Carolina attorney general Daniel McLeod contacted Stephen Pollack at the Civil Rights Division of the U.S. Department of Justice and insisted that federal authorities "fast track" their effort to include the bowling alley under provisions of the 1964 Civil Rights Act. Pollack indicated that the first step was already underway.

Justice Department lawyers would send Floyd a letter immediately—but by regular mail—asking that he voluntarily comply and open his establishment to people of color.

In the meantime Mayor Pendarvis was, if not unreasonable, then certainly reticent. In a meeting with a delegation of students from S.C. State and Claflin a few hours after the White Hall debacle, Pendarvis declined to call a special city council meeting to take up the student grievances. He also told the young people that he would not take the lead in creating a community human relations council.[40]

Wednesday night students assembled on the front of the campus and hurled rocks and bottles at automobiles passing on Route 601, striking several vehicles. They also let loose with some vile language at nearby highway patrolmen, who soon closed the thoroughfare to traffic. Near the Claflin campus, a white resident shot three Claflin students with birdshot because he believed they had strayed too close to his house. They were not seriously injured. Then two young white men, William Carson and Carroll Carson, drove into the main entrance of the S.C. State campus after 11 P.M. (and after highway patrolmen had supposedly halted traffic). One of them fired several shots as they sped into a dead end where the new library was under construction. Forced to make a u-turn, they retreated to the campus entrance as students pelted their auto with bricks, rocks, and bottles. Campus security chief Brantley E. Evans pursued them down Route 601 and shot out one of their tires. They were charged with reckless driving and discharging a firearm on a public street.[41]

THURSDAY, FEBRUARY 8

On Thursday, February 8, there was an eerie mixture of camaraderie, calm, and apprehension on the campus. Tension and anxiety combined with a tightening bond among students, faculty, and administrators that had rarely been experienced at S.C. State—even during the civil rights demonstrations earlier in the decade or during "the Cause" the previous year. The differences between moderates and militants that had been so evident weeks before seemed to blur in the midst of white intransigence, hostility, and opposition.

Classes were held. Acting president M. Maceo Nance circulated a memo to students urging them to stay away from the fringes of the campus, warning them that "your personal safety is in jeopardy." He added that while the faculty and staff supported the grievances, they would not countenance any "violence and destruction" on the part of students. Nance wanted no repeat of the previous evening when students showered vehicles with stones, bricks, and bottles.[42]

Fear and outrage gripped Orangeburg. In the absence of the dissemination of any factual information about what steps—if any—were being taken to resolve the crisis, rumors ricocheted through the black and white communities and added to the already precarious situation. White people worried that black militants Stokely Carmichael and H. Rap Brown might arrive in town at any moment. Accordingly they fully armed themselves and prepared to defend their businesses and homes against the impending black uprising. In the black community word spread that I. DeQuincy Newman, the state field secretary of the NAACP, would discuss the crisis that evening in a speech at Claflin. But there was no truth to it. In the meantime law enforcement

Orangeburg firemen extinguish the bonfire students had ignited on Watson Street in front of the campus on the night of February 8, 1968. Courtesy of Bill Barley

personnel assembled in Orangeburg, led by SLED chief J. P. "Pete" Strom. They were told that students intended to break out of the S.C. State campus and invade downtown Orangeburg.[43]

That evening Strom brought highway patrolmen forward and aligned them near the front of the campus. Students were milling around the open area between Lowman Hall and Watson Street. Several shots rang out about three hundred yards to the northeast near the Claflin campus on Highway 601. They were apparently aimed at the Livingston warehouse located across the highway and railroad tracks. At about 9:30 P.M. some of the young people at S.C. State proceeded to build a bonfire on Watson Street, a short thoroughfare that veered off of Highway 601 in front of the campus. Students collected wood, trash, and sign posts. Much of the fuel for the fire came from a vacant house owned by a white woman named Jenny Brunson located on Watson Street next to the St. Paul's Episcopal Church. Several women students helped ignite the blaze. As the fire crackled in the chilly night air, students hollered, cursed, and taunted the nearby highway patrolmen. They seemed to be enjoying themselves as they let off steam. They even sang the anthem of the civil rights movement, "We Shall Overcome."[44]

Chief Strom decided to have the bonfire extinguished because it threatened overhead utility lines. The call went to the Orangeburg Fire Department. Firemen arrived and doused the blaze. It was about 10:30. Several patrolmen had proceeded up the embankment parallel to Watson Street on the front of the campus to protect the firemen.

Suddenly one of the patrolmen, David Shealy, crumpled to the ground with blood gushing from his face. Other patrolmen immediately assumed the worst. One of them yelled, "Shealy's been shot." Anxiety and concern swept through their ranks. The semiconscious patrolman was placed in a patrol car and rushed to the hospital. As it turned out, Shealy had been hit in the face with a heavy three-foot-long banister rail taken from the Brunson house.[45]

Several minutes elapsed as between one hundred and two hundred students continued to mill around the vacant field, apparently unaware that Shealy had been struck. They continued to yell and curse. A few demanded that the patrolmen get off "their campus." Some persisted in throwing whatever missiles they could lay their hands on. A few of the young men closed to within perhaps one hundred feet of the patrolmen. By then there were sixty-six highway patrolmen on the embankment and along the side of the Brunson house. To their rear and on the other side of Highway 601 and the Southern Railroad tracks were forty-five members of the South Carolina National Guard with M-1 rifles that had *not* been loaded. There were also SLED agents, sheriff's deputies, city policemen, and FBI agents nearby.

THE SHOOTING

Suddenly one of the patrolmen fired a warning shot into the air. That was followed by the "crack, crack" of more shooting and then an eruption of weapons. Students fell to the ground as they turned to run. The firing lasted eight to ten seconds. Then one patrolman blew a whistle. There had been no order to open fire although one lieutenant later recalled yelling, "now."

At least thirty-one students had been hit by bullets and double-ought buckshot pellets. The open area looked like a battlefield with young men crying, moaning, and crawling toward Lowman Hall. Nurse Bernice Daniels at Brooks Infirmary was quickly overwhelmed with bloody students whose injuries ranged from superficial to grave. Most were transported by private vehicles out the rear gate of the campus to the black emergency room at the Orangeburg Hospital. Within three hours three of them had died: Samuel Hammond, Delano Middleton, and Henry Smith.[46]

A few minutes after the shooting, several young men broke into the ROTC armory next to Hodge Hall to obtain weapons and ammunition. Colonel Walter Mebane, the head of the military science program, arrived shortly after that and persuaded them to return the firearms. But many students were terrified that highway patrolmen and the National Guard would invade the campus. Almost simultaneously Chief Strom redeployed law enforcement personnel to the other side of Highway 601 and the railroad tracks. "We didn't have any intention still of letting the students get off the campus and in the town because in our opinion Orangeburg would have been burned."[47]

THREE YOUNG MEN

Samuel Hammond Jr. died at 11:30 P.M. He had been shot once. Born in Barnwell, South Carolina, he was raised in Ft. Lauderdale and was one of the first black students to

Two students—possibly Henry Smith and Delano Middleton—lie on the sidewalk in front of the campus shortly after highway patrolmen opened fire on them on February 8, 1968, in what came to be known as the Orangeburg Massacre. Courtesy of Bill Barley

graduate from Stranahan High School. He was a shy young man with a ready smile who loved athletics and was a freshman on the Bulldog football team. But as much a student as an athlete, he took his academic responsibilities seriously. He sat in the second row of his U.S. history class and carefully compiled notes. His father was a World War II veteran who had attended South Carolina State.

Delano H. Middleton died at 1:10 A.M. He had been shot seven times. A student at all-black Wilkinson High School, he was one of four children of Reather Middleton. She was a longtime custodial employee at South Carolina State. He spent much of his childhood in a four-room house on the outskirts of Orangeburg. He was devoted to basketball and largely uninterested in protests or demonstrations. Following a game of table tennis in the student center, he had walked to the front of the campus more out of curiosity than a passion for civil rights.

Henry E. Smith died at 1:45 A.M. He had been shot five times. A tall, rangy, and energetic young man, he had been an eager participant in "the Cause" and was dedicated to civil rights. While many college students were considered apathetic, "Smitty" was absolutely "anti apathy." He was from Marion, South Carolina, where his mother worked as a maid for a well-to-do white family. He lived with his mother, sister and brother in a shotgun home with an outside toilet. At the time of the shooting, a number of people thought that highway patrolmen mistook Smith for Cleveland Sellers when they opened fire.[48]

Among the casualties that night was one young woman, Louise K. Cawley. Married, twenty-seven years old, and pregnant, she worked on the yearbook and was intensely concerned with civil rights and the destiny of African Americans. She was one of several coeds who had joined young men earlier in the evening on the front of the campus. She helped rush wounded students to the hospital after the shooting. On a third trip to the emergency room, she was stopped, beaten, and sprayed by three Orangeburg police officers. She was then transported to the hospital, where she fell from a table. Louise Cawley suffered a miscarriage a week later.[49]

THE ACCUSED

Cleveland Sellers was one of those who had been injured. Prior to the shooting, he spent most of the evening resting in a men's dormitory. He did not join the crowd of protesters until about 10 P.M., and after the bonfire had been lit. When highway patrolmen opened fire, Sellers was shot in the upper left arm. He went to the college infirmary and then—reluctantly—to the emergency room, where the city's sole black police officer recognized him. Sellers was quickly given medical attention and then escorted to the Orangeburg courthouse. Local officials filed an assortment of charges against him including arson, inciting a riot, assault and battery with intent to kill, destruction of personal property, damaging real property, and grand larceny. (Had he been tried and convicted on all these charges, Sellers would have spent his one-hundredth birthday behind bars.) Sellers was then rushed to Columbia and locked up in the Central Correctional Institution. His lawyer and SNCC's attorney, Howard Moore Jr., posted bond of $50,000, and Sellers was released but prohibited from traveling within five miles of Orangeburg.[50]

In March Sellers was on trial in federal court in Atlanta because a year earlier he had refused induction into U.S. military forces. A jury of nine white people and three black people found him guilty, and he was subsequently sentenced to five years in federal prison. He spent four months of 1968 in several federal prisons before U.S. Supreme Court justice Hugo Black ordered him released on bail while his conviction was appealed.[51]

THREE TRIALS

Cleveland Sellers returned to Orangeburg and to the courtroom of state circuit judge John Grimball in September 1970 for the trial on charges in connection with what had become known as the Orangeburg Massacre. That there was a trial was more than a little remarkable. Had Governor Robert E. McNair not been absolutely adamant, it is unlikely Sellers would have been brought to the bar of justice. Julian S. Wolfe, the First Judicial Circuit solicitor advised against prosecuting Sellers. He wrote McNair in December 1968 and told him so. "I have conferred with Mr. J. C. Coleman [assistant attorney general of South Carolina] . . . and Chief [Pete] Strom, and they too feel it is best that we not attempt the trial of the Sellers case or an alleged criminal assault case." The exchange of correspondence continued for months, and Solicitor Wolfe complained that his heavy workload had precluded the timely prosecution of Sellers. Clearly impatient and frustrated, McNair implored Wolfe to get on with it. "As you know, I have always felt Cleveland Sellers should be tried. It is difficult to send National Guardsmen, Highway Patrolmen and other police into dangerous situations that result in riot and death, and have the ringleader escape any punishment."[52]

The case finally went to trial eleven months later. Sellers was defended by attorneys Fred Henderson Moore and Howard Moore (no relation). Fred H. Moore had been the Student Government Association president in 1955–56 who was expelled for his role in the boycott of classes in the protests against President Turner's policies. He had since earned a law degree at Howard University. Howard Moore's attempts to have the trial shifted to federal court were denied

Most of the initial charges against Sellers had been dropped. But a grand jury had indicted him for participating in a riot, incitement to riot, and conspiracy to incite others to riot. Judge Grimball, however, directed a verdict of acquittal on the charges of conspiracy to riot and incitement to riot that stemmed from the events of February 7 and 8. Grimball pointed out to Sellers's attorneys (with the jury sequestered) "that 30 to 40 agents of the FBI investigated for four months and found nothing against your client." The jury of nine white people and three black people took slightly over two hours to find Sellers guilty of one charge of inciting a riot on Tuesday night, February 6, in the parking lot of the bowling alley. Grimball sentenced him to one year in prison and a fine of $250. After the South Carolina Supreme Court upheld the verdict and the U.S. Supreme Court denied his appeal, Sellers served seven months of the sentence at the Broad River Correctional Facility in Columbia.[53]

U.S. attorney general Ramsey Clark and Stephen Pollack, assistant attorney general in charge of civil rights, decided to seek indictments of the nine patrolmen who admitted that they had opened fire on the students. For eight days in late October and early November 1968, forty individuals including highway patrolmen and students were called or subpoenaed to testify before a federal grand jury of twenty-one white people and two black people. The patrolmen were accused of violating a federal law passed in 1870 to protect newly freed African Americans from Ku Klux Klan violence and terror. Section 242, Title XVIII, of the federal code prohibited anyone acting under the color of law to subject anyone to the deprivation of federally protected rights. The grand jury, however, declined to indict the patrolmen.[54]

Six weeks later Department of Justice officials decided to bring a criminal information against the highway patrolmen. The criminal information was a misdemeanor and did not require a grand jury indictment. The maximum penalty was one year in prison and a fine of $1,000. It was, however, based on the earlier charges that had been filed against the patrolmen. It alleged that the nine patrolmen, "acting under color of the laws of the State of South Carolina, did willfully discharge and shoot firearms into a group of persons on the campus of South Carolina State College . . . thereby killing, injuring and intimidating persons in the said group, with the intent of imposing summary punishment upon those persons and did thereby deprive those persons of the right, secured and protected by the Constitution of the United States, not to be deprived of life or liberty without due process of law."[55]

The ten-day trial of the patrolmen was held in May 1969 in Florence in the courtroom of federal district judge J. Robert Martin Jr. Since February 8, 1968, three of the patrolmen had been awarded promotions in rank. The South Carolina Highway Patrol had also employed its first two African American patrolmen, and they were seated prominently among the spectators. Led by assistant attorney general J. C. Coleman, the State of South Carolina vigorously defended the patrolmen. Coleman argued that the lives of the law enforcement personnel were threatened by an advancing, aggressive mob of riotous students on the night of February 8, and that the patrolmen fired in self-defense to protect their lives. SLED chief J. P. "Pete" Strom and FBI agent Nelson Phillips testified that they heard gunfire from the campus before the patrolmen opened fire. But *Charleston Evening Post* reporter Warren H. Koon, FBI agent Charles DeFord, and three highway patrolmen who had not been charged testified that they heard no shooting from the campus.

Coleman asserted that even if the students lacked firearms, the highway patrolmen were still justified in opening fire. "Let's just say for the purpose of argument that there was no shooting in the crowd. Where does that put us? That still puts us with an on-charging mob, throwing bricks, brickbats, balustrades, possibly iron pipes at the patrolmen. Frankly, I can't see it makes any difference. It was necessary for them [the patrolmen] to get there, to hold the line, to stop this mob from going out and doing further violence."[56]

The prosecution was led by two young Justice Department lawyers, Chad Quaintance and Robert Hocutt. They maintained that the highway patrolmen used excessive force and punished the students, thus depriving them of their civil rights. Quaintance pointed out that several patrolmen had fired repeatedly at the students. "Undisputed facts require verdicts of guilty at least as to the patrolmen who fired bullets or buckshot more than once into the crowd." The prosecution also explained that law enforcement personnel failed to use tear gas or a public address system that were both available to warn to the crowd.

Neither Cleveland Sellers nor any of the nine defendants testified. Judge Martin rejected a defense motion for a directed verdict of acquittal. In his instructions to the jury Martin told them they would have to determine whether or not the patrolmen believed they were in imminent danger, and would any person of "ordinary prudence, firmness, and courage" have likewise believed that in such circumstances their lives were in jeopardy. If the answer was "yes," then the patrolmen had acted in self-defense. If they were not in imminent danger, they could not claim self-defense.

The jury of ten white people and two black people spent less than two hours to return a verdict of "not guilty." But the U.S. Department of Justice and attorney general Ramsey Clark had not realistically anticipated a guilty verdict. Even with the acquittals, they believed the trial of the patrolmen would serve as a warning in the future and under similar circumstances that police officials could not act precipitously. "From a law enforcement standpoint," Clark explained, "I would say that it would have a sobering, stabilizing effect on law enforcement."[57]

There would be another trial involving the highway patrolmen in November 1970. Students and faculty raised funds following the massacre to undertake legal action in support of the families of the slain young men. They organized the Council for Legal Appeal and Defense (CLAD) in late 1968. Civil rights attorney and S.C. State law school graduate Matthew Perry filed a civil suit in federal district court in Columbia. Perry sought $100,000 in damages from the nine patrolmen for each of the three families.

The four-day trial in the courtroom of Judge Donald S. Russell was in many respects a replay of the 1969 trial. Perry argued that the patrolmen violated the civil rights of the students and summarily punished them without benefit of due process. Assistant South Carolina attorney general J. C. Coleman again defended the nine patrolmen and countered once again that they had fired in self-defense. Fourteen witnesses for the students testified that there was no shooting before the patrolmen opened fire. Eight defense witnesses testified that there was shooting prior to the patrolmen discharging their weapons. The all-white jury found the testimony of the defense witnesses persuasive, and they deliberated a mere fifty-three minutes before finding the patrolmen not liable. The Smith, Hammond, and Middleton families never received restitution for their losses.[58]

THE HOURS AND DAYS AFTER THE SHOOTING

On the day after the massacre, Friday, February 9, acting president Nance closed the college and told students to return to their homes and families. "I think under the circumstances the best place for you to be is at home with your friends, relatives, and loved ones." In some instances the college had to purchase bus tickets so that students could leave. In the meantime Governor McNair declared a dusk-to-dawn curfew. With the proliferation of National Guard troops, Jeeps, and armored personnel carriers, Orangeburg took on the appearance of an occupied city.[59]

Inaccurate information flooded the media in the immediate aftermath of the massacre. The first Associated Press report stated that two students had been killed "during a heavy exchange of gunfire." That erroneous account was never retracted or corrected. In a press conference the day after the shooting, Governor McNair added to the misinformation. Calling it "one of the saddest days in the history of South Carolina," the governor placed the blame on "Black Power advocates who represent only a small minority of the total student bodies at South Carolina State College and Claflin College."[60]

McNair then stated that the shooting had happened off campus. He told journalists that students had broken into the ROTC armory and taken weapons before the highway patrolmen opened fire. There had been, McNair claimed, "an extended period of sniper fire from the campus." He added that there would be a full accounting of what had occurred. "It is our intention to make all facts in this case public and to put aside rumor, speculation, and propaganda." In the minds of many people, these initial and inaccurate reports created a lasting impression of what had happened in Orangeburg.[61]

H. Rap Brown, speaking at a New York City news conference on February 10, was the first person to characterize the shootings as "the Orangeburg Massacre." Brown had been active in SNCC and had since come to reject nonviolent tactics in the struggle for racial justice. Referring to Orangeburg Brown declared, "If we are going to be murdered for acting peacefully, we might as well be murdered while trying to kill a few white honkies."[62]

In the meantime and belatedly, the Department of Justice went to court on February 10 to compel Harry Floyd to open his All-Star Lanes to black people. Federal judge Robert M. Martin Jr. issued a restraining order on February 22, and Floyd did not contest it. Students James P. Davis and John Stroman became Floyd's first black customers. The Justice Department also filed suit on February 13 against the Orangeburg Regional Hospital for practicing racial discrimination. In both cases the Justice Department based its legal actions on the Civil Rights Act of 1964.[63]

THE SOMBER CAMPUS

Classes resumed on a grim campus on February 26. A day earlier, on a Sunday afternoon, Roy Wilkins, the executive director of the NAACP, addressed students, faculty members, and people from the community in White Hall Auditorium. While holding Governor McNair accountable for the bloody episode, he also cautioned students against resorting to violence.[64]

There was a solemn memorial service—"A Day of Rain and Tears"—held three weeks to the day after the massacre. Several hundred students and faculty members gathered outdoors in front of White Hall only a few hundred feet from where the shooting happened. A number of students and clergymen spoke in a "cold brisk wind" before the "weary assemblage" slowly made their way to the embankment on the front of the campus, where they placed three garnet and blue wreathes.[65]

Students and faculty were incensed, angry, bitter, and profoundly upset at the gross miscarriage of justice that had occurred on their campus. They were both baffled and enraged that the white community, led by Governor McNair, placed the blame for the tragedy on outsiders and black militants, most notably Cleveland Sellers. In an unsigned column in the *Collegian* the writer tried to put it into perspective. "It is easy to 'put the shoe on the other foot,' but we cannot be convinced that SNCC, Black Power, [Stokely] Carmichael, Cleveland Sellers, etc. are responsible for what took place in Orangeburg, for not one of them set up a segregated bowling alley in our city, nor did they put up 'white' and colored signs at the doctors' offices."

In another editorial, "Must Blood Flow?," Woodrow S. Nathan Jr. could barely contain his rage. "Three black men died. And we ask our governor, 'Did it have to happen? Did the state have to 'murder' three of our students?' He continued, "Must blood flow? Must tears be shed? Must students so elect disorder, boycott classes, etc., as a means toward settling their grievances? Is this the only way to get the ear of the white power structure?"[66]

Shortly after the campus reopened following the Orangeburg Massacre, students organized a memorial service to pay homage to Samuel Hammond, Delano Middleton, and Henry Smith. The ceremony was held February 29, 1968, on the embankment where the shooting had occurred. Courtesy of the Historical Collection, South Carolina State University

Just a few weeks earlier most students were barely concerned about a bowling alley that would not admit them. BACC members were dismissive of John Stroman's attempts to mobilize student protests against Harry Floyd's All-Star Lanes. But the beating, killing, and wounding of their friends and fellow students galvanized the student body and sent waves of concern and fear among parents as their children made it plain that they would not quietly accept what had happened on February 8.

STUDENTS DEMAND JUSTICE

Robert V. Scott, the SGA president, and seven other student leaders met with Governor McNair on March 6. While listening carefully, the state's chief executive made few commitments, and he flatly rejected several requests made by the dissatisfied but courteous young people. He told them that the $8.8 million appropriation President Nance had asked for S.C. State for 1968–69 stood virtually no chance of passage "because of the financial condition of the state," and that there would be no increase in professors' salaries. He did indicate that bonds would be issued for permanent improvements. He also agreed to explore the possibility of dropping criminal charges that had been filed against freshman Arthur Dodson in connection with the pushing, shoving, and broken glass at the entrance to the bowling alley on February 6.

Student leaders met Governor Robert McNair in his office on March 6, 1968, to insist that the Democratic governor offer an effective and sympathetic response to their concerns in the aftermath of the Orangeburg Massacre. Secluded in a room adjacent to the governor's office were armed highway patrolmen, in case violence erupted. Courtesy of Bill Barley

McNair, however, refused to consider their request that charges against Cleveland Sellers be dropped. He also would not withdraw praise he had previously offered for the performance of SLED and law enforcement personnel following the shooting. He suggested that South Carolina attorney general Daniel McLeod and his office might consider the possibility of the state assuming the medical expenses of the injured students. The governor said that any chance of opening the South Carolina National Guard to black men depended on the Department of Defense increasing the state's quota, because the National Guard was already at its maximum enrollment. The student leaders also wanted McNair's support in naming the new physical education facility on the campus in honor of the three slain young men, but he deferred that decision to the president and board of trustees. Additionally they wanted him to use his influence to bring William A. Carson and Carroll Carson to trial. They were the two white men who drove through the campus discharging weapons on February 7. McNair explained "that he had made public statements about this" but that the press barely mentioned it. The campus leaders returned to Orangeburg having derived few meaningful concessions from McNair.[57]

The next day, March 7, a larger and angrier group of S.C. State students descended on Columbia. With BACC now furnishing the initiative, between two hundred and three hundred students traveled on four buses and in automobiles. They went directly to the statehouse and entered the house and the senate galleries as well as the governor's outer office. Some of them were carrying signs: "McNair Is a Son of a Birch," "Orangeburg Massacre—a Police Riot," and "Needed: Quality Education at South Carolina State." Governor McNair refused to meet with the large number of students, and BACC president Wayne Curtis would not agree to meet in the governor's chambers with five or six students. In the meantime six students including BACC member Steve Moore were arrested in the senate gallery for disrupting the legislative body. They were charged with disorderly conduct, but those charges were later dropped.[68]

One week later approximately one thousand students gathered at the capital to protest the massacre and seek redress. Most were S.C. State students. But there were also black students from the University of South Carolina, Benedict College, Allen University, and Voorhees College. A small number of white people joined in the demonstration as well. The statehouse was surrounded by highway patrolmen in full riot gear. McNair agreed to meet with five students as well as psychology professor Roland Haynes and Robert Moore, who was the president of the state conference of the AAUP and a history professor at Columbia College. When Haynes asked McNair what the response of the state might be in a future confrontation, the governor did not mince his words. "I have made myself crystal clear before and I will make it clear again. We will never initiate any confrontation, but whenever the first brick is thrown, whenever the first rock is thrown, whenever the first firebomb is thrown, whenever the first house is set on fire, then it's *our* move."[69]

Another fifteen students with history professor and BACC advisor Rubin Weston were admitted to present a petition of grievances to Lieutenant Governor John West and Greenwood senator John Drummond. The petition was read the next day in the senate and printed in its journal. West took special interest in the S.C. State students. He cautioned them against resorting to violence, but he would also praise them more than once publicly for their determined efforts to work within the system. He would later visit the college at the behest of Weston.[70]

Delegations of students representing the Student Government Association and the Black Awareness Coordinating Committee also met separately with the board of trustees on March 27. However, the concerns of the two student groups were nearly identical. Students also wanted the new physical education building named in honor of the three slain students, but the board demurred on that issue. The trustees did, however, approve the plan to honor the young men with an engraved memorial. (On February 8, 1969, a granite marker was placed on the plaza. It was donated by the Onyx Society of the City College of New York.) Board members also assured concerned students that they were involved in "a diligent search" for a president of the college. Students also wanted more frequent meetings and improved communication between the students and the trustees. The board then agreed to a meeting with the student body the following month during chapel.[71]

And it was primarily students—not faculty and administrators—who made the most critical impact on the governor, lieutenant governor, members of the general assembly, and the board of trustees in the weeks following the massacre. Impressed with their earnest but courteous behavior, John West privately implored governor McNair to

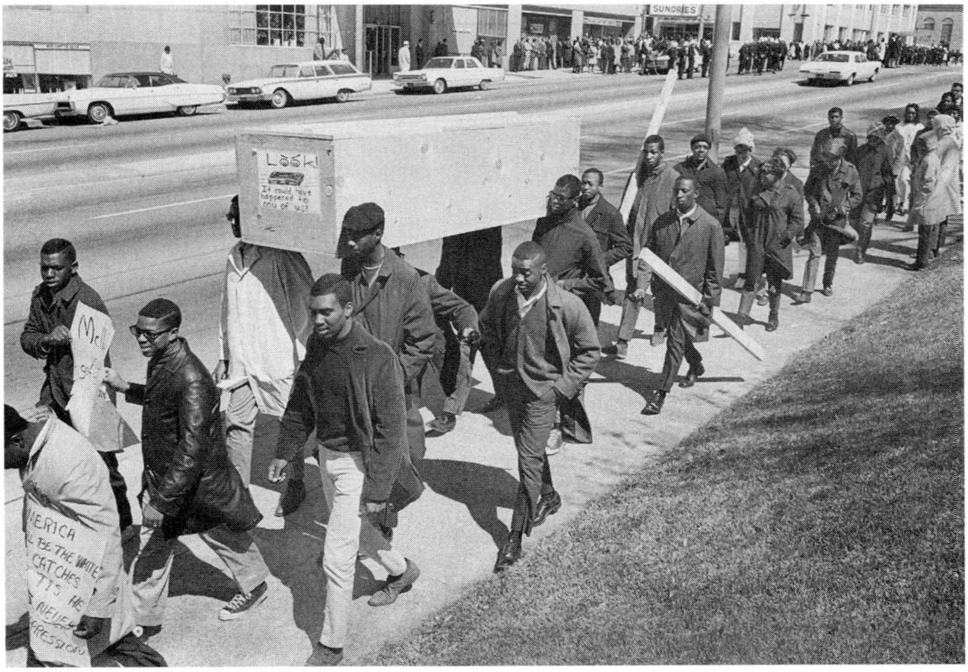

Approximately one thousand students from S.C. State and other colleges and universities marched around the statehouse in Columbia to protest Governor McNair's handling of the events surrounding the Orangeburg Massacre. Courtesy of Bill Barley

respond affirmatively to the demands of the angry but peaceful young people. At least fifty students sent mostly handwritten letters to Lieutenant Governor West in the days and weeks after the shootings. Some called him "stupid" and a "patsy" for Governor McNair. But others sensed in West someone who was sympathetic to their concerns and aware of their anger and anguish. One of those letters came from freshman Leroy Davis, of Orangeburg, and he offered West some advice. "I wish you would get out of your private, segregated world and do something to help our cause. I know not whether you have any children or grandchildren, but if you do, I'm sure you wouldn't want them to be murdered in school. You would do everything in your power to see that the murderers are brought to justice, and you would find the causes and try to resolve them. This is what we are trying to do." Andrew Hugine Jr., another freshman who was a clergyman's son from Green Pond, asked West to help persuade the U.S. Civil Rights Commission to investigate the massacre in the hope that such a probe might help calm racial fears. "Their findings should be made public. I am sure that if the findings, along with those of the FBI, are made public, the facts are presented uncensored, it will do much to quiet racial tension in South Carolina." Possibly political leaders who had convinced themselves weeks earlier that black nationalists had been bent on the destruction of Orangeburg were now taken aback by the persistence of the students to see a wrong righted and their neglected college improved.[72]

THE GOVERNOR RELENTS—SLIGHTLY

The governor, who had initially insisted to student leaders that the state could not offer an increased appropriation for the college, decided that additional funds could be made available after all. He now backed the $8.8 million appropriation that President Nance had requested for the operating budget for 1968–69. McNair had earlier endorsed a $6.5 million bond bill for the institution. The funds would be used to build two dormitories (Sojourner Truth Hall and Mays II), expand the student center, which would include an six-lane bowling alley, and provide other improvements and renovations to the campus. Moreover this bonded indebtedness would be repaid by the state and not the college.[73]

Republican lawmakers, who were in a decided minority in the legislature, angrily opposed the financial boost for S.C. State. Newberry senator Eugene C. Griffith claimed that McNair wanted to "reward violence." House minority leader Jerry M. Hughes of Orangeburg called it "blackmail" and complained to McNair: "You are ramming something down the throats of the people of Orangeburg they don't want."

Although there were no black members of the general assembly in 1968, there were a small number of white Democrats who passionately supported the measures to assist the college. Camden representative J. Clator Arrants appealed to house members "to do what is right." He pointed out: "We're not trying to help outsiders or strangers, but native born citizens of this state. We'll be condemned and chastised no matter what we do. If I must sacrifice what little political career I have on the mantle of hate, fear, and distrust or upon what I think is right, the choice is easy." The financial package that included the assistance to S.C. State overcame Republican filibusters in the house—led by Hughes—and in the senate—led by Griffith—and finally passed on the last day of the legislative session. It is, nevertheless, an unhappy commentary on the state of South Carolina that it took a horrific tragedy to increase significantly monetary support for the college—and even then there was dogged opposition.[74]

THE NEW PHYSICAL EDUCATION COMPLEX

Persistent students succeeded in pressuring the board of trustees and Nance to name the new physical education complex in honor of Henry Smith, Samuel Hammond, and Delano Middleton. For months administrators and trustees resisted. The building, which was under construction, was slated to be named for former state auditor J. M. Smith. Nance had been fond of the late auditor. While serving as business manager, Nance found in Smith a friend of the college who had helped the institution more than once in its financial transactions with the state.[75]

Even before the massacre, there was opposition among students to naming the new building for Smith. John Stroman in a letter to Governor McNair in January said that students ought to have a voice in selecting names for buildings, and he specifically rejected naming the new physical education facility for a white man. He told McNair: "I am sure there is not a building at the University of South Carolina with a Negro's name on it; so, why not keep your name(s) off of our buildings." In his reply McNair indicated that the college trustees were responsible for building names, and Stroman should contact the board.[76]

On April 11 and for the first time in the history of the college, the board of trustees held a public meeting with students in White Hall Auditorium. While virtually ignoring other issues, students continued to insist that the new physical education facility bear the names of the three young men killed in the massacre. But their impassioned pleas notwithstanding, the trustee continued to refuse their request. James A. Rogers, who would be the second-to-last white man to chair the board, defended the October 1967 decision to name the building for Smith. He tried to assuage the displeased students by promising that one of the new dormitories could be named for the three young men. The students were not appeased. Several weeks later the board and Nance finally relented. The new facility would be the Smith Hammond Middleton Memorial Center.[77]

DR. MARTIN LUTHER KING JR.

As if the agony brought on by the deaths of the three young men on February 8 had not been enough, the assassination of Dr. Martin Luther King Jr. on April 4 again plunged the campus into sadness, anger, and trepidation. How, people wondered, could the nation move forward after the loss of a leader so revered by so many? Tragedy compounded tragedy. In June Democratic presidential hopeful Robert F. Kennedy was shot and killed in Los Angeles after winning the California primary. In the meantime the Vietnam conflict continued unabated as hundreds of Americans and thousands of Vietnamese died every month in 1968.

On the campus a memorial service for Dr. King was held on April 7. Two faculty members shared their recollections of King to the quiet gathering. Ernest W. Boston was an assistant professor of English, and he had been a classmate of King at Morehouse College in the mid-1940s. Eloise U. Belcher, an associate professor of English, had no way of knowing that the young man enrolled in a speech class she taught at Morehouse would become one of the nation's great orators. In Atlanta former S.C. State student and faculty member Dr. Benjamin E. Mays, who was the retired president of Morehouse College, delivered the eulogy at the slain civil rights leader's funeral.[78]

Not long after, a reporter for the *Collegian,* Beverly Alford, interviewed Julie Nance, the wife of acting president Maceo Nance, and asked her to reflect on the preceding months. "This year," Mrs. Nance replied, "we have experienced all types of emotions; joy, anger, grief, and fear, but I think grief overshadowed them all." The worst school year in the history of South Carolina State finally came to a merciful end.[79]

THE INVESTIGATION OF THE MASSACRE

In the four judicial proceedings that followed the massacre, exactly one person—Cleveland Sellers—was found responsible for the events that occurred over four February days and nights in Orangeburg. And Sellers had been one of the twenty-eight individuals who had been shot. There had been one series of grand jury hearings and three separate trials with a total of fifty-nine jurors—fifty-two of whom were white men and women.

But there never had been a formal inquiry that resulted in an account of what had transpired in the community and on the campus. As profoundly as people disagreed over what had happened, there was nearly unanimous agreement in 1968 that there should be a thorough investigation followed by the release of a comprehensive and official report to the public. Governor McNair was eager for an investigation and a report. He believed that he and state law enforcement personnel would be exonerated in such an undertaking. In early March McNair "expressed the hope that a public disclosure of the [FBI] findings of the investigation [would] be made as soon as possible." The governor added that such "a full disclosure of the facts is essential because of the concern and confusion over the tragedy and because of the pressing urgency that the facts in this matter be made public."[80] McNair also insisted that SLED, the South Carolina Highway Patrol, and the National Guard would compile reports that would be furnished to the public as soon as possible.

McNair therefore declined an offer by University of South Carolina sociologists that they make an investigation of the shootings. He also failed to follow through on a combined request by the state conference of the American Association of University Professors (AAUP) and the South Carolina Council on Human Relations to create a biracial and blue ribbon investigating committee. He believed, and rightly so, that any investigation that he was associated with would be regarded as a whitewash in the black community.[81]

Other groups and individuals also anticipated a report that would reveal exactly what had happened on the night of February 8. In its own forty-two-page report, written less than three weeks after the massacre, the Southern Regional Council was optimistic that "investigations that were underway by federal and state authorities would, one assumed, eventually resolve conflicts in interpretation and fact about the events at Orangeburg." The Southern Regional Council's report, written by Pat Watters and Weldon Rougeau, was based on interviews with students and faculty, and the SRC's preliminary investigation raised serious and troubling doubts about the versions of what had happened initially that were provided by Governor McNair and the media.[82]

Roy Wilkins, the executive director of the NAACP, called for a "prompt and thorough investigation" in a telegram to Governor McNair. Acting president Nance pleaded for an investigation by the U.S. Commission on Civil Rights into the "Orangeburg incident so that the public will have an opportunity not only to hear the facts but have an opportunity to read what actually took place during that week."[83]

The board of trustees, responding to student concerns and at Nance's request, wanted either the FBI report made public or a separate investigation: "the Board urges upon the responsible officials that the Federal Bureau of Investigation report relating to the Orangeburg disturbances be made public or, in the absence of this, some other appropriate agency make a complete investigation of the incident and make a public report. The Civil Rights Commission might be an appropriate agency and in the event they should decline, a special committee should be formed by the proper governmental authorities for this purpose."[84]

Several weeks later Nance expressed cautious confidence that the release of the FBI report would serve as a significant step in allaying ongoing disagreements over what had happened in February. "We are still hopeful that an investigation will be completed or the results of the Justice Department and the FBI will be made public so that all the facts may be known. This we consider to be a must and every effort should be put forth to see that such is accomplished."[85]

But the FBI never compiled a public or confidential report. Whatever report SLED agents and staff might have written was never made public despite McNair's insistence that it would. The South Carolina Highway Patrol and the National Guard did not write formal summaries assessing their roles in the events in Orangeburg.

The FBI did conduct a wide-ranging, intensive, but flawed investigation. Dozens of FBI agents interviewed highway patrolmen, students, faculty members, and administrators at S.C. State and Claflin as well as residents of Orangeburg. They assembled evidence and subjected it to scientific scrutiny. Their reports, interviews, photographs, and other information amounted to well over three thousand pages of raw data. The FBI furnished this information solely to Department of Justice attorneys, who subsequently used it in the grand jury hearings and the trial of the nine patrolmen. This FBI material was never provided to Governor McNair or to any other state officials. The FBI, moreover, made no attempt to write a summary or draw conclusions based on its analysis of the data it had collected.[86]

But the FBI's long-standing reputation for integrity and objectivity was compromised in its Orangeburg investigation by the close personal and professional relationships between FBI agents and South Carolina law enforcement personnel. FBI agent Charles DeFord and SLED chief "Pete" Strom shared a room at the Holiday Inn on John C. Calhoun Drive during the events in Orangeburg. They sometimes rode together in the same vehicle. The bureau was then obligated to investigate SLED, an agency it had cooperated with for years. Moreover the FBI had a troubled and difficult relationship with the Department of Justice, and the bureau was the investigative arm of that federal agency. Department of Justice attorneys were unaware for three months that three FBI agents were in the immediate area and were witnesses to the February 8 shootings. Attorney general Ramsey Clark and FBI director J. Edgar Hoover also disliked each other and did not cooperate effectively. Finally the FBI was forced to limit its Orangeburg investigation after it had to redirect its manpower and resources following the assassination of Dr. Martin Luther King Jr. in Memphis in April.[87]

There were omissions in the investigation of the massacre. No autopsies were conducted on Henry Smith, Samuel Hammond, and Delano Middleton. There was no coroner's inquest. The FBI did not retrieve or examine the clothing worn by the three young men on the night they were shot until Department of Justice attorneys asked the bureau to do so in October—eight months after they died.[88]

Worse were the intentional efforts of federal authorities in the early months of President Richard Nixon's administration to interfere with the prosecution of the nine highway patrolmen. Deputy attorney general Richard Kleindienst told attorneys with the Civil Rights Division of the Department of Justice "to not crossexamine the Bureau agents because it would be detrimental to the relationship between the Department and the Bureau." Vehement protests by Justice Department lawyers quashed the Kleindienst directive. But according to Hugh Fleisher, an attorney with the Civil Rights Division of the Department of Justice, FBI agents deliberately "falsified the information to protect the troopers" prior to the trial of the nine highway patrolmen in 1969.[89]

NO OFFICIAL REPORT ON THE MASSACRE

In spite of the repeated calls in 1968 for an official report based on a comprehensive investigation of what transpired before, during, and after the shootings in Orangeburg, no such report was compiled at that time. Nor has there been such an account assembled in the nearly five decades that have elapsed since "one of the saddest days in the history of South Carolina"—as Governor McNair characterized it on February 9, 1968.[90]

Lacking such a report, McNair remained convinced for years after that his original assessment of the situation in Orangeburg had been accurate—that black militants posed a grave threat to life and property in Orangeburg. Cleveland Sellers was the chief provocateur. In a 2001 interview, McNair continued to fix blame on Sellers: "he was leading this group, and maybe wanting a confrontation to stir it up, not [to cause] what happened [the shooting], but wanting a confrontation of some kind, to keep the thing going."[91]

McNair continued to believe that as regrettable as the loss of life had been, the actions of the highway patrolmen prevented even greater carnage, mayhem, and destruction in Orangeburg. However, in 2007 the former governor did accept that as the state's chief executive in 1968 he was ultimately accountable for what had occurred. "The fact that I was Governor at the time placed the mantle of responsibility squarely on my shoulders, and I have borne that responsibility with all the heaviness it entails for all those years." McNair died in 2009.[92]

RECONCILIATION?

The passage of time tempered but did not eliminate divisions that separated South Carolinians along racial lines in the aftermath of the massacre. After years of angry and even inflammatory letters to the editor that appeared in the *Times and Democrat* and coincided with the annual memorial service that was held at S.C. State, local white and black leaders took the initiative and formulated a statement: "Orangeburg: Let Us Heal Ourselves." It was published in the newspaper on February 7, 1999. Community residents wrote that each year's memorial ceremony must cease to be an occasion to stoke racial animosity. They appealed for reconciliation. "History cannot be rewritten, but it can and should be used to move forward and rebuild racial relations. Let us stop recreating, but solemnly recall the untimely deaths of those three young men. The annual memorial service must continue to be the foundation for better relations among the races, not the root of increased tension in the Orangeburg community." The statement was signed by 250 black and white residents, and it served as a significant step in breaching the long-exposed racial divide.[93]

Then on the thirty-third anniversary of the massacre in 2001, Democratic governor James Hodges came to the campus and told an audience that included President Leroy Davis Sr.: "We deeply regret what happened here. The Orangeburg Massacre was a great tragedy for our state." Perhaps what is more important, six highway patrolmen—three white men and three black men—sat in that auditorium virtually rubbing elbows with some of those men who still bore the scars caused by highway patrol bullets and buckshot in 1968. Republican governor Mark Sanford issued a written apology in 2005 without visiting the campus.

Scarred Justice, a documentary film on the massacre produced by Bestor Cram and Judy Richardson of Northern Light Productions, premiered at S.C. State on February 8, 2009. Speaking after the film was shown, Orangeburg mayor Paul Miller apologized on behalf of the city for what had occurred in 1968, and especially for the actions of local law enforcement officers who had beaten students on Tuesday, February 6. *Scarred Justice* was subsequently shown nationwide on public television.

In 2010 Calhoun Cornwell, a senior student at S.C. State, wrote and produced *Taking a Stand,* a play that depicted years of student protests in Orangeburg beginning in 1955–56 with the class boycott led by Fred Moore. But Cornwell's production focused on the personalities and the sequence of events involved in the massacre. With a cast made up almost entirely of students, it premiered on the campus on February 8. After a presentation at the Koger Center in Columbia, the play and its author were the subject of a major feature story in the *New York Times.*[94]

"Sol Driven Train," a rock band from Charleston formed in 2001 that features five white men, recorded "Orangeburg" in 2009 on a CD entitled *Believe.* The lyrics were written and sung by Joel Timmons.

> "Have you heard about Orangeburg?
> What happened there 40 years ago?
> There was angry kids, pigs splitting wigs
> They say they just want to go bowling
> Now the church bells are tolling
> down in Orangeburg."

Two decades earlier Frank Beacham, a native of South Carolina and a University of South Carolina graduate, wrote and directed a radio drama based on the people and events involved in the massacre. Broadcast nationwide on public radio stations, it starred David Carradine, Blair Underwood, and James Whitmore.[95]

Born in Orangeburg nearly ten years after the massacre, Jack Shuler grew up barely aware of what had happened in 1968. "The incident"—as it was called—was rarely mentioned by his elders, but when it was brought up, it was discussed in furtive tones. In the early twenty-first century, as a young college professor, Shuler began a quest to determine what the tragedy meant to people in Orangeburg. He conducted wide-ranging interviews with black and white residents, and he shaped their recollections into a personal account, *Blood and Bone: Truth and Reconciliation in a Southern Town,* which was published in 2012.

RETURN TO THE STATUS QUO?

During meetings that had been held following the massacre with Governor McNair, Lieutenant Governor John West, and legislators, students invariably expressed dissatisfaction with the state's financial neglect of the college as well as concern over the selection of a permanent replacement for President Turner. Even before February 8, many students were frustrated at the lack of progress since "the Cause" and the accompanying boycott of classes that had focused so much attention on S.C. State the previous spring semester.

In December 1967 in a column in the *Collegian*—"'The Cause' Is Dead"—Carrie Tyson, who was a white student journalist, complained that too many legacies of the old regime lingered. "Some few shoddy teachers of the old bureaucracy are still around intimidating students." The "antiquated system of class attendance" was still in enforced. Women students could not wear slacks on the front of the campus or downtown. The Student Government Association and its president confined themselves to posturing and petty issues. The grievances continued. The library should open before 3:30 P.M. on Sunday.[96]

Not long after Tyson's dreary assessment appeared and only a few days before he began to lead protests at the All-Star Lanes, John Stroman wrote a letter to Governor Robert McNair. He made no mention of the bowling alley or segregation in Orangeburg. Rather he dwelled on conditions on the campus in the aftermath of "the Cause." "When we arrived here in August," Stroman explained, "we could see several important changes made, but in the last two months, things seem to have turned around and are headed back to the same old problems." More money was required for new facilities and improved programs.

Stroman added that students needed a president who was qualified to lead the college. "The type person we want for our president is altogether different from Dr. Turner." Moreover students wanted to see improvements in the faculty including those white faculty members who had recently been hired. "We appreciate having white instructors on our campus, but not the ones that are less qualified than the Colored instructors that were and still are here." He mentioned without identifying a white faculty member who had taught at six schools in the previous six years and added, "and the way most of the students feel about him, he can make it seven." Students needed instructors who were familiar with "the problems here." He cautioned McNair that if further changes were not forthcoming, then "the Cause" might be resurrected.[97]

McNair quickly replied to Stroman and told him, "I am terribly concerned about State College." The governor insisted that he was well aware of the financial disparities that had existed in state support for the college and for other state colleges and universities. But he stressed that "we have made every effort to provide additional funds" for academic programs and faculty salaries. He informed Stroman that the general assembly had made direct appropriations to S.C. State for capital improvements unlike other state institutions that had to rely on tuition bonds to finance such projects. The governor also assured Stroman that the board of trustees was working intensively to select a new president.[98]

By making an appeal to McNair, Stroman in effect admitted that the South Carolina's chief executive was in a position to make decisions affecting the college and its destiny. Historically governors had intervened directly in college affairs, and that had continued under McNair. He met with students during "the Cause" in 1967, and it was McNair who informed Benner C. Turner in May 1967 that his tenure as president had come to an end. A year later the governor inserted himself directly in the decision to name a replacement for Turner.

SELECTION OF A NEW PRESIDENT

After the board of trustees named M. Maceo Nance Jr. interim president in June 1967, serious jockeying began among rival candidates for the permanent position. The two leading contenders were Nance and S.C. State professor of education Dr. Charles H. Thomas Jr. In October 1967 separate delegations appeared before the board in support of the two men. The South Carolina Task Force for Quality Education essentially represented the state conference of the NAACP. Billie Fleming, I. DeQuincey Newman, and others spoke for Thomas, who was a leading figure in the Orangeburg branch of the NAACP. Lieutenant Governor West also supported Thomas, and the two of them collaborated in March 1968 in composing a fourteen-page letter and statement to Governor McNair outlining Thomas's "thoughts and recommendations on what the role and function of State College should be, now and in the next ten years." The college alumni association, led by Isaac McGraw and Newton Pough, backed Nance.[99]

Following the massacre in February, the trustees continued to accept applications and interview candidates. Several unidentified candidates were invited to return for further discussions. In an unprecedented move, the trustees asked for faculty involvement in the selection process. Three faculty members—Isaac Bracey, George W. Hunter, and Clemmie Webber—were elected by the faculty to work with the trustees. For the first time in college history, black trustees took part in the selection of a president. Samuel Bacote, who was an associate county supervisor with the Farmers Home Administration in Kingstree, had joined I. P. Stanback and Dr. James Boykin as the three black trustees among the eight men on the board.[100]

But if the trustees thought that they would choose the new president, they were wrong. Governor Robert E. McNair, serving as the chairman of the board, convened a meeting of the trustees in his statehouse office on Saturday, June 29, 1968, and told them that Maceo Nance was his choice to be the next president. "He stated that he had arrived at the decision and that the election of Dr. M. Maceo Nance, Jr., as president would serve the best interests of the college at this time, and he recommended to the Board that the election be made at this meeting." The board promptly complied and unanimously supported Nance—and McNair.[101]

McNair liked Nance. They had become acquainted when Nance, as business manager, represented the college in financial matters and negotiations involving state appropriations in Columbia. Nance was a pleasant contrast to the reclusive Benner C. Turner and the somewhat dour Charles Thomas. McNair was even more captivated by Nance after he had telephoned the interim president one day only to find that Nance was out of the office enjoying a game of pool at the student center. He later told Nance, "And I laughed with him, I said, if you hadn't been playing pool with the students, you might never have been president." Nance had the personality and temperament to lead the college. McNair thought Nance's ties to business and legislative leaders as well as to young people would more than make up for any shortcomings in his academic background.[102]

CHAPTER NINE

A New Era

With the blessing of Governor Robert E. McNair and with the acquiescence of the board of trustees, M. Maceo Nance Jr. ended a year as acting president and became the fifth president of S.C. State in June 1968. He was the first graduate of the institution to assume leadership over it. Nance may not have had the Ph.D. so prized in academic circles, but he possessed abundant common sense, a calm demeanor, good humor, and plentiful experience that more than compensated for the lack of a doctorate.

Friendly and neatly attired in a colorful sport coat or tailored suit, Nance enjoyed walking the campus and talking with faculty, students, and staff—something President Turner never had done. Nance would engage in small talk, discussing politics, sports, and campus issues. He learned firsthand what was on the minds of students and faculty members, what interested them, and what troubled them. He could be candid and even blunt on occasion, telling people what they might prefer not to hear.

The new president had the difficult task of guiding the college through the years immediately after the demise of legalized segregation. That challenge was compounded by the animosity and suspicions that lingered in Orangeburg for years following the massacre. It took all the personal and political skills that Nance could muster to deal with black and white people who often mistrusted and sometimes actively disliked each other.

ELIMINATING SEGREGATION IN HIGHER EDUCATION

Early in Nance's presidency, authorities with the Department of Health, Education, and Welfare (HEW) decided that, based on the Civil Rights Act of 1964, the burden to desegregate institutions of higher education rested equally on what historically had been all-white and all-black schools. Federal officials apparently believed that black and white people and their educational institutions shared the responsibility for the imposition and maintenance of racial segregation. Therefore they were equally responsible for eliminating it.

In the wake of that civil rights legislation, many African Americans enrolled in what had been exclusively white institutions of higher education. By the late 1960s administrators and admissions personnel from these former bastions of Jim Crow displayed newfound enthusiasm for recruiting young black people. Nance noted that by 1970 "talented college-bound Black high school seniors are under tremendous pressures from both white colleges and universities, and in many instances, guidance counselors to attend these institutions."[1]

While African Americans showed little reluctance to patronize businesses or facilities or to attend schools that previously had been closed to them, the same could not be said of white people as racial barriers gave way. They did not rush to integrate what had been all-black businesses, neighborhoods, or educational institutions. After all segregation laws had been initiated and enacted by white political leaders in the late nineteenth and early twentieth centuries while African Americans had adamantly opposed the creation of the Jim Crow system. By the 1960s and 1970s, white and black people both were well aware that the separate black educational institutions that had evolved during the era of segregation had been grossly underfunded and were unequal to white schools in facilities, resources, and programs.

Nevertheless federal officials now insisted that black colleges like S.C. State demonstrate that they would welcome and work to enroll significant numbers of white students, thereby desegregating the institution. Two representatives of the Civil Rights Office of the Department of Health, Education, and Welfare visited the campus in early 1970 to assess the commitment and efforts of S.C. State administrators to integrate the college.

In a letter to Nance, Dewey E. Dodds of HEW's regional civil rights office indicated that although S.C. State "freely admitted" students "without regard to race," there were potential problems in the college's compliance with Title VI of the Civil Rights Act of 1964. Among those issues were the lack of photographs of white students in college publications, no inclusionof an equal opportunity statement in printed materials, and the absence of white students in campus organizations, on athletic teams, and in the residence halls. Also S.C. State students who were taking part in student teaching were still assigned to predominantly Negro schools.[2]

Nance's reply reflected the racial realities confronting the college in 1970, and the reality was that not many white people were inclined to enroll as students. Nevertheless Nance promised that henceforth S.C. State publications would include members of the "minority" group as well as an equal opportunity statement. Nance pointed out, however, that in recruiting high school students and organizing "College Day" programs for prospective students, "the response by white students has been less than encouraging." He added that in the past "we have experienced difficulty in placing our student teachers in predominantly white schools," but there were signs that the situation was improving. In college organizations "the small number of white students involved in the undergraduate program, have not shown too much interest in the activities of the campus." There were, however, indications that two white athletes planned to attend S.C. State the next academic year. In conclusion Nance tactfully explained that any changes in the racial composition of the campus were more dependent on "the philosophies and attitudes of our local community" than on the policies of the college. In other words white people in Orangeburg and South Carolina were mostly unwilling to enroll at a college where they would be in the minority. And after that initial flurry of inquiries and recommendations in 1970, nothing more was heard on civil rights from the federal government for ten years.[3]

The number of white undergraduate students never increased significantly in the years and decades that followed. The majority of white people who attended S.C. State were in the graduate program. Some were full-time graduate students, but most

Table 39. Black and White Enrollment

	White	Black	Total
	Fall 1969		
	Male		
Undergraduate	0	845	845
Graduate	22	155	177
	Female		
Undergraduate	2	875	877
Graduate	7	210	217
	31	2,085	2,116
	Fall 1980		
	Male		
Undergraduate	8	1,436	1,444
Graduate	15	124	139
	Female		
Undergraduate	12	1,664	1,676
Graduate	61	317	378
	96	3,541	3,637

Sources: *Annual Report, 1969–1970,* appendix; Presidents' Papers, M. Maceo Nance Jr., Box 35, Folder: Admissions and Records, Dorothy Brown. The 1980 figures exclude special students, students enrolled in a training institute, Orangeburg Regional Hospital nursing students enrolled in S.C. State science courses, and transfer students.

attended on a part-time basis. Two of the first white people to earn degrees at the college in May 1968 were John M. Cronin Jr. and Alfred Schattschneider, who were in the National Teacher Corps program. Four other white graduate students, three men and one woman—Carmella Mancari—received master's degrees in December 1968.[4]

THE FACULTY

Desegregation had a more immediate and meaningful impact on the composition of the faculty. The lack of doctorates among the faculty was a long-standing issue that had hindered accreditation by the Southern Association of Colleges and Schools (SACS). Segregation's demise steadily bolstered the academic credentials of the teaching staff and also led to increased research activity among faculty members. S.C. State employed in increasing numbers white and Asian people who possessed doctorates. Perhaps what is more important, the end of segregation in higher education opened the way

Table 40. Faculty Members with Doctorates

	Total Faculty	Faculty with Doctorates	Percent
1969–70	127	35	27.5%
1976–77	223	100	44.8%

Sources: *Annual Report, 1969–1970*, 48; *Annual Report, 1976–1977*, 26.

for African Americans to earn graduate degrees from predominantly white universities in the South as well as in the North. The pool of potential faculty members with doctorates expanded rapidly in the 1970s and 1980s. In less than a decade the percentage of S.C. State faculty with doctorates increased from slightly more than 25 percent to a little less than 50 percent. Moreover the size of the faculty nearly doubled in the 1970s.

While the faculty became more racially diverse, that was not the case among the other professional and nonprofessional employees. There were fewer white people who were administrators as well as secretaries and maintenance personnel. Of the ten administrators including vice presidents and deans in 1979–80, eight were black men, and two were black women. In secretarial and clerical positions, there were 105 black females, five black males, one white female, and no white males. In service and maintenance jobs, there were two white males, 118 black males, forty-five black females, and no white females.[5]

GENDER

"There is no sex discrimination at South Carolina State College." Or so declared President Nance in a report sent to the American Association of University Women in 1976.

Table 41. Racial and Gender Composition of the Faculty

1979–80		
Black males	97	41%
Black females	81	34%
White males	39	17%
White females	14	6%
"Other" males	5	2%
"Other" females	0	0%
Total	236	

Source: Presidents' Papers, M. Maceo Nance Jr., Box 37, Folder: Commission on Human Affairs, Report on Full-Time Classified and Unclassified Employees.

Table 42. Academic Faculty: Rank and Gender, Fall 1976

Rank	Male	Female
Professor	25	8
Associate professor	34	16
Assistant professor	61	25
Instructor	17	34
Total	137	83

Source: Presidents' Papers, M. Maceo Nance Jr., Box 26, Folder: American Association of University Women, 1976, HC SCSU.

Women on the campus might, however, have taken exception to Nance's easy assurance that they confronted no obstacles because of their gender. There were no women at the highest administrative ranks including vice president for academic affairs, vice president for business and finance, vice president for student affairs, and vice president for development. The highest-ranking women were the head librarian, Barbara Williams, and the director of career planning and placement, Daisy Dunn Johnson. Esther Tecklenberg, a white resident of Orangeburg, had recently been elected as the first female member of the board of trustees.

Men dominated the faculty ranks. With the exception of the dean of women, there was no campus office that specifically met the interests and needs of female students and employees. There had been no programs, lectures, workshops, or seminars devoted to the subject of women. No women had been invited to serve as commencement speakers. But among students women occasionally served as the Student Government Association president, beginning with Catherine Peppers in 1961. Women also had edited the *Collegian* and the yearbook, the *Bulldog*.[6]

Nance did please faculty women with the thoughtful gesture of sending each of them a single long-stemmed red rose on her birthday. Jean U. James, an English instructor, wrote to Nance that the rose was the only greeting she had received that year, "Thank you for the birthday *rose.* This was my only remembrance. Therefore, I can assure you that I was quite pleased."[7]

THE HIGHER EDUCATION ACT OF 1965

As a land-grant institution, the federal government had been a visible presence at S.C. State since 1896. The New Deal programs of the 1930s, the passage of the G.I. Bill in 1944, and the establishment of the ROTC program in 1947 strengthened those ties to Washington. But thanks largely to the Great Society programs instituted by President Lyndon B. Johnson in the 1960s, the role of the federal government in higher education expanded exponentially across the nation in the last third of the twentieth century. The

Higher Education Act of 1965 and its subsequent amendments had a dramatic impact on colleges, universities, and students, and nowhere was that impact greater than at South Carolina State.[8]

The 1965 legislation provided funds for capital improvements, program development, and research projects. Its most important beneficiaries, however, were students. Through Title IV of the law, hundreds and hundreds of S.C. State students—who otherwise would not have attended college—gained access to loans and grants. Prior to the Higher Education Act, some of the nation's college students were able to obtain loans through the National Defense Education Act of 1958 and from federally supported bank loans. Unfortunately many black students did not have access to these funds. Nance expressed disappointment in 1969 because "some of our students [are] unable to participate in the USAF loan fund in that it involves the local banks in their communities and many of the banks will not grant loans to our students.[9]

FINANCIAL AID

Johnson's legislation created Educational Opportunity Grants (EOG), Basic Educational Opportunity Grants (BEOG), and Supplemental Educational Opportunity Grants (SEOG), which by the 1970s evolved into the Pell Grant program. Based on financial need, Pell Grants, named in tribute to Democratic senator Claiborne Pell of Rhode Island, do not require repayment. Family income determined the amount of the grant for eligible students. Students also could qualify for federally supported loans, which required repayment but at relatively low rates of interest. Campus jobs were made available through a federally supported work-study program. For decades S.C. State students had gained financial help by working in the cafeteria, from campus jobs, with athletic scholarships, and through band and choir scholarships. The athletic and band scholarships went almost exclusively to males. Students also continued to receive assistance from hometown civic groups and church congregations.[10]

By 1977–78, 75 percent of undergraduate students received BEOG (or Pell Grants). At the same time, 774 students qualified for loans up to $1,500 per year through the National Direct Student Loan program. Students who entered the teaching profession were eligible to have portions of their loan cancelled. Then there were some former students who could not or would not repay loans. Of 1,914 students who had received loans by 1978, 439 (23 percent) were delinquent. Because the federal government required institutions to exercise "due diligence" in compelling repayment, South Carolina State as well as other colleges and universities retained collection agencies.[11]

Sometimes students, parents, teachers, principals, and members of the clergy appealed directly to President Nance for help in securing financial assistance. Nance, who had a wide range of acquaintances across the state, often intervened to make informal arrangements to aid students. Wilkin Williams, the principal of Robert Smalls Elementary School in Cheraw, asked Nance to help Davida Flemming, who was second in her graduating class at Chesterfield High School in 1972. "Davida's mother has had two brain operations," Williams informed Nance, and Davida had stayed home to care for her siblings. In his response Nance promised that Davida would be assigned a job in the

Table 43. Undergraduate Financial Aid

1969–70	
Federal Assistance	**Students**
EOG	335
National Defense Loans	242
Federally backed bank loans	84
Work-study program	210
Campus Assistance	
Cafeteria	105
Campus jobs	20
Presidential scholarships	25
Alumni scholarships	16
Band/choir scholarships	135
Athletic scholarships	80
Tuition waivers	40
Total	1292
75% received financial aid	
Total funding:	$504,170 or $621 average per student
Undergraduate enrollment:	1,722
1976–77	
Federal Assistance	**Students**
BEOG	2,499
SEOG	1,373
National Direct Loans	815
Federally insured loans	16
Work-study program	604
Campus Assistance	—*
Cafeteria	181
Total Funding:	$4,059,962 or $1,375 average per student
Undergraduate enrollment	3,345

*No other campus aid or scholarship listed. Some students received more than one form of aid. Except for the cafeteria, the figures for 1976–77 do not indicate other forms of campus assistance or scholarships.

Table 44. Family Income Levels of S.C. State Students, 1976

$0–$2,999	22%	$2,999 = $10,161 in 2011 dollars
$3,000–$5,999	22%	
$6,000–$7,499	11%	$7,499 = $25,408 in 2011 dollars
$7,500–$8,999	11%	
$9,000–$11,999	15%	
$12,000+	19%	$12,000 = $40,658 in 2011 dollars

Sources: Tables 45–46, *Annual Report, 1969–1970*, 56–57, appendix; *Annual Report, 1977–1978*, 80, appendix 2.

cafeteria that would pay $1,000 and that she was eligible for an Educational Opportunity Grant (EOG) for $200.[12]

A few months later Elizabeth Freeman wrote Nance to ask for a delay in paying for her schooling until mid-September. She explained that her mother was disabled, and her father was the family's sole source of support. Her mother had cashed in an insurance policy to help finance Elizabeth's education, but the check would not arrive until September. Freeman was "hoping, praying and trusting in you and God that my request will be granted."[13]

John H. Wrighten IV and James Wrighten asked Nance if they could pay $350 in fees for their sister, Gwendolyn Wrighten, in four payments of $87.50 between June 16 and September 16, 1973. Nance agreed to their installment plan. (The Wrightens were the children of John Wrighten III, who had sued the University of South Carolina in 1947 to gain admission to the law school. The elder Wrighten had graduated from the S.C. State law school in 1952.)[14]

The federal grant and loan programs enabled many young people to attend college who lacked the financial resources to do so. But significant numbers of these students also lacked the academic preparation for college. Nance conservatively estimated that between 11 percent and 25 percent of S.C. State students were not ready for the rigors of college work. And it was not because S.C. State admitted every high school graduate who applied to the institution. Approximately one-fifth of the applicants for admission in the 1970s were rejected because they were academically unqualified. In 1975 S.C. State turned down 15 percent of applicants, and it rejected 22 percent in 1976. The Admissions Committee sought "to select applicants with a better chance of succeeding in college."[15]

TITLE III

The weaknesses of the students and the historic lack of funding for South Carolina State were addressed to no small extent through funds generated by Title III of the Higher Education Act of 1965. In 1971 the college instituted a special services project to admit young people to S.C. State who would otherwise not have been accepted because of low rank in their high school graduating class and their low scores on the Scholastic Aptitude Test (SAT). For the remainder of the decade, the institution expended between $50,000 and $65,000 annually of Title III money to provide these students with access to intensive one-on-one tutoring and advisement. Upper classmen with excellent academic records were paid to serve as tutors and mentors for the "at risk" students, and these juniors and seniors attended the lower-level classes that their charges were taking. The PEP Program—Partners in Educational Progress—had 125 students by 1977–78 and was administered by former Student Government Association president, Andrew Hugine Jr.[16]

The Advanced Institutional Development Program (AIDP) was created under a Title III grant of $1.2 million from the U.S. Office of Education in 1975. A large portion of those funds went to programs for teaching basic skills in reading, composition, and mathematics. In 1976, for example, 353 of 1,081 freshmen were at the ninth grade reading level or below, and they were placed in a developmental reading course. AIDP also supported career development and cooperative education efforts as well as specific disciplines including sociology, psychology, and rehabilitation counseling.[17]

With AIDP funds, faculty members in English, history, art, and music devised an interdisciplinary humanities program required for undergraduate students beginning in 1974. With more than 90 percent of those students African Americans from South Carolina, the three-semester sequence of humanities courses was created to foster a greater understanding of and appreciation for peoples of other cultures, ethnicities, and ways of living. Students were introduced to a vast array of topics that included African empires, India's religions, Chinese art, and European philosophers. Managing and discussing so much information that dealt with so many societies over so many centuries was a formidable and difficult task for the faculty who taught the courses and for the students who had to master the material.[18]

Efforts to address the academic weaknesses of students met with mixed success. When the Miller F. Whittaker Library opened in 1969 with its books and bound journals housed in an attractive setting of open stacks—replacing the closed stacks of the Wilkinson Library—library director Barbara Williams, Nance, and faculty members were chagrined that students failed to use the resources of the new library in any larger numbers than with the previous facility.[19]

S.C. State students did not fare well on standardized examinations. Students in the teacher-education program had a notoriously poor record on the National Teacher's Examination (NTE). In 1979 Nance told a group of journalism students that the poor performance of students who took the NTE "damaged the image of the school, and impugned the quality of its programs." In considering accreditation of the master's degree program in speech pathology, Dr. Harold Powell confessed that "one weakness for which we have no solution, at present: Student performance on standardized examinations."[20]

COULD S.C. STATE GRADUATES COMPETE?

In 1976 Nance sent a letter to the presidents of black colleges and universities in which he expressed growing concern over the weaknesses of some of the students who graduated from these institutions at a time when racial barriers were falling. Many of those less-than-well-prepared students expected to be hired by mostly white-owned businesses and corporations or to gain admission to major graduate and professional schools. Nance did not mince words when he wrote that the "view is now increasingly expressed by spokesmen for the business community and graduate schools who claim that the black colleges are producing fewer graduates who are academically well prepared and realistically career oriented with the necessary discipline, attitudes and motivation to compete and survive in the current market for college graduates." Nance proposed that presidents of twenty-two of the historically black institutions meet for a panel discussion that would be held in conjunction with the annual meeting of the Southern Association of Colleges and Schools (SACS) that was scheduled for Atlanta in mid-December. He reminded the presidents of his oft-stated concern that the number of black students at predominantly white colleges and universities continued to increase. Most of the presidents responded warmly and eagerly to Nance's invitation. The panel discussion was held, but it produced no concrete results.[21]

The problem was that S.C. State graduated young people deficient in fundamental skills in composition, mathematics, and critical thinking. This was caused in part by the low rate of academic failures at S.C. State. Of 562 freshmen in 1972, fifty-two, or 9.3 percent, failed in their first semester. In 1977 of 3,205 undergraduates, 386 students, or 12 percent, failed, but only thirty-five, or 1.1 percent, were actually dismissed. The college—administrators as well as faculty members—wanted to give students every opportunity to succeed. Thus they made it difficult for students who compiled poor academic records to "flunk out." In an attempt to help incoming freshmen adjust to college and academic life, and with the acquiescence of the faculty, Nance decided that no student—however miserably he or she did in course work—would be sent home after just one semester.[22]

Students did have to earn a minimum of a 2.0 grade point average to graduate (a C average on the 4.0 point system). But to improve the possibility that weaker students remained enrolled and eventually compiled that sometimes elusive 2.0 GPA, S.C. State instituted a policy of calculating only the highest grade a student received in a particular course that he or she might have to repeat one or more times. For example, if a student failed a required Spanish class but repeated the course the following semester and earned a C on the second attempt, only the C (or 2.0) was calculated in compiling that student's cumulative grade point average. The F that the student initially received remained on the student's permanent transcript, but it no longer figured in calculating the GPA. Without this academic "safe harbor," many students would not have been able to compile the 2.0 GPA needed to graduate.

Faculty members and administrators were reluctant to impose tougher academic demands on students who could not meet the weaker academic requirements. Priscilla Ragin was a junior biology major who took part in a student exchange program with the University of Northern Iowa in 1971. While she admitted to "enjoying myself" among the twelve thousand students (150 were black) in Cedar Falls, she pointed out in a letter to Nance, "There's a stronger educational push here than at State and I can really feel it." Two white students from Iowa, Ellen Ann Hay and David John Capper,

Table 45. High School Class Rank of S.C. State Freshmen, 1973

Percent Rank	Female	Male	Total
90–99%	70	20	90
80–89%	73	32	105
60–79%	120	92	212
40–59%	65	62	127
20–39%	20	48	68
1–19%	59	14	73

Source: *Annual Report, May 1973–May 1974*, 36.

were enrolled at S.C. State that fall. Hay explained in an interview in the *Collegian* that classes were "a little easier" at South Carolina State than at Northern Iowa. But she found smaller classes at State and that "instructors go out of their way to help you" more than at the larger institution.[23]

As frustrated and perplexed as faculty members and administrators often were over the lack of motivation and the absence of intellectual curiosity among many students, there was no overwhelming desire or attempt to increase admission requirements or to rid the college of those students with mediocre academic records. On the contrary administrators and faculty members stayed committed to maintaining educational opportunities for those young African Americans who were unlikely candidates to attend, much less graduate from, many institutions of higher education. They were well aware that many S.C. State students came from abjectly funded public schools and from impoverished homes where matters of the mind were often given little attention.

Sometimes there were unanticipated rewards for staying true to that mission. In 1980 an undergraduate student wrote a long letter to President Nance expressing appreciation for the opportunity to get an education at S.C. State. Thomas Gaither was one of nine children raised by his widowed mother, who was a maid for well-to-do white families on Pawley's Island. Gaither attended predominantly black Howard High School in Georgetown and had expected to become a carpenter. But a guidance counselor told him about S.C. State. "This was the first time that I had ever heard of South Carolina State." He made his way to Orangeburg, but in his first two years his "grades were embarrassing." As those grades improved, he gained confidence and spent two summers on a cooperative education job at the Research Triangle Park in North Carolina. His roommates were black undergraduate students from Duke University, and he had a chance to sit in on classes at North Carolina State. Gaither told Nance what the president already knew. "There are many students like myself, students who entered college unknowledgeable and unprepared and who now have a brighter outlook on life. For this I thank South Carolina State greatly." A letter like Gaither's reinforced the conviction of many people—including Nance, faculty members, and alumni—of the vital role that the institution played despite the dismal academic performance of many students.[24]

Then there were those students who were ready for college. The growing enrollment of well-qualified black students at white colleges and universities notwithstanding, S.C. State continued to draw black youngsters who had compiled good to excellent high school records. Nearly two decades after the 1954 *Brown* decision, the dual system in public education had finally begun to come to an uneasy end in 1970. But many South Carolina communities including Orangeburg had already witnessed the emergence of private "segregation academies" as white parents resisted the integration of public schools. In 1974, 421 of S.C. State's 644 freshmen had graduated in the upper 40 percent of their high school class. Ninety-five of those freshmen finished in the upper 10 percent in 1974, and ninety (of 616) were in the upper 10 percent in 1973.[25]

STUDENT CONCERNS

Maceo Nance was well aware that his ascendancy to the college presidency was due in no small measure to the 1967 student uprising—"the Cause"—that drove his predecessor into retirement. Nance took seriously the legacy of student protests that extended from the boycott of classes led by SGA president Fred H. Moore in 1956 through the civil rights demonstrations of the 1960s. Still Nance sometimes failed to reckon with the determination of young people who were committed to an issue. For months in 1968 Nance and the board of trustees had resisted—before they finally agreed to—student demands that the new physical education facility be named in honor of Henry Smith, Samuel Hammond, and Delano Middleton.

The Black Awareness Coordinating Committee (BACC) kept up the pressure on the administration and on the Student Government Association (SGA) to maintain the momentum for change on the campus. But even at their most militant, BACC members never issued threats, occupied buildings, or incited the sort of ugly confrontations that occurred at Columbia, Berkeley, Cornell, or even nearby Voorhees College. The trauma of the massacre remained too vivid for S.C. State students to brandish firearms or trash campus facilities.

BACC drew up—not demands—but a long list of twenty-four specific issues in March 1969: "Students of S.C. State College, 'Wake Up': These Are Our Gripes, Are They Yours? If So, *Let's Move Now*." Some of the problems they raised reflected the day-to-day concerns of many students. BACC wanted an expanded and improved student center. They wanted longer library hours, and they asked for the abolition of Saturday classes. They wanted a coupon system for the dining hall so that they would pay only for meals they consumed. They wanted the construction of new campus buildings that were higher than three stories.

Other issues that they identified reflected the evolution of black consciousness and a deepening interest in black history and culture. BACC wanted the creation of a school of Black Studies that would include courses in jazz, blues, spirituals, and black history that would replace "that U.S. and European 'brainwash' history.'" They wanted new buildings named after black heroes. Athletes should be allowed to let their hair grow into "afros."

Although their numbers were relatively small, the Black Awareness Coordinating Committee had a high profile on the campus during the early years of M. Maceo Nance's presidency. This is a 1969 meeting of BACC. Courtesy of the Historical Collection, South Carolina State University

Some of their other requests were more problematic. They wanted all black applicants admitted to the college and the elimination of the Scholastic Aptitude Test (SAT). They favored the election of students to the board of trustees. They wanted an end to the requirement that a student have a 2.5 GPA to be eligible to run for Student Government Association president or vice president. The national anthem should not be played "until it truly means something." They also called for higher pay for faculty and staff.[26]

The two dozen issues struck a mostly responsive chord, and many of them were implemented over the next several semesters. Sojourner Truth Hall, a fourteen-story dormitory that housed 432 women, was built, as was the Martin Luther King Jr. Auditorium. There was an expansion of the student center that included a bowling alley, four pool tables, and two ping pong tables. Library hours were extended. Saturday classes were abolished, as were classes that began at 7:35 A.M. The implementation of the humanities program in 1974 was an attempt to put more emphasis on non-Western history and culture.

Rather than sit back in self-satisfied contentment, students continued to press for changes that were mostly channeled through the Student Government Association. With opposition to the Vietnam conflict and the draft intensifying, students appealed for an end to compulsory ROTC for freshmen and sophomore males. ROTC had been a well-received and influential program since its arrival on the campus in 1947. Thomas Speights wrote an editorial in the *Collegian* in May 1969 calling for a voluntary ROTC program. Donald "Sonny" McKeever of BACC was more forceful. "ROTC should be completely kicked off the campus."[27]

To remedy a perennial problem, students wanted a smoother and more efficient registration process. There were complaints that the academic programs of too many students included too many required courses. They appealed for more electives and an option to enroll in classes on a pass/fail basis. They wanted an end to the comprehensive final exams that many faculty members administered. Other issues had less to do with academic matters. Students asked for the establishment of a store on campus to purchase toiletries, snacks, and school supplies. They wanted a campus radio station. They asked for coin-operated cigarette machines in the dormitories. They also wanted coin-operated washing machines and dryers in the dorms. Barbering and hair salon facilities were on their list of "wants."[28]

Nance and the board of trustees were usually more than eager to accommodate the students. The trustees voted to make ROTC voluntary in 1969. Efforts to improve registration were undertaken but did not meet with much success. Mathematics professor Robert Abernathy complained that the newly instituted preregistration process in 1971 was too drawn out and woefully disorganized. A limited pass/fail option was put in place, but not very many students took advantage of it. Sojourner Truth Hall contained a beauty salon and launderette on each floor, and the expanded student center contained a barber shop.[29]

Students certainly did not get everything they sought. There was little reduction in the number of required courses. Faculty members continued to "subject" students to comprehensive final exams. No store was established on campus. Students still had to make their way up Russell Street by foot or automobile to retail outlets. It would be 1985 before FM station WSSB would go on the air. At the request of the administration, the trustees added an additional $5 to student fees "for the purpose of improving the entertainment of our students." Students had wearied of "high-brow" cultural attractions like baritone William Warfield, the National Opera Company, and the Cologne Chamber Orchestra that visited the campus in 1968–69. They wanted more popular and, therefore, more expensive entertainers.[30]

Some of America's most popular musicians soon descended on the campus. Gladys Knight and the Pips, Jerry "the Iceman" Butler, and gospel singer Shirley Caesar appeared in 1971. Roberta Flack sang in early 1972. Comedian Dick Gregory got some laughs in 1973, and Eddie Kendricks, Bill Withers, and Dizzy Gillespie also stopped by that year. The Commodores and the Chi Lites visited in 1975 with Kool and the Gang performing in 1978.[31]

CULTURAL AWARENESS

With the surging interest in the African American experience in the late 1960s and into the 1970s, scholars, writers, and political commentators spoke to students and faculty. Stokely Carmichael and his wife, South African singer Miriam Makeba, visited in 1969 as did political scientist Charles Hamilton. Carmichael and Hamilton had recently coauthored the best-selling and controversial book *Black Power.* LeRoi Jones—Imamu Amiri Baraka—visited in 1971. Georgia state legislator Julian Bond and California congressman Ronald Dellums spoke in 1973 as did Atlanta mayor Maynard Jackson. By 1977 Alex Haley, the author *of Roots,* spoke at Founders' Day just after his book had been transformed into the single most popular television series in American history.[32]

Alex Haley, the author of the best seller *Roots,* spoke at Founders' Day in 1977 and is shown here with President M. Maceo Nance. The ABC network program based on the book was the highest-rated television series in history. Courtesy of the Historical Collection, South Carolina State University

The Black Culture Seminar made possible many of the appearances by scholars and activists. The seminar was presided over by sociology professor Marguerite R. Howie, who had secured a $207,000 five-year grant from the Kellogg Foundation in 1969 to enhance the Department of Social Sciences. Howie astutely included support for the seminar in the grant. Kellogg officials, pleased with the success of the social sciences grant, awarded a second grant of $289,000 in 1974 to the Department of Business Administration for four years to bolster that growing program.[33]

RELIGION

The escalating interest in black pride was reflected in the natural hair styles—the Afro—and the dashikis that were a common sight on the campus by 1970. Yet as committed as many young people were to their culture and their African roots, they also regarded themselves as devout Christians. Most students attended church frequently, and they took part in college religious organizations and activities. Like the larger African American population, most students were Baptists and Methodists. But more than two hundred students indicated no religious affiliation. And no student publicly acknowledged that he or she was Muslim or Jewish. (Civil rights activist Charles "Chuck" McDew, who withdrew from S.C. State in 1960 to take part in the movement full time, later converted to Judaism and went on to graduate from Brandeis University.)

Table 46. Religious Preferences among Students at S.C. State, 1971

Adventist	4
Apostolic	3
Baptist	841
Catholic	51
Episcopal	33
Holiness	31
Lutheran	2
Methodist	530
Pentecostal	3
Presbyterian	23
Protestant	30
None	223
TOTAL	1,774

Source: *Annual Report, May 1971 to May 1972*, 29.

Perhaps not surprisingly little change had occurred in religious affiliations among students since the early twentieth century. A 1906–7 survey had revealed that 620 and 671 students belonged to Baptist and Methodist congregations, respectively (see chapter 2).

FEWER REGULATIONS

By the late 1960s and early 1970s, a generation of students had asserted themselves through the civil rights movement, in opposition to the Vietnam War, and in campus protests. Collegiate officials including those at S.C. State were much less consumed than previous generations of administrators with the control and regulation of personal behavior among students. Barriers between the sexes broke down. Efforts to maintain in loco parentis crumbled. Men and women were given more latitude to socialize informally. Administrators and faculty members at South Carolina State were far less vigilant than their predecessors in closely monitoring and supervising the activities and whereabouts of young people, especially young women.

President Nance and dean of student affairs Oscar P. Butler were flexible, reasonable, and willing to concede greater autonomy to students in their personal conduct. But that did not mean that young people could do as they pleased on campus. There was still a curfew of 12:30 A.M. on weekdays and 1:30 A.M. on weekends for women who resided on campus. At many colleges and universities, interdormitory visitation by men and women was permitted, but not at South Carolina State. And many students complained about it. In the *Collegian* in 1971, "Steppenwolf" called for quick action. "Hue [Student Government Association president Andrew Hugine], you're the prexy, get busy and get that room visitation, man." But Nance would not budge.[34]

Priscilla Ragin, the S.C. State junior who was an exchange student, told Nance in 1971 that interdorm visitation at the University of Northern Iowa "works quite well." The residents of each dormitory set the hours for visitors, and there was no curfew for female students unless parents specifically requested it. Nance was not persuaded, and he replied that "certain innovations and ideas that might work very well in certain environments and not work in others."[35]

When approximately two hundred students led by Ellaway Brown gathered in front of the administration building in 1978 to protest and outline their grievances, the lack of male and female dorm visitation was their first concern. But they also complained that the president-elect of the Student Government Association, Victor E. Nesmith, would not be permitted to take office until a marijuana charge against him was resolved. Students also did not like poor service at the campus book store, the procedure for reserving dormitory rooms, the lack of variety among vegetables served in the dining hall, and the absence of outdoor basketball courts, as well as several other matters.[36]

State representative Kay Patterson of Richland County, whose daughter was a political science major at the college, learned of the demonstration, and he was absolutely unsympathetic with the desire for interdorm visitation, regarding it as nothing more than a pretext for sex. The outspoken legislator asked, "Is that what Hammond Middleton Smith died for? Do you little rural jive-ass punks really think we parents pay as much as $2000 tuition-n-fees per year for you to go up in the girls dormitory and *do it on the floor—free?* If you think that, then your crazy-as-hell. Ain't no way! Hell you kin go to a drive-in theater for $2 and *do it* in the back seat—at a saving of $1998." Excessive language aside, Patterson's attitude represented that of most parents, and Nance was well aware that those parents would not support interdorm visits.[37]

Some students decided that they could not accept such an unfair restriction, and they arranged their own dormitory visits. At 12:15 A.M. on April 18, 1972, a junior, Gene White, was caught in the Bradham Hall room of Ms. Russell Davis, a freshman. The SGA Judicial Board suspended both students for one semester, and that penalty was upheld by the College Judicial Board.[38]

By the 1970s illegal drugs and homosexuality surfaced as major issues. In 1978 Victor E. Nesmith, the president-elect of the Student Government Association, was charged with possession of marijuana. Dean of students Oscar P. Butler, with the approval of President Nance, informed Nesmith that he could not take office until "your guilt or innocence has been proven." Nesmith complained, and many students supported him, that he should hold office unless he was found guilty. But it was to no avail.[39]

The older generation was scandalized at what they perceived to be the breakdown in morality, the lack of respect for the law, and the absence of proper behavior in the younger generation. In an indignant letter in 1970, Charles Drake-Long informed Nance that he had witnessed the "widespread uses of narcotics and practices of homosexuality during homecoming weekend." He saw "alumni supplying heroin" as well as pills and marijuana to students. He charged alumni, faculty members, and ex-faculty members with "contributing to unrestrained, emotionally injurious homosexual practices." Drake-Long identified the specific rooms in Mays and Bethea Halls where the alleged debauchery had taken place, but he failed to explain exactly how he had come to know the details of what occurred in those dormitory rooms.[40]

Nance reacted calmly to Drake-Long's information, and without mentioning whether he took the accusations seriously he explained that there were campus programs underway to address the issue of illegal drugs and that homosexuality was a subject openly discussed at S.C. State. Perhaps to reassure his overwrought correspondent, Nance told Drake-Long that twelve male students "with noticeable homosexual tendencies" had been brought to the attention of Dean Oscar P. Butler, and that one of the young men had been offered counseling.[41]

Greek letter organizations had been a prominent presence on the campus for a half century by the 1970s. Fraternities and sororities permitted generations of S.C. State students to form close bonds, to learn to work together, and to take part in community service projects. But not everyone embraced the Greeks and the influence they wielded at the college. Rebecca Kemp, the editor of the *Collegian,* stirred a storm of controversy in 1969 when she claimed that sororities fostered snobbery and elitism among women while fraternities concentrated on monopolizing campus politics. "When social groups," Kemp wrote, "fail to contribute to the stability and welfare of their members as well as to the unity of mankind in general, they become unnecessary evils."[42]

Fraternity and sorority members did not interpret Kemp's criticism as constructive. Anything less than fulsome praise for Greeks was rejected as unfair. J. deLeon McDuffie Jr. pointed out that Kemp's remarks could not apply to the "men of distinction" who belonged to Kappa Alpha Psi because they worked for, and not against, the progress of the fraternity system. Thalia J. Coleman defended Zeta Phi Beta for their extensive commitment to community service work that included Project Hunger in Beaufort and Jasper Counties as well as their support for the Urban League and United Negro College Fund.[43]

Hazing, however, was a perennial problem among Greek letter organizations. Faculty members complained that students spent too much time on fraternity and sorority tasks, and they believed that hazing and hell week detracted significantly from the academic climate on campus. Greek activities severely hindered the ability of young men and women who were pledges to perform in class and on assignments. They were kept up until late hours, sometimes subjected to physical and emotional stress, and forced to traipse through the campus with Greek paraphernalia. In 1977 the Faculty Senate notified the administration that pledge activities contributed to unresponsive students who slept in class.[44]

Instances of physical mistreatment of pledges occurred. Connie Davis, who belonged to the Pyramid pledge class of Delta Sigma Theta Sorority, complained of hazing in 1976. College administrators in cooperation with representatives of the national sorority intervened, and Alpha Xi chapter of Delta Sigma Theta was suspended for "humiliating, demeaning, and degrading" harassment. Six pledges—Lampados Club members—of Omega Psi Phi fraternity were whipped in front of most of the chapter membership in November 1978. That undergraduate chapter was suspended for two years after the graduate chapter reported the incident. Hazing by Alpha Kappa Alpha members in 1979 earned the sorority a one-year suspension accompanied by required attendance at workshops on the history of the sorority and on hazing. Alpha Lambda chapter of Kappa Alpha Psi was barred from campus for two years in 1980 for hazing six pledges.[45]

Students often complained that faculty members were too demanding, and faculty members routinely questioned the ability and motivation of students. But these tensions and disagreements almost never resulted in physical confrontations. Yet on November 3, 1976, a twenty-six-year-old married student, Thomas Moore, assaulted and struck Gregory Hall, a white English professor. But this was no disagreement between student and professor. They had never even met. Moore was reportedly under the influence of drugs or alcohol or both. A four-member Faculty Discipline Committee suspended Moore from school for one year. He also had been arrested for assault and battery. But Moore apparently forfeited the $100 bond he had posted.[46]

It had always been easy for faculty members, administrators, the media, and the general public to criticize S.C. State students for their actions, attitudes, and poor behavior. But whatever their academic strengths or weaknesses, the vast majority of students were friendly, personable, and pleasant. Although not often enough, they were sometimes singled out for praise. Ernest A. Finney Sr., an administrator at Claflin (and father of the future South Carolina Supreme Court chief justice), was impressed by South Carolina State students who he encountered while dining at the Western Sizzler Steak House in Orangeburg in 1980. "I have never observed during my fifty years of teaching and administration a more orderly, well behaved and disciplined group of students any time or any place."[47]

In a similar vein a local businessman extolled John Blake, a co-op student who he had employed. "He was assertive, cooperative, always willing to take that extra step and never had any problems getting along with his fellow employees." He continued, "If this gentleman is representative of the students attending South Carolina State College then both the College and Orangeburg have much to be proud of."[48]

Even football players—who were not often associated with polite and refined behavior—could be complimented on their conduct. The flight attendant on an Ozark Airlines plane that carried the Bulldog football team to Pocatello, Idaho, for an NCAA playoff game in 1981 sent a handwritten note to Nance "to let you know how much we enjoyed your team." She added, "They were considerate and total gentlemen on the flight."[49]

THE HENDERSON DAVIS PLAYERS

Several student groups and campus organizations won accolades and plaudits during the 1970s and early 1980s. The drama program flourished and increased the visibility of South Carolina State College. Under the direction of Horace D. Flowers II, the Henderson Davis Players traveled widely and earned compliments and awards as they put on an astonishing number of productions that ranged from Greek drama and Shakespeare to plays for children. Flowers, who had a bachelor's degree from Grambling State University and a master's from Florida Atlantic University, was able to mold students who had had little exposure to live theater into talented actors and actresses. But they also learned through the long hours and hard work imposed by Flowers the mechanics of staging productions that included the design and construction of sets, lighting, and costume making.

Summer and Smoke by Tennessee Williams was Flowers's first production, put on in 1967 in White Hall Auditorium, which was not the sort of intimate venue that Flowers (or Williams) might have envisioned for such a play. By March 1969 the Henderson Davis Players were one of twelve colleges and universities invited to the thirteenth annual Yale University Festival for Undergraduate Drama. They performed Lorraine Hansberry's 1959 classic *A Raisin in the Sun.*[50]

With a financial assist from the South Carolina Arts Commission, twenty of the Henderson Davis Players and three technicians toured the state over the course of several months in 1970–71 offering performances of Euripides's *Medea,* James Weldon Johnson's seven Negro sermons in verse, *God's Trombones, Tell Pharaoh,* and a children's production, *The Prince and the Pea.* Their visits included Springfield Baptist Church in Greenville, Mount Pisgah Baptist Church in Sumter, Howard High School in Georgetown, and Lincoln High School in McClellanville. Several hundred people—"most had never seen live drama"—were in attendance at most of the productions. They also put on performances at Voorhees College and the University of South Carolina.[51]

In August 1971 fourteen students and Flowers traveled overseas to the American Festival in Great Britain, where they presented *Medea.* One year later in a trip sponsored by the USO, they toured U.S. military bases in Iceland, Greenland, and Labrador. Thirteen students offered a musical variety show that included excerpts from the Broadway play *Purlie Victorious.* Their mostly male audiences were as small as twenty-five people and as large as five hundred.[52]

The campus community, and especially President Nance, was so won over by the many accolades bestowed on Flowers and the Henderson Davis Players that a first-rate facility to house the drama program was built adjacent to Turner Hall. It opened in 1972. At a cost of $2 million, it included a 350-seat theater, up-to-date sound and lighting systems, work areas for set construction and costume design, dressing rooms, a green room, offices, and storage areas. The Henderson Davis Theater was named for the two individuals—Sara B. Henderson and George Davis—credited with initiating a drama program with the Wig and Mask Drama Society in 1932. By 1948 the Henderson Davis Players were periodically presenting plays on the campus.[53]

Flowers may have been a master at staging dramatic productions, but a financial wizard he was not. He severely tested the patience of administrators with his cavalier approach to purchasing equipment and supplies and arranging travel. He ignored college policies and procedures for securing requisitions and purchase orders. Attempts to get Flowers to adhere to a budget mostly failed. He was summoned to a meeting with Nettie P. Parler, the chair of the Department of Communications; George Hunter, the dean of arts and sciences; and Ashriel I. Mose, the dean of the faculty, in October 1974, and they made it clear that they were thoroughly dissatisfied with "his extensive well documented record of financial mismanagement and untrustworthy acts." Restrictions were imposed on the director and his drama program. In 1975 all monetary matters involving drama were assigned to Malverse Nicholson, the director of development. There would be no off-campus productions permitted until spring 1976, and then only on weekends. Flowers did not contest the allegations but perhaps felt overcriticized and underappreciated after attracting so much favorable publicity to the college. He left S.C. State in 1977.

THE MARCHING 101

Students in the Marching 101 also gained visibility and praise for the college. The band and its director, Clifford D. Watkins, were invited to take part in the Tournament of Roses Parade in Pasadena on January 1, 1970. The estimated cost of transportation for the 105 men and six women in the band was $25,000. To raise that kind of money, President Nance appealed directly to the Orangeburg community for support, and most business people and local leaders responded enthusiastically and generously. It was the first time in the history of South Carolina State that large numbers of white South Carolinians contributed financially to the school. There were large donations that included $1,000 from Bankers Trust, $500 from J. W. Smoak Hardware (trustee Wallace C. Bethea was the owner), $100 from Coca-Cola, and smaller amounts of $25 each from Bill Dukes' Gulf and the Sulton Oil Company. Ann Ramsey Gifts and the Peoples Barbershop each gave $10. The alumni gave several thousand dollars, and

Under the direction of Clifford Watkins and with money raised in large measure by President M. Maceo Nance, the Marching 101 took part in the Tournament of Roses Parade in Pasadena on January 1, 1970. Courtesy of the Historical Collection, South Carolina State University

the faculty and staff contributed over $5,500. Contributions finally totaled more than $35,000.[54]

The band flew to Los Angeles and performed at Disneyland in Anaheim on December 30 before participating in the Rose Bowl Parade on New Year's Day. The only disappointment was that the band did not get to attend the Fifty-Sixth Rose Bowl game, where 103,000 people watched the University of Southern California defeat the University of Michigan, 10–3.[55]

In 1971 the Marching 101 was invited to London for the International Festival of University Bands, and they were also asked to march in the St. Patrick's Day Parade in Dublin on March 17, 1972. The invitations were reluctantly rejected. Each trip would cost at least $60,000, and coming so soon after the big fund-raising push for the Rose Bowl trip, it was unlikely that such a sizable sum could be raised in a relatively short time for one trip, much less two. But in 1975 the band did march in the Macy's Thanksgiving Day Parade in New York City under the guidance of director Isaac Richardson.[56]

THE CONCERT CHOIR

The concert choir also traveled extensively on annual spring trips that gave alumni, church congregations, and high school audiences an opportunity to hear the singers. Director Arthur Evans took the choir to Miami in 1980 on a tour that very nearly ended in tragedy. After a performance at a church on May 17, the choir found itself in the midst of an unfolding urban uprising. Miami exploded in violence and destruction after an all-white and all-male jury acquitted several Miami police officers in the December 1979 beating and death of Arthur McDuffie, a thirty-three-year-old African American motorcyclist.

Rioters attacked the bus carrying the choir. Windows were smashed, and at least one bullet was fired into the vehicle. Choir members and Evans were caught completely unaware, having no knowledge of the jury's verdict a few hours earlier. The students were terrified. "There was blood and broken glass over much of the front of the bus," choir member Lee Plowden later recalled. He was perplexed. "Why did they attack us; we were black just as they were." Several students were injured, and at least one choir member was taken to the hospital after police intervened. The remainder of the choir retreated to their hotel. But the riot swiftly grew from the Liberty City and Overton neighborhoods to other areas of Miami. The choir was forced to move to a second hotel while they waited in safety for repairs to be made to the bus. Miami suffered widespread destruction as fifteen people died and more than 180 were injured over several days and nights.

Once the choir was back in Orangeburg, Plowden looked back not so much in anger or fear, but in appreciation for the bond that choir members formed with each other as they survived such a traumatic event. "The events in Miami were not all bad. The incident did help to bring all of the members of the choir a little [closer] together and show some of the real feelings that we have for each other and our director, Dr. Evans." The next year the choir removed Miami from their itinerary as they visited Charleston; Washington, D.C.; and New York City.[57]

ATHLETICS

Intercollegiate athletics, already a well-embedded feature of campus life, became even more prominent during the last three decades of the twentieth century. South Carolina State joined the newly formed Mid-Eastern Athletic Conference (MEAC) in 1970 as a charter member. Under Coach Willie Jeffries the football team became a powerhouse in the new conference. Men's and women's basketball moved into the spacious confines of the Smith Hammond Middleton Memorial Center after four decades in cramped Dukes Gymnasium. Coach Willie Simon's Lady Bulldogs won the AIAW National Basketball Championship in 1979. The women's track team claimed the AIAW (Association of Intercollegiate Athletics for Women) national title in 1982.

The adoption and enforcement of Title IX of the 1972 Higher Education Act brought a huge expansion in intercollegiate competition among female athletes and forever changed sports for undergraduate men and women across the nation. The athletic program at S.C. State was part of that transformation as new women's teams were formed, scholarships for female athletes increased, and facilities for women's teams were created and expanded. However several men's teams were discontinued as more women joined in intercollegiate competition. Also during the 1970s more racial barriers fell as Bulldog athletic teams began to schedule for the first time games and matches against colleges with a majority of white undergraduates.

Since 1931 S.C. State teams had been members of the Southern Intercollegiate Athletic Conference (SIAC), a black athletic league that had been organized in Atlanta in 1913. In 1969 the presidents of several historically black institutions along the East Coast began preliminary discussions about the formation of a new conference. Athletic officials from these schools took the initiative in 1970 to create the Mid-Eastern Athletic Conference. South Carolina State was the last college invited to become one of the charter members of the MEAC, joining Morgan State, University of Maryland–Eastern Shore, Delaware State, Howard, North Carolina Central, and North Carolina A&T. The conference began competition in 1971. Over the years conference membership has fluctuated as the University of Maryland–Eastern Shore dropped out and North Carolina Central withdrew and then rejoined. Bethune Cookman, Hampton, Florida A&M, Norfolk State, and Savannah State joined.[58]

South Carolina State's departure from the SIAC and entry into the MEAC coincided with the arrival of Willie Jeffries as the head football coach. Oree Banks was dismissed after the Bulldogs lost nine games and won one game by one point in 1972. Banks had succeeded George Bell as head coach in 1965, and he had early success, winning twenty-one games and losing five in his first three years. But his record was 10–18–1 in his last three years.[59]

Athletic director Milton Hunter complimented the likable Banks but thought it was time for new leadership over football. Hunter wrote to the Athletic Committee that "our head coach is a good man, and a hard working man." Nevertheless, "all indications point to the fact that he simply does not know how or what to do for improvement." Hunter suggested that Banks was disorganized and an ineffective recruiter and sometimes failed to answer his correspondence.[60]

The selection of Jeffries was an inspired choice that proved to be more successful than anyone—except maybe Jeffries himself—might have anticipated. In 1972 Jeffries was a $24,000-a-year defensive line coach under Johnny Majors at the University of Pittsburgh. S.C. State, however, came through with an offer the thirty-two-year-old Jeffries could afford to refuse—a $16,000 salary, a home adjacent to the campus, and the use of a used green Plymouth for recruiting.[61]

Like most new coaches, Jeffries exuded confidence. But unlike many men who take charge of a beleaguered team, Jeffries quickly restored the Bulldog program to winning ways. Jeffries was a native of Union, South Carolina, and a 1960 graduate of S.C. State who had been a center on the football team and a pitcher on the baseball squad. He began his coaching career as an assistant at Lancaster's Barr Street High School in 1960. He took over the head coaching position at Granard High School in Gaffney, compiling a 65–7–2 record and winning three state AAA championships in six years, before moving on to become defensive coordinator in 1968 at North Carolina A&T.[62]

Jeffries's success on the field was due largely to his ability to recruit. With that green Plymouth, Jeffries toured South Carolina (and Georgia), landing football prospects who became outstanding players. Some of those young men agreed to join Jeffries in Orangeburg because there was still reluctance on the part of major white football programs in the Atlantic Coast Conference and the Southeastern Athletic Conference as well as the Southern Conference to recruit black athletes. The University of South Carolina, for example, had no black football or basketball players until 1969–70, and Clemson's first black athlete was a football player who joined the team in 1971. Major athletic powers and smaller predominantly white institutions signed relatively small numbers of black athletes well into the 1970s.[63]

But Jeffries's accomplishments as a recruiter had as much to do with his gregarious personality as the racial climate in which he worked. Jeffries was amiable, witty, and persuasive. He was at ease around players, their parents, and the public. He was always armed with a funny story or an amusing anecdote. One of his players once asked the coach if the team would be taking a plane to the next away game. Jeffries dryly replied, "Yeah, we'll be taking a plane, a plain bus."

But under that affable demeanor was a tough, demanding football coach whose no-nonsense approach to preparation for games enabled his teams to compete successfully in the MEAC. He startled some players and angered others when they were told practice began at 5 A.M.—an hour when some undergraduates were just concluding an evening's extracurricular activities. Jeffries had lights installed on the practice field to illuminate the predawn darkness. His players would be in shape and ready to execute. Jeffries would out-coach opponents, and his players would outperform them.

Or maybe not. After the first three games of his first season in 1973, Jeffries's team was winless. They lost to Bethune Cookman and Howard and tied North Carolina A&T. They then reeled off seven straight wins and met Florida A&M in the Orange Blossom Classic in Miami. They lost 23–12. In six years (1973–78) the Bulldogs won fifty, lost

No two individuals—coach and player—better capture the success of the Bulldog football team than Willie Jeffries and Harry Carson, shown here in 1975. Jeffries would be enshrined in the College Football Hall of Fame, and Carson was inducted into the National Football League Hall of Fame. Courtesy of the Historical Collection, South Carolina State University

thirteen, and tied four. They lost Pelican Bowl games in New Orleans to Grambling in 1974 and to Southern University in 1975. But they defeated Norfolk State in the Bicentennial Bowl in Richmond in 1976 and beat Winston-Salem State in the Gold Bowl in 1977.[64]

The 1976 Bulldog team was possibly the best aggregation of football players in S.C. State history. They were 10–1, losing to North Carolina A&T by one point. They shut out seven opponents as the defense yielded a mere twenty-seven points in eleven games. Jeffries's teams won the MEAC in 1974, 1975, 1976 (tied with Morgan State), and 1978. For the first time in school history they played teams from predominantly white colleges and won four of the first five games. They lost to Wofford College 20–0 in 1974 in bitterly cold rain but defeated the Terriers 23–9 in 1975 and 14–6 in 1976. They also defeated Newberry College twice.[65]

Between 1973 and 1978, eleven former Bulldogs signed NFL contracts. Barney Chavous, Harry Carson, and Donnie Shell went on to long and illustrious professional careers. Each of them played in Super Bowls. In 2006 Carson joined Marion Motley (1968) and David "Deacon" Jones (1980) as South Carolina State's inductees to the NFL Hall of Fame in Canton, Ohio. S.C. State is the only college or university in the Palmetto State with former players in the Hall of Fame.[66]

Jeffries's sterling record attracted attention and job offers. After turning down positions including that of an assistant coach with the Atlanta Falcons of the NFL, he accepted the head coaching job at Wichita State in December 1978. He became the first black head coach at a predominantly white university in Division I of the NCAA. He turned the Wichita program around before moving on to Howard University, where he spent five years before coming back to South Carolina State in 1989 for a second stint of thirteen years at his alma mater. Jeffries was not only an outstanding coach. He became a superb ambassador for S.C. State. No one, except perhaps Maceo Nance, moved as effortlessly and engagingly among black and white South Carolinians as Jeffries.[67]

Bill Davis, who had been Jeffries's offensive coordinator, took the helm at S.C. State in 1979 and built on his mentor's success, winning the MEAC in 1980, 1981, 1982, and 1983. His teams went 54–25 in seven seasons. In 1980 the MEAC joined Division I of the NCAA, and its conference champions were eligible for NCAA national tournaments. In 1981 the Bulldogs defeated Tennessee State in overtime 26–25, before falling to eventual national champion Idaho State in Pocatello, 12–41. They defeated Furman in the 1982 NCAA tournament 17–0 in the first meeting between the two South Carolina schools. But the Bulldogs lost the following week to Louisiana Tech, 3–38.[68]

RADIO, TELEVISION, AND ATHLETICS

For decades mainstream media mostly ignored black college sports. There were, for example, no local radio broadcasts of S.C. State football games on a regular basis until 1977, when WOIC in Columbia assembled a statewide network of stations. Bill Terrill, Bobby Gist, and Ernest Robinson handled the play-by-play and color descriptions of the games.[69]

But by the late 1970s black college sports began to gain modest exposure through television. Before the advent of cable and ESPN, the NCAA carefully limited the appearances of major university and college teams through exclusive contracts with ABC television. Teams (and the conferences they represented) that did appear on the network gained more than just exposure for their schools and athletic programs; they reaped large sums of money. When the Bulldogs played at home on an ABC regional broadcast in 1980, they not only defeated Alcorn, 33–0; they shared $399,692 with the Mississippi school and with the MEAC. S.C. State put $157,759 in the bank after allocating 20 percent ($42,105) to the conference. In 1981 ABC paid $422,929 to televise the S.C. State game with Grambling that the Bulldogs won, 30–14.[70]

The options available to television viewers exploded with cable and satellite transmission, and it changed the landscape of college sports. The NCAA lost its monopoly over broadcast rights, and ABC was no longer the sole source of college football on TV. Cable television pioneer and entrepreneur Robert L. Johnson, the founder of Black Entertainment Television (BET), began to televise black college sports including S.C. State football and basketball games. Johnson visited the campus in 1981 and discussed the financial and logistical arrangements for the broadcasts with President Nance and athletic director Milton Hunter. The BET founder then asked to televise the Howard football game on September 25, 1982, on a delayed basis for $1,000.[71]

Ben Jobe took over as head coach of men's basketball after Ed Martin left for Tennessee State in 1968. Jobe was a 1956 graduate of Fisk who had coached at Talladega and Alabama State before coming to Orangeburg. He had also worked with young men in Sierra Leone, where his teams won forty-one games without losing. In four years at S.C. State, Jobe led the Bulldogs to an impressive 76–30 record. His high-powered offenses scored more than one hundred points in fifty games, and that was before the NCAA adopted the three-point field goal. They lost to Newberry College in 1969 in the NAIA District 6 Tournament. But in 1970 they defeated Erskine College and Appalachian State in the District 6 Tournament and advanced to the sixteen-team NAIA National Championship in Kansas City, where they lost to Stephen F. Austin, 100–86. Jobe left S.C. State in 1972 amid controversy when his star player, Tommy Boswell, transferred to Coach Frank Maguire's University of South Carolina team. Jobe followed Boswell to Columbia and joined Maguire as an assistant coach, and he remained at USC for five years.[72]

Tim Autry replaced Jobe. He was a disciple of and former player for the legendary Clarence "Big House" Gaines at Winston-Salem State. Autry arrived at S.C. State after having served as an assistant to Charles "Lefty" Drisell at the University of Maryland. With the assistance of former Bulldog football and basketball standout Samuel Goodwin, Autry's first team won the District 6 tournament and went to Kansas City in 1973 for the NAIA finals. They beat Hastings from Nebraska, 82–71, before losing to Wisconsin Green Bay, 72–55.[73]

Autry compiled a 96–93 record in seven seasons, but his 1978–79 and 1979–80 teams were 20–36, and he stepped down. Men's basketball went into a decline in the 1980s and had a losing record for seven straight seasons (1980–81 to 1986–87) under coaches Johnny Jones (34–45) and Percy "Chico" Caldwell (48–65). In 1981 the MEAC and South Carolina State had joined Division 1 of the NCAA, and basketball competition became more intense than it had been in the NAIA.[74]

As men's basketball faltered, the women's basketball program excelled. Coach Willie Simon was the architect of these superb Lady Bulldog teams, but he had come to the position more by happenstance than by careful planning. Simon was a graduate of Allen University, and he was the head coach of the Bulldog baseball team and an assistant to Willie Jeffries with the football team. He had inherited the baseball team after Ed Martin, who coached baseball as well as basketball, left for Tennessee State. However S.C. State dropped the baseball program in 1974 as a cost-cutting measure but not before Simon produced two bona fide major-league players in Eugene Richards and Willie Mays Aikens. With no baseball to coach, Simon took over women's basketball.[75]

Women had been playing basketball at S.C. State since at least the 1920s. But it was in the 1970s and in tandem with the rapidly expanding women's rights movement that participation and interest in intercollegiate athletic competition among women surged through American society. The NCAA initially ignored women's sports, and

The women's basketball team defeated the University of Dayton in Fargo, North Dakota, to win the Association of Intercollegiate Athletics for Women (AIAW) championship in 1979. They were coached by Willie Simon. Courtesy of the Historical Collection, South Carolina State University

the Association of Intercollegiate Athletics for Women (AIAW) was founded in 1971 to administer competition among women and to sponsor national championships.

Simon brought together some of the most gifted athletes in the history of S.C. State as he created a basketball powerhouse. Margaret English, Joyce Robinson, and the remarkable Roberta Williams won twenty-eight and lost only to Clemson in 1976–77. Williams scored twenty-eight points in that loss to Clemson, but she hit for thirty-three points in a win over the South Carolina Lady Gamecocks and was the Most Valuable Player in the MEAC Tournament. In 1978 Simon's squad went 30–2, defeating Eastern Washington in the AIAW College Division national tournament, before losing to national champion High Point College of North Carolina.[76]

The Lady Bulldogs won the AIAW national championship in 1979 when they defeated the University of Dayton in Fargo, North Dakota. That triumph capped a 33–2 season that included victories over Clemson and the College of Charleston. But they also lost to the University of South Carolina. In 1980 they fell to Iowa's William Penn College in an AIAW tournament game played before a sparse crowd during spring break in the Smith Hammond Middleton Memorial Center.[77]

Willie Simon coached the Lady Bulldogs until 1986–87, winning 271 games and losing sixty-eight, a winning margin of nearly 80 percent. It was the best record ever compiled by a coach at South Carolina State. His 1985–86 team was 24–5 and 13–1 in the MEAC. He had five seasons with twenty or more wins, and three of those seasons had thirty wins.[78]

Women had taken part in track and field periodically in the 1960s. But the women's track team began serious intercollegiate competition in 1977 and won the AIAW

College Division National Championship in 1982. They were coached by Robert "Jet" Johnson and led by Angela Carson, Esme Austin, and Sonia Clark. Carson participated in the long jump and hurdles and was on the relay team. Austin ran the quarter mile and mile relay while Clark was a one-hundred- and two-hundred-meter sprinter.[79]

TITLE IX

But 1982 was the last year that the AIAW awarded championships. The NCAA took over supervision of women's intercollegiate athletics. This was no small irony because the NCAA had stubbornly opposed Title IX and the inclusion of women in athletic competition. Title IX of the Education Amendments of 1972 prohibited educational institutions from excluding anyone "on the basis of sex" from participation "in any educational program or activity receiving federal financial assistance." NCAA administrators and lawyers and the athletics directors at many institutions argued that Title IX *did not* apply to the nation's college and university athletic programs because athletic departments did not receive federal funds. Federal officials—and what is more important, the federal courts—contended otherwise. Women did have the right to take part in intercollegiate athletics on an equitable basis with men because the institutions that sponsored the athletic programs received federal money.[80]

The nation's colleges and universities were thus compelled to provide women athletes with scholarships, facilities, equipment, accommodations, and academic support comparable to those afforded male competitors. In 1977, and before the implementation of Title IX, South Carolina State awarded athletic scholarships to twelve women—eleven basketball players and one tennis player—and 203 to male athletes.

By 1980 colleges and universities were expected to offer athletic scholarship awards to members of each sex in proportion to the number of students of each gender participating in intercollegiate activities on that campus. A delay in the arrival of equipment and uniforms in 1977 led to a postponement of participation by women in outdoor track and field until 1978. In 1981 South Carolina State's women's track and field team won the AIAW College Division National Championship. In 1979 the women's tennis team was organized. The volleyball squad was formed in 1980 and cocoached by Bambi Ware and Hazel Michaux. Former women's basketball player Charlene Myers took charge of the volleyball and women's tennis teams in 1983. She won the MEAC women's coach of the year award in volleyball in 1986 and coached the volleyball team to the MEAC title in 1990.[81]

Charlene Myers Johnson's coaching experience served her well. She became the senior women's administrator and associate director of athletics before she was named interim athletic director in 2003 and then director of athletics in 2004. Johnson's ascendancy in athletics administration mirrored the huge increase by women in intercollegiate sports at South Carolina State.[82]

By the early twenty-first century women's team competition expanded to softball, soccer, bowling, and golf. But to maintain something close to parity in athletic scholarships awarded to men and women, the number of those scholarships allotted to men was reduced. The men's wrestling team had been formed in 1972, and they won the

Table 47. Athletic Scholarships, October 1977

Team	Number of Scholarships	Cost
MEN		
Football	117	$114,394
Swimming	19	$16,269
Track and field	22	$19,950
Basketball	19	$18,776
Tennis	7	$5,549
Wrestling	13	$10,993
Golf	5	$4,537
Total	202	$190,468
WOMEN		
Basketball	11	$9,821
Tennis	1	$921
Total	12	$10,742

Source: Financial Report: Athletics. Harold Jenkins, Vice President for Business and Finance, 15 November 1977, Box 27, Folder: Athletics. Presidents' Papers, M. Maceo Nance Jr., HCSCSU.

NAIA Area 7 Tournament in 1977 and then won the MEAC championship in 1979 and again in 1980 under Coach James Ragland. But wrestling was dropped from the athletic program in 1989. The men's swimming team—the Aqua Dogs—under former swim team member and coach Robert Bradley won the National Black Championship at Hampton in 1981, but the sport was discontinued the next year. Baseball, which had ended in 1974, was briefly revived in 1990 before it was terminated for a second time in 1993.[83]

Not everyone was pleased that the elimination of men's teams opened opportunities for women to engage in intercollegiate athletics. After baseball was dropped in 1974 *Collegian* sports columnist Stanley Bennett asked, perhaps tongue-in-cheek, "But what about our women. Our sweet little pampered, mini skirted people. They are the best fed, best dressed, best looking, and best loved women in the world. I am afraid that they are the world's worst athletes." The Lady Bulldogs who competed for S.C. State in the years that followed Bennett's smart-alecky assessment proved just how wrong he was.[84]

ROTC

For the first time, women began to enroll in the ROTC program in 1972–73, exactly one-quarter century after the ROTC detachment had been established at the college in 1947. South Carolina State was one of the ten colleges and universities—and the

South Carolina State's Bulldog Battalion, shown here in 1973, was one of the first ROTC detachments in the nation to enlist women. From left to right, cadets Mary Bridges, Joyce Leaks, and Patricia Simmons as they depart Miller F. Whittaker Library. Courtesy of the Historical Collection, South Carolina State University

only historically black institution—selected by the Department of the Army for a pilot program to enroll females. S.C. State women were eager to take part in the military as they joined the Bulldog Battalion in ever increasing numbers in the 1970s. Forty-nine women were among the 481 cadets in spring 1973. By fall 1975 there were 214 women in the 639-member cadet corps, and seven had attended summer camp at Fort Bragg that year.[85]

The women cadets were initially regarded as "ladies" and treated deferentially. They were "not eligible for training beyond their normal physical strength." They could not bear arms or take part in marksmanship training. Women were barred from the Rangers and airborne training and field combat training. Dorothy Tucker, an elementary education major from Columbia, was the first woman awarded a four-year ROTC scholarship, in 1973. Women cadets swiftly moved up the leadership ranks. In 1975 two women were in brigade staff positions, another served as battalion executive officer, and two were company commanders. But it was not until 1984 that cadet colonel Gloria Washington became the first woman to command the Bulldog Battalion.[86]

By the time that women began to take part in the military, enrollment in ROTC by S.C. State students had become voluntary. In the midst of the anguish over the Orangeburg Massacre in 1968, some students had demanded an end to compulsory ROTC for freshman and sophomore men. The Vietnam War and the draft had ignited nationwide protests among college students, and South Carolina State was no exception. President Nance and the board of trustees—with some trepidation—agreed to make ROTC optional.[87]

The unpopularity of the Vietnam conflict and an expanding emphasis on Black Nationalism notwithstanding, many administrators, faculty members, and alumni were exceedingly proud of the ROTC program and the commissioned officers it produced. For decades the military served as a desirable career path for African American men who all too often were rejected for employment by corporate America. The U.S. Army represented a viable economic and professional opportunity for a black man with a college degree. But if ROTC participation was voluntary, then many young men might miss that opportunity. If sufficient numbers of S.C. State men rejected ROTC, then there was also the possibility the college would give up the program that President Miller F. Whittaker had worked so diligently to secure in 1947. President Nance admitted in 1970 that "there was much apprehension on our part" for the future of ROTC.[88]

But those fears were ungrounded. Voluntary enrollment in ROTC surged in the 1970s. In 1969–70, 157 freshmen males out of 230 signed up for ROTC. Some of those freshmen may have selected ROTC because the draft remained in place until President Richard Nixon and Congress abolished it in 1971. However, the end of military conscription does not explain the continued growth in the voluntary program over the next decade. The Bulldog Battalion grew to 475 by 1973–74 and to 816 by 1977–78. Part of that growth was due to cross enrollment with Claflin and Voorhees. In 1973–74 there were ninety Claflin and Voorhees students in ROTC at S.C. State, and that number increased to 137 of 639 cadets by 1975–76. The influx of women also bolstered the program.[89]

Attractive scholarships and increased stipends no doubt account for much of the growth in ROTC. In 1977–78 fifty-eight cadets received commissions—eight in the Regular Army and fifty in the Reserve. By 1975–76 eleven officers led by Lieutenant Colonel Burnis L. Hall Jr. served as instructors in the military science program, and they were assisted by seven noncommissioned officers and two administrative assistants. Most freshmen and sophomore cadets did not go on to the advanced corps or receive commissions. In some cases those men and women who had volunteered for the first two years of ROTC became disenchanted with the military. Or the cadre of the Bulldog Battalion became disenchanted with them, perceiving little academic or leadership potential in many of those first- and second-year cadets.[90]

The RQ (ROTC qualifying) test had been an obstacle for many would-be officers in the 1950s and 1960s. A base score of 50 was mandatory for admission to the advanced corps. Some African American army officers complained that the test was culturally biased while other black officers supported the test and the eligibility criteria required

Table 48. ROTC Qualifying Test Results

Year	Number Tested	Number Passed	Percent Passed
1963–64	108	29	26.8%
1965–66	127	49	38.6%
1967–68	107	56	52.3%
1969–70	78	58	74.4%

Source: *Annual Report, 1969–1970*, 31.

for participation in the advanced program of ROTC. The performance of S.C. State students on the test did improve during the 1960s. By the 1970s the RQ test had become one of several factors that included grade point average, SAT scores, and evaluations by the professor of military science that served as predictors of success in the advanced program and leadership potential as a commissioned officer. The RQ test was apparently administered for the last time in 1970–71.[91]

That test was not the only impediment for South Carolina State students who sought a career in the army. Once they had earned their commissions, many young officers performed poorly at the army service schools they attended following graduation. In the five years from 1967–68 to 1971–72, ninety-five officers from S.C. State were evaluated for service school performance. Ten were graded in the upper one-third, twenty-five were in the middle one-third, fifty-four were in the lower one-third, and six failed. Thus over three-fifths (61.7 percent) of those officers finished in the lower third or failed.[92]

Nevertheless the Bulldog Battalion continued to graduate large numbers of students who received commissions in the U.S. Army. From 1948–49 until 1970–71, 598 were commissioned in the Army Reserve while seventy-one received commissions in the Regular Army. By 2010, 2,034 had been commissioned, including 266 women. But some of those commissions went to Claflin, Voorhees, Denmark Technical College, and Orangeburg-Calhoun Technical College students. Fourteen of those commissioned second lieutenants have been promoted to general officers.[93]

CONCLUSION

Having endured and then overcome the trauma of the Orangeburg Massacre, South Carolina State grew steadily during Maceo Nance's first decade as president. Enrollment expanded to over three thousand. Financial support for students swelled. The composition of the teaching staff was transformed with the addition of white and Asian faculty members, and an increasing number of faculty members had earned a doctorate. There was a more open atmosphere on campus as students encountered far fewer restrictions than their predecessors had. More women competed in intercollegiate athletics, and women joined the ROTC program. Small numbers of white students enrolled and then graduated from S.C. State. But as the Civil Rights Act of 1964 formally ended legal segregation and racial exclusion across the South, the matter of South Carolina State College's survival as a historically black public institution remained unresolved.

CHAPTER TEN

Maintaining the Legacy

In January 1981 the Office for Civil Rights in the U.S. Department of Education informed South Carolina governor Richard Riley that the state was in violation of Title VI of the Civil Rights Act of 1964 because it maintained a dual system of higher education among its public colleges and universities. South Carolina was, therefore, obligated to dismantle those vestiges of segregation that had persisted following the legal elimination of separate colleges for black and white South Carolinians. If the state failed to devise and implement a plan to eradicate those remaining elements of segregation, the public colleges and universities would lose federal funds.[1]

The federal government's demand did not come as a surprise to Governor Riley or other state officials. It had been a decade in the making. In 1969 and 1970 the Office for Civil Rights examined segregation in higher education in nineteen states that for decades had supported separate black and white institutions of higher education. Ten of those states were required to develop plans to desegregate their colleges and universities. Surprisingly South Carolina was not one of them. Some commentators speculated that Senator Strom Thurmond's influence in the Nixon administration shielded South Carolina from federal scrutiny.[2]

But after the federal government failed to follow up and compel those ten states to eliminate segregation, in 1972 the NAACP Legal Defense Fund filed a class action lawsuit—*Adams v. Richardson*—against Elliot Richardson, the secretary of health, education, and welfare (HEW) to force HEW to adhere to Title VI and to suspend federal funds to the ten states that HEW had found not in compliance. The Adams case in its assorted appeals and challenges spent nearly two decades in the federal courts before it was finally dismissed in 1990.[3]

In the meantime *Adams* badly split the upper echelons of national black leadership. The National Association for Equal Opportunity in Higher Education (NAFEO) had been founded in 1969, and it represented the 107 presidents of historically black colleges and universities. NAFEO filed an amicus brief in 1973 to dismiss the initial decision in *Adams*. NAFEO contended that the NAACP Legal Defense Fund victory in the 1972 *Adams* decision posed a grave threat to the survival of black institutions. If states in response to that decision entirely eradicated their dual systems of higher education, then the public black colleges and universities would vanish. NAFEO asked that states have the right to maintain historically black institutions.[4]

As a result of the ongoing *Adams* litigation in 1977, federal civil rights officials were required to investigate and evaluate those states that had operated dual systems of higher education. By 1979 they turned their attention to South Carolina and visited six of the state colleges and universities including S.C. State. Then Governor Riley received notification in January 1981 that South Carolina was not in compliance with Title VI.[5]

Anticipating that federal decision, Riley responded quickly and positively. "I believe in desegregation," he declared. He had no intention of challenging Washington or defending the racial status quo in the state's system of higher education. Senator Strom Thurmond pledged to work with Riley, but he was less enchanted with Washington's interest in the Palmetto State. "I'll cooperate with Governor Riley to keep the federal government's filthy hands off the state of South Carolina."[6]

Riley and his staff assembled a blue ribbon committee to formulate a desegregation plan for the state's colleges and universities. The governor asked Bankers Trust chief executive and former University of South Carolina football player W. W. "Hootie" Johnson to chair the committee and James E. Bostic, the chair of the Commission on Higher Education, to serve as vice chair. The twenty-three-member committee included the presidents of the University of South Carolina, Clemson University, Francis Marion College, the Citadel, and South Carolina State College.

But desegregation was too important an issue to be left to educators and academics to resolve. Political leaders would take charge. Thus the panel also included attorney general Daniel R. McLeod; Lieutenant Governor Nancy Stephenson; Senate Judiciary Committee chair L. Marion Gressette; House of Representatives Speaker Ramon Schwartz Jr.; the chair of the House Judiciary Committee, Robert J. Sheheen; the chair of the Legislative Black Caucus, McKinley Washington Jr.; James E. Clyburn, the commissioner of the State Human Affairs Commission; Milton Kimpson, an executive assistant to Governor Riley, and several other people. There were eight African Americans and one white woman on the committee. No faculty members or students were asked to serve.[7]

NEGOTIATING DESEGREGATION

If anyone on the committee entertained the notion that S.C. State should be sacrificed as a black institution for the sake of eliminating segregation and creating a unified system of higher education, they were hastily disabused of that thought by M. Maceo Nance Jr. He made it abundantly clear that African Americans would rally to the cause of the college. "It's the only damn thing in the state we run," Nance proclaimed. "We'll take over the University [of South Carolina] if they want, but the University will not take us over." Somewhat taken aback by Nance's stern defense of the black college, "Hootie" Johnson conceded that "S.C. State is a very important symbol to blacks. They view it as their school and run it with great pride."[8]

But the administrators and supporters of the traditionally white institutions were also unprepared to give up programs or make major concessions in the name of desegregation. When Nance proposed that South Carolina State take over the University of South Carolina–Aiken, a four-year institution, as well as the two-year Orangeburg Calhoun Technical College, there were immediate objections. State senator L. Marion Gressette, whose senate district included both S.C. State and Orangeburg Calhoun Tech, was not in favor of the black college taking over two predominantly white schools. "I don't want to rob Peter to pay Paul. If we need changes, let's do it within each institution."[9]

With the colleges and universities so determined to protect their turf, what realistic chances were there to alter significantly the racial composition of these historically white and black institutions? What new programs, for example, might be created at South Carolina State that would increase the enrollment of white students? At a meeting in Atlanta with "Hootie" Johnson, James E. Bostic, and James Solomon, the regional director of the Office of Civil Rights, William H. Thomas, suggested the creation of an engineering program at South Carolina State. That was unacceptable, however, because Clemson, the University of South Carolina, and the Citadel already had established engineering programs.

Bostic then proposed the development of a doctoral degree in education at S.C. State. But it was quickly pointed out that it would duplicate a doctoral program in educational administration that the University of South Carolina offered. Perhaps—as the discussion continued—the university's program could be transferred to South Carolina State. This possibility created a rich historical irony. When the first graduate programs on the master's degree level had been established at S.C. State in 1947, it was to prevent the enrollment of black students in the graduate programs at the state's white institutions. Now a doctoral program was proposed for S.C. State with the expectation it would attract white students.[10]

That doctoral program became the lynchpin of the desegregation plan, but it first had to weather a storm of controversy. White public school administrators and faculty members in the School of Education at the university—who had not been consulted about the transfer—opposed relinquishing the program to South Carolina State. However, Carl Carpenter, the vice president for academic affairs at S.C. State, who had earned a graduate degree in education at the university, observed that those university faculty members and the state's school administrators too often consulted each other on the selection of public school administrators throughout South Carolina. If S.C. State offered the doctoral degree, it might break the monopoly of white public school officials.[11]

"Hootie" Johnson had to exert considerable pressure on University of South Carolina president James Holderman to move the doctoral program to S.C. State. The Commission on Higher Education later approved the change by a slim 8–7 vote, and that came only after chairman James Bostic warned that the failure to turn the program over to S.C. State would jeopardize the entire desegregation plan.[12]

Having overcome that hurdle, the remainder of the desegregation plan was easier to negotiate. S.C. State would develop a bachelor's degree in nursing, an agribusiness program at the bachelor's and master's levels, and an undergraduate nuclear engineering program. (The nuclear engineering program was suspended for a time because the

Savannah River nuclear plant, which was to be directly involved in the new program, had been scheduled for closure by the federal government.) Funds also would be provided to S.C. State to enhance programs in business and engineering technology, to employ additional faculty, and to increase the salaries of the current members of the faculty so that those salaries would achieve parity with faculty members at Winthrop and the Citadel.

The desegregation plan included commitments by the predominantly white colleges and universities to increase the first-time enrollment of black students from 918 in 1981 to 2,295 in 1985. African American administrators would increase from thirty-two to fifty-two during the same five-year span, and fifty-one additional black faculty members would be employed by those white institutions. There was no corresponding quantitative commitment to expand the number of white students at S.C. State. The new programs in nursing and agribusiness and the doctoral program in educational administration were expected to attract white students.[13]

IMPLEMENTATION OF THE PLAN FOR DESEGREGATION

South Carolina's political and higher education leadership took much satisfaction in completing the five-year plan to desegregate the colleges and universities within the sixty-day deadline imposed by federal authorities. The 359-page plan was submitted on March 9, and federal officials approved its implementation on July 17, 1981. Between 1981 and 1986 South Carolina regularly submitted reports to the Office of Civil Rights (OCR) in the Department of Education documenting the progress that colleges and universities were or were not achieving in eliminating segregation. The general assembly appropriated $19.8 million to fund the plan, and $14 million went to South Carolina State.[14]

In early 1988 the OCR notified Governor Carroll Campbell that the state had fulfilled the commitments set forth in its 1981 plan and had effectively desegregated its state colleges and universities. "The state has substantially complied with the terms of the plan. Accordingly, South Carolina's system of public higher education is now in compliance with Title VI, and no further desegregation measures will be required by OCR." South Carolina was free of further federal supervision.[15]

SUCCESSFUL DESEGREGATION?

In fact South Carolina *had not* achieved meaningful compliance nor had it eliminated the vestiges of segregation in its public institutions of higher education. The number of black students who enrolled for the first time in the traditionally white schools declined by 542 students between 1981 and 1985. The percentage of black students enrolled in the predominantly white colleges and universities increased only 1 percent in five years—from 10 percent to 11.1 percent. The number of black administrators declined from thirty-two in 1981 to twenty-one in 1985. However, the number of black faculty members at the white institutions increased from seventy-six in 1981 to ninety-five in 1985. Each institution's board of trustees did have at least one black member by 1986, and the number of black trustees had increased from fourteen in 1981 to twenty-four in 1986.[16]

The percentage of white students at South Carolina State remained steady at 3.7 percent from 1981 to 1985. In the new nursing program, twenty-four of twenty-eight students were white. There were two white students and sixty-eight black students enrolled as undergraduates in the agribusiness program. The graduate program in education established in 1983 consisted of a doctorate in education and a specialist in education. In 1985 the doctoral program had thirty-nine black students and twenty-seven white students, and the enrollment in the educational specialist program had thirty-five black students and two white students—a total of seventy-four black students and twenty-nine white students in the two programs.[17]

Thus white student enrollment at S.C. State did not increase measurably despite the addition of the enhancement programs. The University of South Carolina lost its Ed.D. program in educational administration, but it retained its Ph.D. program in educational administration. The university also maintained doctoral programs in curriculum and instruction, health education administration, special education administration, and student personnel services. And the university never actually transferred its Ed.D. program to the black institution. No graduate students or faculty members made the move to Orangeburg. Instead S.C. State employed new faculty members and administrators to initiate a new program.[18]

Furthermore the doctoral program at South Carolina State would never represent more than a small white enclave on a campus where most of the students were undergraduates who lived in the residence halls. Doctoral students—white or black—would rarely come in contact with most students in an academic or social setting. But then no political or educational leaders were publicly willing to advocate increasing the number of white students at South Carolina State to the extent that the college might lose its historic legacy. Speaking on the campus at Founder's Day in 1981, Governor Richard Riley reassured the audience. "We must not intentionally do harm to this institution by stripping it of its rightful identity as a black college."[19]

However, the desegregation plan did commit the state to pump $14 million into South Carolina State, which helped remedy long-standing disparities in programs and

Table 49. Average Faculty Salaries by Rank at the Citadel, Winthrop, and S.C. State 1985–86

	# Professor	# Assoc. Prof.	# Asst. Prof.	# Instructor
Citadel	49: $38,124	52: $31,029	48: $26,487	6: $17,625
Winthrop	61: $38,287	54: $30,667	68: $25,384	38: $18,266
S.C. State	46: $38,145	62: $31,012	62: $25,814	58: $20,219

Source: *Final Comprehensive Report on Implementation of the South Carolina Higher Education Desegregation Plan 1981–82 through 1985–86* (Columbia: South Carolina Commission on Higher Education, 1986), table 8, 25.

in faculty salaries. Fourteen new faculty members were employed. More than $2 million was spent over five years to bolster faculty salaries 20 percent to a level comparable to salaries paid at Winthrop and the Citadel.

ACADEMIC PROGRAMS AT S.C. STATE

The three new programs that S.C. State acquired through the desegregation plan—the doctorate in educational administration, the bachelor's and master's degrees in agribusiness, and the undergraduate nursing program—were the most visible manifestations of the ongoing academic changes at the institution during the 1970s and 1980s. The college had eliminated the agricultural program and dropped its courses in agronomy, animal husbandry, and horticulture by 1971. Low enrollments in library and media studies led to the termination of that program in the mid-1980s.[20]

Several of the vocational programs that had been a staple of the college curriculum since its founding were also abolished. Gone were courses in tailoring, masonry, and painting. But the College of Industrial Education and Engineering Technology was still a curious amalgam that provided courses in woodworking, metalwork, and automobile mechanics as well as driver's education while simultaneously offering more sophisticated work in engineering technology. However, the trades courses that did survive were to prepare young men (and women) for careers as teachers in industrial arts rather than to enter the job market as skilled laborers. The programs in civil engineering technology, electrical engineering technology, and mechanical engineering technology required students to have a solid foundation of mathematics, physics, and computer science. That technology program was subsequently accredited by the Accreditation Board for Engineering and Technologies (ABET).[21]

The new undergraduate agribusiness program was less an initiative to promote agriculture and more an attempt to offer students a curriculum that would enable them to pursue careers with businesses and corporations that had connections to agriculture. Agribusiness was not designed to prepare students to be productive farmers. In early 1985, for example, the new program sponsored a talk by Gil Spears, the director of advertising for *Successful Farming Magazine.* He discussed career opportunities in advertising and marketing to an audience of about one hundred students. The agribusiness major was not exactly a brand-new program either. In the mid-1960s, the School of Agriculture had featured an undergraduate program in agribusiness economics and business that was intended to ready students for careers in farm management, for agricultural extension work, and for sales and management positions with business.[22]

The new nursing program also had a predecessor in a cooperative diploma program devised in the mid-1970s between S.C. State and the nurse-training program affiliated with the Orangeburg Regional Hospital. The nursing students—all of them women—would enroll in thirty-one semester hours of course work at S.C. State. Most of those courses were in biology and chemistry. The thirty to thirty-five students lived at the nurses' residence across the street from the Orangeburg Regional Hospital on Carolina Avenue. Those who completed the hospital training program were eligible to take the licensing exam for registered nurses. When the new Department of Nursing

The first graduates of the nursing program under the implementation of the state plan for desegregation are shown with the chair of the nursing program, Judy Bradley, on the right. Courtesy of the Historical Collection, South Carolina State University

was established as part of the desegregation plan in 1986 under the leadership of Judy Bradley, it was for men and women who sought a bachelor of science degree in nursing. Only licensed registered nurses with CPR training who had malpractice insurance were qualified for admission to the new program.[23]

The speech and hearing program and its clinic became one of the most recognized and respected programs sponsored by S.C. State in the last third of the twentieth century. It provided undergraduate and graduate instruction. Over the years it offered speech and hearing evaluations to thousands of students as well as local residents, and it furnished therapy to countless children and adults who had hearing and speech problems.

Dr. Harold Powell was the inspiration behind the program, and he presided over its creation and rapid expansion. A native of Jacksonboro, South Carolina, Powell served six years in the U.S. Air Force before enrolling at S. C State College. He served as the editor of the *Collegian* prior to graduating in 1961. Powell earned a Ph.D. in speech pathology and audiology from Penn State and then returned to his alma mater. Almost immediately he secured $5,000 to begin building and equipping a clinic that would be housed for a time in Nix Hall, the former residence hall for single male faculty.[24]

Freshmen students as well as Felton Laboratory School students were tested for speech and hearing problems. Each weekday afternoon the clinic was also open to the public. Therapy was provided to individuals diagnosed with speech and hearing defects. Those with the financial means were asked to pay for the service while those who lacked funds were treated without cost. Among the clinic's first clients were the parents of seven children who could afford therapy while the parents of four other young people were treated at no charge.[25]

Henry and Esther Tecklenberg had five sons, and one—Michael—had been born deaf. The Tecklenbergs became members of the local business community after they had moved to Orangeburg from Massachusetts. Esther Tecklenberg became a strong supporter of the clinic and an enthusiastic booster of the college after Michael learned to speak with the help of clinic personnel. The Tecklenbergs donated $500 to the speech and hearing program. In 1971 Governor John West appointed Esther Tecklenberg to the college board of trustees. She was the first woman to serve on the board.[26]

The South Carolina Commission on Higher Education (CHE) approved a master of arts program in speech pathology and audiology in 1974. The American Speech and Hearing Association required practitioners to possess a master's degree for certification. Students who held only a bachelor's degree had limited career choices. The first graduate students enrolled that summer. In the meantime demand for the clinic's services mushroomed. By 1975 the clinic provided speech and language screening to 4,235 people and hearing evaluations to 6,010. More than three hundred individuals received therapy. Clinic personnel also screened 2,278 Head Start children at several locations around South Carolina.[27]

Funds from paying clients steadily increased. The clinic's billings totaled $24,023 in 1985. With the assistance of the local Sertoma Club, the clinic offered speech and hearing evaluations to 239 people at the Orangeburg Rose Festival in 1986. Still the situation was not altogether rosy. Dr. Joan A. Lawrence, a faculty member in the speech and hearing program, wrote on behalf of the Clinical Services Committee and complained that faculty members were increasingly unable to keep up with the burgeoning demands made on them and on the clinic. They needed more secretarial and clerical assistance. The telephone system was inadequate, and faculty members were hard pressed to cope with both teaching and clinical responsibilities. Lawrence asked Nance to meet with the committee. Nance politely declined and suggested that the issues be taken to Harold Powell.[28]

THE MUSEUM AND PLANETARIUM

The opening of the I. P. Stanback Museum and Planetarium in 1980 was one of the bright moments in the history of South Carolina State. Although it was built of the red brick that was so familiar among most campus structures, the new facility stood in sharp contrast to bulky and boxy buildings like Lowman, Miller, and Wilkinson Halls. From the front view, the one-story museum and planetarium featured oversized and recessed square windows on the left with a graceful cylindrical two-story wall on the right that housed the planetarium.

The credit for the museum belongs to M. Maceo Nance. In the mid-1970s the president approached artist and art professor Leo F. Twiggs about the possibility of enriching campus life with the addition of a museum. Twiggs was taken aback. "I thought he was joking." But it was no joke. Nance succeeded in raising $100,000 in funding from the S. S. Kresge Foundation and $50,000 from the Francis Ley Springs Foundation. With that seed money, Nance turned to L. Marion Gressette, the majority leader of the state senate. The powerful senator from nearby Calhoun County was receptive to the idea, and nearly $1 million in additional funding was included in the college appropriation for the museum.[29]

While there had been no burning desire on the campus for a museum prior to Nance's brainstorm, Twiggs was eager to capitalize on the project. The Whittaker Gallery in the small and damp basement of the library had been the sole space available to display visiting artistic exhibitions as well as the works of students and faculty members. However, when word of the proposed museum began to circulate, Clemmie Webber, a professor of science education who had long sought a planetarium for the college, successfully lobbied Nance to add it to the museum.[30]

Construction of the $1,125,000 facility began in September 1977. At 16,750 square feet, it included one large and one small gallery, a spacious lobby and reception area, offices, studios for printmaking, ceramics, and sculpture, and storage space. The planetarium had a Viewlex projector capable of depicting the sky on the forty-foot dome from any point on earth from twelve thousand years in the past to twelve thousand years in the future. The structure was named in honor of the chairman of the board of trustees, I. P. Stanback, who was the first African American to hold that position.[31]

Leo Twiggs, already a widely recognized artist for his works in batik, served as the first executive director of the museum. He was determined that the Stanback would serve the entire Orangeburg region as well as the college. To that end he created a community advisory committee that included Clemmie Webber; Arthur and Lois Lusty, a local couple with a passion for the arts; Arthur Rose, who was an artist at Claflin who had served as a mentor to Twiggs during the latter's undergraduate years at Claflin; and Mary Williams, a devoted community leader.[32]

Don Walter, who taught astronomy, directed the planetarium and organized its programs. With eighty-two plush seats that tilted back, visitors could gaze at the stars and planets as they traversed the darkened sky. Narration, music, and images accompanied the dramatic views of this and more distant solar systems that were reflected off the dome.

The first major museum exhibit was "Harlem on My Mind." Twiggs persuaded the staff at the Schomburg Branch of the New York Public Library to donate approximately two hundred enormous black and white photographs to S.C. State and the new Stanback Museum. The photos had originally appeared as an exhibition at the Metropolitan Museum of Art from January to April 1969. The images of prosperous and not-so-prosperous, famous and not-so-famous residents of Harlem in the 1920s and 1930s offered an evocative glimpse into urban life and African American culture.[33]

In its first eight months, the museum and planetarium attracted 10,598 visitors. As pleased as Twiggs was with this warm response, there were matters of concern. The faculty and academic departments had been slow to incorporate the museum into their educational programs. Twiggs found himself overextended as he served as the museum's executive director and curator as well as a faculty member with a heavy teaching load, who was also a working artist.[34]

But most worrisome was a persistent leak in the roof of the planetarium. It left water stains on the dome, created a musty odor, and threatened serious damage to the $250,000 projector and control panel. For a time, despite repeated attempts, it seemed nothing could be done to stem the dripping water. Eventually Luther Battiste and a crew from facilities management managed to seal the leak.[35]

THE RADIO STATION

During the construction of the museum and planetarium, efforts to establish a campus radio station inched ahead. Like the museum the radio station was Nance's idea, although students had raised the issue in their 1978 demands. He asked Charles Roberts, the director of the Instructional Media Center (IMC) to spearhead the effort to establish the station. Roberts, who had no experience in broadcasting, found that it was no simple or quick task to navigate the federal bureaucracy to acquire a license as well as funding for the station. The gestation period lasted six long years from the preliminary discussions in 1979 to the first broadcast in 1985.[36]

To obtain a license from the Federal Communications Commission to operate a nonprofit, public radio station, the college retained Thomas C. Gherardi, a Washington, D.C., attorney who specialized in communications law. Gherardi was responsible for submitting the application for a license and expediting its approval. To obtain the funding to build the station and transmitter, the college sought a grant through the Public Telecommunications Facilities Program of the U.S. Department of Commerce. With the timely intervention of U.S. senator Strom Thurmond, S.C. State was poised to receive an award of $164,000 toward the station's total cost of $219,000. The college would have to furnish the balance of $55,000.[37]

A potentially serious obstacle to the station loomed, however, in the person of Henry J. Cauthen. As the longtime executive director of the South Carolina Educational Television and Radio networks, Cauthen was concerned that a new college station might compete with or interfere with the broadcast signals of public radio stations currently operating in Columbia and Sumter. Maceo Nance rushed to reassure Cauthen that a station at the college posed no conflict with the mission or broadcasts of the public radio network because its "sole purpose [would be] developing a training mechanism for our students in broadcasting." Thus mollified Cauthen did not object to the Department of Commerce grant.[38]

WSSB FM went on the air in 1985. With studios in the basement of Nance Hall and an antenna atop a 225-foot tower behind Bulldog Stadium, the new station broadcast at eighty thousand watts of power—making it one of the most powerful college radio stations in the nation, with a signal that reached several counties in the midlands and lowcountry. Gil Harris was the first general manager, and he was assisted by program director Debra Derr. The station offered an eclectic mix of music ranging from jazz and rhythm and blues to gospel. It also provided locally produced news and information programs as well as broadcasts of the men's and women's basketball teams, and as Nance had promised, it afforded training opportunities in broadcasting for students.[39]

The presence of a museum, planetarium, and radio station on the campus would have astonished earlier generations of faculty and students. For much of its history, S.C. State barely had sufficient infrastructure and funding to provide its students with an adequate education. Most of the credit for the new programs in speech and audiology and in nursing and for the new facilities belongs to Maceo Nance as well as to administrators and faculty members including Algernon S. Belcher, Carl Carpenter, Judy Bradley, Harold Powell, Leo Twiggs, and Charles Roberts.

POLITICAL EMPOWERMENT

Times had changed, and the political winds that had blown across South Carolina for decades shifted radically during Nance's nineteen-year tenure. Thanks largely to the civil rights movement in general and the Voting Rights Act of 1965 in particular, Nance and the college enjoyed access to a political system that had been largely denied to previous presidents and supporters of S.C. State. As Jim Crow withered, black political power grew.

The Voting Rights Act of 1965 enfranchised thousands of black voters. In 1958 there were fifty-eight thousand registered black voters in South Carolina, and that number swelled to 220,000 by 1970. For the first time since John W. Bolts completed a term in the legislature in 1902, there were black members serving in the South Carolina General Assembly. James Felder, I. S. Leevy Johnson, and Herbert U. Fielding were elected to the house in 1970, and they broke the sixty-eight-year white legislative monopoly.[40]

White Democrats and Republicans soon found themselves scrambling to gain the support of black voters. White political leaders saw Maceo Nance as a visible black ally with strong ties to the black community, and for the first time many of these politicians came to recognize that S.C. State was held in high esteem by most of the state's black residents. Leaders like Strom Thurmond and L. Marion Gressette who had spent their earlier political careers extolling the virtues of racial segregation changed course and became fast friends of the college and among its reliable supporters.

Thurmond had voted against the 1964 Civil Rights Act and against the Voting Rights Act of 1965. In opposing the earlier Civil Rights Act of 1957, Thurmond filibustered in the Senate chamber a record twenty-four hours and eighteen minutes. But in 1982 he voted in favor of a twenty-five-year extension of the Voting Rights Act, and he supported the establishment of a national holiday in honor of Dr. Martin Luther King Jr. Gressette had chaired the segregation committee—otherwise known as the South Carolina School Committee—following the *Brown* decision in 1954. Originally a staunch opponent of integration, he became a devoted friend of Nance and an advocate for S.C. State.[41]

Nance himself emerged as a savvy political operator. He had received his indoctrination in South Carolina politics in the 1960s as the college business manager under

President Benner C. Turner. It was Nance who often presented the proposed college budget to house and senate committees. He came to enjoy the "give and take" of legislative negotiations while the reserved Turner, who disliked the rough and tumble world of politics, preferred to remain in Orangeburg.

Assuming the college presidency in 1968 gave Nance the opportunity to plunge into a political system in a state of transition. But Nance had to tread a political tightrope as he sought support from both Democrats and Republicans. As the number of black voters grew in the 1970s and 1980s, conservative white voters abandoned the Democratic Party and joined the once-dormant Republican Party. Republican senator Strom Thurmond led the exodus out of the Democratic Party when he became a Republican in 1964.

No twentieth-century South Carolina politician was of more help or better known for responding swiftly to constituents than Strom Thurmond. The senator would intervene again and again on behalf of the college during the Nance years. It was, after all, Thurmond who had contacted Department of Commerce officials in 1982 to help secure funds for WSSB. Thurmond personally called and then sent a telegram in 1974 to ask the secretary of health, education, and welfare, Casper Weinberger, to approve S.C. State's application for an Advanced Institutional Development Program grant. The senator told Weinberger that help was needed to improve education for low-income students. S.C. State was awarded the AIDP grant. In 1977 Thurmond informed Nance that the college would receive a grant for $45,000 for a training program in speech pathology and a $30,000 grant for dealing with special education students who were "severely mentally retarded" and with students who were "severely emotionally disturbed."[42]

The Republican senator also took S.C. State student Armstrong Williams under his wing as an intern and protégé. A native of Marion County, where his father was a prosperous tobacco farmer, Williams served two terms as the Student Government Association president from 1979 to 1981. His close connection to Thurmond opened doors for Williams among prominent conservatives in the Reagan and George H. W. Bush administrations. Following his internship and graduation, he worked in the Department of Agriculture, and then at the invitation of its newly appointed chairman, Clarence Thomas, Williams moved over to the Equal Employment Opportunity Commission. He went on to establish a Washington public relations firm with Stedman Graham, the longtime consort of Oprah Winfrey. Williams also wrote a syndicated conservative newspaper column while hosting a radio talk show. But some of the luster of Williams's Republican credentials was tarnished when it was revealed in 2005 that he accepted over $200,000 to offer support in his newspaper column for President George W. Bush's educational reform, "No Child Left Behind."[43]

Democratic congressman Butler Derrick also turned to S.C. State in search of an employee. In a "personal and confidential" letter to Nance in 1975, Derrick explained that he wanted to hire "a young black person" at $9,500 per year from Derrick's Third Congressional District. "I prefer that this individual be attractive, intelligent and certified as being able to type at least 60 words per minute." There is no record of Nance's response. White politicians were not bashful about asking Nance for political favors.

Democrat J. Claytor Arrants, a lawyer from Camden, appealed Nance in 1974 to "say a kind word" to Orangeburg house members in support of Arrants's candidacy for speaker of the house. Arrants hoped to replace veteran speaker Sol Blatt.[44]

Nance was quick to contact politicians to insist (and sometimes demand) that they give support to the college and to programs that affected African Americans. When federal funds were slashed from the Department of Education's proposed budget for several programs, Nance sent telegrams to House member Carroll Campbell and Senators Thurmond and Ernest Hollings asking that money be restored for the three programs: the Educational Talent Search, assistance for low-income families, and funds for low-income students attending postsecondary schools. The three legislators cosigned a letter to Secretary Shirley Hufstedler of the Department of Education requesting reinstatement of the funds.[45]

When there was a threatened reduction in funding for Pell Grants in 1981, Nance dispatched appeals to the entire South Carolina congressional delegation. Nance wanted money restored to the level appropriated in 1980. He added that time was critical. Action was needed by April so that the Pell Grants would be available for the fall semester. Among the positive responses that Nance received was one from Democratic representative Kenneth Holland, who pointed out that he had received federal help as a college student—"I am the product of the federal student loan assistance program."[46]

Later in 1981 Nance asked South Carolina's delegation in the U.S. House to support an agricultural bill that included funding for cooperative extension and research work at the black land-grant colleges—usually referred to as the 1890 program. The bill narrowly passed 205–203, and Butler Derrick, Thomas Hartnett, Carroll Campbell, and John Napier promptly informed Nance that they had voted for the bill.[47]

To mobilize support for pay raises for faculty and administrators in 1975, Nance cautioned state senators that they needed to increase compensation more than the miserly amount included in the house appropriations bill. Nance complained that the house measure provided just a 2 percent increase for those earning $15,000 or more per year. This, Nance pointed out, would penalize "middle and upper ranges of people who carry the major responsibility of instruction and leadership." He maintained that their current and proposed salaries were not competitive and that "it seems illogical to offend these employees even more." Nance then raised the dreaded specter of unionization—something almost no southern politician wanted to contemplate. He cautioned that the failure to address the financial needs of public workers might "stimulate an interest in collective bargaining among government employees." Nance continued, "South Carolina is relatively free of this development today, and I presume we prefer it that way." It is difficult, however, to imagine state employees and especially the faculty members and administrators at S.C. State giving even remote consideration to organizing a union. Furthermore state law prohibited labor unions among public workers.[48]

BLACK LAWMAKERS

Nance was the first of South Carolina State College's presidents who could collaborate with elected black state leaders—and he welcomed that opportunity. He personally contributed money to the campaigns of four black men who ran for seats in the state legislature in 1970. Three of them—James Felder, Herbert Fielding, and I. S. Leevy Johnson—won the Democratic primary election, which at the time assured victory in the general election. Only James Clyburn lost. But Clyburn managed to survive that defeat and later moved on to a larger political stage in Washington, D.C.[49]

The three black legislators had barely taken office in early 1971 when they promised Nance that they would work to restore $53,000 that had been cut from the appropriation for S.C. State by the State Budget and Control Board. I. S. Leevy Johnson told Nance, "I called to let you know that you could rest assured that Herb [Fielding], Jim [Felder], and I will fight vigorously to block any such actions on the part of the legislature if it ever reaches the floor." He indicated, however, that the House Ways and Means Committee might in the meantime reinstate the funds.[50]

The black men elected in the 1970s were novices in a political system where seniority gave enormous advantage to legislators who had held office for decades. But the number of black political leaders steadily grew. By 1982 fifteen members of the 124-member South Carolina house were black, and fourteen of them were men. (Juanita White was the only African American woman in the general assembly in that session, and there were no black state senators until the election of I. DeQuincey Newman in 1983. Juanita Googins, a 1957 graduate of S.C. State, had been the first African American woman elected to the legislature in 1974.) In 1981, at the instigation of McKinley Washington, the chair of the legislative black caucus, and with the backing of Nance, the caucus sponsored a one-day conference on the S.C. State campus in January 1982. Edward R. Jackson, the chair of the Department of Political Science and History, coordinated a series of workshops for elected and appointed local leaders who came mostly from the state's rural counties and communities.[51]

Richard E. Fields, a black family court judge from Charleston, wanted the general assembly to elect him to the Ninth Circuit Court in 1978, and he asked the politically well connected Nance for assistance. The S.C. State president arranged a meeting between Fields and senate majority leader L. Marion Gressette. Fields was elected in 1980 and served until he retired from the bench in 1992.[52]

But Nance did not always accede to requests for intervention. Robert C. Nix, a member of the U.S. House of Representatives from Philadelphia and the son of former S.C. State dean Nelson C. Nix, asked Nance as "a personal favor" to have Samuel L. Perry admitted as a student in 1970. Nance respectfully turned Nix down, explaining that Perry's poor academic record and weak score on the college entrance exam prevented his acceptance.[53]

THE BOARD OF TRUSTEES

Nance was every bit as skillful in dealing with the board of trustees as he was with the politicians. He earned the trustees' confidence and then their praise with his firm leadership over the students and faculty, and with his extensive knowledge of the inner workings of the college. The board typically met quarterly in February, May, August, and November, and the trustees granted Nance wide latitude in the day-to-day operations of the institution. They routinely approved requests by Nance. With little debate they dropped compulsory ROTC, approved the decision to join the Mid-Eastern Athletic Conference, agreed to purchase and sell various parcels of real estate, and agreed to forbid interdorm visitation. The trustees did not begin to examine intensively academic issues or financial matters until the 1980s. They were usually content to read the annual reports and to listen to Nance's commentaries. Nance expected the trustees to heed his guidance, and not the other way around.

Nance sharply rebuked I. P. Stanback, the chairman of the board, in 1971 after Stanback—who also served on the Commission on Higher Education—seconded a motion at a CHE meeting that had the effect of endorsing a budget request that did not include an increased appropriation for S.C. State. An irritated Nance wrote Stanback, "As I indicated to you and the board of trustees at the last meeting, we here at the College are completely opposed to the recommendations set forth by the commissioner and his staff." He let Stanback know that the board chairman's conduct put S.C. State in "a very embarrassing position" at a time when the college needed additional funding.[54]

Hugh Lane, the chairman of the board of the Citizens and Southern National Bank in Charleston, joined the S.C. State trustees in 1969, and he suggested to Nance that board members needed access to more information about the college and greater input from its students. "I do not believe the trustees can have a complete involvement unless and until they have a broader knowledge of the academic program and a broader knowledge of the wishes of the majority of the students." He also sought more financial data. Nance did not dispute Lane's points and agreed that the role of the board "in the formulation of the budget perhaps was negligible." But it mattered little. Lane resigned from the board in 1971 to accept an appointment by Governor John C. West to chair the new State Housing Authority.[55]

The board granted Nance a five-year contract in 1973, and they presented him with a framed portrait in a ceremony at the Lace House in Columbia attended by Governor West and his wife, Lois. Five years later, in 1978, on the occasion of his tenth anniversary as president, the board recognized Nance in a resolution that gushed with such extreme words of admiration that they might have embarrassed the usually unflappable Nance. "He personifies intelligent good will. We honor his nobility of character and his fine friendly personality. He is truly one of God's noblemen. He is a most gracious gentleman manifesting the grace of God." Nor did they forget Mrs. Nance. "We rejoice that his wife, Julie, is a most intelligent, lovely and charming person who renders fine service to the College." It almost seemed as if the college had reached a state of idyllic perfection under Nance's leadership.[56]

FINANCIAL ISSUES

Almost, but not quite. Financial management issues plagued the college. Internal audits and state auditors identified problems that seemed to defy solution under Harold A. Jenkins, the vice president for business and finance. Bank statements were reconciled by hand, not by computer, and the drawn-out process lagged thirteen to thirty-three months behind timely completion. Bank deposits went unrecorded. Record keeping was careless. Loans were made to students who had failed to repay earlier loans. Property records were not maintained for equipment purchased through externally funded grants. Property owned by the federal government was not labeled and identified. Accounts were maintained for grants that had not been active since 1969–70.[57]

The finance committee of the board of trustees found deficiencies in 1984 that had been disclosed in two separate and previous audits by outside firms. The S.C. State business office did not have an operations manual, which was customary in most business offices and established the procedures by which transactions would be conducted. The administration promised to prepare such a manual. But the situation was so dire that the finance committee suggested that the business office might need outside professional assistance.[58]

The assorted audits and inquiries indicated a lack of sound business practices combined with a measure of ineptitude rather than blatant dishonesty. But persistent rumors of corruption and outright theft circulated during the Nance years. An investigation by state auditors and by SLED (State Law Enforcement Division) in 1979 uncovered no illegal activity. But Nance did offer one chilling revelation. Harold Jenkins had an ice-making machine at his residence that belonged to the college. He was sent a letter of reprimand, and the ice maker was returned to the campus.[59]

Historically S.C. State had been grossly under funded by a state legislature that was not especially generous to its white colleges and universities. In 1963–64 South Carolina was last among ten southern states in appropriations for higher education based on state tax revenues. But the changing political and racial environment brought vastly increased state appropriations for higher education. By 1973–74 South Carolina had jumped to first among the ten states. Maceo Nance, through his carefully cultivated relationships with influential politicians, was able to tap the state's coffers for more money than the black college had ever received. Funding from the state for S.C. State skyrocketed during Nance's presidency. But S.C. State did not quite achieve a financial nirvana as those increases occurred in such an erratic and disjointed way over nearly two decades that it tested the patience of Nance and of supporters of the institution.

The Commission on Higher Education (CHE), which was established in 1967, created formula funding for colleges and universities in a mostly unsuccessful effort to eliminate inequities in allocating money among the state's institutions. Those colleges and universities—especially the University of South Carolina and Clemson University,

Table 50. S.C. State College Revenue

	1969–70	1981–82	1985–86
Student tuition and fees	$587,457	$1,288,113	$3,618,516
State appropriations	$2,312,479	$12,706,649	$18,877,377

Sources: *Annual Report, 1969–1970,* appendix 6; *Annual Report, 1981–1982,* 69; *Annual Report, 1985–1986,* 55. The annual reports in the mid- and late 1970s lack budget information. The revenues from auxiliary, private, and federal sources are not included.

but sometimes S.C. State—bypassed the commission and continued to appeal directly to legislators for limited state dollars. Moreover fluctuations in the state and national economies made it ultimately impossible to maintain full formula funding. (CHE also waged an uphill struggle to eliminate duplication in academic programs among the state's schools.) The economy dipped precipitously in the mid-1970s and again in the early 1980s, and S.C. State and other institutions saw their budgets slashed.[60]

Nance complained, for example, about the 1981 cuts. Rather than confront Democratic governor Richard Riley, Nance contacted to state auditor Edgar A. Vaughn Jr. to express his unhappiness over the proposed reduction of $265,292 that came on top of a reduction of $350,565 the previous year. Nance was especially irate that funds set aside for program enhancement and faculty salaries as part of the state's desegregation plan were also included in the reduction. Altogether the college would have $1,426,596 less in 1981–82 that it had had in 1980–81 even as enrollment continued to increase. For good measure Nance sent copies of his letter to Vaughn to the members of the Legislative Black Caucus. But the reductions were not restored.[61]

STUDENT FEES

Tuition and fees charged to students more than doubled in the fifteen years between 1970 and 1985. Although African American students were now eligible to attend any state or private college or university, enrollments at S.C. State grew steadily into the 1980s. The decades-old problem of insufficient campus housing persisted into the 1970s. More than four hundred students were rejected in the fall of 1969 because of the lack of rooms. But with the construction of new dormitories and the renovation of sixty-year-old Manning and Bradham Halls, the critical housing shortage was largely alleviated by the late 1970s. The first and second Benjamin E. Mays Halls, Sojourner Truth Hall, and John H. Mitchell Hall as well as Queens Village—apartments for married students—were built. The college also purchased the former Holiday Inn on John C. Calhoun Drive and turned it into South Campus. Some consideration had been given to buying the old Edisto Hotel on Russell Street in 1970, but the $360,000 cost was considered excessive.[62]

HILLCREST RECREATION CENTER

The college also engaged in several other real estate transactions as property was bought, sold, and leased. In 1971 President Nance proposed leasing a large portion of

Table 51. College Fees and Tuition, South Carolina Residents

1969–70	1975–76	1984–86
$230	$250	$525

Sources: Catalog, 1969–70, 24; catalog, 1975–76, 29; catalog, 1984–86, 29.

Table 52. Enrollments

	1969–70	1975–76	1980–81	1985–86
Undergraduate	1,729	2,909	3,493	3,508
Graduate	419	617	517	680

Sources: *Annual Report, May 1970–October 1970,* appendix 1, 25; *Annual Report, 1975–1976,* 59; *Annual Report, 1980–1981,* 72; *Annual Report, 1985–1986,* 37.

the Hillcrest Farm to the City of Orangeburg for use as a community recreation facility. The farm was located about two miles north of the campus between St. Matthews Road and Route 601 and along the Southern Railroad (now the Norfolk and Southern) right of way. The termination of the agricultural program meant the farm was no longer of tangible benefit to the college. The subsequent agreement leased two hundred acres of the Hillcrest Farm to the city for $1 per year for fifty years. With a federal grant of $320,000 and another $130,000 from city funds, the farmland was transformed into soccer and baseball fields and—perhaps what is most important—into an eighteen-hole seven-thousand-yard public golf course. Nance and several other college administrators including Lewie C. Roache and Oliver "Bull" Dawson enjoyed golf, but the Orangeburg Country Club was private and excluded African Americans. By terms of the agreement with the city, S.C. State faculty and staff would enjoy a reduction in fees at Hillcrest, and the college golf team would have a home course. There was at the time a black country club—the Northside Country Club—that had a clubhouse and swimming and tennis facilities, but it lacked a golf course. Prosperous local black men had purchased land off Route 178 about seven miles north of town in the early 1960s and maintained the club until they sold the property in the early 1990s.[63]

Not all the former farm was included in the Hillcrest recreational complex. The college sold slightly more than one hundred acres on the east side of Route 601 to the American Koyo Bearing Company in 1973 for $250,000 for the construction of a manufacturing facility. Combined with state funds, the proceeds from the Koyo sale were then used to purchase for $349,000 seven parcels of land and houses located along Russell Street adjacent to the campus. One of the houses was set aside for use by

Table 53. Faculty

	1969–70	1975–76	1980–81	1985–86
Number	144	225	241	243
Number with doctorate	43	93	101	129
Percent with doctorate	30%	41%	42%	53%

Sources: *Annual Report, May 1970–October 1970,* 15; *Annual Report, 1975–1976,* 33; *Annual Report, 1980–1981,* 28; *Annual Report, 1985–1986,* 9.

the alumni association, and a second home was used for a time for a faculty and staff club. In 1978 the college sold six acres of the Hillcrest Farm for $3,000 per acre to the Orangeburg Association of Retarded Citizens for a new facility on Route 601.[64]

THE CHANGING ROLE OF THE COLLEGE

When Maceo Nance assumed the S.C. State presidency in 1968, the future of the college as a land-grant institution seemed precarious. The agricultural program had been sacrificed on the altar of desegregation. During Turner's administration the agreement with Clemson University officials in 1966 effectively ended S.C. State's undergraduate major in agriculture as of 1971. The Hillcrest Farm was shut down. The separate extension program had ended. Only home economics and industrial education survived as part of the original land-grant mission. Faculty members in agriculture dispersed. The dean, Laler DeCosta, assumed leadership of the cooperative education program. Leon C. Chavous, who taught poultry science, moved to biology and later became the associate administrator of the 1890 extension program. Kailash Mathur, who had been professor of diary science, transformed himself into a professor of biology and nutrition. William Warren went from horticulture to biology. Gabe Buckman, who had been teaching agriculture at S.C. State since 1937, became director of adult education.[65]

Clemson and S.C. State tried for a time to maintain a significant black presence in agriculture education. The two institutions submitted a proposal in 1970 to the Rockefeller Foundation for a ten-year $575,000 grant to collaborate on an undergraduate degree program in agriculture directed toward African Americans. Rockefeller Foundation officials, however, declined to support it. The two land-grant schools did briefly try to sustain a cooperative academic program in agriculture with African American students spending two years at S.C. State before moving to Clemson to complete their degree. In 1971–72 there were seven students enrolled at S.C. State and four at Clemson. Two of the unnamed black Clemson students indicated satisfaction with the agricultural program, but they were unhappy with campus life because they felt excluded from extracurricular activities. The failure of the Rockefeller proposal combined with the lack of student interest and the absence of genuine cooperation on the part of administrators at S.C. State and Clemson doomed the arrangement to extinction.[66]

The future for agriculture at S.C. State had all but disappeared. There was no ongoing research or scientific mission. The black land-grant institutions had never had access to research funds allocated by the U.S. Department of Agriculture. The 1887 Hatch Act provided funding for agricultural research and experimentation, but those appropriations went exclusively to the white land-grant colleges and universities as well as to state experiment stations. From the late nineteenth century to the 1960s, there had never been a pretense of sharing research money with the black or 1890 institutions.[67]

THE 1890 PROGRAM

Just as the agricultural program at S.C. State was about to fade into oblivion, the federal government inaugurated support for research at black land-grant schools with the creation in 1967 of the Cooperative State Research Service (CSRS). Sixteen 1890 institutions including S.C. State initially divided $283,000 into an average of just $17,658 for each school. By 1972 CSRS funding expanded to $8,880,000 with $475,705 allotted to S.C. State.[68]

Then in 1971 the extension program at the 1890 institutions was revived and revitalized with an appropriation of $4,000,000. Thus the land-grant mission of the black colleges and universities that seemed consigned to extinction by desegregation was restored and then strengthened. Congress enacted the Food and Agriculture Act (Public Law 95–113) in 1972, which created a formula based funding for research and extension work at the 1890 schools. Under what came to be known as Evans-Allen funds, the federal money to 1890 institutions swelled to $23,470,000 by 1985.[69]

With substantial research funds available for the first time in the history of South Carolina State, faculty members embarked on an array of projects in the 1970s and 1980s. Botany professor Charles Cottingham was not deterred by the loss of the Hillcrest Farm as he experimented with soybeans, peanuts, sorghum, cowpeas, and tomatoes in an effort to develop plant varieties that would be resistant to the fungus *Macrophomina phaseoli.* With a four-year grant (1972–76) of $136,626, Cottingham carried out his investigation at the Edisto branch of the South Carolina Agricultural Experiment Station at Blackville.[70]

Andrew Koli, an associate professor of chemistry, used a $75,600 grant to investigate mercury contamination in locally caught fish consumed by rural South Carolinians. Miriam Abernathy, a home economics professor, examined nutritional problems among pregnant adolescent girls in the Orangeburg area with a $17,143 grant. Claflin professor S. S. Sandhu collaborated with S.C. State biology professor W. J. Warren with a grant of $201,651 to study pollutants in the drinking water supplies of rural residents in three counties. Kailash Mathur and C. Douglas Poe, both professors of human nutrition and biology, used a $475,705 five-year grant to examine and evaluate the extent of hunger and the nutritional needs among low-income people in Hampton County.[71]

Social scientists also engaged in 1890 research. With a grant of $106,630, economics professor Suresh R. Londhe studied the feasibility and potential methods of organizing supply and marketing cooperatives among low-income farmers. Such cooperatives would conceivably reduce farmer costs in purchasing equipment and materials while increasing their income when they sold crops and livestock. Marguerite R. Howie, a sociology professor, carried out an investigation of communication and transportation problems among poor rural residents of Orangeburg County in an effort to determine why many of those people did not take advantage of services that were available to them. Kathleen Underwood, Robert Phillips, Patricia Gibson, and Wendell White assisted Howie with the $161,000 grant.[72]

S.C. State's five-decade-old extension program had disappeared by 1967, having been absorbed by Clemson University. But with federal support it was rejuvenated in 1971. The new 1890 extension program bore several similarities to its all-black predecessor. It focused on rural families, community development, small-acreage farmers, and young people. Instead, however, of trying to saturate the state with extension personnel—something the Clemson program already had accomplished—the S.C. State extension efforts concentrated initially on low-income residents in Marlboro, Georgetown, Hampton, and Anderson Counties.[73]

Farmers were offered instruction and information on soil testing, seed selection, fertilizers, cultivation, and pesticide control. Altogether 419 families in the four counties grew sweet corn, okra, snap beans, lima beans, watermelons, squash, sweet potatoes, and other produce that sold for an estimated $20,000 in local markets. In Marlboro County seventy-seven families took part in a garden contest with local donors contributing prizes to the five winners. A five-year program to eradicate rats began in 1973. With the assistance of community residents and local leaders, the despised rodents were exterminated in 1,112 homes in the four counties in late 1975 and early 1976.[74]

With the assistance of extension work personnel, 574 families processed three thousand canned products and five thousand pounds of frozen goods in 1976. They learned sewing techniques and were taught methods of home improvement. In 1977 twenty-nine bathrooms were added to homes to replace outdoor toilet facilities, and 128 new windows and seventy-seven new doors were installed. Family members added curtain, rugs, and quilts as well.[75]

Six youngsters joined in a feeder pig program in Hampton County. Each of them was given five bred gilts and one boar so that they could care for and tend the animals and thereby learn lessons in responsibility and thrift. The sale of pigs would augment family income and create "an opportunity to experience the production of top grade feeder pigs and hogs instead of inferior grades." Four young people from Marlboro County traveled to Washington, D.C., in 1977 to visit the nation's capital and for a short course in citizenship.[76]

In the wake of desegregation, Clemson University had assumed control of the 4-H camps around the state. But in 1971 S.C. State regained control of popular Camp Harry Daniels. The two-hundred-acre camp on Lake Marion near Elloree had been the black 4-H camp since its creation in 1944. Black and white youngsters from low-income families who resided in rural counties attended summer camps in the 1970s and 1980s. In 1976, for example, 359 young people ranging in age from nine to sixteen joined in a wide variety of activities that included arts and crafts, programs in nutrition, personal grooming, drug abuse education, and highway safety. They took part in a mini-Olympics with competitions in swimming, badminton, and softball, along with sack races and a tug-of-war. The camp was supervised and operated by a camp director, two assistant directors, an arts and crafts instructor, eight counselors, five cooks, three kitchen aides, and a custodian. The Food and Nutrition Service of the U.S. Department of Agriculture provided much of the food.[77]

Although S.C. State and Clemson each operated extension programs, specialists from both institutions cooperated in training efforts, in coordinating activities, and in providing the latest available information to clients. Training sessions for extension personnel were held on both campuses. The 1890 extension staff offered advice and information to black and white South Carolinians. By 1977, 615 black people and 127 white people took advantage of information on food and nutrition. Suggestions and advice on home furnishing went to 323 black people and 134 white people. But no white women took advantage of information on quilting, while twenty-one black women did.[78]

Farm and home demonstration agents from S.C. State who had labored during the Jim Crow era would have been astonished to learn that 1890 extension staff members openly dispensed political advice. With the civil rights movement having dramatically altered South Carolina's political landscape, extension specialists now urged rural residents and poor people to take an active role in politics. "They are encouraged to register and vote for candidates who are sympathetic toward their cause."[79]

Extension leadership and programs experienced other major transformations as well. The people who were the beneficiaries of extension activities were given for the first time an enlarged role in planning and carrying out those programs. For decades extension directors and county agents had assumed that they knew what services and information people needed, and therefore they dictated the delivery of programs to low-income and poorly educated South Carolinians. That changed. Men and women recognized as community leaders became paraprofessionals who served as liaisons between extension personnel and local clients. Very few of them had graduated from high school, and "some of them have not finished the eighth grade." But with training and guidance they could work closely and effectively with families.[80]

Robert Hurst directed the 1890 research and extension program during the Nance presidency. He was a no-nonsense administrator with a prickly personality that sometimes offended people. In a dispute over office space in the Staley building, Algernon S. Belcher complained to Nance in 1974 that Hurst "became quite abusive" during a telephone call with Belcher, and used "profane" language that so offended the prim vice president for academic affairs that he abruptly hung up the phone on Hurst.[81]

The next year Hurst matter-of-factly informed Nance that the 1890 program could not meet the July 20 deadline to submit a response to an audit of research grants at the college. Hurst explained that a shortage of personnel in that office would delay for two months the reply to U.S. Department of Agriculture CSRS officials. "We are behind in our work." Hurst advised that either additional staff should be hired or the college should postpone the acceptance of future grants until "we are able to catch up with our back work." Nance must have been shocked when Hurst recommended the possibility of returning $650,000 in CSRS funds that would be forthcoming in 1976.[82]

Hurst also tangled with a local poverty administrator in Hampton County in another misunderstanding over office space that drew state senators James M. Waddell and James P. Harrelson into the dispute. Hurst wanted the Committee for the Betterment of Poor People to abandon its quarters in a former elementary school so that the extension program would have room for a food laboratory, a sewing lab, a group assembly room, and staff offices. But the head of the committee, James A. Moore, had the ear of the local politicians, and he resented the intrusion of the 1890 extension program as a "waste" of taxpayers' money run by outside administrators from Orangeburg. The intervention of Waddell and Harrelson helped settle the dispute amicably, but not before Hurst threatened to withdraw the 1890 program from Hampton County. "If we cannot get adequate building space," he warned, "we must discontinue the program there."[83]

Robert Hurst retired from the program in 1986. By that time a newly constructed research facility had been added to the recently renovated 1890 offices located on the campus.[84]

FACULTY RESEARCH

While the 1890 research program supported many of the scholarly and investigative projects undertaken on the campus in the late twentieth century, some faculty members in the sciences pursued research through grants provided by the National Institute of Health. In the 1980s biology professor N. Datta-Gupta worked on oxygen-carrying porphyrin-protein complexes. Roy Isabel, a chemist, undertook a photochemical study of a series of metalloporphyrins ligan photodetachment and substitution. Biologist Leroy Davis studied ribonucleic acid protein synthesis in HISW mutants of salmonellae.[85]

Economics professors Suresh R. Londhe and Patricia Frazier analyzed agricultural programs and methods in the Philippines and Indonesia in the mid-1980s with funds from the Agency for International Development (AID). Londhe worked on sloping agricultural land technology on small upland farms in the Philippines, and he undertook an evaluation of investment opportunities in upland agriculture in Central and East Java in Indonesia. He collaborated with Frazier on an examination of the impact of research and extension on selected root crops in the Philippines.[86]

Following Asa H. Gordon and Lewis McMillan, Stanley Harrold became the third history professor at South Carolina State to publish a book when he completed a biography of abolitionist newspaper editor Gamaliel Bailey in 1986. After Gordon finished *Sketches of Negro Life and History in South Carolina* in 1929 he departed for a teaching position at Savannah State. McMillan's *Negro Higher Education in the State of South Carolina* led to his swift dismissal in 1953. Fortunately Harrold remained on the S.C. State faculty and went on to research and write several more major studies that made him one of the nation's foremost scholars of the antislavery movement.[87]

NANCE STEPS DOWN

Maceo Nance informed the board of trustees on May 1, 1985, that he would retire one year later at the conclusion of the 1986 academic year. Nance left an enduring legacy. Speaking in 1971 at the Columbia Rotary Club, he declared: "The need now is not for *fewer* black institutions but for *better* black institutions." When he stepped down fifteen years later, he could take considerable satisfaction that South Carolina State was a better college thanks to his leadership. State appropriations had increased to a point that the college was supported on parity with Winthrop College, Francis Marion College, and the Citadel. Students as well as the college benefited enormously from the federal government's intrusion into higher education with grants, loans, support for programs, and aid for capital improvements. Enrollments doubled in the 1970s and 1980s as did the number of faculty. The academic preparation of those faculty members improved significantly with over half of them in possession of doctorates. There were impressive additions to the physical plant that included additions to Hodge Hall and Turner Hall, a new classroom building named in honor of Nance, Martin Luther King Jr. Auditorium, the K.o. Donma Administration Building, and a new facilities management building and warehouse named for Dudley Zimmerman and T. J. Crawford. There was also the Henderson Davis Theater, the I. P. Stanback Museum and Planetarium, WSSB, and three new residence halls: Benjamin E. Mays II, Sojourner Truth, and John H. Mitchell. Two women's dormitories of ancient age, Manning and Bradham Halls, had been renovated.[88]

New programs in speech and hearing, agribusiness, nursing, political science, economics, music performance, and music merchandising, as well as the doctoral program in educational administration were among the additions to the curriculum. The office of career planning and development helped students who were now entering fields and taking advantage of job opportunities that previously had been closed to African Americans and to women.

With his genial personality, Nance served as a superb ambassador for the college at a time following the massacre in 1968 when bitter racial feelings prevailed. He effectively inserted himself between black and white South Carolinians and largely gained the confidence of leaders of both races. He regularly spoke to civic, religious, and educational groups across the state. He was elected president of the South Carolina Association of Colleges and Universities in 1970. A heart attack in 1979 prevented him from assuming leadership over the Orangeburg Chamber of Commerce in early 1980. (He had quadruple heart bypass surgery in 1982.)[89]

Nance and the board of trustees continued the policy begun in the mid-1920s of declining to award honorary degrees. Nance did make certain, however, that local white community leaders including state senator Marshall Williams, automobile dealer Cliff Morgan, and the Reverend Roy O. McClain of the First Baptist Church were recognized at various college functions. He likewise invited state and national black leaders to the campus and maintained ties to the South Carolina Conference of the NAACP and to local black churches. Black clergymen rotated service as college chaplains, and they were paid a modest stipend. At Christmas in 1977 Nance drew $2,200 from the college auxiliary fund and donated $200 to each of eleven local churches. Nine were black churches, and two—the Roman Catholic and the Jehovah's Witnesses—had mixed racial membership. This gesture may well have violated the First Amendment provision for the separation of church and state, but it could only serve to enhance Nance's reputation and the standing of the college among area congregations.[90]

While students and faculty were no longer subjected to the array of arbitrary rules and regulations that had been enforced with no regard for due process under President Turner, little of consequence occurred on the campus that escaped Nance's attention or involvement. Although lauded by many people for his warm and pleasant manner, he insisted on making most decisions, large and small. He delegated little authority. Nance, for instance, followed his predecessors' example and for a time routinely approved and rejected the adoption of textbooks by members of the faculty.[91]

Nance was willing to compromise with students, faculty, and politicians. But on some issues—interdorm visits and making major concessions in the name of desegregation—he would not budge. Nance as well as other administrators and members of the faculty grew increasingly exasperated with students who took advantage of the benign campus atmosphere that prevailed by the 1980s. Too many students with weak academic backgrounds were given an opportunity to get an education, and then demonstrated a decided absence of interest in and dedication to their studies. They betrayed a woeful lack of passion for education. Some students skipped classes, taking advantage of relaxed class attendance regulations initiated early in Nance's presidency. By 1985 Nance had come full circle, and in a suggestion reminiscent of the Turner years, he thought it might be necessary to make some college activities once again mandatory. But no action was taken before he retired. He lived in Orangeburg with his wife, Julie, until his death in March 2001. She died in 2012.[92]

Epilogue

South Carolina State University had been established as an all-black institution in the late nineteenth century when white supremacy was matter-of-factly accepted by millions of Americans. In the decades that followed its founding, the college managed to survive neglect, indifference, two world wars, and the financial hardships of the Great Depression. Students and faculty members endured segregation and hostility as they sought to make their way in the larger society. Unfortunately their campus was not an oasis where they could learn in an atmosphere of open expression and creative inquiry. Instead they too often encountered arbitrary authority and mandatory regulations that severely curtailed freedom of thought and action.

By the 1950s and 1960s many students joined young people from across the South as they rose up in peaceful defiance against the American system of apartheid. But S.C. State students also took up the cause on their campus as they protested and boycotted classes in opposition to the unyielding administrative authority that governed their lives. These were not easy struggles. Students were suspended and expelled. Faculty members were fired. Students were arrested again and again. Finally and tragically three young men were killed and twenty-eight injured in 1968.

But those young people eventually triumphed. They helped destroy Jim Crow, and they liberated themselves from the autocratic rule that had denied generations of students their rights and access to due process on their campus. These were monumental achievements that dramatically altered American society and transformed South Carolina State College.

Since the federal government's 1988 declaration that Jim Crow no longer existed in South Carolina's system of higher education, S.C. State has managed to make significant progress as the state's only historically black public institution. It finally has achieved something close to legal and financial parity with South Carolina's other public colleges and universities. For example in 2000–2001, when the state legislature was relatively generous in its appropriations for higher education, S.C. State received $25.3 million. Winthrop got $25.4 million, Lander got $11.3 million, Francis Marion received $16.3 million, Coastal Carolina got $14.7 million, and the College of Charleston received $33.4 million. It is no longer possible to claim that S.C. State is underfunded and treated unequally simply because it remains essentially a black institution.

And the perennial problem of poorly prepared, underqualified, and underpaid members of the faculty has vanished. In 1986, 53 percent of the teaching staff had a

Table 54. Full-Time Faculty at South Carolina State, Fall 2009

Race	Male	Female	Total
Black	73	69	142
White	40	22	62
Asian	18	6	24
Hispanic	1	1	2
All	132	98	230

Sources: *South Carolina Higher Education Statistical Abstract 2010,* Stephanie Charbonneau, ed. (Columbia: Commission on Higher Education, 2010), Full-Time Faculty by Race and Tenure, S.C. Public Colleges and Universities, 2009, 130.

doctorate. By 2011, 80 percent (172 of 213) had earned a terminal degree. A faculty that was once limited by law to members of the Negro race has become far more representative of the racial and gender composition of American society.[1]

Most of the academic programs that are eligible for accreditation and certification by regional and national organizations have achieved that distinction. They include teacher education, speech pathology and audiology, social work, computer science, engineering technology, music, business, and several others.[2]

For the first time in its history, S.C. State has ample academic and residential facilities for learning and living. These up-to-date buildings include Belcher Hall, the Fine Arts Center, Leroy Davis Sr. Hall, and a new computer science, math, and engineering facility. The Andrew Hugine Jr. Residential Suites is a massive housing complex with 772 beds and modern amenities that would make earlier residents of Bethea and Miller Halls weep. The university also purchased the University Village, another large, well-equipped residential facility. But the not-so-fondly remembered Bethea Hall, the raucous men's dormitory, has succumbed to the wrecking ball. Three vintage women's dormitories—Miller, Bradham, and Manning Halls—stand forlorn and vacant. Longtime men's dormitory Lowman Hall has been restored as a sparkling administrative facility. The first phase of the James E. Clyburn Transportation Center has been completed. The I. P. Stanback Museum and Planetarium, the J. I. Washington Dining Hall, and the bookstore have been renovated in the early twenty-first century. The Bulldog football stadium was expanded and became Oliver C. Dawson/Bulldog Stadium featuring Willie Jeffries Field. The lingering and major shortcoming in infrastructure is the library. Forty-year-old Miller F. Whittaker Library badly needs replacement just as thirty-year-old Wilkinson Hall, the first library building, needed replacement by the 1960s.

A century ago students and members of the faculty were instrumental in the design, construction, and maintenance of most facilities at S.C. State. They labored to erect dormitories and academic buildings. They operated the campus farm that yielded commodities for the dining hall and revenue for the college. Today many university operations have been outsourced. UNICCO, a Boston-based service company, manages the buildings and grounds. Sodexo, a multinational corporation headquartered in

France, provides food services. The bookstore is one of 930 campus stores run by Follet Higher Education Group, a billion-dollar corporation.

Although the program in agriculture and the campus farm disappeared with desegregation, the 1890 research and extension program has grown and blossomed as S.C. State maintains its commitment to public service as a land-grant institution. After a lengthy legal dispute in the 1990s involving its construction, the John W. Matthews Jr. Research and Extension Building opened in 2005. The 20,600–square-foot facility contains offices, classrooms, conference rooms, and an auditorium that seats 106 people. S.C. State also continues to operate Camp Daniels, a 267-acre facility near Lake Marion and Elloree, South Carolina. It is scheduled for renovation and expansion to provide a year-round array of workshops, camps, and activities for young people as well as adults.[3]

With a full- and part-time staff of 150 people, the research and extension program operated on a budget of $6,334,038 for 2012–13. The extension program has offices in Orangeburg, Anderson, Marlboro, and Hampton Counties, which serve those and surrounding counties. The extension program shares offices with Clemson extension personnel in Greenwood and Williamsburg Counties. Plans are underway to open an urban extension facility in a neighborhood near downtown Charleston. The extension program also operates a modified Winnebago van equipped with twelve computer stations that travels to rural communities throughout South Carolina.[4]

In keeping with its historic legacy, the extension program is assisting eight small farm cooperatives in Hampton and Allendale Counties by furnishing farmers with equipment and machinery, which they share. The extension staff also offers programs in marketing, animal nutrition, herd health, and soil fertility. In 2012 ninety seventh and eighth graders in six rural communities built their own computers with materials and tools provided by the extension program.

In 2012–13 eighteen South Carolina State faculty members were engaged in a variety of research projects sponsored by the 1890 program. Rahina Mahtab, a professor of chemistry, is leading an investigation in an effort to detect early indications of the onset of Alzheimer's disease. Health science professor Mabel Scott and family and consumer sciences professor Kimberly McClain are conducting research on reducing obesity among children of elementary school age through the use of video games. Sheriase Sanders, a biology professor, is investigating food-borne pathogens. Willie Legette, a professor of political science, has been analyzing how political participation and representation affect the distribution of public services including water, sewer, sanitation, and police and fire protection in rural communities.

Beyond the research supported through the 1890 program, other members of the faculty have embarked on a variety of projects and activities. Stanley Harrold, a professor of history, wrote *Border War: Fighting over Slavery before the Civil War,* which was published in 2010. It was featured by the History Book Club and was a runner-up for the prestigious Lincoln Prize in 2011. English professor Nathaniel Wallace was awarded a Fulbright grant to teach and conduct research at the University of Bergen in Norway in 2011–12, and Shafiqur Rahman, a professor of journalism, received a Fulbright award to lecture in Bangladesh.

By 1980 and for the first time in the history of the eighty-four-year old institution, the board of trustees consisted of a majority of black members. The first woman of color and a 1965 graduate of S.C. State, Jacqueline E. Gilmore, also joined the board that year. By the early twenty-first century, the number of trustees increased to thirteen elected and appointed members. The number of ex officio members had also expanded to include the presidents of the Faculty Senate and Staff Senate as well as the national alumni association. The president of the Student Government Association also took a seat as an ex officio member. Thanks largely to the efforts of President Albert E. Smith and Provost Vermelle J. Johnson, the general assembly designated the institution South Carolina State University in 1992.[5]

In sum there have been very promising developments and genuine achievements in the recent history of S.C. State. Yet these advances have not ushered in an academic utopia—far from it. New obstacles and grave causes for concern confront the university as it moves further into the twenty-first century. Undergraduate enrollment has not grown significantly for a quarter century. While there have been periodic spikes in the number of students, S.C. State has not kept pace with several comparable black and white institutions. North Carolina A&T, Florida A&M, and Fort Valley State have experienced far greater growth since 1985 as land-grant schools. In South Carolina, S.C. State, Lander, and Francis Marion have not seen their enrollments rise as dramatically.

Tuition and fees skyrocketed in the first decade of the twenty-first century, imposing a huge financial burden on students and possibly deterring some young people from enrolling. These costs—excluding housing, books, and other expenses—have increased by 127 percent since 2000. The primary reason for the increased financial load has been the decline in state support for its public colleges and universities. That reduction has been in excess of 30 percent in that decade. Students and their families have been saddled with enormous debts as the legislature has tightened the purse strings. But some young people have found relief through the South Carolina Educational Lottery, which offers Palmetto and Life Scholarships to higher-achieving students who attend public and private four-year institutions in South Carolina. These awards have certainly assisted S.C. State students and the university, but not nearly to the extent that students at other schools have benefited because S.C. State University enrolls fewer of the state's most academically talented young people.

The smaller number of lottery awards among S.C. State students reflects another issue that has long confronted the institution. For decades faculty members and administrators have been frustrated by the weak academic preparation of students and their accompanying lack of commitment to course work and scholarship. Historically many of them have been first-generation students from less than prosperous families. Too often they have been graduates of poorly funded public schools that have left them inadequately prepared for the rigors of college-level work. While some of them do possess the fundamental skills as well as the necessary motivation, too many others are indifferent toward books, classes, and the world of ideas. Still there are other students—often from out of state and from the West Indies, Africa, and Europe—who are eager to engage in academic pursuits and compile excellent records of achievement.

Table 55. Enrollments at S.C. State and Comparable Institutions, 1985–2010

Institution	1985	1990	1995	2000	2005	2010
Coastal Carolina	2,898	4,080	4,199	4,405	6,397	8,203
	2,898*	4,080	4,468	4,653	7,316	8,706
College of Charleston	4,494	6,663	8,582	9,750	9,878	10,121
	5,303	7,726	10,537	11,129	11,332	11,532
Florida A&M	4,662	7,915	9,352	10,707	10,552	11,289
	4,983	8,344	10,306	12,126	12,154	13,284
Fort Valley State	1,701	1,933	2,431	2,212	1,997	3,500
	1,819	2,158	2,978	2,561	2,174	3,728
Francis Marion	3,067	3,647	3,418	2,793	3,500	3,771
	3,434	3,886	3,836	3,567	4,008	4,032
Lander	2,246	2,309	2,539	2,436	2,612	2,996
	2,313	2,309	2,780	2,935	2,703	3,060
North Carolina A&T	4,987	5,726	6,933	6,850	9,735	9,151
	5,712	6,595	7,947	7,748	11,103	10,795
Winthrop	4,065	4,173	4,133	4,649	5,187	4,933
	4,934	5,104	5,308	6,061	6,480	5,998
South Carolina State	3,442	4,615	4,129	3,639	3,888	3,759
	4,046	4,822	4,993	4,525	4,446	4,362

*The upper row for each institution shows the undergraduate enrollment, and the lower figure gives the total enrollment.

Source: National Center for Education Statistics, U.S. Department of Education website, http://nces.ed.gov, accessed 12 June 2012.

Table 56. Tuition and Required Fees, South Carolina State University

2000–2001	2009–10	Percent Increase
$3,724	$8,462	127%

Source: *South Carolina Higher Education Statistical Abstract, 2010*, Stephanie Charbonneau, ed. (Commission on Higher Education, Columbia), Ten-Year Summary of Tuition and Required Fees for Full-Time, In-State Undergraduates, Public Institutions, 109.

Table 57. State Appropriations for South Carolina State University

2000–2001	2005–6	2009–10
$25,346,000	$21,040,000	$16,471,000

Source: *South Carolina Higher Education Statistical Abstract, 2010,* Stephanie Charbonneau, ed. (Commission on Higher Education, Columbia), Ten-Year Comparison of the State Education Recurring Appropriations, FY 2000–2001 to FY 2009–10, 114.

Leadership has been the most serious problem facing South Carolina State University in its recent past—and that may explain in part why there has not been more substantial growth. For nearly three decades, there has not been steady, consistent, long-term leadership. Before 1986 no president served less than fifteen years. Ten presidents or interim presidents have served since 1986. Albert E. Smith served six years, and Leroy Davis Sr. served seven years including one year as interim president. There has been a steady turnover of senior administrators including vice presidents, assistant vice presidents, and deans. There has not been experienced and settled leadership over academic affairs, business and finance, student affairs, the 1890 programs, or fund-raising. The board of trustees has been plagued by a similar absence of stable and reliable leadership, which no doubt helps explain the rapid succession of administrators. Between 1969 and 1990 two men—I. P. Stanback and I. S. Leevy Johnson—chaired the board. From 1990 to 2012 ten men (and no women) have chaired the board. Membership on the board changes frequently, which accounts in part for the rotating chairmen.

For much of its history, S.C. State was buffeted by external forces over which it had little direct control. It was a black institution that functioned in an era of Jim Crow. Had it not been for race and the insistence by white people that black people be excluded from the state's white public colleges and universities, S.C. State would never have existed. For generations people of color were denied access to the political and economic

Table 58. Palmetto and Life Scholarships, 2009

Institution	Palmetto Fellows	Life Scholarships
Coastal Carolina	69	1,139
College of Charleston	504	2,266
Francis Marion	46	908
Lander	42	721
Winthrop	169	1,497
S.C. State	4	308

Source: *South Carolina Higher Education Statistical Abstract, 2010,* Stephanie Charbonneau, ed. (Commission on Higher Education, Columbia), LIFE and Palmetto Fellows Scholarship Disbursements with Enhancements, 103.

levers of power in South Carolina, and that left the college vulnerable. Political ideology and conflicting views on the role of the state and the federal government in higher education have also had an impact on S.C. State as well as on other public colleges and universities. More recently, however, the problems the university has had to reckon with have been the result of internal factors. Some—not all—of the contemporary administrative troubles have been self-inflicted.

Gauging the future is a hazardous enterprise. Yet what will that future hold for a college created in 1896 as a vocational school and teacher-training institute in a segregated society? Do South Carolina's African American residents still claim S.C. State as "their own"? Are white South Carolinians genuinely interested in its welfare and advancement? How should its legacy as a historically black college be perpetuated? What will the state of the institution be in two or three decades? Will its enrollment grow? Will its student body include more Hispanics, Asian Americans, Caucasians, and people from outside the United States? Will S.C. State continue to offer as many graduate and undergraduate programs as it currently does? Should it refocus its mission? How will it resolve its leadership and administrative difficulties?

As serious as these and other challenges are, they do not compare to the obstacles that administrators, faculty members, and students endured earlier in the history of the college. If S.C. State was able to withstand decades of depravation, discrimination, and negligence, then surely it can overcome its more recent conflicts and problems.

Notes

PREFACE

1. Washington, *Class of 1957*, 29–30. (When full publication facts are not included in the notes, they can be found in the bibliography.)

PROLOGUE

1. *First Annual Report of the Board of Trustees of the Colored Normal, Industrial, Agricultural and Mechanical College of South Carolina* (Columbia: Charles A. Calvo Jr., 1896), 18.

2. For more on antebellum education among black Carolinians, see Drago, *Initiative, Paternalism, and Race Relations*, 36–40; and Powers, *Black Charlestonians*, 15–16, 52–55, 150. The slave code was strengthened in 1834. "If any person shall hereafter teach any slave to read or write, or cause or procure any slave to be taught to read or write, such person, if a free white person, upon conviction thereof, shall, for each and every offence against this Act, be fined not exceeding one hundred dollars, and imprisoned not more than six months; or if a free person of color, shall be whipped, not exceeding fifty lashes, and fined not exceeding fifty dollars, at the discretion of the court of magistrates and freeholders before which such free person of color is tried; and if a slave, to be whipped at the discretion of the court, not exceeding fifty lashes; the informer to be entitled to one half of the fine, and to be a competent witness." No. 2639, An Act to Amend the Laws in Relation to Slaves and Free Persons of Color." *Statutes at Large of South Carolina*, ed. David J. McCord, vol. 7 (Columbia: A. S. Johnson, 1840), 468–69.

3. Rose, *Rehearsal for Reconstruction*, 76–78, 87; R. Morris, *Reading, 'Riting, and Reconstruction*, 7.

4. For more on Avery's founding, see Drago, *Initiative, Paternalism and Race Relations*, 42–56. For more on the normal schools, see Lucas, *American Higher Education*, 139–44. Lucas explains that the term "normal" comes from the Latin, *norma*. Such institutions imparted norms or rules for effective teaching.

5. *Survey of Negro Colleges and Universities;* Powers, *Black Charlestonians*, 155.

6. Gore, *On a Hilltop High*, 53.

7. In 1867 South Carolina failed in an attempt to secure land-grant funds from the federal government because Republicans in Congress would not authorize funds to states that had belonged to the Confederacy. For the text of the 1862 Morrill Land-Grant Act, see 12 *Statutes*, 503. The act is also contained in Kerr's *Legacy*, 207–8. For more on the origins of the Morrill Act and on the land-grant institutions that developed because of its passage, see Nevins, *State Universities and Democracy*, 27–30; Shannon, *Farmer's Last Frontier*, 273–74; Eddy, *Colleges for Our Land and Time*, 34–38.

8. *Acts and Joint Resolutions of the General Assembly of South Carolina* (Columbia: Republican Printing Co., 1872), 17–75; Gore, *On a Hilltop High*, 58–62; *Annual Report of the Board of Trustees of the Agricultural and Mechanics' Institute, Reports and Resolutions of the General Assembly of the State of South Carolina, 1872–1873* (Columbia: Republican, 1873), 795–96; *Annual Report of the Board of Trustees of the Agricultural and Mechanics' Institute, Reports and Resolutions of the General Assembly of the State of South Carolina, 1874–1875* (Columbia: Republican, 1875), 804–6; *Reports and Resolutions, 1875–1876*, 1276; *Reports and Resolutions, 1888–1889*, 1: 536–37; *Reports and Resolutions, 1883–1884*, 2: 685; Gore, *On a Hilltop High*, 82–83.

9. Gore, *On a Hilltop High,* 39, 44, 94–95, 105–7.

10. *Catalogue of Claflin University College of Agriculture and Mechanics' Institute, Orangeburg, S.C. 1890–91* (New York: Hunt and Eaton, 1891), 66.

11. Four of the seven trustees of South Carolina College were black during the "Radical Republican" era of its history. See Hollis, *University of South Carolina,* vol. 2, *College to University,* 16–37, 45–61, 63–69, 75–76; and William C. Hine, "Dr. Benjamin A. Boseman, Jr.: Charleston's Black Physician-Politician," in Rabinowitz, ed., *Southern Black Leaders of the Reconstruction Era,* 345.

12. For more on the "integrated" South Carolina College, see Hollis, *College to University,* 61–79. Hollis contends that "the Radical University was not as bad as it has been painted by its critics and that for a limited number the institution constituted not only a symbol of hope but an opportunity for real accomplishment" (61). Also see P. White, "'Free and Open.'" For more on the black men who attended the college, see Fulmer, "Richard T. Greener and the Radical University"; Tindall, *South Carolina Negroes,* 54–57; Simmons, *Men of Mark,* 757–59; Broussard, *African-American Odyssey;* Marszalek, *Court Martial.*

13. Hollis, *College to University,* 82–83; *Acts and Joint Resolutions of the General Assembly of the State of South Carolina, Extra Session of 1877* (Columbia: Calvo and Patton, 1877), 314–15.

14. Hollis, *College to University,* 89–95.

15. Daniel Hollis noted, "Although the [South Carolina] College derived its financial support from the Morrill Act funds, it does not appear that the chief interest of the faculty and students was in the field of agriculture or mechanics." *College to University,* 96. Hollis also points out that legally the A&M institute at Claflin and the Citadel were branches of the university in Columbia but that there "was no coordination among the separate branches" (145).

16. Hollis, *College to University,* 102–20, 128–35; Simkins, *Pitchfork Ben Tillman,* 105; Kantrowitz, *Ben Tillman,* 117–18.

17. Simkins, *Pitchfork Ben Tillman,* 124. Simkins's source for the Tillman quote is the *Charleston News and Courier,* 10 October 1887.

18. For more on Thomas G. Clemson and the founding of Clemson A&M College, see Reel, *High Seminary,* chapters 2–4, 33–93. Hollis, *College to University,* 134–35, 145–53; Simkins, *Pitchfork Ben Tillman,* 120–23; Kantrowitz, *Ben Tillman,* 127–28.

19. Hollis, *College to University,* 154–56.

20. Miller's recollection is contained in "A True History of the Establishment of State College," located in the Historical Collection of Miller F. Whittaker Library. It is also reprinted in Potts, *History of South Carolina State College,* 15–16. Miller represented Beaufort County in the state senate from 1880 to 1882, and Bruce Williams, a former slave, represented Georgetown County in the state senate from 1876 until 1887.

21. Minutes, Board of Trustees, Claflin University, 1870–1915, Special Collections, H. V. Manning Library, Claflin University, Orangeburg, S.C. Claflin's first president, Alonzo Webster, also sent a letter to the Freedmen's Aid Society of the Methodist Episcopal Church complaining about its employment practices. Gore, *On a Hilltop High,* 64, 87–89, 98–99.

22. Gore, *On a Hilltop High,* 70–71.

23. Kantrowitz, *Ben Tillman,* 219.

24. South Carolina Constitution (1895), art. 2. See also Edgar, *South Carolina,* 443–48.

25. South Carolina Constitution (1895), art. 2, sec. 4, part c. See also Kantrowitz, *Ben Tillman,* 222.

26. Miller, *Suffrage,* 9, 10, 15, 17, 19–20. Tindall, *South Carolina Negroes,* 81, 84. Tindall cites the *State* (Columbia), 27 October 1895. Simkins pointed out that if the right to vote had been determined strictly on the basis of literacy, then thirteen thousand white men and fifty-eight thousand black men would have been disfranchised while nearly seventy-five thousand literate black men and more than eighty-five thousand literate white men would have been eligible to vote. Simkins, *Pitchfork Ben Tillman,* 295.

27. Tindall, *South Carolina Negroes,* 285. Tindall cites the *State,* 27 October 1895.

28. Tindall, *South Carolina Negroes,* 285.

29. Miller's recollection of his role in the separation of the A&M school from Claflin and the creation of the A&M College is contained in "True History of the Establishment of State College." The Tillman quote on education is in Kantrowitz, *Ben Tillman,* 216.

30. Miller, "True History of the Establishment of State College."

31. A copy of Miller's leaflet containing these quotations is contained in the Benjamin R. Tillman papers at Clemson University. U. Series/O.S., Box 5.

32. "A Divorce Measure," *State,* 20 November 1895, 1–2; *Journal of the Constitutional Convention of the State of South Carolina,* 577, 580–81; South Carolina Constitution (1895), art. 11, sec. 8.

33. Miller, "True History of the Establishment of State College," 15; South Carolina Constitution (1895), art. 11, sec. 8.

34. Tindall, *South Carolina Negroes,* 87–88. Two white conservatives also voted against the constitution. Thomas Miller twice offered motions to submit the document to voters for their approval, but both motions failed. The constitution went into effect on 1 January 1896 without voters having had an opportunity to accept or reject it.

35. Message of John Gary Evans to the General Assembly of South Carolina, *Journal of the House of Representatives of the State of South Carolina,* 27; L. M. Dunton to John Gary Evans, 6 February 1896, Governors' Papers, South Carolina Department of Archives and History.

36. Miller, "True History of the Establishment of State College," 15. The Orangeburg legislative delegation consisted of Senator William Samuel Barton and house members Laurance Keitt Sturkie, Ilderton Wesley Bowman, Lawrence Summerfield Connor, J. H. Price, and William Otis Tatum.

37. L. M. Dunton to Gov. John Gary Evans, 24 February 1896, Governors' Papers, South Carolina Department of History and Archives.

38. Mrs. L. M. Dunton to Gov. John Gary Evans, 24 February 1896; L. M. Dunton to Gov. John Gary Evans, 27 February 1896, Governors' Papers, South Carolina Department of Archives and History.

39. *Journal of the House of Representatives of the State of South Carolina,* Regular Session, 1896, (Columbia: Charles A. Calvo, 1896), 158, 233, 290, 304–5, 309, 551; *Journal of the Senate of the State of South Carolina, Regular Session, 1896* (Columbia: Charles A. Calvo, 1896), 182, 244, 283, 289, 298, 570; *Acts and Joint Resolutions of the General Assembly of South Carolina,* 1896 (Columbia, 1896), 922–23. Hollis, *College to University,* 204–5.

40. Miller, "True History of the Establishment of State College," 15.

41. *Acts and Joint Resolutions,* 1896, 922–23; *Journal of the House of Representatives of the State of South Carolina,* Regular Session, 1896 (Columbia: Charles A. Calvo), 878, 841–44. The trustees were C. D. Kortjohn, Arthur Kibler, Dr. William R. Lowman, D. J. Bradham, A. G. Brice, and J. W. Floyd. Gov. John Gary Evans also served as a trustee. Kortjohn and Lowman were from Orangeburg.

42. *Plessy v. Ferguson,* 163 U.S. 537 (1896). Packard, *American Nightmare;* Woodward, *Strange Career of Jim Crow.*

43. Record Book No. 1, Board of Trustees of the Colored Normal, Industrial, Agricultural and Mechanical College of South Carolina, 10 April 1896–5 May 1914, 2–5. Historical Collection, Miller F. Whittaker Library, South Carolina State University; Board of Trustees, Claflin University, 1870–1915, 381–83, Special Collections, H. V. Manning Library, Claflin University. Hereafter cited as HCSCSU. Dunton provided the trustees with a guided tour of the A&M school on 10 April, "and every courtesy in my power was extended to them" (382).

44. Record Book No. 1, Board of Trustees, 10 June 1896, 6–7.

CHAPTER ONE: THE EARLY YEARS

1. Tindall, *South Carolina Negroes,* 61.

2. *Thirty Years of Lynching in the United States,* 32–33, 88–89; "Lynching," in *South Carolina Encyclopedia,* 579–80; Tindall, *South Carolina Negroes,* 255–57. Benjamin E. Mays recalled the Phoenix riot and one of the mobs associated with it as his earliest memories. He was four years old. Mays, *Born to Rebel,* 1. For more on the Phoenix riot, see Roper, *Magnificent Mays,* 20–31.

3. Jack Shuler briefly discusses the Brown lynching in *Blood and Bone,* 49–50. Also see J. Moore, *Carnival of Blood,* table A2, 212.

4. Recollections of J. A. Pierce contained in Nelson C. Nix, "Tentative History of South Carolina State College," unpublished manuscript, 146. Historical Collection, Miller F. Whittaker Library. The U.S. census for South Carolina in 1900 listed 782,821 black residents and 557,807 white residents.

5. Nix, "Tentative History of South Carolina State College," 116, 118.

6. Recollections of J. A. Pierce, in Nix, "Tentative History of South Carolina State College," 117–18, 146; *Catalogue and Special Announcements of the Colored Normal, Industrial, Agricultural and Mechanical College of South Carolina, 1896–1897* (Orangeburg: Parks and Cannon, 1897), 5–6; Minutes, Board of Trustees, 28 September 1896, 18–19.

7. Census reports, *Twelfth Census, 1900*, vol. 2, *Population*, part 2, cxii.

8. Newby, *Black Carolinians*, 263.

9. Much of Miller's early life and family history is shrouded in uncertainty. Eric Bargeron, a graduate student at the University of South Carolina, has worked diligently to trace Miller's ancestry. Eric Bargeron to William Hine, e-mail, 13 May 2008. Late in life and while living in Charleston, Miller offered biographical information to Augustus Ladson as one of the interviews of ex-slaves conducted during the New Deal. At the time Miller stated that he had completed a study of Reconstruction, but it was never published. No manuscript apparently survived. Rawick, *American Slave*, 392–96.

10. W. Hine, "Thomas E. Miller and the Early Years of South Carolina State University"; Tindall, *South Carolina Negroes*, 48–49. Marszalek, *Black Congressman in the Age of Jim Crow*, 27, 37.

11. Wilkinson's entry in *Who's Who in Colored America* listed his degree as honorary. *Who's Who in Colored America: A Biographical Dictionary of Notable Living Persons of Negro Descent in America*, 1: 221.

12. *Catalogue and Special Announcements of the Colored Normal, Industrial, Agricultural and Mechanical College of South Carolina, 1896–1897*, 2; *Catalogue of the Colored Normal, Industrial, Agricultural and Mechanical College of South Carolina for 1906–1907* (Orangeburg: Patriot, 1907), 3. Where Hoffman obtained his Ph.D. is unknown. Neither Michigan State University nor Harvard University has any record of his attendance. Hoffman and Wilkinson are listed as faculty members in the *Thirteenth Catalogue of State University, Louisville, Ky., 1892–1893* (Louisville, Ky.: Courier-Journal Job Printing, 1892), 8.

13. Census reports, *Twelfth Census, 1900*, vol. 2, *Population*, part 2, cxii; Schweninger, *Black Property Owners in the South*, 183–84.

14. W. T. B. Williams, "The State Colored College," 3 April 1904, Box 94, Folder 1162, General Education Board, Rockefeller Archive Center, North Tarrytown, N.Y.

15. Newby, *Black Carolinians*, 29, 85–86.

16. Mays, *Born to Rebel*, 37. There were several other private schools available to black youngsters, including Penn Normal, Industrial, and Agricultural School on St. Helena Island (1862–1953), Avery Normal Institute in Charleston (1865–1954), Bettis Academy in Edgefield (1881–1952), Schofield Normal and Industrial School in Aiken (1871–1953), and Mather Academy in Camden (1887–1983).

17. Mays, *Born to Rebel*, 38.

18. *Catalogue and Special Announcements of the Colored Normal, Industrial, Agricultural, and Mechanical College of South Carolina*, 5; W. T. B. Williams, "The State Colored College," 3 April 1904, GEB, Box 94, Folder 1162, Rockefeller Archive Center; Nelson C. Nix, "South Carolina State College: A History to 1937," unpublished manuscript, 1938, 17.

19. Nix, "South Carolina State College," 20, 23; *Thirteenth Annual Report of the Board of Trustees of the Colored Normal, Industrial, Agricultural and Mechanical College of South Carolina, Reports and Resolutions of the General Assembly of the State of South Carolina* (Columbia: Gonzales and Bryan, 1910), 1113; Faculty Log Book, 4 October 1909, 252; Minutes, 30 November 1909, Board of Trustees; *Fourteenth Annual Report of the Board of Trustees of the Colored Normal, Industrial, Agricultural and Mechanical College of South Carolina, Reports and Resolutions of the General Assembly of the State of South Carolina* (Columbia: Gonzales and Bryan, 1910), 2: 1355; *Ninth Annual Report of the Board of Trustees of the Colored Normal, Industrial, Agricultural and Mechanical College of South Carolina, Reports and Resolutions of the General Assembly of the State of South Carolina* (Columbia: Gonzales and Bryan, 1905), 621.

20. Manning, *Black Apollo of Science*, 16–20.

21. *Catalogue of the Colored Normal, Industrial, Agricultural and Mechanical College of South Carolina for 1906–1907*, 14, 49, 63; *Sixth Annual Report of the Board of Trustees of the Colored Normal, Industrial, Agricultural and Mechanical College of South Carolina, Reports and Resolutions of the General Assembly of the State of South Carolina* (Columbia: State, 1903), 897; *Ninth Annual Report of the Board of Trustees of the Colored Normal, Industrial, Agricultural and Mechanical College of South Carolina, Reports and Resolutions of the General Assembly of the State of South Carolina* (Columbia: Gonzales and Bryan, 1906), 627; Board Minutes, 14 May 1902, 112–13.

22. W. T. B. Williams, "The State Colored College," 3 April 1904, GEB, Box 94, Folder 1162, Rockefeller Archive Center. Williams was a Virginian and an 1897 graduate of Harvard. See *Who's Who in Colored America: A Biographical Dictionary of Notable Living Persons of African Descent in America*, 473–74.

23. *Fourteenth Annual Report of the Board of Trustees of the Colored Normal, Industrial, Agricultural and Mechanical College of South Carolina, Reports and Resolutions of the General Assembly of the State of South Carolina* (Columbia: Gonzales and Bryan, 1911), 1363; *Catalogue of the Colored Normal, Industrial, Agricultural and Mechanical College of South Carolina for 1906–1907,* 56.

24. The 1896 legislation creating the college stipulated that the trustees could ask the state to furnish "forty able-bodied convicts" to assist in the construction of the campus. But there is no record that the trustees ever did so. Board Minutes, 21 September 1897, 47; *Catalogue of the Colored Normal, Industrial, Agricultural, and Mechanical College of South Carolina for 1906–1907,* 12, 63.

25. *Annual Report of the Board of Trustees of the Colored Normal, Industrial, Agricultural and Mechanical College of South Carolina, Reports and Resolutions of the General Assembly of the State of South Carolina for 1896–1897* (Columbia: Charles A. Calvo Jr., 1897), 938; *Ninth Annual Report of the Board of Trustees of the Colored Normal, Industrial, Agricultural and Mechanical College of South Carolina, Reports and Resolutions of the General Assembly for 1904–1905* (Columbia: Gonzales and Bryan, 1906), 627; *Catalogue of the Colored Normal, Industrial, Agricultural and Mechanical College of South Carolina for 1906–1907,* 9; *Fourteenth Annual Report of the Board of Trustees of the Colored, Normal, Industrial, Agricultural and Mechanical College of South Carolina, Reports and Resolutions of the General Assembly of the State of South Carolina for 1909–1910* (Columbia: Gonzales and Bryan, 1911), 1358.

26. *Catalogue of the Colored Normal, Industrial, Agricultural and Mechanical College of South Carolina for 1906–1907,* 13, 64; Faculty Log Book, 6 January 1897, 27, 1 November 1909, 254. HCSCSU.

27. Mays, *Born to Rebel,* 38.

28. Mays, *Born to Rebel,* 42; Jelks, *Benjamin Elijah Mays,* 59–60. John Herbert Roper Sr. examined medical records and discusses Ellen Harvin Mays's death more fully than Benjamin Mays was able to bring himself to do. Even a half century following her passing, Mays found it difficult to elaborate on the loss of his young wife. Roper, *Magnificent Mays,* 94–97.

29. *Catalogue of the Colored Normal, Industrial, Agricultural and Mechanical College of South Carolina for 1906–1907,* 10.

30. "By 1899 the [land-grant] colleges were ready to become not just agricultural and mechanical institutions preparing farmers and mechanics, but centers of learning and preparation for all areas of life. The colleges had begun the inevitable step toward becoming universities." Eddy, *Colleges for Our Land and Time,* 87.

31. Eddy, *Colleges for Our Land and Time,* 86.

32. "Address of the Hon. W. D. Mayfield, State Superintendent of Education, at the Dedication of Bradham Hall," *Catalogue and Special Announcements for the Colored Normal, Industrial, Agricultural and Mechanical College of South Carolina, 1896–1897,* 82, 81.

33. For a critical assessment of the Hampton and Tuskegee models, see J. Anderson, *Education of Blacks in the South.*

34. Grant, *Black Protest,* 196, 197, 198.

35. W. E. B. Du Bois, "Of Mr. Booker T. Washington and Others," *Souls of Black Folk,* 48.

36. W. E. B. Du Bois, "Of the Training of Black Men," *Souls of Black Folk,* 78, 81.

37. *Catalogue and Special Announcements for the Colored Normal, Industrial, Agricultural and Mechanical College of South Carolina, 1896–1897,* 68–69, 8–16.

38. Washington was easily one of the most prominent leaders—black or white—in early twentieth-century America, and yet the *Times and Democrat* relegated the story of Washington's visit to four paragraphs on page 3. For more on Washington's tour of the Palmetto State, see Jackson, "Booker T. Washington in South Carolina, March 1909."

39. Faculty Log Book, 25 November, 3 December 1896, 9–11; 12 January 1897, 28–29; 4 November 1897, 52; 19 January 1905, 186.

40. *Catalogue of the Colored Normal, Industrial, Agricultural and Mechanical College of South Carolina 1904–1905* (Orangeburg: W. F. Cannon, 1905), 17; *Catalogue of the Colored Normal, Industrial, Agricultural, and Mechanical College of South Carolina for 1906–1907,* 17.

41. Faculty Log Book, 21 April 1897, 55.

42. Mays, *Born to Rebel,* 38.

43. *Catalogue and Special Announcements of the Colored Normal, Industrial, Agricultural and Mechanical College of South Carolina, 1896–1897,* 3; *Catalogue of the Colored Normal, Industrial, Agricultural and Mechanical College of South Carolina for 1906–1907,* 2.

44. "Miller to Negroes," *State,* 29 November 1897, 5; Faculty Log Book, 3 May 1904, 181; Minutes, Board of Trustees, 6 May 1904, 129; 12 May 1905, 135; *Catalogue of the Colored Normal, Industrial, Agricultural and Mechanical College of South Carolina for 1906–1907,* 30.

45. W. T. B. Williams, "The State Colored College," 3 April 1904, GEB, Box 94, Folder 1162, Rockefeller Archive Center.

46. *Catalogue of the Colored Normal, Industrial, Agricultural and Mechanical College of South Carolina for 1906–1907,* 18; Faculty Log Book, 7 October 1898, 62.

47. Fiftieth Anniversary Program Southern Intercollegiate Athletic Conference [1963], J. D. McGhee, "Intercollegiate Athletic Competition at S.C. State A. and M. College." McGhee was the longtime registrar and public relations director at S.C. State. He wrote a brief history of Bulldog athletics sometime in the late 1930s that was reprinted as part of the fiftieth anniversary of the SIAC in 1963. John Mitchell, oral history, 8 November 1975, Historical Collection, Miller F. Whittaker Library. Mitchell attended the preparatory program in 1897 as a thirteen-year-old and finished in 1903. He returned to the college in 1906 and graduated from the collegiate program in 1910.

48. Faculty Log Book, 9 March 1906, 205; *Catalogue of the Colored Normal, Industrial, Agricultural and Mechanical College of South Carolina for 1906–1907,* 18.

49. *Catalogue and Special Announcements of the Colored Normal, Industrial, Agricultural and Mechanical College of South Carolina, 1896–1897,* 37, 9, 10, 12, 14; *Catalogue of the Colored Normal, Industrial, Agricultural and Mechanical College of South Carolina for 1906–1907,* 20.

50. *Catalogue of the Colored Normal, Industrial, Agricultural and Mechanical College of South Carolina for 1906–1907,* 17–18.

51. Eddy, *Colleges for Our Land and Time,* 64–65; *Annual Report of the Board of Trustees, Reports and Resolutions of the General Assembly of the State of South Carolina* (Columbia: Charles A. Calvo, 1897), 926. As a young man, Wilkinson had applied for admission to the U.S. Military Academy at West Point. He was rejected ostensibly because of his small physical stature. But his race may have been a more important consideration.

52. *Catalogue and Special Announcements of the Colored Normal, Industrial, Agricultural and Mechanical College of South Carolina, 1897–1897,* 38–39; *Eighth Annual Report of the Board of Trustees of the Colored Normal, Industrial, Agricultural and Mechanical College of South Carolina, Reports and Resolutions of the General Assembly of the State of South Carolina, 1905* (Columbia: Gonzales and Bryan, 1905), 1: 567; *Catalogue of the Colored Normal, Industrial, Agricultural and Mechanical College of South Carolina for 1906–1907* (Orangeburg: Patriot, 1907), 44–46.

53. Minutes, Board of Trustees, 13–14 June 1900, 95. For more on Whittaker's life and the episode at West Point, see Marszalek, *Court Martial.*

54. Marszalek, *Court Martial,* 270–72.

55. Minutes, Board of Trustees, 9 May, 2 July 1901. Avery Daniels deserves credit for uncovering much of this information on Mikell.

56. *Who's Who in Colored America: A Biographical Dictionary of Notable Living Persons of African Descent in America,* 302–3.

57. *Sixth Annual Report of the Board of Trustees of the Colored Normal, Industrial, Agricultural and Mechanical College of South Carolina, Reports and Resolutions of the General Assembly of the State of South Carolina, 1901–1902* (Columbia: State, 1903), 903; *Annual Report of the Board of Trustees of the Colored Normal, Industrial, Agricultural and Mechanical College of South Carolina, Reports and Resolutions of the General Assembly of the State of South Carolina, 1896–1897* (Columbia: Charles A. Calvo, 1897), 942; Minutes, Board of Trustees of the Colored Normal Industrial, Agricultural and Mechanical College of South Carolina, 4 December 1908, 159–60; *Fourteenth Annual Report of the Board of Trustees of the Colored Normal, Industrial, Agricultural and Mechanical College of South Carolina, Reports and Resolutions of the General Assembly of the State of South Carolina* (Columbia: Gonzales and Bryan, 1911), 1356.

58. *Annual Report of the Board of Trustees of the Colored Normal, Industrial, Agricultural and Mechanical College of South Carolina, Reports and Resolutions of the General Assembly of the State of South Carolina, 1896–1897* (Columbia: Charles Calvo Jr., 1897), 935, 942; *Thirteenth Annual Report of the Board*

of Trustees of the Colored Normal, Industrial, Agricultural and Mechanical College of South Carolina, Reports and Resolutions of the General Assembly of the State of South Carolina, 1908–1909 (Columbia: Gonzales and Bryan, 1910), 1114, 1123; *Fourteenth Annual Report of the Board of Trustees of the Colored Normal, Industrial, Agricultural and Mechanical College of South Carolina, Reports and Resolutions of the General Assembly of the State of South Carolina, 1909–1910* (Columbia: Gonzales and Bryan, 1911), 1356.

59. *Eighth Annual Report of the Board of Trustees of the Colored Normal, Industrial, Agricultural and Mechanical College of South Carolina, Reports and Resolutions of the General Assembly of the State of South Carolina, 1903–1904* (Columbia: Gonzales and Bryan, 1905), 566–67; *Thirteenth Annual Report of the Board of Trustees of the Colored Normal, Industrial, Agricultural and Mechanical College of South Carolina, Reports and Resolutions of the General Assembly of the State of South Carolina, 1908–1909* (Columbia: Gonzales and Bryan, 1910), 1114, 1123; Minutes, Board of Trustees, 26 March 1908, 153, 167; *Fifteenth Annual Report of the Board of Trustees of the Colored Normal, Industrial, Agricultural and Mechanical College of South Carolina, Reports and Resolutions of the General Assembly of the State of South Carolina, 1909–1910* (Columbia: Gonzales and Bryan, 1911), 961; *Fourteenth Annual Report of the Board of Trustees of the Colored Normal, Industrial, Agricultural and Mechanical College of South Carolina, Reports and Resolutions of the General Assembly of the State of South Carolina, 1910–1911* (Columbia: Gonzales and Bryan, 1911), 1356; Mays, *Born to Rebel,* 38.

60. *Annual Report of the Board of Trustees of the Colored Normal, Industrial, Agricultural and Mechanical College of South Carolina, Reports and Resolutions of the General Assembly of the State of South Carolina, 1896–1897* (Columbia: Charles A. Calvo Jr., 1897), 933, 935, 942; *Third Annual Report of the Board of Trustees of the Colored Normal, Industrial, Agricultural and Mechanical College of South Carolina, Reports and Resolutions of the General Assembly of the State of South Carolina, 1897–1898* (Columbia: Bryan, 1899), 271–72; Nix, "Tentative History of South Carolina State College," 118.

61. Nix, "Tentative History of South Carolina State College," 147–48.

62. *Annual Report of the Board of Trustees of the Colored Normal, Industrial, Agricultural and Mechanical College of South Carolina, Reports and Resolutions of the General Assembly of the State of South Carolina, 1896–1897* (Columbia: Charles Calvo Jr., 1897), 942; *Third Annual Report of the Board of Trustees of the Colored Normal, Industrial, Agricultural and Mechanical College of South Carolina, Reports and Resolutions of the General Assembly of the State of South Carolina, 1897–1898* (Columbia: Bryan, 1899),272; *Sixth Annual Report of the Board of Trustees of the Colored Normal, Industrial, Agricultural and Mechanical College of South Carolina, Reports and Resolutions of the General Assembly of the State of South Carolina* (Columbia: State, 1903), 903; *Eleventh Annual Report of the Board of Trustees of the Colored Normal, Industrial, Agricultural and Mechanical College of South Carolina, Reports and Resolutions of the General Assembly of the State of South Carolina, 1906–1907* (Columbia: Gonzales and Bryan, 1908), 1059–60, 1065.

63. *Thirteenth Annual Report of the Board of Trustees of the Colored Normal, Industrial, Agricultural and Mechanical College of South Carolina, Reports and Resolutions of the General Assembly of the State of South Carolina, 1908–1909* (Columbia: Gonzales and Bryan, 1910), 1: 1114–15; Minutes, Board of Trustees, 30 November 1909, 168–69; 17 January 1910, 170–73.

64. *Thirteenth Annual Report of the Board of Trustees of the Colored Normal, Industrial, Agricultural and Mechanical College of South Carolina, Reports and Resolutions of the General Assembly of the State of South Carolina, 1908–19091* (Columbia: Gonzales and Bryan, 1910), 1: 1114–15; Minutes, Executive Committee of the Board of Trustees, 14 December 1909, 174–76.

65. *Fourteenth Annual Report of the Board of Trustees of the Colored Normal, Industrial, Agricultural and Mechanical College of South Carolina, Reports and Resolutions of the General Assembly of the State of South Carolina, 1909–1910* (Columbia: Gonzales and Bryan, 1911), 3: 1365–66.

66. *Fifteenth Annual Report of the Board of Trustees of the Colored Normal, Industrial, Agricultural and Mechanical College of South Carolina, Reports and Resolutions of the General Assembly of the State of South Carolina, 1910–1911* (Columbia: Gonzales and Bryan, 1912), 2: 953–54.

67. Nix, "Tentative History of South Carolina State College," 119.

68. *Fifteenth Annual Report of the Board of Trustees of the Colored Normal, Industrial, Agricultural and Mechanical College of South Carolina, Reports and Resolutions of the General Assembly of the State of South Carolina, 1910–1911* (Columbia: Gonzales and Bryan, 1912), 2: 960–61; *Fourteenth Annual Report of the Board of Trustees of the Colored Normal, Industrial, Agricultural and Mechanical College of South*

Carolina, Reports and Resolutions of the General Assembly of the State of South Carolina, 1909–1910 (Columbia: Gonzales and Bryan, 1911), 3: 1356, 1366; *Eleventh Annual Report of the Board of Trustees of the Colored Normal, Industrial, Agricultural and Mechanical College of South Carolina, Reports and Resolutions of the General Assembly of the State of South Carolina, 1906–1907* (Columbia: Gonzales and Bryan, 1908), 1: 1065.

69. For more on the South Carolina Interstate and West Indian Exposition, see the files on the exposition contained at the South Carolina Historical Society in Charleston. Also see Chibbaro, *Charleston Exposition;* and Smyth, "Blacks and the South Carolina Interstate and West Indian Exposition"; Thomas J. Jackson, "The Negro Department," The Exposition, 369. The South Carolina Historical Society, Charleston, S.C.

70. A copy of the architect's drawing of the arch is reproduced in the 1906–7 college catalog.

71. Thomas E. Miller to Booker T. Washington, 12 October 1901, *Booker T. Washington Papers,* 6: 238n1. Washington was not alarmed or offended by *The Negro Group* because black people did till the soil and work as menial laborers. See also Smyth, "Blacks and the South Carolina Interstate and West Indian Exposition," 218; Anthony Chibbaro, "South Carolina Interstate and West Indian Exposition Negro Building, Charleston (1901)," in *African American Architects,* 373–75.

72. For more on the controversy over *The Negro Group,* see Roberts and Kytle, "Looking the Thing in the Face," 662–71.

73. Smyth, "Blacks and the South Carolina Interstate and West Indian Exposition," 218. "Emancipation Day at the Exposition," *Charleston News and Courier,* 2 January 1902, 3.

74. "Emancipation Day at the Exposition," *Charleston News and Courier,* 2 January 1902, 3.

75. Chibbaro, *Charleston Exposition,* 7; Nix, "Tentative History of South Carolina State College," 26–27.

76. *Fifteenth Annual Report of the Board of Trustees of the Colored Normal, Industrial, Agricultural and Mechanical College of South Carolina, Reports and Resolutions of the General Assembly of the State of South Carolina, 1910–1911*(Columbia: Gonzales and Bryan, 1912), 2: 953.

77. The Second Morrill Act of 1890 is contained in Kerr, *Legacy,* 211–13. The South Carolina law requiring equal division of Morrill funds is located in "Report of the Code Commissioner," *Reports and Resolutions,* Civil Code of South Carolina, 1910, section 1730, 733.

78. Table 8, *Reports and Resolutions of the General Assembly of the State of South Carolina, 1910–1911* (Columbia: Gonzales and Bryan, 1912), 2: 686–87. See Reel, *High Seminary,* 72–73, 79, 89, 158.

79. *Catalogue of the Colored Normal, Industrial, Agricultural and Mechanical College of South Carolina 1911–1912* (Orangeburg: W. F. Cannon, 1912), 20–21.

80. *Ninth Annual Report of the Board of Trustees of the Colored Normal, Industrial, Agricultural and Mechanical College of South Carolina, Reports and Resolutions of the General Assembly of the State of South Carolina, 1904–1905* (Columbia: Gonzales and Bryan, 1906), 1: 627.

81. *Annual Report of the Board of Trustees of the Colored Normal, Industrial, Agricultural and Mechanical College of South Carolina, Reports and Resolutions of the General Assembly of the State of South Carolina* (Columbia: Charles A. Calvo Jr., 1897), 931, 939.

82. *Annual Report of the Board of Trustees of the Colored Normal, Industrial, Agricultural and Mechanical College of South Carolina, Reports and Resolutions of the General Assembly of the State of South Carolina, 1898–1899* (Columbia: Bryan, 1899), 2: 274–75; *Annual Report of the Board of Trustees of the Colored Normal, Industrial, Agricultural and Mechanical College of South Carolina, Reports and Resolutions of the General Assembly of the State of South Carolina, 1901–1902* (Columbia: State, 1903), 2: 905; *Annual Report of the Board of Trustees of the Colored Normal, Industrial, Agricultural and Mechanical College of South Carolina, Reports and Resolutions of the General Assembly of the State of South Carolina, 1909–1910* (Columbia: Gonzales and Bryan, 1911), 3: 1367; Nix, "Tentative History of South Carolina State College," 30–31.

83. Minutes, Board of Trustees, 10 June 1896, 7; 28 August 1896, 14; 28 September 1896, 18; 28 October 1896, 20–21; 21 September 1897, 40–45; 20 May 1897, 37; 14 December 1909, 175.

84. Gov. Martin Ansel to W. L. Izlar, 6 May 1909; Thomas E. Miller to Gov. Martin Ansel, 10 October 1910, Box 17, Governors' Papers, South Carolina Department of Archives and History.

85. Minutes, Board of Trustees, 20 May 1897, 35. In 1895 Palmer learned that Dunton was preparing to terminate him from the Claflin faculty, and Palmer decided to level charges against Dunton first. See Gore, *On a Hilltop High,* 115–16.

86. Minutes, Board of Trustees, 20 May 1897, 35. Miller's salary was restored to $1,800 in 1898. Minutes, Board of Trustees, 6 January 1898, 56.

87. Minutes, Board of Trustees, 21 September 1897, 45; Minutes, Board of Trustees, 10 March 1899, 69.

88. Mathematics professor Nelson C. Nix and physics professor Robert S. Wilkinson also earned $900 per year. Minutes, Board of Trustees, 21 September 1899, 79–81.

89. Minutes, Board of Trustees, 27 October 1899, 83–88.

90. Minutes, Board of Trustees, 8 March 1900, 99.

91. Minutes, Board of Trustees, 6 June 1906, 141. Miller and Fordham remained at odds. Four years later Miller alleged that Fordham refused to reside in a house the college rented for five single women on the faculty. Shortly thereafter she resigned to accept a teaching position in Kansas City. Thomas E. Miller to Martin Ansel, 17 October 1910, Box 17, Governors' Papers, South Carolina Department of Archives and History.

92. Minutes, Board of Trustees, 10 August 1906, 142; 19 June 1908, 156–57.

93. Thomas E. Miller to Martin Ansel, 22 December 1909, Box 1, Governors' Papers, South Carolina Department of Archives and History; Minutes, Executive Committee of the Board of Trustees, 14 December 1909, 176–77; Faculty Log Book, 23 December 1909, 256.

94. Thomas E. Miller to Gov. Martin Ansel, 31 December 1909, Box 17, Governors' Papers, South Carolina Department of Archives and History.

95. Claude E. Sawyer to Gov. Martin Ansel, 15 January 1910, Governors' Papers, South Carolina Department of Archives and History.

96. Nelson C. Nix to Gov. Martin Ansel, 31 January 1910, Box 17, Governors' Papers, South Carolina Department of Archives and History.

97. Nix, "Tentative History of South Carolina State College," 31.

98. Faculty Log Book, 4 May 1903, 164–65.

99. W. T. B. Williams, "The State Colored College," 3 April 1904, GEB, Box 94, Folder 1162, Rockefeller Archive Center.

100. Minutes, Board of Trustees, 18 October 1906.

101. Faculty Log Book, 31 October 1899, 83; 20 November 1899, 85; 29 November 1898, 66; 6 April 1899, 76; 25 March 1901, 118.

102. Faculty Log Book, 10 January 1905, 185; 20 November 1905, 195; 5 December 1906, 214. Goode's note is contained in the Faculty Log Book.

103. Faculty Log Book, 13 April 1897, 45; 24 February 1904, 177; 31 March 1904, 178; 15 February 1905, 188.

104. Faculty Log Book, 10 January 1899, 68; 26 January 1910, 257; 7 December 1906, 215–18. In the 4–1 vote to suspend Walker, Thomas Miller, Johnson C. Whittaker, Henry Butler, and Louise Fordham voted to suspend him while Robert S. Wilkinson voted no.

105. Faculty Log Book, 6 November 1902, 10 November 1902, 129–38.

106. "Emancipation Day at the Exposition," *Charleston News and Courier,* 2 January 1902, 3.

107. Quote from Meier, *Negro Thought in America,* 249.

108. *Congressional Record,* 51st Congress, second session, 22, 14 February 1891, 2691, 2694. He also spoke a month earlier in support of the Lodge federal elections bill. *Congressional Record* 22 (12 January 1891): 1216. See also S. Smith, *Negro in Congress,* 104.

109. Blease's comments on black education are from Newby, *Black Carolinians,* 83. Newby's source is the *Crisis* 5 (March 1913), 216. Also see Edgar, *South Carolina,* 468; William V. Moore in *South Carolina Encyclopedia,* 79–80; Litwack, *Trouble in Mind,* 269. Blease ran for a seat in the state house of representatives six times and won twice. He ran for lieutenant governor twice and lost twice. He ran for the state senate twice and won both races. He ran for governor six times and won twice. He ran for the U.S. Senate seven times and won twice.

110. Minutes, Board of Trustees, 6 March 1902, 111. In 1902 Blease did endorse the proposed $10,005 appropriation for the college. *Reports and Resolutions of the General Assembly of the State of South Carolina* (Columbia: State, 1903), 1: 898.

111. "Miller Writes His Resignation," *State,* 29 January 1911, 1; Minutes, Board of Trustees, 27 January 1911, 188. See also Burnside, "Governorship of Coleman Livingston Blease," 6.

112. For more on this fascinating case and the people involved in it, see Burke, "Pink Franklin v. South Carolina." After spending most of eight years on a chain gang, Franklin was paroled by Gov.

Richard Manning in 1919. He took a new name—Mack Rockingham—and lived in obscurity with his wife and children in Barnwell County until his death in 1949.

113. *Fifteenth Annual Report of the Board of Trustees of the Colored Normal, Industrial, Agricultural and Mechanical College of South Carolina, Reports and Resolutions of the General Assembly of the State of South Carolina, Regular Session Commencing January 9, 1912* (Columbia: Gonzales and Bryan, 1912), 2: 955–60. There were eighty-eight students in the normal program, 191 in the preparatory program, and eight special students.

114. *Fifteenth Annual Report of the Board of Trustees of the Colored Normal, Industrial, Agricultural and Mechanical College of South Carolina, Reports and Resolutions of the General Assembly of the State of South Carolina, Regular Session Commencing January 9, 1912* (Columbia: Gonzales and Bryan, 1912), 2: 953, 959.

115. Nix, "Tentative History of South Carolina State College," 21; Potts, *History of South Carolina State College,* 23–27; Thomas E. Miller to Gov. Martin Ansel, 17 October 1910, Box 17, Governors' Papers, South Carolina Department of Archives and History.

116. *Reports and Resolutions of the General Assembly of the State of South Carolina, Regular Session Commencing January 9, 1912* (Columbia: Gonzales and Bryan, 1912), 2: 960–61, 954. In 1911 the trustees had again requested $5,000 as a portion of the $18,000 that they asked the general assembly to provide. However, $8,000 of that amount was a special request for the steam heating plant for Bradham Hall.

117. W. T. B. Williams, "The State Colored College, 3 April 1904, GEB, Series 1, Subseries 1, Box 127, Folder 1161; "Report of the Committee to Examine the Financial and Physical Condition of State Colleges," *Reports and Resolutions of the General Assembly of the State of South Carolina* (Columbia: Gonzales and Bryan, 1907), 11: 398; Seaman A. Knapp to Dr. Wallace Buttrick, 19 October 1908. GEB, Series 1, Subseries 1, Box 127, Folder 1162. Savely's comments were contained in Knapp's letter. However, Savely was even more impressed with Claflin than S.C. State because "everything is done on a more expensive and extravagant scale at Claflin University than at the State Industrial School."

118. Katherine Mellow Charron discusses the effort to replace the white teachers with black teachers in the Charleston schools in *Freedom's Teacher,* 92–96. Also see Drago, *Initiative, Paternalism, and Race Relations,* 162.

CHAPTER TWO: THE STRUGGLE TO GROW

1. President's Report, *Nineteenth Annual Report, 1915,* 646.

2. *Who's Who in Colored America: A Biographical Dictionary of Notable Living Persons of Negro Descent in America,* 70.

3. "Local News," *Times and Democrat,* 7 February 1911, 4; "Want Him to Stay," *Times and Democrat,* 18 March 1911, 4. Michael Mounter of the University of South Carolina law school library uncovered this information on Frederick and Miller in the pages of the Orangeburg newspaper. For more on the obsequious Richard Carroll, see Hudson, *Entangled by White Supremacy,* 37–39; and Newby, *Black Carolinians,* 168–84.

4. Robert Shaw Wilkinson to Walter M. Riggs, 28 January 1911; Walter M. Riggs to Robert Shaw Wilkinson, 31 January 1911, Presidents' Papers, Walter M. Riggs, Robert Muldrow Cooper Library, Clemson University. At the time Riggs was thirty-eight years old and Wilkinson was forty-five.

5. Minutes, Board of Trustees, 29 March 1911, 54; C. Alan Brubb, "The Master Executive: Walter Merritt Riggs, 1910–1924," in McKale, *Tradition,* 107. For more on Frederick, see *Who's Who in Colored America: A Biographical Dictionary of Notable Living Persons of Negro Descent in America,* 70. Also see W. Lewis Burke and W. Hine, "The South Carolina State College Law School," in Burke and Gergel, *Matthew J. Perry,* 24–26.

6. For more complete biographical information on Wilkinson, see Weingarth, "Race and Power." Wilkinson's biography in *Who's Who In Colored America* indicates he had an honorary doctorate. *Who's Who in Colored America: A Biographical Dictionary of Notable Living Persons of Negro Descent in America,* 461. Wilkinson was also not listed in Harry Washington Greene's *Holders of Doctorates among American Negroes.*

7. Wilkinson day book, 23 August 1923, HCSCSU.

8. Wilkinson day book, 19 August 1923, HCSCSU. See Tye, *Rising from the Rails,* 43–44, for more on the exclusion of African American passengers from Pullman accommodations. Benjamin E. Mays,

who worked for a time as a Pullman porter, described his efforts (mostly unsuccessful) to gain access to Pullman cars. See *Born to Rebel,* 94–95.

9. *South Carolina Encyclopedia,* 1028–29; *Who's Who in Colored America: A Biographical Dictionary of Notable Living Persons of Negro Descent in America,* 221; Simkins, "Robert Shaw Wilkinson"; Drago, *Initiative, Paternalism, and Race Relations,* 102–3; Oberlin College Alumni files; Archives, University of Louisville Library; Wilkinson day book, 23 August 1923, HCSCSU.

10. Gov. Coleman Blease to Robert Shaw Wilkinson, 22 July 1911, Box 28, Governors' Papers, South Carolina Department of Archives and History.

11. Gov. Coleman Blease to A. L. Dukes, 20 June 1911, Box 28, Governors' Papers, South Carolina Department of Archives and History. *Sixteenth Annual Report of the Board of Trustees of the Colored Normal, Industrial, Agricultural and Mechanical College of South Carolina, 1912* (Columbia: Gonzales and Bryan, 1913), 14–15.

12. Gov. Coleman Blease to W. R. Lowman, 29 November 1911, Box 28, Governors' Papers, South Carolina Department of Archives and History.

13. *Seventeenth Annual Report of the Board of Trustees of the Colored Normal, Industrial, Agricultural and Mechanical College of South Carolina 1913* (Columbia: Gonzales and Bryan, 1914), 5; *Journal of the House of Representatives of the State of South Carolina,* Regular Session, 1914 (Columbia: Gonzales and Bryan), 1447.

14. *Eighteenth Annual Report of the Board of Trustees of the Colored Normal, Industrial, Agricultural, and Mechanical College of South Carolina* (Columbia: Gonzales and Bryan, 1914), 5.

15. President's Report, *Twentieth Annual Report of the Board of Trustees of the Colored Normal, Industrial, Agricultural and Mechanical College of South Carolina 1916* (Columbia: Gonzales and Bryan, 1917), 11.

16. Walter M. Riggs to Robert S. Wilkinson, 28 February 1912; Wilkinson to Riggs, 9 March 1912; Wilkinson to Riggs, 12 March 1912; Riggs to Wilkinson, 20 March 1912; Wilkinson to Riggs, 22 March 1912; Riggs to Wilkinson, 25 March 1912; Riggs to Wilkinson, 9 May 1912; Riggs to Wilkinson, 5 June 1912; Wilkinson to Riggs, 7 September 1912; Riggs to Wilkinson, 15 October 1912; Wilkinson to Riggs, 16 October 1912, Walter M. Riggs Presidential Papers, Series 17, Folders 52, 53, 54, 59, 66, 69, 70, Strom Thurmond Institute, Special Collections, Clemson University; President's Report, *Sixteenth Annual Report of the Board of Trustees of the Colored Normal, Industrial, Agricultural and Mechanical College of South Carolina 1912* (Columbia: Gonzales and Bryan, 1913), 3–5.

17. President's Report, *Seventeenth Annual Report of the Board of Trustees of the Colored Normal, Industrial, Agricultural and Mechanical College of South Carolina 1913* (Columbia: Gonzales and Bryan, 1914), 3, 8. *Twenty-First Annual Report, 1917,* 9–12; *Twenty-Fourth Annual Report, 1920,* 8.

18. *Twenty-Third Annual Report, 1919,* 13, 5, 21; *Twenty-Second Annual Report, 1918,* 25.

19. *Twenty-Second Annual Report, 1918,* 27. William R. Lowman, the secretary of the board of trustees who also served as chair of the local board, was paid an annual salary of $600, which was more than many of the full-time faculty received. Hall, *One-Hundred Years of Education at Savannah State College, 1890–1990,* 33.

20. "Agricultural work is stressed as never before" was a stock sentence that appeared in each annual report submitted by the college Board of Trustees from 1917 to 1921. *Twenty-First Annual Report, 1917,* 3; *Twenty-Second Annual Report, 1918,* 5; *Twenty-Third Annual Report, 1919,* 3; *Twenty-Fourth Annual Report, 1920,* 3; *Twenty-Fifth Annual Report, 1921,* 3. President's Annual Report, *Twenty-First Annual Report, 1917,* 13.

21. P. Claxton, Commissioner of Education, Department of Interior, to President R. S. Wilkinson, 10 September 1911, Presidents' Papers. HCSCSU.

22. Robert S. Wilkinson to P. Claxton, 26 September 1912, Presidents' Papers. HCSCSU.

23. L. A. Kalbach, Acting Commissioner of Education, to R. S. Wilkinson, 19 October 1911; Wilkinson to the Commissioner of Education, 15 November 1911, Presidents' Papers. HCSCSU.

24. President's Annual Report, *Twentieth Annual Report, 1916,* 13; *Twenty-Fifth Annual Report, 1921,* 7; Report of Jackson Davis, "State Colored Normal, Industrial, Agricultural and Mechanical College," General Education Board, Folder 1162, 1904–24, Series 1, Subseries 1, Box 127. Rockefeller Archives, North Tarrytown, N.Y.; Nix, "Tentative History of South Carolina State College," 40.

25. President's Report, *Twenty-Second Annual Report, 1918,* 10.

26. "46 Students Injured as College Dormitory Burns," *Times and Democrat,* 21 March 1916, 4; Nix, "Tentative History of South Carolina State College," 38–39; *Twentieth Annual Report of the Board*

of Trustees of the Colored Normal, Industrial, Agricultural and Mechanical College of South Carolina, Reports on State Officers Boards and Committees to the General Assembly of the State of South Carolina (Columbia: Gonzales and Bryan, 1917), 3–5, 14–19. Two days following the Bradham fire, the residence of S. M. Boston and his family, which was located on the college farm, burned to the ground. That fire originated in a chimney in the kitchen. No one was hurt.

27. "College Suffers Loss," *Times and Democrat,* 24 October 1916, 4; Nix, "Tentative History of South Carolina State College," 38–39; Minutes, Board of Trustees, Faculty Log Book, 27 November 1914, 314; 23 October 1916, 352, HCSCSU.

28. *Twentieth Annual Report of the Board of Trustees of the Colored Normal, Industrial, Agricultural and Mechanical College of South Carolina, Report of State Officers Boards and Committees to the General Assembly of the State of South Carolina* (Columbia: Gonzales and Bryan), 19; Nix, "Tentative History of South Carolina State College," 39–40.

29. *Twenty-First Annual Report of the Board of Trustees of the Colored Normal, Industrial, Agricultural and Mechanical College of South Carolina, Report of State Officers Boards and Committees to the General Assembly of the State of South Carolina* (Columbia: Gonzales and Bryan, 1917), 3–4, 17–18; *Twenty-Fourth Annual Report of the Board of Trustees of the Colored Normal, Industrial, Agricultural and Mechanical College of South Carolina, Report of State Officers Boards and Committee to the General Assembly of the State of South Carolina* (Columbia: Gonzales and Bryan, 1921), 16–17; Nix, "Tentative History of South Carolina State College," 39. The buildings were named after members of the board of trustees: Gov. Richard I. Manning, D. J. Bradham, and William R. Lowman.

30. Faculty Log book, 21 December 1916, 355.

31. Nix, "Tentative History of South Carolina State College" (Tobin recollection); President's Report, *Twenty-First Annual Report, 1918,* 7. At a later date, Boston's remains were removed from the campus and buried in the Orangeburg Cemetery near the Edisto Gardens.

32. President's Report, *Twenty-Second Annual Report, 1918,* 19; President's Report, *Twenty-Third Annual Report, 1919,* 16; President's Report, *Twenty-Fourth Annual Report, 1920,* 9, 16; Memorandum of Conference, 29 June 1920, General Education Board, Series 1, Subseries 1, Box 127, Folder 1162. Rockefeller Archive Center.

33. *Twenty-Third Annual Report, 1919,* 26; *Twenty-Fourth Annual Report, 1920,* 21; President's Report, *Twenty-Third Annual Report, 1919,* 24–25.

34. President's Report, *Nineteenth Annual Report, 1915,* 650–51; President's Report, *Twentieth Annual Report, 1916,* 13–14; President's Report, *Twenty-Fifth Annual Report, 1921,* 16.

35. Faculty Log Book, 15 January 1917, 356.

36. Faculty Log Book, 19 October 1914, 309; 23 November 1914, 311.

37. Faculty Log Book, 10 November 1916, 353, 16 April 1917, 369.

38. *Catalogue of State Agricultural and Mechanical College of South Carolina for 1917–1918* (Columbia, 1918), 19–20.

39. Faculty Log Book, 8 March 1911, 268; 14 April 1915, 332–33.

40. President's Report, *Twenty-Second Annual Report, 1918,* 8; President's Report, *Twenty-Third Annual Report, 1919,* 23.

41. Faculty Log Book, 7, 8, 11 March 1913, 286–88.

42. L. M. Tobin recollections, "Two Decades after the Opening," Nix, "Tentative History of South Carolina State College," 149.

43. Faculty Log Book, 11 April 1916, 348; 12 October 1917, 374.

44. Faculty Log Book, 8 January, 31 January 1913, 281.

45. Mays, *Born to Rebel,* 40–41.

46. Faculty Log Book, 1 May 1914, 305.

47. Faculty Log Book, 19 October 1914, 309.

48. *Catalogue of State Agricultural and Mechanical College of South Carolina, 1918–1919* (1918), 42.

49. *Catalogue of State Agricultural and Mechanical College of South Carolina, 1918–1919,* 41–42.

50. Personnel records, HCSCSU; *Catalogue of State Agricultural and Mechanical College, 1920–1921* (1921), 30.

51. Gordon, *Sketches of Negro Life and History in South Carolina.* The book was reprinted in 1970 by the University of South Carolina Press. Quote from p. xxiii of the preface. Hall, *One-Hundred years*

of Educating at Savannah State College, 1890–1990, 54. *Who's Who in Colored America: An Illustrated Biographical Dictionary of Notable Living Persons of African Descent*, 217–18.

52. Robert S. Wilkinson to Dr. F. W. Butler, 12 December 1923, Folder 98, HCSCSU.

53. Lau, *Democracy Rising*, 131.

54. Nix, "Tentative History of South Carolina State College," 41–42.

55. Nix, "Tentative History of South Carolina State College," 22; *Sixth Annual Report, 1902*, 904.

56. *Sixteenth Annual Report of the Board of Trustees of the Colored Normal, Industrial, Agricultural and Mechanical College of South Carolina, Reports and Resolutions of the General Assembly of the State of South Carolina* (Columbia: Gonzales and Bryan, 1913), 3–4, 10.

57. *Eighteenth Annual Report of the Board of Trustees of the Colored Normal, Industrial, Agricultural and Mechanical College of South Carolina, Reports and Resolutions of the General Assembly of the State of South Carolina* (Columbia: Gonzales and Bryan, 1915), 2: 589–90.

58. Eddy, *Colleges for Our Land and Time*, 144–45; Fosdick, *Adventure in Giving*, 43–50; Harris, "Ray of Hope," 44, 51.

59. Harris, "Ray of Hope," 51; Walter M. Riggs to Bradford Knapp, 6 January 1912, quoted in Harris, "Ray of Hope," 52. There was some concern whether black extension agents could or should work only with black farmers who owned their own land or also with black tenants if white landowners gave their consent. See also Grubb, "The Master Executive Walter Merritt Riggs," 110n23.

60. Harris, "Ray of Hope," 45–47.

61. Quoted in Eddy, *Colleges for Our Land and Time*, 141. See Reel, *High Seminary*, 179–80, 190–93.

62. Eddy, *Colleges for Our Land and Time*, 141; Report of the Board of Trustees of Clemson College, President's Report, *Reports and Resolutions of the General Assembly of the State of South Carolina* (Columbia: Gonzales and Bryan, 1915), 2: 345; Annual Report of the Extension Service, *Reports of State Officers Boards and Committees to the General Assembly of South Carolina* (Columbia: Gonzales and Bryan, 1921), 2: 113–14.

63. Harris, "Ray of Hope," 61, Robert S. Wilkinson to Walter M. Riggs, 27 July 1914.

64. Harris, "Ray of Hope," 61; McKale, *Tradition*, 115–16; Reel, *High Seminary*, 190–92.

65. Act No. 190, *Acts and Joint Resolutions of the General Assembly of the State of South Carolina, Passed at the Regular Session of 1915* (Columbia: Gonzales and Bryan, 1915–16), 382–83; Harris, "Ray of Hope," 67.

66. See Harris, "Ray of Hope," for more on the intricacies of the negotiations between Clemson and the Department of Agriculture, 67–82. W. M. Riggs to Senator Alan Johnstone, 24 February 1915, quoted in Harris, "Ray of Hope," 78.

67. Harris, "Ray of Hope," 82. President's Report, *Nineteenth Annual Report, 1915*, 649.

68. Annual Report of the Extension Service, *Annual Report of the Board of Trustees of Clemson College 1920*, 113–14; President's Report, *Twenty-Fourth Annual Report of the Board of Trustees of the Colored Normal, Industrial, Agricultural and Mechanical College of South Carolina, Reports of State Officers Boards and Committees to the General Assembly of South Carolina* (Columbia: Gonzales and Bryan, 1921), 2: 12. The 1917–18 college catalog listed the extension work personnel: B. Barnwell, Beaufort County; J. Powell, Barnwell County; E. D. Jenkins, Bamberg County; G. W. Daniels, Orangeburg County; J. E. Dickson, Richland County; H. A. Woodward, Sumter County; E. L. Nix, Georgetown County; H. E. Daniels, Darlington County; Mattie J. Battiste, state home economics worker; and Sallie C. Walker, extension work clerk. *Catalogue of State Agricultural and Mechanical College of South Carolina for 1917–1918*, 5–6.

69. President's Report, *Twenty-Third Annual Report, 1920*, 10.

70. President's Report, *Twenty-Fourth Annual Report, 1921*, 2: 12; President's Report, *Twenty-Third Annual Report, 1920*, 11.

71. President's Report, *Twenty-Fourth Annual Report, 1921*, 2: 12.

72. Annual Report of the Extension Service, *Report of the Board of Trustees of Clemson College 1920, Reports of State Officers Boards and Committees to the General Assembly of South Carolina* (Columbia: Gonzales and Bryan, 1921), 113–14.

73. Annual Report of the Extension Service, *Annual Report of the Board of Trustees of Clemson College Reports of State Officers Boards and Committees to the General Assembly of South Carolina* (Columbia; Gonzales and Bryan, 1921), 117.

74. President's Report, *Twenty-Fourth Annual Report of the Board of Trustees of the Colored Normal, Industrial, Agricultural and Mechanical College of South Carolina, Reports of State Officers Boards and Committees to the General Assembly of South Carolina* (Columbia: Gonzales and Bryan, 1921), 15–16.

75. President's Report, *Twenty-First Annual Report, 1917,* 13.

76. President's Report, *Twenty-Third Annual Report, 1919,* 8.

77. *Eighteenth Annual Report, 1914,* 586; *Twentieth Annual Report, 1916,* 6–7.

78. Report of the President of the College 1914, *Annual Report of the Clemson Board of Trustees, Reports of the General Assembly of the State of South Carolina* (Columbia: Gonzales and Bryan, 1915), 2: 326–27.

79. Newby, *Black Carolinians,* 186–87. Newby cites the *Charleston News and Courier,* 17 April 1917, 5.

80. Newby, *Black Carolinians,* 188.

81. Newby, *Black Carolinians,* 188.

82. The figure 683 in the table is from the twenty-fourth annual report (1919–20). The figure of 448 is from the twenty-third annual report (1918–19).

83. *Twenty-Second Annual Report,* 6–7, and *Twenty-Third Annual Report,* 8; Hall, *One-Hundred Years of Education at Savannah State College, 1890–1990,* 34. Miller F. Whittaker personnel record, Historical Collection, South Carolina State University; and Marszalek, *Court Martial,* 269. It is ironic that Miller F. Whittaker received his commission before his father, Johnson C. Whittaker, who had been a cadet at the U.S. Military Academy nearly four decades earlier. The elder Whittaker had been dismissed from West Point after a controversial court martial and trial on trumped-up charges. He received his commission posthumously from President Bill Clinton in 1995.

84. Coffman, *War to End All Wars,* 58; *Twenty-Second Annual Report,* 17.

85. *Twenty-Second Annual Report,* 17–18.

86. *Twenty-Third Annual Report,* 14.

87. *Twenty-Third Annual Report,* 14.

88. Gordon, *Sketches of Negro Life and History in South Carolina,* 215.

89. *Twenty-Second Annual Report,* 4, 11; *Twenty-Third Annual Report,* 10, 12. "Influenza Pandemic of 1918," by Lisa J. Dimitriadis, in *South Carolina Encyclopedia,* 479–80.

90. Typescript, Minutes, Board of Trustees, HCSCSU.

91. President's Report, *Eighteenth Annual Report, 1914,* 2: 590; President's Report, *Nineteenth Annual Report, 1915,* 651.

92. President's Report, *Twenty-Fifth Annual Report, 1921,* 13.

93. President's Report, *Twenty-Fourth Annual Report, 1920,* 11; President's Report, *Twenty-Fifth Annual Report, 1921,* 13; Fosdick, *Adventure in Giving,* vii, 13, 327, 331; Jackson Davis, "State Colored, Normal, Industrial and Mechanical College, 23 January 1920, Series 1, Subseries 1, Box 127, Folder 1162, Rockefeller Archive Center.

94. J. E. Swearingen to A. J. Thackston, 24 January 1920, Series 1, Subseries 1, Box 127, Folder 1162, Rockefeller Archive Center.

95. President's Report, *Twenty-Fourth Annual Report, 1920,* 12–14.

96. Jackson Davis to Dr. E. C. Sage, 12 June 1920, Series 1, Subseries 1, Box 127, Folder 1162, Rockefeller Archive Center.

97. Jackson Davis memorandum, 29 June 1920, Series 1, Subseries 1, Box 127, Folder 1164, Rockefeller Archive Center.

98. President's Report, *Twenty-Third Annual Report, 1919,* 14–15.

99. President's Report, *Twenty-Fifth Annual Report, 1921,* 14.

100. Edgar, *South Carolina,* 484–85.

101. Fraser, *Charleston! Charleston!,* 363; Edgar, *South Carolina,* 481.

CHAPTER THREE: BECOMING A COLLEGE

1. *Twenty-Seventh Annual Report of the Board of Trustees* (Columbia: Gonzales and Bryan, 1924), 8. For more on the Great Migration, from South Carolina, see Hudson, *Entangled by White Supremacy,* 148–75.

2. *Thirty-First Annual Report of the Board of Trustees of the Colored, Normal, Industrial, Agricultural and Mechanical College of South Carolina, 1927* (Columbia: Joint Committee on Printing, 1927), 32.

3. *Twenty-Seventh Annual Report, 1924,* 9; *Twenty-Sixth Annual Report, 1923,* 16.

4. *Acts and Joint Resolutions of the General Assembly of South Carolina, Regular Session, 1929,* 301–19.

5. *Twenty-Ninth Annual Report of the Board of Trustees* (Columbia: Joint Committee on Printing, 1925), 6–7, 3.

6. Robert Shaw Wilkinson to Jackson Davis, 6 October 1924, State Department of Education file, HCSCSU.

7. *Twenty-Eighth Annual Report of the Board of Trustees* (Columbia: Joint Committee on Printing, 1924), 15, 4, 6.

8. Walter M. Riggs to Robert S. Wilkinson, 9 January 1923, Sinking Fund Commission folder, HCSCSU.

9. Robert S. Wilkinson to W. Claude Martin, 5 March 1926, State Department of Education, General Education Board folder, SCSU. Martin was a Democrat from the Orangeburg County town of Branchville. *Biographical Directory of the South Carolina Senate 1776–1985,* 2: 1065.

10. Robert S. Wilkinson to W. Claude Martin, 7 March 1927; Martin to Wilkinson, 10 March 1927, HCSCSU.

11. Robert S. Wilkinson to J. B. Beck, 4 February and 9 February 1931, High School principals folder, Historical Collection, SCSU; *Biographical Directory of the South Carolina Senate 1776–1985,* 2: 1675–76. *Biographical Directory of the South Carolina Senate,* 3: 1676.

12. Robert S. Wilkinson to C. F. Brooks, 1 March 1927, State Department of Education, General Education Board folder, HCSCSU.

13. Robert S. Wilkinson to C. F. Brooks, 1 March 1927; Brooks to Wilkinson, 26 February 1927, State Department of Education, General Education Board folder, HCSCSU.

14. Claude E. Sawyer to Robert S. Wilkinson, 7 January 1930; Robert S. Wilkinson to Claude E. Sawyer, 13 January 1930, Sinking Fund Commission folder, HCSCSU; *Biographical Directory of the South Carolina State Senate,* 3: 1736–37.

15. Charles H. Gerald [secretary to Gov. Blackwood] to Miller F. Whittaker, 26 June 1933, State Department of Education; James C. Shepard to Miller F. Whittaker, 16 February 1933, Sinking Fund Commission, HCSCSU.

16. C. F. Brooks to Robert S. Wilkinson, 11 April 1927, State Department of Education, General Education Board folder, HCSCSU.

17. E. D. Hodge to Robert S. Wilkinson, 20 June 1930; Robert S. Wilkinson to E. D. Hodge, 25 June 1930, Department of Education folder, HCSCSU.

18. Robert S. Wilkinson to E. D. Hodge, 24 March 1931, Department of Education folder, HCSCSU.

19. Blease lost U.S. Senate races in 1914 and 1918 and failed in gubernatorial elections in 1916 and 1922. "Coleman Blease," by William V. Moore, in *South Carolina Encyclopedia,* 79–80.

20. Coleman Blease to Robert S. Wilkinson, 27 December 1926; Wilkinson to Blease, 12 January 1927; 2 February 1927; Blease to Wilkinson, 3 February 1927, State Department of Education folder, HCSCSU.

21. John D. Long, Secretary to Senator Blease, to Robert S. Wilkinson, 14 October 1927; Robert S. Wilkinson to Senator Cole Blease, 30 December 1929; Blease to Wilkinson, 2 January 1930, State Department of Education folder, HCSCSU. Allen University President Robert M. Mance ignited a bitter controversy among African Americans when he invited Blease to deliver an address in 1916 to a black audience on the Allen campus. See Hudson, *Entangled by White Supremacy,* 190–91.

22. *Twenty-Eighth Annual Report of the Board of Trustees* (Columbia: Joint Committee on Printing, 1924), 19.

23. *Survey of Negro Colleges and Universities,* 676; *Catalogue of State Agricultural and Mechanical College for 1928–1929* (Orangeburg, 1929), 6–12; *Thirty-First Annual Report of the Board of Trustees* (Columbia: Joint Committee on Printing, 1927), 17.

24. *Catalogue of State Agricultural and Mechanical College of South Carolina for 1922–1923* (Orangeburg, 1923), 21); *Thirty-First Annual Report of the Board of Trustees* (Columbia: Joint Committee on Printing, 1927), 32.

25. *Catalogue of State Agricultural and Mechanical College of South Carolina for 1928–1929,* 19.

26. *Twenty-Eighth Annual Report of the Board of Trustees* (Columbia: Joint Committee on Printing, 1924), 24; *Thirty-Third Annual Report of the Board of Trustees* (Columbia: Joint Committee on Printing, 1929), 11; "Program: Dedication of Dukes Gymnasium," 26 May 1931, contained in Faculty Log Book II, 267. A. L. Dukes was a local board member who had served for thirty years. See also, "John Henry Blanche, 1908–1960," by Peggy Stevenson Ratliff and Roosevelt Ratliff Jr., in *African American Architects,* 39–41.

27. *Thirty-Fifth Annual Report of the Board of Trustees* (Columbia: Joint Committee on Printing, 1931), 20–21.

28. *Thirty-Third Annual Report of the Board of Trustees* (Columbia: Joint Committee on Printing, 1929),10; *Wilkinsonian,* 1926, 86.

29. *Twenty-Ninth Annual Report of the Board of Trustees* (Columbia: Joint Committee on Printing, 1925), 21; *Thirty-First Annual Report of the Board of Trustees* (Columbia: Joint Committee on Printing, 1927), 24.

30. *Twenty-Seventh Annual Report of the Board of Trustees* (Columbia: Gonzales and Bryan, 1923), 18; *Thirty-Fourth Annual Report of the Board of Trustees* (Columbia: Joint Committee on Printing, 1930), 25.

31. Robert S. Wilkinson to James H. Hope, 6 December 1927; Hope to Wilkinson, 8 December 1927, State Department of Education folder, HCSCSU.

32. James E. Hillman to Robert S. Wilkinson, n.d., State Board of Education folder, SCSUHC. North Carolina officials used the ratings as a basis for teacher certification. S.C. State's C rating ranked it with Florida A&M, Tuskegee, and Morris Brown. Claflin, Morris, and Alcorn received D ratings. Atlanta University, Fisk, Hampton, and Howard received an A rating while North Carolina A&T, Lane, and Clark received B ratings. See Faculty Log Book II, 122, HCSCSU.

33. *Catalogue of State Agricultural and Mechanical College for 1928–1929,* 6–10.

34. "The History of Education in South Carolina: Colonial to Mid-Twentieth Century," by Lewis Jones, in Walker, Richardson, and Parks, *Organization of Public Education in South Carolina,* 25–26; "Education," by Deborah M. Switzer and Robert Green Jr., in *South Carolina Encyclopedia,* 288; Edgar, *South Carolina,* 490; *Catalogue of State Agricultural and Mechanical College for 1928–1928,* 22.

35. *College Catalogue, 1926–1927.*

36. Robert S. Wilkinson to President C. B. Antisdel, 25 September 1925, State Department of Education, High School Principals, HCSCSU.

37. Programs: "State Declamation Contest," 4 May 1928, 16 May 1930, Faculty Log Book II, 175, 232, HCSCSU.

38. Mays, *Born to Rebel,* 101.

39. Mays, *Born to Rebel,* 105. Roper, *Magnificent Mays,* 120–30. Mays's first wife, Ellen Harvin, had died in 1923. See chapter 2.

40. The report was compiled by Arthur J. Klein, the chief of the Division of Higher Education in the Department of Interior's Bureau of Education. *Survey of Negro Colleges and Universities,* 665–80.

41. *Survey of Negro Colleges and Universities,* 675–76.

42. *Survey of Negro Colleges and Universities,* 675. Some of the honorary degrees were used as if they had been earned. For example, W. W. Wilkins, who was an instructor in the vocational program, was awarded an honorary bachelor's degree. Thereafter he was listed as a faculty member with a bachelor's degree.

43. *Survey of Negro Colleges and Universities,* 673.

44. *Survey of Negro Colleges and Universities,* 679–80.

45. *Catalogue of the State Agricultural and Mechanical College of South Carolina for 1930–31* (Orangeburg: 1931), 12; L. Turner, *Africanisms in the Gullah Dialect.* Turner told Darlene Clark, an undergraduate history major at Roosevelt University in the mid-1960s, that she did not have to cross the Atlantic Ocean to become acquainted with African culture and language. She could simply pay a visit to the South Carolina lowcountry.

46. "New Alma Mater," *Collegian,* November 1927, 1.

47. "Should State College Have a Mascot," *Collegian,* February 1927, 1; "Mascot," *Collegian,* March 1927, 1.

48. *Catalogue of State Agricultural and Mechanical College for 1928–1929,* 4.

49. *Catalogue of State Agricultural and Mechanical College for 1923–1924* (Orangeburg, 1924), 19–23; *Catalogue of State Agricultural and Mechanical College for 1925–1926* (Orangeburg, 1925), 24. A copy of the entire booklet "Rules and Regulations Governing Students" is contained in the Faculty Log Book II, 114, HCSCSU.

50. *Catalogue of State Agricultural and Mechanical College for 1923–1924*, 23.

51. Faculty Log Book II, 26 November 1923, 21, HCSCSU.

52. Faculty Log Book II, 2 December 1924, 45, HCSCSU.

53. Faculty Log Book II, 14 April 1926, 104; 14 May 1926, 109.

54. Faculty Log Book II, 28 December 1926, 128; 27 January 1925, 48; Robert S. Wilkinson to William Morgan, 31 March 1928; S. M. Gossett, Onleanis Reid, Lalee Worthy, Wade Witherspoon, and Burnette Gallman to Wilkinson, 2 April 1928. This correspondence is contained in the Faculty Log Book II, 170.

55. Johnson C. Whittaker to Robert S. Wilkinson, 8 March 1928, Faculty Log Book II, 167 HCSCSU.

56. Faculty Log Book II, 18 April 1923, 11, 26 April 1923, 12, 23 November 1925, 76; 1 December 1925, 77.

57. Faculty Log Book II, 22 May 1924, 37; 18 December 1929, 222.

58. *Catalogue of State Agricultural and Mechanical College for 1925–1926*, 24–26.

59. Robert S. Wilkinson to Mr. James Moody, Tupelo, Mississippi, 22 January 1932, Robert S. Wilkinson to Mrs. Josephine Jordan, 27 February 1930, contained in Faculty Log Book II, 278 and 227.

60. In considering the creation of a smoking room in Lowman Hall, the men's dormitory, the Faculty Council estimated that 90 percent of male students smoked. Faculty Log Book II, 15 October 1929, 209.

61. Faculty Log Book II, 8 October 1929, 208; 18 October 1929, 212.

62. Faculty Log Book II, n.d., 193; 22 February 1929, 197.

63. Eleven Junior Women to Robert S. Wilkinson, 29 October 1929, Faculty Council to "Young Women of the Junior Class, 4 November 1929, Faculty Log Book II, 213; Faculty Log Book II, 26 November 1929, 217.

64. *Catalogue of State Agricultural and Mechanical College for 1924–1924*, 21.

65. Faculty Log Book II, 15 October 1929, 209. Mabel James was listed in the U.S. census of 1920 as the adopted daughter of the Robert S. and Marion B. Wilkinson and lived in their home on campus. By 1930 she was living on her own.

66. Faculty Log Book II, 7 January 1930, 223.

67. *Wilkinsonian*, 1925, HCSCSU.

68. Faculty Log Book II, 13 May 1924, 33; 22 February 1926, 96; 30 November 1927, 153.

69. Faculty Log Book II, 13 January 1923, 4; 10 November 1930, 240.

70. Faculty Log Book II, 5 December 1927, 157; 10 November 1930, 240. Female faculty members were to inform dormitory matrons if they would be out after 10:30 P.M.

71. Faculty Log Book II, 21 October 1929, 210.

72. Faculty Log Book II, 17 April 1929, 178; 26 April 1929, 179; 28 May 1929, 181, HCSCSU. Fort went on to earn a Ph.D. in chemistry from the Massachusetts Institute of Technology in 1933. Greene, *Holders of Doctorates among American Negroes*, 149.

73. Faculty Log Book II, 9 January 1928, 161; 17 December 1928, 190; 13 January 1930, 224; 3 February 1930, 224; 19 May 1931, 265. Fitchett and Asa Gordon were among the very few faculty members who published scholarly work.

74. Faculty Log Book I, 6 December 1921, 465; Faculty Log Book II, 23 November 1925, 76.

75. "Christmas Recess Regulations—1927," Faculty Log Book II, 159.

76. "YWCA Christmas Program," *Collegian*, January 1928, 1.

77. "Commencement Program," May 1926, Faculty Log Book II, 111.

78. "Emancipation Day," *Collegian*, January 1928, 1.

79. Faculty Log Book II, Program: Education Week, 16–22 November 1925, 74; Commencement Program, 1926, 111; Declamation Contest Program, 1930, 232. "Yankee Doodle" and the "Star Spangled Banner" were sung at commencement in 1928. Commencement Program, 1928, File: Commencement Programs, HCSCSU.

80. Faculty Log Book I, 11 April 1921, 450; Faculty Log Book II, 24 January 1923, 6. It is not certain that Douglass Day was celebrated each year. Faculty Log Book II, 12 March 1928, 168. "Negro History

Week," *Collegian,* February 1927, 1, and "College Celebrates Negro History," *Collegian,* February 1928, 1. For more on Carter G. Woodson, see Dagbovie, *Black History,* 203, 209.

81. "College Celebrates Negro History Week," *Collegian,* February 1928, 1; "Negro History Week Starts Feb. 3," *Collegian,* January 1929, 1.

82. Franklin, "Courses concerning the Negro in Negro Colleges," 138.

83. *Catalogue of State Agricultural and Mechanical College for 1923–1924,* 18; "College Celebrates Negro History Week, *Collegian,* February 1928, 1.

84. T. J. Crawford recalled this anecdote in his alumni column in the *Collegian,* December 1966.

85. Faculty Log Book I, 7 November 1921, 462; 50th Anniversary Program, Southern Intercollegiate Athletic Conference; 1963, McGhee, "Intercollegiate Athletic Competition at S.C. State A. and M. College."

86. Faculty Log Book II, 18 October 1928, 183; 29 October 1928, 184.

87. Faculty Log Book II, 28 November 1927, 152; 28 March 1929, 198.

88. Faculty Log Book II, 18 October 1928, 183; 26 May 1929, 201; 4 November 1929, 214; 27 September 1930, 239; "Football Financial Statement," 1928, Faculty Log Book II, 189.

89. *Catalogue of State Agricultural and Mechanical College for 1923–1924,* 18; *Wilkinsonian,* 1925, 80–81; *Wilkinsonian,* 1926, 82. The names of the players appeared only in the 1926 yearbook. "Football Season Review," *Collegian,* December 1927, 4; New Athletic Facilities, Collegian, January 1928, 4; 50th Anniversary Program, Southern Intercollegiate Athletic Conference, McGhee, "Intercollegiate Athletic Competition at S.C. State A. and M. College."

90. *Catalogue of State Agricultural and Mechanical College for 1928–1929,* 18; *Thirty-Fifth Annual Report, 1930–1931* (Columbia: Joint Committee on Printing, 1931), 15; 2007 *Bulldog Centennial [Football] Media Guide* (Orangeburg, 2007), 70; *Wilkinsonian,* 1925, 86; 50th Anniversary Program, Southern Intercollegiate Athletic Conference, McGhee, "Intercollegiate Athletic Competition at S.C. State A. and M. College"; *Wilkinsonian,* 1926, 83; *Thirty-Sixth Annual Report, 1931–1932* (Columbia: Joint Committee on Printing, 1933), 12.

91. Faculty Log Book II, 6 November 1926, 102; Debate program, 175. U.S. Marines were dispatched to Nicaragua in 1927 to prop up the government of Anastasio Somoza against a popular uprising led by Augusto Sandino and his Sandinista supporters. The Marines departed in 1933. Nugent, *Habits of Empire,* 297.

92. W. C. Bethea to Robert S. Wilkinson, 20 January 1926, State Department of Education folder, HCSCSU; Faculty Log Book II, 12 March 1928, 175; 28 January 1926, 87. "Marian Anderson," *Collegian,* December 1927, 1.

93. *Catalogue of State Agricultural and Mechanical College for 1923–1924,* 18; *Catalogue of State Agricultural and Mechanical College for 1928–1929,* 19; Editorial, *Collegian,* January 1929, 2.

94. *Thirty-First Annual Report, 1926–1927* (Columbia: Joint Committee on Printing, 1927), 18; *Catalogue of State Agricultural and Mechanical College for 1928–1929,* 19. "Omegas," *Collegian,* January 1928, 3; Manning, *Black Apollo of Science,* 40–41; *Bulldog,* 1940, 63–67.

95. Faculty Log Book II, 12 March 1924, 27; Program: "Omega Psi Phi" 25 March 1928, 175; 14 April 1924, 29.

96. "Rules Governing Fraternity Activities on the State College Campus." Faculty Log Book II, January 1932, 277; *Thirty-Fifth Annual Report of the President* (Columbia: Joint Committee on Printing, 1931), 27.

97. *Catalogue of State Agricultural and Mechanical College for 1923–1924,* 22; *Thirty-First Annual Report, 1926–1927* (Columbia: Joint Committee on Printing, 1927), 32; *Catalogue of State Agricultural and Mechanical College for 1928–1929,* 19; *Thirty-Fifth Annual Report of the President* (Columbia: Joint Committee on Printing, 1931), 14.

98. *Thirty-First Annual Report, 1926–1927* (Columbia: Joint Committee on Printing, 1927), 29.

99. Drago, *Initiative, Paternalism, and Race Relations,* 102; "Marion Birnie Wilkinson," by Cherisse R. Jones, in *South Carolina Encyclopedia,* 1028.

100. J. Johnson, *Southern Ladies,* 13–15, 53; Kibibi Mack, *Parlor Ladies and Ebony Drudges,* 57–58, 105–6; Drago, *Initiative, Paternalism and Race Relations,* 193.

101. J. Johnson, *Southern Ladies,* 54, 93–94.

102. J. Johnson, *Southern Ladies,* 92–93.

103. J. Johnson, *Southern Ladies,* 181–85.

104. J. Johnson, *Southern Ladies*, 187–90.

105. J. Johnson, *Southern Ladies*, 192; Hudson, *Entangled by White Supremacy*, 32–33, 108.

106. *Twenty-Sixth Annual Report, 1921–1922*, 9–10; *Thirty-Sixth Annual Report, 1931–1932*, 12–13.

107. *Twenty-Seventh Annual Report, 1922–1923*, 8–9.

108. *Twenty-Seventh Annual Report, 1922–1923*, 8–9; Harris, "Ray of Hope," 190–91.

109. *Twenty-Eighth Annual Report, 1923–1924*, 28; Robert S. Wilkinson to E. H. Shinn, 25 February 1930. Folder: Extension Work Matters, HCSCSU. Shinn was an official in extension work at the U.S. Department of Agriculture.

110. *Twenty-Eighth Annual Report, 1923–1924*, 27.

111. *Twenty-Eighth Annual Report, 1923–1924*, 27; *Thirty-Third Annual Report, 1928–1929*, 26–27.

112. *Thirty-Third Annual Report, 1928–1929*, 25–27.

113. *Thirty-Third Annual Report, 1928–1929*, 28–29.

114. Narrative summary of Annual Report of Dora E. Boston, State Supervisor of Negro Home Development." Folder: Extension Work Matters, 1926–32, HCSCSU.

115. Robert S. Wilkinson to C. McGowan, 5 January 1928, Folder: Extension Work Matters, 1926–32, HCSCSU.

116. *Thirty-Third Annual Report, 1928–1929*, 29.

117. Nettie L. Kerner, 1929 and 1930 Annual Reports of Home Demonstration Agent. Folder: Extension Work Matters, 1926–32, HCSCSU.

118. Dora E. Boston, State Supervisor of Negro Home Demonstration, 1928 Narrative Summary of Annual Report, Folder: Extension Work Matters, 1926–32, HCSCSU.

119. *Thirty-Fourth Annual Report, 1929–1930*, 17.

120. *Thirty-Fourth Annual Report, 1929–1930*, 18–19.

121. Program: "A Pageant and Garden Party: 'The Feast of the Tomato.'" Folder: Extension Work Matters, 1926–33, HCSCSU.

122. E. H. Shinn to Robert S. Wilkinson, 21 October 1930; Wilkinson to Shinn, 27 October 1930, 19 February 1931; Wilkinson to Shinn, 4 March 1931, Folder: Extension Work Matters, 1926–33, HCSCSU.

123. *Bulletin*, 1924—No. 37, *Land-Grant College Education 1910–1920;* Robert S. Wilkinson, "Education in Negro Land-Grant Colleges," 80–81, 87–89.

124. *Thirtieth Annual Report, 1925–1926*, 10; *Thirty-First Annual Report, 1926–1927*, 27.

125. Dora E. Boston to Robert S. Wilkinson, 3 August 1928, Folder: Extension Work Matters, 1926–33, HCSCSU.

126. Robert S. Wilkinson to Dora Boston Daniels, 7 August 1928, Folder: Extension Work Matters, 1926–33, HCSCSU.

127. Dora Boston Daniels to Robert S. Wilkinson, 5 September 1928, Folder: Extension Work Matters, 1926–33, HCSCSU. Wilkinson replied cordially to Boston asking her who she thought might replace her as home demonstration supervisor. "If you have a recommendation to make, I would be pleased to receive it." He offered her "best wishes for future happiness and welfare." Wilkinson to Daniels, 24 September 1928.

128. Lonny I. Landrum to Robert S. Wilkinson, 4 December 1930. Folder: Extension Work Matters, 1926–33, HCSCSU.

129. Robert S. Wilkinson to E. W. Biggs, 2 March 1931, Folder: Extension Work Matters, 1926–33, HCSCSU.

130. Robert S. Wilkinson to Lonnie Landrum, 3 March 1931; Landrum to Wilkinson, 7 March 1931. Folder: Extension Work Matters, 1926–31, HCSCSU.

131. Marian B. Paul to Robert S. Wilkinson, 5 March 1931; Lonnie Landrum to Robert S. Wilkinson, 28 May 1931. Folder: Extension Work Matters, 1926–33, HCSCSU.

132. Robert S. Wilkinson to W. W. Long, 6 January 1931. Folder: Extension Work Matters, 1926–31, HCSCSU.

133. Robert S. Wilkinson to Rosa B. Cooley, 7 January 1931. Folder: Extension Work Matters, 1926–31, HCSCSU.

134. Robert S. Wilkinson to H. E. Daniels, 1 May 1930. Folder: Extension Work Matters, 1926–33, HCSCSU.

135. C. W. Warburton to Robert S. Wilkinson, 28 March 1931. Folder: Extension Work Matters, 1926–33, HCSCSU.

136. Robert S. Wilkinson to W. W. Long, 27 March 1931; Long to Wilkinson, 28 March 1931; Wilkinson to Long, 30 March 1931. Folder: Extension Work Matters, 1926–31, HCSCSU.

137. Robert S. Wilkinson to J. E. Dickson, 5 March 1929, 7 March 1929. Folder: Extension Work Matters, 1926–33, HCSCSU.

138. Robert S. Wilkinson to J. E. Dickson, 7 March 1929. Folder: Extension Work Matters, 1926–33, HCSCSU.

139. A. J. Collins, President of the State Colored Fair, to W. W. Long, 18 March 1931 (copy), Long to Collins, 19 November 1931. Folder: Extension Work Matters, 1926–33, HCSCSU.

140. Robert S. Wilkinson to W. W. Long [n.d.], Folder: Extension Work Matters, 1926–33, HCSCSU. In an earlier letter to J. B. Blanton, the principal of Voorhees College in Denmark, S.C., Wilkinson explained that he had previously agreed to take part in the State Colored Fair—which received state funding—provided reforms were implemented. "The agreement, however, was not kept, and our extension forces were withdrawn. We shall never return until a radical change is made." Robert S. Wilkinson to J. B. Blanton, 6 November 1929, Folder: Extension Work Matters, 1926–33, HCSCSU.

141. Robert S. Wilkinson to D. W. Watkins, 16 February 1931. Folder: Extension Work Matters, 1926–33, HCSCSU. Wilkinson's emphasis. Columbia's black newspaper, the *Palmetto Leader,* carried an obituary for Seymour Carroll when he died. *Palmetto Leader,* 20 March 1943. There is a brief biography of Carroll in *Who's Who in Colored America: A Biographical Dictionary of Notable Living Persons of Negro Descent in America,* 37.

142. E. D. Jenkins to Robert S. Wilkinson, 22 August 1930, Wilkinson to Jenkins, 7 October 1930. Folder: Extension Work Matters, 1926–33, HCSCSU. Jenkins contended that he had been conducting extension work since 1905. See "Statement of Local Agent E. D. Jenkins, Bamberg County, South Carolina, Outlining Briefly Developments Resulting from His Work in Farm Demonstration Extending over a Period of Twenty-Two Years in One Locality," 1927. Federal officials claimed he had been appointed on 29 August 1913. See J. A. Evans, Associate Chief, Extension Service, to Edmund Douglas Jenkins, 20 December 1930, Folder: Extension Work Matters, 1926–33. Jenkins asked Wilkinson if perhaps his son, Robert, could be appointed to replace him as Bamberg's agent so that his family would have some income. E. D. Jenkins to Robert S. Wilkinson, 22 August 1930, Folder: Extension Work Matters, 1926–33, HCSCSU; Harris, "Ray of Hope," 195–99.

143. Robert S. Wilkinson to E. W. Sikes, 11 April 1931; Sikes to Wilkinson, 20 April 1931. Folder: Extension Work Matters, 1926–33, HCSCSU.

144. Harris, "Ray of Hope," 199–200.

145. Robert S. Wilkinson to W. W. Riggs, 19 April 1923; Riggs to Wilkinson, 21 April 1923, Correspondence: President's Office, 1923–32, HCSCSU.

146. Ascoli, *Julius Rosenwald.* Rosenwald also donated money to Jewish organizations, the YMCA, the University of Chicago, and the Museum of Science and Industry in Chicago.

147. Hoffschwelle, *Rosenwald Schools of the American South,* appendix 2, 238. In addition, the black and white taxpayers of South Carolina through state appropriations contributed $1,706,000 to the Rosenwald schools.

148. Ascoli, *Julius Rosenwald,* 396–97.

149. See chapter 3.

150. *Twenty-Eighth Annual Report, 1923–1924* (Columbia: Joint Committee on Printing, 1924), 9; Minute Book B, Board of Trustees, 23 October 1923, 52–53; Robert S. Wilkinson to J. B. Felton, 2 October 1924, State Department of Education folder, 1924–34; Robert S. Wilkinson to Julius Rosenwald Fund, 13 November 1928, Rosenwald file, HCSCSU; Gorman and Stickell, "Partners in Progress."

151. George Arthur to Robert S. Wilkinson, 15 November 1928; M. C. James to George Arthur, 20 November 1928; Robert S. Wilkinson to George Arthur, 20 December 1928. Rosenwald Folder, HCSCSU. In 1929 the gifts included a shooting game, a wood clarinet, a military set, and a kiss-me doll in a trunk.

152. George R. Arthur to Dr. C. B. Smith, Chief of Extension Service of the U.S. Department of Agriculture, George Arthur to Robert S. Wilkinson, n.d., Robert S. Wilkinson to George Arthur, 12 November 1920, Rosenwald Folder, HCSCSU. Ascoli, *Julius Rosenwald,* 295, and Manning, *Black Apollo of Science,* 125–26, 137–38

153. Robert S. Wilkinson to George R. Arthur, 2 April 1929; George R. Arthur to Robert S. Wilkinson, 18 July 1929; George R. Arthur to Robert S. Wilkinson, 5 April 1930, Rosenwald Folder, HCSCSU.

154. Robert S. Wilkinson to J. B. Felton, 4 July 1928; Robert S. Wilkinson to J. H. Hope, 15 May 1929; J. B. Felton to Robert S. Wilkinson, 30 April 1931, Department of Education Folder, S. L. Smith to Robert S. Wilkinson, 15 October 1930, Rosenwald Folder; "Contributions to Library Fund," *Collegian,* April 1927, 2.

155. Folder: "W. W. Wilkins, Agricultural Education." The journals that Wilkinson kept are included in the folder. HCSCSU. The Rosenwald Fund also purchased vehicles used in other states for vocational education.

156. Ascoli, *Julius Rosenwald,* 374, 383; Robert S. Wilkinson to George R. Arthur, 13 March 1930, George R. Arthur, 5 April 1930, Rosenwald Folder, HCSCSU.

157. James D. Anderson makes the strongest case that northern wealth was intent on maintaining the racial status quo by promoting teacher training and agricultural and industrial skills in institutions such as Hampton and Tuskegee. *Education of Blacks in the South.* Also see Spivey, *Schooling for the New Slavery.*

158. Fosdick, *Adventure in Giving,* vii, appendix 3, 329–32.

159. The quote is from "Report to General Education Board Special Meeting at Gedney Farms Hotel, October 12–14, 1922," section 6, 24, Box 331 of the GEB papers. See E. Anderson and Moss, *Dangerous Donations,* 96.

160. Anderson and Moss, *Dangerous Donations,* 95–97.

161. Robert S. Wilkinson to Jackson Davis, 6 October 1924, Report of Jackson Davis, 28 October 1924, Series 1, Subseries 1, Box 127, Folder 1162, Rockefeller Archive Center.

162. *Thirtieth Annual Report, 1925–1926,* 24.

163. Wallace C. Bethea, F. Limehouse, E. D. Hodge, and Charles F. Brooks voted aye, while Adam H. Moss and A. L. Dukes dissented. Minute Book B, Board of Trustees, 24 September 1926, 69–70; *Thirty-First Annual Report, 1926–1927,* 20; *Thirty-Second Annual Report, 1927–1928,* 20.

164. *Thirty-Second Annual Report, 1927–1928,* 29.

165. "R. S. Wilkinson Improves," *Palmetto Leader,* 17 January 1925, 1. Wilkinson had fallen ill in South Carolina in 1925, but he sought medical care in New York City. Claude E. Sawyer to Robert S. Wilkinson, 7 January 1930, Sinking Fund Folder; Wilkinson to Amanda S. Roberts, 30 December 1930, State Department of Education Folder, HCSCSU.

166. Wilkinson had been raised in the African Methodist Episcopal Church. Robert S. Wilkinson to Bishop A. S. Thomas, 29 July 1929, Sinking Fund Commission Folder. Several obituaries were included in the faculty log book: Faculty Log Book II, 282–92. HCSCSU.

CHAPTER FOUR: THE GREAT DEPRESSION

1. Minute Book B, Board of Trustees, 15 March 1932, 89. Miller F. Whittaker to Charles F. Brooks, 10 May 1932, Sinking Fund Commission file, HCSCSU.

2. B. E. Mays to W. C. Bethea, 27 May 1932, "Permanent Facts about State A&M College," Sinking Fund Commission folder, HCSCSU.

3. Minute Book B, Board of Trustees, 30 May 1932, 90.

4. Personnel File, HCSCSU; Marszalek, *Court Martial,* 263–71. For example, in 1926 Whittaker took charge of the college when Wilkinson left for a week in Washington, D.C. Robert S. Wilkinson to W. C. Bethea, 9 May 1926, Department of Education file, HCSCSU.

5. *Thirty-Sixth Annual Report,* 8; *Thirty-Eighth Annual Report, 21–22*; Miller F. Whittaker to John H. Hope, 29 June 1933, State Department of Education file, HCSCSU.

6. Minute Book B, Board of Trustees, 15 March 1932, 89; Miller F. Whittaker to Verd Peterson, 21 February 1933, State Department of Education file, HCSCSU.

7. W. Jack Bryant to Senator James F. Byrnes, 13 April 1932, Extension Work, Box 1, Folder 1. HCSCSU. Bryant was local pharmacist who felt compelled to support the black college. See also, Harris, "Ray of Hope," 305. Such a loss in federal money would have been a disaster for Clemson as well.

8. Postal telegrams, 19, 20, 22 April 1932. South Carolina's six house members were Hampton Fulmer, Thomas McMillan, Butler B. Hare, Fred H. Dominick, W. F. Stevenson, and Allard H. Gasque. Fulmer was from Orangeburg and chairman of the House Agriculture Committee. Extension Work, Box 1, Folder 1; Telegram: L. A. Kalbach, Chief Clerk, U.S. Office of Education, to M. T. [*sic*] Whittaker, 22 May 1932, Extension Work, Box 1, Folder 3. HCSCSU.

9. J. B. Felton to Miller F. Whittaker, 4 April 1933, State Department of Education file. Eventually Wilkins did receive at least partial compensation. See Felton to Whittaker, 10 June 1933, State Department of Education file, HCSCSU.

10. A. W. Beattie to Miller F. Whittaker, 25 April 1933, State Department of Education file, HCSCSU; *Thirty-Eighth Annual Report, 1933–1943,* 5.

11. Typed manuscript, Faculty Log Book III, 19 September 1932, 23.

12. Miller F. Whittaker to Jackson Davis, 22 March 1933; Miller F. Whittaker to Walter B. Hill, 4 April 1933, GEB file, State Department of Education, HCSCSU; Report by Walter B. Hill, 31 March 1933; W. W. Brierly to Miller F. Whittaker, 17 May 1933, Series 1, Subseries 1, Box 127, Folder 1163, Rockefeller Archive Center.

13. Miller F. Whittaker to Walter B. Hill, 8 November 1932; Hill to Whittaker, 12 November 1932; Whittaker to Hill, 16 November 1932, GEB file, State Department of Education, HCSCSU; *Thirty-Sixth Annual Report, 1931–1932,* 14; *Thirty-Seventh Annual Report, 1932–1933,* 16.

14. *Thirty-Seventh Annual Report, 1932–1933,* 10; Miller F. Whittaker to E. W. Sikes, 7 November 1932, Sinking Fund Commission file. See also Minute Book B, Board of Trustees, 27 October 1932, 93, 23 May 1933, 94. HCSCSU.

15. Robert S. Wilkinson to Benjamin M. Sawyer, 5 February 1932, Sinking Fund Commission file, HCSCSU.

16. *Thirty-Seventh Annual Report, 1932–1933,* 22–23.

17. *Thirty-Seventh Annual Report, 1932–1933,* 22–23; Minute Book B, Board of Trustees, 23 May 1933, 94; Circular Letter to Students from William J. Spann, Registrar, 10 June 1933, Sinking Fund Commission file, HCSCSU; *College Catalogue, 1930–1931,* 10–11. Johnson C. Whittaker had served as principal of the high school until his death in 1931. The position had not been filled by the time the high school closed in 1933.

18. *Thirty-Sixth Annual Report, 1930–1931,* 7; *Forty-Third Annual Report, 1938–1939,* 6.

19. *Fortieth Annual Report, 1935–1936,* 6; Eddy, *Colleges for Our Land and Time,* 153.

20. Fosdick, *Adventure in Giving,* 302–9.

21. Miller F. Whittaker to Jackson Davis, 14 June 1932, GEB file, State Department of Education, HCSCSU; *State Agricultural and Mechanical College Catalogue, 1934–1935,* 8–10.

22. *State Agricultural and Mechanical College Catalogue, 1939-1940,* 8-9. According to one contemporary account, recipients of GEB fellowships were "selected in an almost haphazard way." There were no formal application forms or admission tests administered. College presidents recommended faculty members, and the GEB staff reviewed the recommendations, accepting most while rejecting some. Fosdick, *Adventure in Giving,* 304.

23. Jackson Davis to Robert S. Wilkinson, 24 March 1931, GEB file, State Department of Education, HCSCSU.

24. *Thirty-Seventh Annual Report, 1932–1933,* 19. E-mail, Gayle Collier, University of Michigan Registrar's Office, to William C. Hine, 4 February 2009.

25. GEB Series 1, Subseries 1, File 669.1, Rockefeller Archive Center. The five other presidents were from Prairie View in Texas, Delaware State, Arkansas at Pine Bluff, Florida A&M, and Virginia State.

26. Orr, "Analytical Study of the Conference of Presidents of Negro Land-Grant Colleges," 35, 39.

27. Orr, "Analytical Study of the Conference of Presidents of Negro Land-Grant Colleges," 88–89, 91, 101, 104–5; *Forty-First Annual Report, 1935–1936,* 7. *Collegian,* December 1936.

28. *Thirty-Ninth Annual Report, 1934–1935,* 9; *Forty-Second Annual Report, 1937–1938,* 6.

29. Fred McCuistion to Miller F. Whittaker, 14 April 1938, contained in the *Forty-Second Annual Report, 1937–1938,* 42. North Carolina A&T and Florida A&M were among the schools that had achieved the A rating.

30. Hayes, *South Carolina and the New Deal,* 29.

31. J. E. Sirrine, Chair, State Planning Board, to Miller F. Whittaker, 29 September 1933; "Application for Loans from the Federal Emergency Administration of Public Works for Permanent Improvements at the State Agricultural and Mechanical College of South Carolina," 28 September 1933. Relief Folder, HCSCSU. Bethea was the General Manager of J. W. Smoak Hardware. *Baldwin's City Directory,* 79.

32. Miller F. Whittaker to B. Kortjohn, Administrator, Orangeburg Emergency Relief Administration, 16 October 1933; Miller F. Whittaker to B. Kortjohn, Local Civil Works Administrator, 24 February 1934, Relief Folder, HCSCSU.

33. Student Relief Work Form submitted to South Carolina Emergency Relief Administration, February 1934, Relief Folder; Rosa Lee Irby to Miller F. Whittaker, 14 February 1934. Relief Folder, 1933–34, HCSCSU.

34. P. V. Jewell to Miller F. Whittaker, 7 February 1934. Relief Folder, 1933–34, HCSCSU.

35. Miller F. Whittaker to Leo Favrot, 2 November 1938; Interview: Walter B. Hill, Fred McCuistion, W. A. Schiffley, and Miller F. Whittaker, 12 October 1936, GEB, Series 1, Subseries 3, Box 479, Folders 5102 and 5101, Rockefeller Archive Center. Fosdick, *Adventure in Giving*, 274–75.

36. Jackson Davis to Leo Favrot, 2 November 1936, GEB, Series 1, Subseries 3, Box 479, Folder 5101, Rockefeller Archive Center.

37. Miller F. Whittaker to Leo Favrot, 19 November 1936, GEB, Series 1, Subseries 3, Box 479, Folder 5101, Rockefeller Archive Center; Favrot to Whittaker, 28 November 1936; Whittaker to Favrot, 13 December 1936; W. W. Brierly to Whittaker, postal telegram, 19 December 1936, Folder 1, Library Building, HCSCSU.

38. Miller F. Whittaker to Leo Favrot, 13 January 1937, Folder 1, Library Building; Whittaker to W. W. Brierly, 10 June 1937; Minute Book B, Board of Trustees, 22 December 1936, 106, HCSCSU.

39. Minute Book B, Board of Trustees, 28 October 1937, 111. There was an additional delay of several months pending the outcome of a lawsuit over the constitutionality of the bond bill. Miller F. Whittaker to W. W. Brierly, 13 December 1937, Folder 2, Library Building, HCSCSU.

40. J. L. M. Irby to Miller F. Whittaker, 13 September 1937; George E. Lafaye to Whittaker, 29 September 1937, Folder: Miller Hall, HCSCSU.

41. Miller F. Whittaker to Kline Iron Works, 22 June 1938; Whittaker to John Miller, 22 June 1938, Whittaker to Lafaye and Lafaye, 7 February 1938, Folder 1, Library Building, HCSCSU.

42. Miller F. Whittaker to J. C. Heslep, 4 January 1938; Whittaker to H. L. Eargle, 19 April 1938, Folder 1, Library Building, HCSCSU. Eargle was a superintendent with J. C. Heslep.

43. Miller F. Whittaker to J. C. Heslep, 19 April 1938; Heslep to Whittaker, 28 April 1938, Folder 1, Library Building, HCSCSU.

44. "The New Library at State College," *Collegian*, February 1939, 1; "Founder's Day Celebrated," *Collegian*, March 1939, 1.

45. Miller F. Whittaker to W. W. Brierly, 14 February 1939; Brierly to Whittaker, 21 February 1939; Whittaker to Edwin Embree, 16 February 1939; Embree to Whittaker, 23 February 1939, Folder 2, Library Building; Whittaker to F. R. Foster, 5 January 1939 and passim, Folder 1, Library Building, HCSCSU.

46. See Whittaker's correspondence in 1939, 1940, and 1941, Folder 2, Library Building, Minute Book B, Board of Trustees, 30 October 1940, 134, HCSCSU.

47. *Twenty-Seventh Annual Report, 1923–1924*, 9.

48. "Statement of Justification and Revenue Anticipation," 6 November 1936, Folder: Miller Hall, HCSCSU; *Forty-First Annual Report, 1936–1937*, 11, 24.

49. Booklet: "Specifications," 15; "Application for Grant, Federal Emergency Administration of Public Works," 12 January 1937; Booklet: "Specifications: Boy's Dormitory for the Colored Normal, Industrial, Agricultural and Mechanical College at Orangeburg, South Carolina." Lafaye and Lafaye, Architects, 2, 9–10; Miller F. Whittaker to J. T. Liles, U.S. Employment Office, 6 December 1937.

50. "Report of Chief G. H. Fischer, the Orangeburg Fire Department," Minute Book, Board of Trustees, 26 October 1936, 104; Miller F. Whittaker to Lafaye and Lafaye, 3 January 1937; Stanley H. Wright, Regional Engineer for FERA of Public Works to Miller F. Whittaker (via Lafaye and Lafaye), 15 January 1937; George E. Lafaye to Miller F. Whittaker, 13 April 1938. Folder: Miller Hall, HCSCSU.

51. Miller F. Whittaker to Lafaye and Lafaye, 19 April 1938. Folder: Miller Hall, HCSCSU. There were several other letters also complaining of construction defects. Miller Hall was formally completed and accepted by the trustees on 28 June 1938. *Forty-Second Annual Report, 1937–1938*, 33; *Forty-Third Annual Report, 1938–1939*, 7.

52. Hayes, *South Carolina and the New Deal*, 64–70.

53. *Forty-Second Annual Report, 1937–1938*, 33; *Forty-Third Annual Report, 1938–1939*, 20; *Forty-Fourth Annual Report, 1939–1940*, 10; Minute Book, Board of Trustees, 23 April 1940, 131. HCSCSU.

54. Miller F. Whittaker to Leo Favrot, 2 November 1938, Interoffice Memo: Dr. Robert J. Havighurst to Leo Favrot, 9 November 1939, GEB, Series 1, Subseries 3, Box 479, Folder 5102, Rockefeller Archive Center.

55. Miller F. Whittaker to Leo Favrot, 14 November 1938; "General Education Board Grant in Aid"; W. W. Brierly to Whittaker, 4 January 1939, GEB, Series 1, Subseries 3, Box 479, Folder 5102, Rockefeller Archive Center.

56. Undated memo from Robert J. Havighurst, GEB, Series 1, Subseries 3, Box 479, Folder 5102, Rockefeller Archive Center.

57. Miller F. Whittaker to Fred C. McCuistion, 5 August 1939; McCuistion to Whittaker, 8 August 1939, GEB, Series 1, Subseries 3, Box 479, Folder 5102, Rockefeller Archive Center.

58. Miller F. Whittaker to Fred C. McCuistion, 14 December 1939. The comments about Whittaker are written in pencil in the margin of Whittaker's letter. Whittaker to Arthur R. Mann and Jackson Davis, 17 June 1940, GEB, Series 1, Subseries 3, Box 479, Folder 5104, Rockefeller Archive Center.

59. Report of L. H. Foster, 15 March 1939, GEB, Series 1, Subseries 1, Folder 1164, Rockefeller Archive Center.

60. Interview: Jackson Davis with James H. Birnie, 8 August 1938, GEB, Series 1, Subseries 1, Box 127, Folder 1163, Rockefeller Archive Center. *Forty-Third Annual Report, 1938–1939,* 19. James Birnie was the son of the second wife of Richard Birnie. Information courtesy of Dr. Barbara Williams Jenkins.

61. Proposal: Marine Biology Laboratory, 3, August 1938, GEB, Series 1, Subseries 1, Box 127, Folder 1163, Rockefeller Archive Center.

62. Birnie, "Report," 10. Just, who made a name for himself as a marine biologist, had already received grants from the Rosenwald Fund and the GEB for study and research in Italy and Germany. See Manning, *Black Apollo of Science.*

63. Interview: Jackson Davis with James H. Birnie, 8 August 1938, GEB, Series 1, Subseries 1, Box 127, Folder 1163, Rockefeller Archive Center.

64. Interoffice Correspondence: Jackson Davis to W. W. Brierly and others, 19 September 1938; W. W. Brierly to James H. Birnie, 23 September 1938, GEB, Series 1, Subseries 1, Box 127, Folder 1163, GEB.

65. Rosa B. Cooley to Trevor Arnett, 1 May 1936, GEB, Series 1, Subseries 3, Box 479, Folder 5103, Rockefeller Archive Center. For more on the establishment and development of the Penn School, see Rose, *Rehearsal for Reconstruction;* Cooley, *Homes of the Freed.*

66. Interview: Leo Favrot, Miller F. Whittaker, J. B. Felton, and W. A. Schliffley, Orangeburg, S.C., 11 September 1936; W. W. Brierly to Miller F. Whittaker, 21 October 1936, GEB, Series 1, Subseries 3, Box 479, Folder 5103, Rockefeller Archive Center.

67. NYA Form: "Proposed Work Plan College and Graduate Aid." N.d., probably 1939, Folder: NYA, 1939–40, Relief Agencies, State Department of Education file, HCSCSU; Hayes, *South Carolina and the New Deal,* 60–61.

68. Attalee Pickens to Miller F. Whittaker, postcard, 19 September 1940. Folder: NYA, 1939–40, Relief Agencies, South Carolina Department of Education file, HCSCSU.

69. Juanita Williams to Miller F. Whittaker, 19 February 1941. Folder: NYA, 1939–40, Relief Agencies, South Carolina Department of Education file, HCSCSU.

70. Francis Pendarvis to Miller F. Whittaker, 5 September 1940. Folder: NYA, 1939–40, Relief Agencies, South Carolina Department of Education file, HCSCSU.

71. Mary McLeod Bethune to Miller F. Whittaker, 20 May 1940; Miller F. Whittaker to Mary McLeod Bethune, 30 May 1940. Folder: NYA, 1939–40, Relief Agencies, South Carolina Department of Education, HCSCSU.

72. Lynwood Smith, Director of Student Work and Related Training for the NYA, to Clarence E. Clinkscales, Assistant to President Miller F. Whittaker, 1 November 1940; Miller F. Whittaker to William A. Huey, Supervisor of Educational Aid for the NYA, 18 July 1939; Draft report in pencil in response to a request to provide data to the NYA on academic averages from Roger L. Coe, State Youth Administrator, 23 January 1940. Folder: NYA, 1939–40, Relief Agencies, State Department of Education file, HCSCSU.

73. Hayes, *South Carolina and the New Deal,* 61; Miller F. Whittaker to Mary McLeod Bethune, 18 May 1940; Miller F. Whittaker to William A. Huey, 15 August 1939, Folder: NYA, 1939–40, Relief Agencies, South Carolina Department of Education, HCSCSU.

74. "Official Rules and Regulations Governing Students," revised February 1935, Faculty Log Book III, 89. HCSCSU.

75. Faculty Log Book III, 3 October 1934, 77. See the exchange between Nevin Austin and President Miller F. Whittaker, Faculty Log Book III, November 1935, 109. HCSCSU.

76. Faculty Log Book III, 16 May 1933, 49; 3 February 1934, 66; 16 May 1936, 147, HCSCSU.

77. Faculty Log Book III, 15 July 1932, Memo: N. C. Nix to Miller F. Whittaker, 21, 57. HCSCSU.

78. Faculty Log Book III, 18 December 1934, 79. HCSCSU.

79. Faculty Log Book III, 7 November; 5 December 1935, 107, 111. HCSCSU.

80. "Cabot Lodge Debating Union," *Collegian,* November 1936, 3.

81. Editorial, *Collegian,* October 1933, 2.

82. Editorial, *Collegian,* November 1935, 2.

83. K. W. Green, "The Negro as a Problem in America," *Collegian,* March 1935, 3.

84. K. W. Green, "Racketeering and Organized Crime," *Collegian,* January 1937, 3. Seven people were killed in a violent confrontation in the Anderson County town of Honea Path in September 1934 as efforts by the United Textile Workers to organize failed. See Bass and Poole, *Palmetto State,* 81–82; and Edgar, *South Carolina,* 505.

85. Program: "Presenting Thomas E. Miller," 15 May 1933, Faculty Log Book III, 55. HCSCSU.

86. *Thirty-Sixth Annual Report, 1931–1932,* 6, 44–45; *Thirty-Seventh Annual Report, 1932–1933,* 36.

87. "Negro History Week," *Collegian,* February 1934, 1. In February 1939, the *Collegian* observed that Negro History Week extended from February 5 to 12, but that most of the month would be devoted Negro history programs. "Negro History Week Observed at State College," 1.

88. "Negro History Week," *Collegian,* February 1934, 1.

89. "Negro History Week," *Collegian,* February 1936, 1; "Outstanding Negroes of South Carolina," *Collegian,* February 1937, 1; Faculty Log Book III, Programs for 1936, 161. HCSCSU.

90. "Founder's Day," *Collegian,* March 1938, 1; *Forty-First Annual Report, 1936–1937,* 8, 21.

91. "Easter Service," *Collegian,* May 1938, 1.

92. Faculty Log Book III, 14 September 1936, 175; *Forty-First Annual Report, 1936–1937,* 5. HCSCSU.

93. For more on the Jones Bankhead Act of 1935, see Harris, "Ray of Hope," 314–17; Kerr, *Legacy,* 73–76; and Eddy, *Colleges for Our Land and Time,* 153.

94. For the annual increases in the federal funds, see the budgets included in the annual reports. Watkins had replaced Clemson's first and longtime director of extension work, W. W. Long.

95. Robert S. Wilkinson to J. B. Pierce, 5 January 1929, Wilkinson Presidential Papers, Extension Work Matters; Directory of Federal and State Departments and Agencies, compiled by the National Emergency Council, Lawrence M. Pinckney, Director, 1 April 1939, 28–38, Miller F. Whittaker Miscellaneous File, HCSCSU.

96. "Population," in *South Carolina Encyclopedia,* 744.

97. The Directory of Federal and State Departments and Agencies, 1939, contains the list of black and white extension personnel. See 30–31, 34. See Narrative Summary, *Annual Report, 1931–1932,* 2.

98. Narrative Summary, *Annual Report, 1931–1932,* 15; *Thirty-Ninth Annual Report, 1934–1935,* 15.

99. Narrative Summary, *Annual Report, 1931–1932,* 4–5, Narrative Summary, *Annual Report, 1939–1940,* 8–9. See Harris, "Ray of Hope," 395.

100. Narrative Summary, *Annual Report, 1931–1932,* 14.

101. See Harris, "Ray of Hope," 320. For the statistics mentioned by Whittaker, Harris cites letters from Whittaker to Secretary of Agriculture Henry Wallace, 6 March, 8 March 1937, Box 486, File A–G, S.C., Entry 3, RG 33, National Archives and Records Administration.

102. Personnel file for Marian B. Paul; Marian Baxter Paul to Harry Daniels, 9 December 1930; Robert S. Wilkinson to Paul, 11 December 1930, Extension Work, Box 1, Folder 4, HCSCSU; *Hill's Columbia City Directory, 1930,* 668.

103. In addition to annual reports, Paul and Harry Daniels provided monthly accounts to President Whittaker and the extension authorities at Winthrop and Clemson. Paul's comments are taken from the February 1933 report. Extension Work, Box 2, Folder 1, HCSCSU.

104. Narrative Summary, *Annual Report, 1931–1932,* 8, 39.

105. Narrative Summary, *Annual Report, 1931–1932,* 3; Marian B. Paul, Monthly Report, April 1933, Extension Work, Box 2, Folder 1, HCSCSU.

106. "Handbook for 4-H Girls." Extension Work, Box 2, Folder 1, HCSCSU. Paul utilized information for the handbook taken from the U.S. Department of Agriculture as well as material prepared at Winthrop College; Narrative Summary, *Annual Report, 1931–1932,* 24–27.

107. Marian B. Paul, Narrative Summary, *Annual Report, 1931–1932,* 37. Extension Work, Box 2, Folder 1, HCSCSU.

108. Marian B. Paul, Narrative Summary, *Annual Report, 1931–1932,* 19. Extension Work, Box 2, Folder 1, HCSCSU.

109. Narrative Summary, *Annual Report, 1931–1932,* 18, 29.

110. The Paul and Dickson comments are from Harris, "Ray of Hope," 414–15. Harris cites Marian B. Paul, Narrative Summary, *Annual Report, 1932–1933,* 4; J. E. Dickson, "Historical Appraisal of Extension Work in Richland County [1939]," 1. Dickson Collection, South Caroliniana Library, University of South Carolina, Columbia, S.C.

111. Harry Daniels, Monthly Report, February 1933. Extension Work, Box 2, Folder 5. HCSCSU; *Thirty-Ninth Annual Report, 1934–1935,* 18–19.

112. Marian B. Paul, Narrative Summary, *Annual Report, 1931–1932,* 7. Box 2, Folder 1. HCSCSU.

113. Marian B. Paul, Narrative Summary, 1938–39, 1. Harris points out in "Ray of Hope," 409n75, that the first sentence in this quote is taken from Thomas Pearce Bailey, *Race Orthodoxy in the South and Other Aspects of the Negro Question,* 37.

114. Narrative Summary, *Annual Report, 1931–1932,* 45.

115. *Forty-First Annual Report, 1936–1937,* 6.

116. Whittaker cited *Clemson Bulletin* 302 as his source for Frayser's study. Miller F. Whittaker, "A Study of Occupational Opportunities of Negroes by the Land Grant Colleges." *Proceedings of the Thirteenth Annual Conference of the Presidents of Negro Land-Grant Colleges,* 14–17.

117. Personnel files for Alfred W. Shute and Buelah Shute, HCSCSU.

118. Edwin R. Embree to Miller F. Whittaker, 29 April 1932; W. W. Long to Whittaker, 7 May 1932, Miscellaneous file, Miller F. Whittaker, HCSCSU.

119. H. W. Barre to Miller F. Whittaker, 12 May 1932; A. F. Woods to Whittaker, 16 May 1932, Miscellaneous file, Miller F. Whittaker, HCSCSU.

120. H. W. Barre to Miller F. Whittaker, 28 May 1932, "Cooperative Agreement between the South Carolina Experiment Station and State A. and M. College," 24 May 1932, Miscellaneous file, HCSCSU.

121. George R. Arthur to Miller F. Whittaker, 15 June 1932, Miscellaneous file, HCSCSU.

122. Lowman was born in 1866 in Lexington County. He was an 1888 graduate of the College of Physicians and Surgeons in Baltimore. He was a senior partner in the Lowman Drug Company. He was also a physician with the Atlantic Coast Line Railroad and a vice president of the Edisto National Bank. Obituary, *Times and Democrat,* 6 July 1925, 1. Genealogy file, Orangeburg Historical Society.

123. "Bethea Ends Long Service with College," *Times and Democrat,* 4 December 1966, 1. Dr. Eugene Atkinson graciously provided his file on Bethea. Bethea stepped down as board secretary in 1966 and retired from the board after his last six-year term expired in 1970. He died in 1982.

124. W. C. Bethea to Jackson Davis, 5 July 1926; W. W. Brierly to Bethea, 2 December 1926, State Department of Education file, HCSCSU; *Forty-Fourth Annual Report, 1939–1940,* 14.

125. Robert S. Wilkinson to Gov. John G. Richards, 10 May 1927, Correspondence, President's Office, HCSCSU.

126. W. Hine, "Civil Rights and Campus Wrongs," 329; Grose, *South Carolina at the Brink,* 193

127. *Biographical Directory of the South Carolina House of Representatives,* vol. 1, *Session Lists,* 477, 481, 509, 530, 537, 554.

128. Robert S. Wilkinson to E. D. Hodge, 5 December 1930. President's Correspondence, Sinking Fund Commission, HCSCSU; *Thirty-Eighth Annual Report, 1934–1935,* 18.

129. Minute Book B, Board of Trustees, 25 June 1935, 100; 20 May 1936, 103.; *Fortieth Annual Report, 1935–1936,* 24. HCSCSU.

130. Minute, Book B, Board of Trustees, 28 June 1938, 119. HCSCSU.

CHAPTER FIVE: THE SECOND WORLD WAR

1. "Answers from Students," *Collegian,* February 1939, 4.
2. "Editorial Comment," *Collegian,* April 1941, 2.

3. "We Are at War," *Collegian,* December 1941, 1.

4. "We Are at War," *Collegian,* December 1941, 1. As far as can be determined, "The Double V" was first coined by a correspondent of the *Pittsburgh Courier.*

5. "Editorial Comment"; John L. Pendarvis, "Problems Facing the American Negro," *Collegian,* November 1940, 2, 4. Frustrated by the War Department and its secretary, Henry Stimson, to deal with racial discrimination in the military, Hastie resigned his position in January 1943.

6. While the creation of the Fair Employment Practices Commission (FEPC) was an important civil rights milestone, the agency proved to be far from effective in eliminating racial discrimination during the war. See Garfinkel, *When Negroes March.*

7. In 1943 Viola Duvall earned an annual salary of $645 as the chair of the Burke High School Science Department. The lowest paid white teacher in the district earned $1,100 a year. R. Scott Baker shows how the State of South Carolina rushed to adopt the National Teachers Exam (NTE) to maintain salary inequities. Baker, *Paradoxes of Desegregation,* 44–62. Also see Lau, *Democracy Rising,* 129–30.

8. "Editorial Comment," *Collegian,* 7 March 1941, 2.

9. "Editorial Comment," *Collegian,* March 1942, 2.

10. "Governor Appoints 120 Negroes to County Selective Service Boards," *Collegian,* November 1940, 1; Carroll was the head of the American Humane Education Society. The three black men who assisted in the registration of black males for the Selective Service in Orangeburg were attorney and S.C. State graduate Shadrach Morgan; John Burgess, who was in charge of the itinerant agriculture and vocational teachers; and E. Horace Fitchett, a professor of sociology at Claflin. *Annual Report, 1941–1942,* 10. Under the Selective Service Act of 1940, forty-three million men registered for the draft. There were 6,443 local draft boards, and 250 African Americans served nationwide on those boards. See Kennedy, *Freedom from Fear,* 632–33.

11. "Should College Students Be Drafted?" *Collegian,* November 1941, 2.

12. *Annual Report, 1942–1943,* 5, 7, 10.

13. Miller F. Whittaker to W. A. Schiffley, 19 April 1943, 26 April 1943, Selective Service file, 1942–46, Miller F. Whittaker papers, HCSCSU; *Annual Report, 1944–1945,* 7.

14. For Whittaker's letters to Local Board 62 in Orangeburg, see the Selective Service file, H. W. Crawford (24 April 1942), E. Melvin Adams (28 January 1944), Gabe Buchanan and Thomas J. Crawford (27 April 1944), Oliver C. Dawson and Dudley M. Zimmerman (12 June 1945). By 1943, black people represented 10.6 percent of the U.S. population, but only 6 percent were in the military. For more on the draft during World War II, see Kennedy, *Freedom from Fear,* 634; Litwack, *How Free Is Free?,* 59. John Hope Franklin, a historian with a Ph.D. from Harvard, was discouraged from enlisting by military recruiters.

15. *Annual Report, 1941–1942,* 21.

16. Carriebelle C. Wright to Miller F. Whittaker, 1 October 1942, File: Students General, General Files, HCSCSU.

17. *Annual Report, 1940–1941,* 6; *1943–1944,* 21; *1944–1945,* 34. For correspondence involving the lack of housing, see for example File: Work, 1942–43, General Files, 1942–42. HCSCSU.

18. *Annual Report, 1940–1941,* 24; *1944–1945,* 10, 12, 19.

19. *Annual Report, 1942–1943,* 11; Minute Book B, Board of Trustees, 7 December 1942, 142–43. When the war ended so did Saturday classes, and the college returned to a thirty-six-week academic year. *Annual Report, 1944–1945,* 16.

20. *Annual Report, 1942–1943,* 8–9, 7. Minute Book B, Board of Trustees, 7 December 1942, 142. The federal government leased the facilities for the training courses at an undisclosed rate.

21. *Annual Report, 1942–1943,* 12.

22. *Annual Report, 1942–1943,* 10–11.

23. *Annual Report, 1942–1943,* 25.

24. Minute Book B, Board of Trustees, 25 April 1944, 150, 29 August 1944, 152; 25 May 1945, 156, 25 September 1945, 157. *Annual Report, 1944–1945,* appendix B, South Carolina House of Representatives Committee Report, 127.

25. *Annual Report, 1941–1942,* 5; Minute Book B, Board of Trustees, 19 May 1942, 139.

26. *Annual Report, 1942–1943,* 21, 25; *Annual Report, 1943–1944,* 20.

27. *Annual Report, 1944–1945,* 9–10; Minute Book B, Board of Trustees, 24 April 1945, 155.

28. *Annual Report, 1944–1945,* 33.

29. *History of the American Negro,* 186–87; "Robert N. C. Nix, Sr.," *Biographical Directory of Congress,* 1774–2005: HTTPS: www.GPO.GOV/pdsys/pkg/GP-CDOC-108hdoc222/GPO-CDOC-108hdoc pdf accessed 3 March 2017; "Robert C. Nix, Jr., Groundbreaking Judge," New York Times, 26 August 2003, www.nytimes,com/2003/08/26/us/r-n-c-nix-jr-75-groundbreakingjudge.html accessed 2 March 2017; *Annual Report, 1944–1945,* 8.

30. *Collegian,* May 1940, 1.

31. Harold W. Crawford, Editorial, *Collegian,* December 1941, 2.

32. Webber, *College Soda Shop,* 20, 25–27.

33. Eugenia Dean, "Campus Etiquette," *Collegian,* November 1940, 3.

34. "Eugenia Dean, "Campus Etiquette, Collegian, December 1940, 3, 2. Dean admitted that the restrooms on the segregated rail coaches were filthy. "At best the restroom is [uninviting] . . . but keep it as clean as possible."

35. *Collegian,* January 1943, p. 2.

36. File: Students Dismissed, 1942-42, Miller F. Whittaker papers, HCSCSU.

37. Rev. J. D. Bryan to Miller F. Whittaker, 11 July 1942; Whittaker to Bryan, 20 July 1942, File: Students Dismissed, General Files, 1942–43, HCSCSU.

38. Miller F. Whittaker to Matthew Perry, 1 July 1942, File: Students Dismissed, General Files, 1942–43, HCSCSU.

39. W. M. Kinney to Miller F. Whittaker, 23 September 1942; Whittaker to Kinney, 25 September 1942. Kinney had complained three weeks earlier that he had been charged fifty cents for a room key deposit that was not mentioned in the catalog. "Now if your printed matters in your catalogue is not dependable and you can't guarantee her a reserve room without paying the $.50 in advance please send me by return mail the $35.00." Kinney to Whittaker, 1 September 1942, File: Students General, General Files, 1942–43, HCSCSU.

40. Lyles Perry, "A Student Thinks Seriously," *Collegian,* November 1940, 1, 4.

41. Photographs of the May Queen and her attendants were prominently displayed in the *Collegian.* See May 1937, 1; May 1940, 3; and May 1941, 3, for example. On the appearances by Benjamin E. Mays, see *Collegian,* April 1941, 1; May 1942, 3; and April 1943, 1.

42. Lillian Waring, "Campus Clubs and Greekdom," *Collegian,* January 1939, 3; 28 March 1941, 2–3. The Greek letter organizations on the eve of World War II were Alpha Kappa Alpha, Alpha Phi Alpha, Phi Beta Sigma, Kappa Alpha Psi, Omega Phi Psi, and Delta Sigma Theta.

43. Cooke spoke on 26 January 1941, *Collegian,* March 1941. Schuyler performed in December 1942, *Collegian,* January 1943, 1. Lewis's visit was in December 1945. *Collegian,* December 1945, 1.

44. "The Student Speaks," *Collegian,* December 1941, 2.

45. Luther "Pepsi Cola" Bligen, "Sports Review," *Collegian,* February 1943, 4; May 1943, 6.

46. *Collegian,* October 1941, 1; Minute Book B, Board of Trustees, 17 February 1945, 154.

47. Webber, *College Soda Shop.* An advertisement in the *Collegian,* January 1941, 4: "Sodas, Sandwiches, Cigarettes, Magazines, Newspapers." The Webbers opened the Riverside Soda Shop on lower Russell Street on the corner at Windsor Street.

48. Webber, *College Soda Shop,* 51. The advertisement for the State Theater appeared in the *Collegian,* December 1940, 3.

49. "State College Observes 50th Anniversary," *Collegian,* April 1946, 1–2; Minute Book B, Board of Trustees, 2 April 1945, 159.

50. Miller F. Whittaker to W. C. Bethea, 19 February 1943, General Files, Trustees, HCSCSU. Whittaker wrote an identical letter to the chairman of the board, Charles F. Brooks.

51. *Annual Report, 1940–1941,* 10, *Annual Report, 1942–1943,* 7, Minute Book B, Board of Trustees, 25 May 1943, 143; *Annual Report, 1943–1944,* 5–6, Minute Book B, Board of Trustees, 28 July 1943, 144; 4 August 1943, 145; 22 September 1943, 146; 13 October 1943, 147.

52. Charles F. Brooks to Miller F. Whittaker, 10 May 1943; Whittaker to Brooks, 13 May 1943; Brooks to Whittaker, 16 July 1945, File: Trustees, Presidential Papers, Miller F. Whittaker, HCSCSU.

53. Charles F. Brooks to Miller F. Whittaker, 1 October 1946. File: Trustees, Presidential Papers, Miller F. Whittaker, HCSCSU.

54. Charles F. Brooks to Miller F. Whittaker, 10 January 1946, File: Trustees: Presidential Papers, Miller F. Whittaker, HCSCSU.

55. Julian C. Wolfe to Miller F. Whittaker, 30 September 1946; Charles F. Brooks to Miller F. Whittaker, 8 April 1947, File: Trustees, Presidential Papers, Miller F. Whittaker, HCSCSU.

56. Miller F. Whittaker to Gov. Strom Thurmond, 31 January 1948; Charles F. Brooks to Whittaker, 16 January 1947, File: Trustees, Presidential Papers, Miller. F. Whittaker, HCSCSU.

57. William C. Hine interview with Thomas J. Crawford, 9 March 1989.

58. William C. Hine interview with Thomas J. Crawford, 9 March 1989.

59. *Annual Report, 1940–1941,* 11.

60. *Annual Report, 1944–1945,* 13. At least one farm demonstration agent, R. C. Bacote in Marion County, was drafted for military service. G. W. Dean replaced him. See Harry E. Daniels, *Annual Report, 1942,* 2.

61. Harris, "Ray of Hope," 462–63. Harris cites Marian B. Paul's *Annual Report, 1942* on 131, 29, 30, 56–57, 76–77.

62. Harry E. Daniels, *Annual Report, 1942,* 32. To conserve fuel and tires, Farm and Home Week had been combined with 4-H Conservation Week.

63. Harry E. Daniels, *Annual Report, 1942,* 1.

64. Marian B. Paul, *Annual Report, 1945,* 29; Harry E. Daniels, *Annual Report, 1942,* 14, 35.

65. Harry E. Daniels, *Annual Report, 1942,* 35–43.

66. Marian B. Paul, *Annual Report, 1945,* 43.

67. Marian B. Paul, *Annual Report, 1945,* 43.

68. Harry E. Daniels, *Annual Report, 1942,* 35.

69. Harry E. Daniels, *Annual Report, 1942,* 20–21. Edgar, *South Carolina,* 530.

70. Marian B. Paul, *Annual Report, 1945,* 1. *South Carolina State Bulletin,* 1945–46, 76–77. For the Bankhead-Flannigan Act, see Eddy, *Colleges for Our Land and Time,* 237.

71. Marian B. Paul, *Annual Report, 1945,* 10.

72. *Annual Report, 1943–1944,* 22. For more on the legal struggle of black South Carolinians to secure a legal education in the Palmetto State, see Burke and Hine, "South Carolina State College Law School," in Burke and Gergel, eds., *Matthew J. Perry,* 17–60. Bailey told Houston that his primary intention in his application to the University of South Carolina was to gain financial support from the state in order to attend the New York University law school. Houston approved of this tactic because it fit with Houston's overall strategy to undermine Jim Crow by making it too expensive for states to create separate educational facilities on the graduate and professional levels or to expend funds on the education of black residents outside of South Carolina. Ultimately, Houston believed, states would be compelled to admit black students to white educational institutions.

73. Tushnet, *NAACP Legal Strategy against Segregated Education,* 70–77; and Sullivan, *Lift Every Voice,* 231–33.

74. Press Release "Solomon Blatt Declares USC to Keep Status," 28 August 1938. NAACP Papers.

75. J. Nelson Frierson to Leonard T. Baker, 14 February 1936, Office of the President, 1935–36, Box 1, Folder: Law School, South Caroliniana Library, University of South Carolina.

76. *State* (Columbia), 18 June 1939. *Journal of the Senate, First Session of the 83rd General Assembly of South Carolina,* 445, 566, 720 (1939).

77. Bailey mentions a letter he wrote to Dean J. Nelson Frierson on 27 April 1938 in Bailey to President J. Rion McKissick, 18 May 1938; Bailey to Board of Trustees, 27 June 1938, NAACP Papers. Charles B. Bailey interview by W. Lewis Burke, 11 November 1997.

78. *Annual Report, 1944–1945,* appendix B, "Report of Committee to Study Present and Post War Needs at State Agricultural and Mechanical College," 26.

79. *Annual Report, 1944–1945,* "Report of the Committee," 28–29.

80. *Annual Report, 1944–1945,* "Report of the Committee," 27–28.

81. *Annual Report, 1944–1945,* appendix 3, W. H. Calcott Report, 43–47.

82. *Public Higher Education in South Carolina,* 1.

83. John E. Brewton coordinated the effort as the director of the Division of Surveys and Field Services. Henry Harp was the assistant director. The Citadel, Clemson, the University of South Carolina, Winthrop College, the Medical University of South Carolina, and S.C. State were the six institutions that were evaluated.

84. *Public Higher Education in South Carolina,* 367–68.

85. *Public Higher Education in South Carolina,* 358, 418–19.

86. D. Hine, *Black Victory;* Sullivan, *Lift Every Voice,* 282–86; Edgar, *South Carolina,* 515–16.

87. Lau, *Democracy Rising,* 134–44; Frederickson, *Dixiecrat Revolt and the End of the Solid South 1932–1968,* 42–46; Sullivan, *Lift Every Voice,* 283–85; Richards, "Eminent Lieutenant McKaine," 16–17.

88. Lau, *Democracy Rising,* 146–53.

89. Lau, *Democracy Rising,* 151.

90. Annual Report of the State Supervisor of the Home Demonstration Program, 1946, Marian Paul, 1, Annual Reports, Extension Program, HCSCSU.

91. Miller F. Whittaker to Benjamin E. Mays, 21 July 1946; Mays to Whittaker, 17, 26 July 1946, Personnel files, E. B. Winston, HCSCSU. For more on Winston, see *Who's Who in Colored America: An Illustrated Biographical Dictionary of Notable Living Persons of African Descent Living in the United States,* 368. Years later in his autobiography, Mays described Tallmadge's racial views as "vile and vicious." But in what some African Americans surely must have thought was divine intervention, Tallmadge died suddenly before taking office. Mays, *Born to Rebel,* 221.

92. Nalty, *Strength for the Fight,* 204–6; Sullivan, *Lift Every Voice,* 319–20; Steve Estes, "Woodard, Isaac, Beating of," in *South Carolina Encyclopedia,* 1045–46.

93. John H. Wrighten to the dean of the law school, 30 June 1946; John H. Wrighten to E. G. Siebels, Chairman, Board of Trustees, University of South Carolina, 17 August 1946. In his letter to Siebels, Wrighten declared that "on or about the 6th day of July 1946, I received a letter from President Norman H. Smith of the University of South Carolina informing me that the University was unable to act favorably upon my application and has refused me admission solely on account of my race and color." Wrighten asked that the board overrule the president. Papers of the NAACP, Part 3, Campaign for Educational Equality: Legal Department and Central Office Records, 1913–50, Series B. While at Avery, Wrighten had applied to the College of Charleston, and he was rejected. See Drago, *Initiative, Paternalism, and Race Relations,* 231–32.

94. See Summons and Complaint, Civil Action No. 1670 in the District Court of the United States for the Eastern District of South Carolina dated 8 January 1947, Record Group 21, National Archives, Southeast Region; *Wrighten v. Board of Trustees of the University of South Carolina et al.,* 72 F. Supp. 949 (E.D.S.C. 1947).

95. *Wrighten v. Board of Trustees of the University of South Carolina et al.,* 72 F. Supp. 953 (E.D.S.C. 1947).

96. *Acts and Joint Resolutions of the General Assembly of South Carolina,* 1947, Act No. 286, Section 70. The general assembly had appropriated $523,000 to S.C. State for the fiscal year beginning on 1 July 1947, with the stipulation that the college offer courses in the law, medicine, pharmacology, and other disciplines in higher education. Sixty thousand of the $523,000 was for the graduate program and the law school.

97. Miller F. Whittaker to J. B. Felton, 27 May 1947, Folder: Department of Education, Presidents' Papers, HCSCSU.

98. Court transcript: 28–30, 34. See also "Negro Avers No S.C. Law School for Race Exists," *State,* 6 June 1947, 1; Alderman Duncan, "Federal Judge Takes USC Law School Case under Advisement," *State,* 7 June 1947, 1, 4.

99. Lau, *Democracy Rising,* 175–78; Sullivan, *Lift Every Voice,* 350–51. Democratic leaders attempted to "conform" to Waring's ruling that black voters must be permitted take part in Democratic primary elections by admitting black people to the Democratic Party while compelling them to take an oath to "support the social, religious and educational separation of the races." Waring rejected this evasion in 1948, and thirty-five thousand black voters cast ballots in the 1948 Democratic primary election. Edgar, *South Carolina,* 519–20.

100. *Wrighten v. Board of Trustees of the University of South Carolina et al.,* 72 F. Supp., 972; *State* (Columbia), 13 July 1947. For more on Waring, see Tinsley E. Yarbrough, *Passion for Justice.*

101. Bethea notified the other board members as well as Gov. Strom Thurmond, and they all approved of the decision to hire Turner. Minute Book B, Board of Trustees, 18 July 1947, 170; C. F. Brooks to Miller F. Whittaker, 28 July 1947, Presidents' Papers, HCSCSU. For a brief biography of Turner, see *Who's Who in Colored America: An Illustrated Biographical Dictionary of Notable Living Persons of African Descent in the United States,* 32 supplement.

102. Report of Attorney Harold R. Boulware to NAACP, 1 October 1947. Papers of the NAACP, Part 3, The Campaign for Educational Equality: Legal Department and Central Records, 1913–50, Series B. Also see *Annual Report, 1947–1948.*

103. Thurgood Marshall to John Wrighten, 29 September 1947, Papers of the NAACP, Part 3, The Campaign for Educational Equality: Legal Department and Central Office Records, 1913–50, Series B.

104. Thurgood Marshall to Harold Boulware, 3 March 1948, NAACP Papers, Group II, Series B, Container 204, Library of Congress. Wrighten further angered Marshall in 1949 when he wrote a letter to Judge Waring's wife asking for financial assistance to attend the law school at S.C. State. John Wrighten to Mrs. J. Waties Waring, 6 February 1949; J. Waties Waring to Thurgood Marshall, 8 February 1949; Thurgood Marshall to John Wrighten 21, February 1949. Marshall informed Wrighten that his appeal to Mrs. Waring was "in extremely bad taste."

105. Transcript of newspaper column, 24 May 1947, *Norfolk Journal and Guide.* Modjeska Simkins Collection, South Caroliniana Library, University of South Carolina, Columbia.

106. Thurgood Marshall to Frank A. DeCosta, 1 July 1947, NAACP Papers, Part 2, The Campaign for Educational Equality: Legal Department and Central Office Records, 1913–50, Series B. Library of Congress, Washington, D.C.

107. Julian Wolfe to R. H. Jennings, 7 March 1948, Wolfe to Charles N. Plowden, Chair of the House Ways and Means Committee, 29 December 1947 and copies to "quite a few personal friends—JSW," Presidents' Papers, Folder: Trustees, HCSCSU.

108. Minute Book B, Board of Trustees, 21 April 1948, 175; 8 December 1948, 179.

109. Gov. J. Strom Thurmond to Miller F. Whittaker, 19 March 1948, Whittaker papers, Presidents' Papers, HCSCSU; I. S. Newby, *Black Carolinians,* 351.

110. Altschuler and Blumin, *G. I. Bill,* 135, 137. See chapter 5, "White Veterans Only," in Katznelson, *When Affirmative Action Was White.*

111. The G. I. Bill permitted 2,232,000 veterans to attend college including 64,728 women (2.9 percent) at a cost of $5.5 billion. Olson, *G. I. Bill,* 43, 75. *State Agricultural and Mechanical College Bulletin,* 1948–49, 106.

112. *Annual Report, 1945–1946,* 7, 27; *Annual Report, 1946–1947,* 9; "News Release," 29 August 1946; Miller F. Whittaker to L. H. Foster (President of Virginia State College), 26 September 1946, Whittaker circular letter to state elected officials, 30 January 1948, Presidents' Papers, HCSCSU.

113. *Annual Report, 1946–1947,* 30.

114. Mary J. Miller, Dean of Women, Annual Report to Miller F. Whittaker, 15 March 1945, Presidents' Papers, HCSCSU; *Annual Report, 1949–1950,* 43.

115. J. R. Porter, Dean of Men, Annual Report, 1946–47, to Miller F. Whittaker, *State Agricultural and Mechanical College Bulletin,* 1948–49, 23.

116. Miller F. Whittaker to James Brailsford, Hugo Sims Jr., Charlton B. Horger, Marshall Williams, and Solomon Blatt, April–May 1947, File: State of South Carolina, Presidents' Papers, HCSCSU.

117. Blatt's reply was handwritten on the bottom of Whittaker's letter to him of 2 May 1947, and then the letter was returned to Whittaker.

118. Julian S. Wolfe to David W. Robinson, 13 August 1947. Folder: Trustees, Presidents' Papers, HCSCSU. By the end of the year, Wolfe resigned from the board of trustees because he had been elected solicitor of the First Judicial Circuit.

119. Hugo S. Sims to Miller F. Whittaker, 27 January 1948, Presidents' Papers, HCSCSU. *Biographical Directory of the South Carolina Senate, 1776–1985,* 2: 1467–68.

120. Minute Book B, Board of Trustees, 25 May 1937, 107; Miller F. Whittaker to F. G. Clark, President of Southern University, 16 July 1947, Presidents' Papers, HCSCSU.

121. Miller F. Whittaker to F. G. Clark, 16 July 1947, Presidents' Papers, HCSCSU; Cox, "From Racial Uplift to Personal Advancement," 85–86; Neiberg, *Making Citizen Soldiers,* 167.

122. *Annual Report, 1947–1948,* 10–11.

123. Report of the President of the College, 1 October 1946 to 20 May 1947, Presidents' Papers, HCSCSU. In 1944 Fraser Metzger, the dean of men at Rutgers University, explained the benefit of ROTC a bit more bluntly than did Whittaker: "They [male students] come to us at supercilious and sophomoric stage of their development and seriously need restraint and guidance such as the Army is so well equipped to render." Neiberg. *Making Citizen Soldiers,* 12.

124. *Annual Report, October 1948 to October 1949, 11–12; Annual Report, October 1949 to October 1950,* 22–23.

125. Berman, *Politics of Civil Rights in the Truman Administration,* 117, 67–71; Frederickson, *Dixiecrat Revolt and the End of the Solid South 1932–1968,* 65–66.

126. Frederickson, *Dixiecrat Revolt and the End of the Solid South 1932–1968,*56. Quote in Berman, *Politics of Civil Rights,* 62.

127. Daily Presidential Calendar, 22 October 1946, Harry S. Truman Presidential Library, Independence, Missouri, www.trumanlibrary.org/calendar, accessed 2 March 2017; Berman, *Politics of Civil Rights,* 125–26.

128. Berman, *Politics of Civil Rights,* 129–33; Frederickson, *Dixiecrat Revolt and the End of the Solid South 1932–1968,* 184.

129. For more on her life, see E. Williams and Stadiem, *Dear Senator.* Also see Bass and Thompson, *Ol' Strom,* 273–86. The Bass and Thompson book was published before Essie Mae Washington Williams publicly acknowledged that Strom Thurmond was her father.

130. E. Williams and Stadiem, *Dear Senator,* 113. Willie Earle was alleged to have killed a white taxi cab driver. He was removed by a mob from the Pickens County jail and killed. Thirty-one white men, mostly cab drivers, were tried for Earle's lynching in May 1947. They were all acquitted. *South Carolina Encyclopedia,* 279.

131. E. Williams and Stadiem, *Dear Senator,* 129–51; Robert J. Moore, "Matthew J. Perry's Preparation," in Burke and Gergel, eds., *Matthew J. Perry,* 67.

132. E. Williams and Stadiem, *Dear Senator,* 116.

133. E. Williams and Stadiem, *Dear Senator,* 145.

134. E. Williams and Stadiem, *Dear Senator,* 145–48. Essie Mae Washington also informed Thurmond that her mother, Carrie, had died of kidney disease a few days before the election at the age of thirty-nine. He was shocked and saddened. "'Ohh . . .' he bleated, like a wounded animal. 'Ohh . . .' He didn't cry, but tears filled his eyes." 144.

135. E. Williams and Stadiem, *Dear Senator,* 110.

136. E. Williams and Stadiem, *Dear Senator,* 112–15.

137. File: "Students General," Miller F. Whittaker to Mr. and Mrs. Theo Barnes, 18 February 1948; File: "Students General," January–February 1949, Presidents' Papers, HCSCSU.

138. File on Students Gambling, File: "Students General," February 1949, Presidents' Papers; Folder: "Students Not Accepted," 1947–48, Presidents' Papers, HCSCSU. M. Maceo Nance Jr., interview with William C. Hine, 14 March 1989. Nance later confided that he and the other vets should first have approached Whittaker with their grievance rather than holding a public demonstration.

139. Miller F. Whittaker to Solomon Blatt, 7 November 1946. Folder: "Students General," Presidents' Papers, HCSCSU.

140. Lau, *Democracy Rising,* 156–73. Also see Hughes, "We Demand Our Rights"; and Gellman, *Death Blow to Jim Crow,* chapter 5, 213–53.

141. Lau, *Democracy Rising,* 166–69.

142. Miller F. Whittaker to Louis E. Burnham, Organizational Secretary, Southern Negro Youth Congress, September 1946, "The Southern Negro Youth Congress Summons You to—the Southern Youth Legislature." Promotional flier, File: Debate and Drama, Miller F. Whittaker papers, Presidents' Papers, HCSCSU. The Rev. Adam Clayton Powell was scheduled to be the featured speaker, but he withdrew shortly before the legislature met. Lau, *Democracy Rising,* 166, 170–71. The Du Bois and Robeson quotes come from Lau.

143. *Collegian,* November 1946, p. 2. This issue is contained in the folder Debate and Drama, Miller F. Whittaker papers, HCSCSU.

144. Lau, *Democracy Rising,* 170–71.

145. For more on the life of Paul Robeson, see Duberman, *Paul Robeson.*

146. The Rev. T. A. Gideon to M. F. Whittaker, 18 January 1947. The text of the letter is contained in L. McMillan, *Negro Higher Education,* 26.

147. For a brief history of Seneca Junior College, see L. McMillan, *Negro Higher Education,* 22–36.

148. C. F. Brooks to Miller F. Whittaker, 16 May 1947, Miller F. Whittaker, Presidents' Papers, HCSCSU; *Annual Report, September 1946 to September 1947,* appendix 5, 25–26. In 1978 the Seneca

Family Life Center opened on the campus of what had been the Seneca Junior College. See Felder, *Civil Rights in South Carolina*, 174.

149. Miller F. Whittaker to Leo M. Favrot, 20 January 1939; Favrot to Whittaker, 27 January 1939; Portion of 1942 Survey of Colleges of the Central Jurisdiction for GEB—Done by Division of Surveys and Field Studies of George Peabody Teachers College. Series 1, Subseries 1, Box 127, Folder 1164, Rockefeller Archive Center.

150. Summary of Interview: Fred McCuistion with C. J. Martin, 2 October 1950. McCuistion had been to Orangeburg and talked with Turner, who had just assumed the presidency. Thad L. Hungate, Controller, Teachers College of Columbia University, to McCuistion, 9 March 1950, Series 1, Subseries 1, Box 127, Folder 1164, Rockefeller Archive Center.

151. Summary of Interview with Benner C. Turner, Fred McCuistion, 13 March 1951. Series 1, Subseries 1, Box 127, Folder 1164, Rockefeller Archive Center.

152. "Using Claflin for S.C. State Expansion Urged," *State* (Columbia), 10 March 1956, B-1.

153. Minute Book B, Board of Trustees, Local Board, 19 April 1949, 180, 20 June 1949, 182, 16 November 1949, 186.

154. "College Mourns Beloved President Whittaker," *Collegian*, December 1949, 1; *Savannah Tribune*, 24 November 1949.

155. The Orangeburg Lutheran Church possesses the original architectural drawings of Whittaker and Blanche.

156. Examples of these memos are scattered through Whittaker's general files in the 1940s. HCSCSU.

157. Minute Book B, Board of Trustees, 16 November 1949, 186.

CHAPTER SIX: SEPARATE BUT EQUAL?

1. *Savannah Tribune*, 10 August 1950; Richard Reid had a concise summary of Turner's life and tenure at S.C. State. "S.C. State's Fourth President: Dr. Benner C. Turner," *Times and Democrat*, 21 June 2008, B7. See also Potts, *History of South Carolina State College*, 97–123; *Who's Who in Colored America: An Illustrated Biographical Dictionary of Notable Living Persons of African Descent in the United States*, supplement, 31; Boyce, "I Am Leaving and Not Looking Back," 152–67.

2. E. D. Grizzell to Gov. J. Strom Thurmond, 2 December 1949, Governors' papers, Box 5, Folder 35, South Caroliniana Library. Thurmond's papers have since been moved to Clemson University.

3. Interview: William C. Hine and M. Maceo Nance, 14 March 1989. In 1950 Nance was the property custodian for the ROTC program. He would become Turner's successor in 1967.

4. Fortunately J. S. Nicholson, who was an aide to Governor Thurmond, attended the board meetings on May 25 and August 2, and he took notes in pencil of what transpired. Governors' Papers, Box 5, Folder 35; the minutes of the board meetings do not contain any discussion of the candidates. Minute Book B, 25 May 1950, 191, 1 August 1950, 193; Nance interview, 14 March 1989. The information on Thomas Fraser comes from *Science Education* 43, no. 1 (February 1959), 3–4.

5. Because the Republican Party was virtually nonexistent statewide, Byrnes's victory in the Democratic primary election in July 1950 assured his win in the November general election. Biographer David Robertson has written: "Byrnes is arguably among the most experienced and least known of the 'wise men' who exercised great political power just below the office of the president during the Roosevelt, Truman, Eisenhower, and Nixon administrations." Robertson, *Sly and Abel*, xi. See also "Byrnes, James F.," by Cole Blease Graham, in *South Carolina Encyclopedia*, 114–15; "The Year of the Billbat," *Time Magazine*, 6 January 1947, 23–27; Richards, "James F. Byrnes," 300–301.

6. R. E. Grier, "S. C's Largest Crowd Sees Byrnes Take Office," *State*, 17 January 1951, 1–2; Robertson, *Sly and Abel*, 504. Kluger, *Simple Justice*, 334–35.

7. Undated speech manuscript, Gov. James F. Byrnes, James F. Byrnes papers, Folder 870, Robert Muldrow Cooper Library, Clemson University; Kluger, *Simple Justice*, 334–35.

8. Byrnes, *All in One Lifetime*, 407–8.

9. Doak S. Campbell to Benner C. Turner, 11 January 1952, General Education Board Records [GEB], Series 1, Subseries 3, Box 479, Folder 5098, Rockefeller Archive Center.

10. James F. Byrnes to John Foster Dulles, 12 March 1952, GEB Records, Series 1, Subseries 3, Box 479, Folder 5098, Rockefeller Archive Center.

11. Miller F. Whittaker to Robert Calkins, Associate Director of the General Education Board, 2 July 1947, 30 July 1947. W. W. Brierly to Miller F. Whittaker, 10 October 1947. Brierly told Whittaker: "I am sorry to have to inform you that it was not found practicable to present these requests to the Board for favorable consideration." GEB Records, Series 1, Subseries 3, Box 127, Folder 1164, Rockefeller Archive Center.

12. James F. Byrnes to John D. Rockefeller III; a copy of the letter is contained in the John Foster Dulles papers, selected correspondence, James F. Byrnes folder, Box 58, Seeley G. Mudd Manuscript Library, Princeton University; Summary of interview: Robert D. Calkins, Benner C. Turner, W. C. Bethea, and Fred McCuistion (a GEB staff member), 11 December 1951, GEB Records, Series 1, Subseries 3, Box 479, Folder 5097, Rockefeller Archive Center.

13. Telephone interview and memo, Gov. James F. Byrnes and Robert D. Calkins, 11 February 1952, GEB Records, Series 1, Subseries 3, Box 479, Folder 5098, Rockefeller Archive Center.

14. Robert D. Calkins, interoffice memo, 13 February 1952, GEB Records, Series 1, Subseries 3, Box 479, Folder 5098, Rockefeller Archive Center.

15. Robert D. Calkins to Gov. James F. Byrnes, 21 February 1952, GEB Records, Series 1, Subseries 3, Box 479, Folder 5098, Rockefeller Archive Center.

16. Gov. James F. Byrnes to John D. Rockefeller III, 14 February 1952, John Foster Dulles papers, Selected Correspondence, 1952, James F. Byrnes folder, Seeley G. Mudd Manuscript Library, Princeton University. At Rockefeller's request Robert Calkins dictated the memo that became the substance of Rockefeller's reply to Byrnes. Memo: Calkins to Rockefeller, 21 February 1952; Rockefeller to Byrnes, 21 February 1952, GEB Records, Series 1, Subseries 3, Box 479, Folder 5098, Rockefeller Archive Center.

17. Purks's emphasis. Summary of interview, J. Harris Purks and Gov. James F. Byrnes, 25 February 1952, GEB Records, Series 1, Subseries 3, Box 479, Folder 5098, Rockefeller Archive Center.

18. B. C. Turner to Robert D. Calkins, 11 March 1952; Summary of telephone call, J. Harris Purks to Gov. James F. Byrnes, 12 March 1952, GEB Records, Series 1, Subseries 3, Box 479, Folder 5098, Rockefeller Archive Center.

19. Gov. James F. Byrnes to John Foster Dulles, 12 March 1952, Dulles to Byrnes, 19 March 1952, John Foster Dulles papers, Selected correspondence, 1952, Box 58, James F. Byrnes Folder, Seeley G. Mudd Manuscript Library, Princeton University.

20. General Education Board Minutes, 3 April 1952, 52045–47, GEB, Rockefeller Archive Center. In a letter to the author, Rusk explained that he had no recollection of that specific meeting. "I do not remember the details of the discussion we had over the grant to South Carolina State College, but I can assure you that it was not made lightly and included a full discussion of the circumstances of the college and the prospects for its future. Dean Rusk to William C. Hine, 14 August 1988. In author's possession.

21. J. Harris Purks interview with Benner C. Turner, 19 March 1952, GEB Records, Series 1, Subseries 3, Box 94, Folder 1164, Rockefeller Archive Center.

22. Private black institutions such as Tuskegee, Atlanta University, Spelman, Morehouse, and Fisk were each the recipients of millions of GEB dollars. See Fosdick, *Adventure in Giving*, 327–35.

23. Benner C. Turner to Robert W. July, Assistant Director of the GEB, 2 December 1954, GEB Records, Series 1, Subseries 3, Box 479, Folder 5098, Rockefeller Archive Center.

24. Ethna Beulah Winston, *Who's Who in Colored America: An Illustrated Biographical Dictionary of Notable Living Persons of African Descent in the United States,* 568; L. K. McMillan to Miller F. Whittaker, 15 September 1946; McMillan to Whittaker, 9 April 1947, Presidents' Papers, Miller F. Whittaker, HCSCSU. At $450 McMillan was the highest paid member of the summer school teaching staff.

25. Moss, "Negro Teachers in Predominantly White Colleges," 456–57. See also Greene, *Holders of Doctorates among American Negroes,* 23–26.

26. Atwood, Smith, and Vaughn, "Negro Teachers in Northern Colleges and Universities in the United States," 562. See also, Moss, "Negro Teachers in Predominantly White Colleges," 457. In 1946 *Phylon* listed by name, institution, and discipline fifty-one black faculty members who taught at white institutions. Of that number, twenty-two were full-time appointments, and nine of the fifty-one were women. Reid, "People and Places."

27. *Annual Report, 1951–1952,* 48; *Annual Report, 1958–1959,* 23; *South Carolina State College Catalogue 1958-59*

28. Compiled from college catalogs and the 1960 *Bulldog* yearbook.

29. Edward Ferguson Jr. to James H. Green, 26 October 1956. The letter was published in the *Annual Report, 1956–1957,* 85; *Annual Report, 1951–1952,* 11; *Bulldog,* 1960. Greene, *Holders of Doctorates among American Negroes,* 107, 189–90.

30. *Annual Report, 1950–1951,* 49; Gov. James F. Byrnes to John D. Rockefeller III, 14 February 1952, John Foster Dulles papers, Selected Correspondence, 1952, James F. Byrnes folder, Seeley G. Mudd Manuscript Library, Princeton University. Byrnes told Rockefeller: "Their [S.C. State's] first need is increased compensation for the faculty, and I have induced the Legislature to give them an additional $100,000 for this purpose." *Annual Report, 1951–1952,* 11.

31. *Annual Report, 1955–1956,* 70; Benner C. Turner to Felton G. Clark, President of Southern A&M College, 26 September 1952, File: Land-grant colleges, Presidents' Papers, Benner C. Turner, HCSCSU; *Annual Report, 1956–1957,* 57.

32. J. M. Godard, Executive Secretary of the Southern Association of Colleges and Schools, to Benner C. Turner, 5 December 1952, File: Southern Association, Presidents' Papers; Turner to Adam H. Moss, 6 December 1954, File: Association of Sec. Schools and Other Rating Agencies, Presidents' Papers, HCSCSU.

33. The visiting committee consisted of Dr. William A. Alexander, the chair, and a professor of education at the University of Miami; Dr. Ernest Becker, the assistant superintendent of schools for the Parish of New Orleans; Dean R. F. Thomason of the University of Tennessee; and President A. E. Manly of Spelman College. The three white men stayed at the Eutaw Hotel, and Manly resided with President Turner. Their visit was 9–12 November 1954. Benner C. Turner to William A. Alexander, 2 December 1954, and Turner to Adam H. Moss, 6 December 1954, File: Association of Sec. Schools and Other Rating Agencies, Presidents' Papers, HCSCSU.

34. *Annual Report, 1957–1958,* 15, 24. Turner cited a letter from Dr. Donald Agnew, Executive Secretary of the Southern Association of Colleges and Universities, 13 December 1957.

35. *Annual Report, 1950–1951,* 61; "Savannah River Site," by Rick D. Boulware, in *South Carolina Encyclopedia,* 843.

36. *Annual Report, 1954–1955,* 30; *Annual Report, 1951–1952,* 14; *Annual Report, 1950–1951,* 49. The renovations to Lowman Hall, which was built in 1917, were undertaken in two phases. The board of trustees authorized $84,500 to begin the process in 1951, and then the board asked for a loan of $60,000 from the Sinking Fund to complete the rehabilitation. *Annual Report, 1951–1952,* 6, 14; State College Minute Book, Board of Trustees, special meeting, 28 February 1952, 2. HCSCSU.

37. State College Minute Book, Board of Trustees, local board, 27 August 1953, 10. HCSCSU.

38. State College Minute Book, Board of Trustees, special meeting, 27 May 1953, 9; local meeting, 27 August 1953, 10. HCSCSU. *Annual Report, 1954–1955,* 62–63.

39. *Annual Report, 1951–1952,* 51.

40. Interview: William C. Hine with M. Maceo Nance, 14 March 1989; Interview: William Hine with Dr. Franklin Roosevelt Jackson, 20 July 1990. L. McMillan, "Negro Higher Education as I Have Known It." McMillan taught at S.C. State in the late 1940s. For a time he also taught at Claflin and taught courses at Allen University in Columbia and Morris College in Sumter.

41. Personnel file, Lewis K. McMillan, HCSCSU; Greene, *Holders of Doctorates among American Negroes,* 66.

42. McMillan spoke to students in a lyceum program and then wrote an article for the *Collegian* about his postwar trip to Germany. He reported that one of the daughters of the German family had lost her husband during World War II and that the father had died just as the war came to an end in 1945. The family endured hunger and privation in the aftermath of the conflict. Lewis K. McMillan, "On Going Back to Germany," *Collegian,* December 1949, 3, 8.

43. L. K. McMillan to B. C. Turner, 31 December 1951; Turner to McMillan, 4 January 1952, Presidents' Papers, Benner C. Turner, HCSCSU.

44. L. McMillan, *Negro Higher Education,* ix.

45. See L. McMillan, *Negro Higher Education,* 201–2.

46. L. McMillan, *Negro Higher Education,* 60.

47. L. McMillan, *Negro Higher Education,* 81, 94, 116.

48. L. McMillan, *Negro Higher Education,* 186.

49. L. McMillan, *Negro Higher Education,* 199.

50. L. McMillan, *Negro Higher Education,* 221.

51. *Lighthouse and Informer,* 21 February 1953.

52. The AAUP, after a delay of three years, proceeded to investigate McMillan's case. McMillan had informed AAUP officials of his meeting with Turner prior to the book's publication. Warren C. Middleton to President B. C. Turner, 25 January 1957; B. C. Turner to Dr. Lewis K. McMillan, 6 May 1953. Presidents' Papers, B. C. Turner, HCSCSU. The trustee's minutes indicate that Turner recommended that the McMillan's contract not be renewed. He also recommended that the football coach and athletic director be terminated as well as English professor Cordella J. Blount. State College Minute Book, Board of Trustees, 30 April 1953, 8.

53. Lewis K. McMillan to the Trustee Board, n.d., copy, Series 1, Subseries 3, File 1194, Rockefeller Archive Center.

54. J. M. Godard, Executive Secretary, Southern Association of Colleges and Schools, to B. C. Turner, 20 May 1953; B. C. Turner to J. M. Godard, 22 May 1953; J. M. Godard to Lewis C. [*sic*] McMillan, 13 July 1953 (copy), Leo Koutouzos, Research Member, American Academic Freedom Project, to President B. C. Turner, 27 May 1953 and Turner to Koutouzos, 5 June 1953; Presidents' Papers, Benner C. Turner, HCSCSU. See also Patrick Murphy Malin, Executive Director, American Civil Liberties Union, to President B. C. Turner, telegram, 25 May 1953; Richard H. Ullman, Editorial Chairman, *Harvard Crimson,* to Mr. Benner C. Turner, 17 May 1953, Presidents' Papers, B. C. Turner, HCSCSU.

55. Howard K. Beale to President B. C. Turner, 5 August 1953, Presidents' Papers, B. C. Turner, HCSCSU. Beale had taken a keen interest in academic freedom. See his two studies *Are American Teachers Free?* and *History of Freedom of Teaching in American Schools.*

56. Warren C. Middleton to Dr. Benner C. Turner, 25 January 1957; Turner to Middleton, 5 February 1957; Middleton to Turner, 18 June 1957; Turner to Middleton, 21 June 1957, Presidents' Papers, HCSCSU.

57. B. C. Turner to W. C. Bethea, 21 June 1957; W. C. Bethea to Warren C. Middleton, 21 June 1957 (draft). In 1960 Louis Joughin wrote Turner to say that they had received no reply to a letter to McMillan. "For this reason we are closing the file on the Orangeburg State College–McMillan case at this time." Louis Joughin to Dr. B. C. Turner, 21 November 1960, Presidents' Papers, B. C. Turner, HCSCSU.

58. Reference Staff, Anne Killheffer, Stratford Public Library, to William C. Hine, 24, 27 April 2006, e-mail. "Connecticut Death Index, 1949–2001," database, Familysearch (https://familysearch.org/ark:61903/1:1:VZ53-3NQ: accessed 14 November 2015, Lewis K. McMillan, 7 July 1974; from "Connecticut Death Index, 1949–2001," database, Ancestry (http.//ancestry.com: 2003); citing Bridgeport, Connecticut, Connecticut Department of Health, Hartford.

59. Benner C. Turner to J. F. Drake, 24 November 1952. File: "Land-grant colleges," Presidents' Papers, Benner C. Turner, HCSCSU.

60. Benner C. Turner to Jerome H. Holland, 3 July 1954. File: "Information," Presidents' Papers, Benner C. Turner, HCSCSU. Holland was the President of Delaware State College, and he had asked Turner about the tenure policy at S.C. State.

61. The policy on tenure was published in the *Annual Report, 1956–1957.* The emphasis was in the published policy. The tenure policy was approved by the trustees at their 14 April 1955 meeting. State College Minute Book, Board of Trustees, 14 April 1955, 27.

62. R. C. Henderson, Chairman of the Faculty Study Commission, to President B. C. Turner, 4 April 1956. The resolution accompanied Henderson's letter. Minute Book, Board of Trustees, 12 April 1954, 39.

63. See W. Hine, "Civil Rights and Campus Wrongs."

64. "NAACP Asks Reorganization of Schools in Orangeburg," *Times and Democrat,* 31 July 1955, 1; James E. Sulton and Ruby Sulton, 31 July 1955; James E. Sulton and Ruby Sulton, interview by William C. Hine, 20 July 1994; "List," NAACP Records, Group III, Series A, Container 279, Folder: Reprisals, South Carolina, General, 1956–59, Library of Congress, Washington, D.C.; *Hill's Orangeburg City Directory, 1956;* Klarman, "How Brown Changed Race Relations," 88.

65. "Preserving Separate Schools," *Times and Democrat,* 24 August 1955, 4; "Citizens Group to Meet," *Times and Democrat,* 29 August 1955, 1.

66. *Times and Democrat,* 29 August 1955. For more information on the Citizens' Councils and their opposition to desegregation, see N. McMillan, *Citizens' Council.* There is a brief discussion of the Citizens' Council in Orangeburg on p. 271.

67. The sole contemporary summary of these events is Edward Gamarekian's "The Ugly Battle of Orangeburg," in *Reporter* 24 (January 1957), 32–34. Harvey to Shell Oil Co., Inc., 29 September 1955, NAACP Records, Group II, Series A, Container 508, Folder: Reprisals, South Carolina cases, 1955.

68. To "encourage" support for the selective-buying effort, photographer Cecil J. Williams was asked to shoot photos of those black people who continued to patronize the white businesses that were off limits. Much to the consternation of the offenders, the photos were subsequently posted on a board in the basement of Trinity United Methodist Church, the church where NAACP president Matthew McCollom served as pastor. A. M. Rivera Jr., "Organize S.C. Boycott against White Pressure," *Courier* (Pittsburgh), 24 September 1955, 1; "Orangeburg Condemned by NAACP Official [i.e., Roy Wilkins]," *Times and Democrat,* 18 September 1955, 1; "$10,000 Reported Offered for NAACP Membership List," *Times and Democrat,* 22 September 1955, 1; NAACP Collection, James M. Hinton, President, South Carolina State Conference of NAACP Branches, "Orangeburg Teaches a Lesson thru Economic Boycott," 13 October 1955, Group II, Series A, Container 508, Folder: Reprisals, South Carolina, General, 1955; William C. Hine interview with James and Ruby Sulton, 20 July 1994.

69. Lau, *Democracy Rising,* 216.

70. William C. Hine interview with Fred H. Moore, 21 July 1994.

71. William C. Hine interview with Ruby and James Sulton, 20 July 1994; William C. Hine interview with Fred H. Moore, 21 July 1994; NAACP Collection, James M. Hinton, President, South Carolina State Conference of NAACP Branches, "Orangeburg Teaches a Lesson thru Economic Boycott," Group II, Series A, Container 508, Folder, Reprisals, South Carolina, General, 1955. With the campus newspaper, the *Collegian,* carefully supervised by faculty and administrators, students subsequently published an underground newsletter, the *Free Press,* edited by campus journalist Rudolph Pyatt. Unfortunately no copies of the *Free Press* apparently survive.

72. Report to the Board of Trustees: Factors Related to the Recent Student Strike at South Carolina State College, 9–12 April 1956; William C. Hine interview with Fred H. Moore, 21 July 1994. Since early in the presidency of Robert S. Wilkinson the dining hall had been operated as a private concession under the authority of the college. Marion Birnie Wilkinson, the widow of Robert, ran the dining hall for nearly four decades before turning its day-to-day operations over to her daughter, Helen R. Sheffield. Mrs. Sheffield had taught chemistry while her husband, Frederick, taught French. Students also objected to the college sending laundry to Kirkland's Cleaners because it was also among the white businesses that black people were avoiding. Those in attendance at the local board meeting included W. C. Bethea, Charles Jones, Adam Moss, James Moss (the college attorney), T. J. Crawford, and Helen Sheffield. Minute Book, Board of Trustees, 26 March 1956, 36. For a student's recollections of these events, see Washington, *Class of 1957,* 76–85.

73. Timmerman quotes from J. White, "Managed Compliance," 231, and Quint, *Profile in Black and White,* 132. Quint pointed out that 525 Democrats attended the convention, and two of them were black; "Resolution for NAACP Announced," *Times and Democrat,* 26 October 1955, 1; "Investigation of the NAACP Announced," *Times and Democrat,* 25 January, 1956, 1; "Investigation of NAACP Proposed," *Times and Democrat,* 23 February 1956, 1; "Legislature Passes Ban against NAACP," *Times and Democrat,* 14 March 1956, 1; "NAACP Activities in State College to Be Investigated, *Times and Democrat,* 17 March 1956, 1; "Act Signed Barring NAACP Members from Jobs, *Times and Democrat,* 18 March 1956, 1. See also *Southern School News,* 12 April 1956, 12; and Quint, *Profile in Black and White,* 53, 104–5.

74. R. C. Henderson to President B. C. Turner, 4 April 1956, Minute Book, Board of Trustees, 26 March 1956, 36; 25 April 1956, 37–39. Only one unnamed professor declined to sign the petition. In addition there were five faculty members on leave, and the ROTC officers were not asked to sign. Tom MacRae, "Turner Denies Report of 'Effigy' Hanging," *Times and Democrat,* 27 March 1956, 1; "State College Students Voice Several Protests," *Times and Democrat,* 29 March 1956, 1; "State Teachers Join NAACP in Views," *Times and Democrat,* 7 April 1956, 10; Editorial: "Again, a Loss, in Race Relations," and "Demonstration Expected at State College," *Times and Democrat,* 8 April 1956, 4, 8; "State College Trustees to Investigate Strike," *Times and Democrat,* 25 April 1956, 1; Tom MacRae, "Moore Is Expelled from State College, *Times and Democrat,* 26 April 1956, 1; copy of letter from Benner C. Turner to W. C. Bethea, 4 April 1956: Folder: CNIAMC [Colored Normal, Industrial, Agricultural and Mechanical College], Box 26, Governors' Papers, George Bell Timmerman, South Carolina Department of Archives and History. In the editorial on April 8, the *Times and Democrat* expressed disappointment that the faculty would permit itself to be misled by the NAACP. Just as white moderates were willing to

disavow the Ku Klux Klan, the newspaper wondered why moderate black people would not condemn "militant groups [like the NAACP] with a publicity axe to grind."

75. SLED officers were to cooperate with the Orangeburg Police Department and the Orangeburg sheriff in the effort to identify the subversive elements on the campus. "State College Demonstration Fails to Come Off Yesterday," *Times and Democrat,* 9 April 1956, 8.

76. "Students at State College on 'Strike,'" *Times and Democrat,* 10 April 1956, 1; "Some Students Return to Class in 2nd Day of State Strike," *Times and Democrat,* 11 April 1956, 10; "State College Students Go 'on Strike,'" *State* (Columbia), 11 April 1956, 1; "Students Hit Surveillance," *State* (Columbia), 11 April 1956, 15-A; "Orangeburg Students Bow to Ultimatum by School President," *News and Courier,* 14 April 1956, 1, 9; U.S. teletype report, Folder: CNIAMC, Box 26, Governors' Papers, George Bell Timmerman, South Carolina Department of Archives and History (SCDAH). F. Moore, "School Desegregation," 57. A photograph of Turner hanging in effigy captured by Cecil Williams appeared in the *Baltimore Afro-American,* 14 April 1956, 6. Murray Kempton, a *New York Post* columnist, visited the campus and reported on the protest as well. "Education in Revolt," *New York Post,* 27 March 1956.

77. Folder: CNIAMC, Box 26, Governors' Papers, George Bell Timmerman, SCDAH; William C. Hine interview with Fred H. Moore, 21 July 1994. Moore later explained that William N. Smith "allowed his animosity toward Turner to escalate.'' William C. Hine telephone interview with Rudolph Pyatt, 25 August 1994. Students declined to discuss the strike or their grievances with white journalists. See also Gore, *On a Hilltop High,* 199–204.

78. Report to the Board of Trustees on Factors Related to the Recent Student Strike, Minute Book, Board of Trustees, 25 April 1956, 37–39.

79. Minute Book, Board of Trustees,25 April 1956, 38; Folder: CNIAMC, Folder 26, Governors' Papers, George Bell Timmerman, SCDAH; Tom MacRae, "Moore Is Expelled from State College," *Times and Democrat,* 26 April 1956, 1; W. G. Barber, "Student President Is Expelled from S.C. State College," *News and Courier,* 26 April 1956, 1; William C. Hine interview with Fred H. Moore, 21 July 1994; William C. Hine telephone interview with Rudolph Pyatt, 25 August 1994.

80. Marie R. Vernon, Dean of Women, to B. C. Turner, 29 May 1956, copy in the President's Report, October 1955 to April 1956, Presidents' Papers, Benner C. Turner, HCSCSU.

81. Fourteen carbon copies of the identical letters to the students and fourteen carbon copies of the identical letters to the parents are contained in File: Students General, 1955–56, Presidents' Papers, Benner C. Turner, HCSCSU; William C. Hine interview with Fred H. Moore, 21 July 1994; Benner C. Turner to R. Daniel, 30 June 1956, Folder: Students—General, Presidents' Papers, Benner C. Turner to Dr. Howard G. Royal, 4 February 1957, Folder: Trustees, Presidents' Papers, Benner C. Turner (Royal was a trustee from Aiken), HCSCSU; John McCray, "Unrest Mounts at S.C. State," *Afro-American* (Baltimore), 6 October 1956, 3; William C. Hine, telephone interview with Rudolph Pyatt, 25 August 1994.

82. List: "Students at the End of the Academic Session 1955–1956 Requested Not to Return to the College." Turner's initial list contains the name Barbara Anderson. But the name Barbara Brown appears on subsequent lists and in correspondence. Mr. and Mrs. Rudolph A. Pyatt Sr. to B. C. Turner, 8 June 1956, File: Students General, 1955–56, Presidents' Papers, Benner C. Turner, HCSCSU.

83. Mrs. Roosevelt Brown to B. C. Turner, June 1956, File: Students General, 1955–56, Presidents' Papers, Benner C. Turner, HCSCSU. Mrs. Brown was no kin to the student Roosevelt Brown, who had been suspended.

84. Alice Pyatt's recollection is contained in Marvin Ira Lare, ed., *Champions of Civil Rights and Human Rights in South Carolina,* vol. 1, *Dawn of the Movement Era, 1955–1967* (Columbia: University of South Carolina Press, 2016), 67–77.

85. B. C. Turner to Alice Pyatt, 31 May 1956, Turner to Robert Daniel, 25 June 1956, Folder: Students —General, Presidents' Papers, Benner C. Turner, HCSCSU.

86. Benner C. Turner to R. Daniel, 30 June 1956, Folder: Students—General, Presidents' Papers, Benner C. Turner; William C. Hine telephone interview with Rudolph Pyatt, 25 August 1994. Editorial: "Powell and State A&M," *Times and Democrat,* 3 July 1956, 3.

87. "Orangeburg Students Bow to Ultimatum by School President," *News and Courier,* 14 April 1956, 1,9.

88. John H. McCray, "Need for Changing," *Afro-American,* 26 May 1956, 4.

89. William N. Smith to President B. C. Turner, 9 May 1956, Personnel file, HCSCSU.

90. Minute Book, Board of Trustees, 30 May 1956, 40; *Afro-American* (Baltimore), 26 May 1956, scrapbook, HCSCSU.

91. Minute Book, Board of Trustees, 31 October 1956; Cassandra Maxwell file, HCSCSU; William C. Hine interview with Lewie C. Roache, 16 August 1990.

92. "Charges" attached to Minutes of the Executive Committee of the Board of Trustees, Minute Book, Board of Trustees, 20 February 1959, 53. Those who attended the hearing were R. Beverly Herbert, Bruce White, W. C. Bethea, President Turner, Nettie Parler, Cassandra Maxwell Birnie, and college attorney James Moss. Dr. Louis Joghan, an observer for the AAUP, and George Hopkins, an observer for the State Department of Education, also attended. Apparently Florence Miller was not at the hearing.

93. Minute Book, Board of Trustees, 15 May 1959, 54.

94. John H. McCray, "Students Again Assail B. C. Turner," *Afro-American* (Baltimore), 2 June 1956, 5; "Tension Still Rules S.C. State Campus," *Afro-American,* 16 February 1957, 3.

95. John McCray, "Probing What Doesn't Exist," *Afro American,* 4 August 1956, 4; Quint, *Profile in Black and White,* 53. "Committee to Investigate State College Completed, *Times and Democrat,* 4 July 1956, 8; "NAACP Probe Set Wednesday," *Times and Democrat,* 17 July 1956, 1; "NAACP Probe Open Today at State College," *Times and Democrat,* 18 July 1956, 1; "McFaddin Named Chair of Group Probing NAACP Here," *Times and Democrat,* 19 July 1956, 1.

96. *Annual Report, 1955–1956,* 80–81. In 2010 Student Government Association president Zachary Middleton, with the support of a petition signed by five hundred students, asked the board of trustees to award an honorary degree to Fred H. Moore. The trustees declined by tabling the motion.

97. William C. Hine telephone interview with Rudolph Pyatt, 25 August 1994; John H. McCray, "Unrest Mounts at S.C. State," *Afro-American,* 6 October 1956, 3.

98. Benner C. Turner to George H. Williams, Acting Dean, Harvard Divinity School, File: Students —General, Presidents' Papers, Benner C. Turner, HCSCSU; https:www.nytimes.com/2016/10/12/us/benjamin-payton-dead.html?_r=0 , accessed 3 March 2017; William C. Hine telephone interview with Rudolph Pyatt, 25 August 1994.

99. William C. Hine interview with Fred H. Moore, 21 July 1994.

100. F. Roosevelt Jackson to President Benner C. Turner, 20 May 1953, File: Student Council, Presidents' Papers, Benner C. Turner, William C. Hine interview with Dr. Franklin R. Jackson, 20 July 1990.

101. President Benner C. Turner to F. Roosevelt Jackson, 30 October 1952, File: Student Council, Presidents' Papers, Benner C. Turner, HCSCSU.

102. F. Roosevelt Jackson to Benner C. Turner, 27 October 1952; Turner to Jackson, 29 October 1952, File: Student Council, Presidents' Papers, Benner C. Turner, HCSCSU.

103. The three young men were permitted to finish the fall semester, which concluded in late January, and were suspended for the spring term. Monroe and Sanford were freshmen, and Sanford and Sims were married. Faculty Log Book, 21 January 1951. HCSCSU.

104. Etta Rowe, Guidance Report on Advisees, School of Education, 1952–53, File: Guidance Program, Presidents' Papers, Benner C. Turner, HCSCSU.

105. Hattie R. Dingle, Guidance Report on Advisees, School of Education, 1952–53, File: Guidance; M. Maceo Nance to Benner C. Turner, 31 July 1957, Folder: College Finance. Presidents' Papers, Benner C Turner, HCSCSU.

106. Minutes, Department of English meeting, 17 April 1957, File: English Dept., Failures, first semester, 1954–55, Mrs. Conyers Williams to President Benner C. Turner, 1 July 1955, File: Students General, Presidents' Papers, Benner C. Turner, HCSCSU.

107. Minutes, College of Arts and Sciences, 13 April 1955, File: Arts and Sciences, Presidents' Papers, Benner C. Turner, HCSCSU.

108. *Annual Report, 1953–1954,* 47–48.

109. *Annual Report, 1953–1954,* 48. *South Carolina State College Catalogue 1954–1955,* 24–25.

110. *Annual Report, 1955–1956,* 31; *Annual Report, 1956–1957,* 31–32.

111. An additional nine cadets passed conditionally while six failed outright. *Annual Report, 1954–1955,* 26–27; *Annual Report, 1956–1957,* 32–34.

112. *Annual Report, 1957–1958,* 25–26.

113. *News and Courier,* 9 June 1954, quoted from Baker, *Paradoxes of Desegregation,* 132. Baker and Henry Lesesne discuss the University of South Carolina's racial reasons for the adoption of entrance examinations. Lesesne, *History of the University of South Carolina,* 120–23.

114. Baker, *Paradoxes of Desegregation,* 133–34; Lesesne, *History of the University of South Carolina,* 122.

115. Klarman, "How Brown Changed Race Relations," 88. Klarman points out that "a significant shift in Southern political opinion took place in the interval between *Brown* (May 1954) and the emergence of the Montgomery Bus Boycott on to the national stage (late February 1956)." 116.

116. Orr, "Analytical Study of the Conference of Presidents of Negro Land-Grant Colleges," 2, 19–20, 149–50. The presidents in attendance at Michigan State were Rufus B. Atwood of Kentucky State, R. Daniel of Virginia State, and E. B. Evans of Prairie View A&M; Turner. W. T. Gibbs also attended as a proxy for F. D. Bluford of North Carolina A&T. Also see File: News Articles, no date, Presidents' Papers, Benner C. Turner, HCSCSU.

117. Kirkland W. Green to Benner C. Turner, 22 October 1953, File: Arts and Sciences, Presidents' Papers, Benner C. Turner, HCSCSU.

118. See course listings for history in college catalogs for 1937–38, 1941–42, 1943–44, 1944–45, 1948–49, 1953–54, 1956–57, 1957–58.

119. Benner C. Turner to Lane L. Bonner, 8 November 1954, File: Information, Presidents' Papers, Benner C. Turner, HCSCSU.

120. George W. Hunter to Benner C. Turner, 3 November 1954; Howard Jordan Jr. to Benner C. Turner, 3 November 1954; Kirkland W. Green to Benner C. Turner, 5 November 1954; James H. Green to Benner C. Turner, 6 November 1954; G. J. Penn to Benner C. Turner, 8 November 1954; Frank M. Staley to Benner C. Turner, n.d.; Benner C. Turner to Lane L. Bonner, 8 November 1954, File: Information, Presidents' Papers, Benner C. Turner, HCSCSU.

121. Interview, William C. Hine with Matthew Perry, 1995. Perry explained that because of the institution's embarrassing legal name, he never put the diplomas for his bachelor's degree or his law degree on the wall of his office.

122. Thomas A. Babb to Benner C. Turner, 25 April 1953; Turner to Babb, 28 April 1953, File: Legislature, Presidents' Papers, Benner C. Turner, HCSCSU.

123. *Journal of the House of Representatives, Second Session of the 90th General Assembly, 1954,* 82, 1234 (House Bill 1800); *Acts and Joint Resolutions of the General Assembly of the State of South Carolina, Regular Session, 1954,* 674.

124. Marian B. Paul to Jackson Davis, 16 September 1946, Series 1, Subseries 3, Box 479, Folder 5099, Rockefeller Archive Center.

125. Interview: Miller F. Whittaker and Robert D. Calkins, 27 June 1947, New York City, GEB, Series 1, Subseries 3, Box 479, Folder 5099, Rockefeller Archive Center.

126. Marian B. Paul, "Proposed Demonstration Home," Miller F. Whittaker to Fred McCuistion, 31 October 1949, Series 1, Subseries 3, Folder 5100, Box 479, Rockefeller Archive Center.

127. Sherman Biscoe, "A Way to Better Rural Homes: South Carolina Demonstration House," *U.S. Department of Agriculture Extension Service Bulletin,* no. 505, April 1956, 6–9. Copy: HCSCSU.

128. Press Release, "S.C. Demonstration House Speeds Up Rural Home Improvement Program," Sherman Briscoe, Information Specialist, U.S. Department of Agriculture, 30 November 1953, Washington, D.C., Series 1, Subseries 3, Box 479, Folder 5100, Rockefeller Archive Center.

129. Sherman Briscoe, "A Way to Better Rural Homes," 10–12.

130. Press Release, "S.C. Demonstration House Speeds Up Rural Home Improvement Program," Sherman Briscoe, Information Specialist, U.S. Department of Agriculture, 30 November 1953, Washington, D.C.; Marian B. Paul, Annual Report Home Demonstration Work, 1958, 31.

131. Marian B. Paul, Annual Report Home Demonstration Work, 1958, 8.

132. Marian B. Paul, Annual Report Home Demonstration Work, 1958, 7.

133. Marian B. Paul, Annual Report Home Demonstration Work, 1958, 7.

134. Marian B. Paul, Annual Report Home Demonstration Work, 1958, 7.

135. Marian B. Paul, Annual Report Home Demonstration Work, 1958, 10–11.

136. Marian B. Paul, Annual Report Home Demonstration Work, 1958, 11–14.

137. Marian B. Paul, Annual Report Home Demonstration Work, 1958, 37.

138. Marian B. Paul, Annual Report Home Demonstration Work, 1958, 38.

139. Marian B. Paul, Annual Report Home Demonstration Work, 1958, 42.

140. Marian B. Paul, Annual Report Home Demonstration Work, 1958, 26.

141. Marian B. Paul, Annual Report Home Demonstration Work, 1958, 23–24, 26–27.

142. Wayman Johnson, "History, Growth, and Transition of the 4-H among Negroes in South Carolina" (Orangeburg, 1970), 86–100. HCSCSU. See also Harris, "Ray of Hope," 489–500.

143. Report of the President of the College, June 1959 to October 1959, 5–6, 19, 22–23, Presidents' Papers, Benner C. Turner, HCSCSU.

144. *Annual Report, October 1950–October 1951,* 31; Report of the President of the College, June 1959–October 1959, 55.

CHAPTER SEVEN: CIVIL RIGHTS IN THE COMMUNITY AND ON THE CAMPUS

1. The Greensboro sit-in was not the first. But it did inspire the sit-in movement that swept the South in the spring of 1960. Aldon Morris points out that there were at least sixteen sit-ins between 1957 and 1960: *Origins of the Civil Rights Movement,* 188–215. For more on civil rights in Orangeburg, see W. Hine, "Civil Rights and Campus Wrongs." Oppenheimer, *Sit-In Movement of 1960,* 168–73. Cecil Williams, an Orangeburg photographer, also has provided an account of the era through his marvelous photographs. C. Williams, *Freedom and Justice;* and C. Williams and Dubose, *Orangeburg 1968.*

2. Editorial: "A Word of Caution," *Times and Democrat,* 26 February 1960, 4; "Mayor Issues Warning to Protest Paraders," *Times and Democrat,* 2 March 1960, 1, 5; "Negro 'Sit-Down' Held at Library," *State,* 2 March 1956, 1; Zinn, *SNCC.* Zinn discusses Orangeburg on pp. 23–24. The system of racial segregation that students challenged in the 1960s often bore little resemblance to the "separate but equal" doctrine the U.S. Supreme Court sanctioned in 1896. Many public facilities including lunch counters, restaurants, hotels, parks, golf courses, and bowling alleys did not provide separate accommodations or services for black people. White public officials and business owners excluded African Americans entirely rather than segregating them.

3. "Negro Demonstrators Arrested," *Times and Democrat,* 16 March 1960, 1; Gus Chigges, "425 Negro Protesters Jailed," *State,* 16 March 1960, 1, 5; NAACP Collection, Group III, Series A, Container 290, Folder: Sit-Ins, South Carolina, 1960–63, Library of Congress, Washington, D.C.; Oppenheimer, *Sit-In Movement of 1960,* 170–71.

4. Harrison E. Salisbury, "350 Negro Demonstrators Held in South Carolina Stockade, *New York Times,* 16 March 1960, 1; Gus Chigges, "425 Negro Protesters Jailed," *State,* 16 March 1960, 1, 5.

5. Branch, *Parting the Waters,* 283. Branch cites the Oral History Collection of the Civil Rights Documentation Project, Moorland-Spingarn Research Center, Howard University, Washington, D.C., as his source for McDew's comment. McDew, however, seems to have suffered a lapse in memory. By 1960 David "Deacon" Jones was no longer enrolled at South Carolina State.

6. *Times and Democrat,* 16, 17 March 1960; NAACP Collection, Group III, Series A, Container 279, Folder: Reprisals, South Carolina General, 1960–65. Quotation from Dan Wakefield, "Eye of the Storm," *Nation* 190 (7 May 1960), 404–5.

7. The Faculty Council members in attendance were Algernon S. Belcher; M. Maceo Nance; A. I. Mose; Marie Vernon; Henry Vincent; Theodus Gay; R. C. Henderson; and Major Harold Jenkins. Council members who were absent were Howard Jordan; Frank M. Staley, J. D. McGhee. Minutes, 16 March 1960, Faculty Log Book III.

8. Faculty Council Minutes, 16 March 1960, Faculty Log Book III.

9. "State Students Get Stiff Warning on Demonstrations," *Times and Democrat,* 18 March 1960, 1.

10. Minute Book, Board of Trustees, 17 March 1960, 57.

11. "15 Negro Students Found Guilty," *Times and Democrat,* 20 1960, 1, 10; "Both Sides Seek Best Trial Method," *Times and Democrat,* 21 March 1960, 10; "More Negro Students Go on Trial," *Times and Democrat,* 28 March 1960, 5; "22 More Negro Demonstrators Found Guilty," *Times and Democrat,* 29 March 1960, 5; "27 More Students Tried," *Times and Democrat,* 1 April 1960, 6; "More Negroes Found Guilty," *Times and Democrat,* 6 April 1960, 6; "More Negroes Found Guilty," *Times and Democrat,* 9 April 1960, 5; "Fifty More Negro Students Sentenced in Local Court," *Times and Democrat,* 23 April 1960, 6; "More Negro Students Fined in Local Court," *Times and Democrat,* 30 April 1960, 8; "Ninety-One More Negro Students Convicted by Magistrate Culler," *Times and Democrat,* 8 May 1960, 12; Oppenheimer, *Sit-In Movement of 1960,* 171; Press Release, "NAACP Hails Court's Ruling in Protests," 25 October 1963, NAACP Records, Group III, Series A Container 290, Folder: Sit-Ins, South Carolina, 1960–63.

12. Bob McHugh, "Negro Demonstrators Are Given Sentences," *State,* 20 March 1960, 1B; Minute Book, Board of Trustees, 4 August 1960, 61.

13. Zinn, *SNCC,* 18.

14. Zinn, *SNCC,* 33; Ransby, *Ella Baker,* 239–53.

15. Curry, *Deep in Our Hearts,* "Wild Geese to the Past," 19–20.

16. Ransby, *Ella Baker,* 262; Curry, *Deep in Our Hearts,* Casey Haden, "Fields of Blue," 340. "Chuck said that before he could do what he did, he had to be willing to die." See also Howard Zinn, *SNCC,* 171–74; "Charles McDew," in *Encyclopedia of African American Civil Rights,* 334.

17. Oppenheimer, *Sit-In Movement of 1960,* 171–72; Isaac Williams interview with William C. Hine, 21 June 1995.

18. C. Williams, *Freedom and Justice,* 151. Williams has a photo of the lunch counter minus the seats; *Times and Democrat,* 22–27 October 1960, 3, 5–15; Press Release: "Orangeburg Negroes Gird for Showdown," 11 October 1963, Press Release, "Orangeburg Arrests Protested by NAACP," 25 October 1963, NAACP Collection, NAACP Records, Series A, Container 279, Folder: Reprisals: South Carolina, General, 1960–65, Library of Congress.

19. "Jennings and Bethea Head Local Conservative Organization," *Times and Democrat,* 3 August 1962, 1.

20. Minute Book, Board of Trustees, 5 October 1963, 74.

21. Isaac Williams interview with William C. Hine, 21 June 1995.

22. "James Baldwin Opens President's Lecture Series, *Collegian,* November 1962, 1, 6.

23. The SACS committee was chaired by Dr. William M. Alexander, a professor of education at the University of Miami. Dr. Ernest Becker, the assistant superintendent of schools for the Parish of New Orleans, and Dean R. F. Thompson of the University of Tennessee served on the committee as well. The three white men were lodged in the Eutaw Hotel on Russell Street while Manly stayed at the president's residence. Folder: Southern Association, Presidents' Papers, Benner C. Turner, HCSCSU; *Annual Report, 1954–1955,* 36–37.

24. Dr. Donald Agnew, Executive Secretary of the Commission on Colleges and Universities of the Southern Association of Colleges and Schools, to Benner C. Turner, 16 January 1957, published in the *Annual Report, 1956–1957,* 21–22; *Annual Report, 1957–1958,* 15.

25. *Annual Report, 1960–1961,* 51–52.

26. "Gov. Hollings informed the Board [of Trustees] of his efforts to have the College accredited by the Southern Association." Precisely what those efforts involved is unknown. The board meeting took place in the governor's office. Minute Book, Board of Trustees, 10 December 1959, 56. HCSCSU.

27. *Annual Report, 1960–1961,* 12–13, 51–53; *Annual Report, 1961–1962,* 48–50.

28. *Annual Report, 1956–1957,* 22, 77–78.

29. *Annual Report, 1957–1958,* 33, 52; *Annual Report, 1960–1961,* 52.

30. *Annual Report, 1957–1958,* 15, 51; Minute Book, Board of Trustees, Local Committee, 10 August 1955, 31; HCSCSU. *Annual Report, 1960–1961,* 21.

31. *Annual Report, 1950–1951,* 54; Benner C. Turner to W. C. Bethea, 19 November 1954, Folder: Trustees: Presidents' Papers, Benner C. Turner, HCSCSU.

32. *Annual Report, 1960–1961,* 16, 54; *Annual Report, 1961–1962,* 10–11, 23; *Annual Report, 1962–1963,* 63; *Annual Report, 1963–1964,* 12. The laboratory school had been named for J. B. Felton, the longtime white administrator who supervised the Negro public schools for the State Department of Education.

33. *Annual Report, 1961–1962,* 9–10.

34. *Annual Report, 1962–1963,* 58–60.

35. Minute Book, Board of Trustees, 27 February 1961, 64.

36. Minute Book, Board of Trustees, 11 September 1964, 79; *Annual Report, 1964–1965,* 42.

37. *Annual Report, 1955–1956,* 69; *Annual Report, 1956–1957,* 23–24, appendix 6, 92; Minute Book, Board of Trustees, 31 January 1957, 42; 22 May 1958, 48. HCSCSU.

38. Harvey Gantt transferred from the architecture program at Iowa State University to Clemson (Lau, *Democracy Rising,* and Lesesne, *History of the University of South Carolina*). While it would not be accurate to suggest that the first black students at these historically white institutions were warmly greeted, they certainly did not encounter the violence that accompanied the desegregation of the University of Mississippi and the University of Georgia.

39. *Annual Report, 1950–1951,* 24–25, 58. In a letter of 22 March 1955, Turner referred to Hervey as "Dear John." File: School of Law, 1955–56, Presidents' Papers, Benner C. Turner, HCSCSU.

40. For more on the S.C. State law school and its faculty and students, see "South Carolina State College Law School," in Burke and Gergel, *Matthew J. Perry,* 17–60.

41. Personnel file, Peter H. Whittaker, HCSCSU.

42. William C. Hine interview with Judge Matthew J. Perry, 19 June 1995; Burke and Hine, "South Carolina State College Law School," 38; Baker, *Paradoxes of Desegregation,* 84.

43. Baker, *Paradoxes of Desegregation,* 85; *Annual Report, 1952–1953,* 58.

44. Burke and Hine, "South Carolina State College Law School," 36.

45. There is a list of the published and reported civil rights cases heard in federal and South Carolina courts handled by the graduates of the South Carolina State College law school. See Burke and Hine, "South Carolina State College Law School," 44–49.

46. John G. Hervey to Benner C. Turner, 18 March 1955, Turner to Hervey, 22 March 1955, File: School of Law, 1955–56, Presidents' Papers, Benner C. Turner, HCSCSU.

47. John G. Hervey to Leo Kerford, Dean, 6 November 1963, copy in State College Minute Book, Board of Trustees, 75, HCSCSU.

48. In Turner's *Annual Report, 1964–1965,* 30, he stated that the board of trustees at its November 1965 meeting "directed the College Administration to discontinue operation of the School of Law." But the minutes of that meeting as well as other meetings of the board from 1964 to 1966 make no mention of and indicate no vote on closing the law school. For more on Robert McC. Figg and the reluctance to admit black students at the university's law school, see Lesesne, *History of the University of South Carolina,* 149.

49. See Burke and Hine, "South Carolina State College Law School," 39. Gore, *On a Hilltop High.* See LeMarquis DeJarmon's essay "Voting—One Hundred Years to the Beginning."

50. *Annual Report, 1964–1965,* 30.

51. *Annual Report, 1947–1948,* 9; *Annual Report, 1946–1947,* 20; *Annual Report, 1956–1957,* 46; *Annual Report, 1952–1953,* 26.

52. Pete Daniel, "The Hidden Story behind the Sherrod Case: USDA Racism." History News Network, 2 August 2010: http://www.hnn.us/articles/129618.html, accessed 2 August 2010.

53. Daniel, "Hidden Story."

54. *Annual Report, 1954–1955,* 6–8; *Annual Report, 1955–1956,* 6–7.

55. F. Marcelleus Staley to Benner C. Turner, 7 October 1955; S. M. Pinckney to Benner C. Turner, 12 October 1955, File: School of Agriculture, 1955–56, Presidents' Papers, Benner C. Turner, HCSCSU. Staley stated it was twelve acres of land, and Pinckney indicates the college was using ten acres.

56. F. Marcelleus Staley to Benner C. Turner, 30 May 1956, File: School of Agriculture, 1955–56, Presidents' Papers, Benner C. Turner, HCSCSU.

57. F. Marcelleus Staley to J. I. Washington, 2 July 1952 (copy), File: School of Agriculture, Presidents' Papers, Benner C. Turner, HCSCSU.

58. *Annual Report, 1956–1957,* 53–54; *Annual Report, 1962–1963,* 24.

59. *Annual Report, 1962–1963,* 24.

60. *Annual Report, 1964–1965,* 14–15.

61. *Annual Report, 1966–1967,* 11–15. The ten Clemson officials were Victor Hurst, vice president for academic affairs and dean of the university; J. W. Jones, director of resident instruction in the College of Agriculture and Biological Sciences; W. J. Lanham, head of the Department of Agricultural Economics and Rural Sociology; L. H. Davis, head of the Department of Agricultural Education; A. W. Snell, head of the Department of Agricultural Engineering; U.S. Jones, head of the Department of Agronomy and Soils; R. F. Wheeler, head of the Department of Animal Science; T. L. Senn, head of the Department of Horticulture; B. D. Barnett, head of the Department of Poultry Science; and F. I. Brownley, dean of the Graduate School.

62. See Algernon S. Belcher to Benner C. Turner, 16 December 1966 (copy) and Memorandum of Understanding between South Carolina State College and Clemson University, [no date], appendix 3, *Annual Report, 1966–1967.*

63. Harris, "Ray of Hope," 573, 599.

64. Harris, "Ray of Hope," 621.

65. Oral history interviews: Sara Aiken Waymer, Altamese B. Pough. Conducted by Carmen V. Harris, William C. Hine, and Barbara Williams Jenkins, Miller F. Whittaker Library, 20 May 1988.

66. Quoted from Harris, "Ray of Hope," 574.

67. Quoted from Harris, "Ray of Hope," 595. "Grievances of Negro County Extension Agents," Attachment to Isaac E. McGraw to George Nutt, 14 July 1965.

68. Oral history interviews, Altamese B. Pough; Harris, "Ray of Hope," 591.

69. Harris, "Ray of Hope," 589; Oral history interviews, Altamese B. Pough and Sara Aiken Waymer.

70. Harris, "Ray of Hope," 626. Harris cites Responses to Various Issues Raised in the Penn Center Report, 2–3, Series 32, Box 29, Folder 5. Strom Thurmond Institute, Clemson University.

71. Harris, "Ray of Hope," 650–51, 669–70, 673. Clemson was so pleased with the Brown appointment that they issued a press release. T. J. Crawford noted Cunningham's promotion in his column "Alumni Corner" in the *Collegian,* December 1966. Crawford also noted that Quincy Benbow, the assistant agent in Marlboro County, had resigned to take a position with the U.S. Agency for International Development (AID) in Ghana.

72. W. Johnson, "History, Growth, and Transition of the 4-H among Negroes in South Carolina," 100–101; Harris, "Ray of Hope," 628.

73. W. Johnson, "History, Growth, and Transition of the 4-H among Negroes in South Carolina," 101–2; Harris, "Ray of Hope," 633–34.

74. Harris, "Ray of Hope," 672; William Hine interview with Sara Aiken Waymer, 14 April 2010.

75. For more on the comparison of graduates of S.C. State and Clemson, see Harris, "Ray of Hope," 649–52.

76. Harris, "Ray of Hope," 548, 629, 644.

77. Minute Book, Board of Trustees, 12 November 1959, 55; 10 December 1959, 56. *Collegian,* February, April, May 1960.

78. Minute Book, Board of Trustees, 16 May 1961, 65; 22 May 1964, 17; 19 May 1965, 81. The visitors submitted their annual reports to the trustees, and those reports were received as information.

79. "Bill to Appoint Negro to College Board Approved," *State* (Columbia), 23 February 1966, 11A; *Journal of the House of Representatives of the Second Session of the 96th General Assembly of the State of South Carolina, 1966* (Columbia: State Budget and Control Board), 293, 357, 463–64, 478, 975.

80. "Bill to Include Alumnus on Trustee Board of College Passes," *Collegian,* May 1966, 1; "Meet the New Trustees at South Carolina State," *Collegian,* October 1966, 1; Minute Book, Board of Trustees, 11 May 1966, 84.

81. William C. Hine interview with T. J. Crawford, 9 March 1989. Philip G. Grose points out that McNair desegregated the boards and commissions of several state agencies with interim appointments that were later confirmed by the general assembly, including those of Mental Health; Public Welfare; Probation, Parole and Pardon; the Criminal Justice Academy; and South Carolina State College. . . . But this was not the case with S.C. State," Grose, *South Carolina at the Brink,* 147.

82. Minute Book, Board of Trustees, 11 May 1966, 84; "W. C. Bethea Relinquishes Secretarial Duties of Trustees of State College," *Collegian,* December 1966, 1; Atkinson, *Interesting and Influential People of Orangeburg,* 36–38.

83. *Annual Report, 1947–1948,* 18; Financial Report, Oliver C. Dawson, Faculty Book Log Book Faculty Log Book V , HCSCSU. Each team was to receive 28 percent of the receipts with each coach provided 1 percent. But only 1,039 tickets were sold, and the receipts totaled $3,129.81 while the expenses for the game were $6,809.40. There was a net loss of $3,679.59.

84. Much of the athletic information and many of the statistics come from the Bulldog Media Guides prepared over the years by Sports Information director Bill Hamilton and his staff.

85. Personnel File, Lawrence Simmons; "A Letter from the Coach," *Collegian,* May 1953, 11.

86. Isaiah Barnwell, "State's Athletic Program Revamped," *Collegian,* October 1955, 7–8; *Bulldog,* 1954, 128; *Bulldog,* 1955, 160–61.

87. Faculty Athletic Committee—H. W. Crawford, M. Maceo Nance, and F. Marcellus Staley—to President Benner C. Turner, 10 February 1960, Turner General Correspondence, 1959–60, Athletic file, HCSCSU.

88. F. Marcellus Staley to Roy D. Moore, 26 September 1956, copy, Turner General Correspondence, 1956–57, Athletic file, HCSCSU.

89. "State Bows to Allen," *Collegian,* October 1955, 7–8; "State–Fla. A. and M. Broadcast," *Collegian,* November 1959, 7.

90. "State Wins Pumpkin Classic," *Collegian,* December 1963, 6; "Bulldogs Smash Tigers in Pumpkin Classic, *Collegian,* December 1966, 3. The Benedict rivalry was revived in 1999 when Benedict resumed intercollegiate football, and the two teams played intermittently in the twenty-first century with the Bulldogs winning all six of the contests. According to the 1966 recollection of alumnus John Dorman recorded by Thomas J. Crawford, the first game with Benedict was a S.C. State victory in 1912. But Dorman remembered a S.C. State loss in 1914 in a game played at the Orangeburg Fairgrounds when a S.C. State safety was distracted by a passing horse-drawn fire engine and a Benedict receiver got behind him and scored. T. J. Crawford, "Alumni Corner," *Collegian,* December 1966, 3.

91. F. Marcellus Staley, Chairman of the Faculty Athletic Committee, to Benner C. Turner, 4 August 1959, Turner General Correspondence, 1959–60, Athletic file, HCSCSU.

92. "Allen Surprises State," *Collegian,* October 1963, 5.

93. "Letter," *Collegian,* September 1963, 2.

94. "Head Football Coach George Bell Resigns," *Collegian,* April 1965, 1.

95. "John Devlin, Sophomore Fullback, Dies," *Collegian,* September 1965, 5.

96. www.youtube.comwatch?v=E7C/sRPJx-8.

97. Faculty Athletic Committee (H. W. Crawford, Secretary; M. Maceo Nance; Frank M. Staley, Chair) to Benner C. Turner, 10 February 1960, Faculty Athletic Committee file, Turner General Correspondence, 1959–60, HCSCSU. There is an interview of approximately 18 minutes with Coach Martin conducted by James Haney that was uploaded on You Tube in 2007 in which Martin discusses his life and career. Date uploaded 4 March 2017.

98. "Wright Nation's Top Scorer among Small Colleges," *Collegian,* February 1958, 5; "Team Enjoys Trip by Plane," *Collegian,* March 1958, 5; *Bulldog,* 1958, 204. For more on race and college sports, see Martin, *Benching Jim Crow.*

99. *Bulldog,* 1958, 204; Lindberg Moody, "Lindy's Views," *Collegian,* February 1961, 5; "State College Bulldogs are S.I.A.C. Champs," "Bulldogs Participate in First NCAA Tournament," *Collegian,* March 1961, 1, 7.

100. "Lindberg Moody Drafted by Two Pro Teams," *Collegian,* April 1962, 1; "Ernest 'Sonny' Jackson Plays with the NAIA-NCAA All Stars," *Collegian,* April 1963, 5; "Bill Morgan Signs Up with Globetrotters," *Collegian,* October 1963, 1.

101. *Bulldog,* 1964, 226. The 1964 *Bulldog* was dedicated to that year's basketball team. Martin, *Benching Jim Crow,* 70–72.

102. See news.vanderbilt.edu/2002/02professor-ed-martin-remembered-as-strong-advocate-for-children-and-youth-60269, accessed 4 March 2017.

103. *Bulldog,* 1961, 124–25; "Jeffries Is College's Top Pitcher," *Collegian,* May 1958, 7; *Bulldog,* 1962, 128, 120.

104. *Bulldog,* 1961, 128–29. Aflamingo was the formal ball held by Alpha Phi Alpha Fraternity each spring.

105. *Bulldog,* 1963, 236–37; "Robert Bradley to Spend Summer as Seasonal Park Ranger," *Collegian,* May 1964, 3.

106. *Bulldog,* 1961, 112, 128, 129, 180; *Bulldog,* 1962, 121; "LBJ Praises Green Beret Killed in Vietnam," *Jet Magazine,* 27 December 1966, 8.

107. *Annual Report, 1948–1949,* "Bulldogs Win 24th Annual SIAC Tennis Tournament," *Collegian,* May 1950, 7; *Bulldog,* 1954, 133.

108. Photo, *Collegian,* November 1954, 3; *Bulldog,* 1962, 113.

109. "Joe Louis Visits Campus," *Collegian,* March 1950, 7; *Bulldog,* 1962, 138; *Bulldog,* 1963, 243.

110. *Bulldog,* 1948, 90–91.

111. *Bulldog,* 1960, 164–65, *Bulldog,* 1961, 130; *Collegian,* May 1964, 4.

112. "Wilkinson Memorial Organ Rededicated at Vesper Services," *Collegian,* May 1961, 10.

113. Leon Gibbs, "State's ROTC Band Plays at State Capitol," *Collegian,* October 1952, 1; *Bulldog,* 1953, 72.

114. F. Abraham, Chair of the Music Department, and Shellie Thomas Jr., band director, to Howard Jordan Jr., Dean, School of Education, 28 January 1955, File: Music Dept.; Benner C. Turner to

J. I. Washington, 18 April 1955, General Correspondence, 1954–55, Presidential Papers, HCSCSU; "First Annual 'S' Day Held October 1," *Collegian*, October 1955, 1.

115. Foster directed the Florida A&M band from 1946 until he retired in 1998. He died in 2010 at age ninety-four. http//www.famu.edu/index.cfm?/a=marching100&p=dr.williamp.foster, accessed 4 March 2017. "FAMU Rolls over S.C. State," *Collegian*, November 1958, 6.

116. "Band Back," *Collegian*, September 1963,1.

117. "The Marching 101 Band to Appear on National TV," *Collegian*, December 1965, 1.

118. The 1896 legislation creating the college stipulated that the president and "corps of instructors" were to be of the Negro race. That legal requirement remained in effect until the passage of the 1964 Civil Rights Act.

119. Robert Moore, who taught history at Columbia College, provided copies of correspondence involving the 1967 controversy on the S.C. State campus that came to be known as "the Cause." At the time, Moore was the president of the state branch of the Association of University Professors (AAUP), and he would also serve on the 1967–68 Blackwell Committee. That correspondence includes four letters all dated 18 February 1967 to Felix C. Robb, the director of the Southern Association of Colleges and Schools (SACS). One of the letters was cosigned by Wirth, Fanning, and Morrison. There are also three separate letters to Robb from Wirth, Fanning, and Morrison that discuss the circumstances that led to their terminations at S.C. State.

120. Morrison, Wirth, and Fanning to Robb, 18 February 1967; Morrison to Robb, 18 February 1967, copies from Moore file.

121. See discussion of the tenure policy in chapter 5, Annual Report, 1955–56; Minute Book, Board of Trustees, 14 April 1955, 27.

122. For more on the student protests and what came to be known as in the spring of 1967 as "the Cause," see W. Hine, "Civil Rights and Campus Wrongs," 325–31; and Grose, *South Carolina at the Brink*, 187–93; "College Students May March on Governor," *Times and Democrat*, 8 March 1967, 1, 11.

123. "Student Unrest May Force College to Suspend School," *Times and Democrat*, 4 March 1967, 1; Student Handbook, 1965–66, 49; W. Hine, "Civil Rights and Campus Wrongs," 325–26; Grose, *South Carolina at the Brink*, 187.

124. Isaac Williams interview with William C. Hine, 21 June 1995; "Class Boycotts Continue at S.C. State," *Times and Democrat*, 5 March 1967, 1, 3A; W. Hine, "Civil Rights and Campus Wrongs," 328.

125. Williams interview with W. Hine; "Proposals" and "Reactions to the Proposals." These documents were in the possession of Mr. Williams. Jack Bass, "3 Students' Rehearing Calms Campus," *Charlotte Observer*, 1 March 1967, 1-B; Jack Bass, "Students Continue Class Boycott as College Considers Shut Down," *Charlotte Observer*, 7 March 1967, 1-C.

126. "Proposals," *Times and Democrat*, 8 March 1967, 1; *State*, 7 March 1967.

127. Benner C. Turner, "Memorandum to All Faculty Members," 6 March 1967. Papers in possession of Isaac Williams. See Grose, *South Carolina at the Brink*, 188.

128. Minutes, Board of Trustees, 2 March 1967, 87.

129. I. Stanback, Dr. James Boykin, Wallace C. Bethea, and Elliott Elam attended the meeting as well as John Cauthen, Algernon S. Belcher, Henry Vincent, and Maceo Nance. Minute Book, Board of Trustees, 8 March 1967, 87. "Students Given until Friday to End College Boycott Here," *Times and Democrat*, 9 March 1967, 1; W. Hine, "Civil Rights and Campus Wrongs," 327; Grose, *South Carolina at the Brink*, 189.

130. Nichols reference was to the new Carolina Coliseum, which was under construction at the University of South Carolina. "State College Students Vow They'll Stand Fast," *Times and Democrat*, 10 March 1967, 1; Paul Clancy, "Students Are Told to Return to Classes," *State*, 9 March 1967, 1, 8; "S.C. State Boycott Leaders" (photo), *State*, 10 March 1967, 7-B.

131. Hine interview with Williams, 21 June 1995; W. Hine, "Civil Rights and Campus Wrongs," 328–29.

132. *Times and Democrat*, 9 March 1967; *State*, 4, 9 March 1967; W. Hine, "Civil Rights and Campus Wrongs," 329. McNair had defeated Republican candidate Joseph Rogers by seventy-two thousand votes in a contest in which most of the ninety-two thousand black voters supported McNair.

133. William C. Hine interview with Gov. Robert E. McNair, 23 January 2001; Hine interview with Williams, 21 June 1995.

134. William C. Hine interview with Judge Matthew Perry, 19 June 1995. Grose, *South Carolina at the Brink*, 190–91.

135. See Grose, *South Carolina at the Brink*, 194–95. Grose cites the *State*, 8 March 1967.

136. Grose, *South Carolina at the Brink*, 195. Grose cites the *State*, 23 April 1967.

137. At a 22 March 1967 meeting of the trustees, Turner asked that he be permitted to resign, but the trustees voted unanimously to reject the offer. Minute Book, Board of Trustees, 22 March 1967, 87. W. Hine, "Civil Rights and Campus Wrongs," 329–30; Grose, *South Carolina at the Brink*, 191–92. One unnamed commentator wryly observed that if Turner remained, "we might as well provide a year-round dormitory for Pete Strom and his agents in the State Law Enforcement Division (SLED)." "Agreement Told at State College," *Times and Democrat*, 11 March 1967, 1, 2; Frank K. Myers, "S.C. State College: What Does the Future Hold?" *Times and Democrat*, 30 April 1967, 1; Paul Clancy, "Unrest Still Grips State," *State*, 23 April 1967, 3E.

138. Hine interview with McNair, 23 January 2001. Minute Book, Board of Trustees, 10 May 1967, 87. The board agreed to pay Turner through 31 December 1967.

139. Personnel file: Etta B. Rowe, Benner C. Turner to Etta B. Rowe, 10 February 1958, HCSCSU.

140. Hine interview with Gov. McNair, 23 January 2001.

141. Historian Richard Reid conducted research on Turner's later years and uncovered this information. Reid also learned that Turner's death certificate listed him as a white man. Richard Reid, "S.C. State's Fourth President: Dr. Benner C. Turner," *Times and Democrat*, 12 June 2008, B7.

CHAPTER EIGHT: 1968

1. Minute Book, Board of Trustees, 31 May 1967, 93; HCSCSU. William C. Hine interview with M. Maceo Nance, 14 March 1989.

2. "Howell to Head Faculty Study Commission," *Collegian*, May 1961, 5.

3. *State Agricultural and Mechanical College Bulletin*, "Faculty Study Commission Number," Orangeburg: 1952, iv. For a time in the early 1950s, the college published the proceedings of the commission. Emphasis added.

4. *State Agricultural and Mechanical College Bulletin*, "Faculty Study Commission Number, Orangeburg: 1952, 4, 13–14. President Turner sent letters to absent faculty members and administrators informing them that there would be $5 deducted from their paycheck for missing FSC meetings. Several such letters appear in the personnel file of business manager J. I. Washington, HCSCSU.

5. John K. Cauthen to Dr. Roland E. Haynes, Chairman, Faculty Senate Guidelines Committee, 1 September 1967, Robert Moore files.

6. Minutes, Committee on South Carolina State College [the Blackwell Committee], 14 July 1967, Moore file.

7. Faculty Senate Guidelines Committee, Roland E. Haynes, Chair, to John K. Cauthen, 29 August 1967; Cauthen to Haynes, 1 September 1967, Moore file. The Faculty Senate Guidelines Committee included Roland E. Haynes, chair; Rubin F. Weston, cochair; Marguerite R. Howie; secretary; Oliver C. Dawson; Bernice Middleton; Clemmie E. Webber; Leroy E. Anderson; Omeda R. Livingston; and Harold Powell. The Blackwell Committee consisted of Gordon W. Blackwell, president, Furman University; Walter D. Smith, Winthrop College; John F. Potts, president, Voorhees College; Walter P. Cox, Clemson University; Leroy E. Anderson, director of institutional research, S.C. State; Henry N. Vincent, dean of students, S.C. State; Rubin F. Weston, chair of Social Sciences, S.C. State; Marguerite R. Howie, professor of sociology, S.C. State; Robert V. Scott, president of the Student Government Association, S.C. State; Marcella Peron, student, S.C. State; Robert J. Moore, professor of history (and president of the state conference of the AAUP), Columbia College; and Webster Myers, University of South Carolina.

8. Minutes, Committee on South Carolina State College [Blackwell Committee], 15 September 1967, 4. The minutes are contained in the papers of Gordon Blackwell, Special Collections, James B. Duke Library, Furman University.

9. Article 2, section 2, Constitution of the Academic Faculty and Faculty Senate, South Carolina State College, adopted 29 August 1967. Contained in the Blackwell Committee Report, Orangeburg, February 1968, 1–16.

10. Article 2, section 3, Constitution, 3–4.

11. Constitution of the Faculty and Faculty Senate, Educational Policies Council, 5–6, 11–12.

12. "South Carolina State College Regulations on Academic Freedom and Tenure," Blackwell Committee Report (Orangeburg: 1968), 17–21. The statement was approved by the Faculty Senate on 9 October 1967.

13. "Regulations on Academic Freedom and Tenure," Blackwell Committee Report, 20–21.

14. "Student Handbook," 1962–64, 50–52.

15. Student Regulations, "The Student Handbook," Blackwell Committee Report, 57.

16. Student Regulations, "The Student Handbook," Blackwell Committee Report, 64–65.

17. Student Regulations, "The Student Handbook," Blackwell Committee Report, 65–66.

18. Student Regulations, "The Student Handbook," Blackwell Committee Report, 39.

19. Student Regulations, "The Student Handbook," Blackwell Committee Report, 40.

20. Student Regulations, "The Student Handbook," Blackwell Committee Report, 38–48.

21. The *Times and Democrat* ran the supplement devoted to S.C. State on 17 September 1967.

22. Bass and Nelson, *Orangeburg Massacre,* 3, 12–13.

23. Rebecca Kemp, Editorial: "Now It's Up to You," *Collegian,* September 1967, 7.

24. Editorial: "Emphasis BACC," *Collegian,* November 1967, 2.

25. Letters to the Editor, *Collegian,* December 1967, 2–3. Emphasis in the original Edwards letter.

26. Editorial, *Collegian,* December 1967, 2. Emphasis in the original editorial.

27. Editorial, *Collegian,* December 1967, 2.

28. For more on the life and civil rights career of Cleveland Sellers, see his marvelous memoir *River of No Return.* For his recollections of King, see 163–67.

29. Bass and Nelson, *Orangeburg Massacre,* 24–25.

30. Bass and Nelson, *Orangeburg Massacre,* 22–27. Mancari encountered an apartment owner who would not rent to black people. "No niggers live here, you can be sure of that," she was told. *Walking on the Grass,* 71.

31. Bass and Nelson, *Orangeburg Massacre,* 27–28.

32. Bass and Nelson, *Orangeburg Massacre,* 28–29; Grose, *South Carolina at the Brink,* 204–5.

33. Bass and Nelson, *Orangeburg Massacre,* 30–34; Grose, *South Carolina at the Brink,* 202; "BACC's members repeatedly refused to get involved in the bowling alley issue. They believed, and I supported them, that integration was an irrelevant issue." Sellers, *River of No Return,* 209.

34. Bass and Nelson, *Orangeburg Massacre,* 30–32; Grose, *South Carolina at the Brink,* 204–5.

35. Nelson and Bass, *Orangeburg Massacre,* 36–40; Grose, *South Carolina at the Brink,* 206–8.

36. Bass and Nelson, *Orangeburg Massacre,* 10, 62–64, 49.

37. Grose, *South Carolina at the Brink,* 209.

38. Bass and Nelson, *Orangeburg Massacre,* 48–49.

39. Bass and Nelson, *Orangeburg Massacre,* 50–51.

40. Bass and Nelson, *Orangeburg Massacre,* 51–53.

41. Bass and Nelson, *Orangeburg Massacre,* 55–58.

42. Bass and Nelson, *Orangeburg Massacre,* 60–61; Grose, *South Carolina at the Brink,* 215–16.

43. Bass and Nelson, *Orangeburg Massacre,* 64–69; Grose, *South Carolina at the Brink,* 215.

44. Bass and Nelson, *Orangeburg Massacre,* 69–73.

45. Grose, *South Carolina at the Brink,* 222; Bass and Nelson, *Orangeburg Massacre,* 77–78.

46. Bass and Nelson, *Orangeburg Massacre,* 81–98; Grose, *South Carolina at the Brink,* 215–24.

47. Bass and Nelson, *Orangeburg Massacre,* 95; Grose, *South Carolina at the Brink,* 224, for the Strom quote.

48. Bass and Nelson, *Orangeburg Massacre,* 125–46; Sellers, *River of No Return,* 218.

49. Bass and Nelson, *Orangeburg Massacre,* 95–96; Sellers, *River of No Return,* 221–22.

50. Sellers, *River of No Return,* 222–24.

51. Sellers, *River of No Return,* 226, 241–44; Bass and Nelson, *Orangeburg Massacre,* 126.

52. Quotes from Grose, *South Carolina at the Brink,* 234–35. "Orangeburg Massacre" was apparently first used by SNCC leader H. Rap Brown in comments to the media in New York City shortly after the shootings. *Daily Defender* (Chicago), 12 February 1968.

53. Bass and Nelson, *Orangeburg Massacre,* 206–10, 214.

54. Bass and Nelson, *Orangeburg Massacre,* rev. ed., 155; Grose, *South Carolina at the Brink,* 231.

55. Conviction on the criminal information was later increased to life in prison if a victim died. The nine patrolmen who admitted firing their weapons and who were tried were Lieutenant Jesse A. Spell, Sergeant Henry M. Addy, Corporal Norwood Bellamy, Patrolman John W. Brown, Corporal Joseph H. Lanier, Patrolman Colie M. Metts, Patrolman Edward H. Moore, Patrolman Allen J. Russell, and Sergeant Sidney C. Taylor. Bass and Nelson, *Orangeburg Massacre,* rev. ed., 157.

56. Coleman was assisted by Orangeburg solicitor Julian Wolfe (who had been a member of the S.C. State board of trustees two decades earlier), and attorneys Frank Taylor and Geddes H. Martin Jr. Klyde Robinson, the U.S. attorney for South Carolina, declined to participate in the prosecution of the patrolmen because he did not believe it had legal merit. Bass and Nelson, *Orangeburg Massacre,* rev. ed., 154, 159–85; Grose, *South Carolina at the Brink,* 232–33.

57. Bass and Nelson, *Orangeburg Massacre,* 185–89. The authors noted that the jury actually took less than thirty minutes to reach their verdict but remained out for another hour for the sake of appearances.

58. See "CLAD Newsletter," February 1969, Folder: CLAD, Box 45, HCSCSU; "Witness: No Cause Given," *State,* 10 November 1970, 1B, 10B; Ginny Carroll, "Plaintiffs Rest Case in Orangeburg Trial, *State,* 12 November 1970, 1B, 10B; "Orangeburg Civil Suits to Be Resumed," *State,* 13 November 1970, 12A; Ginny Carroll, "S.C. Patrolmen Cleared of Liability in Slaying," *State,* 14 November 1970, 1-B; Grose, *South Carolina at the Brink,* 233–34. Judge Russell was a former governor as well as the former president of the University of South Carolina. Six potential black jurors were dismissed.

59. Bass and Nelson, *Orangeburg Massacre,* rev. ed., 80; Grose, *South Carolina at the Brink,* 224.

60. Bass and Nelson, *Orangeburg Massacre,* rev. ed., 81–82.

61. Bass and Nelson, *Orangeburg Massacre,* rev. ed., 81–82.

62. "Brown Terms Killing of Three Students 'Orangeburg Massacre,'" *Chicago Daily Defender,* 12 February 1968, 4. See Shuler, *Blood and Bone,* 108–9. Although the massacre did not receive widespread or long-lasting media coverage, it was not quite forgotten. Martha Biondi examines the impact that it had on black students on other campuses in 1968. Biondi, *Black Revolution on Campus,* 32–33.

63. Grose, *South Carolina at the Brink,* 226–27; Bass and Nelson, *Orangeburg Massacre,* rev. ed., 90–91.

64. "Wilkins Challenges McNair: Stand Up as a Man and Admit Killings a Mistake," *Collegian,* March 1968, 3.

65. "Memorial Services Held for Slain Students," and Betty Edwards, "A Day of Rain and Tears," *Collegian,* March 1968, 1 5.

66. Woodrow S. Nathan Jr., "Why Must Blood Flow?," *Collegian,* March 1968, 4.

67. "SGA Committee Meets with Gov. McNair," *Collegian,* March 1968, 2. The other campus leaders were Alexander Nichols, vice president of the SGA; Albertha Mitchell, acting secretary; Bobby L. Williams, business manager and treasurer; senior class president Otis Williams; junior class president Clifford Stanley; sophomore class president Alex Palmer Jr.; and freshman class president Richard S. Whitney.

68. Carrie Tyson, Linda Anderson, Charles Lewis, "State College Students Stage Massive Protest," *Collegian,* March 1968, 7; Bass and Nelson, *Orangeburg Massacre,* rev. ed., 92–93; Grose, *South Carolina at the Brink,* 229–30. The other five students who were arrested were Eddie Sharperson, Ann Albert, Al Hazel, Sonya Fordham, and William Torey.

69. Bass and Nelson, *Orangeburg Massacre,* rev. ed., 94.

70. Bass and Nelson, *Orangeburg Massacre,* rev. ed., 95.

71. Minutes, Board of Trustees, 27 March 1968. The SGA representatives were Robert V. Scott, president; Alexander Nichols; vice president; Bobby Williams, treasurer; Marcella Johnson, recording secretary; Bobby Poole (position unidentified); Otis Williams, senior class president; Clifford Stanley, junior class president; Alex Palmer, sophomore class president; and Richard Whitney, freshman class president. The BACC representatives were Sandra Lunn, Alfred Hazelton, John Stroman, William Toney, Wayne Curtis, and John Wilson. Plans for the 8 February 1969 memorial service were announced in the *Collegian:* "Memorial Lecture Planned for Three Students Slain a Year Ago," January 1969, 1.

72. The Davis and Hugine quotes are from Grose, *Looking for Utopia,* 142. Grose has an excellent account of West's involvement with S.C. State students and faculty members.

73. Bass and Nelson, *Orangeburg Massacre,* rev. ed., 95–96; Grose, *South Carolina at the Brink,* 229–31.

74. Bass and Nelson, *Orangeburg Massacre,* rev. ed., 96–97; Grose, *South Carolina at the Brink,* 230–31.

75. Mancari, *Walking on the Grass,* 188–89.

76. John Stroman to Gov. Robert E. McNair, January 1968, McNair to Stroman, 17 January 1968, The correspondence is reprinted in *BACC Speaks,* February 1968, 2.

77. James A. Rogers address to students, 11 April 1968, Folder: Board of Trustees, Box 1. Much of what Rogers told the students was based on information in a letter Nance provided Rogers on March 29. See "Trustee J. A. Rogers Explains Choice of J. M. Smith as Name for New P.E. Facility," *Collegian,* May 1968, 12. The J. M. Smith family asked the trustees to rescind their decision to name the building after the late auditor. Minutes, Board of Trustees, 17 October 1968, HCSCSU.

78. "State College Family Mourns Death of a Leader," *Collegian,* May 1968, 1.

79. Beverly Alford, "The Lady behind the Man," *Collegian,* May 1968, 8.

80. Grose, *South Carolina at the Brink,* 231.

81. Bass and Nelson, *Orangeburg Massacre,* rev. ed., 86–90; Grose, *South Carolina at the Brink,* 227–28.

82. Pat Watters and Weldon Rougeau, "Events at Orangeburg: A Report Based on Study and Interviews in Orangeburg, South Carolina, in the Aftermath of a Tragedy," 25 February 1968, Southern Regional Council, Atlanta, Georgia. The report did praise the *Charlotte Observer,* the *Los Angeles Times,* and NBC News for their coverage of Orangeburg.

83. Bass and Nelson, *Orangeburg Massacre,* rev. ed., 85; M. Maceo Nance Jr. to William L. Taylor, Staff Director, U.S. Commission on Civil Rights, 28 March 1968. The letter is misfiled in Folder: U.S. Civil Rights Comm., Box 33, HCSCSU.

84. Minutes, Board of Trustees, 27 March 1968. HCSCSU.

85. Annual Report of the President, M. Maceo Nance, May 1968, 8.

86. Based on a Freedom of Information request in 1988, the FBI released its Orangeburg file to the Historical Collection of Miller F. Whittaker Library at South Carolina State University. The file is, however, severely redacted (with information and names blacked out).

87. Bass and Nelson, *Orangeburg Massacre,* rev. ed., 146–47; Grose, *South Carolina at the Brink,* 228–29.

88. FBI file, Orangeburg Massacre, File 44 389101, Section 8, Series 110782, HCSCSU.

89. O'Reilly, *"Racial Matters,"* 256–57. Kleindienst's quote is from p. 257, and Fleischer's quote is from p. 256.

90. Grose, *South Carolina at the Brink,* 224.

91. Gov. Robert E. McNair interview with William C. Hine, 23 January 2001, transcript, 22. Oral Histories of the Orangeburg Massacre, HCSCSU.

92. Grose, *South Carolina at the Brink,* 239. McNair agreed to meet Frank Beacham in 1992 for an interview. Beacham had written and produced a radio drama on the massacre that had been broadcast nationally. McNair was polite but unwilling to discuss the massacre in any detail. He engaged in "polite banter without substance." The governor continued to maintain that he had acted properly in Orangeburg. See Beacham, *Whitewash.* Chapters 8 to 13 deal with the massacre. For Beacham's interview with McNair, see 95–96.

93. For that statement, "Orangeburg: Let Us Heal Ourselves," see *Times and Democrat,* 7 February 1999, 9A. It is reprinted in the appendix of W. Moore and Burton, *Toward the Meeting of the Waters.* See also in that volume William C. Hine, "We're Not There Yet," 373–80.

94. Bass and Nelson, *Orangeburg Massacre,* rev. ed., 219–20; *Scarred Justice: The Orangeburg Massacre 1968,* Boston: Northern Light Productions, 2009; Patrick Healy, "A Time of Darkness Illuminated on Stage," *New York Times,* 20 October 2010, C1, 5.

95. Beacham, *Whitewash,* 85.

96. Carrie Tyson, "The Cause Is Dead," *Collegian,* December 1967, 2.

97. John Stroman to Gov. Robert E. McNair, January 1968, *BACC Speaks,* February 1968, 2.

98. Gov. Robert E. McNair to John Stroman, 17 January 1968, *BACC Speaks,* February 1968, 2. Stroman also emphasized that students should play a role in determining the names of new buildings constructed on the campus.

99. Minutes, Board of Trustees, 19 October 1967, Minute Book, 93. HCSCSU. West's support for Charles H. Thomas Jr. is discussed by Grose, *Looking for Utopia,* 143.

100. Rubin F. Weston to Bruce W. White, chairman of the Board of Trustees, 3 April 1968; Algernon S. Belcher to White, 5 April 1968, Folder: Board of Trustees, Box 1, M. Maceo Nance papers, HCSCSU.

101. Minutes, Board of Trustees, 29 June 1968, HCSCSU. With this meeting, the board stopped keeping minutes in ledgers or journals, as it had done since 1896, and began to maintain those minutes in separate files.

102. William C. Hine interview with Gov. Robert E. McNair, 23 January 2001, transcript, 36–37, Orangeburg Massacre Oral History, HCSCSU. Following the appointment of Nance, Charles Thomas left S.C. State. According to James L. Felder, Thomas joined the Republican Party, and President Richard Nixon appointed him to serve as an equal opportunity officer with the U.S. Postal Service in Washington, D.C. Felder, *Civil Rights in South Carolina,* 152.

CHAPTER NINE: A NEW ERA

1. President's Report to the Board of Trustees, May 1970–October 1970, 1, HCSCSU.

2. Dewey E. Dodds, Chief, Educational Branch, Office of Civil Rights, Department of Health, Education, and Welfare, to M. Maceo Nance Jr., 9 March 1970, photocopy contained in *Annual Report, October 1969–May 1970,* appendix 5, HCSCSU.

3. Nance to Dodds, 4 May 1970, photocopy contained in *Annual Report, May 1970–October 1970,* appendix 3, HCSCSU.

4. Seventy-Second Annual Convocation program, 26 May 1968; Seventy-Third Annual Convocation program, 18 May 1969. The four white men who received degrees were Charles T. Haskell, Thomas N. Hyde, Michael D. Woodson, and Henry V. Zaleski. See also Folder: Graduate School, Box 5, HCSCSU.

5. Presidents' Papers, M. Maceo Nance Jr., Box 37, Folder: Commission on Human Affairs, Report on Full-Time Classified and Unclassified Employees. HCSCSU.

6. Presidents' Papers, M. Maceo Nance Jr., Box 26, Folder: American Association of University Women, 1976, HCSCSU.

7. James's emphasis on "rose." Jean U. James to M. Maceo Nance Jr., undated, Folder: Complimentary letters, Box 1, HCSCSU.

8. The Higher Education Facilities Act of 1963 that Johnson signed only two weeks after John F. Kennedy's assassination was a key stepping stone to the 1965 measure.

9. *Annual Report, May 1969 to October 1969,* 2. USAF was United Student Aid Fund.

10. Thelin, *History of American Higher Education,* 324–26. Brubacher and Rudy, *Higher Education in Transition,* 235–36.

11. *Annual Report, 1977–1978,* 59. Students with automobiles had their grant reduced by $675, 56.

12. Wilkin Williams to M. Maceo Nance Jr., 19 January 1973; Nance to Williams, 22 January 1973, Presidents' Papers, Box 16, Folder: Student Accounts, HCSCSU.

13. Elizabeth Freeman to M. Maceo Nance Jr., 14 August 1973, Box 16, Folder: Student Accounts, HCSCSU. There is no record of Nance's reply.

14. John H. Wrighten IV and James L. Wrighten to M. Maceo Nance Jr., 9 May 1973, Box 16, Folder: Student Accounts, HCSCSU.

15. Nance's estimate came in response to a questionnaire. Survey of College Presidents, May 1980, Presidents' Papers, M. Maceo Nance Jr., Box 33, Folder: Surveys and Questionnaires, HCSCSU; *Annual Report, 1977–1978,* 38.

16. *Annual Report, May 1971–May 1972,* 16; *Annual Report, May 1974–May 1975,* 10; *Annual Report, 1977–1978,* 19.

17. *Annual Report, May 1974–May 1975,* 7; *Annual Report, 1976–1977,* 35, 65; *Annual Report, 1977–1978,* 44–47. Reading levels were based on Nelson-Denny Reading test scores.

18. *South Carolina State College Catalogue 1974–75* (Orangeburg, 1975), 93–94. The members of the faculty who participated in the humanities program compiled the textbooks used in the three courses.

19. *Annual Report, October 1969–May 1970,* 54.

20. *Annual Report, 1977–1978,* 24. Presidents' Papers, M. Maceo Nance Jr., Box 31, Folder: Journalism. R. Scott Baker convincingly demonstrates that the NTE was adopted by South Carolina's political and educational leaders after black teachers won salary equalization lawsuits in the 1940s. State education

officials used the NTE results to determine qualifications and pay scales for black and white teachers. Baker, *Paradoxes of Desegregation*, 172–74, 178–79.

21. Nance's invitation was sent in response to a request by Andre G. Beaumont, managing director, College Placement Services, 4 October 1976, Presidents' Papers, M. Maceo Nance Jr., Box 26, Folder: College Placement Services, HCSCSU.

22. "Academic Rules Change," *Collegian*, February 1972, 1; *Annual Report, May 1972 to May 1973*, 32; *Annual Report, May 1977 to May 1978*, 15.

23. Priscilla Ragin to M. Maceo Nance Jr., 8 October 1971, Folder: Students General, Box 57; Ellen Hay, "An Exchange Program," HCSCSU. *Collegian*, October 1971, 2; Burbette Moorer, "Iowa Girl Tells of Experiences at S.C. State," *Collegian*, September 1972, 4.

24. Thomas Gaither to M. Maceo Nance Jr., 14 July 1980, Presidents' Papers, M. Maceo Nance Jr., Box 39, Folder: Student General, HCSCSU.

25. Edgar, *South Carolina*, 544–45. For a brief discussion of Orangeburg's Wade Hampton and Willington Academies that merged into Orangeburg Preparatory School, see Shuler, *Blood and Bone*, 32–34. *Annual Report, May 1973–May 1974*, 36; *Annual Report, May 1974–May 1975*, 27, 60.

26. "Students of S.C. State College, 'Wake Up': These Are Our Gripes, Are They Yours? If So, *Let's Move Now*." Emphasis in original. Presidents' Papers, M. Maceo Nance Jr., Box 12, Folder SGA, HCSCSU.

27. Editorial: "Non Compulsory ROTC for State," *Collegian*, May 1969, 2. McKeever is quoted in the editorial.

28. Presidents' Papers, M. Maceo Nance Jr., Box 12, Folder: SGA, HCSCSU.

29. M. Maceo Nance Jr. to Andrew Hugine Jr., 20 June 1969, Box 12, Folder: SGA; Robert O. Abernathy to M. Maceo Nance Jr., 8 December 1971, Presidents' Papers, M. Maceo Nance Jr., Box 8, Folder: Mathematics and Computer Science, Minutes, Board of Trustees, 19 June 1969; M. Maceo Nance Jr., Presidents' Papers, Box 15, Folder: Founders Day, 1974, HCSCSU.

30. Minutes, Board of Trustees, 19 June 1969; M. Maceo Nance Jr. to Andrew Hugine Jr., 20 June 1969; Box 12, Folder: SGA; Box 5, Folder: Programs, Presidents' Papers, HCSCSU.

31. *Bulldog*, 1971, 104–6; Roberta Flack photo, *Collegian*, February 1972, 9; *Bulldog*, 1973, 122, 171–73; *Bulldog*, 1975, 184; *Bulldog*, 1978, 192.

32. *Bulldog*, 1969, 53; "70s Will Unite Black People Says Black Nationalist Writer," *Collegian*, February 1971, 4; *Bulldog*, 1971, 75; Thimuelle Robinson, "Register and Vote Says Julian Bond," *Collegian*, September 1972, 1; *Bulldog*, 1973, 171–73; *Bulldog*, 1977, 170.

33. Howie, *Research Projects and Programs in Progress at South Carolina State College*, 29–30. See also Folder: Social Sciences, Box 6, HCSCSU.

34. "Steppen Wolfe's Comments," *Collegian*, February 1971, 4.

35. Priscilla Ragin to M. Maceo Nance Jr., 8 October 1971, Nance to Ragin, 28 October 1971, Folder: Students General, Box 57, HCSCSU.

36. "About 200 Students Join in Protest," *Collegian*, May 1978, 5; *State* clipping, 25 April 1978, contained in Folder: U.S., State Senators, Representatives, Box 46, HCSCSU.

37. "Release," Kay Patterson, District 73, Richland County, 29 April 1978. Folder: U.S., State Senators, Representatives, Box 46, HCSCSU.

38. M. Maceo Nance Jr., Presidents' Papers, Box 15, Folder: Student Discipline, HCSCSU.

39. "About 200 Students Join in Protest," *Collegian*, May 1978, 5.

40. Charles Drake-Long to M. Maceo Nance Jr., 1 November 1970, Presidents' Papers, Box 7, Folder: Dean of Student Affairs, HCSCSU.

41. M. Maceo Nance Jr. to Charles Drake-Long, 6 November 1970, Presidents' Papers, Box 7, Folder: Dean of Student Affairs, HCSCSU.

42. Rebecca Kemp, Editorial: "Black Greekdom an Unnecessary Evil," *Collegian*, November 1969, 2.

43. Letters to the Editor: Thalia J. Coleman and Joseph deLeon McDuffie Jr., *Collegian*, January 1970, 2.

44. Algernon S. Belcher to M. Maceo Nance Jr., 3 May 1977, Folder: Dean of Student Affairs, Box 25, HCSCSU. For more on Greek life in the 1950s, see Washington, *Class of 1957*, 54–56.

45. Louise K. Riddick, Director of South Atlantic Region, Delta Sigma Theta to Johnnie Sharpe, advisor, 8 March 1976, Folder: Sororities, Box 60; Oscar Butler to Walter Funderburk, 19 January 1981,

Folder: Omega Psi Phi, Box 39; DeLoris A. Oliver to Oscar Butler, 20 March 1979, Folder Sororities, Box 46; Butler to M. Maceo Nance Jr., 13 June 1980, Folder: Fraternities, Box 36, HCSCSU.

46. The Faculty Discipline Committee that heard the Moore case consisted of George Hunter, Nettie Parler, Amelia Roberts, and Milton Hunter, who served as chair. M. Maceo Nance Jr., Presidents' Papers, Box 24, Folder: Student Discipline, HCSCSU.

47. Dr. Ernest A. Finney to M. Maceo Nance Jr., 21 April 1980, Presidents' Papers, M. Maceo Nance Jr., Box 33, Folder: Students General, HCSCSU.

48. R. A. Berry, Plant Manager, Starflo Corporation to William Shuler, Cooperative Education Coordinator, 31 December 1979, Presidents' Papers, M. Maceo Nance Jr., Box 34, Folder: Cooperative Education and Career Planning, HCSCSU.

49. Suzy Mayfield, Ozark Airlines Flight Attendant, to M. Maceo Nance Jr., 14 December 1981, Presidents' Papers, Box 38, Folder: Athletics, HCSCSU.

50. Eloise U. Belcher to M. Maceo Nance Jr., 27 February 1969, Presidents' Papers, Box 5, Folder: English Department. Mrs. Belcher was the faculty coordinator of the drama program, and she asked Nance for $1,700 to support the trip to Yale.

51. M. Maceo Nance Jr., Presidents' Papers, Box 17, Folder: Communications Center, HCSCSU.

52. M. Maceo Nance Jr., Presidents' Papers, Box 19, Folder: Henderson Davis Players trip to England; Folder: H-D Players, 1971–72, HCSCSU.

53. Program: Henderson Davis Theater, 1972, 12–13; Folder: Trustees, Box 51; *Collegian,* January 1973.

54. M. Maceo Nance Jr., Presidents' Papers, Box 12, Folder: Rose Bowl Band; Folder: Band list of contributors, HCSCSU.

55. M. Maceo Nance Jr., Box 12, Folder: Rose Bowl Band, HCSCSU.

56. Clifford Watkins to Walsh, Manager, Silverdale Travel Limited, 1 September 1971; Program, "The Marching 101 Band," 9 April 1970, Box 16, Folder: Band and Choir, Box 63, Folder: Marching 101, M. Maceo Nance Jr., Presidents' Papers, HCSCSU.

57. Lee Plowden to M. Maceo Nance Jr., no date, received 24 July 1980, Presidents' Papers, Box 39, Folder: Department of Music and Fine Arts, HCSCSU. Plowden's letter to Nance is an excellent firsthand description of what it was like to be caught up in an urban riot.

58. Victor E. Kerr, Chair, Athletic Committee, to Talmadge L. Hill Sr., Morgan State University, 16 March 1970, Presidents' Papers, M. Maceo Nance Jr., Box 20, Folder: MEAC General. Kerr informed Hill that South Carolina State accepted the offer "to fill [the] remaining berth in the Mid-Eastern Athletic Conference." 2010 Football Media Guide, South Carolina State University, 60. Morgan State, North Carolina Central, and University of Maryland–Eastern Shore withdrew in 1980. Both UMES and Morgan State subsequently returned. North Carolina Central rejoined in 2010 as Savannah State became a member. Bethune Cookman entered the conference in 1979 with Florida A&M, but FAMU withdrew briefly from 1984 to 1986. Coppin State joined in 1985 while Hampton and Norfolk State entered in 1995 and 1997. Winston-Salem State made an abbreviated entry in 2007 only to withdraw in 2010.

59. 2.0.10. Football Media Guide, South Carolina State University, 67–68.

60. Milton Hunter, Athletic Director, to the Athletic Committee (Victor E. Kerr, chair; George W. Hunter, secretary; Roy J. Isabel; and Col. Harold A. Jenkins), Presidents' Papers, M. Maceo Nance Jr., Box 9, Folder: Athletics, HCSCSU.

61. The *Times and Democrat* published a five-part series on Coach Willie Jeffries by Bob Gillespie: "Legend of the Fall," *Times and Democrat,* 2, 3, 4, 5, 6, August 2010, B1–B2.

62. Football Program, Howard University vs. S.C. State, 27 September 1975.

63. In 2010 Jeffries pointed out that the current Bulldog head coach, Oliver "Buddy" Pough, operated in a more competitive recruiting environment than Jeffries had in the 1970s. Pough had to deal with Furman, Presbyterian, the Citadel, Coastal Carolina, and Charleston Southern and other institutions that Jeffries had not had to contend with. Bob Gillespie, "Legend of the Fall," *Times and Democrat,* 5 August 2010, B1–B2; Lesesne, *History of the University of South Carolina,* 150–51; Martin, *Benching Jim Crow,* 138–46.

64. 2010 Media Guide, 67.

65. 2010 Media Guide, 67.

66. 2010 Media Guide, 79–80.

67. Jeffries' coaching successes at Wichita and Howard were marred by NCAA investigations, and both schools were put on probation for recruiting and eligibility violations. Bob Gillespie, "Jeffries' Move to Wichita State Paves Way for Black Coaches," *Times and Democrat,* 5 August 2010.

68. 2010 Media Guide, 60, 67–68.

69. WWDM in Sumter initially won the rights to broadcast the games. Norman Thompson, Sports Director of WOIC, to Milton Hunter, 13 June 1977, Presidents' Paper, M. Maceo Nance Jr., Box 27, Folder: Athletics, HCSCSU.

70. Harold A. Jenkins to President Walter Washington, Alcorn State, 10 November 1980; Jenkins to Joseph R. Johnson, President, Grambling State, 6 January 1982, Presidents' Papers, M. Maceo Nance Jr., Box 37, Folder: Athletics, HCSCSU. Black college sports began to receive long overdue attention in 1968 when Howard Cosell of ABC Sports brought the story of Coach Eddie Robinson and his Grambling State Tigers to the nation's sports fans in his documentary *Grambling College: 100 Yards to Glory.*

71. Robert L. Johnson to Milton Hunter, 12 June 1980, Box 33, Folder: Athletics; Johnson to M. Maceo Nance, 11 February 1981, Box 37, Folder: BET; Johnson to Nance, 20 September 1982, Box 41, Folder: BET, Presidents' Papers, M. Maceo Nance Jr., HCSCSU.

72. Jobe left USC to become the head coach at the University of Denver. In 1980 he signed on as an assistant coach with the Denver Nuggets of the NBA. Men's Basketball Media Guide, 1971–72," 6–7, 46; Denver Nuggets Basketball Program, 1980–81, Box 37, Folder: Athletics, Presidents' Papers, HCSCSU.

73. Men's Basketball Media Guide, 1973–74, no page numbers, HCSCSU.

74. Men's Basketball Media Guide, 1988–89, 15, HCSCSU.

75. Richards played eight years for the San Diego Padres, and Aikens spent his eight-year career with the California Angels, Kansas City Royals, and Toronto Blue Jays. www.baseball-almanac.com/players, accessed 5 March 2017.

76. Women's Basketball Media Guide, 1977–78, 13.

77. Basketball Media Guide, 1983–84, 14, 19–20; *Bulldog,* 1979, 256.

78. Women's Basketball Media Guide, 1986–87, 6.

79. *Bulldog,* 1983, 347.

80. "NCAA Draft on Implementation of Title IX of the Education Amendments of 1972." The draft was a response to the Department of Health, Education, and Welfare (HEW) position that Title IX did apply to intercollegiate athletics. Box 22, Folder: Athletics. AIAW officials opposed the NCAA takeover of women's intercollegiate sports. Marion Freeman, the chair of the Faculty Committee on Intercollegiate Athletics at the University of Minnesota, appealed for support of the AIAW in 1980 because the NCAA had been opposed to Title IX, but now it had "decided to become a shepherd for women." Marion Freeman to M. Maceo Nance Jr., 22 February 1980. The S.C. State Athletic Committee declined to take a stand in the controversy between the NCAA and the AIAW, preferring instead to "continue to study the issue." Victor E. Kerr Jr., Chair of the Athletic Committee, to Algeron S. Belcher, 28 February 1980. Box 33, Folder: NCAA, HCSCSU.

81. *NCAA Newsletter,* no. 3 (15 February 1980), Box 33, Folder: NCAA. *Bulldog,* 1978, 282; 1979, 264–66; 1981, 327.

82. 2011 S.C. State Media Guide, 93.

83. Mary Hill, the senior women's administrator in the Department of Intercollegiate Athletics, provided valuable assistance in assembling information on the initiation of women's team sports at S.C. State. E-mail, Mary Hill to William Hine, 23 September 2011. See also *Bulldog,* 1988, 302–3; 1981, 326; 1982, 286–87.

84. Stanley Bennett, "Women Get Their Place; Sports Loses," *Collegian,* September 1974, 11.

85. The other nine schools in the pilot project were Eastern Kentucky, Penn State, Florida State, Indiana University, Louisiana State University, Texas A&M, Hawaii, South Dakota State, and Arizona State. "Army ROTC for Women Being Offered," *Collegian,* May 1972, 12; *Annual Report, 1972–1973,* 38–39; *Annual Report, 1975–1976,* 42–45. Of the 639 cadets in 1975–76, thirty-seven were Claflin and Voorhees students. One of the seven women at summer camp was a Voorhees student.

86. *Annual Report, 1975–1976,* 42–45; *Bulldog,* 1973, 127; 1984, 226; "Dorothy Tucker First Black Female to Get 4-Year ROTC Scholarship," *Collegian,* January 1973, 3.

87. "Non-compulsory ROTC for State," *Collegian,* May 1969, 2; Minutes, Board of Trustees, 19 June 1969. HCSCSU.

88. *Annual Report, May 1970–October 1970*, 7.

89. *Annual Report, 1975–1976*, 42–47; *Annual Report, 1976–1977*, 30; *Annual Report, 1977–1978*, 25–36. There was no breakdown provided for cross enrolled students or for women in 1976–77 or 1977–78.

90. *Annual Report, 1975–1976*, 44–45.

91. C. Johnson, *African Americans and ROTC*, 178. The criteria for qualification for the advanced program are listed in *Annual Report, 1971–1972*, 42–43. Those criteria included a 2.0 GPA, a military science grade point average of C, recommendations from the chair of the department of the student's major, physical qualification, and an aptitude and desire for military training.

92. *Annual Report, 1971–1972*, 42. There is an error in figures compiled in the annual report. It indicates that twenty officers were evaluated and that 50 percent or ten failed or were in the lower one-third for 1971–72. But only three are listed in the middle one-third, and none are listed in the upper one-third: a total of thirteen, and not twenty.

93. *Annual Report, 1971–1972*, 40–42. "The History of Army ROTC at S.C. State University," ROTC webpage, South Carolina State University website, http://www.scsu.edu/armyrotc/thehistoryofarmy rotcatsouthcarolinastateuniversity.aspx, accessed 20 September 2011.

CHAPTER TEN: MAINTAINING THE LEGACY

1. Copies of correspondence between the Office for Civil Rights within the Department of Education and state officials are contained in *South Carolina Plan for Equity.* William H. Thomas, Regional Director, Office for Civil Rights, to Gov. Richard W. Riley, 7 January 1981. Although Title VI made no specific reference to colleges or universities, it did forbid financial assistance to any program or activity that discriminated on the basis of race, color, or national origin. Loomis, "State Policy and Planning," 46–54, 140–44. See also Halpern, *On the Limits of the Law.*

2. Bass, *Something's Happening in South Carolina*, 11.

3. Kenneth Adams, a Mississippi student, was the first plaintiff listed alphabetically in the suit against Richardson. The courts eventually ruled that Congress had not permitted the suit against the federal government and that the suits should be filed against individual states and institutions, Loomis, "State Policy and Planning," 53–54.

4. Loomis, "State Policy and Planning," 50–52; Preer, *Lawyers v. Educators*, 193–222.

5. Loomis, "State Policy and Planning," 129–30. See also Samuel , *Is Separate Unequal?*, 84–86.

6. Bass, *Something's Happening in South Carolina*, 19.

7. *South Carolina Plan for Equity*, 207–8.

8. Bass, *Something's Happening in South Carolina*, 20–21. Loomis, "State Policy and Planning," 149–50.

9. Loomis, "State Policy and Planning," 154.

10. Loomis, "State Policy and Planning," 151–52.

11. Bass, *Something's Happening in South Carolina*, 21–22; Loomis, "State Policy and Planning," 165.

12. Loomis, "State Policy and Planning," 155–57.

13. Loomis, "State Policy and Planning," 161–63, Bass, *Something's Happening in South Carolina*, 27.

14. *South Carolina Plan for Equity;* Loomis, "State Policy and Planning," 155–59.

15. LeGree Daniels to Gov. Carroll Campbell, 9 February 1988. Contained in Loomis, "State Policy and Planning," 171.

16. Loomis, "State Policy and Planning," 161–63.

17. *Final Comprehensive Report on Implementation of the South Carolina Higher Education Desegregation Plan*, table 9, 33.

18. Loomis, "State Policy and Planning," 157.

19. Bass, *Something's Happening in South Carolina*, 23.

20. Library science had been one of the post–World War II programs created at S.C. State to prevent black students from enrolling at the state's white institutions.

21. As late as the mid-1960s, the college catalogs indicated that vocational courses provided students the opportunity to become journeyman craftsmen and technicians. *College Catalog, 1964–1965*, 173–74. *South Carolina State College Catalogue 1964–65*, 173–74; *South Carolina State Collge Catalogue Number 1969–70*, 200–203, listed six woodworking courses, five courses in auto mechanics, six courses in masonry, five tailoring courses, and three courses in masonry. See *Annual Report, 1985–1986*, 8 for ABET accreditation.

22. *Annual Report, 1985–1986,* 14; *South Carolina State College Catalogue 1964-65,* 68–69.

23. *South Carolina State College Catalog 1979–80,* 69; *South Carolina State College Catalog 1986-87,* 148–51.

24. Funeral program, Dr. Harold Powell, 10 May 2010.

25. *Annual Report, October 1969–May 1970,* 34–35.

26. Undated *Times and Democrat* newspaper story by Joyce Milkie. M. Maceo Nance Jr., Presidents' Papers, Box 15, Folder: Trustees, HCSCHC.

27. *Annual Report, 1971–1972,* "Report of the Vice President for Academic Affairs," 14–15, 22; *Annual Report, 1973–1974,* 12, 15–16; *Annual Report, 1975–1976,* 16, 22–23.

28. *Annual Report, 1985–1986,* 11; Dr. Joan A. Lawrence to M. Maceo Nance Jr., 4 March 1983, Nance to Lawrence, 7 March 1983, Presidents' Papers, M. Maceo Nance Jr., Box 43, Folder: Department of Habilitative Science, HCSCSU.

29. Telephone interview, William Hine with Leo Twiggs, 6 December 2011.

30. Telephone interview, Hine and Twiggs, 6 December 2011.

31. Folder: Art Program, Box 32, M. Maceo Nance Papers, Presidents' Papers, "Dedication of the I. Stanback Museum and Planetarium," 27 April 1980, HCSCSU.

32. Leo Twiggs to M. Maceo Nance, 9 December 1980, Folder: Art Program, Box 39, M. Maceo Nance Papers, Presidents' Papers, HCSCSU.

33. Leo Twiggs to M. Maceo Nance Jr., 9 December 1980, Folder: Art Program, Box 39, Folder: Art Program, Box 40. HCSCSU.

34. "First Year Report," Leo Twiggs, July 1981, Folder: Art Program, Box 40, HCSCSU.

35. Leo Twiggs to M. Maceo Nance Jr., 30 June 1982, 9 June 1983, Folder: Art Program, Box 40; Don Walter to Leo Twiggs, 8 June 1983: Folder: Art Program, Box 43, HCSCSU. The museum and planetarium was not built with adequate and sensitive humidity controls in the heating and air-conditioning system, and that led eventually to an infestation of mold that required painstaking and costly removal in the early twenty-first century. Telephone interview: Leo F. Twiggs with William Hine, 6 December 2011.

36. Telephone interview: Charles Roberts with William Hine, 17 January 2012.

37. Algernon S. Belcher to M. Maceo Nance Jr., 31 January 1979, Folder: A. V. Center, Box 31. Thurmond and his staff were renowned for their efficient and effective constituent services, and the senator's office had contacted the Public Telecommunications Facilities Program staff almost immediately after Nance requested the assistance. Senator Strom Thurmond to M. Maceo Nance Jr., 29 June 1982, Folder: Instructional Media Center (I.M.C.), Box 42, Presidents' Papers, HCSCSU.

38. Henry J. Cauthen to Public Telecommunications Facilities Program, U.S. Department of Commerce, 8 July 1982; M. Maceo Nance to Cauthen, 9 July 1982; Charles Roberts to Nance, 6 January 1983, Folder: I.M.C., Box 43, Presidents' Papers, HCSCSU.

39. *Annual Report, 1985–1986,* 21–22.

40. Bolts represented Georgetown, and his departure left the general assembly all white until 1970. Tindall, *South Carolina Negroes,* 61; Edgar, *South Carolina,* 541; Bass and Poole, *Palmetto State,* 135. By 2007 there were thirty-five black members of the general assembly: twenty-seven in the house and eight in the senate.

41. Bass and Poole, *Palmetto State,* 135; Grose, *Looking for Utopia,* 125.

42. Strom Thurmond to M. Maceo Nance Jr., telegram, 30 January 1974. Telegram copy: Thurmond to Caspar Weinberger, 28 January 1974. Folder: U.S. Senators, State Senators, and Representatives, Box 14; Thurmond to Nance, telegram, 3 June 1977, Folder: Habilatative Sciences, Box 29, HCSCSU.

43. Bass and Thompson, *Ol' Strom,* 256–61.

44. Butler Derrick to M. Maceo Nance Jr., 4 April 1975; J. Claytor Arrants to Nance, 26 September 1974, Folder: U.S. Senators, State Senators, Representatives, Box 14, HCSCSU.

45. Copy: Carroll Campbell, Ernest Hollings, and Strom Thurmond to Secretary of Education Shirley Hufstedler, 19 June 1980, Folder: Urban League, Box 33, HCSCSU.

46. M. Maceo Nance Jr. to Ernest F. Hollings, J. Strom Thurmond, Floyd Spence, Carroll A. Campbell, Kenneth L. Holland, Thomas F. Hartnett, John Napier, and Butler Derrick, 18 March 1981. Holland to Nance, 27 March 1981, Folder: Financial Aid to Students, Box 35, HCSCSU.

47. Butler Derrick to M. Maceo Nance Jr., 6 January 1982; Thomas Hartnett to Nance, 22 December 1981; John L. Napier to Nance, 22 December 1982; Carroll Campbell to Nance, 18 December 1981, Folder: Grants Coordinator, Box 42, HCSCSU.

48. M. Maceo Nance Jr. to Senators L. Marion Gressette, Robert C. Lake, Hyman Rubin, and Marshall B. Williams, 8 April 1975, Folder: U.S. Senators, State Senators, Representatives, Box 14, HCSCSU.

49. Telegrams: M. Maceo Nance Jr. to I. S. Leevy Johnson, Herbert Fielding, James Felder, and James Clyburn, June 1970, James Felder to Nance, 4 June 1970. Folder: Blacks Running for Political Office, Box 57, HCSCSU.

50. I. S. Leevy Johnson to M. Maceo Nance Jr., 11 February 1971, Folder: Blacks Running for Political Office, Box 57, HCSCSU.

51. McKinley Washington to M. Maceo Nance Jr., 23 December 1981, Folder: Outside Conferences and Conventions, Box 39. The conference was held in Staley Hall on 9 January 1982. HCSCSU.

52. Richard E. Fields to M. Maceo Nance Jr., 7 March 1978, Folder: U.S., State Senators, Representatives, Box 46, HCSCSU.

53. Robert C. Nix to M. Maceo Nance Jr., 31 July 1970, Nance to Nix, 4 August 1970, Folder: Pressure cases, Box 51, HCSCSU.

54. M. Maceo Nance Jr. to I. Stanback, 15 December 1971, Folder: Trustees, Box 15, HCSCSU.

55. Hugh Lane to M. Maceo Nance Jr., 7 May 1970; Nance to Lane, 8 May 1970, Folder: BOT, Box 51, HCSCSU.

56. M. Maceo Nance Jr. to Elliott Elam, Secretary of the Board of Trustees, 8 June 1973, contained in the Minutes, 4 December 1973; Minutes, Board of Trustees, 3 May 1978.

57. J. Leonard Gattison, Internal Auditor, Response to 30 June 1980 Audit. Folder: Internal Auditor, Box 44; Report of Herbert Walker Jr., Director of Internal Audit, 3 March 1982. Folder: Internal Auditor, Box 42, HCSCSU.

58. Minutes, Board of Trustees, 2 May 1984.

59. Minutes, Board of Trustees, 5 September 1979.

60. N. Morrison, *History of the College of Charleston,* 123.

61. M. Maceo Nance Jr. to Edgar A. Vaughn Jr., 15 December 1981. Folder: Black Caucus, Box 37, HCSCSU.

62. *Annual Report, October 1969–May 1979,* 5; Minutes, Board of Trustees, 6 October 1969, 7 May 1975; 18 February 1970. The married student apartment complex was named for former S.C. State queens: Lottie Washington Russell, 1939–40; Juanita Vaughn Eaton, 1946–47; Barbara A. Vaughn, 1956–57; Mildred Gilmore Brevard, 1960–61; and Gerry Maxine Watson, 1972–73. Minutes, Board of Trustees, 18 February 1976.

63. Minutes, Board of Trustees, 21 October 1971; special meeting, 5 January 1972; SCSU Review, December 1971, contained in Folder: SCSU Review, Box 49, Presidents' Papers, M. Maceo Nance, HCSCSU; Potts, *History of South Carolina State College,* 167. Potts credits Nance with leading the effort to purchase the land for the Northside Country Club. Also see Middleton and Barnes, *Knowing Who I Am,* 71.

64. Minutes, Board of Trustees, 2 May 1973; 4 October 1973; 20 February 1974; 4 May 1977; 15 February 1978.

65. *College Catalog, 1970–71,* xxiii–xxvii; *College Catalog, 1974–75,* xxv–xxx; *Bulldog,* 1982, 106, 108; *Bulldog,* 1985, 221; "35 Added to Faculty at SCSC," *Collegian,* October 1971, 5.

66. M. Maceo Nance Jr. and R. C. Edwards, "Joint Proposal Bachelor of Science in Agriculture," to George Harrar, President, the Rockefeller Foundation, 28 December 1970; Jesse Perry Jr. to Nance, 8 March 1971, Folder: Agriculture Phased Out, Box 10; Draft by W. C. Brown, "Cooperative Programs: S.C. State and Clemson." Brown was the associate director of the Institute for Higher Educational Opportunity at the Southern Regional Education Board (SREB). Brown had been the director of athletics at S.C. State. Folder: SREB, Box 13, HCSCSU.

67. Neyland, *Historically Black Land-Grant Institutions,* 108, 111, 114, 144; Kerr, *Legacy,* 115.

68. Neyland, *Historically Black Land-Grant Institutions,* 111, 116; Mayberry, *Development of Research at Historically Black Land-Grant Institutions,* 53–54, 94.

69. Congressman Frank E. Evans of Colorado and Senator James B. Allen of Alabama had consistently advocated passage of the legislation during the 1970s. Neyland, *Historically Black Land-Grant Institutions,* 116, 146, 162–64; Kerr, *Legacy,* 154–55.

70. Howie, *Research Projects,* 9–10.

71. Howie, *Research Projects,* 10–12, 16.

72. Howie, *Research Projects,* 13–15.

73. The most complete discussion of extension work in the 1970s is contained in two annual reports: *Annual Report, 1976–1977*, 47–53; and *Annual Report, 1977–1978*, 62–78.

74. *Annual Report, 1977–1978*, 74; *Annual Report, 1976–1977*, 51.

75. *Annual Report, 1976–1977*, 50–51; *Annual Report, 1977–1978*, 76.

76. *Annual Report, 1977–1978*, 74–75.

77. Robert Hurst to Evelyn D. Harris, 25 June 1974 (the letter is mistakenly dated 1954), Folder: Research and Extension, Box 54; Folder: 1890 Research and Extension, Box 44, *Annual Report, 1976–1977*, 52–53.

78. *Annual Report, 1977–1978*, 77–78.

79. *Annual Report, 1976–1977*, 49.

80. *Annual Report, 1977–1978*, 78.

81. Algernon S. Belcher to M. Maceo Nance Jr., 31 October 1974, Folder: Vice President for Academic Affairs; Robert Hurst to Nance, 31 October 1974, Folder: R. L. Hurst, Research and Extension, Box 54, HCSCSU.

82. Robert L. Hurst to M. Maceo Nance Jr., 25 July 1975; Hurst to Edwin C. Miller, Deputy Administrator, Evaluation and Analysis, Cooperative State Research Service, 20 July 1975, Folder: Dr. R. L. Hurst, Research and Extension, Box 56, HCSCSU.

83. The correspondence involving Hurst, Moore, Waddell, and Harrelson is contained in Folder: Dr. R. L. Hurst, Research and Extension, Box 56, HCSCSU.

84. *Annual Report, 1985–1986*, 30–31.

85. *Annual Report, 1985–1986*, 43.

86. Interview: William C. Hine with Suresh R. Londhe, 13 March 1990. Londhe, et al. *Adoption and Economic Viability of the Sloping Agricultural Land Technology on Small Upland Farms, Eastern Visayas, Philippines*; Suresh R. Londhe, "Economic Evaluation of Alternative Investment Opportunities in Upland Agriculture, Central and East Java, Indonesia"; and Patricia Frazier, "Economic Evaluation of the Impact of Research and Extension on Selected Root Crops in the Philippines."

87. See Harrold, *Subversives; Rise of Aggressive Abolitionism;* and *Border War.* Shortly after history professor and chair of the Department of Social Sciences Rubin F. Weston left South Carolina State for Central State University in 1970, he completed *Racism in U.S. Imperialism.*

88. Transcript of speech delivered at the Columbia Rotary Club, 25 October 1971. Nance's emphasis. Folder: Speeches, Box 49, HCSCSU.

89. Gordon W. Blackwell to M. Maceo Nance, 7 October 1970, Folder: S.C. Association of Colleges and Universities, Box 7; Folder: newspaper clippings, *State*, 20 October 1985, Box 49,

90. The Rev. Chappelle Davis received $1,000 as a member of the Chaplain's Corps in 1974–75. Oscar Butler to M. Maceo Nance Jr., 27 August 1974, Folder: Student Affairs, Box 54; Folder: Orangeburg Area Churches, December 1977, Box 27, HCSCSU. Nance seemed to select the churches attended by the largest number of S.C. State students and faculty members. The black churches were New Mount Zion, St. Paul Baptist, Faith Tabernacle Deliverance Temple, Trinity United Methodist, Mount Pisgah Baptist, St. Luke United Presbyterian, Greater Faith Baptist, William Chapel AME, and St. Paul's Episcopal.

91. In 1969 A. E. Lockert Jr., the dean of industrial engineering, asked Nance for approval to change several textbooks. In 1971 Algernon S. Belcher sought Nance's approval for a change in economics and political science textbooks, Folder: School of Industrial Education, Box 45; Folder: Department of Social Sciences, Box 8, HCSCSU. It is not clear whether Nance continued to determine textbook selection through his presidency. Often the college bookstore had an inventory of unsold textbooks in various disciplines and did not want to absorb a loss by having faculty members adopt new books before the previous books were sold.

92. Algernon S. Belcher to O. Butler, 22 November 1974, Folder: V. For Academic Affairs, Box 54; Minutes, Board of Trustees, November 1985.

EPILOGUE

1. *Annual Report, 1985–1986*, 9; website, South Carolina Commission on Higher Education, Faculty Data, "Full Time Faculty Based on Terminal Degree as Defined by SACS in Their Teaching Area," 12 June 2012.

2. The complete list of accredited programs is contained in the South Carolina State University Undergraduate Catalog, 2012–14, inside cover, for list of accredited programs.

3. The information and data on the current 1890 programs are courtesy of Delbert H. Foster, Louis Whitesides, Janie Grant, and Tomeko James.

4. By comparison Clemson University's budget for public service activities for 2012–13 is $65,910,976.

5. By 2012 the ex officio members of the board also included the chairs of the board of visitors, the University Advancement Foundation, the University Foundation, and the Real Estate Foundation.

Bibliography

MANUSCRIPT COLLECTIONS AND ARCHIVES

Claflin University, H. V. Manning Library, Archives, Orangeburg, S.C.

Annual reports
Catalogs
Minutes, board of trustees

Clemson University, Strom Thurmond Institute, Special Collections, Clemson, S.C.

Presidents' papers: Walter M. Riggs, Enoch W. Sikes
Benjamin R. Tillman papers
Strom Thurmond papers (the Thurmond papers were relocated to Clemson from the South Caroliniana Library at the University of South Carolina since this project began).

Historical Collection, Miller F. Whittaker Library, South Carolina State University, Orangeburg, S.C. (HCSCSU)

Annual reports, 1897–2012
College catalogs and bulletins, 1897–2011
Collegian
Faculty log books, 1896–1937
FBI file, Orangeburg Massacre
"History, Growth, and Transition of the 4-H among Negroes in South Carolina," Wayman Johnson, 1970.
"Tentative History of South Carolina State College," Nelson C. Nix, 1937
Office of the President files: Athletics; Correspondence; Departments;;Extension work; Financial; Personnel; Students
Oral Histories: John Mitchell, 8 November 1975; The Orangeburg Massacre
Photographs
Scrapbooks and newspaper clippings
Yearbooks: *Bulldog; Wilkinsonian*

Library of Congress, Washington, D.C.

National Association for the Advancement of Colored People records

Princeton University, Seeley G. Mudd Manuscript Library, Princeton, N.J.

John Foster Dulles papers, selected correspondence

Rockefeller Archive Center, North Tarrytown, N.Y.

General Education Board records

South Carolina Department of Archives and History

Governors' papers: John Gary Evans, Martin Ansel, Coleman Blease, George Bell Timmerman

PUBLISHED WORKS

African American Architects: A Biographical Dictionary, ed. Dreck Spurlock Wilson. New York: Routledge, 2004.

Altschuler, Glenn C., and Stuart M. Blumin. *The G.I. Bill of Rights: A New Deal for Veterans.* New York: Oxford University Press, 2009.

Anderson, Eric, and Alfred A. Moss, Jr. *Dangerous Donations: Northern Philanthropy and Southern Black Education, 1902–1930.* Columbia: University of Missouri Press, 1999.

Anderson, James D. *The Education of Blacks in the South, 1860–1935.* Chapel Hill: University of North Carolina, 1988.

Ascoli, Peter M. *Julius Rosenwald: The Man Who Built Sears, Roebuck and Advanced the Cause of Black Education in the American South.* Bloomington: Indiana University Press, 2006.

Atkinson, Gene. *Interesting and Influential People of Orangeburg.* Charleston: History Press, 2010.

Atwood, R. B., H. S. Smith, and Catherine O. Vaughn. "Negro Teachers in Northern Colleges and Universities in the United States." *Journal of Negro Education* 18, no. 4 (Autumn 1949): 559–67.

Bailey, Thomas Pearce. *Race Orthodoxy in the South and Other Aspects of the Negro Question.* 1914. New York: Negro Universities Press, 1969.

Baker, R. Scott. *Paradoxes of Desegregation: African America Struggles for Educational Equity in Charleston, South Carolina, 1926–1972.* Columbia: University of South Carolina Press, 2006.

Baldwin's City Directory, Orangeburg South Carolina 1940. Charleston, S.C.: Baldwin Directory, 1940.

Bass, Jack. *Something's Happening in South Carolina.* Atlanta: Southern Education Foundation, 1982.

Bass, Jack, and Jack Nelson. *The Orangeburg Massacre.* Cleveland: World, 1970.

———. *The Orangeburg Massacre.* Rev. ed. Macon, Ga.: Mercer University Press, 2002.

Bass, Jack, and W. Scott Poole. *The Palmetto State: The Making of Modern South Carolina.* Columbia: University of South Carolina Press, 2008.

Bass, Jack, and Marilyn W. Thompson. *Ol' Strom: An Unauthorized Biography of Strom Thurmond.* Marietta, Ga.: Longstreet, 1998.

Beacham, Frank. *Whitewash: A Southern Journey through Music, Mayhem and Murder.* New York: Frank Beacham, 2002.

Beale, Howard K. *Are American Teachers Free? An Analysis of Restraints upon Freedom of Teaching in American Schools.* New York: Charles Scribner's Sons, 1936.

———. *A History of Freedom of Teaching in American Schools.* New York: Octagon Books, 1966.

Berman, William C. *The Politics of Civil Rights in the Truman Administration.* Columbus: Ohio State University Press, 1970.

Biographical Directory of the South Carolina House of Representatives, session lists, ed. Joan S. Reynolds, Robert E. Rector, and David K. Bowen. Columbia: University of South Carolina Press, 1974.

Biographical Directory of the South Carolina Senate, 1776–1985, 3 vols., ed. N. Louise Bailey, Mary L. Morgan, and Carolyn B. Taylor. Columbia: University of South Carolina Press, 1986.

Biondi, Martha. *The Black Revolution on Campus.* Berkeley: University of California Press, 2012.

Birnie, Cassandra Maxwell."Race and Politics in Georgia and South Carolina." *Phylon* 13, no. 3 (1952): 236–44.

Booker T. Washington Papers, ed. Louis R. Harlan and Raymond W. Smock. Urbana: University of Illinois Press, 1977.

Bowles, Frank, and Frank A. DeCosta. *Between Two Worlds: A Profile of Negro Higher Education.* New York: McGraw Hill, 1971.

Boyce, Travis D. "I Am Leaving and Not Looking Back": The Life of Benner C. Turner." Ph.D. diss., Ohio University, 2009.

Branch, Taylor. *Parting the Waters: America in the King Years, 1954–1963.* New York: Simon and Shuster, 1988.

Broussard, Albert S. *African-American Odyssey: The Stewarts, 1853–1963.* Lawrence: University of Kansas Press, 1998.

Brubacher, John S., and Willis Ruby. *Higher Education in Transition: A History of American Colleges and Universities, 1636–1976.* New York: Harper and Row, 1976.

Burke, W. Lewis. "Pink Franklin v. South Carolina: The NAACP's First Case." *American Journal of Legal History* 54 (July 2014): 265–302.

Burke, W. Lewis, and Belinda F. Gergel, eds. *Matthew J. Perry: The Man, His Times, and His Legacy.* Columbia: University of South Carolina Press, 2004.

Burnside, Ronald D. "The Governorship of Coleman Livingston Blease of South Carolina, 1911–1915." Ph.D. diss., Indiana University, 1963.

Byrnes, James F. *All in One Lifetime.* New York: Harper and Brothers, 1958.

Charron, Katherine Mellow. *Freedom's Teacher: The Life of Septima Clark.* Chapel Hill: University of North Carolina Press, 2009.

Chibbaro, Anthony. *The Charleston Exposition.* Charleston: Arcadia, 2001.

Coffman, Edward M. *The War to End All Wars: The American Military Experience in World War I.* Madison: University of Wisconsin Press, 1986.

Committee on South Carolina State College (Blackwell Committee), Orangeburg, S.C., 1968.

Cooley, Rosa B. *Homes of the Freed.* New York: New Republic, 1926.

——. *School Acres: Adventures in Rural Education.* New Haven, Conn.: Yale University Press, 1930.

Cox, Marcus S. "From Racial Uplift to Personal Advancement: African American Attitudes toward the Military Service in the Deep South, 1941–1973." Ph. D. diss., Northwestern University, 2001.

Curry, Constance. *Deep in Our Hearts: Nine White Women in the Freedom Movement.* Athens: University of Georgia Press, 2000.

Dagbovie, Pero Gaglo. *Black History: "Old School" Black Historians and the Hip Hop Generation.* Troy, Mich.: Bedford, 2006.

DeJarmon, LeMarquis. "Voting—One Hundred Years to the Beginning." In *Legal Aspects of the Civil Rights Movement,* ed. Donald B. King and Charles W. Quick, 59–77 Detroit: Wayne State University Press, 1965.

Drago, Edmund L. *Initiative, Paternalism, and Race Relations: Charleston's Avery Institute.* Athens: University of Georgia Press, 1991.

Duberman, Martin Baum. *Paul Robeson: A Biography.* New York: Ballentine, 1989.

Du Bois, W. E. B. *The Souls of Black Folk.* New York: Vintage Books/ Library of America, 1990.

Eddy, Edward, Jr. *Colleges for Our Land and Time: The Land-Grant Idea in American Education.* New York: Harper and Brothers, 1957.

Edgar, Walter. *South Carolina: A History.* Columbia: University of South Carolina Press, 1999.

Egerton, John. *Speak Now against the Day: The Generation before the Civil Rights Movement in the South.* Chapel Hill: University of North Carolina Press, 1994.

Encyclopedia of African American Civil Rights: From Emancipation to the Present, ed. Charles D. Lowery and John P. Marszalek. New York: Greenwood, 1992.

Felder, James L. *Civil Rights in South Carolina: From Peaceful Protests to Groundbreaking Rulings.* Charleston: History Press, 2012.

Final Comprehensive Report on Implementation of the South Carolina Higher Education Desegregation Plan 1981–82 through 1985–86. Columbia: Commission on Higher Education, 1986.

Fosdick, Raymond B. *Adventure in Giving: The Story of the General Education Board.* New York: Harper and Row, 1962.

Franklin, John Hope. "Courses concerning the Negro in Negro Colleges." *Quarterly Review of Higher Education among Negroes* 8, no. 3 (July 1940): 138–44.

Fraser, Walter J., Jr. *Charleston! Charleston! The History of a Southern City.* Columbia: University of South Carolina Press, 1989.

Frederickson, Kari. *The Dixiecrat Revolt and the End of the Solid South 1932–1968.* Chapel Hill: University of North Carolina Press, 2001.

Fulmer, Henry G. "Richard T. Greener and the Radical University." *Ex Libris* (1995): 34–37.

Garfinkel, Herbert. *When Negroes March: The March on Washington Movement in the Organizational Politics for FEPC.* New York: Antheneum, 1973.

Garmarekian, Edward. "The Ugly Battle of Orangeburg." *Reporter,* 24 January 1957, 32–34.

Gellman, Erik S. *Death Blow to Jim Crow: The National Negro Congress and the Rise of Militant Civil Rights.* Chapel Hill: University of North Carolina Press, 2012.

Gilmore, Glenda Elizabeth. *Defying Dixie: The Radical Roots of Civil Rights: 1919–1950.* New York: W. W. Norton, 2008.

Gordon, Asa H. *Sketches of Negro Life and History in South Carolina.* 1927. Columbia: University of South Carolina Press, 1970.

Gore, Blinzy. *On a Hilltop High: The Origin and History of Claflin College to 1984*. Spartanburg: Reprint Company, 1994.

Gorman, Bob, and Lois Stickell. "Partners in Progress: Joseph B. Felton, the African American Community and the Rosenwald School Program." *Carologue* 18, no. 3 (Fall 2002): 14–20.

Grant, Joanne, ed. *Black Protest: History, Documents, and Analyses 1619 to the Present.* New York: World Library, 1968.

Greene, Harry Washington. *Holders of Doctorates among American Negroes.* Boston: Meador, 1946.

Grose, Philip G. *Looking for Utopia: The Life and Times of John C. West.* Columbia: University of South Carolina Press, 2011.

——. *South Carolina at the Brink: Robert McNair and the Politics of Civil Rights.* Columbia: University of South Carolina Press, 2006.

Hall, Clyde W. *One-Hundred Years of Education at Savannah State College, 1890–1990.* East Peoria Ill.: Versa, 1991.

Halpern, Stephen C. *On the Limits of the Law: The Ironic Legacy of Title VI of the 1964 Civil Rights Act.* Baltimore: Johns Hopkins University Press, 1995.

Harris, Carmen V. "A Ray of Hope: Blacks in the South Carolina Extension Service, 1915–1970." Ph.D. diss., Michigan State University, 2002.

Harrold, Stanley. *Border War: Fighting over Slavery before the Civil War.* Chapel Hill: University of North Carolina Press, 2010.

——. *The Rise of Aggressive Abolitionism: Addresses to the Slaves.* Lexington: University Press of Kentucky, 2004.

——. *Subversives: Antislavery Community in Washington, D.C., 1828–1865.* Baton Rouge: Louisiana State University Press, 2003.

Hayes, Jack Irby, Jr. *South Carolina and the New Deal.* Columbia: University of South Carolina Press, 2001.

Hill's Columbia City Directory, 1930. Richmond, Va.: Hill Directory, 1930.

Hill's Orangeburg City Directory, 1956. Richmond, Va.: Hill Directory, 1956.

Hine, Darlene Clark. *Black Victory: The Rise and Fall of the White Primary in Texas.* Millwood, N.Y.: KTO, 1979.

Hine, William C. "Civil Rights and Campus Wrongs: South Carolina State Students Protest, 1955–1968." *South Carolina Historical Magazine* 97, no. 4 (October 1996): 310–31.

——. "Thomas E. Miller and the Early Years of South Carolina State University." *Carologue* 12, no. 4 (Winter 1996): 8–12.

History of the American Negro, South Carolina Edition, ed. A. B. Caldwell. Atlanta: A. B. Caldwell, 1919.

Hoffschwelle, Mary S. *The Rosenwald Schools of the American South.* Gainesville: University Press of Florida, 2006.

Hollis, Daniel Walker. *University of South Carolina.* Vol. 2, *College to University.* Columbia: University of South Carolina Press, 1956.

Howie, Marguerite Rogers. *Research Projects and Programs in Progress at South Carolina State College.* Orangeburg: South Carolina State College, 1974.

Hudson, Janet G. *Entangled by White Supremacy: Reform in World War I Era South Carolina.* Lexington: University Press of Kentucky, 2009.

Hughes, C. Alvin, "We Demand Our Rights: The Southern Negro Youth Congress 1937–1949." *Phylon* 48, no. 1 (March 1987): 38–50.

Jackson, David H., Jr. "Booker T. Washington in South Carolina, March 1909." *South Carolina Historical Magazine* 113, no. 3 (July 2012): 192–220.

Jelks, Randal Maurice. *Benjamin Elijah Mays: Schoolmaster of the Movement; A Biography.* Chapel Hill: University of North Carolina Press, 2012.

Jenks, Christopher, and David Reisman. *The Academic Revolution.* Garden City, N.Y.: Doubleday, 1968.

Johnson, Charles S., Jr. *African Americans and ROTC: Military, Naval and Aerospace Programs at Historically Black Colleges, 1916–1973.* Jefferson, N.C.: McFarland, 2002.

Johnson, Joan Marie. *Southern Ladies, New Women: Race, Region, and Clubwomen in South Carolina, 1890–1930.* Gainesville: University Press of Florida, 2004.

Jones-Branch, Cherisse. "'To Speak When and Where I Can': African American Women's Political Activism in South Carolina in the 1940s and 1950s." *South Carolina Historical Magazine* 107, no. 3 (July 2006): 204–24.

Journal of the Constitutional Convention of the State of South Carolina. Columbia, 1895.
Journal of the House of Representatives of the State of South Carolina. Columbia: 1896.
Kantrowitz, Stephen. *Ben Tillman and Reconstruction of White Supremacy.* Chapel Hill: University of North Carolina Press, 2000.
Katznelson, Ira. *When Affirmative Action Was White: An Untold History of Racial Inequality in Twentieth Century America.* New York: W. W. Norton, 2005.
Kennedy, David M. *Freedom from Fear: The American People in Depression and War, 1929–1945.* New York: Oxford University Press, 2005.
Kerr, Allen. *The Legacy: A Centennial History of the State Agricultural Experiment Stations.* Columbia: University of Missouri Agricultural Experiment Station, 1987.
Klarman, Michael J. "How *Brown* Has Changed Race Relations: The Back Lash Thesis." *Journal of American History* 81, no. 1 (June 1994): 81–118.
Kluger, Richard. *Simple Justice: A History of* Brown v. Board of Education *and Black America's Struggle for Equality.* New York: Vintage Books, 1977.
Land-Grant College Education, 1910–1920, Part 2, U.S. Department of the Interior, Bureau of Education, U.S. Government Printing Office, Washington, D.C., 1920.
Lau, Peter F. *Democracy Rising: South Carolina and the Fight for Black Equality since 1865.* Lexington: University Press of Kentucky, 2006.
Lesesne, Henry H. *A History of the University of South Carolina, 1940–2000.* Columbia: University of South Carolina Press, 2001.
Litwack, Leon. *How Free Is Free? The Long Death of Jim Crow.* Cambridge, Mass.: Harvard University Press, 2009.
——. *Trouble in Mind: Black Southerners in the Age of Jim Crow.* New York: Alfred A. Knopf, 1998.
Londhe, Suresh R., et al. *Adoption and Economic Viability of the Sloping Agricultural Land Technology on Small Upland Farms, Eastern Visayas, Philippines.* Orangeburg: South Carolina State College, 1989.
Loomis, Frederick D., Jr. "State Policy and Planning Systems: Responses to the Legal Mandate to Desegregate Higher Education in Virginia and South Carolina," Ph.D. diss., Pennsylvania State University, 1994.
Lucas, Christopher. *American Higher Education: A History.* 2nd ed. New York: Palgrave McMillan, 2006.
Mack, Kibibi Voloria C. *Parlor Ladies and Ebony Drudges: African American Women, Class and Work in a South Carolina Community.* Knoxville: University Press of Tennessee, 1999.
Mack-Shelton, Kibibi Voloria. *Ahead of Her Time in Yesteryear: Geraldyne Pierce Zimmerman Comes of Age in a Southern African American Family.* Knoxville: University Press of Tennessee, 2010.
Mancari, Carla. *Walking on the Grass: A White Woman in the Black World.* Macon, Ga.: Mercer University Press, 2001.
Manning, Kenneth R. *The Black Apollo of Science: The Life of Ernest Everett Just.* New York: Oxford University Press, 1983.
Marsh, Charles. *God's Long Summer: Stories of Faith and Civil Rights.* Princeton, N.J.: Princeton University Press, 1997.
Martin, Charles H. *Benching Jim Crow: The Rise and Fall of the Color Line in Southern College Sports, 1890–1980.* Urbana: University of Illinois Press, 2010.
Marszalek, John P. *A Black Congressman in the Age of Jim Crow: South Carolina's George Washington Murray.* Gainesville: University Press of Florida, 2006.
——. *Court Martial: A Black Man in America.* New York: Charles Scribner's Sons, 1972.
Mayberry, B. D. *Development of Research at Historically Black Land-Grant Institutions.* Tuskegee, Ala.: Tuskegee Institute, 1990.
Mays, Benjamin E. *Born to Rebel: An Autobiography.* New York: Charles Scribner's Sons, 1971.
Meier, August. *Negro Thought in America, 1880–1915.* Ann Arbor: University of Michigan Press, 1970.
McKale, Donald, ed. *Tradition: A History of the Presidency of Clemson University.* Macon, Ga.: Mercer University Press, 1988.
McMillan, Lewis. *Negro Higher Education in South Carolina.* Orangeburg, S.C.: Privately printed, 1952.
——. "Negro Higher Education as I Have Known It." *Journal of Negro Education* 8, no. 1 (January 1939): 9–18.

McMillan, Neal R. *The Citizens' Council: Organized Resistance to the Second Reconstruction 1954–1964.* Urbana: University of Illinois Press, 1971.

Middleton, Earl, and Joy Barnes. *Knowing Who I Am: A Black Entrepreneur's Struggle and Success in the American South.* Columbia: University of South Carolina Press, 2008.

Miller, Mary J. ed. *The Suffrage: Speeches by Negroes in the Constitutional Convention.* N.p.: n.p., n.d.

Moore, F. Henderson. "School Desegregation." In *The Angry Black South*, ed. Glenford E. Mitchell and William H. Peace III, 52–72. New York: Corinth Books, 1962.

Moore, John Hammond. *Carnival of Blood: Dueling, Lynching and Murder in South Carolina, 1880–1924.* Columbia: University of South Carolina Press, 2004.

Moore, Winfred B., Jr., and Orville Vernon Burton, eds. *Toward a Meeting of the Waters: Currents in the Civil Rights Movement of South Carolina during the Twentieth Century.* Columbia: University of South Carolina Press, 2008.

Morris, Aldon. *Origins of the Civil Rights Movement: Black Communities Organizing for Change.* New York: Free Press, 1984.

Morris, Robert C. *Reading, 'Riting, and Reconstruction: The Education of Freedmen in the South 1861–1870.* Chicago: University of Chicago Press, 1981.

Morrison, Nan. *A History of the College of Charleston 1936–2008.* Columbia: University of South Carolina Press, 2011.

Moss, James Allen. "Negro Teachers in Predominantly White Colleges." *Journal of Negro Education* 27, no. 4 (Autumn 1958): 451–62.

Nalty, Bernard. *Strength for the Fight: A History of Black Americans in the Military.* New York: Free Press, 1986.

Neiberg, Michael S. *Making Citizen Soldiers: ROTC and the Ideology of American Military Service.* Cambridge, Mass.: Harvard University Press, 2000.

Nelson, Jack. *Scoop: The Evolution of a Southern Reporter.* Jackson: University Press of Mississippi, 2012.

Nevins, Allen. *The State Universities and Democracy.* Urbana: University of Illinois Press, 1962.

Newby, I. A. *Black Carolinians: A History of Blacks in South Carolina from 1895 to 1968.* Columbia: University of South Carolina Press, 1973.

Neyland, Leedell W. *Historically Black Land-Grant Institutions and the Development of Agriculture and Home Economics.* Tallahassee: Florida A&M Foundation, 1990.

Nugent, Walter. *Habits of Empire: A History of American Expansion.* New York: Alfred A. Knopf, 2008.

Olson, Keith W. *The G.I. Bill, the Veterans and the Colleges.* Lexington: University Press of Kentucky, 1974.

Oppenheimer, Martin. *The Sit-In Movement of 1960.* Brooklyn, N.Y.: Carlson, 1989.

O'Reilly, Kenneth. *"Racial Matters": The FBI's Secret File on Black America, 1960–1972.* New York: Free Press, 1989.

Orr, Clyde E. "An Analytical Study of the Conference of Presidents of Negro Land-Grant Colleges." Ph. D. diss., University of Kentucky, 1959.

Packard, Jerrold M. *American Nightmare: The History of Jim Crow.* New York: St. Martin's, 2002.

Potts, John, Sr. *The History of South Carolina State College.* Orangeburg: South Carolina State College, 1978.

Powers, Bernard E., Jr. *Black Charlestonians: A Social History, 1822–1885.* Fayetteville: University of Arkansas Press, 1994.

Preer, Jean L. *Lawyers v. Educators: Black Colleges and Desegregation in Public Higher Education.* Westport, Conn.: Greenwood, 1982.

Proceedings of the Thirteenth Annual Conference of the Presidents of Negro Land-Grant Colleges, November 18–20, 1935, Washington, D.C.

Public Higher Education in South Carolina: A Survey Report. George Peabody College for Teachers, Nashville, Tenn., 1946.

Quint, Howard. *Profile in Black and White: A Frank Portrait of South Carolina.* Washington, D.C.: Public Affairs, 1958.

Rabinowitz, Howard N., ed. *Southern Black Leaders of the Reconstruction Era.* Urbana: University of Illinois Press, 1982.

Ransby, Barbara. *Ella Baker and the Black Freedom Movement: A Radical Democratic Vision.* Chapel Hill: University of North Carolina Press, 2003.

Rawick, George P., ed. *The American Slave: A Composite Autobiography.* Supp., series 2. Westport, Conn.: Greenwood, 1977.
Reel, Jerome V. *The High Seminary: A History of Clemson Agricultural College of South Carolina 1889–1964.* Clemson: Clemson University Digital Press, 2011.
Reid, Ira De A. "People and Places." *Phylon* 7, no. 4 (Fall 1946): 382–87.
Richards, Miles. "The Eminent Lieutenant McKaine." *Carologue* 7, no. 3 (Fall 1991): 6–7, 14–17.
——. "James F. Byrnes on the Democratic Party Nomination for Vice President, July 1944." *South Carolina Historical Magazine* 109, no. 4 (October 2008): 295–305.
Roberts, Blain, and Ethan J. Kytle. "Looking the Thing in the Face: Slavery, Race, and the Commemorative Landscape in Charleston, South Carolina, 1865–1910." *Journal of Southern History* 77 (August 2012): 639–84.
Robertson, David. *Sly and Abel: A Political Biography of James F. Byrnes.* New York: W. W. Norton, 1994.
Rogers, Ibram H. *The Black Campus Movement: Black Students and the Racial Reconstruction of Higher Education, 1965–1972.* New York: Palgrave McMillan, 2012.
Roper, John Herbert, Sr. *The Magnificent Mays: A Biography of Benjamin Elijah Mays.* Columbia: University of South Carolina Press, 2012.
Rose, Willie Lee. *Rehearsal for Reconstruction: The Port Royal Experiment.* Indianapolis: Vintage, 1967.
Samuel, Albert L. *Is Separate Unequal? Black Colleges and the Challenge of Desegregation.* Lawrence: University Press of Kansas, 2004.
Savage, Barbara D. *Your Spirits Walk beside Us: The Politics of Black Religion.* Cambridge, Mass.: Harvard University Press, 2008.
Schweninger, Loren. *Black Property Owners in the South 1790–1915.* Urbana: University of Illinois Press, 1990.
Sellers, Cleveland, with Robert Terrell. *The River of No Return: The Autobiography of a Black Militant and the Life and Death of SNCC.* New York: William Morrow, 1973.
Shannon, Fred A. *The Farmer's Last Frontier: Agriculture, 1867–1897.* Vol. 5 of *The Economic History of the United States.* New York: Holt, Rinehart, and Winston, 1945.
Shuler, Jack. *Blood and Bone: Truth and Reconciliation in a Southern Town.* Columbia: University of South Carolina Press, 2012.
Simkins, Francis Butler. *Pitchfork Ben Tillman: South Carolinian.* 1944. Reprint, Baton Rouge: Louisiana State University Press, 1967.
——. "Robert Shaw Wilkinson." In *Dictionary of American Biography,* 229–30. New York: American Council of Learned Societies, 1936.
Simmons, William J. *Men of Mark: Eminent, Progressive and Rising.* 1887. New York: Johnson, 1970.
Smith, J. Clay, Jr. *Emancipation: The Making of the Black Lawyer 1844–1944.* Philadelphia: University of Pennsylvania Press, 1993.
Smith, Samuel Denny. *The Negro in Congress 1870–1901.* Chapel Hill: University of North Carolina Press, 1940.
Smyth, William D. "Blacks and the South Carolina Interstate and West Indian Exposition." *South Carolina Historical Magazine* 88, no. 4 (October 1987): 211–19.
South Carolina Constitution, 1895.
The South Carolina Encyclopedia, ed. Walter Edgar. Columbia: University of South Carolina Press, 2006.
The South Carolina Plan for Equity and Equal Opportunity in Public Colleges and Universities as Approved by the U.S. Department of Education, South Carolina Commission on Higher Education, Columbia, S.C., 1981.
Spivey, Donald. *Schooling for the New Slavery: Black Industrial Education, 1868–1915.* Westport, Conn.: Greenwood, 1978.
Statutes at Large of South Carolina, ed. David J. McCord. Vol. 7. Columbia: A. S. Johnson, 1840.
Sullivan, Patricia. *Lift Every Voice: The NAACP and the Making of the Civil Rights Movement.* New York: New Press, 2009.
Survey of Negro Colleges and Universities, ed. Arthur J. Klein. U.S. Department of the Interior, Bureau of Education, U.S. Government Printing Office, Washington, D.C., 1928; reprint, Negro Universities Press, 1969.
Thelin, John R. *A History of American Higher Education.* Baltimore: Johns Hopkins University Press, 2004.

Thirty Years of Lynching in the United States, 1889–1918. New York: National Association for the Advancement of Colored People, 1919.

Tindall, George B. *South Carolina Negroes 1877–1900.* Columbia: University of South Carolina Press, 1952.

True, Alfred Charles. *A History of Agricultural Extension Work in the United States, 1785–1923.* Washington: D.C.: U.S. Department of Agriculture, Miscellaneous Publication No. 15, 1928.

Turner, Jeffrey A. *Sitting In and Speaking Out: Student Movements in the American South 1960–1970.* Athens: University of Georgia Press, 2010.

Turner, Lorenzo Dow. *Africanisms in the Gullah Dialect.* Chicago: University of Chicago Press, 1949.

Tushnet, Mark V. *The NAACP Legal Strategy against Segregated Education, 1915–1950.* Chapel Hill: University of North Carolina Press, 1987.

Tye, Larry. *Rising from the Rails: Pullman Porters and the Making of the Black Middle Class.* New York: Henry Holt, 2004.

Walker, John, Michael D. Richardson, and Thomas I. Parks, eds. *The Organization of Public Education in South Carolina.* Dubuque, Iowa: Kendall Hunt, 1992.

Washington, Philemon. *The Class of 1957: Golden Anniversary Reunion South Carolina State University.* Orangeburg: South Carolina State University, 2007.

Webber, Clemmie Embly. *The College Soda Shop.* Orangeburg, S.C.: Cecil Williams, 2005.

Weingarth, Jean. "Race and Power: The Myth and Mystique of Robert Shaw Wilkinson." Ph. D. diss., University of South Carolina, 2011.

Weston, Rubin F. *Racism in U.S. Imperialism: The Influence of Racial Assumptions on American Foreign Policy, 1893–1946.* Columbia: University of South Carolina Press, 1972.

White, John W. "Managed Compliance: White Resistance and Desegregation in South Carolina, 1950–1970." Ph.D. diss., University of Florida, 2006.

White, Pamela Mercedes. "'Free and Open': The Radical University of South Carolina." Master's thesis, University of South Carolina, 1975.

Who's Who in Colored America: A Biographical Dictionary of Notable Living Persons of African Descent in America, 1930–1931–1932, ed. Thomas Yenser. Brooklyn, N.Y.: Thomas Yenser, 1933.

Who's Who in Colored America: A Biographical Dictionary of Notable Living Persons of Negro Descent in America, ed. Joseph J. Boris. New York: Who's Who in Colored America, 1927.

Who's Who in Colored America: An Illustrated Biographical Dictionary of Notable Living Persons of African Descent, 7th ed., ed. G. James Flemming and Christian E. Buckel. Yonkers-on-Hudson, N.Y.: Christian E. Buckel, 1950.

Wiggins, Sam P. *Higher Education in the South.* Berkeley, Calif.: McCutchen, 1966.

Williams, Cecil. *Freedom and Justice: Four Decades of the Civil Rights Movement as Seen by Black Photographer of the Deep South.* Macon, Ga.: Mercer University Press, 1995.

Williams, Cecil, and Sonny Dubose. *Orangeburg 1968: A Place and Time Remembered.* Orangeburg, S.C.: Cecil Williams, 2008.

Williams, Essie Mae Washington, and William Stadiem. *Dear Senator: A Memoir by the Daughter of Strom Thurmond.* New York: Regan Books, 2005.

Wolters, Raymond. *The New Negro on Campus: Black College Rebellions of the 1920s.* Princeton, N.J.: Princeton University Press, 1975.

Woodward, C. Vann. *The Strange Career of Jim Crow.* 3rd ed. New York: Oxford University Press, 1974.

Yarbrough, Tinsley E. *A Passion for Justice: J. Waties Waring and Civil Rights.* New York: Oxford University Press, 1987.

Zinn, Howard. *SNCC: The New Abolitionists.* Boston: Beacon, 1964.

Index

About the Author

William C. Hine, now retired, was a professor of history at South Carolina State University for forty years. His scholarship has been published in several journals including *Agricultural History, Labor History,* and the *Journal of Southern History.* Hine co-authored with Darlene Clark Hine and Stanley Harrold the widely adopted college history textbook *The African American Odyssey.*